PARIS JOURNAL

1944–1965

Books by Janet Flanner

PARIS JOURNAL: 1965–1971 (*1971*)

PARIS JOURNAL: 1944–1965 (*1965*)

MEN AND MONUMENTS (*1957*)

PÉTAIN: THE OLD MAN OF FRANCE (*1944*)

AN AMERICAN IN PARIS (*1940*)

THE CUBICAL CITY (*1926*)

PARIS JOURNAL

1944–1965

JANET FLANNER
(GENÊT)

Edited by William Shawn

A Harvest Book

Harcourt Brace Jovanovich
New York and London

Printed in the United States of America

Harvest edition published by arrangement with The New Yorker Magazine, Inc.

Library of Congress Cataloging in Publication Data

Flanner, Janet, 1892–
Paris Journal.

(A Harvest book; HB 359–360)
Reprint of the ed. published by Atheneum, New York.
Includes index.
CONTENTS: [v. 1] 1944–1965.—v. 2. 1965–1971.
1. Paris—History—1944– 2. France—Politics and government—1945– 3. Paris—Intellectual life.
I. Title.
DC737.F55 1977 944'.361'082 76-45462
ISBN 0-15-670950-3 (v. 1)
0-15-670951-1 (v. 2)

First Harvest edition 1977

A B C D E F G H I J

To my editor, William Shawn,

with admiration, gratitude,

and more than affection

PARIS JOURNAL

1944–1965

1944

December 15

This is a period of high visibility in France. The surface of Paris today consists of fundamentals, as it has before during the country's crucial mutations. The good and bad that lie at the base of French life are now being temporarily pressed to the top. Today is a general French date, like the date after the French Revolution, like the date after the fall of Napoleon. On such a calendar, it seems evident, 1918 was no date at all.

What, each according to his station in life, the citizens of Paris, four months after its liberation, hope that they will live to see in the way of a revived and reformed France, and what, rich or poor, they know they cannot live through again are doubtless clearer now than they will be later, when normal living and forgetfulness begin to dim the scene. Existence in Paris is still abnormal with relief, with belief. The two together make for confusion. The population of Paris is still a mass of uncoördinated individuals, each walking through the ceaseless winter rains with his memories. Government, because it is a novelty after four years of occupation, seems so intimate that each citizen feels he can keep his eye on it in vigilant curiosity. News, too, is intimate, as if the globe had shrunk to suit the size of the one-sheet French newspapers. Large events, when reduced to a paragraph, seem personal, and battlefronts on which millions of men of various nationalities are struggling assume, in print, the intense, direct interest of a family affair in which three of its members are involved, since France metaphysically considers that she has three armies—her soldiers, her deportees, and her tortured civilian dead. No Parisian, worker or capitalist, patriot or turncoat, important or obscure, has enough of everything. Nourished by liberation, warmed by the country's return to active battle, Paris is still, physically, living largely on vegetables and mostly without heat. France, which was the strained and straining leader of Europe for so many years that finally she no longer had the strength to lead herself, is now probably the most fortunate survivor of an Old World that is being destroyed into something new.

For five years Europe has been the victim of cannibalism, with one country trying to eat the other countries, trying to eat the grain, the meat, the oil, the steel, the liberties, the governments, and the men of all the others. The half-consumed corpses of ideologies and of the civilians who believed in them have rotted the soil of Europe, and in this day of the most luxurious war machinery the world has ever seen, the inhabitants of the Continent's capital cities have been reduced to the primitive problems of survival, of finding something to eat, of hatred, of revenge, of fawning, of being for or against themselves or someone else, and of hiding, like savages with ration cards. The desperate economic competition which will arrive with the peace will be scarcely less bloodthirsty. The country whose men, machines, and municipalities are the least wrecked physically; the country lucky enough to have unweary, educated brains, young or old, which will volunteer their services to public life, like youthful corporals or middle-aged colonels volunteering for a dangerous, unrewarded front-line mission; the country which, above all, has in readiness a leader not identified with military defeat or, even worse, what peacefully led up to it—that country should have the best chance for survival. At this moment of semi-liberation in Europe, with the end of hostilities surely situated somewhere across the Rhine, in a field or village not yet in history's view, France seems the Continental nation most favored for the future. As *Combat,* a former underground newspaper that has assumed great importance here, has just declared, this is the time, in France, for harsh intelligence. As *Figaro,* which represents a new, noble-hearted Right, has just stated, the French must rethink many things which up to now they have failed to think to a conclusion. As the Communist *Humanité* repeats in its slogan, which sounds strangely like an imperial throwback, it is now or never for the "French Renaissance."

Until the Renaissance gets under way, mouths and hands are more important than intellects and hopes. The shortages of food and employment are equally great; there is a nice balance between the empty factories and the nearly empty stomachs. When the Germans disappeared from Paris in August, the black market began to disappear, too. This has not turned out to be the blessing one might have expected. The black market, and even the gray market—the constant bartering, selling, and haggling that went on among friends—devastated what was left of French morale and cheapened the value of time, since it consumed hours of each day, but it also saved French lives. The black market was built upon the French peasant's classic cupidity and the Vichy government's stupidity in thinking that it is a farmer's social duty to grow things whether they profit him or not. Because the French peasant was paid parsimoniously low official prices in an attempt to keep consumer prices down, he found that he was receiving only a fraction of what it cost him to produce what he sold. Therefore, humanly, he not only lied to the authorities about the quantity he could bring to market but, inhumanely, he undersupplied even his assessed regional share for the needy. And while the Parisian, in the four years of the occupation, was losing, on the average, forty pounds in weight because of inadequate rations, the peasant was selling his surplus on the black market at profits which, if he had big herds, flocks, and fields, made him a franc millionaire. Now, as one of the money-minded *nouveaux riches,* he fears the inflation he helped to create. Thus nowadays a cow in the bush seems a better bet than thirty thousand francs in the hand. The peasant has stopped selling, the black market is drying up, and Parisians, who expected to fill up on something more than freedom after the liberation, are still underfed. This week's fat-and-flesh ration for a family of three in Paris is a half pound of fresh meat, three-fifths of a pound of butter, and nine twenty-fifths of a pound of sausage. On this much food the family of three will not starve, but neither will any member of it feel full. Since the breakup of the excellently organized black market, substitute arrangements have come into being and with them have come hijacking, robberies, connivances, and Chicagoesque gangs drawn from the Mauvais Maquis, which was composed of thugs who had nothing to do with the original Maquis (the Communist Maquis Rouge) or the subsequent non-political Maquis Blanc and who have done the properly sacred Maquis legend harm. It is nothing now for helpless officials to announce that en route from Normandy to Paris two tons of butter have melted from a six-ton truckload. For that matter, whole trainloads of food have been reported lost, including the locomotive.

The first of the two major attacks by the Consultative Assembly on de Gaulle's Cabinet to date was made by slightly hungry Deputies, who asked questions about supplies. Last year, under the Nazis, the Deputies pointed out, there were turkeys for those who could pay a thousand francs for them. This year there were only bombed bridges, too few freight cars, and blasted railroad tracks. The Germans departed on and with two-thirds of the country's railway equipment and two-thirds of the country's trucks. This year, too, on the war maps, there is a great food-producing slice of France which even the Deputies may have forgotten about, since it is never mentioned and is still controlled by the Germans—from the lamb-grazing pasture lands above Bordeaux up into southern Brittany, secondary butter-and-egg basket of the country. Anyway, even if there were quantities of food in Paris, there would be nearly no fuel with which to cook it. The coal is in the north. There can be no transportation without coal and no coal without transportation. Two months of continuous rain have so swollen the rivers and canals that coal barges are tied up to the banks. Because of the lack of coal, there is no electric power for the city's factories, so they remain closed and the men have no work to do. But if they were open, who would fill all the jobs? Eight hundred thousand of the most skilled French factory workers are still labor slaves in Germany, working against the Allies. Because of the lack of electricity, a dozen of the Métro stations have been closed in an effort to force people to walk and reduce the number of passengers. The government has just announced that no public buildings will be heated before January 1st. The Academicians, old and wise men, have just announced that they will not hold their end-of-the-year annual meeting until some nice day next spring.

Then, because of the coal shortage, there is a gas shortage. Gas for cooking is rationed to an hour and a half for luncheon—it is on between noon and one-thirty—and an hour for supper, between seven and eight. There is no gas to heat the breakfast coffee of burned barley. Parisians rich enough to buy sawdust by the ton, and black-market gasoline for trucks to deliver it, can store a winter's supply of several tons of sawdust in half of an apartment and keep the other half warm with special sawdust-burning stoves. With equally special low-current electrical attachments, the newly invented stone-lined stoves here can be heated during the night, after which the hot stones give warmth most of the next day. But these attachments are no longer available. For nearly everybody in Paris, the only available commodity is the cold. Except for the first winter after the defeat, this is the most uncomfortable winter of the war. Nevertheless, to the freed Parisians, dining in their overcoats on a meagre soup of carrots and turnips, the only obtainable vegetables, Paris seems like home for the first time since the Christmas before the war.

The second attack by the Consultative Assembly on the de Gaulle Cabinet was on the question of *Epuration,* as the cleaning up of the collaborationists is called. The appetite of many people in France for justice, too, is unsatisfied. Certainly there are families to whom the word "justice" will lose all meaning, except to serve as a mocking epitaph for the tombs of sons, husbands, and even daughters and wives—provided their bodies could be found to be buried—unless some traitor's life is taken (legally and quickly, by a firing squad) in payment for each patriot's life (taken slowly, behind locked doors and in agony). During the early, idealistic, inexperienced days of the resistance, a member of a group was trusted never to betray his comrades, who therefore did not disband and disperse if he was caught. Statistics later proved that the average member could not resist the Nazi tortures more than twelve hours, which was all, finally, that his comrades asked of him, the half day being sufficient for them to hide. *Le Franc-Tireur,* the resistance paper that has remained most faithful to the memory of the dead, has just candidly demanded a thousand heads and five thousand arrests to wipe out the old score. On the other hand, eloquent, calm pleas against repeating what in France's Revolutionary days was called *Le Terreur* have been made, usually by good citizens not in mourning. There sometimes seem to be few who are not. In two families your correspondent knew well, an only son, in each instance a Sorbonne student, was killed in the street fighting on the Place St.-Michel during the liberation of Paris. A fashion editor's daughter, a delicate, blond figure in the early intellectual resistance, lived through a year's solitary confinement in a cell in the Santé Prison and today is a slave factory worker in Germany. A French Catholic poet, great-nephew of a cardinal and betrothed when the war broke out to an American Jewish girl, officially declared himself an *Enjuivé,* or Semitic sympathizer, then lived in hiding for four years without ration cards. He is now an eighty-five-pound skeleton. The son of an anti-Nazi refugee German woman intellectual, who aided the son to flee to England and the R.A.F., became a parachutist and made jumps in France to obtain information for the British about the resistance. Just before the Nazis left Paris, they captured him in the suburbs, and before taking him off, they tortured him, mutilating his hands. Behind the cushions of a French police car into which the Germans put him after the torture, he left a blood-stained note addressed to his mother. She does not know who mailed it to her. One of the best-known women journalists of Paris, who refused to be party to the collaboration of her old paper, *Le Matin,* is crippled by rheumatic fever from having lived for years, without a job, in an unheated house. A Jewish singing teacher developed such severe chilblains on her hands in the Jewish concentration camp at Drancy that they turned black. They are still too swollen for her to play scales for her pupils. A White Russian, sister of a famous painter, became a seamstress, a Communist, and a sufferer from tuberculosis in the course of the war. A composer of modern music who had been aiding the resistance was deported, after being arrested by the Gestapo at a house where he had called by mistake and where the Germans were seeking a man he did not know and who had already fled. In the Rue Jacob, where a printer was seized, to be shot, for setting type for an underground resistance paper, Gestapo agents discovered a wedding list left in the shop by a matron who had ordered invitations for her daughter's marriage; all the people on the list were arrested. One American woman, in her château near Chartres, had to quarter the officers of the local German command in her downstairs rooms for two months while she hid five men of the Maquis on an upper floor; the two groups never met, but her hair began to turn white. One music-loving New Yorker with a small country cottage not far from Paris hid and fed, by her own labors on her patch of land, one singer and one church organist wanted by the Gestapo for helping the Maquis, one French poet wanted by the Paris police, and one Polish deserter from a German artillery regiment camped on a farm above her little valley. In the past week, three friends from the old days have written your correspondent letters on black-edged stationery but have not said what their loss is.

French politics, unfortunately, will have to start up again soon. Local elections for the Municipal and General Councils will be held in February, the first balloting since the liberation and the first in the country's history in which women will cast their vote. To make it easier for them, they are being registered as they pick up their December food-ration cards. They will outvote the males of France by four million. Two and a half million Frenchmen are, of course, disfranchized, being still sealed inside Germany. So far, General de Gaulle has no political party; instead, he has popularity. What program he has is social; his slogan is *"Rénovation,"* which means reforming France out of the nineteenth century into the twentieth. Even people who are against him believe that he has been the savior of France. The grand old political parties have not yet raised their heads or voices to say what they think of *rénovation*. Nobody in France any longer has the courage to describe himself as a conservative and at the other end of the line there is also lacking a party of revolution. The Communists are now, realistically, the party for construction. The Communists, who were the great heroes of the resistance, are also, as the result of their excellently organized underground years, the best-organized party in France. They have just accepted affiliation with the weakened Socialist group, as a healthy man might take on an invalid wife. French Communism seems to be something very different from what it was in the old international days, since now it is avowedly pro-French. On the extreme right is what remains of the rich owner class, who seem readier than they were during the Front Populaire for a sort of belated New Deal. This they describe as Saint-Simonisme, which calls for a Christian, responsible élite, with precepts laid down by the French social philosopher of more than a century ago, Claude-Henri Saint-Simon.

There has been a great national deviation from morality as the result of the French people's contact with the Nazi doctrines and of the French people's unhappy, defeated, introverted contact with itself. The materialism of the nineteenth century, the *enrichissez-vous* of the Bourbon revival, the formal corruption of the kings named Louis all established habits which the Third Republic inherited and which now only silent anti-democratic French imbeciles can suppose began with the Third Republic's first ballot. Citizens who vote have to have political parties to vote for, but what France needs most, now that she clearly has a leader without a past, is not the salvation offered by any one political party but a revival of morality, to be practiced alike by the governing and the governed.

1945

January 1

The most appropriate decoration on the rare Parisian Christmas tree this year was ribboned tinfoil, which American bombers cast into the suburban air when towns like Le Pecq, Achères, and Poissy were being softened up for the liberation of Paris. These fragments, intended merely to interfere with German radio-detection devices, were salvaged by trinket-hungry French children and ended up as décor for the wartime holiday whose slogan was still "Peace on earth."

Charity drives are now under way to help the many thousands of French who have lost only their homes and not their lives and whose dwellings are now debris-filled cellars in Le Havre, Dieppe, Caen, Rouen, and other towns where, without the added melodrama of enemy sadism, the victorious push of the Allies was enough to bring ruin. The drives are for food, but there is little for anyone to give, and for clean old clothes, of which there seems to be none. A motion has been made in the Consultative Assembly to set up a Ministry of Victims of the War. A Ministry of Prisoners, Deportees, and Refugees already exists. Under its sponsorship was celebrated, in the days between Christmas and New Year's, *La Semaine de l'Absent,* in honor of that twentieth of France's population which is still prisoner, one way or another, in Germany. The posters for the absent ones bore nothing but de Gaulle's Lorraine Cross, made of twisted barbed wire. These are the images, these are the texts, these are the greetings from life which took the place of 1944 Christmas cards in Paris.

January 17

Liberated Paris is now occupied by snow. Parisians are colder than they have been any other winter of the war. They are hungrier than they have been any other winter of the war. They are the hungriest they have been since the Prussian siege of Paris, when their grandparents ate mice. Because there is still a lack of coal to transport anything, even coal, the citizenry is still waiting, muffled to its ears, for its single sack per person due last August. Electricity has just been ordered turned off all over France from morning till evening, except for an hour at noon, perhaps for the women in dark kitchens to see what little they are cooking. For fear that the plumbing will burst, the water is turned off in many Paris apartment houses and office buildings except between noon and two o'clock, too late to do most people any good. Passenger trains pulled by steam engines have been suppressed. Only trains pulled by Diesel engines or electricity will now operate. People who must travel a distance of more than a hundred kilometres must get a permit, which will probably take them more time than if they walked.

Owing to the paper shortage, announced by a paper trust which was able to find enough for the Nazis during the occupation, Parisian newspapers, which were already limited to one sheet, are now down to a half-size sheet. There is even a shortage of salt. Lacking salt, whatever Normandy butter could be stored is turning rancid. Lacking salt, Breton peasants don't kill their pigs, which makes for a lack of *charcuterie,* the secondary meat ration in France. Lacking everything but rain in the autumn, Ile-de-France farmers were unable to pull their sugar beets out of the mud, so that there is a shortage of sugar and there may soon be a shortage of cows, because to feed a French cow on beet root now costs a hundred francs a day, which used to be the price of dinner at the Ritz. Because of the beet-root shortage, many a French cow will not live to see the pleasant spring or her pretty calf. As one butcher gloomily declared, it will be not slaughter but a double assassination. Owing to the grain shortage and the fact that under the Germans the French were eating in their bread some of what their horses usually ate in the manger, many an old French horse will not be allowed to last out the winter, either. However, owing to the gasoline shortage, even last month's ration of horse meat has not yet been brought to town.

Milk is now available only to what the ration books classify as "J-1," which means *"Jeunesse Première,"* or babies of from one to three, who are also in line this month for their one annual dried banana, if it arrives. January also entitles "J-2" (children of from four to fourteen) and "J-3" (adolescents up to twenty-one) to four eggs apiece, which their parents, if they can afford it, will probably buy on the black market at thirty francs each. Clinics, filled with pneumonia victims from otherwise charming homes, lack drugs and heat. The nurses lack thermometers, the surgeons lack light to operate, the dentists, lacking electricity, for once cannot drill. There is no plaster-of-Paris in the hospitals to set the record number of bones that are being broken because of falls on icy streets. Otherwise, French doctors say, people's bones are almost too soft to break, because of decalcification due to undernourishment in general and especially to the lack of fish, which the Nazis forbade the Bretons to fish for in the pre-invasion Channel waters. The invasion is over, but there is still no fish in Paris. There is nothing of lots of things which could be called normal, even in war.

Little is left even of some of the more orderly high hopes which fluttered in French hearts as the French flags fluttered overhead on the day of liberation. Paris is free, and no one forgets it for a minute, since nothing much else has happened to remember. Because the person of General de Gaulle is still sacrosanct, the editorials do not criticize him, but every day they carp at his provisional government as if he had nothing to do with it, which is beginning to seem to be the case. His Assembly is one of the strangest on earth today, since it contains, among others, representatives of four political groups named after four Left Wing newspapers. Each of these groups has six delegates and represents the editorial faith of one of the four powerful anti-Pétain, pro-patriot underground papers of the occupation—*La Libération du Nord, La Libération du Sud, Le Franc-Tireur,* and *Combat.* It is as if New York had a couple of Leftist congressmen whose party was called *PM,* or as if the isolationist senator from Illinois had had to drop the Republican tag and come right out and say that he belonged to the Chicago *Tribune.* The Assembly also contains a hundred and five other patriot delegates who could but do not unify themselves into a majority—two groups called Those of the Resistance and Those of the Liberation (the leading ex-underground groups, now organized to the extent of even having offices and telephone numbers), as well as the Socialist resistance group of twenty-one delegates, now, as before the war, the largest single party; the Communist Resisters; and, for the first time, a labor-union group, the Confédération Générale de Travail, which is the French C.I.O. Alone of the old domineering, inefficient, middle-of-the-road pre-Munich parties, the Radical Socialists have squeezed themselves into the picture by officially declaring that their prewar party policy was "one of dastardliness and desertion." The drollest fact about the de Gaulle political scene is that it is the arch-conservatives like Louis Marin, of the old Fédération Républicaine, who have now gone underground, like yesterday's revolutionaries.

Newspapers, no matter what their size, have never before been so highly regarded in France as they are today. In clandestinity, news was dangerous and rare and precious, and Parisians still don't have enough of it. The most remarkable new journalistic figure in France is Albert Camus, an editorial writer on *Combat.* He was born in Belcourt, a modest suburb of Algiers, thirty-one years ago. He majored in philosophy at the University of Algiers and became a neo-Sophist whose wisdom consisted of thinking that life was ridiculous. In this mood he wrote some not very wise poems and an interesting novel called "L'Etranger," which revealed a Hemingway influence in style but not in substance, since the point of the book was that the hero did not know anything about himself. Camus wrote a play, "Le Malentendu," which was produced in Paris under the Germans last spring and featured a man who so misunderstands himself that he commits a meaningless murder. Everything Camus writes today in *Combat* is incised with meaning. An ill young man (he is tubercular), he watches the available fragments of French news with the extra attention of the invalid, too intelligent and objective to presume that he will ever get the full story.

Of all the revolutions in the professions, whose reforms the resistance had hoped would become part of a changed, cleansed republic after the liberation, the journalists' revolution is the only one which seems to have succeeded, perhaps because, being active, intrepid, and young, they established their setup before anyone, in the early excitement of freedom, had time to think twice and stop them. They gained their two major objectives—the right, as journalist patriots without printing plants, to take over the printing plants of the nonpatriot Paris press, whose owners had fled when the liberation came; and the right, as a new, thinking political nucleus, to become delegates to the Assembly in that new, free France for which they had resisted and bled. Since freedom arrived, they are the only examples here of someone's having reached for the moon and got it. So the new Republic has started off with something the old did not have—the most intelligent, courageous, and, *grâce à Dieu,* amateur press which venal, literate France has ever known. The new press of Paris alone lives up to the resistance slogan, "*Les Durs.*" It is indeed hard, and pure.

A new crime has just been created, by ordinance. It is called *l'indignité nationale* and it certainly covers a multitude of collaborationist sins. Roughly, to have committed national indignity, a Frenchman need only have belonged to "that government in authority"—and recognized by Washington—between June, 1940, and the provisional government of today; or have sung songs, spoken poetry, or even helped organize the former government's many artistic galas. The punishment for anyone found guilty of national indignity is equally comprehensive and is called *dégradation nationale.* National degradation will consist of being deprived of nearly everything the French consider nice—such as the right to wear decorations; the right to be a lawyer, notary, public-school teacher, judge, or even a witness; the right to run a publishing, radio, or motion-picture company; and, above all, the right to be a director in an insurance company or bank. As time goes on, fewer collaborationists are going to be shot and more of them, in their national degradation, will be looking for jobs.

February 21

The brightest news here is the infinite resilience of the French as human beings. Parisians are politer and more patient in their troubles than they were in their prosperity. Though they have no soap that lathers, both men and women smell civilized when you encounter them in the Métro, which everybody rides in, there being no buses or taxis. Everything here is a substitute for something else. The women who are not neat, thin, and frayed look neat, thin, and chic clattering along in their platform shoes of wood—substitute for shoe leather—which sound like horses' hoofs. Their broad-shouldered, slightly shabby coats of sheepskin—substitute for wool cloth, which the Nazis preferred for themselves—were bought on the black market three winters ago. The Paris midinettes, for whom, because of their changeless gaiety, there is really no substitute on earth, and who are what our seventy-two-hour-leave soldiers are out to catch or be caught by, still wear their home-made, fantastically high, upholstered Charles X turbans. Men's trousers are shabby, since they are not something which can be run up at home. The young intellectuals of both sexes go about in ski clothes. This is what the resistance wore when it was fighting and freezing outdoors in the *maquis,* and it has set the Sorbonne undergraduate style. Nothing is left of the proletariat male and female Zazous (opposite numbers to our zoot-suiters), who had their own special resistance sartorial getup—nothing, that is, except the long, crook-handled umbrella which all French women now carry, rain or shine. That was only a part of the strange chic of the female Zazous, along with no hat, an artful, absolutely terrific pompadour, a strict, tailored suit with a full skirt for bicycling, and, hanging from the neck, the inevitable cross. It was not a de Gaulle Lorraine cross; it was a Christian cross. Second-hand shops are now full of them and nobody can explain what they signified. Male Zazous were like the long-coated zoot-suiters except for their pantaloons, which were skintight; no one can explain that either.

The more serious normalities of traditional Paris life go on, in readjusted form. Candy shops display invitations to come in and register for your sugar almonds, the conventional sweet for French baptisms, but you must have a doctor's certificate swearing that you and your wife are really expecting. Giddy young wedding parties that can afford the price pack off to the wedding luncheon two by two in *vélo-taxis,* bicycle-barouches which are hired for hundreds of francs an hour. The other evening your correspondent saw a more modest bridal couple starting off on their life journey together in the Métro. They stood apart from everyone else on the Odéon platform, the groom in his rented *smoking* and with a boutonnière, the bride all in white—that is, a white raincoat, white rubber boots, white sweater and skirt, white turban, and a large, old-fashioned white nosegay. They were holding hands. American soldiers across the tracks shouted good wishes to them.

The year's first French literary prize has just been awarded and been tossed back into the donors' ladylike faces. It is the Prix Fémina-

Vie Heureuse, or the Fémina Happy Life Prize, unquestionably, despite its faded title, second in importance only to the Prix Goncourt, and it was given to the writers of twenty-one clandestine booklets published by the Editions de Minuit during the occupation. Good writing was one thing the intellectual resistance did succeed at. However, the midnight-edition writers, or such of them as are available, have not only scorned the happy-life prize but have insulted the jurors to boot. In a round-robin letter they accuse the prize-givers of never having "busied themselves to combat the invader or his accomplices. It is derisory for them to give an award of this sort to writers who were and are still fixed on the sublime goal of the Rights of Man and of whom some—let us not forget them—were killed or deported by the Germans." The letter was signed by, among others, Elsa Triolet, François Mauriac, Claude Aveline, Jean Guehenno, Louis Aragon, Jean Cassou, Claude Morgan, Paul Eluard, and Vercors. One major character who did not sign was M. Alaud, the little Place d'Italie printer who risked his life to print their works. His regular commercial specialty was printing black-edged funeral notices, and he was never suspected of also printing for the lyric heroes of death. The midnight-edition group is genealogically the descendant of Dada and then of Surrealism.

In the resistance's best writing, patriotism and talent together attained heights which are an important part of the new literary horizon of France. All the members wrote fiercely, with a finesse sharpened by danger and despair, all celebrated what they called *"l'époque des prisons,"* and all signed false names. The two who burned brightest in those dark years were Aragon, who signed himself François la Colère, and Paul Eluard, who wrote under many names or none at all. By the exciting extensions of his imagination, in "Le Musée Grévin," a poetical chamber of horrors in which the waxen figure of the Vichy Marshal (*"cette vieille terreur aux traits de macaron"*) appears, and in "Les Yeux d'Elsa," a group of poems addressed to his wife, Elsa Triolet, Aragon broke new ground for his rhymed anger and tenderness. Eluard's most celebrated creation is his poem "Liberté," written in 1942, which was secretly circulated through imprisoned Europe as a clandestine classic. As a dolorous feat, the "Trente-trois Sonnets Composés au Secret," by Jean Cassou, who called himself Jean Noir, remains unique. He composed them while in prison, where, since writing materials were forbidden, he was forced to incise them in his memory. Cassou was an unremarkable literary figure before the war; prison unlocked his talent. Under the nom de plume of Forez, even Academician François Mauriac contributed some stirring lines on the state of the French nation's soul. Elsa Triolet's popular novel "Le Cheval Blanc," one of the few works not on the Germans' Otto list, or proscription index—nobody knows who Otto was—established her as the leading new talented writer among French women.

Malraux avoided Otto by publishing his last volume, "La Lutte avec l'Ange," in Switzerland. The most popular freak piece of fiction and the most contentious, since its hero is a Siegfriedian German of the type the French saw few of, still remains "Le Silence de la Mer," a hymn signed by Vercors, the resistance name of Jean Bruller, publisher of the Midnight Editions. Before the war he published *cahiers* of his own unimportant drawings and he is now preparing another one. He wishes to be known as an artist rather than a writer, although he is a better writer. He was such an excellent resistance publisher that his twenty-one booklets, clandestine though they had to be, were elegantly printed on vellum paper, in numbered, limited, subscribed editions. Each booklet, which originally sold for twenty-one hundred francs, is now worth up to fifty thousand to collectors. A faithful reprint edition of all twenty-one booklets, on the same paper and at the original price, is now being published. Each volume bears, as a headpiece, the phrase "Printed by Alaud, clandestine printer." Each ends with a tailpiece which says, like a memo to history, "This volume achieved publication under the Nazi oppressor."

March 7

Paris, for the first time since the liberation, seemed herself again the morning after de Gaulle's recent speech to his Consultative Assembly. For the first time the Paris newspapers were in full critical cry. The brilliant clamor of the dissenting editorial opinions was a treat. It was like listening to the intelligent, uproarious voices of dear old friends and dear old enemies. To enable the journals to give full attention to the General's long-awaited speech, they were allowed, also for the first time, an extra ration of paper, so that they could print four pages instead of the usual two. The august mutism of the General had up to then constrained the French press and people to a polite taciturnity of their own; being mere citizenry, they were waiting for the oracle to speak up first. If the volubility which has followed the speech continues, Paris will seem gustier, more nearly normal, and closer to reality than it was. After any significant parliamentary debate in the days before the war, the friends and enemies in the press were always against each other and for somebody. In their reaction to the de Gaulle speech, the editors were still not for each other, but they were unanimous in being against de Gaulle. They were at odds only in their reasons.

The tipoff to the General as to what at least two papers expected of him was given the morning before his speech by the Communist *Humanité* and the Socialist *Populaire* in a jointly written three-quarter-page *mot d'ordre* which demanded, in large type, the old, familiar resistance program—immediate nationalization of big banks, later nationalization of natural resources, key industries, and transport and insurance companies, and the confiscation of all traitors' earthly goods, "not as vengeance but as a moral exigence." Inevitably, neither was satisfied with what the General offered, though it sounded revolutionary. *L'Humanité* sniffed at nationalizations in which the de Gaullist state would hold fifty-one per cent of a company's stock but the old directors could continue to own a forty-nine-per-cent interest. As for traitors' fortunes, *L'Humanité* declared itself "profoundly ulcerated" to see that the two hundred families of the Banque de France appeared to be above the law. It also said that if state ownership was Communism, then Louis XI was a Communist, because he founded the French post office. The Socialist *Populaire* declaimed against the collaborationist bourgeoisie which had saved its investments but lost its honor.

Combat, perhaps the most intelligent of the resistance papers in its criticism of the General, said it had been "filled with fears and reservations as to what he might say, though by his words he encouraged our dearest hopes. When he ends words and starts acts, he will obtain the gratitude of the entire country." De Gaulle's speech was received coldly and almost without applause by all the resistance, trades-union, and Leftist benches.

If this had been the General's opening speech to his nation, it would have been historic. In its elegant, démodé vocabulary, which stiffened his ideas into classic stateliness, his address would have been perfectly suited to the Académie. The grand type of French he spoke and thought in put him two hundred years away from his listeners on the radio. In his formal phraseology, he impatiently deplored the lack of good brains for big tasks. He quoted Shakespeare. He spoke of the "twelve million handsome babies" which France must have in the next ten years, "for if the French people do not multiply, France will be nothing but a great light which is extinguished." He spoke of never having lulled France with illusions, spoke of the wisdom of seeing large and looking high, of his attempt to measure his own words, and of his desire that others should measure theirs. It was a splendid speech—to read afterward. When spoken in the Assembly, it pleased neither reformers nor conservatives, both of whom wish, for very different reasons, that he would stop talking and start doing, so that at least one side can know where it stands with him.

Never, perhaps, has the French journalist written with a greater sense of responsibility than he has in his criticism of de Gaulle. The magnitude of the General's legend, his intellectuality, and his integrity seem precisely what has broken many editorial hopes and hearts.

The great disappointment to the man in the street and the woman in the kitchen was that de Gaulle did not say a word in his speech about butter. The last time the French around here had butter was Christmas Eve. The food situation is frightful. Parisians are already talking about "going down into the streets," which is their phrase for rioting, and they might really do it if they had enough physical and mental energy. The four years of Nazi occupation produced a general torpor. This torpor has plainly affected the Food Ministry, which has just promised more meat next July. Parisians can now recite by heart the number of bombed bridges still unrepaired and the number of trains and trucks being used to feed the armies at the battlefronts. The statistics they would like some news on are the twenty-five thousand tons of black-market butter and the ten million francs of black-market profit that changed hands in the past six months; they would like to hear why the bombed bridges hold up legal comestibles while the black-market trucks cross the rivers as if by miracles. The French realize that the black-market butter, even if diverted to legal channels, would not spread one slice of bread per citizen per day, but what they want, and quickly, is some symbolic act of justice, invention, efficacy, and administrative gumption.

Butter has taken on political qualities. By New Year's Day certain butterless French were already muttering that they had had more food when the country was occupied by the Germans than they had had under the Allies. This slur was attributed to the ten thousand Fifth Columnists that were rumored to have been filtered back into Paris by the Germans. It is now rather generally admitted that the French have less of everything under the Allies, that the little France has she manages badly, and that there are forty thousand Fifth Columnists in Paris. Friction between the Americans and the French has been steadily mounting. The worst of it is that there is always a great deal of truth in every unpleasant claim made by either side. And it is no lie that the occupiers of a country are never popular, either those who want to stay forever or those who are dying to get back home. Good Americans here criticize those French who think their country can remain great no matter how picayunely they find it convenient to act. Good Frenchmen criticize those American Army officers who knowingly frequent the same fashionable salons the Germans frequented. One of the reasons for supposing that the war will soon be over is that all three of us old Allies have been getting along together as badly as we usually do in peace.

Two extremely curious plays that ran under the baffled Nazis have persisted into the liberation. The weightier of the pair is the Atelier Theatre's "Antigone," once by Sophocles, now put into modern dress and modern psychology by Jean Anouilh, a well-known dramatist. It is extraordinary that the Germans, with their power complex, should have permitted the presentation of this power classic which for two thousand years has been proving that individual rebellion is a good idea. The fillip of anachronism which modern dress and mode always give to the classics is especially thought-provoking in "Antigone." The two best scenes in the Anouilh version would astonish Sophocles; they feature fascinating conversations between Œdipus's daughter and a police detective. The second, far more original occupation piece is "Huis Clos," now about to reopen at the Vieux-Colombier. The title is a legal term meaning "behind closed doors;" the author is Jean-Paul Sartre, now in America. Sartre is certainly the most creative stylist to emerge during the occupation. His astonishing play is set in Hell, which in this case is a cheap hotel room. One of this hell's special tortures is a lack of mirrors for two women, the unhappier of whom is a throwback to Sappho. The general torment is that each damned soul depends on the others for proof of his or her eternal infernal individuality. Sartre is a member of the Café de Flore literary group, which has replaced the Deux Magots as the Left Bank intelligentsia center.

The Flore is the only café which looks like, though it does not taste like, old times: male and female intellectuals, jargon, no fresh air. And now no alcohol. In Montmartre, a place called the Chansonnier Dix Heures is nightly packed with appreciators of its political ballad singers, who spare nobody. One night when your correspondent was there, a song entitled "The Stars and Stripes," which jeers at the American overfeeding of German prisoners, and an impiety called "Hallelujah, the Pope Is a Republican," referring to the Vatican's recent liberalisms, gave the greatest joy. You need a strong head and legs to stay up late in Montmartre now, for you have to walk home after the last Métro, which stops running at eleven-fifteen.

The most dramatic announcement this week in Paris was that Marshal Pétain's properties have just been seized by what used to be his state.

March 30

Hannibal's crossing of the Alps with elephants is the only military transportation miracle which, to historical-minded Parisians, seems comparable, in its exciting strangeness, to our Allied amphibicaerial feat of crossing the Rhine with glider scows in the sky and ocean boats assembled on the land beneath. *Le Canard Enchaîné,* the cafés' favorite satiric gazette, rushed into print with a cartoon showing a goggle-eyed Rhineland grasshopper—*"les sauterelles"* was occupied-Paris slang for the Nazis who laid waste the French land—peering in terror at the parachute-filled spring clouds and exclaiming, *"Tiens!* It's raining men!" In keeping with the extravagance of the good news, the paper-starved Paris newspapers began spreading themselves onto two tabloid-size sheets instead of the standard one tabloid-size sheet, or onto a single, old-style big page, or they added a picture section showing Nazi prisoners, hands held high, springing through the concrete dragon teeth of their invincible Siegfried Line. The Paris journals acted as though they were drunk on ink; no two headlines agreed on what town the Allied troops were closest to. It was as if the editors had shut their eyes and confidently pinned a tail on the donkey—Cassel, Münster, Nuremberg, Danzig, Vienna—*qu'importe?* To Paris, the prodigy of Allied speed—part victory, part gasoline—was breathtaking.

The German radio, once an occupied necessity, is now a joy to Parisians. Until recently, the Cologne, Stuttgart, and Vienna stations were the three biggest the Nazis operated. After the Americans had taken Cologne and the Russians had closed in on Vienna, those two stations were combined, and if you dialled one you got either—meaning neither, geographically, since doubtless the new transmitter was in heaven knows what sheltered area. Thus, on the Tuesday Cologne fell, the Cologne station was still emitting soothing German waltzes. Last week, during which the Allies advertised that they had dropped eighty thousand tons of bombs on dilapidated Germany, the *Köln-Wien* station intermittently informed whatever German listeners were still able to hear it over the deathly uproar that "there are only weak enemy fighter groups over the Reich." However, after the Allies crossed the Rhine in their Noah's Ark flotilla of so-called buffalo, alligator, and duck boats, the German radio moved rapidly from alarm to self-pity to treachery against the *Partei*. One weekend commentator moaned, "Somebody has failed at his duty. The fact that so many depots of oil, food supplies, and munitions fall intact into the enemy's hands proves it." The most treacherous statement, for which a month ago the Germans not only would have cut the commentator off the air but would have cut his voice from his shoulders, was what purported to be a quotation from the *Völkischer Beobachter,* Hitler's and the Nazi Party's own newspaper. It went as follows: "It has become very difficult to feel like a National Socialist and to profess that one is one. We have no illusions about this." From disillusion to democracy will doubtless take no more time than will be required for the *Völkischer Beobachter* editor to turn his coat.

April 19

The death of President Roosevelt caused a more personal grief among the French than the deaths of their own recent great men. On the demise of both old Clemenceau and Marshal Foch, their grief was a nationalistic, patriotic emotion, since these men, the one with his sabre-sharp tongue, the other with his sword, had saved France. The sorrow the French felt at losing Roosevelt seemed like someone's private unhappiness multiplied by millions. Friday morning, when the news was first known here, French men and women approached the groups of Americans in uniform standing on street corners and in public places and, with a mixture of formality and obvious emotion, expressed their sorrow, sometimes in French, sometimes in broken English. On the Rue Scribe, a sergeant in a jeep held up traffic while he received the condolences of two elderly French spinsters. In the Jardin des Tuileries, an American woman was stopped beneath the white-flowering chestnut trees by a French schoolboy who, with trembling voice, spoke for his father, a dead Army officer, to express his father's love for the dead President. At the outdoor flower stalls of the Place de la Madeleine, a patriarchal flower vendor gave a passing and startled paratrooper a free pink tulip, with the statement "Today they will be sending beautiful flowers for your great man. How sad." A café waitress naïvely touched the sublime when she said of his death, *"C'est ennuyeux pour toute l'humanité."*

Since the American system for filling the Presidential chair when it is left vacant by death was unknown to most French citizens, the journals here carried an official explanatory paragraph headed *"Monsieur Truman Sera Président Jusqu'en 1948"* and quoted our Constitution.

The Paris press wrote of F.D.R. with sober magnificence and sincere superlatives. Under the spirited Gallic headline "*Vive Roosevelt!,*" the *Libération-Soir* spoke of "the unjust destiny and yet the ancient grandeur of the event." *Le Monde,* in an editorial entitled *"Après Roosevelt,"* began by saying, "The great voice which directed American political destinies has been silenced, but its echo continues in French souls." In conclusion, it praised "his charm, his beautiful and great words," and said, "Let us weep for this man and hope that his wise and generous conception of the human communities remains like a light to brighten the path for all men of good will." De Gaulle's Minister of Foreign Affairs said, "It is not only appropriate but necessary to express the depth of the sadness of the government and of the French people. Roosevelt was one of the most loved and venerated men in France. He takes with him the tenderness of the French nation."

The increasing malaise, now that Roosevelt must be absent from the peace, and the unexpected return last Saturday of thousands of

French prisoners liberated from Germany, juxtaposed fear and happiness in a mélange that Parisians will probably always remember in recalling that historic weekend. On Saturday, eight thousand French male prisoners were flown back from Germany in American transport planes, which afterward tumultuously circled the city while the men were being unpacked from trucks outside the newly decorated reception center in the Gare d'Orsay. On its walls these weary men saw an astonishing series of modernistic bas-reliefs depicting their welcome return to the freedom of what explanatory signs called *"la liberté d'aimer"* and the liberty to play, to sleep, to work, to eat, to drink, and to breathe freely. Few of the prisoners, in their hasty flight from the German Army and their later flight with the Americans in the skies, had heard our sad news. When they did hear it, one thin, bitter blond Frenchman said, *"Voyez-vous.* We've come home too late."

The next day, the first contingent of women prisoners arrived by train, bringing with them as very nearly their only baggage the proofs, on their faces and their bodies and in their weakly spoken reports, of the atrocities that had been their lot and that of hundreds of thousands of others in the numerous concentration camps our armies are liberating, almost too late. These three hundred women, who came in exchange for German women held in France, were from the prison camp of Ravensbrück, in the marshes midway between Berlin and Stettin. They arrived at the Gare de Lyon at eleven in the morning and were met by a nearly speechless crowd ready with welcoming bouquets of lilacs and other spring flowers, and by General de Gaulle, who wept. As he shook hands with some wretched woman leaning from a window of the train, she suddenly screamed, *"C'est lui!,"* and pointed to her husband, standing nearby, who had not recognized her. There was a general, anguished babble of search, of finding or not finding. There was almost no joy; the emotion penetrated beyond that, to something nearer pain. Too much suffering lay behind this homecoming, and it was the suffering that showed in the women's faces and bodies.

Of the three hundred women whom the Ravensbrück *Kommandant* had selected as being able to put up the best appearance, eleven had died en route. One woman, taken from the train unconscious and placed on a litter, by chance opened her eyes just as de Gaulle's color guard marched past her with the French tricolor. She lifted an emaciated arm, pointed to the flag, and swooned again. Another woman, who still had a strong voice and an air of authority, said she had been a camp nurse. Unable to find her daughter and son-in-law in the crowd, she began shouting "Monique! Pierre!" and crying out that her son and husband had been killed fighting in the resistance and now where were those two who were all she had left? Then she sobbed weakly. One matron, six years ago renowned in Paris for her elegance, had become a bent, dazed, shabby old woman. When her smartly attired brother, who met her, said, like an automaton, "Where is your luggage?," she silently handed him what looked like a dirty black sweater fastened with safety pins around whatever small belongings were rolled inside. In a way, all the women looked alike: their faces were gray-green, with reddish-brown circles around their eyes, which seemed to see but not to take in. They were dressed like scarecrows, in what had been given them at camp, clothes taken from the dead of all nationalities. As the lilacs fell from inert hands, the flowers made a purple carpet on the platform and the perfume of the trampled flowers mixed with the stench of illness and dirt.

May 11

In Paris the war ended the way it began—with marching. It began with the French soldiers marching off to the war and it ended with the French civilians marching around into the peace. A frenzied spirit of enlistment seemed to take hold of the people of Paris the moment peace ceased being a rumor and became a fact, and by the hundreds of thousands they settled into restless ranks and began their parade. They started marching on Tuesday afternoon at three o'clock, just after the voice of General de Gaulle announced the great news over the government's street loudspeaker system, and thousands were still marching at dawn the next morning. The crowds marched in the sunshine and on into the night with the collective, wandering rhythm of masses who are not going anywhere but are feeling something which their marching together expresses. V-E Day here was like an occupation of Paris by Parisians. They streamed out onto their city's avenues and boulevards and took possession of them, filling them from curb to curb. They paved the Champs-Elysées with their moving, serried bodies. Around the Arc de Triomphe the marchers, pouring in from the spokes of the Etoile, solidified into a dangerous, living, sculptural mass which was swayed and pushed by its own weight until the marchers, limping and dishevelled, disengaged themselves to march back down the avenues and boulevards, in the dusty, beautiful spring heat.

The babble and the shuffle of feet drowned out the sound of the stentorian church bells that clanged for peace, and even the cannon firing from the Invalides and from the precincts of the Louvre were audible on the nearby Place de la Concorde only as rumbling explosions, muffled by the closer noise of feet and tongues that were never still. The people in the crowds seemed to draw nourishment from each other, and the strength to go on down one more street, up one more avenue. Except for whatever food they may have brought from home and carried in their pockets, the marching masses lived on air and emotion. Restaurants were closed, apéritifs were scarce, beer was feeble. Peace and spring found the Parisians as badly victualled as they had been during the war and the winter, but now no one thought or cared about being hungry. All anyone cared about was to keep moving, to keep shouting, to keep singing snatches of the "Marseillaise"—"*Le jour de gloire est arrivé . . . marchons, marchons.*"

By midnight, on side streets near the Rond Point, the crowds had thinned enough for long lines of boys and girls, arms high and holding hands, to run, to crack the whip, to curvet and stretch out in antics, like long lines of noctambulistic paper dolls. Youth dominated the day and the night. It was youth that shouted with delight at the occasional skyrockets which cometed through the night sky, and it was youth, earlier in the day, that had screamed with joy at the giant American planes which roared above the tops of the chestnut trees on the Champs-Elysées and flirted deafeningly around the Obelisk. It was young Paris that was on foot and underfoot. It was the new postwar generation, running free and mixed on the streets, celebrating peace with a fine freedom which their parents, young in 1918, had certainly not known. And those Frenchmen, with their old ribbons and medals, who had fought through the last war were the quietest, the least free-moving of the Parisians among the street crowds during this week's peace. As one of these tired, middle-aged French veterans said, "That great world insomnia which is war has come to an end once again."

France and the rest of Europe are tired to death of death, and of destruction. Much of the comfort which should have arrived automatically with the peace has been lost in the news of the German concentration camps, which, arriving near the end of the war, suddenly became the most important news of all its nearly six years of conquests, defeats, campaigns, and final victories. The stench of human wreckage in which the Nazi regime finally sank down to defeat has been the most shocking fact of modern times. Only dreadful natural phenomena like the earthquake in Lisbon in the time of Voltaire or the gases and ashes of Pompeii in the time of Pliny the Younger seem to have so horrified the world. The shooting is over, but the concentration-camp prisoners are now returning, or are being advertised for by families still waiting in vain at railway stations with diminishing hope. In *Le Monde,* under the brief heading "RECHERCHE," an advertisement has just been run that said, "Any persons having known Mmes. Marie-Louise Roure and Adrienne Baumer, deportees at the camp of Ravensbrück, and Louis Baumer, deported from the camp at Compiègne in June, 1944, are begged to furnish their information to Monsieur Remy Roure." The Nazi program of non-military destruction has not been affected by the peace; it is still continuing in the bodies of the camp prisoners now home but still sick or still crazy or still mutilated or still stone-deaf from blows on the head or still malodorous with running sores.

The vigilant resistance newspaper *Le Franc-Tireur* has demanded that returned prisoners who are strong enough be selected to serve as jurymen in the still to come trials of collaborationists, of which the trial of Marshal Pétain, in June, will be the climax. The same paper has also had the disagreeable courage to say what thousands of prisoners' families know is the truth—that the Ministry of Prisoners and Deportees functions, as it has functioned from the start, with inefficiency and confusion. Many prisoners have arrived without being met by officials, or even by their unnotified families, at the railway stations; the Ministry has not provided trucks, or even ambulances, for transportation; and the pitiful thousand francs each prisoner receives as a government gift on returning home is doled out by an office which sportily observes *La semaine anglaise* and so is closed Saturdays to penniless prisoners who for years have lost all count of money, let alone time. Furthermore, the wretched Spanish Republican prisoners who were plucked out of prewar French concentration camps by the Nazis and sent off to Germany are, on their return to La Belle France, being popped back into the same old French camps again.

Some of the best and most highly educated brains of France, after imprisonment in Germany, are now being returned, ripened by isolation, suffering, hope, and misinformation. When a questionnaire was submitted to a select group of such men a few days ago, three trenchant reactions turned up repeatedly: No. 1, since they, the prisoners, had been informed in Germany that France was overrun by famine, anarchy, and civil war, they were relieved to find France merely suffering as usual from political party wrangles at the expense of national unity; No. 2, it was their opinion, formed in prison camp, that fear and lack of faith are what push any nation into self-destructive attitudes, such as Munich and Collaboration; and No. 3, it was their opinion, formed since leaving prison, that the post-liberation Frenchmen are "too inclined to easygoingness, immorality, and selfishness."

None of the Paris newspapers thought of the great and simple headline "VICTORY," which both the Paris *Herald Tribune* and the *Stars & Stripes* used on their front pages on the historic Tuesday, May 8th. Most of the French dailies described Germany rather than the Allies in the favorite headline, which proclaimed, "L'ALLEMAGNE A CAPITULE." General de Gaulle's paper, *Les Nouvelles du Matin,* gave over its front page to a fancy drawing of a female figure symbolic of France, with wings, laurels, Allied flags, and the headline "LA GUERRE EST FINIE." *France-Soir's* headline was a great white "JOUR-V" on a deep black band. The Socialist *Populaire* used as its headline "LE REICH NAZI ABBATU." The Communist *Humanité* had no Tuesday headline at all, since it ignored the victory that day but celebrated it Wednesday, Moscow's V Day, with a seven-tier headline—or more headlines than anyone in Paris had ever seen before—which declared (we translate), "VICTORY! ACCLAIMED ALL DAY YESTERDAY BY THE PEOPLE OF PARIS IN CELEBRATING THE MILITARY TRIUMPH OF THE UNITED NATIONS OVER HITLERISM. IN INNUMERABLE PARADES, IN IMPROVISED MASS MEETINGS, EVERYWHERE WAS DECLARED THE WISH TO CRUSH THE RESIDUE OF HITLERISM. FROM ONE END OF THE LAND TO THE OTHER, BUT ONE UNANIMOUS CRY: PETAIN TO THE GALLOWS! VIVE LA FRANCE! VIVE LA REPUBLIQUE!" The incorrigible *Canard Enchaîné,* Paris's favorite satiric gazette, celebrated the victory by publishing a cartoon of Hitler, dead and gone to heaven, where he starts the New Order by pinning a Jewish star of David on God's chest.

At half-past-ten Monday night, in the Allied Servicemen's Club in the Grand Hotel, an orchestra leader whose men had just finished playing and singing "And the tears flowed like wine" suddenly shouted to the dancers that the war was over, that tomorrow was V Day in Europe. A wild groan of joy went up from the men in uniform. Then they began capering extravagantly, their girls in their arms, to the tune of "Hallelujah." Afterward, tumbling out onto the boulevards, they started spreading the news to all Joes and to anyone French who would listen. But that night it was only the Americans, the optimists from across the Atlantic, who believed the good news about Europe.

Next morning, though, the French papers announced that at 3 p.m. the great news would be officially true. At that hour all Paris was dressed in its not very fine best and standing on its handsome boulevards waiting in the sun for the "Marseillaise" and the pronouncement of its leader de Gaulle. And then his for once impassioned, excited voice proclaimed victory, which had come at last.

Europe's Five and a Half Years' War is all over but the peace.

May 24

Now that not only Paris but all Europe is liberated, it seems reasonable to view Paris as what is left, after another plague of German war, of the city that was once the civilized, intellectual capital of so-called French Europe. Paris is not gay; it is restless, anxious, cantankerous, and probably convalescent. The theatres are packed; the shops and groceries are still empty. Parisians either have money to throw away and little to throw it away on, or they have next to nothing and manage to live on it. There are three classes: first, the formerly comfortable *rentier* class, with incomes that now buy a tenth of what they did; second, the working class, which, with the highest wages in French history, is now striking all over France for increased wages to meet increasing prices (in the northern coal mines, however, where production had fallen off anyway because the miners were on a vegetable diet, the strikes are really to get meat); and third, the inflation-money class, both new rich and old rich, who are part of the financial phenomenon of accruing cheap millions and scarce goods the way floating leaves and logs are part of the phenomenon of a river in flood. Class No. 3 looks, so far, like the class of survivors.

The first new American movie to reach film-famished Paris was "Mrs. Miniver," whose sweetness and light were given a peculiar twist by the fact that the opening night was a gala charity affair to raise money for the sick, sad women returning from the concentration camp of Ravensbrück. The only other big American movie that has been seen since the liberation is Charlie Chaplin's "The Dictator," which Paris, after four years of one, did not find funny. Maurice Chevalier has been packing the midtown ABC, which is again offering, as before the war, picked night-club talent on a music-hall basis. Ciro's has been taken over as a private night club by French officers, who, since the Americans and British have taken over everything else, had to have some place to go. Ciro's has the best entertainment in town, including old, familiar faces like the fabulous Charles Trénet and the fascinating Edith Piaf and her tough songs.

July 26

Certainly it is incorrect to call Marshal Pétain's trial for treason, in the Palais de Justice, one of the greatest trials in history. The trial is turning out to be merely one of the greatest lessons in history, pedagogically speaking, the French people have had since June, 1940. It was then that there began the particular chapter of French history whose details most French citizens are only now learning about, five years later. The lesson is being recited ad lib by expert witnesses like ex-Premiers Paul Reynaud and Edouard Daladier and ex-President Albert Lebrun in the court sessions, and next morning the French newspapers are giving the text to the ignorant citizens. Each sad passage is headlined in a manner that history books perhaps should copy. "Audience Instructed" was one of *Paris-Presse's* opening headlines, followed by a subhead explaining that "the disastrous events of the year '40 are still not fully known except by a small number of initiates." In the same didactic spirit, *La Voix de Paris* ran the headline *"Révélation Sensationelle de Daladier,"* plus a subhead that gave Daladier's government's figures on

France's 1939 air force, and then, in the article that followed, went into the Marshal's previous request for a reduction of armament appropriations, his lack of interest in those military modernities like tanks and anti-tank guns, his peacetime domination of the French Army chiefs, and so on. *Le Monde* featured Reynaud's revelations about those last, complicated, disorderly days of the Republic in Bordeaux, under a subhead saying "Prisoner Pétain's Plot to Seize Power Via an Armistice." Other journals have featured the fact that, in Bordeaux, Pétain had ready in his pocket, like an extra handkerchief, a tentative list of names for his prospective autocratic cabinet. The collaborating policy arranged at the Montoire meeting between Hitler and Pétain also got a big front-page play. Even the Battle of Verdun was slipped into the court lesson and into the reporting of it, together with the little-known fact that, according to General Joffre, its hero was not the pallid, handsome, prisoner Marshal, alive and in his armchair before the jurors, but a minor, now-dead general named Nivelle. And, finally, the French armistice of 1940 hit the front page, after the Marshal's unattractive, sour, stammering, black-robed chief defense advocate, the *bâtonnier* Payen, angrily inquired if anyone present in court so much as knew the armistice terms, and after the charming, smiling Presiding Judge Mongibeaux leaned down from his bench, rather like an elegant host catering to his guest's whims, to ask if perchance there was a copy of the armistice in the house. At that point, the terrifying old Prosecutor of the Republic Mornet, who wants Pétain's head and has said so, leaped up from his box to recite by heart those armistice clauses that gave to the Nazis the right to occupy two-thirds of France. "That's unfair!" the defense screamed. "You've no right to begin with the worst part." "I have a right to begin where I choose and my good memory dictates," the prosecution snarled back. The red and black robes recalled the face cards in the trial scene of "Alice in Wonderland," but in the Paris trial scene there was no gentle humor, no awakening from a dream.

The general outline of French history from 1940 to today, most of the details and anecdotes, and certainly more documentation than has yet been cited in court have long been familiar to all the American journalists who have been sitting on their press bench with pencils idle in the heat and, listening, have refreshed their memories. There are four reasons why the French did not until now know their own facts. In June, 1940, when France was falling, people and newspapers were fleeing Paris, as if to avoid the country's collapsing on them physically. In the confusion, the June events were only fragmentarily or inaccurately known. After Pétain settled firmly into power in Vichy, he was at first too beloved for anyone to tell the truth and later it became too dangerous to tell. At the time of the Riom trial, at which some of the witnesses in today's court were then prisoners, audaciously giving the same news of France's fall (as a means of expressing faith in America), the excellent underground Riom reports were sent out to the United States but had little circulation in France. And after the liberation last summer, when the truth about France's past could have been told, the exalted French were interested only in her future. Anyhow, there was a paper shortage, which would have prevented printing this vast stale news even if anyone had been interested in doing it. Now, during these long, hot hours of Pétain's trial, the old news is datelined afresh; it is as good as, it is worse than, new. The French absorb it hungrily or cynically, as proof of this or as negation of that. It embodies everything that French democracy is now facing.

There are already three important rumors about the way the trial will end, and all are untrue. The first two are that the French penal code forbids the execution of a man over seventy and that the special legal weight of a high court such as the one Pétain is being tried in makes impossible a reprieve of the death sentence. The third false rumor is that General de Gaulle is against the death sentence. Many Parisians say that they would be satisfied if the old man's buttons were cut away—that is, if he suffered military degradation, a punishment perhaps worse than death to him—since they are sick to the depth of their souls of eternally hearing about Le Maréchal.

Under the complicated but fair system by which the French Ministry of Information parcelled out the tickets to the courtroom, which seats only about six hundred, your correspondent's first ticket was for Tuesday, the second day of the trial. The initial visual impression was not of the white-faced Marshal but of the picturesque, scarlet-colored opening of the court that had assembled to try him. This began with the filing in of the five red-robed judges, black velvet hats in hand, and ended with the entrance, loudly announced, of *Monsieur le Procureur Général*. Preceded by a major domo (a sort of kindly, bald court butler in a worn dress suit), Prosecutor Mornet rushed into the room, past the red-robed Bench, and toward his private little pulpit—a torso bent almost horizontal with age, eagerness, and speed, his pointed gray beard and peaked nose leading, his blood-colored robe trailing behind like a sanguine silhouette from a sketchbook of Goya. One's mental impressions of the court accumulated more slowly. To an American, whose judges are supposed to be impartial arbiters, the active, witty, worldly, and openly anti-Pétain comments of handsome Presiding Judge Mongibeaux seemed a strange foreign novelty. It seemed equally odd that once a deputy juror interrupted witness Reynaud to back him up in some statement; that two resistance jurors jumped to their feet to protest angrily against what they called Pétain's *bâtonnier's* insults to their cause; that the same *bâtonnier* accused Reynaud on the stand of calumny, then of "remaking his political virginity"; that both Prime Ministers were allowed to quote what somebody said somebody else had said; that both were allowed to talk by the hour, often of events long before their political time; and, above all, that they were allowed to interpret their own part, their nation's part, the Marshal's part in any event whatever—that they were, indeed, encouraged to stand, with the eyes and ears of the world watching and listening, while they mixed memoirs and politics into their lecture on, and version of, recent French history. It would appear that this peculiar academic treatment, in this particular place and court, was clearly the only procedure by which the final verdict could be reached. As Daladier declared on the stand, with the brutal candor of an *Homme d'Etat* newly sworn for that afternoon to the whole truth, "There is no connection between justice and politics."

During Reynaud's endless testimony that day, he spoke, among a thousand other things, of the fact that the poet Paul Valéry, once Pétain's friend, had delivered the address of welcome when the Marshal was finally received into the French Academy. Tuesday, just before midnight, the body of Valéry, who had died bravely of cancer, was escorted, to the beat of muffled military drums, through dark streets to a flambeaux-lighted outdoor catafalque, where it lay, keeping its own last nocturnal vigil over that great view of Paris between the Trocadéro hill and the Tour Eiffel. Valéry was the greatest living French poet, as Pétain had been the greatest living French Marshal; they were of the same vintage and at one time they had been equally appreciated, each for his special flavor. While in Vichy, Pétain dismissed Valéry from his post in that curious institution of scholarly Paris exiles, the Centre Universitaire Méditerranéen of Nice. De Gaulle later reinstated him. In 1943, the elderly poet joined the clandestine littérateurs of the resistant Comité National des Ecrivains. On that Tuesday night, there were only a handful of us waiting on the curb as, in a sudden red flare of Bengal lights, like an apotheosis, the dead poet was carried from the Church of St.-Honoré-d'Eylau. Two once-great old men of France had just been lost forever, and a period of French history had indeed come to its end.

August 3

It is extraordinary that the treason trial of Marshal Philippe Pétain reached its sixth day in the Palais de Justice before it bumped into a few completely objective facts. Up to then the trial had been coasting along on the airy, wary personal opinions of some of the most famous and least disinterested politicians in France—those who had been running the country during the already culpable nineteen-thirties, before the Marshal took over at Vichy. The little-known, fact-giving witness was General Paul Doyen, who had been the French president of the Wiesbaden Armistice Commission until he was sacked, early in the occupation, by the Vichy crowd for telling them that they not only should but could resist German post-armistice pressure. The important facts, which, the General declared, made "a recitation painful to French ears," featured Germany's unprotested illegal annexation of Alsace-Lorraine, which, though it happened in August, 1940, was still news to Paris in July, 1945. They also included the ensuing Nazi demand for all French war material in North Africa, as feed for Desert Rat Rommel's campaign against Wavell in Tripoli, and the Vichy Government's promise to comply, which General Weygand was able to sabotage by slowdowns. And they detailed the subsequent German demand for the Levant airfields, plus the port of Bizerte, and Vichy's compliance, which by this time no one, either military or civil, could slow down. The climax of General Doyen's declarations was that the Marshal, after kicking out Dauphin Pierre Laval in early December of 1940, "thereafter had at Vichy a free road to defend what could be defended of France" against the Germans, but that "of his own choice he had elected otherwise."

The importance of Doyen's testimony (aside from his revelation that the elegant Marshal, during the first Christmas at Vichy, which was to have been so amical, referred to Laval as "a dung heap") lay in the fact that it was indeed fact, based on the Wiesbaden documents, and that it dealt with the Pétain of the occupation, surely the period in which the charge of treason will have to be localized if it is to be made truly legal. One of the weaknesses of the prosecution up to then had been that its political witnesses had droned on about the prewar anti-republicanism of the Marshal, as if that in itself was a crime during the Third Republic, which unfortunately it was not. The prosecution's other great weakness had been that it had achieved only a single, oblique reference to that historic telegram from President Roosevelt which requested Pétain's aid for our invading Allied troops in North Africa, and to the Marshal's reply that he would resist any invasion, and to his not resisting the Germans when they invaded his unoccupied France a few days later, on November 11, 1942. To the French populace, confused by its old mixed love and hate for the Marshal and addled by the current tarradiddles in court, that November 11th has become Treachery Day just as significantly as July 14th became Independence Day.

One thing the populace has certainly disagreed with the prosecution about is the delay in calling to the stand some of the resistance families that lost men and women in the struggle, tortured or shot by Pétain's militia or sent by them to die more slowly, scarred and starved, in Nazi concentration camps. One such resistance relict presented herself early this week on the sidewalk before the Palais de Justice gate. She was a middle-aged country mother, sweating in her heavy mourning in the afternoon heat. She told the Palais guard that one of her sons had been beaten to death by Vichy legionnaires, that the other had perished in the concentration camp of Nordhausen, and that she wanted to speak to the Marshal. When an American reporter urged the guard to let her enter (so-called "spontaneous witnesses" are admitted to this strange high court), the guard refused, saying, "She might assassinate him. Then his death would be my fault." Later that same afternoon, Colonel Charles Chaudrey, the resistance hero celebrated under the *nom de guerre* of Grégoire, did indeed speak to Pétain in court. Chaudrey pointed an accusing finger at Pétain and cried, "If there remains in him even a little love for France, let him, before he pays with his life, fall to his knees upon her land and ask its pardon!"

* * *

For the American press, the most ticklish moment in the trial came during the reading of the pro-Pétain letter from Admiral Leahy, our former ambassador to Vichy. To this communication, which interrupted one of the many installments of Reynaud's uncomplimentary evidence against the Marshal (the defense had shrewdly cut in with Leahy's praise, to prove Reynaud wrong), the sly little mouse-faced politician came back with a gallant pun. "Ambassadors are polite enough to forget the truth. *C'est la courte mémoire qui fait la courtoisie diplomatique.*" The Parisian press seemed almost bashful about acknowledging the existence of the Leahy note. Both *France-Soir* and *Ce Soir* lied about it politely. The first briefly described it as "a rather reticent letter, which could cut both ways." The second was more thorough, explaining, truthfully enough, that the defense considered that it had had a big stroke of luck in the Leahy document but that all Leahy really had said was that Pétain should have resisted the Germans more, even if France suffered more. Only *Le Monde* actually quoted the Leahy letter intact, but it did so without comment, which its conservative readers could easily make for themselves.

What with the touchiness of Franco-American relations and the French people's angry memory of what they called our State Department's misleading backing of Vichy in the early days, it is just as well that the populace here never reads *Le Monde* and so missed Leahy's choicer paragraphs, translated into lovely French. Example: "*J'avais alors et j'ai maintenant la conviction que votre but principal était le bien et la protection du peuple abandonné de France . . . Avec l'expression de mes sentiments personnels et avec les vœux que votre activité dans la période d'occupation par l'ennemi puisse être évaluée à sa juste valeur par le peuple français, je demeure très sincèrement à vous,* Leahy."

Pétain was in no position to have the best lawyers in the land come running to his help, but his trio of defenders still seems peculiarly, unnecessarily poor, lacking tact, teamwork, grace, and, with one exception, brains. His chief, *bâtonnier* Payen, has a scattered, jerky mind, and an unfortunate tic which makes his mouth pop open and shut like a bullfrog's. Pétain's second man, *maître* Lemaire, raises unimportant legal points in the loud, declamatory voice of the Comédie-Française. The youngest Pétain defender, *maître* Isorni, has brains, but they don't seem at their best at the bar, where his bad habit of continually interrupting everybody seems to distress even his client, as Judge Mongibeaux classically and courteously calls old Pétain. All that can be said for the defense is that no one, at any rate, has yet accused the pro-Pétain trio of having had anything to do with the resistance. Yet all the court's major anti-Pétainist witnesses have had to admit, under cross-examination, that once they were pro-Pétain, in that they trusted what is now constantly called his prestige and authority. As Léon Blum thoughtfully told the court, "There is a Pétain mystery." The judges now trying Pétain for his life once perforce swore allegiance to him as their Unoccupied France chief of state. Even old Prosecutor Mornet had to admit, after first denying the fact with an indignant screech of "Infamy!," that he had accepted an invitation to sit on Pétain's scandalous Riom trial bench, though he later refused to take his seat. And even the two juries, one chosen from the resistance, the other from those rare parliamentarians who in Bordeaux had voted against giving the Republic to the old, autocratic Marshal, even the juries—like those of the French Revolution, out to get heads—are packed and proud of it. So far, the trial has tarnished everyone it has touched. An atmosphere in which all the men seem faintly fallible and all the methods slightly illegal has established itself as the natural air to breathe in the small, stuffed, shoddy courtroom.

Of all the testimony of the big political figures, what Léon Blum had to say against Pétain was the most intellectual, clear (if complex), and unequivocal. All the politicians were asked by the Presiding Judge if they thought Pétain had committed treason and what they thought treason consisted of. Blum's definition was best: "An absence of moral confidence was the base of the Vichy Government, and that is treason. Treason is the act of selling out."

Taking advantage of one of the admirable, odd privileges given to them in this high court, entitling them to insist upon hearing from anyone they chose, the resistance jurors insisted on summoning the newly returned Pierre Laval. Laval's name is a well-known palindrome—as the French say, it reads the same forward and backward, so how can you tell if he's coming or going—and Parisians wagered that Laval, being too dangerous to both the defense and the prosecution, would not be called to talk. He was called, and he talked. He entered the courtroom as if its complete silence were dangerous to him. He carried his gray hat and his worn brown briefcase in his hand, in confusion and in a low voice asked where the witness stand was, and, when he saw that it was only a carved, cane-seated parlor chair, deposited his hat and briefcase on the seat and stood erect. He was at first unrecognizable. The fat of his face is now gone. His oily, Moorish hair is now dry and gray and his mustache is the color of tobacco juice. His crooked, stained teeth make a dark, cavernous background for his large lips. Until he spoke, he was some other man who had been announced as the infamous Pierre Laval. The buxom dandy of other days had turned into an unprosperous stranger, a worn, brown-skinned, worried-looking country fellow, with watchful, inelegant, careful gestures. Above his habitual white string tie, his large, low white collar ruffled around his thin neck, which was hung with loose wattles like those of a brunette turkey cock. His rumpled, gray-and-white-striped suit was so large for his frame that it looked borrowed. The moment he started speaking, the interesting phenomenon ended. His voice, his vocabulary, his alert and vulgar mentation were the same as ever.

For thirty-nine minutes by the clock, Laval talked without a stop and without ever answering Judge Mongibeaux's opening inquiry, "When did your political relations with Marshal Pétain begin?" The only insulting thing Laval said about the Marshal was that Pétain had never known anything about politics. Then, like any successful black-market businessman telling another how he got his start, Laval confided, "Politics has to be learned. It's not something you just catch on to. It has to be studied to be good. You've got to learn it all the way up. Now, me, I began at the bottom and took on every job on the way to the top." He also recited a confidence about the Duke of Windsor, then the Prince of Wales, with whom he must have had, years ago, a curious conversation about the problem of Mussolini and the Abyssinian War. " 'You ask your father about it,' I kept telling the Prince," said Laval. " 'You go ask your father the King and he will tell you.' But the Prince, he kept saying that his father was a king and so wasn't a politician. Pétain was like that. War and Les Invalides were his element." Inflexible, wax-faced, motionless as usual, Marshal Pétain, from his worn black-leather easy chair, watched his former Dauphin's back. The two men did not speak, upon finding themselves together in the same high court. But once, when Laval turned, with the Vichy Dauphin smile, to say something nice about the old man, the Vichy chief of state lifted his white hand in an almost imperceptible contemptuous, familiar gesture of greeting. It was their unofficial *rencontre* at their treason trial.

August 17

The Pétain trial ended the day after the end of that World War in which Vichy had played its paltry part. The B.B.C., in London, erroneously reported riots before the Palais de Justice. Actually, Paris was calm while waiting for the verdict and deeply satisfied when it came. The French people felt that out of the lengthy legal complexities which for twenty-one days had stretched justice almost to the breaking point, out of the parade of overimportant political witnesses and too obscure generals, out of all the documents read aloud and the phrases of praise and vilification that were cited, out of all that issued from the mouths of the old Marshal's defenders and his prosecutor, it was what Marshal Pétain himself had said or written during his period of power at Vichy, and the kind of justice he had established there, that in court condemned him. It is certain that never before has an illustrious and complex old figure on whom so many millions of words have been spent been condemned on so few, and all those his own. In Prosecutor Mornet's *réquisitoire,* on the eighteenth day of the trial, there were a half dozen outstanding determinants against Pétain, among them excerpts from his radio pronunciamentos in the early Vichy days: "All our miseries have come from the Republic. . . . The responsibility for our defeat lies with the democratic political regime of France. . . . A strong state is what we wish to erect upon the ruins of the old, which fell more under the weight of its own errors than under the blows of the enemy. . . . You have only one France, which I incarnate." His letters to Hitler, only recently made known and therefore especially shocking to the public, told even more terribly against him. On the anniversary of his only meeting with the Führer, at Montoire, where Pétain offered the policy of collaboration, he solemnly wrote Hitler, "France preserves the memory of your noble gesture." And after the tragic British failure in the Dieppe Commando raid, he wrote Hitler, "I thank you for having cleansed French soil." Later, under Nazi pressure for greater conformance to the anti-Jewish laws, the Marshal fell so low as to write von Ribbentrop, "In future, all modifications of our laws will be submitted to your approbation." As the prosecution brought out—and this was the only moment during the trial when the Marshal's face looked like a marble mask of shame—a hundred and twenty thousand Jews were thereafter deported from France and only fifteen hundred lived to return.

On the nineteenth day, the defense's supposed trump card was played and came to nothing. The trump card was the theory of the Marshal's *double jeu*—though he had openly cabled President Roosevelt, "I have learned with stupefaction of your troops' aggression in North Africa," he had also telegraphed in code to Admiral Darlan, ordering him to aid us. A letter from General Juin, read in court, proved that the Marshal had indeed belatedly ordered the go-ahead in code but had also cancelled it the same way because he was "in relations with Hitler."

From the very first day of the trial, Pétain's haughty opening declaration that he would not deign to talk and that the special high court lacked legal authority to try him—he who had founded a no less special high court at Riom, where Daladier and Blum had had to talk and talk speedily to save their lives—told against him. The last straw was the Marshal's strange insistence that he, too, had been among "the first of the resistants," for, he asked, had he not held France for de Gaulle to recover, and what recovery could the General have effected for a France in ruins wrought by lack of German collaboration? Among the many ruins of France today are the graves of the Gaullistes whom the old man of Vichy ordered hunted down as rebels. As Blum said on the witness stand at the trial, "I never knew Pétain. *Il y a en lui un mystère*"—a puzzle. The sole great importance of the *procès Pétain,* supposedly one of the greatest trials in history, is that it tore into a half-dozen clear pieces, for those who were willing to look and learn, the legend of the *mystique autour du Maréchal,* that unrepentant old man of unrepublican France.

October 11

There was also something mysterious about the Laval trial held in the same august court: why was it the scene of such a loosing of passions? Judges, juries, lawyers, deputies, prosecution, a youthful visitor or two in the little gallery, and, above all, the accused himself, hemmed in in his narrow aisle on the crowded floor, all shouted as they undoubtedly never had before in public. It was probably sheer hatred of Laval, the physical as well as the symbolic *summum malum* of France's occupation, collaboration, and shame, that loosed the outcries against him. And there was something left in Laval that made him scream back. Physically and mentally, he completely dominated the court both when he was in it—sweating and thinking and swearing—and when he was out of it, when he took his victory with him to his cell and the court dragged on, dull and defeated. He had his judges, prosecutor, and attackers beaten three different ways; he, the single traitor, was more intelligent, wise, and intuitive than all of them rolled together. His superior brain guided even his cheapest gibes. As a former lawyer and Minister of Justice, he knew the law better than the Bench seemed to. As a former deputy, he knew all about the mentality of deputies who made up the vituperative parliamentary jury. As a politician with an amazing memory, he knew the policies he had made and recalled them verbatim while the politically ignorant court scuffled through its reference papers for information. When he started to talk, he was like quicksilver: no one could control him; his phrases, flashy or weighty, rolled in all directions through the court, separating, then coagulating, but always slipping through the fingers.

Throughout Laval's trial, the whole Paris press demanded his death, deplored the scandalous fashion in which it was being led up to, and noted each paradoxical pickle his maneuvers put the court into. The best cartoon on the trial was run in the disrespectful weekly *Le Canard Enchaîné*. It showed two troubled lawyers talking, and the caption was "Do you think he will be able to pull himself out of all this?" "Who?" "Mongibeaux, the judge."

For five full days the French press, from Left to Right, groaned when it thought about what the foreign press bench at the trial was going to say about the affair. Yet the French press was harsher toward its own countrymen than any of the four English-language Paris papers. As angry a French sample as any was one Paris editorial which summed up, "The astuteness of Pierre Laval, that old war horse quick to exploit any situation; the feminine nervousness of a judge inclined to the vapors and attacks of nerves; the senile peevishness of a prosecuting attorney already discredited for his part in those other trials; the unimaginable lack of propriety of the jurors, who have forgotten what the most elementary decency is like—these are the elements of the scandal that is dishonoring our high court. It is enormously painful to speak in these terms of the highest magistrates in France. However, it must be said because it is true."

The pessimists' morning paper, *Combat,* which rejoices in a gloomy view of things, croaked as its contribution, "The Laval trial has the prospect of turning France's stomach. Yesterday's séance was even more odious than the two before. This time it was sordidness and mediocrity at loggerheads in the midst of incoherence. How could it be otherwise when we are watching magistrates who not only cannot control the prisoner but cannot even control themselves? For four years people have dreamed of the Laval trial. We too dreamed of it. Dreamed of settling an account. But we never imagined that Laval's trial could be as comic as it was the day before yesterday, as odious as it was yesterday, and as ridiculous as it will be tomorrow. On our manner of judging Laval, we ourselves are being judged."

There were also moments of wit and sheer fun in the trial, as when Laval coolly replied to the judge, whose question he refused to answer because the judge had already imprudently answered it himself, "As the victim of a judiciary crime, Monsieur le Premier Président, I do not aspire to be also the accomplice." And there was a roar of laughter when the nervous judge, making an elegant attempt at regaining lost authority, requested the sheriff to bring in a string of witnesses and the underling returned with nothing but the explanation "There aren't any witnesses anywhere, Monsieur le Premier Président. Perhaps we forgot to order any." There was also some fretful gaiety over the occasional tardiness of the Resistance jurors in turning up for duty; many of them were busy running for deputy in the forthcoming elections. They were and are literally running—on five new tires, three new inner tubes, and three thousand litres of gasoline allotted by the government to each of the dozen or more contending political parties, while country doctors and priests often have to walk miles to save men's lives and shrive men's souls. There were three women jurors among the Resistants, all of whom were widowed by the Laval-Pétain-Darnand-Maurras militia. The best known of the trio was the Communist Mme. Gabriel-Péri, whose dark beauty was like an allegorical portrait of Grief waiting upon Justice. And it must be noted, finally, that it was the parliamentarians, not the Resistance jurors, who conducted themselves with so experienced a lack of public dignity.

* * *

Late on the third turbulent afternoon of his trial, Laval refused to return to court after some parliamentary jurors had called him foul names and promised him "twelve balls in the skin"—or execution before the dozen rifles of the firing squad—and after the judge, as Laval put it, had submitted him to "outrageous treatment," so the prisoner was forced by legal etiquette to send a formal written declaration, announcing his refusal, by a sheriff, who carried it from the prisoner's cell in the basement of the Palais to the court, upstairs. According to the press, when the note was received by the judge, it bore, legally enough, not only Laval's signature but the sheriff's postscript, "Cost—nine francs." The next morning, Laval was reported by Palais gossip to have said to his guard, "Anyhow, I wager I slept better last night than Mongibeaux." It was this sort of realistic insouciance which drove the high court crazy.

Laval's refusal to return to the court, even to hear his sentence on the fifth day, made it necessary for his defense lawyers to go down to his cell at dusk to announce the fatal news. They arrived beside his cot during one of the shutdowns of electrical current that are a daily occurrence in Paris because of the coal shortage. His cell was lighted by a small flare. When he saw their sad and shadowed faces, he gently said, or so they later declared, "Am I the one who should try to cheer you up?" Twenty-four hours later the Paris papers, no longer querulous, grimly announced that Pierre Laval was installed in one of the death cells in the suburban prison of Fresnes. He was already dressed in a drill suit, his head had been shaved, and he was wearing leg chains.

October 20

To the sound of the groans of long-unused machinery and in a flaky cloud of rust, things are beginning their slow improvement here. But as General de Gaulle recently, and harshly, said, it will take the French people a full twenty-five years—"a whole generation of furious work"—even to resuscitate France. The general opinion is that the gigantic task of the country's complete recuperation cannot conceivably be concluded until around 1975, and that it will probably be 2000 before Europe, whatever it will be like politically then, will have recovered physically from its losses in people and cities, and from its memories of its losses in beauty.

The brightest spot in the Parliamentary pre-election hodgepodge has been an odd party called the Union Monarchiste, whose candidates have consisted of an anomaly listed as a Socialist Monarchist, one female Traditionalist, one plain Monarchist, one plain Royalist, and one Young Royalist. The candidates are not relatives of the Comte de Paris, the only royal pretender family; the candidates are merely little politicians who would like to see monarchy restored in France. The Party's boulevard posters advised French voters to keep their liberties, "like the English, Swedish, Norwegians, Danish, Belgians, and Dutch, all citizens of democratic monarchies," denounced all three French Republics, and ended with an exhortation to "rise against all tyrants!" That is exactly where, a hundred and fifty-three years ago, the First Republic came in.

October 25

Never before in living memory has a bitterly contested French election made a trio of rivals so happy as the Communists, the Socialists, and the new Popular Republicans are right now. One way or another, all of them have just won in France's first national election since before the war. The world waited over the weekend, with unusually flattering attention, to see how France would choose. France chose three things, all different. Madame La Quatrième République is starting out like a woman with three hands, two Left and one Right, the Communists and Socialists being on the side closer to her newly reawakened revolutionary heart and the Popular Republicans on her other, purse-carrying side. The Sunday elections killed the Third Republic, for the people voted enthusiastically to abolish its constitution of 1875. Probably nobody but the meticulous General de Gaulle has even reread the old constitution lately; no newspaper reprinted it for final inspection; and no candidates who were against it ever quoted from it to show what was wrong. The single sad post-election cartoon showed Marianne, symbolic figure of the now late Third Republic, gazing pitifully at the baskets of votes against her that were being brought to her deathbed, from which she wailed, "And not one love letter in the lot!"

During the campaign, tomatoes were twice thrown at ex-Prime Minister Edouard Daladier, the diehard Radical Socialist ex-chief, by country audiences on whom he was pressing his candidacy for reëlection. Léon Blum was not only still too fatigued by his Buchenwald captivity but also too wise to put himself in Daladier's position. He ran his Socialist party—into second place—but he didn't make the political error of running himself for office. The French citizen was sick of the old, bitterly disappointing, though perhaps well-meaning public faces left over from before the war. As de Gaulle had pointedly and brutally said, France wants the "new and reasonable."

If the voters acted calmly, those they were voting for did not. The harshest and most significant ill-feeling was that which developed between the Communists and Socialists, who were supposed to be blood brothers. On their ability or inability to make a majority together hangs France's immediate future, which will consist of either severe structural reforms or else a bourgeois sigh of relief. The Socialists accused the Communists of all the old types of election malpractice—stealing ballots, menacing Socialist Party members, and, above all, dropping Communist leaflets on Limoges from a couple of airplanes, though private flights over France are still forbidden—and where the gas for the planes came from the Socialists couldn't guess, unless it came from de Gaulle's Communist Minister of Air. To all this the Communists offered their usual disciplined, hermetic silence. To the bourgeoisie, however, they did make a startling reply by letting a great dead artist speak for them. In their victory edition of *L'Humanité,* among the snapshots of their winning candidates, they put Daumier's lithograph of a Gulliver-sized figure of France sweeping out with a broom the bedizened, Lilliputian bourgeois figures cluttering the French landscape like fat, fancy little insects. This is the true meaning of the election. The main plank in Blum's campaign platform was his condemnation of the French bourgeoisie as the lost, inadequate political directors of France. The Socialists want not revolution but radical change. The Communists want changes which will be revolutionary, including, to begin with, the nationalization of credit, which means "Down with the Banque de France." The rightist Popular Republicans want what they carefully call reasonable change. It is their last chance.

Whatever the new political government turns out to be, the government itself has already turned into a postwar monster. As fast as the Allies hand back the Paris hotels which they requisitioned for war, the swelling French state absorbs them as offices for peace.

Ministers mingle with chambermaids in the service of *étatisme,* and fifty thousand Parisians cannot find a place to live. Before the war, seven hundred thousand French worked for the state as functionaries; now two million are busy at it. Louis XIV said, *"L'état, c'est moi."* Now the state, unfortunately, is beginning to be everybody in all France.

December 5

Because of the worst drought Europe has known in a hundred and fifty years, Paris electricity, which has been trying to do on limited water power what it failed to do on no coal, is now rationed more severely than it was last winter. The working hours of factories not producing necessities have been cut nearly in half, and so has the pay of their workers. Two hours a day are clipped from the time department stores are allowed to burn their lights, and two hours from the salesclerks' pay. Misery is again adding itself to penury. The Métro service has been reduced one hour daily, and at night the street lights, which for a brief moment after the war comforted everyone again, are once more dimmed. Householders who had no coal last year now have a seven-day supply for each person in the family for the entire winter and are saving it for the week when they fall sick. Everybody's five-year-old chilblains have started up again. Smart, chilblained Parisiennes beg transatlantic travellers for American vaseline the way smart New Yorkers used to beg for Paris perfume. There was supposed to be a small ration of coffee beans, but what has shown up instead is a stock of old powdered coffee. However, at least French women have just been given their first cigarette ration since Marshal Pétain's virile Vichy decision that only men should smoke. Many French women do not want to smoke anyway, and their hundreds of thousands of accumulating packages of Gauloises are already weakening our soldiers' black market in American brands.

This winter's rationed food for the French costs double last winter's, but necessities are less necessary and cheaper on the black market. For the first time since the Nazis tried to call in all French firearms, game is legally on sale for the approaching holidays. A dozen dainty, dead skylarks, worth fifty francs before the war, sell at only a hundred and eighty now, and a cock pheasant fetches only around six hundred. Live game is plentiful; it is the cartridges to kill it with that are rare. One literary Parisienne, browsing in her attic among prewar books, found two boxes of prewar cartridges. For twenty shells, a neighborly crack shot brought her back in trade two pheasants, a kilo of country butter, and a roast of veal. Gas stations are open again and rejoice the motoring eye, but gas is short. Because trucks lack gas, the monthly wine ration, which had been increased to two litres a person, has been reduced to one. International trains are beginning once more to creep across Europe, whose landscape is too old-fashioned, too cruelly beset by barrier mountains, by mist-producing boundary rivers, and by windy weather to be hospitable in winter to modern man in the air. Even the wing-minded American Army is taking to slow trains. From Paris to the Nuremberg trials is now a thirty-hour, sit-up train jog. The deadly necessity of getting planes into the freezing clouds to fight is now finished. In the depressing fog of the first winter's peace in Europe, man has come down to earth again and is moving about slowly.

Two winters ago, Paris pre-Christmas shop windows were bare. Last winter, the little they showed was not for sale. This winter they are full, in special neighborhoods, for the special, full purses of the nouveaux-riches. Behind glass, in the Faubourg-St.-Honoré, luxury is purchasable, and without ration tickets—soft sweaters for both sexes, fur-lined gloves, or dreamy silk nightgowns at nightmare prices. In the windows of the Au Printemps department store, catercorner from our most popular Army PX, the traditional mechanical-doll tableaux and the live clowns, all back in action for the first time in five years, have necessitated the same old traditional line of policemen and ropes to handle this season's mobs of dazed French children, the smallest of whom stare silently at the first toy of their lives. Only those who have seen toys in their pretty past cry out with recognition. Paris is not the same and probably never will be, but under disheartening conditions it is making its first effort. After all, Christmas is a civilized fête, however little it has now to do with peace on earth.

Albert Camus's fashionable philosophic play "Caligula" opened a month ago at the quaint neighborhood Théâtre Herbertot. Camus was formerly editor of *Combat,* the most intelligent, stimulating newcomer that the resistance has given to French journalism. He has abandoned his fascinating editorializing about France and against the United States in order to write plays. "Caligula" is a drama about what one Roman did in Rome, and it illustrates the new, modish philosophy of existentialism developed by that other talented ex-*Combat* journalist, Jean-Paul Sartre. As nearly as can be made out by dullards who would have thought that an important new French philosophy must be founded on something more than a "disgust for humanity," Sartre's form of existentialism is, indeed, founded on a disgust for humanity. It also gives a fresh twist to the old Gidean "*acte gratuit,*" which, for Sartrians, leads to what they call the necessity for choice, and has as its main premise a belief that there are two kinds of existence, one in the world and one in your mind, and as its slogan "*l'être et le néant*" ("being and nothing"). This belief leads to an anti-humanistic dualism and to a phenomenology which considers God a pure phenomenon—a notion thought up by the late Edmund Husserl, who has, along with other German philosophers, tremendously influenced the postwar French philosophers. These, now that Paul Valéry, with his theory of the apparent light of man's intelligence, is dead, regard Catholic Jacques Maritain as the last living example of French Christianism and have discarded deduction and rationalism and embraced mass responsibility and the doctrine that an autobiography of the thought of the thinker takes the place of thought.

Sartre, who did a remarkable series of articles as a roaming reporter in the United States last summer, used to teach in Paris at the Lycée Henri Quatre and today instructs his disciples mostly at the St.-Germain-des-Prés Café de Flore. In his Spanish War story called "The Wall," about a prisoner who was not shot, he has produced the finest short story of the resistance. He is also the author of a novel called, simply, "Nausea" and is already the best-known new Frenchman throughout Europe. Sartre is automatically fashionable now among those who once found Surrealism automatically fashionable.

Europe, warring and warred-upon for six years, is bankrupt but neglects to say so. Its editions of paper money say so for it. In Budapest the pengö is unofficially quoted at twenty-four thousand to the dollar. French peasants refuse gold sovereigns and American eagles. Gold, as a tangible value, has been out of style for so long that nobody knows what it is worth any more, or cares. Today peasants want bushels of paper money. It is a sign of the times. Industries want more money with which to make goods, premiers of governments want more money with which to govern, children prattle about thousand-franc or thousand-lire or thousand-mark notes. The war, which destroyed so much of everything, was also constructive, in a way. It established clearly the cold, and finally unhypocritical fact that the most important thing on earth to men today is money.

1946

January 3

On New Year's Day here this year there was more food on the plate, if less hope in the heart, than there was last year. A year ago there were still empty stomachs and heads were light not only with hunger but with desperate notions of a better world to come. The three most important things that have happened to France since last January 1st have been disillusion, devaluation, and the continued dominance of General Charles de Gaulle. All these happenings have been normal to the times. France today has little chance for the abnormal.

Achieving what amounted to a total surprise to the Paris population, the shops at Christmastime were suddenly filled with practically everything but the money to buy it with. Along with diamond bracelets, there were inelegant rabbit-skin moccasins—at the price of a midinette's weekly wage—for the icy, unheated home. There were grapefruit for the first time since 1939, at what a laboring man got then for four days' work. The butcher shops were crowded with the old-time, statuesque figures of sacrificial lambs, marble-white with fat and at such high, though legal, prices that the butchers have threatened to close up shop and hand the whole business back to the government, which has already taken back bread. Before the October elections, de Gaulle's government derationed bread, thus trading bread tickets for votes in a smart political move which elected its deputies, who are now faced once again with a wheat shortage. Under the new rationing, the government will give each person only three slices a day more than the Nazis gave in 1942, the worst of all years for those poorer French who practically live by bread alone. All over Europe, government has become a sort of harried, shabby, food-spotted maître d'hôtel fumbling over the menu of what its people will eat next and wondering who will pay the political and financial bill.

It is a pleasure to report not having seen the late Jean Giraudoux's last play, "La Folle de Chaillot," at the Athénée; its wildfire popularity, which makes seats almost impossible to buy, is an encouraging sign of revived public intelligence. The piece is already established as probably the most influential success of the modern French theatre. For several days after its première, the play was a topic for the editorial columns of nearly every newspaper in town. The theatre critics wrote of it with exaltation. In their various emotional and ideological flights, they compositely declared that one felt in the presence of a miracle; that it was a high French moment which the world envies France, the peak of Giralducien art, a lesson which we will never forget, the ghost of Beaumarchais, and an anticipation of the revolution which is coming. Provided the revolution does not come within the next fortnight and upset things, a few thousand of us who reserved our seats way back in '45 plan to go and see for ourselves.

January 30

The only flash of brightness that General de Gaulle's resignation brought was a political witticism which was not even true: "What we now have is a de Gaulle government without de Gaulle." Otherwise, his striding out of the Presidency left French morale in a state of empty gloom. This past fortnight has obviously been the worst here since the war ended. In Paris, the sense of crisis has been greater than in any other peacetime period since the February 6th riots of 1934, when there was at least the effervescence of fresh political hopes. The malaise is quieter but deeper now. There is no feverish surface reaction that might stir citizens into doing anything. The four years of occupation, the obedience to hundreds of orders, and the thousands of hours the French have spent in queues seem to have taken the old, violent, animated crowd spirit out of them. This is perhaps a good, perhaps a bad, thing; anyway, it is a new thing for Parisians. They act like people who know that there is nothing they can do except stand, as usual, and wait. The French are waiting to be governed.

Nobody, except possibly a few state librarians, believes that the General is really abandoning power in order to write his memoirs. A month before he resigned, the Bibliothèque Nationale, at his request, sent him a cartload of volumes by or on Mme. de Sévigné and the Duc de La Rochefoucauld, both of them certainly the wrong track for a well-educated military Frenchman who might want to brush up on the near coup d'état of General Boulanger (and his failure) or the successful coup d'état of President Louis Bonaparte (and his subsequent failure). Millions of French and the entire German Army found it difficult to believe that de Gaulle meant what he said when, in June, 1940, he declared that he would keep on fighting. It may well be that he was telling the truth again in January, 1946, when he said he would fight no more. De Gaulle is probably an entirely self-made democrat, having originally been an honorable Tory of the sort who would have done well in England a hundred years ago, and he must have decided, in recent months, that he could not give himself another complete education and become one-third Communist and one-third Socialist, like the Assembly he had to work with.

The editorials of respectful adieus to General de Gaulle were marked by a heroic, elegiac tone, as if it were still he and not his critics who set the style. On the Left, his captious Socialist admirer Léon Blum said that his departure was "dolorous" and "perilous for France, since it created a void equal to his services and the place he had held in the nation's life." Over toward the Right appeared statements and phrases such as "He retired with his dignity intact. He remains one of the high summits of our history . . . his romantic heroism . . . his ascetic scruples . . . his lack of Machiavellism." The General is still France's unknown soldier. No two people who have worked with him, and no two who have analyzed him from afar, seem to have come to the same conclusion. He has been earnestly described as a male Joan of Arc, as a Hapsburg type born too far north, as an inspiring, almost royal figure, and as the last great Republican legitimist. It has also been said that his blazing sincerity and lack of adaptability were against him. In his favor it has been admitted that he has an amazing sense of timing, his only political gift. Perhaps the cruelest and truest comment is that his leaving now is the greatest service he could render to France. In a tragic, ironical way, he symbolizes her shame, her defeat in the war. Now that he is off the scene, France can move on and try to forget.

It isn't often that the clear-cut success of a play here—or anywhere else, for that matter—can be estimated by the amount of confusion it arouses. It is a real tribute to say that this is the case with Jean Giraudoux's "La Folle de Chaillot," which means "The Madwoman of Chaillot," to begin with. People are already addled, on their way in to see it at the Athénée, because they have heard far too much about its snob, revolutionary, and intelligentsia importance. They are completely muddled, on their way out, because it is impossible for them to believe that they've just been through all they have and that it gave them such a delightful time. The plot goes as follows: Aurélie, an elderly female from the Chaillot section of Paris, who enjoys the privilege of sitting in her tatterdemalion finery on the terrace of the Chez Francis Café, there overhears a goldbrick promoter planning to fleece the public once more by selling it shares in a petroleum company which, this time, will claim to have struck oil in the very foundation of Paris—its sewers. Calling to her aid her friends, who include, among others, a waiter, a hat-check girl, a ragpicker, a sidewalk singer and juggler, a deaf-mute beggar, and a half-drowned young man who has been rescued from an attempted suicide for love, she plans to save society by eliminating the stock market. That is Act I. Act II (there is no Act III) consists of the elimination. After taking counsel with three other lady lunatics, from three other sections of Paris—one lunatic is accompanied by an invisible dog she loves—and after ascertaining from a genial city-waterworks employee that the eerie basement room she lives in has a secret door which leads down to the sewers, Aurélie decides to give a party. She invites the petroleum-company promoters, their high-society lady friends, their press agents, and their government lobbyists to visit her and their subterranean oil fields, and, after the last businesslike crook and pal have disappeared underground, she simply locks her secret door. That is all. Or anyway, all there is to the much-discussed revolutionary implication of the play.

The love theme is fancier. It involves Aurélie's thinking that the young near-suicide is her own youthful, untrue love, Adolphe, come back to betray her again, which delusion, in a dream sequence, gives the play a sort of mid-last-act happy ending. It is just after the petroleum promoters have disappeared underground to die that up the sewer staircase march three dead Adolphes in attractive cerements—a sort of Seducers Corporation, perhaps, since they state that they represent all the perfidious Adolphes ever on earth. The play ends with the café-terrace mountebank crew swarming in to take the four lady lunatics off to a really pleasant party, and with Aurélie's philosophic comment that "these are the people who are actually worth while." It might be added that the promoters, society ladies, and lobbyists, on their death march, are followed by two other strange companies, listed on the program as The Friends of Vegetables and The Friends of Animals. Perhaps their role was to attract the gnats that the audience strained at and the camels it swallowed.

What makes this play more remarkable than even the plot may lead one to suppose is the work of four greatly gifted people involved in it. Its production is a brilliant tour de force by Louis Jouvet, possibly the most creative actor-manager in Europe today. He plays a minor part, that of the ragpicker. There are fifty-seven characters in "La Folle de Chaillot" but only one real role, that of Aurélie, a nearly endless monologue, recited with a lifetime of technique by the elderly, energetic Marguerite Moreno. She dates from near the founding of the Third Republic and is a notable surviving example of that early vintage of gifted Frenchwomen in which her friend Mme. Colette was the literary champagne. In a program note on Moreno, Colette writes, "Her name has often figured in my books, like a clover leaf pressed between the pages." As the old lunatic, Moreno wears a startling makeup—the white face of a clown, with the wise, black, saucer eyes of an owl. Her foolish finery—such as her great hat, with its mad white bird, her sumptuous, silly dress of red-and-green silk, with torn black lace drooping at half-mast—and the astonishingly beautiful basement room are the careful, *démodé* romantic creations of the painter Christian Bérard. His old-fashioned, elegant white dress for the dog-loving lunatic is like a page of embroidery from Marcel Proust. One of the other lunatics is played by Lucienne Bogaert, now almost unrecognizable, like many once beautiful sights in Paris.

The fourth artist concerned is, of course, the author, the late Jean Giraudoux. American theatregoers who recall the charming, anachronistic titillation of his "Amphitryon 38" might be less surprised at the fantasy of his last piece than at the heavy, symbolic political significance Paris gives it. Maybe Paris is right. Just before his death, in 1944, Giraudoux prophesied, correctly, that his play could be appropriately produced late in 1945. Thus his bitter whimsy about a righteous madwoman suppressing a wicked big-business oil company runs full tilt into the beginning of 1946, just when the country's big-money gas and electric companies, following the banks and mines, are being scheduled for nationalization; just when the arrest of the big-money gentleman who owns the Paris Métro has been demanded by the Left press; and just when thirty-one of the big-money French insurance companies have been jerked up against the law for having insured the big-money black-market food racketeers against any possibility of loss—a pretty whimsical idea in itself. Giraudoux's play is no Beaumarchais "Barber of Seville," in respect to revolution. But it is an oddly fashionable sign of the tensely speeded up French evolution from Right to Left, from what remains of the bourgeoisie to what is coming from *le peuple*.

May 22

During the three weeks in which the Big Four failed to get on with the peace, Paris took a big step forward toward what must be one base for it—prosperity. The intentions of our quadripartite statesmen toward the Senusi tribes in Cyrenaica are still obscure, but anyhow the Galeries Lafayette and seven hundred and ninety-nine other Paris shops have just placed on sale the first postwar men's, women's, and children's shirts, pajamas, and underwear. New underdrawers are vital to a civilized reconstruction of Europe, and as a part of the peace which diplomats had nothing to do with, they seemed wonderful. The garments were sold one to a customer, under the category *"Articles Utilitaires,"* were priced cheaply from a hundred and twenty-five to two hundred and fifty francs (a franc is now worth four-fifths of a cent), and took only one textile ticket off the family ration card. There were not nearly enough to go around. Under the planned-economy program of the Ministry of Industrial Production, they were made up by the shops themselves from cotton woven only this year in the north, which is France's spinning center, and every garment looked like an advertisement for the Communist Party. On each was stamped, along with the French cock, the phrase *"Renaissance Française"*—the French Communists' postwar slogan. It was as though the New Deal, during America's depression, had sold drawers marked "For the Forgotten Man."

The inexpensive and unexpected underclothes are only part of the astonishing revival in Paris, which, starting tentatively with New Year's gifts, has snowballed modestly. Until recently, Parisians and their show windows were both shabby. Now the windows, at least, are excellently dressed. Articles that spring from good taste and that look luxurious, homely necessities, and small comforts, all of which had become merely memories to Parisians because of the lean war years, are now suddenly pushing back into circulation and, taken together, give a surface impression that Paris is struggling back to what looks and feels something like subnormal, at least. In other words, Paris is now like a thin, ill, handsome old woman with some natural color flushing her cheeks as she fumbles to her feet. Paris is still possessed of her remarkable habit of survival. She has already received two great boosts from outsiders, pulling in opposite directions—the recent American loan and the earlier impulse toward disciplined work which came from Russia. The strictly European countries cannot aid one another. All of Europe, France included, is sick, weak, and physically and morally hungry in varying degrees. It is precisely in her stomach that Paris has recovered least. Parisians can now lunch off a legal menu in a very modest restaurant for three hundred francs, if they can afford it. The white-collar and the working classes cannot.

As if seeing new historical sights, one's eye instinctively makes its list of cheering novelties as one walks the streets. For one thing, there are almost twice as many newborn babies on view this year as last. These new citizens can be seen all over town, bundled up for protection against drafts in the Métro, spread out on their mothers' knees to the faint sun in the Tuileries Gardens, or rumbling along the sidewalks in what is left of French baby carriages, which, as transport vehicles for everything except babies, took a terrible beating during the war. It has been announced with satisfaction that one of the Ministry of Industrial Production's next offerings of utility articles will feature inexpensive baby carriages.

Transportation for adults has already expanded. There are now five thousand taxis in Paris, and they are available even for healthy or unimportant people. Last month, you had to be pregnant, ill, or on top-level official business to get a taxi, and you had to apply first to the nearest police station. These liberated taxis are too few to accommodate all, but at least they officially are cheap. It costs about twenty-five francs on the clock to drive from the Opéra to St.-

Germain-des-Prés. The catch is the *pourboire*. The proper tip would be around fifteen francs. The Invalides aviation station for plane passengers bound to and from the suburban flying fields is being hustled to completion; it was started only three months ago. Twenty-seven more of the closed Métro stations have just been reopened, which means a saving of miles and hours of walking. Some of the antique green autobuses have lumbered back on the job, all with new routes and numbers, thus mixing confusion with satisfaction. Now that Parisians are off their feet more than they have been for six years, a ration ticket for having shoes resoled is to be distributed. Five-horsepower Simcas, France's midget motorcars, are now rolling out of the company's Nanterre plant at the rate of forty a day and can be seen passing through the streets en route to Belgium, Switzerland, Holland, and Denmark. The French will not be allowed to buy them until later, and then the price will be 92,000 francs. The new eleven-horsepower Citroëns will cost 121,180 francs, precisely. France has tripled her exports in the past four months, which may be encouraging reading for Americans, but the inflated banknotes that have been appearing in steady volume are gloomy reading for the French. Despite the upward swing of business, another new banknote is just out—a fancy, five-hundred-franc note stamped with a portrait of the melancholy poet Chateaubriand holding his head, as well he might.

Fifty-three Paris theatres and five music halls are going full blast—a sign of the continued restless tension, the hunger for unreality, and, indeed, the plain hunger that still obtains. It is cheaper for a modest bourgeois couple to nourish their imaginations at a theatre than their stomachs at a black-market restaurant. The Folies-Bergère has just put on an eye-popping new show, with the best-dressed girls and the best-looking undressed girls that it has assembled in ages.

The new comedy hit is Marcel Achard's "Auprès de Ma Blonde," at the Théâtre Michodière, starring Yvonne Printemps and her husband, Pierre Fresnay, in five stages of contented marital love. This is absolutely satisfying second-rate theatre animated by an enormous cast, all playing perfectly, as if with first-rate material. The chronology, which runs in reverse, starts in 1939 with rich old M. and Mme. Chose happily celebrating their golden wedding anniversary, and from then on goes back to 1889, when they ran away together, penniless, to get married. The disagreeable children they subsequently produced provide the rest of the plot. The play has three virtues and one error. The error is that Mlle. Printemps' role never permits her to sing. The first virtue is that the play allows her to start the evening as a gray-haired, deaf, but dexterous old *grande dame* and then romp back into turbulent, blond youth. The second virtue is that four of the acts take place in the same salon, which marches backward in its décor from prewar chromium-steel modern to 1899 Lalique, the room and its changing appearance thus acting like a living personality. The third virtue is that the ladies' costumes were created by Mme. Jeanne Lanvin, *la grande couturière*. With needles and braid, she has written a sort of brief, feminine French history on satin and wool.

June 12

When the Opéra put on a gala ballet night last month for the Big Four conferences here, it hung a sign over the box office timidly requesting the public to wear evening clothes "to the extent to which it may be possible." The invitations for the Galerie Charpentier's recent evening première of its modern-art show, "Cent Chefs-d'Oeuvre des Peintres de l'Ecole de Paris," peremptorily told those invited that dressing up was "acutely desirable." This dressy upper crust was asked free. So many of the lower crust were eager to pay the five hundred francs' admission in order to be seen in the upper crust's company—and probably in order to see the pictures, too—that a riot squad was called to handle the crowd that choked the Faubourg St.-Honoré, and half the élite, including Cabinet Ministers, were unable to squeeze in among the art.

Another controversial art exhibition has opened at the Orangerie. It is the first big postwar government show and bears the long, explicative title "Chefs-d'Oeuvre des Collections Françaises Retrouvés en Allemagne par la Commission de Récupération Artistique et les Services Alliés." The Allied Services referred to are the United States Army's Monuments, Fine Arts, and Archives Sub-Commission, and the art recuperated from Germany was looted during the Occupation from the houses of famous Jewish collectors in Paris and for the most part handed over to those noted connoisseurs, Hitler and Göring. Since these pictures came from private collections, the public has been interested in the first chance it has had to see gems like Vermeer's "Astronomer," which went to the Führer; Fragonard's "Girl with China Doll," which Göring held out on Hitler; van Gogh's "Bridge at Arles," which Göring gave to Frau Emmy; and Lancret's "Le Repas de Chasse," which bears a bullet hole it got when it was shot up in the Reichsmarschall's loot train during the battle for Berchtesgaden. Privileged citizens who used to admire these pictures when dining *en famille* with the Rothschilds or the other noted collector-owners were doubtless even more interested to learn from the catalogue that "Creation of the World," which has always been ascribed to Patinir, and "Adam and Eve," which generations of students have been told was by Cranach, are not the real thing but merely belong to the respective schools of those painters. Out of three portraits which have always been considered Bronzinos, two are now merely attributed to him. A picture long catalogued as an elder Breughel, an "Infanta" that people thought was by Velásquez, and a portrait of the little Princess Henrietta Maria of France for which Van Dyck has been given credit for centuries are in a similar fix. The exhibition has developed political aspects, too—the world being what it is today and what it was yesterday—because the catalogue fails to give the owners' names. This omission is being interpreted as, first, a sop to fear of Communism, since the owners are rich, and, second, as a sop to fear of a revived Fascism, since the owners are also Jews.

The French state proudly takes the view that these looted pictures are a part of the patrimony of France herself and has insisted on bearing the very considerable cost of assembling, packing, and restoring them to their owners' hands in Paris. Some liberal art circles here think that a third sop (one to democracy) is now indicated—that out of thankfulness to the French Republic for its respect for religion and private ownership, gifts should be made to the state's public museums of some of these invaluable, authentic masterpieces, which the taxpayer could then enjoy on any Sunday afternoon. Léon Blum's wisest postwar aphorism is that the prewar stupidity and selfishness of the bourgeoisie and of the rich cost them the political leadership of France. Their now giving a portion of their possessions to the state and of their brains to its problems might save them from having to give their heads and all the rest later on.

June 26

In June seasons before the war, one of the big French racing fixtures was called the President of the Republic Race. When it was run this year it was still called that, but it should have been renamed, to be politically up to date, the President of the Provisional Government and Minister of Foreign Affairs Race, these being the titles under which the newly elected Georges Bidault functions as chief of the French state, following the latest Communist-Socialist-M.R.P. (Popular Republican Movement) upheaval. This tripartism had a definite effect on most of the activities that went on during what developed into a hoity-toity June season—the first in seven years. Most of the social events were class-conscious and charitable, and the finger of the French Red Cross was in nearly every pie. The Red Cross got off to a bad start with an announcement of its prices for a concert to be given by Toscanini and the Milan Orchestra—eight thousand francs a seat (a stenographer's monthly wages), which people indignantly called an *insulte à la misère,* or plain gouging. It probably did better with its Pré-Catalan gala evening in the Bois, for which the ladies were requested to wear masks. Thus a few square inches of black satin on the face substituted for the fabulous costumes that used to swathe the demoiselles from head to foot in the famous prewar *bals masqués*. But the Red Cross failed with its Nuits Foraines, a three-night gala at the Théâtre des Champs-Elysées, the parterre of which was boarded over so that a street fair could be installed. For one reason and another, the Nuits Foraines came in for considerable criticism. Memories are long here. Among the war-aid organizations that worked in France during the Occupation, the American Quakers and the French Salvation Army are more popular in retrospect than the French Red Cross.

The most indestructible talent in Paris is still that of Jean Cocteau, whose new ballet, "La Mort de l'Homme," has just been given its première by the Roland Petit Ballet, at the Champs-Elysées Theatre. It was one of the high moments of the season. The audience felt the same sense of astonishment that Cocteau aroused with everything he laid his pen, pencil, or imagination to between the two World Wars. The passage of time seems neither to wither nor even to interrupt the hothouse ripeness of his talent. What his startling new romantic ballet contains is this: A youth in his mansard room awaits his beloved, who arrives and refuses him, pointing to a gibbet that suddenly becomes visible beside his garret window. He hangs himself. At this moment the garret walls disappear, to be replaced by the nocturnal Paris sky, lighted and dated by the Tour Eiffel and its prewar Citroën sign. Then Death enters, wearing a gaunt mask, which, when lifted, reveals that Death is the beloved girl. She places the mask on the youth's face and gently dances him away from human view. Finis. The ballet was hailed as a triumph, even for the prodigious Cocteau. Characteristically, he rehearsed it to jazz, to obtain the rhythm he wanted, but had it danced to Bach. As the moribund youth, Jean Babilée, a popular, handsome new French dancer, leaped and died with perfection.

It would be ungrateful to deny that a regime of civilized, almost willful perfect taste and artistic creation was maintained in prewar Paris by what was known as *Tout Paris,* which consisted of perhaps a hundred individuals out of a population of two million. This special, experienced crew were the patrons of fine clothes, just as they were the patrons of fine arts, and they collected early Chanels precisely the way they collected early Picassos. It has seemed fair enough to wonder, rather morbidly, whether this dominant small set of internationally overpublicized Parisians would still have the strength to manipulate the selective sense of this city after a war that brought greater changes than any which their immediate privileged ancestors survived. This year's June season has given the answer. Those who once succeeded in making their particular kind of season go have finally started to fade from the picture, and their particular kind of season is fading out with them. They are finished. They are the ones who are now démodé. For a long time they helped keep Paris the so-called civilizing capital of Europe and did a whale of a lot for the dressmaking trade. This trade, with its multiple beautifying ramifications, was the second largest exporting industry in France and gave employment to two million workers. The chic in an evening gown today costs twenty-five thousand to forty thousand francs. Some of the elegant women who helped set the style in the June season of 1939 are, in 1946, wearing the same '39 gowns. Only the black-market *nouveaux riches* can afford to dress all new all over. The best report on the Paris of today was written by Balzac, in his "Scènes de la Vie Parisienne." There has been a season, true enough, this year, and it has been an active one. The race tracks, the opera, the good theatres, the costly bars, and the hotels have all been packed. But it is a new Paris and a new public, both now only two years old. And temporal power, and all that goes with it, has completely changed hands too. The latest Cabinet of Ministers under whom France is living comprises six former professors, six lawyers, three journalists, three metal workers, three white-collar workers, two miners, two electricians, one engineer, one pharmacist, one broker, and one lonely rich industrialist.

In the midst of the new, Paris is also certainly leaning heavily on its past. The result is not a mixture but a blend. The greatest exposition of French tapestries—which is at the same time one of the greatest art expositions—ever held here has crowds of citizens queuing up at the Musée d'Art Moderne, on the Quai du New York. The show begins with the famous fourteenth-century "Saint John the Evangelist" tapestries, formerly hung on gala days in the Angers Cathedral, and ends with tapestries patterned on Lurçat's "Modern Roosters," which wear leaves instead of feathers. Two women have been influential in the making of tapestries based on modern French paintings. One is Miss Alice B. Toklas, Miss Gertrude Stein's friend, whose early grospoint embroidery of footstools based on designs made for her by Picasso showed new possibilities in tapestry. The other is Mme. Marie Cuttoli, wife of the senior senator from Algiers. Her early sponsorship of tapestries based on paintings by Braque, Dufy, Matisse, Léger, Le Corbusier, Miró, Rouault, and Lurçat has resulted in some of the most interesting tapestries in today's show, which includes everything through the rich years of French weaving—the blue-backed *milles fleurs,* the Gothics (with their unicorns), the Aubussons, and the fat nude and hatted females of the early nineteen-hundreds. Lurçat has taken up tapestry-making himself and the show also includes a reproduction of his workroom—with his designs, graphs, looms, threads, and wools—and exhibits of what Gobelin and other manufacturers are doing to revive one of the great, agreeable industries of France.

July 25

Paris has certainly been animated. Crowds have gathered on the boulevards in the past week to shout, "Death to

Daladier!," which they maybe didn't mean, and "We want our twenty-five per cent!," or the big general wage increase, which they are very serious about. The government is now asserting that it will authorize only an eighteen-per-cent boost, though it is unable to deny that the cost of living, dying, and being ill has certainly gone up forty per cent in the past year. The latest figures give eighteen thousand francs a month as the average H. C. of L. for a Paris couple with two children. Schoolteachers, who last month held a parade protesting their salaries, earn nine thousand francs a month and cannot afford any children other than those in their classes. Inflation is covering Europe like a magnifying glass. Seen through it, objects swell to twice their size in necessity or desirability and the piles of paper money grow to distorted heights. The inflation in the United States is regarded as even more grave. The dollar has fallen on the black market here from three hundred to a hundred and ninety francs. At this rate, it soon will not pay expatriate Americans to be dishonest.

The recent meetings of the Assembly were the most violent that the Fourth Republic has yet weathered. They were important because the Assembly majority refused to unseat deputies the people had elected. They were important because, for the first time in a crisis, there was no babble about France's past glories. There was, instead, both inside the Assembly and among the men on the street, a unifying feeling of war guilt—the guilt of brainy, weak statesmen, the guilt of greedy, middle-class businessmen, the guilt of partisan workers, all of whom, a family of forty million, had let their house fall.

August 1

A throwback to the Treaty of Versailles days was furnished by two of General de Gaulle's recent speeches, the first of which was given against the carefully selected backdrop of the Vendéen countryside, from which Clemenceau came, and the second at Bar-le-Duc, which was Poincaré's country. The first speech was on France's *politique intérieure,* the second on her *politique extérieure,* topics which let the General cover a lot of ground. What he said in his second speech not only was offered in the talented, pungent literary style that is characteristic of all the General's versions of French history but contained classic evaluations of the new world balance of power, evaluations which make some of the Peace Conference practices look like a reckless game of teeter-totter, with the twenty-one big and little boys trying to outweigh each other at opposite ends of the board. "Lucidity and strength of soul are what we have need of," de Gaulle boldly began, "in order to consider frankly, and realistically, the situation of the world and the position of France. The peace of France depends primarily upon the determining of the destiny of Germany. As a result of France's wounds, the equilibrium of the world has been compromised. Whatever Germany has been through, she remains Germany still—a large nation, a mass of people living in the heart of Europe—who, though she is in the depths today, remembers her days on the heights and whom the daemon of war might one day tempt again if she has the chance to regain her greatness by mating her ambition with that of someone else. She must be permitted neither to tempt nor to be tempted. If not, woe to the sons and daughters of mankind! Nobody in the United Nations should have in the back of his mind the idea of using the renaissance of Germany as a threat against another nation. As a result of the thirty years' war we have just been through [as a military man, de Gaulle always considers that the armed peace of 1918–39 was merely an interim diplomatic battle between the first and second sessions of one World War], a cyclone has passed over the face of the world, and with the collapse of Germany and Japan and the weakening of Europe, Soviet Russia and the United States of America today are alone in the front rank. Rich in their men and their resources, which are all within their territories and naturally protected, in the case of one by immense oceans, in the case of the other by its own space, both are drawn toward expansion, which, according to eternal custom, is clothed in the mantle of doctrine but is in the end an unfolding of power. The emergence of these two new world powers coincides with the discovery of terribly powerful methods of destruction. The United States of America's just and good proposal to place fissional activity under international control is a duty toward humanity that overrides the interests and claims of every regime and nation. And if this duty be not fulfilled, clouds of danger will cast their shadow over every living thing."

To Gertrude Stein's old friends here, her death was the last chapter in her private history's concordance with the important things going on in France. She had lived in France for forty years, had worked for it during its two greatest wars, and had received public acclaim here during the period between them; she had met and welcomed our Army during the liberation; and she left the scene only as international statesmen began talking over the second peace. All the French newspapers, in their obituaries, mentioned the friendship she and her faithful companion, Miss Alice B. Toklas, had for Picasso and Matisse. As a matter of fact, it was the ladies' unchanging good relations with modern paintings rather than with modern painters that best demonstrated the solidity of their jointly operating critical faculties. As they frequently chorused, painters were to be admired for their paintings, not for their characters; first-class painters often had difficult characters, and only third-class painters had really good characters. Most American collectors eventually bought modern French art as they might have bought cut flowers from a florist's shop. Miss Stein pulled hers fresh from the stem, in the ateliers where they grew, four decades ago. Today, her collection is as remarkable for its ripeness as for its freshness. Miss Toklas says that she has no idea what Miss Stein wanted done with her pictures; she says Miss Stein never made any plans for her art, she just enjoyed it.

August 21

Paris now belongs to the peacemakers. It may not be the kind of Paris some of the Conference delegates expected or want. Mostly, its theatres are dark, its restaurants locked up, its little shops closed. Three-quarters of a million Parisians, or over a quarter of the population, finally succeeded, with difficulty, in getting themselves and their luggage out of town by Assumption Day, and wherever they managed to go, they will stay until August is out. There hasn't been such an exodus since the tragic one of 1940. What with the worry about Munich in 1938 and the fear of war in 1939, most people here have not drawn a carefree breath in eight years. Nobody has yet forgotten what happened during those years, but this month there has been at least a readiness for a change of scene. This is the first big postwar holiday. All classes have participated. On the front doors of little shops are pasted bits of paper, in cramped script, advising *"Notre Gentille Clientèle"* that, at the request of the employees, the shops will be shut until September. On Thomas

Cook's door is a large sign warning de-luxe travellers that accommodations in *wagons-lits* are no longer available except a month in advance. Taxi drivers have been asking you if you wanted to ride down to the Riviera with them and their wives for four thousand francs per passenger. Only the French can afford to go there, however. Paris is dear, the seashore is dearer, but for once the franc is strong. It is the legal-rate dollar and pound in this year's tourist's pocket that are in the doldrums. British pleasure travellers are allowed seventy-five pounds a year to spend outside their island, and that has not carried the British far in their brief tourist invasion here. To Americans, this is the memorable summer when Paris shopkeepers can say proudly, for the first time in this century, "It may be expensive for you in dollars, Madame, but it's not expensive for us in francs." It is the summer of the Peace Conference, of the sound franc, of the slowly dying black market, of the reviving supply of goods.

The Congress of Vienna, which gave Europe its longest recent peace, concerned itself with the balance of power in Europe. If anything is clear about this present Paris Conference, it is that the balance now being sought is a balance of the world. At the Congress of Vienna, all the winning parties saw eye to eye, except, of course, as to how much each ought to get; they believed in the same over-all fundamentals—in kings, Christianity, the supreme importance of Europe, and a settled, three-class society of the rich, the middling, and the poor. It is the difference in what Byrnes and Molotov, taking them as chiefs and symbols, believe in that makes this Peace Conference a battleground of opposing ideologies.

One can report with pleasure, the Louvre has been holding a small and exquisite de Goncourt exposition which offers a review of a literary age of logic, sensibility, and comprehensible gossip, and which commemorates a coterie of modern geniuses who are still the chief ornament of today's French letters. There are portraits, photographs, private letters, pink waistcoats, walking sticks, first editions, cartoons, and even the tables and chairs that belonged to men and women like de Maupassant, Zola, Coppée, Flaubert, Huysmans, Dumas, Hugo, George Sand, Heredia, and Renan. It also tells, beneath Flaubert's portrait, what the de Goncourts said of him: "Tall, with big shoulders, with big, beautiful eyes popping out of slightly swollen lids, drooping mustache, and a mottled complexion specked with red." De Maupassant also went into details about Edmond de Goncourt: "He has long, grayish hair, which looks discolored, a slightly whiter mustache, and singular eyes, spread out by strangely dilated pupils," as indeed they may well have been, busy staring with astonishment at his great generation, living for talent, for the perfected word, for the fight for civilized ideas, in a Paris of top hats, bustles, peace, candelight, and time to think.

October 1

In the corridors, there is a strong feeling that the reason the Peace Conference conclusions appear abnormal, spongy, and unstable is that the new balance of power in Europe is now being balanced by a couple of powers that are not European—Russia and the United States. For once, here is something that is not the peace delegates' fault. The situation is, axiomatically, part and parcel of the strange, unidealistic, second twentieth-century peace which this last war, essentially one of gigantism in manpower and production, has loaded onto the U.S.S.R. and the U.S.A., the only two states big enough to take it. Because of sheer size, they have become the world's bosses. They have set up the chimera of absenteeism as the new order for Europeans, some of whom may be the most civilized creatures on earth but all of whom are now reduced to sitting quiet and worried in their cities or on their land and nodding like yes men to a pair of enormous, newly grown-up outsiders. Europe has lost the right to maintain her own power balance because no sooner had it been reëstablished by peace, after one war, than uncontrolled Germany upset it and the world by rushing us all into battle again. Nevertheless, to anyone familiar with Europe (including England) in the thirties, which were doubtless one of Europe's rottenest periods, owing to the reckless policies pursued by the main democracies (policies in which, as proof of our coming responsibilities, we distant Americans shared), there is something sickly in the spectacle of Europe's becoming a conglomerate, largely literate colony, eyed by Russia, which cares, and indifferently tended by the United States, which, except commercially, really is not interested. After two thousand years of Europe's dominating civilization, a nervous shiver runs down the spine of any thoughtful American at the Peace Conference when he realizes that the twenty-one nations' voices are actually silent, that the Big Four's voices are not even a strong and constant quartet, and that the Big Three's voices are not always a powerful trio, because what counts is only the voices of the Big Two, the voices of the East and the West. The world seems to have lost two points on its compass. The earth's surface is changing. Europe is contracting; the U.S.S.R. and U.S.A. areas of influence are expanding. It is as if Europe were slowly entering a new ice age.

1947

January 2

France's Christmas gift to herself was her Fourth Republic, generously presented a few hours before the dawn of December 25th. In making this gigantic nocturnal offering, the presiding chairman of the Council, as the Chamber is now called, said to the weary councillors, "I salute the birth of the Fourth Republic. My best wishes to it are that its new constitution, adopted by the people, may affirm our Republic and our democracy. Long live the Republic! Long live Liberty!" There was applause. The Fourth Republic, like the Third, is a result of a defeat by the Germans. (In 1870, a revolutionary Paris Commune was in the offing, a prophetic counterpart of the Communist Party that functions today in the Parliament in elected and orderly quasidominance.) France's newborn Third Republic was so rich that it immediately paid its war debt to the enemy Prussians and could have paid it twice; the Fourth Republic starts so poor that it has already borrowed from a transatlantic friend. The Third Republic was founded on the curious notion that it would conveniently collapse as soon as the next Bourbon could be maneuvered up to the throne. The Fourth Republic has in part been set up to shut out General de Gaulle, the only massive figure still visible, though faintly, on the French landscape. As the newest European republic makes its difficult first motions of life in a France whose violent idealism created Europe's first modern republic, the belated suspicion is stirring among French citizens that perhaps republics, though conceived strictly on paper, take after each other, in hereditary fashion, much as kings do, and that by some law of genetics the Fourth Republic, when it is a few years old, may begin looking and acting like its parent, the so-called harridan Third Republic, which was no beauty.

In one way, certainly, the two republics will differ. The late No. 3 was so infested with political parties—anywhere from a half-dozen major groups to three dozen or more minor schismatic rivals—that government, enfevered by the multitudinous political bacilli, was constantly dropping weakly in its tracks. In No. 4, the parties are few and hardly count anyway. What does count is its two grim, directly opposite political directions, Left and Right, or Communist and M.R.P., with literally equal strength, so this time the government may not fall, simply because it may not even be able to get going. The Fourth Republic, by a triumph of balloting and the democratic process, can sit perfectly paralyzed by what temporary Premier Léon Blum has described as "those two great parties whose simultaneous presence in government is at once indispensable and impossible." A sardonic Deputy, discussing the semi-existence of the two minority parties, the Socialists and the Radicals, whose thin shadows of strength will be thrown, respectively, to the Left and the Right in efforts to create majorities, declared that in a full-length anatomical portrait of the new government the head and both arms would belong to the M.R.P., the neck, heart, lungs, and left foot forward would belong to the Communists, the Socialists would have the stomach and left leg, the minor Left Wingers would be punished by having the right leg, and the reactionary, pro-Church P.R.L. (Parti Républicain de la Liberté) and its hangers-on would have the right foot, including the Pope's great toe. The First Republic, with the great words "Liberté, Egalité, Fraternité," produced a portrait of man's invisible regions. In the Fourth Republic, what the French have retained of this sacred trio is a too exact equality between Left and Right. Some impulse, whether shock, force, or weakness, will most probably cause France to move, eventually, in one direction or the other.

The Paris theatre scene has been enlivened by the non-commonplace—not necessarily successful as entertainment but distinguished because it comes from important pens. One item is André Gide's translation of "Hamlet," playing to dutiful, admiring crowds at the Théâtre Marigny. Because Gide now ranks as a demigod, no one has had the pluck to say that his translation of the poetic masterpiece not only lacks wings but is downright flat-footed modern prose. For "Get thee to a nunnery," Gide substitutes what sounds like an address tossed to a taxidriver—*"Au couvent."* For the tragedy's great epitaph line, "Good night, sweet prince," he offers merely *"Bonne nuit, gentil prince."* (According to Cassell's bilingual dictionary, *"un gentil enfant"* means "a nice, amiable child.") Since, because Gide's name is attached to it, the play's the thing at the Marigny, little attention has been paid to the production, which is one of those athletic, hearty, hasty "Hamlets," with everyone but the ghost going on- and offstage on the run. Jean-Louis Barrault, as the nice, amiable prince, is remarkable in the death scene, to which he gives an oddly cinematographic effectiveness.

Another special item has been the Théâtre Antoine's program of two lengthy playlets by the Existentialist Jean-Paul Sartre. Both deal with torture, the first in France and the second in our Deep South. The opening piece, "Les Morts sans Sépulture" ("The Unburied Dead"), shows two sides of the French Resistance: first, the patriots' side, through a group of captives in jail, including the inevitable pretty girl, and a philosophic analysis of their arrogant human pride in enduring agony without screaming, let alone squealing on comrades still at liberty; second, the captors' side, in the room next door, where Vichy Frenchmen do the torturing right in front of the audience's startled eyes. In the Vichy group is another inevitable character, the neat, blond sadist who loves his work and the music of "Tosca." He sees to it that the patriots, after they have argued themselves into being spared, are shot anyway. This sort of masochistic entertainment, once idly popular at the Grand Guignol, has now been reclassified as part of recent French history. Sartre's second playlet, "La Putain Respectueuse" ("The Respectful Prostitute"), must be the world's only funny play about a Deep South lynching of a Negro. It is a brilliant, disturbing mixture of melodrama, farce, and deadpan reporting on the Bilbo mentality. The trollop of the title, who at first tries to save the Negro, falsely accused of having accosted her, furnishes the only truthful, and thus the only moral, element, which is finally nullified because of her eager, noisy desire to be recognized socially by the family of the local senator—the uncle of the leading lyncher—at whose request she finally bears false witness against the Negro. This unhappy victim is played, with poetic postures of fright surely never seen in our Cotton Belt, by Habib Benglia, an ebony mime formerly famous at the Folies-Bergère. In addition to the extraordinarily lifelike, funny, kind, ebullient, coarse-mouthed, rattlebrained figure of the whore, there are characterizations of American male prudery, false patriotism, hypocrisy, sentimentality, and what looks to foreign eyes like all-around national infantilism. These are the spicy, comical ingredients in Sartre's deadly skit, the main weakness of which is that it wavers between being a real satire on the Southern U.S.A. and a sort of shapeless exaggeration of it. As a consequence, the play has an amateur quality. This quality may also be due to Sartre's having met so few authentic Southern-gentleman lynchers on his recent American lecture tour.

France's second New Year of the peace opens with an Eastern war. The new Republic's preamble to its constitution states that it will "undertake no war with a view to conquest and will never employ force against the liberty of any people." That is precisely what it appears to be doing in Indo-China.

January 16

Léon Blum's now completed thirty-one days as France's pro-tem chief are, like his prewar Popular Front period, peculiar, very personal islands on the map of modern French history. As proof that he is, perhaps fortunately, a poor politician, both times he was on intimate terms with the French populace, ordinarily in contact with their politicians only through the ballot. Blum, a bookish intellectual who wandered into politics straight out of his library, has social aims that are humanistic rather than revolutionary. His recent governmental announcements to the nation read like confidential correspondence with a group of friends. Almost every other night for four weeks, he carried on what sounded like one side of a long, interesting conversation with France. Before New Year's, when he began begging the French to help him save the franc by being unselfish, it was the quality of his mind and hopes, against the background of all his years of public life, that—after the first moment's surprise—animated a good will that spread from house to neighborhood, from factory (after a few misgivings) to shop, from farm to suburb, and pretty well all over France. The famous five-percent price cut that he offered was no dry financial program but a typical, even cozy, proposition of friendliness. Everybody expected that this year's living costs would jump a mile high, which is just where Blum himself jumped them to balance the budget, but then he also brought them down an inch, which was what no one had expected.

Of all France's old, prewar figures who have again become active, Blum alone has really come full circle. He was a young Jewish littérateur in Paris during the Dreyfus affair, which first divided modern France into Left and Right and into Catholic and anti-clerical. During the period of his Popular Front, which marked the triumphant emergence of the Left, his allies the Communists, then also enjoying their first important party victory, refused to accept any Cabinet appointments or participate in power. It was during that period that his name began to serve as the nobler half of the premature collaborationists' slogan "Better Hitler than the Jew Blum." While Hitler was still having the best of it, the Nazis sent Blum to Buchenwald for his triple crime of being French patriot, Socialist, and non-Aryan. Blum has now made his final, elderly reëntry into, and, it appears, his weary, promised exit from, politics at the exact moment when his former allies the Communists not only are the leading Communist party of Western Europe—and by a narrow margin the leading party of France—but have at last acquired an appreciation of power and office, summed up in 1946's loudest, largest political demand, *"Thorez au Pouvoir."* Blum's scholarly humanism, his love for France, which has been more like a political romance than an expression of professional patriotism, his now weak and outdated Socialist Party (its once potent "Mystique of the Left" has moved east), his experience with the hatred that in his youth sent one French Jew to Devil's Island and in his old age sent millions of Jews of many nations to barbed-wire camps—all these elements, embodied in one leading Frenchman, seem finally to have completed their orbit. Blum's disappearance from the French political scene will be, on a small scale, like the disappearance of Roosevelt, except that there will be no funeral. A recent poll of the country showed that thirty-four per cent of the population is still devoted to General de Gaulle. He and Blum both now seem to be far removed from the governing of their land. But they are the two most popular men in France.

Politically, everything here moves sidewise rather than forward. Calculated horizontally, French Socialism, whatever it seemed like in the old days, is now practically the dead center, or pure middle-of-the-road democracy. The Socialist Vincent Auriol has just been elected first President of the Fourth Republic. While the election was going on in the Salle du Congrès at Versailles, many a rich man in Paris had his Versailles man on the phone for reassurance that the chances were favorable for Auriol's winning on the first ballot. And when he came in victorious, Paris big money probably broke open a good bottle of wine for dinner in relief. However much Socialism means to French capitalism as a breather, Auriol's election means to the already weak Socialist Party that a good active Party man has now become a eunuch politically. The new French President has even less political power than the presidents had before the war.

The voting was dramatic. Just as some people always cry at weddings, some people in Europe now feel that it is a good time to cry at elections—with joy, to be in a place where mankind is still casting a free ballot. For the handful of Americans packed into the galleries, it was a sobering lesson to see the many women deputies calmly treated as if they were deputies and not women, and equally impressive to see the Negro deputies from Guadeloupe and other dark colonies striding with simplicity up the little staircase that led to the two green faïence electoral urns in front of the Speaker's desk.

The mounted horse guard, their trumpets playing, trotted the President's car from Versailles to his new residence in the Elysée Palace in the Rue du Faubourg-St.-Honoré. A fringe of French people lined the streets to watch the modest Presidential procession, but few cried *"Vive la République!"* The people seemed satisfied but quiet. France must wish to remain a republic, since this is her fourth use of the formula.

For six days, through this Tuesday, Paris was without French newspapers, because of a strike about which nobody knew the facts, because there were not any newspapers to give them. To fill in, the M.R.P. Party shrewdly put out a miniature, throw-away newspaper, its back page solemnly carrying a few square inches on horse racing, Admiral Byrd in the Antarctic, and food rationing, as well as a midget column called "News of the Entire World." Its front page was a scoop the size of your hand—the first excerpts seen in Paris of M.R.P. President Maurice Schumann's wishful-thinking speech on Germany, delivered at the Cleveland Council of World Affairs. France, as a little Latin country now ranking only a cut above Italy, knows that she will accept what the Ministers' Conference decides in

March, in Moscow, about the Rhineland, the Ruhr, and the Saar, just as Italy has accepted what they recently decided, in New York, about Trieste.

The only spot on earth France can still act big is in Indo-China, where, even if she were not losing the war, she has already lost face. Ever since England agreed, however reluctantly, after the first World War, to President Wilson's idealistic platform of free determination for small nations and Ireland promptly stepped aboard, one aftermath of this second World War has been inevitable. What with the British Empire losing ground in India and Egypt, and with fighting in Palestine; with the recent revolt (under British influence, the French say) in the French colony of Syria, and with the war against the Vietnam Republic (under Russian influence, the French say); with the Dutch Pacific colonies in unrest; with mutterings audible everywhere around the palm-tree fringes of the commercial globe; with notions of freedom having spread a long way in one generation—the problem of what attitude the white races should take toward their own and other white peoples' colonies is the most awkward, most important philosophical question in Europe today. The French Left favors liberty for everybody in Indo-China except the French capitalists' Banque d'Indochine. The fellow-traveller journal *Le Franc-Tireur* the other day declared, "One can fight against organized armies, conquer them, and make treaties. But one does not fight against a whole people when this people rises above itself and decides to risk the utmost suffering." France has been fiddling around in Indo-China, or "has interested herself in this territory," as the Rightist editorials elegantly put it, since the time of Louis XVI, when he slipped an alliance round the Emperor of Annam. From Louis XVI to the first President of the Fourth Republic is a long time for the French to have been in Indo-China without making friends.

March 20

For a period of thirty-one days, ending this past Monday, the capital of France functioned without any French newspapers to give it news of itself, let alone of the rest of the world. Though theatre box offices suffered a sympathetic slump while the newspapers were not being printed, Paris night clubs were crowded with the kind of people who crowd night clubs the world over, no matter what may be going on outside the doors. The newest night-club hit here is a man called Yves Montand. He looks like a young Abraham Lincoln, sings workingmen's songs, of which the best is "C'est la Grande Cité" (the Great City being the Paris of the factories), uses his hands passionately, as if he were making a political speech, and was the French Frank Sinatra for young working Parisiennes, who are more restrained and respectful than bobby-soxers, when lately he sang at two music halls, the cheap Montparnasse Bobino and the Boulevards' A.B.C. He is now out of his modest admirers' reach, at the costly, champagne-drinking Ambassadeurs. Montand is a protégé of the famous *populo* singer La Môme Piaf. His name is really Yves Livi, and he is really Venetian by birth, with an Italian-Armenian mother and an Italian-Canadian father. Before he became a singer, he had been a barber, a dock laborer, and a factory hand. He is planning to go to New York soon.

The most acclaimed motion picture now showing on the Paris boulevards is the recently released Italian film "Sciuscià," pronounced "Shoosha," which, in turn, is the way Italian bootblacks pronounce "shoeshine," a word they picked up from the occupying American troops. "Sciuscià" is one more of those remarkable European films that have been made with a poverty of equipment and with rich emotion and are putting the slicker, emptier Hollywood productions to shame. The leading actors in "Sciuscià" are Roman bootblacks—a pair of incredibly talented, thin-legged ragamuffins picked out of real life on some shabby piazza. The film's love theme is their passion for a dapple-gray race horse, which they manage to buy through black-marketeering. They are arrested and sent to a Rome reform school, and the tragedy of the story and the precise, quick-paced artistry of the film lie in the fact that in this juvenile prison youthful events lead with the inexorability of the old classics to the poisoning of their friendship, to the ending of one boy's life, and to the ruining of the other boy's existence, no matter how long he might stay alive. The two boys undergo the complete human disaster that is usually harvested only by the adult man. This bootblack film provides the most informative, alarming, and concise picture of poverty-ridden, demoralized postwar European childhood that has yet been seen here.

* * *

For the past two months, there has been a climate of indubitable and growing malaise in Paris, and perhaps all over Europe, as if the French people, or all European people, expected something to happen or, worse, expected nothing to happen.

April 10

Until a fortnight ago, there was a popular after-lunch comic radio program called "Suivez le Guide" ("Follow the Guide"), done by the French music-hall comedian Max Régnier, assisted by Edward Stirling, formerly of the local Stirling English Repertory Players. Régnier acted as a French guide in current affairs, and Stirling followed him, in carefully slow French with a British accent. For saying nothing more than what Robert Schumann, Finance Minister, had already just said about the startling state of the French franc, though making it sound much funnier, Régnier and his program were taken off the air by the state-owned, state-censored Radio Diffusion Française. The program chief was thrown out, the Radio Diffusion chief angrily resigned, and the Paris press, as usual, burst into editorials, though since "Suivez le Guide" had been apolitical, Paris for once did not have to divide into opposite camps. Instead, it united in the old-fashioned and futile cry of "Down with the censors! Up with liberty!" André Philip, Minister of National Economy, said in a speech the other day in Bordeaux that "in reality we are menaced by a total catastrophe on both the economic and the financial plane." If Régnier gets back on the air, he should guide his comments away from these words. Nothing could make them funny.

Nobody can pretend that these are not sober days for France, as well as for other old seats of European civilization. Two months ago, it looked as if there were only one chance in a hundred that the Leftists would make bloody trouble in the streets of Paris, and only two chances in a hundred that the Rightists would make it; it also looked as if the chances were seventy-five in a hundred that for the next two years or so, while the United States, Great Britain, and Russia found out where they all stood, France would be able to worry along in her present strained but tenable condition. De Gaulle's Easter speech at Strasbourg has changed all the percentages. His success has worried everyone—except, that is, his followers. No one, not even he or they, can be sure what their newly formed League for the Betterment of France will bring—not so much with it as against it. On the whole, the French citizenry, from experience, is suspicious of a man who feels that he alone can manage history. For the past six months, France has been in the undignified position of an elderly lady doing the splits, her Right leg extended in one direction, her Left in the other, while everyone wondered how long she could hold it. The image called up by de Gaulle's league is prettier but more disquieting: the single savior on the white horse. Millions of French who had continued to admire de Gaulle, if only for his useful past, are now preparing to fear him—a painful, perplexing change of sentiment that will further addle and exhaust the country. The notable speeches he recently made at Bruneval and Strasbourg were spoken, respectively, on a picturesque hillside and in the shadow of a cathedral. According to the present laws of France, he will still have to talk in the National Assembly to make it count. The General's remarkably suggestive posters publicizing his Strasbourg speech showed France covered not by her hills and rivers and towns but by a photomontage of the sea of devoted de Gaulliste faces that had been lifted up to him when he addressed his thousands, al fresco, at Bruneval. Thus all France, according to his posters, is populated with his followers.

August 20

The Galerie Maeght has just held a show of Surrealist art, the first psychopathic aesthetic exhibition since the war. The de-luxe catalogue was idiotically priced at five thousand francs a copy. It was decorated with black velvet, on which reposed a plastic breast, the work of Marcel Duchamp. The show's japeries were stale *derniers cris*. In place of the prewar Dali taxicab with a shower in its roof and ivy as a passenger, there was, in one room of the gallery, a leaky ceiling that dripped upon a billiard table and the visiting art lovers. There were peepshows with tin cans and pebbles as the objects to be peeped at, and a fine Max Ernst painting of a phenomenal California rainbow. There were no Dalis, since he is apparently cross with the Surrealists, or they with him—though not so cross that they have refrained from copying his superior painting technique and paranoid perspectives as well as they know how. In the midst of the crisis in civilization, the intelligentsia Surrealists are still raking in cash through the inspiration of their private, patented muse—a composite of Marquis de Sade, Machiavelli, Maldoror, Narcissus, Mammon, and Moscow. Picasso has been more generous. He has presented ten pictures, painted in the past fifteen years, to the Louvre. The gift celebrates his happiness, in the autumn of his life, over the birth of a son last April.

The most interesting play of the theatrical season that ended last month proved to be "Les Bonnes," by Jean Genet, today's most discussed young poet and the newest member of that theatre-loving, inner artistic circle still dominated by the eclectic, lyric Cocteau, to whom the footlights have always served as evening stars. Genet's drama is about two tenebrous, visionary servant-girl characters who set out to murder their employer. Their dark plan is to poison the lady of their house, but it goes awry when the dominant domestic, through an insane form of social wish fulfillment, begins pretending that she, the slavey, has turned into the bourgeois mistress and that her sister is her servant. In her fit of *folie de grandeur* and double identity, she fatally serves poison to herself.

The season's most captivating operetta was equally dualistic at moments, but funny—the Opéra-Comique's "Les Mamelles de Tirésias," the ironic old Apollinaire fairy tale, now decorated with enchanting music by Poulenc. As the title implies, the bosoms of that classic heroine are major characters in the plot. Its climax occurs when they zoom off like balloons, whereupon Tirésias instantly grows a beard and, by parthenogenesis, becomes both father and mother of a stageful of baby soldiers, chorusing from cribs. Thus sterile, weak France, of which the heroine is a symbol, is repopulated, and indeed rearmed, to music, and her beard is allowed to drop off, her bosoms come back home, and the audience goes home, too, delighted with one of the few doses of national criticism that have caused mirth.

The same cannot be said for Albert Camus's new novel, "La Peste," whose important, dreadful theme is today's moral corruption and its spread through the social body. Perhaps it is a good sign of *mea culpa* that the Paris public bought up the first edition on the day it reached the bookshops. The reaction has been mixed. Those who enjoyed Camus's small, dry "L'Etranger" admiringly accept, in this broader work, the new protagonist pattern that both Camus and Sartre (increasingly the most influential pair of thinking authors since the war) have now set. In accordance with this pattern, human mediocrities are used, like a very common denominator, to decipher the problem of present-day life. It is their dateline rather than their dimensions that gives them importance. Mostly, they are people without personality, boldness, or the capacity to make shapely decisions—young citizens who are small, citified, ignoble, and monotonous, and who clamber clumsily among the little altitudes of their tragedies, which never seem higher than a Left Bank apartment house. The lack of tension in this modern school of fiction is old-style Russian, like Chekhov in the country; domestic minutiae are put down somewhat as they were in the nineteenth-century "Adolphe" of Benjamin Constant, but the moderns' attention is on their organs, not their emotions. This new French novel style represents the greatest break yet with the Balzac style, though Balzac's most important theme was also the pestiferous corruption of French society, long before the Third and Fourth Republics put their hands into the grab bag.

1948

April 2

On the surface, France has improved so much in the last six months that all that is lacking is the belief that the vital, invisible underpinnings of state and society can hold the improvements in place. The average Frenchman can now find in the shops nearly everything he wants except the means of paying for it. In midtown Paris shop windows, perfect taste, which is the supreme French luxury, has at last reappeared. On the farms, the hedges have been trimmed and the ditches have been cleaned out, the farmers having profited from what may be the last year of German-prisoner farm labor. By day, in the limpid spring sunshine, Paris looks her old, beautiful self, reclining full length in the greenery by the Seine. By night, the city is lighted but largely deserted; restaurants are half empty and cafés are closed for lack of clients. Parisians dine at home, on soup, and go to bed. The rise in the birthrate here may be accidentally patriotic, but it is also alarming, considering the world shortage of food. Since the recent freeing of the franc and of the prices of most edibles and other goods, the frantic black-market bustle for necessities to eat and wear has quieted down. Paris is hovering around a new norm; the new heavy tax increases, the special fiscal levies, and the seizure of five-thousand-franc notes have combined to produce an odd, un-Gallic stoicism that is a substitute for morality. The anti-inflationary government, still insisting that the sellers' margin of profit is too wide, is using pressure to hold retail prices down, and has made a first public example of the vegetable marketman. In the spinach basket in his grocery shop or on his lettuce cart by the curb, he is forced to placard his cost price as well as his selling price. The fixers and the middlemen in the gray market—the nibblers rather than the producers—are the only business groups making big money. Factory workers say that wages must go up; factory owners say that prices cannot come down any farther without economic suicide. For political reasons, both sides exaggerate their difficulties, which are nevertheless real, and which are opposite. It is this absolute diametricism that is cutting France into two bleeding, anemic, and perhaps impermanent parts.

Many important items are still rationed. Except for doctors, taxi-drivers, and other specialists, the French do not get a drop of gasoline. Because the government acutely needs tourist dollars, gasoline flows in fountains for American tourists, as well as for abashed American journalists (French journalists get nearly none), for whom the liberated franc makes life nice and cheap anyway. The French operate on costly black-market gasoline coupons that trickle down from the Brittany fishing ports, where fishermen make more money by selling them than by putting out to sea in their motorboats and catching fish. The farmers also oblige, by selling their tractor-gasoline coupons. Parisian adults have had no butter ration since Christmas and this month their quarter-pound monthly coffee ration is to be skipped, but they received a government Easter present—a rationed tin of sardines, at thirty times the prewar price. Wine is finally unrationed, but some of it is watered, or what the French call baptized, wine and spoils quickly. Compared with conditions a half year ago, there is more choice in everything and more comfort everywhere, except in the average French pocketbook. France is in a curious, momentarily excellent position of recovery. The goods are here, but the marts need faith and buyers with cash. There is a lot of intelligent skepticism as to what tomorrow and tomorrow will be in France, in Europe, and on this earth. France is like someone who has unexpectedly climbed a very high hill and stands breathless and poised on the crest.

French anxiety about the coming Italian elections is so grave that Italy is being spoken of with respect, possibly for the first time since the civilized Julius Caesar conquered all tribal Gaul. Only the Communists still refer to the Italians as "*Ces macaronis-là,*" a phrase they will, naturally, drop at once if the Italian Communists win. The French are also worrying about the possibility of their having their own spring elections, which could force the Communists and General de Gaulle's Rally Party into a final, or temporarily final, struggle at the polls, and perhaps in the streets. Lots of Frenchmen fear that if the General is elected, he will not be able to do much good, because retaliatory Communist strikes and sabotage could do so much harm. André Malraux, who, a fighter on the Republican side in the Spanish War, had been earlier admired for that great and Left-tinged book, "La Condition Humaine," on his youthful life with the Red revolutionary forces in China, is now the General's right-hand man. There is no left-hand de Gaulle man. At a recent private luncheon party here, Malraux talked brilliantly and rapidly and uninterruptedly for exactly two hours—or about twenty thousand words—on the General's political plans. He speaks with a strange, indirect tenacity, his sallow-skinned skull, with its sombre eyes, tilted to one side, apparently seeing nothing but his own thoughts, the expression of which is punctuated by his constant, nervous, maladive gestures and sounds—his dry little cough, his rubbing of his nose, his shuffling of his shapely feet. The main points he made in his remarkable monologue about his and the General's beliefs were these: The French bourgeoisie is finished; there is only one test for a class's fitness to rule—its ability to wage war; the French bourgeoisie did not defend itself in 1940; though the General draws his support from the Right, his political platform is for the workers, who, as all intelligent men now know, must have a better life; within six months, or perhaps only three months, after the General comes to power, he will have to have succeeded in giving the workers specific advantages, which must be so evident to everybody that even the Communists cannot deny them; and the Right will have to aid him in maintaining these working-class ameliorations. If de Gaulle could not do all this and in this period of time, Malraux said, he and the General would deserve to be shot, and probably would be. He figures that the unchangeable hard-core Stalinist French Communist voters amount to only six per cent of the electorate, and that there is an additional twenty per cent of what might be called fluctuating Communists, who are already worried about the Muscovite terror of liberty. The General believes that he already has forty per cent of France's voters and that some of the remaining thirty-four per cent, or the shilly-shally voters, can be drawn to him, and that, besides, things are weighted in his favor because he has the Army behind him. The east, including Alsace-Lorraine, is overwhelmingly for the General. In the west, he claims a majority. In any Communist insurrection, Marseille would become the Communist capital; the General must try to gain in the south. He is speaking at Marseille on April 18th, the Italian election day.

A new Sartre play, entitled "Les Mains Sales," is opening in a few days at the Théâtre Antoine. According to reports, it should restore the author to the pontifical level from which he has slipped lately. It is said to be a story of politics in the mythical Balkan country of Ilyria, where a young idealist assassinates his idolized political chief to prevent him from soiling his hands with ignoble political exigencies, only to discover that the government itself would have wiped out his chief, and thus kept the youth's hands, too, clean—in his case, of blood. Because of the times we live in, Sartre's "The Soiled Hands" will doubtless be no less popular than "Le Procès," André Gide's sonorous, impressive adaptation of Kafka's bitter myth "The Trial," now playing twice a week in Jean-Louis Barrault's Théâtre Marigny repertory. This is, visually, a rich, imaginative production, a synthesis of various somnambulistic states of mind. The finale is startling; Barrault, as the small, confused, innocent M. Joseph K. is led off to his beheading while treading air, being held aloft in eternal space by the polite, strong arms of his two giant, top-hatted executioners.

The Czechs never rated the Prague-born Kafka as one of their own, because he wrote in the hated German language. "Le Procès" is now arousing a belated nostalgic interest among members of the city's Czech colony. Since the new Putsch, the radio has had a lot to tell them about what is going on at home, if they will only listen. The main propaganda programs are at night. At nine, an anti-Communist news report, in Czech, comes from the B.B.C. in London, once more a seat of exiles, telling what is happening under the occupation and what the world thinks of it. At nine-fifteen, a Communist talk comes on, in French, from Prague. One of its recent anti-American items was the bland announcement that the American occupation forces in Germany were about to ship the Sudeten Germans there back to their Czech homes, a piece of propaganda calculated to arouse fury and fear in both the Right and the Left Czechs. So far, letters coming into France from Czechoslovakia have not been censored. A Czech in Paris has just received a letter from her sister in Prague relating her nine-year-old son's report on his first class under a Communist teacher. He reported that the teacher had said, "Children, you all know that in America people live in holes dug in the ground and are slaves for a few capitalists, who take all the profit. But in Russia everyone is very happy, and we in Prague are very happy, too, owing to the government of Klement Gottwald. Now, children, repeat loudly with me, 'We are very contented and approve the Gottwald government.' "

On the first day of the Prague Putsch, there were heartbreaking telephone calls from Paris to Prague, mostly young people calling parents still brave enough to talk out loud for a few precious minutes. One Prague mother, sobbing, shouted to her son that she would lock the door in his face if he tried to return, that Czechoslovakia was lost for a hundred years, that he must stay away and make his life elsewhere, and farewell, farewell forever, oh, my dear son. Since then, the son has learned that he will be condemned to death *in absentia* as a traitor if he does not return to undergo his military service. His father has had to sign as guarantor of his son's good faith in this matter, and can therefore be taken as his substitute into the Czech Army or before a Communist firing squad. The staple newspaper photograph of the long queues of Czechs lining up to view Masaryk's body lying in state was printed large on the front page of many of the morning papers. The Communist *Humanité* ran the picture, in pygmy form, on page 3, next to the fiction serial.

May 26

The Season is well under way—those May and June weeks that before the war were given over by Paris to a concentrated flowering of its civilized talents for fashionable marriages, masked balls, steeplechases, gourmet dinners, and theatre galas, and to the budding out of ladies in fine new clothes, which were in themselves part of the rich annual industrial harvest that the city lived upon. This year, the Parisians are less important to their Season and the vacation months to follow than the American tourists, a hundred thousand of whom are expected and will be profoundly welcome. The tourists are regarded as shiploads of precious material not specified in the Marshall Plan. Tourist dollars are desperately needed, to an extent that only the finance ministers of Western Europe can calculate.

The imported or otherwise special theatrical entertainment

customary during the Season has again turned up, if not in quite the usual sedate form. The old Marigny Theatre, picturesquely squatting in its midtown park of chestnut trees, at the moment in ruddy flower, is now the city's most catholic postwar entertainment center. Following Jean-Louis Barrault's success there with the repertory including works by Gide, Molière, and Shakespeare, with tickets priced at less than four hundred francs, came a week of frenzied *jazz-hot* concerts, with orchestra seats at eight hundred francs and with the house packed as it never had been for "Hamlet." The event, called *"La Grande Semaine du Jazz"* and organized by Le Hot Club de Paris and patron swells like Princesse Amédée de Broglie and the Duc de Brissac, offered American Negro masters like Coleman Hawkins, Howard McGhee, and Slam Stewart. It turned out to be a struggle between the diehard New Orleans style and bebop. The latter, judging, by what most of those present could hear of it over the catcalls of the French younger set, lost. Among the new French jazz talents on display were Claude Luter and his Lorientais and the recent Riviera Jazz Festival's prize trumpeter, Aimé Barelli, the finest French jazzman to come along since Django Reinhardt.

Major literary news concerns André Malraux, still considered the most talented and modern-minded novelist in France. A new book of his has been published, but it is one that few can buy. It is called "Le Musée Imaginaire," is an exposition of Malraux's new theory of obscure, realistic, reproductive art, and costs twenty-five hundred francs, or a tenth of an average, worried family's monthly income. It is a de-luxe collectors' volume, with a hundred and fifty-five illustrations, ranging from a gold Greek mask of Agamemnon to a giant pink face by Rouault. The kernel of Malraux's contemporary, revolutionary theory is that the reproduction of art, via photography and printing, produces what he calls modern man's "imaginary museum." "Today," he goes on to say, "the history of art is what is photographable." To him, photographs "at last make art a world heritage and permit its inventory." He deplores our habit of museums, institutions only two hundred years old, which have given us—as well as him, up to now—"our relation with art. The nineteenth century lived on museums. We still do." He says that photography, as a recorder of life, "in thirty years passed from Byzantine immobility [in daguerreotypes] to the frenetic baroques . . . of modern motion pictures." One of Malraux's few almost positive statements is his definition of modern art: "It is the search through form for an inner scheme that then takes—or not—the form of objects but in which objects are only the expression." The most indisputable line in the book is a quotation from that experienced old aesthete, Picasso: "Who are the younger artists? I am."

June 14

Another crisis has just arisen, over foreign policy and the results of the London Six-Power Conference, in which many French feel that France figures not as one-sixth but as about one-twelfth. The recent attempt by the American Congress to renege on the plans of Secretary Marshall, a move that dazed all western Europe, reminds the French of the reneging on the ideals of President Wilson after his Versailles Peace Treaty. The United Nations already reminds the French of the League of Nations; the possible withdrawal of the Allies from Berlin reminds them of their own withdrawal from the Ruhr in 1925; any Anglo-Saxon desire to lift Germany out of the beggar class reminds them of the Dawes Plan, the Hoover Moratorium, and American bank loans to Berlin; and, most frightening of all, any plan for unifying western Germany instead of isolating each of its provinces reminds them of Germany's organizing genius, which Parisians can see at work again, as it was during the Occupation, simply by shutting their eyes, and can hear, like an echo of the rhythm of Nazi feet along the Champs-Elysées. No sooner was the Six-Power London accord announced than the Communists plastered the boulevards with a Party poster, which, for once, was generally popular: *"L'Allemagne d'Abord? Non!"* ("Germany First? No!") If Bidault and his foreign policy fall in the near future, they will carry Schuman and his Third Force government with them. This would probably lead within the year to a government of the Fourth Force—the coming to power of the mystique and person of General de Gaulle.

Two of the best-known new literary figures, Jean-Paul Sartre and David Rousset, have founded a political party, heaven help us—Le Rassemblement Démocratique Révolutionnaire—and a bimonthly one-sheet newspaper, *La Gauche,* which, coming from professional writers, seems poorly written. Sartre's political ideas are less clear, if more optimistic, than his novels. His talent, his scholarly mind, his French essence, and his hypersensitivity to Europe's dilapidation give momentary importance to his political hopes, which concern that still unresolved trio of human problems, liberty, work, and lasting peace. "Hunger," he says poetically in *La Gauche,* "is already a demand for liberty." His rather less concrete goal is that "consumers and producers . . . may be conscious of their democratic revolutionary humanism." Rousset, whose remarkable book "L'Univers Concentrationnaire" recounts his survival in Nazi concentration camps, is more harshly definite on what Le Rassemblement is not. It is not Marxist, Trotskyist, or Socialist, but it welcomes all men from such, or any, faiths who are disorganized by deceptions and by political play and who have almost lost hope that "by democratic conduct humanity can demonstrate that it is not necessarily dedicated to self-destruction and barbarism." The Sartre-Rousset party declares that it expects to collect, in the next six months, a hundred thousand followers. If words were all, its followers should number millions, from all over this earth.

A mere handful of a hundred and thirty upsurging intelligent Deputies of many parties, and including the president of the Foreign Affairs Committee, have formally laid before the Parliament a resolution demanding "the immediate meeting of a European constituent assembly, having as its mission the founding of the permanent institution of a 'Federated Europe.'" Whatever else happens in Parliament, now or tomorrow, this is the one vital political proposal of the moment, of the year, of the century.

June 23

The most worried, wearied, unthanked, and necessary public servant in any government today is its Minister of Foreign Affairs. He is like a mother-in-law—in the bosom of the family, yet not of it. Essentially, he is related to a world outside, a go-between harried by what the family thinks is its due and by what the neighbors say it deserves, which is invariably a lot less. In the difficult last two months, Georges Bidault, still in his forties, has started to become an old man. The cynosure of all eyes in Parliament during its recent foreign-affairs crisis, and the butt of most of its discontents, he looked, as he sat engulfed in his great chair of office, like someone whom history had indeed dilapidated. His shining black hair had begun to grow white; the small, lively dynamo that supplies his physical energy appeared to be running down. His three years of peace as France's leading diplomat of the younger generation seemed to have cost him more than the long years of war, during which he functioned as President du Conseil National de la Résistance, the bold and successful chief of the underground forces in France.

The recent political crisis was the most protracted one in the history of the Fourth Republic; actually, it was composed of a series of smaller crises, each of which bubbled to the Parliamentary surface and broke in an explosion—if only of talk—that warned of national anxieties and agitations. As the talk grew more tense, the daytime hours did not suffice for it, and Deputies took to arguing all night and voting at dawn; in all Paris, for those hours, only Parliament and the Montmartre night clubs were up and hard at it, with some of the city's too few taxis working both stands, carrying the dissimilar, tired stragglers home. A typical Parliamentary rebel against the London Conference decision to put western Germany back on her feet (which was, of course, the main cause of the French foreign-affairs crisis) was the antique, Right Wing republican Louis Marin, an experienced anti-Teutonite who also rebelled, in his heyday, against France's accepting the Versailles Treaty. Of the London Conference plan, he cried, "We French are asked to sign it with our eyes closed, like the caged nightingales that are blinded so that they will sing better." Parliament was practically unanimous in its two classic Gallic fears: fear of France's naked lack of military security, and fear that control of the Ruhr, where in the past Germany has repeatedly rearmed right under everybody's nose, will probably be inadequate. The French feel that, on these matters, the Anglo-Saxons brushed France aside like the tertiary power she has become precisely because of German aggressions. There is no question but that the French have a fixation on the Germanies of 1870, 1914, and 1939. Only one Deputy gave precedence to the danger from the Soviet machinations in ruined Germany. "The London accord," he declared, "raises the fearful silhouette not only of a new German Reich but of a German-Russian Reich." The grimmest and most up-to-date Parliamentary comment was made by Paul Reynaud, surely an expert on German aggression, since he was Premier of France when it fell in 1940. Reynaud briskly begged his compatriots to try to

forget Bismarck, and even Hitler, "because the atomic bomb has changed all that."

Ever since finishing its debate on the Conference, Parliament has been occupied with the inflation and the recent series of Communist-led strikes in protest against it. As the leading country of the remains of Western Europe, France is now trying to face up to a problem created not only by the second World War but by the first. France's inflation really began thirty years ago. Apparently, something is going to be done about it, at last—doubtless something that will hurt. In all the intervening years, no political party here has ever been courageous, patriotic, or sadistic enough to hurt the French voter in his pocketbook. Today, from the Skagerrak down to the Mediterranean, only the Swiss franc and the Portuguese escudo are hard money. It would seem that modern men have been smart enough at making money but that now they can't control the delightful stuff. French industry is producing at such a high rate that even Americans are investing in it. Business, however, is bad. Rich people can make more money, but lesser citizens cannot afford to buy or are hesitant about buying because they think prices may go down. France's fight against inflation will be waged with enormously increased taxes, with some magic schema that will hypnotize the French into paying them, and, most important, with austerity. This last, up to now, only the British have had the national character to support on the necessary great, dreary scale.

The vanguard of the biggest influx of American tourists since the great season of 1929 is now becoming visible and audible everywhere in Paris. They are as welcome as they are valuable. For everybody's pleasure, Notre-Dame, the Place de la Concorde, Ste.-Chapelle, and other architectural gems are once again being given their prewar evening floodlighting, which makes them stand out like well-proportioned ghosts of history. In the windows of the fine shops in the Faubourg St.-Honoré, the merchants, in a joint effort, have set up insouciant still-lifes illustrating the seven deadly sins. Two of those illustrating the deadly sin of greed feature fresh bananas and oranges. The most artistic is one in Lanvin's window, audaciously illustrating the sin of envy with a headless, and therefore brainless, female figure elegantly attired in court brocades and decked with real jewels. On the Left Bank, where entertainments are simpler, the St.-Germain-des-Prés quarter has become a campus for the American

collegiate set. The Café de Flore serves as a drugstore for pretty upstate girls in unbecoming blue denim pants and their Middle Western dates, most of whom are growing hasty Beaux-Arts beards. Members of the tourist intelligentsia patronize the Rue de Bac's Pont-Royal Bar, which used to be full of French Existentialists and is now full only of themselves, often arguing about Existentialism.

July 8

The Grande Nuit de Paris, which topped off the Grande Semaine, was magnificently handled by government and municipal functionaries, against whose inefficiencies the citizens rail during the duller weeks of the year. Everybody coöperated except the weatherman, who produced sprinkles for the preliminary outdoor fête, which centered around the Tour Eiffel. The tower, floodlighted for the first time, looked like a solid-silver pillar of lace rising into the sky. Down on the earth and among the tower's four feet, trained elephants performed, along with other distinguished acts from the Cirque Bouglione. The star of the lot was an elderly matron named Maria, who, the Bougliones swear, was the favorite elephant of France in the reign of Louis XV, whom she has presumably never forgotten. At two o'clock in the morning, a burst of fireworks was launched from the Pont d'Iéna, below the great amphitheatrical setting of the Chaillot Palace. Earlier, in the Chaillot Theatre, at modest admission prices, there was vaudeville, with chorus girls from the Folies-Bergère acting as ushers. For people who could afford three thousand francs for a 2 A.M. supper in the heavenly upper reaches of the Tour Eiffel, the entertainment included Hollywood stars, among them Edward G. Robinson and Ingrid Bergman.

That night, all the historic monuments of Paris were floodlighted, and Napoleon, atop the column in the Place Vendôme, shone like an enormous lamp on what is left of Ritz society. Autobuses, which nowadays normally stop running at nine, for the first time since the Occupation ran until two. Even the Métro stayed up, staggering around under the city. Cafés had special permission to keep open until two and to open again at four, for late revellers. For all the Grande Semaine activities, including its Grand Prix race, its evenings of ballet at the Opéra, its lighted fountains in the gardens of Versailles, pouring beauty over the night, and its elegant social affairs

(for those who could still afford them), Parisians emerged from their worries and their homes; they spent some money, were cheered up, and, for once, had a good, prewar time. Today, more than ever, government is a form of applied psychology. Hope has to be advertised to the people. The Grande Nuit de Paris was a good advertisement of what Paris used to be like and may one day be again.

August 11

Even in Paris there has been excitement over the summer's humid hot weather, because of the prodigal wheat crop it ripened throughout the land and the hopes everywhere for that long-unseen luxury, white bread. Nevertheless, in view of the stormy political climate in and outside France, Paris, as the capital of what is still the Fourth Republic, seems tired. Lately, the Fourth has looked frail enough to fall, as the three earlier Republics fell. The timid, unpopular new Government of Premier Marie has led, owing to his pious name, to rude, contemptuous puns, such as "the government of the immaculate deception." The Schuman Government that preceded it was nothing but a Parliament-sitter, keeping an eye on the coalition of the little parties while the four big ones—Communist, M.R.P.-ist, Socialist, de Gaullist—carried on their doctrinal fights in real life outside, among their four kinds of French citizens, each of which, since liberation, wants France to be run in an ideological pattern that cannot be reconciled with the ways of the three others. This is not logically possible; this is why the Fourth Republic's survival has been in actual danger; this is why Finance Minister Paul Reynaud's eruption into the scene with his demand for exceptional powers—to save the franc, which, after all, everybody lives on—is also temporarily saving the Fourth Republic. In himself, though physically no bigger than a mouse, he possesses the power of the catalytic agent. As Finance Minister, he can go on being himself—before the war the smartest tax collector of modern France—and the four ideological parties can go on being different, attacking each other and also him, the tarnished Premier of 1940, who handed over the fallen Third Republic to Marshal Pétain. Today, Reynaud sits with idealist, Socialist Léon Blum strangely at his side. "We must save the Republic," the wise old Talmudic patriot said—with the truthfulness that has lately helped ruin his Party—adding as a whispered Party afterthought, "for without it Socialism is impotent." His Socialism has now lost its prestige, just as it has lost its working-class cohorts and voters, who slipped off elsewhere, to Left and to Right. Over the last year, as if today's Parliament were Utopia, the Socialists uniquely, under Blum's idealism, have helped everybody but themselves. The French Socialist Party's present decline is a loss in moderation to all Europe.

October 5

General de Gaulle is very pituitary these days, to judge by his increased appearance at his recent, and important, press conference. It was appropriately held beneath crystal chandeliers, in the elegant old Rue François Premier mansion that has become the headquarters for his French Rally Party. Time, weight, and, evidently, the General's glands are giving his visage a heavy, royal outline; he looks more like a man of dynasty than of destiny. His military voice, which sometimes soars to a treble, and his finical, old-fashioned phraseology make him seem like an eccentric middle-aged monarch. In certain respects, he seems to have improved. There is a closer, quicker, more dynamic connection between his ideas, his words, his remarkable memory, and his convictions. The sense of disaster in present French politics, and the General's own special apocalyptic nature and his growing following, now estimated at forty per cent of voting France, made the content of his press meeting, transmitted by him to us journalists in his special party jargon, headline news. He and his party refer to his followers as "the Companions" and to the Communists as "the Separatists." "The Legality" is their name for the government he would head when and if called to power "by the people's will." He told the press that the Separatists could have representation in his Legality but could not actually have any vote, lest they turn it into what he calls "the Illegitimacy." He used the word "Association" to describe his plan for coöperation between capital and labor, adding that workers must be given an interest in production. Nobody knows whether this means profit-sharing, a fact that may indicate that his main backers are not—as his Leftist opponents claim—the rich industrialists. They would, presumably, long since have rassled some sort of definition out of him on this vital point. For the rest, he was vehemently, intelligently explicit about what has been wrong with every government since he ceased governing.

The General claimed that his party had already realized ten million francs on the sale of its fifty-franc stickers, or stamps. The stickers, an idea of his propaganda chief, the novelist André Malraux, show two Lorraine crosses below the female bust and arms of Rodin's winged Republic, part of a larger group designed as a monument for Verdun. Other political groups have had a lot of free fun with the General's stamps. The Leftist newspaper *Franc-Tireur* prints each day a parody stamp, depicting the General with an umbrella for a body, accompanied by the request that readers cut it out and send it to the General's headquarters, which thousands have done. The Communists' excellent weekly intellectual magazine, *Action*, printed a stamp, in three sections, showing the tall General snipped into three parts and lying flat on his back. Jokes aside, the Parliament's decision to have no major popular elections in the autumn and merely minor ones next spring means that the only way de Gaulle can soon come to power would be by a *coup d'état,* with his hypothetical forty per cent of the French voters at his heels. Against them and their determination to save France by what they are convinced would be an honorable republic would rise that third of France made up of Separatists, who are determined that France become what Moscow now calls a Socialist democracy; i.e., Communist. The French Communist Party's political bureau has just announced its latest Moscow order and slogan: "The French people will never make war against the Soviet Union." In case of a de Gaulle *coup d'état,* the French people would probably fight one another. France is the only European country that is talking about a possible civil war. It's a change, anyway.

France is in a dangerous condition. Her strength is flowing away in choleric politics and falling money. Paper money is worth no more than the total of the national morality behind it. Only voluntary unselfishness and farsighted sacrifices can really help. In the end, France will probably go bankrupt, which will, at any rate, settle things. The French franc is now back on the dollar black market and underselling itself by a clear third. There have been strikes in French mines, banks, government offices, and transportation, gas, and electricity services. At the moment of writing, sections of Paris are without water while the waterworks workers are spending the day protesting against something. Within the month, high prices have become fantastic and, as always, contagious. In the countryside, fertilizer has jumped twenty per cent. In Paris, a ride in the Métro has jumped a hundred per cent. Squeezed by these increases, French life stumbles along.

November 4

The dramatic, unexpected turn in our Presidential election caused extreme surprise, gave great satisfaction, and certainly aroused sentiment here. According to the French calendar, the election took place on Le Jour des Morts (All Souls' Day), a day on which the French celebrate the memory of their dead. To Paris, the election of the Democratic Party and President Truman was a gesture by millions of Americans in remembrance of Roosevelt. For the average citizen here, the main question about the two candidates and their platforms—ideologically indistinguishable to most Continentals, now expert only at evaluating political extremes—was which of the two, the familiar Democrat or the new Republican, would do what for—or with—Europe. This is the attitude of Paris, or any other Western foreign capital, toward Washington today—an acute, vital curiosity as to what our dominant political personalities and elected bodies may decide about the rest of the world.

December 24

France has not fallen during 1948, perhaps less to the surprise of the French than that of everybody else. Looking back on the year, this is the main good news. France apparently cannot knock herself out; she can be knocked out only by some outside force. Though battered by the body blows of her own politics and some of her own people, France is too well fleshed—her land is rich—to do more than stagger sometimes and worry everybody. But she does not fall. The chaotic politics of her republics have not killed her yet, and she is now on Republic No. 4. Unfortunately, what this fourth one has achieved is the logical paradox of twentieth-century European democracy, a mixture of freely elected parties—roughly Left, Center, and Right—in sufficient balance to paralyze one another. The chief political fact of 1948 is that this set trilogy has wavered somewhat. The Socialists, wandering too close to Center, have nearly collapsed, and that is the year's political tragedy, for they are the natural New Dealish bulwark against both reaction and Communism. Communism's supposed loss in popularity is equally important, if equally true. One way or another, France's middle, and muddling, Third Force government has grown a bit stronger. At General de Gaulle's recent monster mass meeting in Vél' d'Hiv, he and his Party chiefs sat high up in a central tribune, with his lesser chiefs sitting below and his rank and file sitting lowest of all, in an obvious hierarchy. If he should come to power in the 1949 spring elections, he could give the French a very odd, unrepublican republic indeed.

1949

April 15

The Marshall Plan's European Recovery Program being one year old, Minister of Finance and Economic Affairs Maurice Petsche recently made a happy-birthday speech over the radio. It was addressed to the United States, but it was really intended for the ears of the French nation. He was explicit; he thanked the Americans for the millions of tons of coal that have kept the wheels of French industry turning; the cotton that the French mills weave two days out of three; the wheat that has lately supplied a quarter of the French bread; and the gasoline on which French trucks roll one day out of two. "All this merchandise," he said with emotion, "has been given us gratis by the American government. A great lifting of the heart goes from us toward the generous American people and toward its leaders."

In this fourth year of peace, France, along with its neighbors in Western Europe, has definitely turned the corner and is rattling down the highway that always had, still has, and, democrats hope, will continue to have some deep political ruts, since only the Communists here guarantee to steam-roller everything smooth. It is now expected that most of what remains of the black market, which has persisted ever since the Occupation, will disappear before the end of this month, when milk, butter, cheese, and maybe fats, oil, and chocolate will be available without ration tickets—at a stiff boost in price, naturally. The franc is soaring, the dollar slumping; there is talk that unloaded black-market dollars may even fall below the legal rate. The Quai d'Orsay's Economic Department of Foreign Affairs has asked the neighboring countries to be ready on May 1st with their money-stabilization plans. American journalists here say they are filing only sixty per cent as much news as they were sending from France a few months ago. This is itself banner news. What it implies is that France is now forty per cent less a headline worry to herself and others than she was when this fourth year of peace began.

Jean-Paul Sartre's Existentialism has often been attacked as a philosophical underminer of postwar French morale, but his latest work of fiction, "Death in the Soul," now being serialized in his monthly magazine, *Les Temps Modernes,* is a novel of high, anguished patriotism. In it, he grieves, like an author and a man, for the loss of one he loved, with all her faults; he grieves for France after her rapid fall in 1940. The novel, the fourth lengthy installment of which is appearing in the current issue, is the third book in "The Road to Freedom," a projected tetralogy on France and some of the French in the past decade. "La Mort dans l'Ame" opens with Sartre's familiar, confusing horizontal technique of aligning unconnected characters and early and late patches of the same event. He starts with a Spanish Republican, in New York, glad that France has fallen; a young White Russian, in Cannes, and his decision to join de Gaulle if his cancerous elderly French mistress will let him; and a Parisian defeatist's bitter pleasure as he notes the handsomeness of the German army marching into Paris. It is only when Sartre backtracks in time and finally focusses on some aimless French soldiers, recumbent and alfresco somewhere at dawn, waiting for day and defeat, that his perspective contracts, and then he stands over his characters with a magnifying closeness. "Where are we?" he asks, speaking for them. "In the grass. Eight citizens in a field, eight civilians in uniform, rolled two by two in one Army blanket, in a vegetable garden. We have lost the war. It was confided to our care and we lost it. It slipped through our hands and was lost somewhere in the North, with a sound of breaking." The schoolmaster Mathieu, from "The Reprieve," the preceding novel in the series, is among this eight, for whom the entire Battle of France consists of exactly fifteen minutes of useless fighting.

At least in its first four installments, "Death in the Soul" is often as dull and as talkative as life, with the virile grossness of speech that is typical of the last war's war books in both the United States and France and that makes many women readers in either language feel civilian and pacifist indeed. But Sartre's new novel also contains enriching formulations and a civilized thoughtfulness that mark it as French. More than any other French writer, he is credited with the sensitivity, talent, philosophy, and patience required to reduce modern history to the size of the individual man.

The artist Christian Bérard recently died—as he had lived for many years—while working, after midnight, in the Marigny Theatre, which houses Barrault's Repertory. His décor for Molière's "Les Fourberies de Scapin," now on view there, is, in a way, his Transfiguration Scene. The single set is a perfect example of his precise sense of stage architecture as a three-sided public shelter for well-rehearsed emotions and actions, with his solid constructions given imaginative perspective by his characteristic, artfully blurred, painter's details, which have always made his scenery look like something seen far off and through time. He was an Ile-de-France painter, and a climatic Paris gray was his favorite color. The décor of "Les Fourberies" is gray, as are the costumes, which are so elegant that they look like portraits of period clothes. Bérard was an authority on Molière and was France's greatest living theatre artist; he more and more used the stage as his easel, to the detriment of his studio canvases. Of late, his attachment to his infrequent paintings, even when he was working on commission, was such that he was inclined to think that they were never finished, so he kept them with him against the day he would add another loving brush stroke. He was a mature eccentric even when he was a good-looking, unbearded youth, and at his death, when he was forty-six, he had become a Paris legend of untidiness and fashionable taste. He was a painter who made his own style and influenced his own time.

April 28

Josephine Baker has returned to the Folies-Bergère as its leading lady. She is still excellent French star material. Her voice continues to be as sweet and reedy as a woodwind instrument. At the beginning of her long Paris career, she looked Harlem; then she graduated to Creole; she has now been transmuted into Tonkinese, or something Eastern, with pagoda headdresses, beneath which her oval face looks like temple sculpture. Her show consists principally of her changing her costumes, which are magnificent. The finale is exceptional. At the top of a high purple staircase, as a well-dressed Western Mary Queen of Scots, wearing a white train that stretches from the flies down to the footlights, she is beheaded, and from behind a veil (to hide her loss) she immediately sings Schubert's "Ave Maria" (written more than two hundred years later), in Latin. Then the whole theatre is turned into a French Gothic church by the appearance of phosphorescent stained-glass windows, which glow above the boxes and the balcony, while the stage is filled with phosphorescent stained-glass-window figures—a regular Folies-Bergère chorus from the clerestory of Chartres Cathedral. This Scottish finale is probably the most spectacular anachronism ever seen on a Paris stage.

May 11

Visitors who want jazz-night-club life will certainly find it on the Left Bank, in the St.-Germain-des-Prés quarter, which has become what Montparnasse used to be. Claustrophilia is the St.-Germain fashion, with the *boîtes* in basements—some of them authentic eighteenth-century cellars that are still unventilated, after all these years. The best new club of the kind is in the basement under the Vieux-Colombier Theatre, with the gifted Claude Luter's *jazz-hot,* and black French African natives singing home songs. The Rose Rouge Club, on the Rue de Rennes, features Les Frères Jacques, a troupe of talented young actors who have become the star entertainers of Paris. Their singing and pantomiming, in sweaters and top hats, of the grammarian Queneau's recent French literary classic "Exercises in Style"—ten ways, tough or refined, of relating the same silly story about a man with an unusual hat on an autobus—is very comic. The Club St.-Germain and the Tabou, the first of the troglodyte caverns called Existentialist—meaning merely jive—are still feverishly popular. There are also Sunday-vespers jam sessions at the old Right Bank Bœuf sur le Toit, now on the Rue du Colisée.

It is sad to have to announce the death of Louis Moysès, known to *tout Paris* as Moïse, founder and patron spirit of the various incarnations, on various streets, of the Bœuf, of which that on the Rue Boissy-d'Anglas during the fabulous nineteen-twenties and early thirties was the celebrated peak. This Bœuf collected the most brilliant figures of a brilliant epoch—the best-known international painters, writers, poets, poseurs, actors, and eccentrics; English milords, dressmakers, and dilettantes; the most talked-of women; the most openhanded millionaires; and the most entertaining parasites. Dadaism, Cubism, and Surrealism all flourished there, amid evening clothes. One member of the Bœuf's famous piano-playing team, Wiener and Doucet, used to read Rimbaud from a book propped on the music rack while he whacked out early boogie-woogie variations on Bach fugues. All that was long ago. One of the Bœuf's writers was tortured to death by the Gestapo, one perished as a slave laborer in the bombing of Hamburg, one committed suicide to avoid being shot as a collaborator of the Nazi Otto Abetz. The Bœuf poets have become bestsellers or Communists. Its greatest painter has become an international political figure. Many other habitués have merely become settled and stout. After the Boissy-d'Anglas's establishment, the Bœuf ran downhill. Few Paris newspapers mentioned the death of M. Moysès, so only a handful of the old Bœuf hedonists rose early enough to go to his funeral, at 9 A.M., in the Neuilly cemetery.

May 26

After a month's refreshing vacation, the French Parliament has just reassembled to deal with a couple of tedious problems that have plagued France intermittently for centuries: how to get the money to balance the national budget and how to stop a war. The war against the insurgent natives in French Indo-China has been dragging on for two and a half years, practically ignored by French politicians and little noticed by most other French citizens, unless, of course, the citizens have had sons fighting, and perhaps dying, there.

As for the war in French Indo-China, *Le Figaro,* politically ever the arch-conservative, has just admiringly stated that Annam's ex-Emperor Bao Dai, who is obligingly pro-French and who recently returned to the country as a mediator from voluntary exile, "conducts his political action like a sportsman." The Socialist *Populaire* and many middle-of-the-road French frankly favor the fighting nationalist Ho Chi Minh, who wants the French Army to get out and stay out, and the colonials to be independent. The Communist *Humanité* is loyally for the Communist rebel government, is especially against the Banque d'Indochine (and Wall Street), which it says are at the bottom of everything, and damns what it calls the Dirty War—"*La Salle Guerre.*" Before the Parliamentary vote on the weighty Indo-Chinese matter—when it was decided that Cochin China and Annam and Tonkin be joined to form the new state of Vietnam, a decision on which a French Indo-China truce may yet be wangled and the war stopped—only fifty Deputies bothered to attend the debates. One of the fifty (who is also a noted professor of anthropology) wearily and wisely remarked, "In any case, in a few months the Communist Chinese armies will have reached the northern frontier of Indo-China."

Prices are dropping in shops and restaurants. So is the recently boosted franc. In 1926, the recalling to the premiership of the strict Raymond Poincaré started, within a few hours, a stiffening of the franc toward a value (twenty-five to the dollar) that it maintained, with only occasional fluctuations, till the beginning of the next war. Today, though, probably only the minting once more of the pre-1914 continental silver coins could check the European inflation that two wars have produced. With astounding ingenuity, France has pieced together a new prosperity, based on a falling paper money. Big business is coming back into politics, and politics is again becoming a cloak for shrewd horse-trading combines, operating under new names. The small, smart, city-type Paul Reynaud, now head of the Independent Republican Party, and Pierre-Etienne Flandin, who was Minister of Something-or-Other in everybody's Cabinet, including Pétain's—these, along with similar long-dormant figures in the discredited Radical Socialist Party (that well-to-do manufacturer of politics and policies for France during most of the Third Republic), are jockeying to get back into the seats which they held so competently, within their limitations, and out of which the convulsion of the war finally threw them. The new French political look of 1944–45 has, understandably, been lost in the revival of bourgeois prosperity, which was thought necessary to fight France's share of Communism in Europe, and the French reform parties that came out of the war searching, as usual, for a brave new world must now, to keep alive, look around for ways of being practical. If the Third Force government falls in the present crisis, the elements out of which the Third Force was itself constructed, plus the more practiced, intense elements that have rallied around it, may well be able to repeat France's interwar phenomenon of the too famous *cabinets des cadavres*—government by the same deadpan faces, in changing official chairs.

It is a remarkable tribute to France that she must now be credited with having in four years, amazingly, recovered from the war. It is a pity that she seems also to have recovered from the spirit of the Liberation.

October 7

The summer is over, and the drought with it. The greatest harm the drought has done is to shake the French peasants' confidence in the necessity for rain. This year's sugar beets are, it is true, unusually small, but they contain an unusually large amount of sugar. This summer's Burgundy grapes are scarce, but they are especially sweet and will make another vintage wine—the fifth in a row. Fruits, notably pears, have been abundant; the lack of rain was made up for by sunlight and the absence of destructive winds. The wheat was more plentiful than it was last year, even though it was short-stalked. Potatoes did suffer. Ile-de-France farmers are digging only twice the weight of potatoes they planted, though an eightfold return is normal. And the farmers cannot compensate for the arid pastures of August and the one crop of meadow hay instead of the customary three. Cattle were slaughtered because they could not be fed. The French government, having turned groceryman, like all governments, has subsidized butter—which it calls "a demagogic victual"—so as to permit a three-per-cent price cut, to stifle the age-old political complaints, from the Left, of high prices. French cigarettes de luxe have just been cut fifty francs, or fourteen cents, a pack, and American cigarettes, at fifty cents a pack, in francs, will be sold in government tobacco shops beginning in November—too late for the tourist trade. The Queuille Cabinet's crisis was provoked by the Socialists' demanding both lower food prices and higher wages for underpaid workers, which workers generally are also insisting upon before prices gather strength for the new jump expected as a result of international devaluation. The cost of food has already risen. According to the official index, it was up four per cent in September.

Another Leftist political undercurrent was set going by the Communist Party's private "vote" for peace on its International Day of Struggle for Peace (Sunday, October 2nd), which culminated in a monster rally around the voting urns set up for the sabbatical balloting in the Parc des Expositions, near the Porte de Versailles. *L'Humanité* next day claimed (as usual) that the rally was attended by "hundreds of thousands of Parisians." The vote was a very successful propaganda sprout of spring's World Congress of the Partisans of Peace. Six Communist mayors were temporarily suspended by the Minister of the Interior for helping local voters to vote, and the Minister of Education publicly warned schoolteachers to eschew any connection with "this illegal referendum." The ballots were printed in September by the Party's elaborate presses and carried the words "I Vote for Peace." The conservative *Figaro* commented that to expect anybody to vote for anything but peace was as silly as to expect anybody to vote for a plague.

The British were the first tourists to make the rounds of the Continent, several centuries ago; then the Germans began travelling in hordes, accompanied by their Baedekers; and finally came the Americans, preferably to Paris, accompanied by their dollars. Without the Germans, with few British as compared to those of the *milord* days, and with only a hundred and sixty thousand invaluable dollar citizens from the States, the 1949 season has nevertheless been a spectacular one for European travel, with an estimated six million people—mostly Europeans—footloose at one time or another. There was also a rich mixture of exotic voyagers, such as Arab chiefs in linen robes, Hindu wives wearing diamond nose buttons, Chinese, Israelis, Turks, and an extra-heavy contingent of elegant South Americans. Even the upper-class French, who rarely go anywhere (except into occasional exile), have been travelling outside their own land. In preparation for an expected three million Catholic pilgrim-tourists to Italy next year (which is an Anno Santo), who will put that country at the top in tourism, Rome's mayor recently concluded an investigation into why his city has been running second to Paris. He discovered that the answer is noise. Noise was suppressed for a time, by Mussolini, and the Demo-Christian Republic has for political reasons feared to bring the matter up again, but it will now take steps. For tourists are the most cherished big business in Europe today.

Not only was the Paris tourist season the best in all Europe but it is continuing, thus turning into the longest one on record. Paris hotels, chic or shabby, Right Bank or Left, are still packed with summer leftovers. The Paris hotels, which, in comparison with those of London or New York, were always cheap, have gone up formidably in price, owing to taxes, wage scales, and the postwar French system of high profits to replace lost capital. Last year, the Government Tourist Bureau feared that Paris's rising hotel rates would scare off tourists or at least make them scream. The only outcry right now is from frustrated travellers who can't squeeze in anywhere, regardless of what they are willing to pay. This summer's mass travel in Western Europe was probably a logical enough result of its recent history. For six years, almost nobody travelled except soldiers and those segments of the population that made an exodus in fright or in fatal, forced emigrations. Some people travelled then because they were ordered to, while others, shut in, yearned in vain to move about. And there were not enough trains, food, or, most important, money, all of which now seem to abound. It is difficult to believe that Europe could change so miraculously and become the great, pleasurable, money-making and money-spending touring ground that it has been this season, exactly one decade after the war season of 1939.

The liveliest revue in Paris features that oldest of old tourist favorites, Mistinguett, in the smallest, funniest, lowest-priced show of her endless career. She must be almost the age of the Third and Fourth Republics combined, and her famous legs have long since assumed the impersonal rank of public statuary. Her show, entitled "Paris S'Amuse," is housed in the little A.B.C. Music Hall, with tickets at from a hundred and twenty to six hundred francs—thirty-four cents to a dollar seventy—and with costumes that are also strictly cotton-grade. Mistinguett is an amazing sight; she still has her lovely, white, sharp-looking teeth, her handsome blue eyes are still empty of thought, and her voice still tintinnabulates on pitch, like a nice, weathered sheep bell. Her dancing has become a series of gingerly skips. To judge by the topical songs she sings about herself, she is still hard-working, still rich, and still growing richer. Big Paris revues such as those she used to star in were traditionally nude and dull. With elderly showmanship, she has seen to it that the sketches in her current revue have satire and good acting, and she has, further, arranged that her chorus girls be buttoned up to the neck.

October 23

Paris has too many automobiles for comfort and is about to have many too many more. During the last fortnight, the Municipal Council's Police Committee announced that there are now twice as many cars in town as there were in 1945, that they are producing the worst traffic bottlenecks in this ancient city's vehicular history, and that two-thirds of the injuries in the Paris Police Department are suffered by the unfortunate traffic squad; and the thirty-sixth annual Salon de l'Automobile has just opened at the Grand Palais to sell more automobiles.

Sixty-four canvases by Picasso, painted during the last two years, have recently been on view at the Maison de la Pensée Française. Since a dozen of these pictures, in his latest distorted manner, are almost recognizable as portraits of children, a list of his offspring is tacked on the gallery wall for the art-lover's information. According to this, his eldest son, who was the model for the lovely harlequin-boy portraits in the early nineteen-twenties, is now thirty and is not represented in this show. Nor is an eleven-year-old daughter. However, his new little son, Claude, and his baby daughter, Paloma, both by his handsome mistress, Françoise Gilot, repeatedly figure in it, as does the mother. A portrait of Paloma, "Infant in Her Perambulator," with the pram wheels and the babe's eyes and nose going off in unexpected directions, might well frighten any child beyond the pram stage into fits. There are two equestrian studies of Claude, both called "Child on a Rocking Horse." Three portraits of the children's mother show a new, more benevolent family style—a normal full-face likeness of a pretty and blond woman, overlaid by a kind of green curtain of traditional Cubist lines. There are also a few magnificently astringent still-lifes, one of which is the hit of the show. Its subject matter sounds absurd but looks both rational and poetic—a stuffed owl perched by a study table and clutching a long spear. In these still-lifes, the genius of Picasso's composition and line serves once more as the signature of the modern master.

At the city's Musée d'Art Moderne there is a retrospective exposition of ninety paintings and drawings by Fernand Léger, done since 1905. It covers all his periods, from cubes through mechanics, tubes, architecturals, dynamics, objects in space, and the American epoch. His latest is husky ladies wearing tights and riding bicycles. The major opus in this new vein is called "Leisure."

France has been like her old self again; that is, without a government for more than two weeks and torn by an angry, noisy, doctrinary, disputatious crisis in Parliament. The Socialists provoked it by insisting on higher wages for a small section of underprivileged workers. The Socialists then tried to calm things by proffering as Premier their own unpopular Minister of the Interior, Jules Moch, who was bound to be offensive to the Left, because last autumn he loosed the Army on France's striking miners—an act the proletariat still recalls as unforgivable. Probably the Socialist Party has stretched itself too far, it being now like a rainbow, with red radical members on one end and true-blue nationalists on the other. The third party in size for more than a year, it has been first in its parliamentary job, which is to serve as a willing minority that, when added to a minority even smaller, like former Premier Henri Queuille's Radical-Socialist Party, tots up (with a little extra help) to a working majority by which France can be governed. Georges Bidault's Popular Republican Party (M.R.P.), second in size, has been unable to get minority help, because it is considered too pro-Church. The Communists, who are the leading party, have also been unable to get minority aid, for reasons too many to enumerate. France has therefore been governed by minorities, elected by a minority of her citizens. Those who lost the elections have been running the country. When this anomaly blows up, as it just has, it takes time for it to be put together again.

November 4

During the better part of October, France had no government. Nor is it certain that things will be improved politically by the earnest new Premiership of Georges Bidault, of the Popular Republican (M.R.P.) Party. In his opening declaration to Parliament, he spoke sadly of "the indifferent eye turned by a tired nation" on democratic (and quarrelsome) institutions like the one he was speaking to. For, after all the fuss, he came to office with practically the same political program as that offered by the Socialist Jules Moch, the most bitterly rebuffed of October's "designated" but not "invested" Premiers. For a minute, it looked as if Bidault, an ex-Premier himself—from the provisional government set up after the Liberation—might have to make up his cabinet almost exclusively of other ex-Premiers, of many political varieties.

Parliament's expert cynics now prophesy that the moneyed bourgeoisie, strengthened by its recent astonishing recovery, is determined to crack its way back into political power. If it succeeded, the actual boss party would again be the Radical Socialists—in which businessmen are as thick as plums—the party that was longest in power in the prosperous heyday between wars and that brought, along with its valuable energy, get-rich-quick scandals and political atrophy. Since the war, the Radical Socialist Party has lain doggo, and time has washed away some of its stains. Surely the answers to the questions now before Parliament, which include the freeing of wages frozen in wartime, the renewal of collective bargaining, and a review of the privileges of strikers whose actions affect public economic safety, concern employers no less than employees. The French think that what France is going to have to face up to is another general election, and soon. Any regime between now and then may be merely a precarious government of day-to-day events.

A series of unflattering analytical anti-American articles, intended principally as merely pro-French, has caused surprise and chagrin in both nations' official circles here since it began to appear in the dignified *Monde*. As a revised, postwar version of the august *Temps,* this newspaper usually achieves, as a diurnal miracle, the accuracy of a lexicon in its writing style, a total absence of humor, and editorials as heavy as bars of gold. Pierre Emmanuel, the author of the articles, the subject of which was what he terms *"L'Amérique Impériale,"* is a youngish French poet and philosophy professor, whose first unsatisfactory visit to the United States apparently occurred, in the company of his parents, when he was aged four. As a polemicist, he has a manner that is an uneven mixture of insults and fiery critical judgments. In one *Monde* gibe, he coarsely remarked, apropros of our President's reported approval of the Vatican's excommunicatory decree against militant Moscow, "And nobody even cracks a smile on seeing the former suspenders merchant transformed into a defender of the faith. 'Hello, Pope!' says Mr. Truman." Emmanuel added, "For five years, American propaganda has been based only on fear [of Communism], a panic sign of impotence. Production-consumption is the diptych of American existence. America kills itself with work. It is a continent hostile to anyone who thinks. Publicity hammers the American brain just as propaganda does [in Russia]. Old countries like France, Italy, and England remind America of its inferiority complex." Emmanuel excoriated Americans for taking to drink and sex. Indeed, he said, America's interest in sex has been its most obvious donation to postwar Europe, where "even in the land of Stendhal, *le phallus est en passe de devenir un dieu,*" a statement that must have astounded the polite *Faubourg* no less than it did the Marshall Plan administrators here.

Mme. Colette has recently been chosen president of the Goncourt Academy—the first woman ever to receive this literary honor. The ovation given her on the opening night of "Chéri," her own dramatization of her famous novel, at the Théâtre de la Madeleine was also unique. Elderly, arthritic, ensconced in a stage box, from which only her head was visible—her still mordantly witty face surrounded by its nimbus of radiant hair—she received the acclaim of what is left of the three generations of *tout Paris* she has known: of French government representatives, members of her own and other academies, the leading poets, writers, and artists, and less prosperous admirers, high in the gallery, who have loved her sad love stories of the froufrou days of gay Paris before the First World War. As for the critics, they paid their homage in their reviews of the play, even though the novel's sombre nuances and emotional flow were lost under the spotlights and the theatre's rigid necessity for three acts. As the leading, fading cocotte of the play, Valentine Tessier seemed more a fine actress than a convincing demimondaine. As Chéri, the old-fashioned gigolo, the romping Jean Marais appeared not to know the more romantic tricks of the trade.

Paris critics were, on the other hand, unanimously severe with the modern amoralities of Tennessee Williams' "Un Tramway Nommé Désir," produced, with the addition of odd blackouts and Negro dancers, in a very free French text by Jean Cocteau, at the Théâtre Edouard VII. Arletty, theretofore known as a comedienne, played the sad, mad Blanche. The piece is a hit with the public, at least. The farther this New Orleans play goes afield, via foreign-language productions in Rome, Brussels, Sweden, and

Paris—and even in the English of London—the less, apparently, its meaning resembles the meaning it had in New York.

November 16

In the small back room of a new Left Bank bookshop called La Hune, a James Joyce exhibition is going on. It is almost as weighty, concise, and personal as his greatest book, "Ulysses," around which it is, properly, built. Joyce died in a final exile, in Zurich, in 1941. His library, his manuscripts, and other possessions that were found in his Paris flat after his death, and were to be sold for back rent, were lovingly and illegally salvaged by his friends Paul Léon and Alexander Ponizowski, both of whom later died in a concentration camp, after being deported by the Germans. Joyce's Paris relics figure with especial vividness in the exhibition; they have been arranged with "piety and skill" by those of his Paris friends who survive, led by the catalytic Mrs. Maria Jolas and Léon's Russian widow, Mme. Lucie Noel. As was recently so accurately remarked by the literary critic George Slocombe, "No writer since Shelley had more friends. Joyce was the most reticent literary genius of this century. Of all his years of exile, he lived longest and perhaps most happily in Paris. It was here that 'Ulysses' was first published in book form, here he wrote 'Finnegans Wake,' here he gained world celebrity."

This compact collection contains examples of all his printed works in all known editions and translations; examples of his notebooks and of his published and unpublished manuscripts, in his uncertain, cryptic script; most of the consequential things that have been written about him or to him (such as letters from André Gide and T. S. Eliot)—all these knowingly gathered by people who knew him and know one another—together with photographs of him and of them, and of his family and their dwelling places, plus a curious gallery of battered oil paintings of his Irish ancestors that he usually carried around with him on his European odysseys. Three courageous American women publishers have notable places in the photograph gallery. They are the Quaker Harriet Weaver, of the Egoist Press, whose generosity permitted Joyce to finish "Ulysses," in twenty years; Margaret Anderson, who was the first to print it—or sections of it—in her *Little Review* and was haled into court by John Sumner for obscenity; and Sylvia Beach, of Shakespeare & Co., who first published it as a book. The exhibition is to be open until Christmas, after which the major part of it, including the family portraits, will be put up for sale—to an American university, many Americans here hope. It is the Complete Joyce, which should be kept intact as a reference library for time to come.

There has lately been a dog show, in midtown Paris; a cat show, becomingly held in the old-fashioned gilt purlieus of the Continental Hotel; a canary show, trilling in the lake pavilions of the Buttes Chaumont; an inexplicable boa constrictor, which was discovered comatose in the gutter of the Quai Voltaire beside the second-hand bookstalls; and General de Gaulle, stentoriously addressing a press conference in the Quai d'Orsay. He literally distinguished himself by saying loudly, "I am de Gaulle," then added the identification that he was the non-politician who was summoning the French to a national renovation—to be led by him, apparently, but only as a savior. He ended by saying tactlessly to the journalists, "I do not know how extensively your objectivity can deploy itself." His eighteenth-century Versailles court style of French and its vocabulary seemed more elegant, mordant, and unaccommodating than ever before. He accused the Anglo-Saxons of having recently fed Germany nothing but an apple of discord and said that a basic settlement in Europe could be obtained only by setting up cultural and economic relations between the French and Germans, the two dominant European nations, without interference such as there had lately been from Washington and London. As for the North Atlantic Pact, he thought that in case of trouble, American aid for France would eventually arrive, "but we would be dead by then, and such aid interests us relatively little." He favored the proposed change in the voting system which is agitating Parliamentary circles at the moment and by which the Communists would lose, according to their screams, a third of their representation—just how is not clear. But with voting changes would come a new election, which no political party except de Gaulle's craves. The betting is that he would steal a great many of the Popular Republican (M.R.P.) voters.

December 8

Paris has no bobby-soxers. Its popular *chansonniers* have to satisfy people who demand a more mature version of life and love than crooning and mooning. Yves Montand, who was trained by Edith Piaf, has now retrained himself and has been delighting adult crowds at the old vaudeville house L'Etoile, where he follows the acrobats and constitutes the entire last half of the bill. A former factory hand, he wears a kind of overalls on the stage. He has learned to make, in the best sense, a perfect show of himself—of his virile, suburban personality, his gift for miming and deftly timed gestures, his carefully clumsy dancing, and his happy hedonist's voice. His songs are short stories of sentiment and character. The favorites are "Clémentine," which is about a best girl; "Paris," about a lonely country boy newly arrived in the city; and "Les Feuilles Mortes," about lovers whose spring has changed to dead leaves.

December 28

By peering around, by glancing back, by peeking forward, Parisians already have a notion of what the new year of 1950 looks like, as the half-century date comes into focus. Some of the significant features, large and small, that make up the present approximation of the immediate future would seem to be the following. No. 1, Politics: The French government may fall. It is a question of passing a budget, a question of money in general, a question of taxes in particular. In this continuing crisis, if as many as three hundred and eleven deputies could agree long enough to vote their lack of confidence in the government, the Chamber of Deputies would also fall. France would be right back where she has been several times since the Liberation—back at the polls and a general election, which could do the Fourth Republic little good. No. 2, Good Cheer: The French called this the first prewar Christmas since the war. It was the first Christmas without rationed foods, except for coffee, and that was available in large quantities, as usual, on the black market. It was the first Christmas when there was every kind of merchandise that the heart could desire. Mostly, the French bought fine food for their stomachs. The poorer ones didn't spend much money except with the butcher and baker, dedicating their holiday purse to Maman's art in the kitchen and a gala dinner at home. No. 3, Forgiveness of Sins: A bill providing amnesty to collaborators with the Germans—if neither murder nor any other crime was involved—has been introduced in Parliament. If passed, this will make a very happy 1950 for eight thousand alleged collaborationists still in jail. No. 4, Music: For the past month, the Opéra and the Opéra Comique have been closed. The orchestras are striking for as much money as they would get if they played in a musical-comedy theatre, where musicians are paid a third more for playing less well. As state employees, musicians in the two Opéra orchestras can be given raises only by the Minister of Finance, who is too worried over the national budget to receive flute players and the like. No. 5, Iron Curtain News: Latest echoes from the Wroclaw trial have it that the guilty were, according to their lawyers, "led astray" by cosmopolitanism, by Sartrism (i.e., the ism of Jean-Paul Sartre), by American literature (no writer named), by Wall Street money, by Bevin, by Truman, by de Gaulle, and by Coca-Cola. No. 6, Intelligentsia: A book is about to be published here, as well as in the United States, called "The God that Failed." It is a collection of articles written by André Gide, Stephen Spender, Louis Fischer, Richard Wright, Arthur Koestler, and Ignazio Silone, who give the reasons for their disillusionment with the Communist Party—at one time they were all either Party members or fellow-travellers. No. 7, E.C.A.: This new year sees the beginning of the end of Marshall Plan aid, as originally timetabled. The E.C.A. and the possibility that disgruntled Washington legislators may close it down completely sooner than scheduled are far and away the most prevalent topics for editorializing in the Paris press, and such a move would drastically change the face of the New Year. For the most part, the editorials take the form of thanks mixed with questions. The thanks are for what America has given. The main question is: When is America going to start to receive? She has given Europe her money and her goods. When will she begin buying European goods? And what are Europeans supposed to buy from America with their shrunken money? A dollar deficit sometimes seems to be the only thing that the potential United States of Europe so far have in common. French editorial writers largely agree, in effect, that the Marshall Plan dollars were at first a warm, fertilizing wind from the west, causing postwar business to sprout again in the war-caked area of Western Europe. What they think is urgently needed now is a great wind that will blow in both directions across the ocean—and blow good and hard, like a splendid gale, for the rest of the twentieth century.

Jean Genet's "Journal du Voleur" has recently been published for the first time in a relatively cheap edition—that is to say, at nearly triple the price of the average novel. Ever since he was first published, in 1943, his works have mostly been privately printed and de luxe, enjoying those lavish publishing favors that make a book not so much forbidden to all as too costly for most. This new edition of one of his major writings puts him within range of general criticism. Genet was discovered during the war by Cocteau. By Genet's account, he was born illegitimate, raised in an orphan asylum, trained in a reform school, and became a thief. The commentary value of his "Diary of the Thief," a novel that is certainly unique in French literature, is its unsalvational viewpoint. He believes that society is not a mixture of good and evil but is a field with a fence across it—on one side are the evil, the outcasts, the misbegotten or desperate poor who for centuries have made criminality their special form of civilization, frame of survival, and group education. To his special damned land, to his country of wretched city alleys, abandoned only during protracted visits to prison, Genet gives his loyalty, his imagination, his fervid romanticism, and his talent as a remarkable novelist and writer of the French language; he creates, indeed, a sort of chauvinism, or patriotism, that until now has precluded an affection for, or even contact with, any other scene, as if he were a regional writer to whom no more interesting place exists on earth. His books, peopled by jailbirds, pimps, traitors, prostitutes, and vicious youths on whom, like a street light, the bright glare of his lubricity suddenly shines, are *sui generis*. They are nothing like the noted eighteenth-century picaresque writings of Restif de la Bretonne, nor are they remotely similar to the calculated tableaux of the Marquis de Sade, which were padded out, between the acts, by philosophizing. Genet writes of criminality and wickedness as naturally as Conrad wrote of the sea or as Hardy wrote of the landscapes of Wessex. Undoubtedly the least sought after of Genet's works is his brochure "L'Enfant Criminel," published a few months ago. It is a brief description of the brutalities of the French reform schools he knew when he was an adolescent, and it was written to be read by him on a national radio program called "Carte Blanche," accepted, and then turned down. In contemporary French letters, Genet is the lone *fleur du mal*.

1950

January 11

The old *Nouvelles Littéraires,* which, if only from pleasant habit, is still everywhere in France the most cherished of the Paris literary weeklies, brought out a stately 1900–50 number at the beginning of the year, to commemorate what important men have been thinking, creating, writing about, or appreciating as readers during the past half century. This special issue's focal point was the tabulation of a poll taken by the editor among two hundred notable *personnalités françaises,* who were asked to select Les Dix Phares (The Ten Lighthouses), or the ten brains that gave the greatest amount of light in that period. Einstein, one of three foreigners selected, won the place of honor at the top of the list, with the approval of seventy per cent of the voters. Behind him came Bergson, Proust, Debussy, Gide, Valéry, Prince Louis de Broglie, Freud, Picasso, and, last, the poet-diplomat-playwright Claudel, with a score of fifty-two per cent.

Some of the illuminators chosen by a smaller number of the voters were Hemingway ("to represent the American influence on French literature"), General Eisenhower, Marshal Foch, Rilke, Renoir, Rodin, César Franck, and Fleming—the discoverer of penicillin. By all odds the queerest light under a bushel basket, designated by only one admirer, was the witty, deaf, poison-pen, anti-Semitic, anti-republican, pro-Fascist, royalist old Charles Maurras, of the defunct *Action Française,* now finishing his life in a Lyons prison as a Nazi collaborator.

Of the many letters of explanation printed along with the nominations, one of the most interesting was from Maurice Schumann, Popular Republican Deputy and skillful, cultivated French politician. His contribution to the *Nouvelles* attained a cultural, philosophic, and literary tone that could well make the average Washington congressman's eyes bulge. "When I received your inquiry," Schumann wrote to the editor, "I began to think out loud, and the result is the following. My choice is Péguy, Bergson, Alain, Debussy, Picasso, Claudel, Maritain, Mauriac, [René] Grousset, and Mme. Curie. I am in no way certain that these ten are the most characteristic and important of the terminating half century, but I feel and I know that they built my universe. The only lecture by Mme. Curie that I was privileged to attend, even though I was incapable of comprehending it, extended my horizon forever after. Thirty-six years ago, the real Picasso already showed that he knew how to draw like Ingres. Mauriac had almost finished his famous novel 'L'Enfant Chargeé de Chaînes.' With surprise, I note that by instinct I have excluded from my list Barrès, Gide, Valéry, and even Proust. Did they enlighten me or lead me astray? I shall not know until my children are mature in their turn. All this merely confirms my idea that today the men of my generation are essentially 'survivalists,' a fact that condemns them to tragedy but confers upon them a singular dignity."

Coca-Cola has finally reached the diplomatic level here. According to the French newspapers, the United States Ambassador, David Bruce, in line with duty, recently demanded an audience of Premier Bidault to talk Coca-Cola. (He had already consulted Finance Minister Petsche on the same refreshing subject.) Last year, consideration of what the Communists gloomily called the "Coca-Colonization of France"—the projected distribution of the beverage on an enormous scale—was discussed by the French Cabinet and was mentioned, usually without affection, at several meetings of Parliamentary committees. This year, the Communists have a brand-new damnation of our national drink. They declare that the Coca-Cola distribution organization will double as a spy network. This harrowing conclusion is based on the fact that the head of the Coca-Cola bottling concession for North Africa, whose offices are in Casablanca, is Mr. Kenneth Pendar, who four years ago wrote a book called "Adventure in Diplomacy," which described his war work in that country as a vice-consul—work that included such unobjectionable tasks as making household arrangements for President Roosevelt and his party during their conference visit there. Today, the Communists see spies everywhere, and to them Coca-Cola is just plain Wall Street hemlock.

There has also been an equable but almost equally inhospitable editorial on Coca-Cola in *Le Monde.* After noting that American chewing-gum wrappers strew Paris boulevards, that our tractors plow French fields, that du Pont stockings sheathe Parisiennes' legs, that Frigidaires chill gourmets' foods, that anyhow Coca-Cola has been selling slightly in France ever since 1919, and that some new concessions for it will be assigned to, and thus will give profit to, French firms like Pernod and the Glacières de Paris, *Le Monde* penetratingly pointed out why many intelligent wine-drinking French shiver at the prospect of also drinking two hundred and forty million bottles of Coca-Cola a year, this, according to *Le Monde,* being Coca-Cola's official quota for France. "What the French criticize is less Coca-Cola than its orchestration," *Le Monde* ruminated, "is less the drink itself than the civilization, the style of life of which it is a sign and in a certain sense a symbol. For the implanting of Coca-Cola in a country is generally accompanied by advertising in the American manner, with red delivery trucks promenading publicity, neon lights, and walls covered with signs, placards, and advertisements." It should be added that an American Coca-Cola official here has since declared to the Paris *Herald Tribune,* "We don't plan to hang any red signs on Notre-Dame or the Eiffel Tower," the second of which, as a matter of fact, used to bear a gigantic, blinking red advertising sign that spelled "Citroën." "Certain very sound citizens," *Le Monde* continued sadly and wisely, "consider that, since many French customs have already regrettably disappeared, those that still persist should be defended. For it is now a question of the whole panorama and morale of French civilization."

Paris has sartorially revolutionized its traffic police and has turned traffic itself upside down in an effort to speed the circulation of automobiles through a city in which some of the streets have always been too narrow—even for a couple of the King's cavalrymen abreast. To heighten the traffic policemen's visibility at night, on the main avenues they now wear elegant white capes, white gauntlets, and a heavy white band around their kepis, which make them both chic and noticeable. As an experiment, a few of those on the Place de la Concorde have also been equipped with what looks at night like a magic wand—a glass baton, powered by an electric battery, that turns white for "Go" and red for "Stop." Since most motorists stop anyway to get a good look, the practice so far has been unfair to the theory. The shakeup in the traffic rules has given Paris twenty-nine new one-way streets, including the Rue de Rivoli, and a few more precious parking spots. In general, the system has been easy to follow. It is mostly the exact contrary, as to directions and turnings, of what it was before. On the day the new system went into effect, the Place de la Concorde, which was the most radically affected, was transformed into a motorized merry-go-round about the Egyptian Obelisk (thirteenth century B.C., period of Ramses II). The uproar of horns was so tremendous that pedestrians lined the square to jeer at and, for once, enjoy them.

January 25

"Le Deuxième Sexe," a long, thoughtful work by Mme. Simone de Beauvoir on the peculiar, even awkward place in civilization that first nature and then man have put the human female, was recently published here. It will eventually be published in the United States, where it should interest readers of the Kinsey Report. The American male would surely be cheered to read of his sex's age-old, uninterrupted, systematized position of superiority over the little woman, though, naturally, he would have to leave her and his home and come to Europe to live to get much out of the situation now. Some of the book might seem archaic to American women (whom the author is not writing about), because the difference between the average American male and the average American female has been reduced to a minimum by our un-European way of life. Mme. de Beauvoir is discussing the maximum, as she finds it in France. French publishing figures show that French readers are not interested in reading books about sex, which hers basically is. The Kinsey Report in French hasn't sold at all. Freud's works were influential but never popular. Mme. de Beauvoir's book has received some rough, unjust reviews. Yet it is a serious, provocative study, unlike any ever produced by a French *femme de lettres* before.

Mme. de Beauvoir has been a philosophy teacher and is a novelist and an editor, and in "The Second Sex" she functions as all three. Her volume is carefully documented, though perhaps there are too many case histories of frigid and unhappy women and not enough of contented women. Its quotations from world literature, including novels—there are few from science—are numerous and scholarly. The book is a dry, wry job, written straightforwardly by an intelligent, determined woman, a practiced writer, and a watchful observer who, having inherited three thousand years of European civilization, has something conclusive on her mind that she wants to say. Her opening premise, which would certainly not be everybody's, is: "One is not born a woman; one becomes it. No biological, psychic, or economic destiny [makes woman] but the ensemble of civilization, which elaborates this intermediate product, between the male and the capon, that is called feminine." More mildly, she thinks that woman's defects and limitations are precisely what society has desired of her and has perfected in her; that her character, such as it is, is the result of her situation; that sex has been hard sledding for most females, and that this is the fault of man and nature; that "the eternal feminine" is hocus-pocus and a male alibi; and that the battle of the sexes should be not denied but explained. A long philoanalytical chapter entitled "Justifications" was to this *deuxième-sexe* reader the most interesting part of the book.

Not in a quarter century have the food markets of Paris been fuller or more tempting. In the Rue du Faubourg-St.-Denis, there is a two-hundred-yard stretch of food shops and street barrows. The hucksters shout their prices and the shop apprentices have become barkers, standing at the shop doors and bawling about the luscious wares inside. In the *charcuteries* there is a mosaic of every known dainty—turkey pâté, truffled pigs' trotters, chicken in half mourning, whole goose livers, boar's-snout jelly, and fresh truffles in their fragile bronze husks. In the poultry shops, there are Strasbourg geese and Muscovy ducks. In the entrail shops, there are indescribable inner items and blood sausages. At the fish stalls, there are costly deep-sea oysters and enormous, hairy sea spiders, to be buried in mayonnaise. The street barrows are filled with bearded leeks and potential salads. The Rue du Faubourg-St.-Denis is not a rich district of the city, but these days it offers a Lucullan supply. Food is still what Parisians buy if they can. It is a nervous means of getting satisfaction, a holdover from the lean years of the Occupation. As for other commodities, also here in abundance, people say they cannot afford them. Prices in the annual January white sales have dropped, and in men's shops shorts, pajamas, and shirts have been marked down from twenty to sixty per cent, but no one is buying. Bankers sourly declare that only a conventional postwar depression will jostle prices and things and people down to normal again, at which point people will buy an undershirt and lay it away, instead of buying pâté de foie gras and eating it.

May 3

There has been considerable literary talk about, and certainly substantial spiritual refreshment in, the revival of Church faith and practices, which started during the sadness of the Occupation, as if postwar French life offered almost the same melancholy and material discouragement as the war years. Among the major contributors to the reanimated Catholic faith are the posthumous books of a Parisian Jewess, Mlle. Simone Weil, who was converted to a personal, perhaps unorthodox Catholicism. Her first book, which was printed two years back and has since gone through several editions, was called "La Pesanteur et la Grâce" ("Weight and Grace"), a title that expresses what was her belief—that the weight of original sin is the law of creation and divine grace consists of man's de-creating himself and losing his ego. Her second book, "L'Enracinement" ("The Roots of the Matter"), was published last year, and the third, "L'Attente de Dieu" ("Waiting for God"), is now on the press. The Weil books have touched the lay-religious soul more than any other personal confessional since Amiel's "Journal," that celibate revelation of Swiss ethics that came out of the last century. The Weil offerings are more apostolic and Pentecostal, though Mlle. Weil's gift of tongues, if fiery, was hasty and not literary. Sure of an early death from semi-starvation and tuberculosis, she did not bother to leave her report of her "inner purification" in any more polished form than a series of notebooks. She was a Parisian, a pupil of Alain, was a University of Paris graduate in philosophy, fantastically erudite in classical languages, and a schoolteacher outside Paris until the Occupation race laws drove her to the Unoccupied Zone; was non-Communist but militant Left; had worked in the Renault factory to detach herself from her intellectualities; and had labored in the fields, where she insisted on living solely on wild blackberries. She followed her parents to New York, then soon afterward went to

London to broadcast for the French Resistance, there refused to eat more than her French friends in France received on their meagre ration cards, and there dwindled away, aged thirty-four, in 1943.

Mlle. Weil endlessly talked mysticism in a monotonous voice, and suffered almost uninterruptedly from headaches. She became so Christian that she was once in trouble with the Church for resenting the inclusion of the Jewish Old Testament in the Bible. To the general reader, her first book seems to be her best, and its oddest, most affecting chapter is the one called "Le Moi" ("The Ego"). Her illuminated idea was that the "I," the personality, the ego, must be shed and effaced. (There is also a thought-provoking chapter entitled "Effacement.") She says many strange things that the psychoanalysts, whom she scorned, have rarely said so well, such as: "We really possess nothing on this earth except the power to say 'I.' This is what we must give over to God—that is to say, destroy. Absolutely no other free act is permitted us. Though nothing should be gained from victory, one supports death for a victorious, not for a defeated, cause. . . . If you help unhappy people and are ill-treated afterward, you are merely carrying a frail part of their unhappiness. . . . Pharisees were people who relied on their own force to be virtuous."

Business is bad in Paris. Owners make profits, all right, but unexpected new jumps in the prices of materials whittle their profits down. When workingmen win their strikes for higher wages, the increase goes into the next new price, and in the end everybody is a consumer, carrying an increasing burden. It will be an aesthetic blow for Paris itself and a tragedy for the myriad workers involved with the *haute couture* if the big dressmakers do not pull out of their current financial doldrums. Skirts are short again, but dressmakers' faces are as long as trains.

Spring has been like leftover winter here, with rain, sleet, and winds until May Day, when the traditional wild lilies of the valley, gathered from neighboring woods, were green, scentless, and very expensive on their stems. But in the forests the chill rain and clouds finally produced some compensating joys. For those willing to trudge among the trees to find them, there has been a wondrous mannalike crop of morel mushrooms, which look like flaccid sponges, are the gourmet's delight, and are considered the finest table gift hereabouts. And the neighborhood nightingales, which had been mute under April tempests, burst, in relief, into great choruses of churring, trilling, and musical pining under the welcome full moon, white and virile, with its man's face showing extra plainly, that brought in the first nights of May.

May 18

Foreign Minister Robert Schuman's surprise project to pool France's and Germany's steel and coal production has so enraged the French coal and steel magnates and the French and German Communists that they are all fit to be tied—for once, in the same bundle. In one way, at least, the Schuman project has pleased many Frenchmen, even those who, owing to caution, hatred, or memory, think Germany should always be pushed down and never helped up so that she can stand again on her own, and probably France's, feet. The average Frenchman is pleased because he believes the Schuman proposal of a Franco-German pool is the most creative of all the postwar ideas so far, second in importance only to the Marshall Plan and superior to it in realism, since Schuman's proposal literally means business, whereas Marshall's kind notion is regarded as meaning charity. Psychologically, too, the Schuman project has given local spirits a lift; it has been inspiring for Frenchmen to see their defeated France, once mistress of Europe, actually taking a positive, unwobbling step forward on her worn old high heels, without an initial friendly push from England, more recently the balancer of Europe—a push that France has waited for since the war's end. Indeed, many French feel that Schuman has at last furnished an answer to France's most worrisome peace problem: whether France should try to make a Europe without England or not try to make a Europe because of England?

Of course, many French also think that the Schuman plan may just possibly provide the answer to the even older German postwar problem, for it obviously gives new hope to Western Germans, already impatient after five years of fairly benevolent, bumbling, and costly Allied occupation, so unlike the Germans' own years of cruel, well-planned, locustlike occupation of all Europe, from Poland to the Atlantic and the Mediterranean. In the past hundred and fifty years, France has tried everything with the Germans except helping them, which to the French has never seemed natural; she has conquered them and been conquered by them, has paid them and attempted to get paid by them, has been occupied by them and has occupied them, has been overharsh with them and contemptuously loose with them. Schuman's shrewd plan is regarded by some people as the first intelligent French effort to control modern Germany's vigorous industrial genius, which is always working on what look like baby carriages but turn out, when put together, to be cannons. No people in France, or anywhere else in Western Europe, are as hysterical about the possibility of a war with Russia as the Americans, or at least those Americans on holiday here, whose Fifth Avenue or Golden Gate would probably be the last to face hand-to-hand fighting with Russian soldiers, if such a muscular anachronism is conceivable in any next, scientists' war. But the French would like to feel that if there is, God save us, to be another war, the German cannons will not this time be pointing in France's direction. To the French, the Schuman plan seems a bid for business, salvation, consideration, and even a protracted peace.

June 1

Right now, Paris is a refined boom town. For its natives, there is too much to see and hear—a blend of intellectual entertainment and honkytonk. Hotels are jammed to the bathtubs with tourists from all latitudes, with enough cash for everything, from Furtwängler's magnificent and high-priced concerts (Berlin conductors and orchestras are ever the dearest in Paris: *aber warum?*) to the Folies-Bergère and its chocolate-tinted American Peters Sisters. In the latest European version of themselves, they descend through the theatre's ceiling as crooning, overweight parachutists. At the Opéra, also at extra-high prices, Flagstad has been heard in "Götterdämmerung," and Max Lorenz merely seen, except in the last act, for which he saves his voice. One modest item in this vast grab bag has been the exquisite performance, at the suburban Château de Sceaux, of Lully's "Idylle sur la Paix," with a libretto by Racine. This was only its third presentation since its première in 1685. Most of us went as far as we could by subway, then trekked a few hearty miles through Le Nôtre's lovely topiary gardens, with their pollarded linden trees imitating arches and walls. In their day, Louis XIV, for whom the idyll was written, and his guests arrived in greater comfort, in gilded coaches. He had momentarily beaten all his Spanish, Austrian, and English royal neighbors, including his relatives, and had burned Heidelberg University, and France, in its apotheosis, was starting a short breather of peace within his fifty years of almost continuous war. So there, last week, sat a few hundred of us in the château's battered orangerie while singers chanted to us, as once to him, "Let him reign!," which has too often seemed the theme song of this Continent, now including Russia. This highly enjoyable Lully-Sceaux concert of ancient music was produced and broadcast by the national radio broadcasting units.

This is the season for France's political parties to clean house in the privacy of their annual caucuses, to discover what they think about their rivals and themselves, as well as about what they have done during the Parliamentary winter and what they had best hustle and do about pending bills before the summer vacation. The Anarchists' Federation (which is apparently merely Trotskyite), Bidault's M.R.P., and the Socialists have already held their official huddles. The forty-second annual Socialist Congress, which met at the dingy Left Bank Palais de la Mutualité, was the most important, because, as the entire Paris press commented, it was the first in fifty years without the guiding presence of its late perennial leader Léon Blum, and its duty was to find a new leader. "No one can succeed Blum except the entire party itself!" cried one zealous delegate on the opening day. "Everyone has confusedly felt this. It was good to have it so stated," gravely editorialized the Party's *Populaire* next morning. The Party, noted usually for its many noisy divisions of conscience, actually integrated itself to a rare degree. For one thing, though bitterly anti-Communist, it demanded, with what it regards as realism, a Chinese Communist delegate to the United Nations. It voted to uphold the Bidault government but to continue disdaining, as it has done since February, to take part in it. This was a sort of blow to the government, but one that it will probably weather. Anyhow, the real crisis this spring for the government, as well as the parties, is the approaching electoral-reform bill, which advocates a complex new proportional-representation method of voting. This reform, for reasons that are also complex, would hit Communist candidates the hardest but could also upset every party's calculations.

At the moment, Communist propaganda is enjoying the most extraordinary success, especially among non-Communists, that it has ever had in France. The Party's Partisans of Peace, whose first meeting was held here only a year ago, is now its most powerful official spearhead against the Atlantic Pact and its implementation, and it is also the greatest magnet for attracting international millions of men of all beliefs, all frightened of atomic war. The Partisans of Peace recently met in Stockholm, where it formulated the snowballing "Stockholm Appeal for the Absolute Interdiction of Atomic Weapons." Point No. 1 demands "the establishment of rigorous international control [or just what America long ago asked] to assure application of this interdiction." The third, and last, point is "We call on all men of good will in the world to sign this appeal." The appeal was widely reprinted here, with a coupon providing space for a signature and the signer's address, and gives a Party address to send it to. The Stockholm Communist appeal has already been signed by a hardly credible galaxy of prominent anti-Communist Frenchmen. This past week's signatures alone, received and headlined by *Les Lettres Françaises,* the Communist literary gazette, included such eminent public figures as André Mornet, former Attorney General of the Republic; Paul Mongibeaux, president of what corresponds in France to our Supreme Court, who was the judge at Pétain's trial; the two presidents of Parliament; illustrious members of the Goncourt and French Academies; and a mass of university professors, popular writers, star actors, and famous artists, including Picasso, unique in the week's list of signers for being already known for his Leftist sympathies. Fifty per cent of the population of Calais have signed, some French towns signed en bloc, eight thousand signed in Casablanca, nine Swiss communal councils signed in a body, nearly five thousand British civil servants signed, forty thousand Chinese signatures came in in fifteen days (surprising only for the speed), and still according to *Les Lettres Françaises,* sixteen thousand *"New-Yorkais"* signed in Madison Square Garden. The new Stockholm appeal is really old; it was an American appeal when it was first launched—and refused by the Soviets. Now it is offered by the Soviet Communists everywhere, who thus brilliantly impound the credit. Masses of cautious Frenchmen evidently regard it as Russia's first offer to consider a commission of atomic control, and as men of good will they have eagerly signed it as a kind of contract. Or so they hope.

June 21

France was shaken by the distant, duplicated tragedy in the Persian Gulf that recently befell two Saigon-Paris planes. They perished off the shore of the same remote island of Bahrein on June 13th and June 15th. As one commentator said, "In this double rendezvous with death, at a fixed hour, at a selected point, there is something that chills the blood. Something in man protests. He can accept the accident. But the coincidence terrifies him." The Left newspapers had something more positive to ruminate about. By chance, the sad news from Bahrein was synchronized with other information from the East, which the Socialist *Populaire* had just received. While everyone was wondering what was suddenly wrong with the Saigon-Paris run, *Le Populaire* told what at least was wrong with Saigon; a feature story headlined Saigon as "THE CHICAGO OF THE FAR EAST" and described it as complete with lupanarian dance halls and dens of vice and a Hotel Continental whose French boss had apparently just celebrated with a champagne dinner his second billion francs of profit. According to *Le Populaire,* Saigon's glory is, however, a French gambling casino called Le Grand Monde, which is reported to run the local gold and piastre traffic. *Le Populaire,* which is violently anti-Communist, also related that to avoid being bombed in France's Indo-Chinese war by the Communist Ho Chi Minh, Le Grand Monde pays him a million seven hundred thousand francs daily—on top of the five and a half million francs' casino-privilege money it daily pays the French government. Similar scandalous news, given earlier to *Franc-Tireur* by its Saigon reporter, François-Jean Armorin, led to his being beaten up and his life's being threatened by the vice ring, or so his last published reports said. There can be no question of further danger for him now. He was killed in the second air crash, en route to Paris with more news.

The Big Six are now meeting here to discuss the Schuman-Monnet Franco-German coal-and-steel pool—really a Big Six minus one, owing to the withdrawal of the British Labour Party from participation in the project. Ten of the Western Europe Socialist Parties are for it, leaving the British as the old-fashioned dissenters. Most French citizens feel that the Schuman Plan, if made to work, could establish new Franco-German relations, a new spirit of Western union, and, lastly, a new French prestige, which is what they usually mention first.

July 6

For the sixth time in two and a half years, the Socialists have toppled a French government. Everybody is understandably cross with them except the thousands of ill-paid state and civil employees, who make up the greater part of the Socialist Party and whose proposed salary increase is what the Socialist deputies are standing pat on as their price for Parliamentary coöperation. Whatever government turns up next will have some prickly problems. It must balance the budget and then unbalance it enough to find some loose cash for these underpaid functionaries and for France's disgracefully underpensioned war cripples.

Delegations of war cripples from the First and Second World Wars have just gathered from all over France and, after a tragic, hobbling parade down the Rue Montmartre, held a strange seven-hour bivouac, ending at midnight, on the Place de l'Opéra, with tents, campfires, chow, card playing, songs, reminiscences, and, of course, attendant ambulances. Their slogan was *"Ajustez Nos Pensions!"* A quick twenty-five-per-cent increase was the adjustment they had in mind. The *mutilés* claim that, what with the high cost of living and the government's delay in classifying them according to its complex system, old soldiers are being paid sixty per cent less than they were getting right after the First World War. All the cripples wore their medals, and many wore blue poilu helmets from World War I. A few were the faceless men, or *gueules-cassées,* wounded before the days of widespread plastic surgery. Some had rolled up a World War II khaki trouser leg to show a metal limb; others, blind or legless, were in basket chairs pushed by their wives. A straw effigy representing L'Argentier, the symbol of all Ministers of Finance, was burned in front of the Opéra steps. At midnight, people coming out of the boulevard cinemas met the bemedalled cripples, straggling, limping, or being wheeled back to wherever they came from.

The Grande Nuit de Paris fireworks on the Tour Eiffel, which served the whole city as a fabulous chandelier, were the finest ever seen here. Hundreds of thousands of people packed the bridges and squares from as far down at Notre-Dame to as high up as the hills of St.-Cloud to watch them. The *feux d'artifice* were created by the famous French pyrotechnician Maître Ruggieri, who has long gone without a first name and who puts on the annual July 14th fireworks in Paris and recently staged displays at the Montevideo Carnival, at Haiti's centenary celebration, and at the Monte Carlo investiture of Prince Rainier III. Shrouded in smoke, the Maestro personally operated his Tour Eiffel display from the second balcony, employing a twelve-button panel that set off the eighteen hundred component parts of the varicolored conflagration. Until eleven-thirty, the Tour, covered by a patina of floodlights, looked as if it had been freshly painted white. Then it was suddenly darkened, and from all three of its balconies burst an apotheosis of fireworks in showers, balls, streamers, rockets, and what looked like silver and gold clouds of burning snowflakes. To the handful of us gaping near the base of the Tour—oddly, the only empty space—the finale was a magical, thunderous bombardment of explosives, going off in artfully patterned flames, and above them the Tour seemed to rock peacefully in the night sky.

July 19

From France's vast fund of experience with wars—Western and Eastern, won and lost—the French people, out of friendliness toward us and worry over the grim Korean events, have been pouring advice into the ears of Americans here, and into their own newspapers. Paris gentlemen whom one hardly knows talk to one like Dutch uncles and military experts combined. Paris newspapers that have loyally supported their government's and their Army's unsuccessful policies in the Communist Ho Chi Minh-Chief of State Bao Dai war in Indo-China—now in its fourth year, and thus serviceable to them as a presumed prototype for our Korean war—have been particularly explicit in telling us what our errors are. And, indeed, errors are what they should be expert on. Paris café strategists have begun explaining what is really going on at the Korean front. Last week's most bruited corner-*bistro* rumor was that the American Army, as a brilliant ruse, would let itself be pushed from Korea, so that Japanese soldiers could take its place, in what would then become a kind of proxy war between mere natives, with

Uncle Sam and Stalin white-man spectators. This gathered such momentum that the Japanese Premier, Shigeru Yoshida, was forced to declare that his country can go to no war right now, since it is still occupied as a result of the last one.

In an editorial entitled "Sodome et Gomorrhe," *Le Monde,* which always regards the United States as insensate, like Lot's wife in her last phase, pointed out "Europe's increasing fear on seeing the result of American intervention in Korea." "Anguished Europe," it went on, "asks itself if it must again undergo the infernal cycle of invasion-occupation-landing-liberation, worsened by the presence of the Russians, who would be far more terrible than the Germans were. Furthermore, Europe is alarmed at the revelation of American military weakness. Europe placed all her security on American arms, neglecting," *Le Monde* admitted angrily, "to build up her own, only to perceive that there is no American Army and that it takes only a few North Koreans to put in check the nation that Europe thought the most powerful on earth." *Le Monde* added, perhaps for our comfort, that the grave lesson of Korea would doubtless bring about repercussions in Washington similar to those that followed Pearl Harbor.

The Academician François Mauriac, in an editorial in *Figaro,* took the most transcendental tone toward Americans: "Should I say all that I think? The American people must revise their whole concept of life if they mean to save human liberty. A people cannot be at the same time the most happy and the most powerful in the world. Between the power of the nation and the happiness of individuals, Russia, for her part, has made her choice." Americans, "on whom weighs the heaviest responsibility that any people has ever assumed," are, Mauriac said, learning the harsh lesson that any great policy, and especially one of such grandeur as saving the world, demands arms behind it. He took issue with Admiral Nimitz's statement that the early, rapid victories go to an aggressor and the final, slow victories to a democracy, and contended that "on the contrary, Soviet Russia shows no haste. She advances a pawn on the chessboard after taking her time, which can be weeks, months, or years, and then watches the reactions of her adversary, which are doubtless those she expected. A man of medium intelligence," he added helpfully, "can obtain an idea of her possible moves by looking at a map of the world."

For centuries, the French have been experts on the subject of prestige. They consider that if America is pushed out of Korea—and French military men say that they believe this can be avoided only by a *contre-offensive de grand style,* for which we lack the necessary men and material—the lowering of our standing in the Orient will change the pressure-politics map of Europe so drastically that no one can precisely envision what that change would be. As prestige experts, the French are more alarmed at what is happening to us in Korea than they are at what has happened to them in Indo-China.

November 2

The first hoar-frost has finally blackened the flowers in the Tuileries Gardens, where a palette of extended French autumn was lying undisturbed. Weather prophets have warned that the Seine will likely freeze over before the year is out. The winter of 1950 has come in cold but peaceful—in Europe, at least—after a summer of sultry fears of another world war. The harvests have been good in the French countryside. With a feeling of relief, Paris has started its winter routine. The weekly ballet nights at the Opéra have begun again, and the Colonne, Lamoureux, Pasdeloup, and Conservatoire Orchestras have tuned up for their weekly musical rivalry. The Comédie-Française, apparently with one eye on the thermometer, is opening its season with a new production of "Le Conte d'Hiver"—Shakespeare's "The Winter's Tale." This is definitely a revival. It was first played here, in French, in 1631. The reconvened Parliament, occasionally the most interesting public spectacle in town, has just held its first all-day-and-all-night sessions, one of them signally historic and all of them marked by that violent disparity of views and casual absenteeism of members that seem normal to democratic chambers everywhere today. Frequently, there were more visitors in the not too commodious galleries than there were deputies on their benches, though a government of France was turning her history topsy-turvy by voting that Germany should be rearmed.

Until the concrete, complicated rearmament scheme known as the Pleven Plan was adopted by Parliament, idealists here had hazily hoped that a federated Western Europe, that elusive twentieth-century goal, would somehow or other be founded on peace, balloting brotherhood, and fine phrases. The new French plan offers a United Western Europe founded on Ruhr coal and steel (the

Schuman Plan), plus a Western European army of nationals who, in accordance with a new ideal, would fight with instead of against one another. In one respect, René Pleven's plan rises magnificently above the memory of the old melees. His is the second French project for Germany in modern history—the first was the Schuman Plan—in which the French motivation has not been *"La Revanche,"* a patriotic slogan that was most popular after 1870, when French revenge seemed a pleasant possibility, and that has behind it a deeper French feeling that goes back to Waterloo, for which Blücher is still remembered and hated here, though Wellington has been practically pardoned and forgotten.

Obviously, many citizens, recalling what Hitler's labor battalions, theoretically trained with shovels, were able to do to them in 1940, are confounded in 1950 by the idea of France's handing any German even a popgun, in whatever federated wrappings. Also, the special Gallic satisfactions in the Pleven Plan, such as its ranking of the German soldiers as helots, without patriotic perquisites or their own military leaders, were badly shaken during the Parliamentary debates by news from West Germany that, aside from Chancellor Adenauer and the rich industrialists, the Germans did not want to be armed at all, *danke sehr*. Nevertheless, to the three-quarters of the French who are not Communists and who are, generally, realists, the Pleven Plan has a strong appeal. It seems a genuinely creative and hopeful diplomatic idea for a new relationship with Germany and for a modern Western Europe. The military risk seems realistically minimized by the Pleven Plan's being built on top of the Schuman Plan for the handling of the Ruhr's coal and steel, which the French also consider a creative and hopeful idea. For, as the French bitterly realize today, what modern European wars are prepared on and fought for is industry, or dialectic ideas on how to run industry. Despite the setback the Pleven Plan received in Washington, the French feel that with these two contributions France has become once more the planning brain of Western Europe, or as much of a planning brain as she can be with England so standoffish and America so powerful.

1951

February 20

The French, as you hear them talking now in Paris, seem certain that General Eisenhower and Premier Pleven, while visiting each other's lands a few weeks ago, presented, in turn, the most valuable gift that lies in the power of such simple, democratic plenipotentiaries. Each gave the gift of explanation. The French, on their various levels, profoundly appreciated the gifts of both, and are still inspecting and analyzing them. To what Eisenhower had to say, Parisians have paid their strangest, sincerest compliment; his brain, they say, did not smell military, even in this crisis in history. They feel that he spoke as a great and modest humanitarian. And the French even understand themselves better after what Pleven said about them in Washington. This is a treat for them. Nobody had properly explained them to themselves since the Great Debate began. The facts of life in a continuing crisis, or of death in an invasion, have changed little, but now these facts are being looked at as part of a possibly—just possibly—controllable destiny, rather than as mere fate. To the humble French, Europe still remains a matter of geography, not ideology. France cannot move off the map, away from the prospect of supplying some more of the most beautiful ruins, architectural and cultural, of modern history. Many middle-class French see Europe as faced with the choice between the Soviet threat of peace and the American threat of war. Many educated French see Europe as in danger of sliding from the sheer weight of history into a hegemony: a state of tight physical union such as was aimed at, through conquest, first by Napoleon and then by Hitler, and is now aimed at ideologically by the Soviet, a hegemony such as only the Union of Western Europe could have made—or may now belatedly make—painless, noble, and voluntary.

There is still a good deal of anti-Americanism here, brash or subtle. Many French bitterly accuse America of being whatever those particular French can be sure it is because of never having been there, including too young. It is those same French who weakly make excuses for elderly France, as if she were a handsome old lady of privilege who had gone off to live upstairs in furnished rooms, in a mansion that had once been hers and was still elegant in all the world's eyes and had all Europe as its topiary garden. To those disappointed French, France seems to await a history that will be supplied to her painfully by one of the two colossal foreigners bearing down on her from East and West. There is one statement that Americans here are becoming aware that they never hear. They never hear the French explain how it happens that France, with her superior old culture and knowledge of how Europe should be handled, finds herself in such a position that ignorant, amateur, bumbling Americans have been called in to do the job.

Eisenhower is reported to have said, smiling, that he wasn't surprised by the Communists' demonstration against him in front of the Hotel Astoria here but that he was surprised there was no counter-demonstration. According to the government order of that day, January 24th, "The Communists' proposed demonstration against him who was chief of the army of liberation for France is treachery and a scandal not to be tolerated." It added that any foreigner taking part (and the foreigner might have been an American who had come only to counter-cheer) would be expelled from France the next day; any participating French civil functionary of "permanent" grade would be disciplined and any such functionary of "temporary" grade would be dismissed; any employee of a nationalized industry would be suspended or fired. These are orders that now apply to any unlicensed demonstration in Paris. They are probably what kept thousands of French and foreigners from going to the Champs-Elysées to shout *"Hourra pour Aike!* Hurray for Ike!" in a melee in which twenty-five hundred Communists were arrested and five journalists were so beaten up by the police that the Chief of Police apologized.

When Pleven mentioned French "neutralism" during his visit to Washington, he put the word into a wider circulation than it had previously known. It was coined in Paris more than a year ago by the Academician Professor Etienne Gilson, of the Collège de France. Gilson is the most erudite, most venerable exponent of medieval Catholic philosophy, France's greatest authority on Thomas Aquinas, and possibly the greatest living Thomist. In a series of articles published in *Le Monde,* he first used the word *"neutralisme"* in his attack upon the Atlantic Pact. (French journalism now regards *Le Monde* as neutralism's editorial center.) Neutralists claim to be not defeatists but believers in the proposition that Europe is sick from many wars and another war would kill her, and that only America and Russia, rotting with wounds, would survive. Gilson recently went further. He resigned his Collège de France chair, stating that he would live in North America—in French Canada, by preference—rather than remain in France to face another war and another occupation. His decision and departure made a big stir in intellectual circles. In November, when he was at Notre Dame University to give a series of lectures, he made some comments about neutralism, which were later firmly opposed in an open letter by Professor Waldemar Gurian, of the same institution. This letter was printed over here in the weekly *Figaro Littéraire,* causing additional intellectual commotion. Although the daily newspaper *Figaro* is the center of Paris antineutralism, its editor, Pierre Brisson, who rarely editorializes, created a third climax in January with his brief antineutralist editorial headed "Les Insexués," The Asexuals. In conclusion, he harshly said, "The wild volition to avoid war makes no sense unless it is affirmed virilely, with readiness to make a supreme effort. Neutral France does not exist. There are neutral men, in the sense that they are *insexués.* They are few. It is not by them that we expect the country to be saved." Brisson doubtless speaks for more French than does the relayed voice of Thomas Aquinas.

According to intimates of André Gide's household in the Rue Vaneau, as the great writer lay there dying—and aware that he was dying—he said calmly, "If anyone asks me a question, make sure I am conscious before you let me reply." Thus, at the age of eighty-one, did he protect his genius for lucid responsibility as his final, most valued earthly possession.

Of those candid critical obituaries that are a sort of philosophic specialty of literate French journalism the morning after a great French figure dies, that of *Figaro's* devotedly Catholic editorialist

François Mauriac was judged perhaps the most masterly. Under the title "Un Destin," he wrote, in part, "Let us not gild his mortal remains. Let us not pretend to have misunderstood the redoubtable instruction of the immoralist. If what we Christians believe is true, today Gide knows what we all will soon know. What does he know? What does he see?" Mauriac asked these questions suddenly, evidently seeking at his editorial desk at midnight to determine precisely the knowledge and sights of immortality that Gide, who was born a Protestant and became an anti-Christian agnostic, had always derided. "He was the writer farthest from art for art's sake," Mauriac continued. "He was a man engaged in special combat for two causes, of which the more apparent was scandalous—to excuse, even to legitimatize, a certain kind of love. Worse, in his youth he broke with the moral law as taught by both Christian churches. No one could have staked his bet against Christianity with more sang-froid and reasonableness than Gide did. Few would have dared to overthrow Bossuet's tribunal of conscience, which condemns all crimes. This Gide accomplished with a tranquillity, a serenity, and a joy that were frightening. We must be living in a casual epoch indeed when his being awarded the Nobel Prize caused no stupefaction, no terror. His literary work? It remains among the most significant of our time. The Gidean critical spirit was incarnated in the *Nouvelle Revue Française,* which he helped to found. 'Les Nourritures Terrestres,' 'L'Immoraliste,' 'Si le Grain ne Meurt,' and his 'Journal' will long preserve as human leaven the ferment that it was his mission to provide. He followed his own path, wrapped in his famous long cape, with a constant solicitude for culture and dignity, with the noble tread of a grand seigneur of great race. Gide was not a poor sinner but a strange pilot."

Gide received the homage of Paris lying on an iron bed in his Rue Vaneau study, wearing one of the heavy sweaters but without the cape and the high, homemade cap—almost like a fez—that he used for many years to protect his chill flesh against the cold. He will be buried near his family's Normandy property at Cuverville, which he so lovingly described in "La Porte Etroite."

March 1

All that Parisians finally understood about Parliament's several mixed-up electoral-reform projects was that their government could fall among, and because of, them. French citizens are groaning in anticipating of March 15th, the last day for paying their income tax. "Ulcerated by the bigamy" of his Radical Socialists in making strange political bedfellows of de Gaullistes, the Radical Socialists' grand old man, Edouard Herriot, has, at the age of seventy-eight, chastely resigned the leadership of his Party. Everybody in Paris walked during this Monday's bus and Métro workers' strike, which was pretty close to total. Prices on practically everything have suddenly leaped alarmingly, including bus and Métro tickets. Everybody is worried and nobody talks of anything else. Compared to 1950 prices, knitting wool is up 65 per cent, workmen's blue jeans 25, kitchen pans 8, paper 60, shoes 15, coffee 55, ladies' hats 20, and pork chops 50. The weather has been dramatic, with tempests, wind, sun, and downpours all taking their turns within the hour, for several hours daily and day after day. Now all is blanketed down by fog. On the hucksters' flower carts on boulevard corners, the first vernal Parma violets are selling cheap and gay at four hundred francs the big bouquet—a fistful of scented purple that shades in with the city's lavender mists.

March 22

For nine days recently, France was without a government. In other political crises and stalemates here since the Second World War, Léon Blum was sought out for consultation, even by politicians to whom Blum's Socialism was anathema, for they admitted his qualities as counsellor, his skill at arbitration, his political experience, and, indeed, the value of his annoying ideals. In the past few weeks of confusion, he has been much missed, if only because he might have kept his party in line and prevented its members from saying one thing in Parliament and voting another—like everybody else. Until his death last year, Blum was the brains—and for much of his career he was the body as well—of contemporary French Socialism. He was more assailed in peace and longer imprisoned during the war than any other noted French leader. He would no doubt have been surprised at his obituaries in other countries, and even in his own, which mourned him as France's grand old man.

Blum died, aged seventy-seven, in his suburban cottage near

Jouy-en-Josas, a year ago, on March 30th. He was both a loved and a hated figure. He was known the world over as the great leader of modern French Socialism, and yet he was an unsuccessful politician. He was also the political figure who—because of his long life, his Jewish origin, his humanitarian aspirations, and his intellectual refinement; because of the schizoid conflict between his acute national patriotism and his devotion to international visions like Socialism itself, pacifism, and unrevolutionary proletarianism; and, above all, because of his prescience as a social reformer—personified the whole complicated, struggle-ridden, sad history of the French Third Republic.

Like Blum, the Third Republic began its life at the time of the Franco-Prussian War and the Commune, moved through the anti-Semitism and anti-libertarianism aroused by the Dreyfus Case (in which Blum and the rest of the liberal element in France fought and suffered), endured the first German world war of aggression (in which Blum's Socialist pacifism failed and France won), then rose to the peak of novelty, for both him and the state, when he became the first Socialist, first Jewish Premier of the very money-loving, very Catholic republic during its Front Populaire government. And, for both him and the state, the Third Republic ended, as it had begun, with an aggressive German war, during which, as a significant symbol of France's defeat, an old Blum, the perfect quadruple hostage—Socialist, liberty-loving intellectual, Frenchman, and Jew—was imprisoned in the Nazi concentration camp of Buchenwald.

Blum's character, interests, and talents made him, until he was forty-eight years old, the most unlikely future important politician then to be found in any fashionable literary salon in Paris. Like George Bernard Shaw, he was of the vintage of comfortably well-off ethical intellectuals who espoused Socialism as a means toward justice for all, and especially the working poor. Born in the drab Rue St.-Denis, Blum always cited its humbleness, as though it were a political birthright, to his working-class followers, with whom he certainly had no other earthly connection. His father's ribbon business early lifted the Blums into the prosperous bourgeoisie and its neighborhoods, and lifted little Léon into private *lycées,* with classmates like the privileged André Gide and with prizes in Greek and Latin. Maybe Blum was a born Socialist. At the tender age of five, he asked his capitalist father how he could bring himself to sell ribbons for more than he paid for them. As a matter of record, Blum was converted to Socialism in college, by Lucien Herr, librarian of the ultra-conservative Ecole Normale Supérieure (radicalism must have been in the air everywhere), who also converted Jean Jaurès and the poet Charles Péguy. After graduating from the Sorbonne, where he majored in literature and law, Blum, then twenty-three, precociously became a member of the Conseil d'Etat, whose judicial position is among the highest in the country. It is devoted to upholding, among other legalities, the French system of private property and capitalism, which Blum dialectically wished were in limbo. He continued this career in the magistracy for twenty-six years. His only known radical rebellion was the wearing of a derby to court instead of the regulation top hat.

As a member of the magistracy, Blum at first received an annual salary equivalent to eight hundred dollars, so, to earn a little more money, he became a journalist in his hours outside the court—specifically, a horse-race columnist and a book and theatre critic. He began to frequent the finical literary salons of Countess Anna de Noailles, the poetess, and of Mme. Caillavet, Anatole France's mistress. While still in his early twenties, he joined the staff of the *Revue Blanche,* a staff that included Marcel Proust and Gide. It became the great intelligentsia monthly magazine of Europe, with contributors like Verlaine, Mallarmé, de Gourmont, and Anatole France. Debussy was its music critic. Together, Blum, Gide, and Proust fought for Ibsen, introduced Tolstoy to the French, and claimed to be intellectual anarchists. "Intellectual anarchism" was a fashionable parlor-pink term, which later they sheepishly said meant, mostly, anti-Victorianism. Just as Blum's years in the Conseil d'Etat gave him a knowledge of the technical functioning of the French state, so his early bookishness gave him a knowledge of the shifting social climate of the French mind; both were invaluable to him in party politics and in his work as a political reformer. He thus dually developed the prodigious braininess that was characteristic of the Third Republic's outstanding political leaders.

Blum was the last of the notable politicos who in their youth participated in the Dreyfus Case, which in the late eighteen-nineties convulsed France, bewildering the Parliament and the people, making a fool, knave, and liar of the Army, overthrowing ministries, and almost toppling the Republic. It started with the Army's erroneously and illegally convicting Captain Alfred Dreyfus—the first Jewish officer ever appointed to its General Staff—of selling military secrets to the Germans, and sentencing him for life to Devil's Island. It developed into one of the most tragic, funniest, and most violent political medleys of spies with false mustachios, gullibilities, idiot experts, loyally lying officers, and dangerous confusions that any modern civilized European state ever suffered through, with the Army, which had started by convicting Dreyfus, finishing by being itself convicted. (It also led, later, to the disestablishment of the French Catholic Church.) Blum served as an unpaid, volunteer legal clerk to the lawyer who defended Zola in the libel suit brought against him in 1898 for his famous "J'Accuse," the Dreyfusard pamphlet that finally split the Case, the army, and France wide open. With the wretched Dreyfus, still in chains on his Devil's Island, as a focal point, two diverging lines cut deeper and deeper into French society. The anti-Dreyfusards, anti-Semites, anti-republicans, conservatives, diehards, Army, and Church were massed on one line, claiming the existence of a wicked Jewish syndicate. On the other line were pro-Dreyfusards, republicans, liberals, libertarians, anti-clericals, anti-militarists, and believers in *les droits de l'homme*. The Right and Left division then drawn still cleaves France. The fairly young Army officer Philippe Pétain, on duty in Paris, was on the anti-republican side, which eventually led him, by then Maréchal, to Vichy, where he ordered the Riom trial of Léon Blum. In "Souvenirs sur l'Affaire," his book on the Dreyfus Case, written years after it was over, Blum wondered, in one of his best-known paradoxes, if the finally vindicated Jewish captain, who, ironically, turned out to be a typically dull, confused, loyal, military-minded man of his time, would have been a Dreyfusard if he hadn't been Dreyfus. The Dreyfus family never forgave Blum.

Blum's books usually plunged him into trouble. Published when he was twenty-nine, his "Les Nouvelles Conversations de Goethe avec Eckermann," a fantasy in which the Sage of Weimar plans a new character for Faust as a modern Socialist French deputy, was stimulating enough to annoy many French. "Du Mariage," which appeared when he was thirty-four, declared his opinion that permitting sexual experience for women before wedlock, as society permits it for men, would make for solider marriages. This incredibly advanced feminism naturally horrified the French, especially French mothers. Even the Socialists wished Blum would merely talk, and not publish. Blum was one of the early enthusiasts who helped reëstablish Stendhal at the beginning of the century. In 1914, his "Stendhal et le Beylisme" appeared. The trouble this book stirred up was purely literary.

In the summer of 1914, the assassination of Jaurès, Blum's friend and god and the dominant chief of the Socialist Party, belatedly pushed Blum, almost as though he were performing a penance, into Socialist Party work, which he had always refused to engage in for Jaurès. On the eve of the First World War, the powerful German Socialists hastily sent delegates to Paris to ask the French Socialists a question that millions of frightened European workers thought could elicit the miraculous answer on how to prevent a war: Should the French and German Socialists combine—dragging with them, perhaps, all the other workers—and pacifically refuse to be mobilized? When the talks were over and war had been declared, both the French and the German Socialists patriotically stepped into uniform, and the vaunted major ideal of seventy-five years of anti-military European Socialism was drowned in blood. Refused by the Army because of his bad eyes, Blum took the post of executive secretary to the Socialist Minister of Public Works. In 1919, the carnage ended, he was elected Socialist deputy from the Seine, and he finally began his Parliamentary career.

Almost immediately, Blum performed one of his two greatest feats, the significance of which he certainly could not have known at the time. Just before 1920's most important postwar Party congress, which was to be held in Tours, French Socialism, which still had a family relationship with Russian Marxism, began wondering what on earth had been going on in Moscow since the bloody Bolshevik Revolution—and how about Moscow's sending complete details? In answer, Moscow sent a sharp inquiry as to what on earth poky, unrevolutionary French Socialism had been doing, especially about establishing the dictatorship of the proletariat. On top of this, the Bolsheviks sent a dictatorial telegram—it was later known by the name of its signer, Grigoryi Zinoviev (afterward liquidated)—preparing the way for the laying down of twenty-one autocratic points the French Socialists, along with Socialists everywhere else, would have to concede to if they wanted to be admitted into the new, glorious Third International. One point was that they would have to throw out of their Party the French Socialist Charles Longuet, who was the husband of the unhappy Jenny Marx, and so Karl Marx's son-in-law. During the ensuing wild meeting in Tours, Blum led the opposition to the Bolshevik demands, and lost. Three-fourths of the delegates, led by Marcel Cachin, walked out, to found what is now the French Communist Party, and, as the majority, legally took with them the Socialist Party's newspaper *L'Humanité,* founded by Jaurès, and the Socialist Party's funds. Blum was the leader of the Socialist Party's penniless remains. He became, at that moment, its brains. He was then forty-eight. Without him, his historic rebellion against Cachin, and his minority, the leadership of the organized French working class might have become predominantly Communist after the First World War, instead of after the Second. Under Blum, France's working class became predominantly Socialist. His action gave the Third Republic twenty years of grace.

The electoral triumph of Blum's Socialist-dominated Front Populaire in the nineteen-thirties was, like all the reform periods in France, a reaction against a period of excessive political corruption. Financial scandals had shaken the country. In 1933, Center and Right governments had fallen like leaves from a calendar as their politicos' complicity was established with the notorious swindler Serge Stavisky, who had sold forty million francs' worth of worthless bonds to the French people. On the night of February 6, 1934, thousands of outraged Parisians of all classes rioted in the Place de la Concorde, shouting, *"A bas le Parlement! A bas les voleurs!"* Troops fired on the crowd, and seventeen or perhaps eighteen citizens were killed. Paris was in an uproar. Over the weekend, groups of Fascist *Croix de Feu* and the royalist bully-boys, *Camelots du Roi,* roamed the streets. Parliament and the very theory of Parliament descended to their lowest status in history. In reaction, finally, rose the notion of a Front Populaire, or bloc of Left Wing parties, which were to be united in reform—and ambition. As chief of the Socialist electoral campaign in 1936, Blum, at the age of sixty-four, became a familiar sight to thousands of French who had never laid eyes on him before. Especially in the turbulent, smoky mass meetings that packed the gigantic Vélo d'Hiver, Blum became a star attraction—a magnetic, though in some ways ill-equipped, political platform speaker, physically well proportioned, medium tall, agile, and looking only middle-aged; in attire somewhat foppish, with pince-nez, a small walrus mustache, and gray spats; and with a high, fastidious voice and the diction of a literary purist. These last two qualities were offered without embarrassment to listening factory hands accustomed to noisy demagogy. In the general elections, the Socialists won their first great victory. With a hundred and forty-six deputies out of the Chamber of Deputies' six hundred and eighteen, they became the largest party. In June, Blum was made Premier of his Front Populaire government, supported chiefly by Radical Socialists and Communists. The Front Populaire was Blum's second great achievement, even though it was, on the whole, a failure, being too experimental in form and too mixed politically.

For the workers, Blum's great social reforms were the forty-hour week and paid vacations, innovations that embittered the French owner class. In what he considered were the interests of peace, and perhaps at England's insistence, he refused to intervene in the war in Spain; this soured many European idealists, including members of his own party, and it infuriated the Communists. On taking office, he had meticulously stated that his was not a Socialist government but a mixed government wherein pure Socialism, in fairness to his non-Socialist partners, could not be put into practice. One year later, he was overthrown by the conservative Senate, which refused him the extensive fiscal powers that the Chamber of Deputies had just voted him. He and the Front Populaire, in various versions, dragged on into 1938, but it had long since shot its bolt. In 1936, surrounded on the Boulevard St.-Germain by a mob of *Camelots du Roi* who were accompanying the funeral cortege of the royalist historian Jacques Bainville, Blum, who chanced by, was dragged from his car and attacked, and his face and neck were badly cut. Inspired by the class hatred his regime and reforms aroused, the rich accused Socialist Blum of being rich, of having a fortune hidden in Swiss banks, of possessing a fabulous collection of silverware in his modest Ile St.-Louis apartment. This last rumor, he patiently explained, was the result of his having bought some second-hand packing cases to store books in during the First World War. The packing cases had previously been used for silverware and therefore were marked "*Fragile. Argenterie.*" None of his enemies believed him. The old Dreyfus Case cry of anti-Semitism had been revived after he became Premier. Indeed, in the days preceding the election won by the Front Populaire, certain conservative and Fascist French had openly shouted, "Better Hitler than the Jew Blum!" Starting in June, 1940, Paris, and then all of France, had Hitler, and had him until August,

1944. Blum was arrested by the Nazis.

After being imprisoned in various châteaux, Blum, early in 1942, appeared before Pétain's special Riom court, created at Hitler's demand; he was accused of having helped cause the military defeat of France by inadequate rearmament during his Premiership. Blum's fearless, witty protests that he had at least provided all the armament requested by Marshal Pétain's inadequate armament program, and his attacks on the legality of the court, both backed up with similar statements and attitudes by his fellow-prisoner, ex-Premier Edouard Daladier, resulted, after twenty-four sessions, in the accuser Pétain's seeming to become the guilty party in the trial—or so Hitler commented in disgust as he called the trial off.

Following another period of imprisonment in France, Blum was sent to the German concentration camp of Buchenwald early in 1943, bravely accompanied by the lady who went there to become his third wife, the first two having died. Blum was so walled off in a private house on the edge of the camp that he did not know anything about the horrors around him till months later. In "Le Dernier Mois," his last book, he recounts the shocks and confusions of being carted around by the S.S. for three weeks in April, 1945, from one camp to another—Regensburg, Schönberg, Dachau, Innsbruck, Präger Wildsee—as his guards fled with their valued prisoner before the oncoming Americans. Blum was suffering from sciatica and from the pain of knowing that his life could be saved only in trade for immunity for Martin Bormann, chief of the Nazi chancellery. Blum and his wife were rescued in May, a few miles from Dobbiaca, Italy, near the Austrian border, by the American Ninth Army.

In the summer of 1949, two months after an intricate intestinal operation, Blum was again receiving political and press visitors at Jouy-en-Josas with his same old spirit. Attired in a fine green dressing gown and scarlet silk neckerchief—he was always an elegant, if eccentric, dresser—he repeatedly bounded from his couch, as if fresh ideas acted on him physically, even in his invalid state. His voice had grown thinner and more like a high reedy musical instrument, but his mentality was vigorous and flourishing. One afternoon, among other things, he said sadly to this writer that what he had wished to see in postwar France was, naturally, a labor government like England's. He reaffirmed his faith in traditional Socialism—no revolution but evolution and gradualism (the Socialists' basic law is gradual change), and free speech for all. He loudly, scathingly denounced the dictatorship and terrorism of Communism, as if he wanted his enemy the French Communist Party to hear him. He spoke of France more with reminiscence than with immediate hope. He felt that the Fourth Republic was merely repeating the Third Republic, as if French history had begun, in a senile way, to stutter its old thoughts, having refused to learn anything new—and appropriate to the middle of the twentieth century—after France's most terrible, most instructive war.

Surrounded by friends, visitors, and his books, Léon Blum, sprightly and hollow-eyed in his handsome dressing gown, seemed an intimate historical figure, an erudite Frenchman who had seen history, made history, and suffered from history.

March 29

This has been a remarkably quiet, orderly two weeks of strikes, well handled by the government and the unions. Both have had plenty of experience. Strikes, which have been legal in France since the law of March 21, 1884, are called *grèves,* for the Place de Grève (now the Place de l'Hôtel de Ville). The Place de Grève was the old city center where workers came to get jobs or to protest, usually unsuccessfully then, against low wages. The recent strikes have been of the same type—strikes for more pay—and not political strikes, which doubtless would have included violence.

These quiet strikes brought quietude indeed to Paris, beginning as they did in the transport services here before spreading over the whole of France and into most of the major industries and bureaucracies. At the Gare St.-Lazare, normally the busiest station for commuters, the uninhabited glass-arched open-air train shed and the empty converging tracks looked as lifeless as a draftsman's sketch. Underground, Métro trains rumbled around town occasionally, and those who rode on them rode free, because ticket sellers and ticket takers had been called out. As substitutes for the city's green buses, which were totally immobilized, Minister of Transport Pinay supplied a few Army camions, operated by white-gaitered soldiers, to pick up passengers on the Concorde, and installed here and there a spasmodic service of those luxury autos usually seen filled with white ribbons, flowers, and wedding parties. (The ex-wedding cars charged more than the buses, which vexed the French, who remain economical even in a national emergency.) The government also asked Parisians driving their cars to give lifts to the rest of us, hopefully standing on street corners in the March wind and rain. Mighty few gave anyone a lift, even down the Champs-Elysées, which was jammed morning and evening by erstwhile Sunday drivers driving to their offices. As the number of Paris taxis is limited by the high price of gasoline and is inadequate even in normal rush hours, most of us walked during the strikes. On the whole, young women managed the best. They fell back on their German Occupation experience and bicycles, and independently scorched all over town, or they dug out their ski trousers and boots, which were all the style here that cold winter after the Liberation, and strode off to work looking as if they were headed for the mountains.

The strikes, of course, killed the Easter-holiday plans and non-motoring foreign tourist trade. On Good Friday, a group of lucky English tourists stuck in Calais by the railway strike were invited by a young French locomotive engineer, who was headed for Paris to see his wife, to climb aboard his unscheduled train if they were going his way. Half way home, he ran out of coal, and he refuelled at some unattended, strikebound railroad coalyard. He eventually larruped into the Paris *gare,* with himself and the English pleased as Punch. The strikes were not unpopular, even among Paris non-strikers, who, with a devotion to work as disciplined as the strikers' devotion to non-work, rose by the hundreds of thousands an hour earlier in the morning and bedded down an hour later at night, so as to walk from one end of Paris to the other, be on the job on time, and complete their regular stint—almost uselessly, since almost no business was transacted. When the government finally announced that, according to its statisticians, the cost of living had gone up twelve and a half per cent since August, the non-strikers also heaved sighs of relief, for it seemed as if their plight, too, had been noted.

April 26

Although Parisians are familiar, by hearsay, with the untrammelled, picniclike public spectacle called a New York welcome, they were downright bewildered by reports of the millions of waiting people, the acute emotionalism, and the extreme partisanship that were assembled on Manhattan's streets while ticker tape streamed from skyscrapers, in the greatest and most frenzied ovation in the city's history—all for General MacArthur. About the only thing the French are sure of is that it could not have happened here. With such tension and such differing views and with even a fraction of such a crowd on the Champs-Elysées, paving stones, not paper streamers, would have been thrown, and the result would have been a bloody riot. Tempers and sensibilities seem to be keyed up everywhere these days. The Paris papers say that Marshal Pétain (at the age of ninety-five still France's most controversial military figure) is probably dying in his fortress prison on the distant Ile d'Yeu. At the mere mention of his name this week in the Chamber, such a storm of outcry, invective, and desk-banging broke out that what the deputy who had the floor was trying to say was never heard, and neither was the voice of Speaker Herriot trying to restore calm.

The Truman-MacArthur crisis and the vast American civilian population's determination to decide for itself which man's military strategy will best serve history has certainly caused worry here, but it has caused no confusion of opinion as to which man is right. The French are solidly for Truman. Not one Paris newspaper has taken anything but the President's side. All the papers—except, naturally, those put out by the Communists—eulogized the General for his earlier military exploits, admired the careful omission of incitement in his address to Congress, which they think was simply a more magnificently worded version of his previous garrulous insubordinations, and disagreed, in real alarm, with his thesis on expanding the war in China. What has become in the United States the Greater Debate—between Republicans and Democrats arguing about war in the Far East—to the French still seems a matter that concerns not just two inflamed American political parties but at least ten of the sixty United Nations and the chances of life or death in Western Europe.

On July 8th, Paris will be two thousand years old and will begin her celebration of the *Bimillénaire,* which this year is the town's biggest summer fête. Julius Caesar conquered Gaul in 51 B.C.—actually two thousand and two years ago, of course. July 8th has been haphazardly chosen as the birthday because the weather ought to be nice.

June 20

In the elections just held, the first French national elections in five years, the citizens have voted in six and a half different directions, everybody hoping to get, from one direction or another, some things he wants very badly. Studying what it is the people want and how many of them, according to the urns, want it, is perhaps the easiest method of reading the election results. There were six winning parties, or groups, figured on the basis of seats gained in the National Assembly, and of these General Charles de Gaulle's Rassemblement du Peuple Français is on top, with a hundred and seventeen deputies sitting for him among the Assembly's six hundred and twenty-seven. De Gaulle's victory, much feared and much hoped for, has been achieved, but it is no landslide, and, since it may turn out that the government will be formed by a coalition of Center parties, his extreme Right-wing party may not even participate. Moreover, because he owns no daily French newspaper to come out with headlines saying he won, no paper has said it; in fact, all the papers noted his winning total obscurely—the conservative *Figaro* putting him at the bottom of the list. The things badly wanted by the fifth of the French electorate that voted for de Gaulle are order, a chance to put France back on her feet (and on a pedestal), a strong hand against pressure from the United States, the suppression of the Communists in the French government (his party, in its special language, calls them "separatists"), and, above all, that *mystique* of single, male leadership that European history has so often recorded and that this century has had considerable sad experience with. Indeed, what de Gaulle's voters want from him is precisely what he has, so far, offered—history and himself. In an electoral radio speech, he spoke of History, with a capital "H," having imposed on him "the responsibility of intervening to show the path and lead the nation. . . . After the difficult victory of 1945, I gave the republic back to the people. . . . The R.P.F. is formed around me for the good of the people." Something his working-class followers also want is his Capital-Labor Association program, despite the fact that he has never told them much about it, and despite the fact that at the first hint of it capital knew enough to dissociate itself from him in horror. An R.P.F. booklet presents the Capital-Labor

Association (it opens by mentioning first the French phalansterian Fourier and then Pope Leo XIII's famous encyclical on social justice, "Rerum novarum") as being against the class struggle and in favor of profit sharing by employees, as a "new" wrinkle in employer-employee relations, but with strict managerial authority and with protection of capital investment. His voters also appear to want, as part of their *mystique,* the picture they get, at a distance, of his very exceptional character, including his egotism (to them it seems a distinguished inheritance rather than a political acquisition), his personal probity, his majestic vocabulary (taken from the religious orator Bossuet), his heavy, dynastic-looking face, and his reiterated views on legitimate republicanism, according to which, if he had won his landslide, he would have aspired to be elected, through the legal devices of referendum and dissolution, President of France and to function also as Premier, a combining of offices that at the moment is forbidden.

The liveliest part of the campaign was the battle of the billposters—a political-advertising technique new to everyone but the Communists and really an imitation of the very successful posters that have been put up since early this spring by the anti-Communist organization calling itself Paix et Liberté. That organization's prize campaign poster was a vivid, Dufy-colored one of the Tour Eiffel, shown rocking under the weight of a hammer-and-sickle flag flying atop, and bearing the warning *"Pas ça!"* The Communists considered it such effective anti-Communist propaganda that they hastily printed American flags to paste over the Soviet emblem. De Gaulle's tricolor posters were the noblest-looking and the most artistic typographically, his publicity man being the novelist André Malraux, recently turned art authority. One showed the tortured, handsome face of La Marseillaise (from one of the François Rude statues of the Arc de Triomphe), with the words *"De Gaulle vous appelle, pour que la France soit la France."*

The elections were held on Sunday, June 17th. Exactly eleven years before—on Monday, June 17, 1940—Maréchal Pétain announced to the French over the radio that France had fallen. Paris newspapers did not mention the significance of the election date, and most of the voters seemed to have forgotten it. They remembered the Maréchal himself on Sunday night, though, when the radio announced that the very ill prisoner was to be transferred from the Ile d'Yeu fortress to a mainland *résidence surveillée,* where he would be hospitalized. On the anniversary of what he tragically began then—the dilapidation of French republicanism—nearly half the electorate voted for the two political extremes of authoritarianism.

The Paris bimillenary celebration, or two-thousandth birthday party, has so far been a struggle between hedonistic outdoor fêtes, arranged against historical architectural backgrounds, and the grim weatherman. The magnificently conceived Louvre Court concert was called on account of rain, like a baseball game. (It was given ten days later.) The Henri IV concert, held in his Place des Vosges, with its *souper* under the arcades, for living French nobles personifying their own or somebody else's ancestors, was interrupted by the worst thunderstorm in even the common people's long memories. The historical art shows, which are being held indoors, have proved safer. The expositions have been extraordinary in their variety, their specialties and oddities interesting both residents and tourists, and the organizing imaginations behind them deserve a vote of thanks. The following is a sketchy listing of what one can see if one's eyes and feet hold out: Charpentier's rich Plaisir de France paintings; the Palais de Glace's First Salon of Hunting and Venery, which is fascinating; pre-Gobelins tapestries, shown at the Musée des Gobelins; the art of glass, at the Pavillon de Marsan, which is fine; Conquests of Photography, at the Muséum d'Histoire Naturelle; the Palais de New-York's show of women painters and sculptors, which is only pretty good; chefs-d'œuvre of the Louvre's French school, at the Petit Palais; Napoleon and his Family, in a show of arms, trophies, uniforms, souvenirs, and so on, at the Invalides; Sèvres table services, in Sèvres; a great Toulouse-Lautrec show, including unfamiliar early, serious works, at the Orangerie; and, if one can get to the suburban Sceaux between showers, an exposition of water colors of "the environs of Paris," beginning with Corot and coming down to the present. Horse racing and steeplechasing have started, hotels are jammed (principally with North and South Americans, most of whom have brand-new Paris umbrellas), the great Paris buildings and squares and fountains are floodlit every night, prices are high, and it is a big tourist season.

Jean-Paul Sartre's new play, "Le Diable et le Bon Dieu," at the Théâtre Antoine, is the season's "must" play. It takes four hours to perform. Sandwiches are sold between acts, as if the Antoine were

Bayreuth. Sartre's theme is the antique one of man's terrible indecision about whether to be good or evil, combined with the more modern one of where good and evil themselves come from, and he did well to put the Devil first in his title. For Goetz, his rich-fleshed, rich-minded German warrior protagonist, fighting with men in battles near the city of Worms and with his conscience on the edge of the Reformation, is more alive as a man, more interesting as a character, wittier to listen to, and far better as a stage figure when the Devil is leading him, in the first act, than he is, after he has turned to God—literally on the throw of dice, in the spirit of a gambler changing his system—in the subsequent two acts, which are lifeless, loquacious, and argumentative, and include eleven tableaux. Goetz is really a dialogue in himself—Shavian, shocking, blasphemous, coarse, and human in Act I, and then, in the following acts, talkative in the dreary medieval, Maeterlinckian theatrical manner as he hunts for the good. Goetz is never Faustian, at least; there is no mean merchandising of an old soul for youth and pleasure. Goetz is apparently meant to be a premature modern, with an outstanding talent for doing and enjoying evil, who, as the result of a cerebral whim, changes his métier to following godliness, for which he lacks the genius that is faith. He returns, finally, to the Devil and butchery, with the excuse that goodness does not pay on earth and that God has not let him work a miracle—like a trick of legerdemain—and this top-ranking blasphemy seems the only conclusion that could bring the curtain down. It is admirable that the philosopher Sartre has been able to put into a theatre the Manichaean problem of good and evil in man, but certainly something is the matter with the play as a play. It arouses outspoken dissatisfaction in everybody, and everybody goes to see it. Pierre Brasseur, as Goetz, gives one of the greatest Act I performances of our time.

July 19

One of the greatest summer art shows of the many given in recent decades by the French government is "Le Fauvisme," currently at the Musée National d'Art Moderne. The Fauves, or Wild Beasts (their brilliant colors supposedly snarled), received their name in the Salon d'Automne, in 1905, when the paintings by Derain, Vlaminck, Marquet, Van Dongen, and so on looked much the way the paintings of their leader, Matisse, still look—some with broken green brush strokes like fallen leaves, and all with the savage shock of the bright colors that attract civilized man's eye to nature's most exciting flora and fauna. There was also visible a determination to wipe out the studio painting of the past and start fresh, for the nth time. Before the Fauves, the Impressionists were damned, and after them the Cubists. France has specialized in violent political revolutions; these groups were responsible for revolutions in modern art, with vermilion blood shed on the palette.

The Fauve exhibition has an impressive scope, which includes a preliminary explanatory room of paintings by the influential pre-Fauve artists Manet, Gauguin, van Gogh, and, above all, Cézanne, who was little thanked at the time. Then the show moves into its strength in the wonderful first-rateness of the hundred or more Fauve canvases—Derains of his vivid Collioure period, Braques still as gay as zinnias, Seine scenes of running purple water by Vlaminck, lovely Camoins, Marquets, and Manguins, and fifteen of Matisse's greatest, most famous paintings. Intense interest has been shown in his Pointilliste 1903 "Luxe, Calme, et Volupté," which once threw Parisian art-lovers into a rage; the 1906 study for "Le Luxe," with its strange duck-egg-colored female nudes; "La Gitane," with her green breasts and nose; a 1907 portrait of Mme. Matisse that looks like a Picasso of 1922; and an 1899 landscape of the city of Toulouse, featuring the innocent pink-lavender that the Wild Beasts all later used—the naïve rainbow color that European man had shut his eyes to as being in a kind of suburban bad taste.

There is still enormous pleasure in viewing these great beginnings of twentieth-century modern art in Paris, where the colors became part of the gray city's brighter history—these pictures produced before the Wild Beasts moved into duller colors and stiffer formulas, leaving old Matisse today the last, as he was the first, practicing Fauve.

August 1

It is more than a week now since ex-Marshal Philippe Pétain died, an unpardoned nonagenarian state prisoner on the Ile d'Yeu. Some few people thought his death could be tinder for trouble in France, though just what dangerous phoenix might rise from his ashes they seemed not to know. The announcement of the death itself, which had been long expected and which he long resisted, was received by the vast majority of Parisians with flat calm, some indifference, and a feeling of general relief, both for him and for themselves. He was so very old. As long as he still breathed, whenever they read or even thought about him, which in the past few years was admittedly not often, he symbolized the corrosive, demoralizing years of occupation that France's citizens wanted to forget and that most of them, perhaps to an alarming degree, have succeeded in putting out of mind. By his death on an island few ever saw, he was finally detached at a distance, separated at last from their postwar existence in France, where their political emotions, interpretations, troubles of conscience, loyalties, disillusions, and memories of him good and bad reached their logical climax of partisanship and grief in his trial for treason, a courtroom condensation of all humiliations for them, for France, and even for him, the Verdun general, sobriqueted victorious, of a former, better war. No nation could rise to the same pitch twice without additional, reanimating events. Pétain's dying brought little of it back, except in the newspapers.

Had Pétain's funeral rashly been held in Paris, the French, who are sentimentally and politically sensitive to such black-trimmed processions, might have reacted more positively, at least for those few brief hours. Even his well-known wish to be buried "at the head of my soldiers" lying at Verdun—a solemn desire that to many French who no longer bothered to be bitter about him seemed a permissible last indulgence, and that to some seemed almost a command from the deep past where they had first heard of him, with gratitude then—failed to fulfill newspaper prophecies that "Pétain burial honors will split France." Except for his former trial lawyers, still briskly and unsuccessfully pleading on his behalf any cause they can find, and the small remaining emotional band of demonstrative pro-Pétainists, the public accepted without demur the official statement that no one had the authority to allow his return to the mainland of France, living or dead. The ex-Marshal's death and burial on an island gave him, in very different historical circumstances, a greater exile, and far less legend, than St. Helena furnished to Napoleon.

One thing about Pétain's death is sure. Of the many dicta he enunciated in his trembling old radio voice, so often heard from Vichy, the one the newspapers quoted most often, as substitute for *de mortuis*—and the one the French most resent today—was his statement that history alone would judge him. Probably seven or eight out of every ten French were automatically pro-Pétainist at first. It is a similar huge aggregate, now anti-Pétainist, who think that history already has judged him, and that they, the French people, were the historians. They think that they have lived his history, for they heard a lot of it from his trial, despite his silence, learned even more about his Nazi colleagues from Nuremberg and Dachau, and can hear further volumes just by listening to their own memories. They think he chose wrongly at every turn, and that a leader's choices, not his intentions, are what write the line of a nation's history. Nearly without exception, the Paris papers listed the main tragic chapter headings—1940, *le shakehand* at Montoire with Hitler and "collaboration with honor," which included anti-Semitism; 1942, the command to resist as aggressors the American liberation forces in North Africa, and concurrent permission for Nazi troops to take over his Free Zone on their way to seize the French fleet at Toulon; 1943, when the Grand Maquis was forming, his radio voice quivering, *"Parents français!* Do not give your children bad advice [i.e., do not encourage them to join the anti-Nazi resistance]. Counsel them to go work in Germany." Apropos Verdun, even his press obits here mentioned what it has taken two wars to make generally known—that if he bravely bled France at Verdun, he also advised retreat and was withdrawn by General Joffre, leaving General Nivelle to say what were supposedly Pétain's most famous words, "They shall not pass," for it was Nivelle who was in charge to win the final hemorrhage of victory.

For those of us who saw Pétain at his trial, the visual memory of him is of his sitting silent in the belated dignity of total uncollaboration at last—with the Palais de Justice assemblage, in any case. From time to time, he lifted his bare hand and flapped his gloves like a fan to protect his face from the myriad focussing retinas of cameras, as if they were multiple-eyed modern insects. An anti-republican, he disapproved of any republic. It is characteristic of the recent republics here that there was no government in office for the important event that was his death (nor any government since, either), but also typical of the viable republicanism of the French people that they have easily met both happenings without losing stride.

One of the important events in the lively posthumous literary career of Henri Beyle, who changed his name to Henry because he liked the letter "y" and to Stendhal because he worked for a French government that did not like political-minded authors, was the Academy's award of this year's Grand Prix Littéraire to Henri Martineau, France's foremost Stendhalian. It was given to him for his thirty years' labor of deciphering and annotating Stendhal's madly illegible manuscripts; for the new minor volumes and text expansions that resulted; for his re-editing and correcting of all earlier printed works, the first complete, definitive Stendhal, published in seventy-nine volumes; and for Martineau's voluminous explanatory writings over the years, of which the latest is his new tome, "L'Œuvre de Stendhal: Histoire de Ses Livres et de Sa Pensée." Martineau, whose blue-painted Librairie du Divan is a landmark on the Place St.-Germain-des-Prés, was a Vendéen doctor until he took up with the Bibliothèque de Grenoble, the city where Beyle was born, which he hated and where his manuscripts have come home. Only fourteen of Beyle's books were published in his lifetime. Grenoble has thirty-two signed manuscripts, plus masses of loose papers and marginalia (such as his annotated copy of Destutt de Tracy's "Commentaire sur l'Esprit des Lois de Montesquieu," recently bought in America) in which he indulged his passion—almost as great as his love for secrecy—for scrawling enigmatic notes about anything on whatever was handy. His opening plan for "Vie de Henry Brulard," another of his pseudonyms, since it is really his autobiography (in his notes, though, he always referred to himself as Dominique), is scribbled in his copy of "Clarissa Harlowe." Martineau says of all the material in Grenoble now there is nothing left unpublished but a handful of leftover pages of "Lamiel," Beyle's unfinished last novel, whose final five hundred words, rushing from his pen a few days before he collapsed in the Boulevard des Capucines, were written with such speed, sickness, and malformation that only their general intention has been deciphered.

For a novelist who became the first master of modern psychology at the wrong time; who was a known worshipper of Bonaparte but published his marks of genius, "Le Rouge et le Noir" and "La Chartreuse de Parme," under Louis-Philippe, no Bonapartish regime; who thought passionate writing "horrible style" and read daily at breakfast from the Code Napoléon, *"pour prendre le ton,"* and yet in those novels created two of the century's most passionate love affairs—for this kind of writer, who also rather ungratefully calculated that he might be appreciated around 1880, or perhaps even 1935 (writing in 1835 as we might write bitterly today of fame in

2051), Stendhal really had a lot of kudos and cash in his lifetime. These details Martineau sets down in full, along with other engrossing, less well-known, material. After all, "Le Rouge et le Noir" had favorable, if not enthusiastic, reviews. Stendhal received twenty-five hundred silver francs, or five hundred dollars, for writing "La Chartreuse de Parme" in seven glorious weeks. Its first edition sold out at the equivalent of three dollars a copy in a period when laborers were laboring for a few sous a day. Balzac gave it a seventy-page puff, still a record, saying, "Where I work in frescoes, you create Italian statues," but adding that the style was often negligent. And Goethe wrote in his "Conversations with Eckermann," "I do not like reading M. de Stendhal, but I cannot help it. I recommend you to buy all his books." Today's Book-of-the-Month Club's publicists might well wonder what more Beyle, with Balzac and Goethe as boosters, could have expected from the year 1880. In 1882, he was posthumously accorded Paul Bourget's famous essay that called him the modern master, and, sure enough, the fastidious cult of Beylisme took root. And in 1935 Martineau was ready to publish ten volumes of Stendhal's journals.

Martineau says Stendhal was pleased with his atrocious handwriting, which he hoped would keep people from prying into his secret papers. For further mystification, he also misspelled, using "k," which was another of his favorite letters, for "q" and "c," "s" for "z," "i" for "y," and also vice versa. He used mixed anagrams, muddles, and abbreviations, such as "Mero" for "Rome," "Téjé," with the stress on the final "e," for "Jesuit," "Tolikeskato" for "Catholiques," and the fraction ⅓ as a pun for the politician Thiers. And though he never kept dates straight or added very well, he computed his age at fifty-three as $5 \times 10 + \sqrt{9}$. Martineau's book has a diverting chapter on "Lucien Leuwen," Stendhal's earlier unfinished novel, lately published for the first time in English in the States. Martineau told your correspondent that the "Leuwen" manuscript is "very instructive," rich in marginalia of gossip, pen portraits, and Beyle's advice to himself and remarks on his health, with asides, in passages on Leuwen's love life, concerned with how Italian coffee troubled Beyle's intestines, how champagne at lunch made him drowsy, and what he thought about wearing spectacles for the first time. As Stendhalians devoted to Beyle's peculiarities are fond of relating, he genially stole the novel's idea from a manuscript called "Le Lieutenant," featuring a Lucien Leuwen, that had been sent him for friendly criticism by Mme. Jules Gaulthier, one of the many ladies he loved and who understandably failed to fall in love with him. Beyle worked over her idea under various titles, including "Le Télégraphe," which had just been invented and which fascinated him. It is amazing how interest in his unsuccessful sex life and squabbles over who his character models were still agitate Stendhal scholars here. The two latest issues of the *Revue des Deux Mondes* contain articles on some vain vacation flirtations of his. The magazine *Le Divan* berates some Stendhalians' notion that Korasoff, Julien Sorel's Russian prince in "Le Rouge et le Noir," was founded on the Marquis Astolphe de Custine, a Restoration acquaintance of Beyle's and an aristocrat lately identified as an astute traveller; his anti-Russian observations were recently published as a book in America, with an introduction by Lieutenant General Walter Bedell Smith, head of the Central Intelligence Agency. Since 1882, the Stendhalian cult here has had time to grow pretty finical.

August 23

After thirty-two days of being without a government, the French find it nice to have one again. They think it ought to last just about thirty-two days, too. Actually, it will probably survive the current *petite* session of Parliamentary powwows and Parliament's seven weeks of autumn holiday. After that, say the de Gaulliste deputies, who already have named it "the vacation government," their General will push out Premier René Pleven's present setup and install his own. There has never before been such a huge Cabinet—a result of the government's effort to obtain a majority—as there is now, even in Léon Blum's Front Populaire regime, which had an Under-Secretary of State for Leisure. According to that cynical old cartoonist Sennep, this one includes several Ministries of Blah-Blah-Blah, or plain gab. It is a tragedy for French democracy, already split into pro-Communist and anti-Communist camps, that it now has a second violent split, on state aid to Catholic schools, with the anticlericals and Socialists bitterly against and the clerical Popular Republicans obstinately for—and with all parties glumly admitting that what France unquestionably needs is a thousand new schools of one sort or another. Today's *problème scolaire* is a revival of the question of the separation of Church and State, considered buried in the early nineteen-hundreds; is another stale battle in the Wars of Religion; is one more struggle between the two types of Frenchmen—a duality that has made modern France.

The death of Louis Jouvet was, if one may say so, the popular event of the month. It interested and affected the population of Paris to an extent that nobody—probably not even he, expert as he was on public reactions—would have thought likely. It was suitably dramatic. Stricken at rehearsal in his Théâtre de l'Athénée, he lay on a cot in his managerial office there for two days and two nights, in a speechless, recumbent pose, while completing his act of dying. Then the cot in the office became his bier, while thousands of Parisians, after work hours, stopped the traffic in the Rue Caumartin as they queued up to climb the little staircase backstage to give him, in their fashion, their final respectful applause. He was the only present-day intellectual French actor who was popular with the masses. Not once but day after day the newspapers devoted whole pages to him, retracing his career and attainments as if he had been a leading governing figure, which in a way he was—the governor of the French theatre, the actor-manager who acted and managed so that the great French classics, the fantasies of Giraudoux, the décors of Bérard became part of people's lives when the curtain rose. Giraudoux's most imaginative play, "The Madwoman of Chaillot," on which the author practically worked himself to death, was produced posthumously. Then Bérard was fatally stricken in the Théâtre Marigny. Now the third of the trio that made an epoch in the French theatre has died where he belonged—in the Athénée.

Seven years ago, on August 25th, Paris was liberated. The liberation itself began earlier on the streets, in the emergence of French men and women of the Underground. "L'INSURRECTION FAIT TRIOMPHER LA REPUBLIQUE A PARIS, LES TROUPES ALLIEES SONT A SIX KILOMETRES DE LA CAPITALE," the clandestine Resistance newspaper *Combat* jubilated in headlines on its first public copy to come from the press, on August 21st. *Combat* has just printed a photograph of that euphoric front page, along with some less happy up-to-date comments. *Combat* is, it should be noted, anti-Communist, even anti-Socialist, and Albert Camus, author of "The Plague," was among its first brilliant editors. "Since 1944," *Combat* commented sadly, "the world has changed. Only the inquietude remains the same. What seemed easy in August, 1944—liberty, security, social justice—has run up against the permanent obstacles of oppressive capitalism, intolerance, and privilege. We still have faith in man, in man only, in his good sense, in his good will." There are many, many French, even of Rightist political views, who, as they look back over those seven years, agree about these disappointments, which they think have come not from others but from their own leaders.

September 5

Bread is going up to fifty francs a kilo, a shock for the French, who eat about a metre of it a day.

Another bread shock has been even worse—the mysterious madness, agonies, and deaths from poisoned bread in the village of Pont-St.-Esprit, near Avignon, composing a medieval nightmare tale. It seems that the lethal bread came from Briand's Bakery, the best in town, on August 17th. The mystery was not solved until August 31st. By that time, four Spiripontains, as the villagers are called, had died in anguish, thirty-one had gone raving mad, five were in grave danger, and two hundred were sick. Even cats, dogs, and ducks that ate crumbs of the bread had fits. People seized with the affliction acted possessed; they saw monstrous visions, and burned with inner fires. Charles Graugeon, aged eleven, tried to strangle his mother. Mme. Paul Rieu needlessly attempted suicide, for she died anyway. Mme. Marthe Toulouse tried to leap into the Rhone to quench the fiery serpents inside her. One citizen fired his shotgun at the monster he thought pursued him. A peasant named Mizon, who missed buying his favorite evening *petits pains* at Briand's on August 17th, came by for them the next morning, went mad, and died on August 20th. In the insane asylums of neighboring Nîmes, Avignon, Montpellier, and Marseille, where the frenzied Spiripontains were sent, they frightened even the other lunatics. Only one photograph of a victim appeared in the press. It was of a M. Guignon, being carried to an ambulance, his legs and arms raised to fight off whatever he thought he saw, his elderly face, with open, distorted mouth, looking like a Gothic carving of an old man screaming in Hell.

The slow solving of the mystery, followed with palpitating interest by the French, was like a detective story. It started with a rumor of a mass political poisoning, developed into a fascinating study of the functioning of provincial authorities, and ended in a sort of Balzac formula. Professor Jean Olivier, chief toxicologist of Marseille, suspected poisoning from the chickling vetch, *Lathyrus sativus,* which produces lathyrism, or spastic paralysis. Then he discovered the presence in the bread of rye ergot, *Claviceps purpurea,* that little black abortion on grain heads that comes in wet weather and, it has been claimed, contains, among dozens of other chemical elements, about twenty alkaloid poisons, three of them virulent. The Montpellier 14th Brigade Mobile of the country police did a brilliant, slow job of deduction. Little grain is raised or ground in the Spiripontains' Département du Gard. There were twenty-three suspects, the mills in two nearby wheat-raising *départements.* Finally, one miller, Maurice Maillet, of the mill at St.-Martin-la-Rivière, in the Département de la Vienne, confessed that he had ground into his wheat granary scrapings of ergot-bearing rye, furnished to him by a dishonest local baker (it seems the baker's cashbooks were not even in order, which also shocked the French), who had bought the diseased grain illegally from unscrupulous peasants. Maillet, who now says his conscience pained him, sent the sack of bad flour to Pont-St.-Esprit "because I did not know anybody personally there." The Balzacian dénouement was, of course, cupidity. The two men were avoiding twenty francs sales tax per kilo on the grain, were dealing in spoiled goods for profit, and were using more rye in wheat flour than the law allows. Maillet has been arrested for homicide and "involuntary wounding" of others.

September 19

This is one of the moments when its being a small world after all is just what is making everyone so nervous. It was the shrinking of Europe's strength in two world wars and, in the last, the shrinkage of its size on the map that have necessitated the new intimacies on the Continent, the rallying of the Anglo-Saxon neighbors across Channel and Atlantic, and today's conferences in Washington and Ottawa, precisely planning (if possible) against a third world war that would shrink Europe to zero. It is exactly the smallness of this world, Parisians feel, and the terror of being reduced to nothing that have at last forced a kind of idealism onto the *conférenciers,* the ideal being a united Europe.

In Paris, there is a warranted feeling of pride and relief that at the Washington conference both the Americans and the British finally accepted the Schuman and Pleven European plans. They are French conceptions, they can be used as starters, in the lower materialistic depths of coal, steel, and permitted German soldiery, toward a basic communal Continental structure. They are also the only new international European notions anybody has thought up since the British put forth their balance-of-power scheme at the Congress of Vienna after Napoleon was defeated. As near as the French can make out (and there was one moment when the Washington Conference reached such a state that Premier Pleven had to tell Parliament he had just buzzed Schuman on the transatlantic phone to ask him to explain what on earth was going on), the acceptance of the Schuman-Pleven plans was due largely to the man who was not there. This was General Dwight Eisenhower, who frankly, almost optimistically, stated in July that he thought joining Western Europe together was the key to the whole thing.

With bitter realism, the French recognize—indeed, it is the Schuman-Pleven thesis—that the one proof of any federation will lie in the relations of the Big Three with the Bonn government. In other words, the developing destiny of what is left of Allied Western Europe will principally depend on its relations with the half of Europe's old attacker, Germany, that is left. This in particular makes it seem a remarkably small world. In a profound editorial, *Le Monde* just stated, "Politics and economics count less than the spirit. Europe will be no more if she does not forge a common soul."

A small book of a hundred and twenty pages entitled "Et Nunc Manet in Te, Suivi de Journal Intime" constitutes for French readers the final shock of the sort that André Gide's obstinate candor about his private life unceasingly furnished during his writing career. The booklet also probably constituted a shock to Gide's regular French publisher, La Maison Gallimard, for the new work has just come off the presses of the Editions Ides et Calendes, of Neuchâtel, Switzerland. To judge by the 1947 copyright, it was at the moment of his receiving the Nobel Prize, and also of his first grave alarm about his health, that he sent the manuscript abroad, to be published only after his death. Actually, thirteen copies were at that time privately printed, and distributed by him among his friends, according to his secret communicative custom.

The book consists of two parts. The first, "And Now It Remains to Thee," a tag from Virgil, was written after the death of Gide's wife, Madeleine, whom he called Emmanuèle in his many journals. She was also his cousin. This part of the book explains what he calls the secret conjugal tragedy of his life and of their existence together. The second part, the "Journal Intime," fills in all the blank spaces indicated by asterisks in those portions of his published "Journals" that deal with her between 1916 and 1938, when she died, thus amplifying also what was so obviously cut short in "Si le Grain Ne Meurt," a book of his memoirs up to the time of his betrothal. These revelations provide the inner sight without which, he declares in his posthumous record, the diaries are blind. This new book will unquestionably spill a great deal of ink here, from bitterly dissentient pens of literary critics, moralists, pro- and anti-Gideans, Catholics, Protestants, and perhaps plain, ordinary well-read French people, who may easily think that this whole recent confessional production might better have been blotted out. Gide's printed candor about his erotic tastes has long since ceased to surprise or shock his accustomed readers. In his posthumous book, it is the living man standing behind the admired novelist that will shock and surprise them anew. "Intoxicated by the sublime," or so he wrote in it, "convinced that the best of me was what communed with her," he made a white marriage, on the extravagant Puritan notion that only males are naturally carnal, wives being sexless—a special, civilizing dispensation of nature, which allows gentlemen to maintain intact the ideals of pure womanhood. With his wife, Gide recounts, he wanted an ethereal love, "the more ethereal, the more worthy of her."

Actually, the new book contains elements of a peculiar dramatic plot—the wife's silence and the husband's opposite, egotistic assumption, which combine into a human experience so unlike any hitherto intelligently recorded that even Gide, as an artist, apparently recognized that his story could never be believed as fiction but only as fact. The tragic high point for both Gides came when she set fire to all the letters he had written her over thirty years, which she considered "her most precious possession on earth" and which he loudly mourned as "the best of me, which disappeared and which no longer counterbalances the worst." "Perhaps there never has been a more beautiful correspondence," he lamented. The undeniably tender spiritual connection between them, or what could have remained of it by that time, thereafter grew feebler, without that earlier ink to live on. Madeleine-Emmanuèle died without their ever having discussed or mentioned what their lives together had not been. Gide was crowned as a literary figure in more ways than one during his lifetime. This last book adds thorns to his laurels—thorns that, because he is no longer alive to wear them, will cause pain principally to his admirers.

October 2

The winter art season has opened with an exposition at the Galerie de l'Elysée of Maurice de Vlaminck's oils. Here are his hallucinated landscapes, dreamy in overrich color beneath the strange, sugary-white frosting that always fills his skies. For the first time, he has added to his regular repertory, exhibiting a pair of odd journalistic still-lifes. One is composed of a revolver, a bottle marked "Poison," and an out-of-print Paris newspaper that used to specialize in crime news. The other shows a tin of salmon, a copy of *L'Humanité,* a knife, and some bread. Nobody in charge at the gallery seemed to know what these pictures mean beyond what they show, which is a revolver, etc., and a tin of salmon, etc.

As a young man, Vlaminck was one of the boldest of the Fauves, whose inflammatory colors inspired him to write in a youthful art magazine, "Ah, to burn the school of the Beaux-Arts with my cobalts and vermilions!" When he first took up painting, he was a music teacher (like all the members of his needy suburban family), a professional bicycle racer on the Paris-Bordeaux run, and a novelist whose works were published in the Orchid Books Series and included "D'Un Lit à l'Autre" ("From One Bed to Another") and "Ames de Mannequins" ("Souls of Dummies"), the latter a fantastic account of some wretched Russian émigrés living in poverty on the rim of Paris. Unfortunately, Vlaminck's own poverty was similar while he was doing the best painting of his life, as a young Fauve. Because canvases cost money and his paintings were then bringing none in, he wiped off many of his superb pictures of the Seine with a handful of grass and started others on the same *toiles*. A few of his Fauve paintings still exist, most of them in modern museums. The loss of the others becomes even sadder when one thinks of them in comparison with the almost lithographic landscapes he has been painting ever since.

November 29

The weekly *Figaro Littéraire* has just enjoyed the honor of printing three long fragments of Marcel Proust's early writings, theretofore unpublished, and, indeed, unpublishable until recently, when his energetic niece and heir, Mme. Gérard Mante, finished piecing these and other bits together into nine hundred pages—precious old scraps, one might say, strangely used to make a brand-new garment for somebody deceased. This new opus, which is entitled "Jean Santeuil," the name given by Proust to himself as the observer in the chronicle, was written between 1898 and 1910 and is clearly a preliminary use of material he later transformed into the romantic and creative carved Gothicism that begins, under the shadow of the Cathedral of Chartres, with "Du Côté de chez Swann." As the opening of the unfinished, unorganized "Jean Santeuil," Proust wrote, "Can I call this book a novel? It is less perhaps and much more—the essence itself of my life. . . . This book was not written, it was reaped." The *Figaro* fragments constitute about a tenth of the work. The first two are like long short stories.

"En Bretagne," the first of the series, contains one forty-line sentence that, like a layer cake, predicts the complex and more refined *madeleine* teacake to come. The "Bretagne" fragment also features that familiar summer-hotel seascape to come, this time in an imaginary village called Kerengrimen, where Proust, his sensibilities already stretched out like a telescope toward the lives of the other guests, focusses on the fatal love story of a middle-aged writer called merely C., who is prophetically like the mature writer-to-be P. For, as Proust suffered from asthma and jealousy, C. suffers from phthisis, a psychosomatic accompaniment of jealousy in love, which is his actual malady and of which he cures himself, only to die of his physical illness.

The second story, "Un Amour de Jean Santeuil," is almost the real thing, is almost pure Proust. Here he is close to "A la Recherche du Temps Perdu"—adolescence in the Champs-Elysées gardens, where the tantalizing Gilberte is tentatively incarnated as Marie Kossichef, a maddening little Russian, where the servant Françoise is nowhere visible among the trees, but where a St.-Germain duchess *is* visible. Proust's mother's bourgeois goodness has not yet been transfigured by her death, but her refusal to come to his room to kiss him good night when he was a boy, and his loneliness for her, which leads him to the miracle of hearing her voice over the long-distance telephone—these are there, though the literary style they were finally preserved in is absent. Proust's early style was rather like Flaubert's. The flamboyant Parisian style he derived, oddly, from Ruskin's "Bible of Amiens," from which English writers got so much less, had not yet been chiselled, just as Illiers, where his uncle lived, had not yet come to be called Combray but is called Etreuilles. However, all the elements of the anguished, carefully drawn-out Proustian life are there: the tempests of unrequited, jealous love, the slow, humid sufferings from rendezvous never kept, and the false, bright garden weather of elegant worldly life shining all around. "Un Amour de Jean Santeuil" is fascinating in its own right, and to Proust-lovers it is like an orchid plant, niched in the hothouse, and in leaf but not yet in bloom.

The third piece, "L'Affaire Dreyfus," must have cost Mme. Mante a lot of trouble to stick together. Its only coherence is the court reporting by Proust, then a young, well-to-do, observant Jew and genius, suffering both for the cause of justice and for the cause of race, who humbly carried sandwiches and a canteen of coffee to the Palais de Justice, where he daily attended the trial. From what he saw, he sketched his first really elaborate, full-length portrait. It was of the anti-Dreyfusard figure General de Boisdeffre, with his stiff leg, his shabby civilian topcoat, and his cheeks "embroidered with red like certain mosses covering autumn walls." Proust gave far less to his picture of the martyred Colonel Picquart, whose truthfulness saved the Dreyfus cause, seeing him only as a gallant spahi, dismounted and without weapons, walking into the ambush of the law.

General de Gaulle's R.P.F. Party has been worrying all the French who did not vote for him last June by its silence—by the fact that although it has the greatest number of Assembly seats, it has done little with them. At a recent three-day R.P.F. caucus on future policy in Nancy, where public speeches were made, the General and his right-hand man, André Malraux, both spoke without soothing anybody. Malraux received an ovation for describing the General as "the single figure toward which one day all the humiliated French will turn—all the innumerable humiliated French of yesteryear and the awesome crowd of those humiliated yesterday." The General himself said, "Because the Americans give us arms, we do not have to be their subjects." He also spoke against the creation of a united European army before there should be a politically united Europe, and was hostile to the Schuman Plan for the European coal-and-steel pool. He made it clear that his R.P.F. deputies would fight both these pillars of French foreign policy when they come up soon in the Assembly. "It is probable that under the formidable pressure of events, common sense and patriotism will lead others onto the road that we have taken," the General said. "I declare that we are not inclined to refuse any helping hand. We aim at serving the country but certainly not at having a monopoly on good ideas or good actions." He also called for constitutional changes that would strengthen the executive branch of the government and his party's position in the Assembly. So now the French know the General means to do one of two things with his dominant party. In a new turn in policy, he means to support any political party that agrees with him and he means, as he has been understood to mean in the past, to take the leadership of the Assembly, if he is given enough power so that the other parties, hot or cold, would *have* to agree with him.

December 5

An astonishing concert of ultramodern music was recently given in the gloomy little Salle d'Orgue of the austere Conservatoire. There were songs set to "Mélodies en Langue Imaginaire," by Mlle. M. Scriabin, a relative of old A. Scriabin, whom she has left far behind. The chief interest, however, was in two examples of quarter-tone music—"Fragment Symphonique" and "Fugue No. 1," composed by Ivan Vyschnegradsky. They were played on four pianos, two tuned at concert pitch and the other two a quarter tone higher. At first, the music sounded like dialogue delicately off key. Then—to this listener, at least—the auditory experience became a surprising and liberated pleasure, comparable to the experience of hearing Debussy's whole-tone-scale music for the first time. It was nothing like hearing the stiffer diatonic music or the work of any of the twelve-tone composers. Vyschnegradsky's quarter-tone music is iridescent, savory, and richly tactile—a sort of supersensory production, which, though received through the ears, involves the other senses. Being a music of fractions, it is refined, calculated, curiously unequivocal, and balanced. It seems there was a Paris concert of it in 1937, when one of the critics referred to the composer's "attractive dissonant relationships between a tonic and its half-sharped fourths." Quite so. Rachmaninoff, Honegger, and Messiaen were early admirers of Vyschnegradsky. His "Ainsi Parlait Zarathoustra," performed by the Brussels Philharmonic Society after the Second World War, is considered his major work. Now living in Paris, he composes on a specially constructed, two-tiered, quarter-tone piano. He was born in St. Petersburg, studied harmony with a pupil of Rimski-Korsakov, and is the son of a director of the Imperial Russian Orchestra. Today, Vyschnegradsky is an invalid, as a result of his confinement in the Nazi prison camp at Compiègne. It is said that Stokowski will present his "Fugue No. 1" in America this coming year.

1952

January 2

The year ended with a significant clash between a couple of leading churchly and laic literary minds, a clash that has already become a *cause célèbre*. It consisted of an exchange of open letters between men who had been friends until the ink started to flow—François Mauriac, the noted ultra-Catholic novelist and editorialist of the daily *Figaro,* and Jean Cocteau, the noted, frequently pagan poet. On the surface, the quarrel centered on "Bacchus," Cocteau's new play, lately given a *Tout-Paris* opening by the Jean-Louis Barrault repertory troupe at the Théâtre Marigny, which Mauriac walked out on, offended by what he considered its frivolous sacrileges. Like Jean-Paul Sartre's recent "Le Diable et le Bon Dieu," Cocteau's piece, despite its mythological name, deals with the Martin Luther period in Germany and the so-called heresy of the new, free, Renaissance European mind, boldly seeking the liberty of personal truth. The two plays are also alike in that neither is its author's best. Cocteau's is adroit and stimulating; Sartre's is profound and, except for its splendid first act, boring. Mauriac's letter, which started the trouble, was run on the front page of the weekly *Figaro Littéraire* and looked like an encyclical, except for some relieving, very human and malignant opening touches, such as "Thou art at once the hardest and most fragile of creatures. [Both letters of rupture were, oddly, written in the second person singular, usually consecrated to expressions of love.] Thy hardness is that of an insect, thou hast its resistant shell. Nevertheless, if one squeezed a little too much—But no, that I shall not do." More loftily, he continued, "At the Marigny the other night, I suffered for the real Cocteau, the invisible Cocteau whom God knows and loves." With this, Mauriac started on his real sermon, reprimanding Cocteau for having used in his play a buffoon bishop and a cynical cardinal to represent the ever-noble Holy Church, and for having willfully composed subversive statements. Mauriac then went into redemption, Hell, saints, and God—not as a drama critic writing to a dramatist in a literary weekly but as a sacerdotal authority giving warning from a Sabbatical pulpit.

Cocteau's answering letter, obviously hastily written, was in print a few hours later, in the afternoon daily *France-Soir*. His letter was called "Je t'Accuse," recalling Zola's famous denunciatory letter in the Dreyfus case. Each of Cocteau's nineteen paragraphs began "Je t'accuse . . ." "I accuse thee, if thou art a good Catholic, of being a bad Christian," he said. He also accused Mauriac of being uncultivated, since the subversive statements Mauriac charged him with composing were taken from the Thomist Jacques Maritain, from Napoleon, from a medieval Archbishop Elector of Mayence, and from followers of Calvin. "I accuse thee of seeing only the ignoble in our world, and of limiting nobility to another world, which escapes us as incomprehensible. . . . At our age [both have turned sixty], one is no longer beautiful, but one can have a beautiful soul. I accuse thee of not having cared for thy soul. Thou canst insult me again," Cocteau concluded, deftly turning the other cheek. "I shall not answer. Adieu."

January 30

It is the dark-skinned antique peoples on the south shore of the Mediterranean who have been making sanguinary news lately, instead of the pale men of Europe, as is usually the case. That the Egyptians dared dream of breaking off diplomatic relations with Britain was less of a shock to Parisians than that they had dared burn Shepheard's Hotel, a caravansary that had come to seem an impregnable outpost of European civilization, with security and deft native service. The bloody Egyptian crises, flaming in the wake of the last fortnight's uprisings, deaths, repressions, and general strike in the French protectorate of Tunisia, which, in turn, followed on the touch-and-go situation in Morocco last November, have certainly stirred up Paris opinion. One type of Parisian thinks that a good, firm Metropolitan French hand is needed with the Tunisian rebels, who want a constitution. But the majority of Paris thinks that previous French governments are partly responsible for today's violence, because of their dangerous dawdling over decisions that might have soothed the natives—though they might also have vexed the French settlers. It appears that over the years the hundred and fifty thousand settlers in Tunisia developed the notion (without legal foundation, as the new young French Premier, Edgar Faure, has courageously made clear—too late) that, as co-inhabitants, they should enjoy equal power with the three and a third million Tunisians in any home rule, even that concerned with strictly Tunisian affairs. As for the government's dealing with the Moroccan upheaval, His Majesty Mohammed V, Sultan of Morocco, who refers to himself with a capital letter in the first person plural, in 1950 wrote to the French requesting talks on a new *modus vivendi;* in 1951 he had to write again, stating, "And for these negotiations We are still waiting." More recently, when His Majesty Sidi Mohammed el-Amin Pasha Bey, officially titled Possessor of the Kingdom of Tunis—a cultivated old gentleman whose dress uniform includes red trousers, a waistcoat, and jewels—received Jean de Hautclocque, cousin of the late General Leclerc, as French Resident General of Tunis, he said candidly, "You are the fourth Resident I have received since the war. Instead of changing Residents, the French ought to change their policy."

Parisians have shown enormous interest in the personality of the rebel leader Habib Ben Ali Bourguiba—now detained—whom few had ever heard of before he roused all Tunisia. His photographs show a violent, flat-nosed peasant face, rather than the more familiar aquiline beak of the elegant sherifian type. Until his followers began being arrested last week, he had twenty thousand disciplined militants behind him, and nearly half a million declared supporters. Frenchmen who knew him when he was studying law and political science in Paris, in preparation for his career of rebellion, say he is a born agitator, an intellectual, and an autocratic idealist who aims at victory but will accept martyrdom. He was born of modest parents in the coast town of Monastir, is now forty-eight, has long been married to a Frenchwoman ten years his senior, and, at one time or another, has spent four years in prison for his political activities. He became president of the Neo-Destour Party (*"destour"* is the Arabic word for "constitution"), which is Western-minded, Wilsonian, Kemalist, and plebeian. It was formed in the early nineteen-thirties, after a split in the Vieux Destour, or Old Turban, Party, which remains Koranic, Pan-Islamic, Oriental-minded, and conservative. Both Destourian groups are bent on independence. Those who know Habib Bourguiba say his personal tragedy is that his fine French education turned him from a Mussulman into an agnostic who believes in no prophet. They say he harangues mobs better in French, with Voltairian citations, than in Arabic, with flowery Koran couplets. As an eager intellectual, he fatally achieved the metropolitan cerebrations of those against whom, as a Tunisian, he vainly rebels today.

On May 21, 1890, Vincent van Gogh came from Arles, where he had been in a lunatic asylum for a year, to the small gray hamlet of Auvers-sur-Oise, near the river town of Pontoise, outside Paris. His brother Theo had sent him there for possible healing by the village physician, Dr. Gachet. Gachet had known Cézanne when Cézanne painted there, and, being himself a painter, was familiar with the crazed souls of artists. Vincent approvingly wrote Theo on June 4th, "The Doctor seems certainly as sick and bewildered as you and me. I am working on his portrait, the head very blond, with a white cap . . . a blue coat, and a cobalt-blue background, leaning on a red table with . . . purple flowers. He is absolutely fanatical about this portrait." The Doctor was less bewildered than Vincent, for late in July van Gogh borrowed an innkeeper's gun—to shoot crows, he said—and killed himself. He was buried in the churchyard at Auvers-sur-Oise.

Dr. Gachet's son, M. Paul Gachet, recently gave the white-capped portrait of his father—and the white cap, too, along with some other touching souvenirs of van Gogh and Cézanne—to the Louvre, and the pathetic little collection has just been put on public view at the Museum of the Jeu de Paume. In addition to the portrait, the collection contains works by Sisley, Pissarro, Renoir, Monet, and their friends. There are sixteen pictures in all. The only truly great items are three van Goghs—a self-portrait he brought with him from Arles, the Gachet portrait, and a picture of the back of the little Gothic church in whose yard he was eventually to lie. This trio of pictures has been on view before, but the Doctor's white cap—in a glass case, along with van Gogh's bamboo pens, for drawing, and his last palette, on which the colors are all smeared in diagonals, typical of his brush strokes in his wheat fields (it is shown next to Cézanne's palette, smeared with curlicues and cones of color, like his bathers' shadows)—gives them their earthly, intimate setting. In the glass case, too, is the Doctor's death sketch, in charcoal, of van Gogh's face—a fine likeness, sad and peaceful. The Doctor also did a portrait of van Gogh in bronze, perhaps from memory, with the bearded head placed in profile in a kind of dish—very strange. Given their present connection with the Doctor and his past, the paintings seem to lack the garish, art-show quality of long-viewed public collections.

For nearly a hundred and fifty years, Benjamin Constant's novelette "Adolphe" has been regarded as unique in lesser French letters, because it is the first example in romantic French literature of the delicate tragedy of the lady pursuing the gentleman, and of the inability of the gentleman, rather than the lady, to say yes or no. "Adolphe" is no longer unique, owing to the recent discovery of another minor Constant chef-d'œuvre, apparently lost in a trunk for more than a hundred years. It has now been published as "Cécile," though it might as well have been called "Adolphe the Second." It is even shorter than "Adolphe," being unfinished, but still more powerful, in its taut, nerve-racking, polite way, because it features two ladies pursuing one gentleman—Constant himself. One of the ladies is his eventual second wife, the Hanoverian Countess Charlotte de Hardenberg, who is the Cécile of the booklet, and the other is that Bonapartist exile and general brilliant holy terror of Europe, Mme. de Staël, whom he disguises as a Mme. de Malbée. His Charlotte was an obedient Germanic angel, but Mme. de Staël once quarrelled with him all night and all the next day, and she post-chaised after him over every frontier of the western Continent.

"Cécile," to a greater degree than "Adolphe" (both are true stories), is a rare record of the new manners of liberty after the Revolution, and of how they affected the domesticities and divorces that had just come into style among well-bred, well-educated Europeans, who, turning from the upholstered conventions of the past, stepped boldly out of doors into a whole dangerous new modern world—our modern world. It was evidently written around 1810 and then dropped and lost as inconsequential. It is supposed that it was preserved in one of Constant's many mislaid trunks scattered over Europe; one of them is known to have finally reached his widow in Switzerland. All that is sure is that the manuscript, of twenty finely written big double pages, turned up in some Constantiana that a present-day member of the family, Baron Rodolphe de Constant-Rebecque, recently deposited in the Bibliothèque de Lausanne. It would be reckless to say that "Cécile" is more fascinating than "Adolphe," but it is definitely more Constant.

June 3

The Congress for Cultural Freedom's month of international twentieth-century masterpieces, presented and mostly paid for by well-intentioned wealthy Americans, has finally come to its end, accompanied by the same mixture of general criticism and individual satisfaction it started with. Cold or hot, Paris owes thanks to the festival's program director, Nicolas Nabokov, for "Wozzeck," which it had been waiting twenty-five years to hear and which, together with the vertiginous peak of pleasure furnished by Stravinsky's evening with his symphonies, was the signal modern musical event of all the postwar seasons here. The Congress's modern-art exposition was justly ticked off for its paucity of French Fauves, but nobody hallooed the inclusion of two rarely viewed Picasso Cubist portraits—one of Wilhelm Uhde and the other of a "Jeune Fille à la Mandoline"—from the London collection of Mr. and Mrs. Roland Penrose. Benjamin Britten's new Melville opera, "Billy Budd," proved tedious and tactless. It was sung in English, and the only phrase that got across was "Down with the French!," which roused an icy breeze of laughter. A revival of the Gertrude Stein-Virgil Thomson opera "Four Saints in Three Acts," vigorously conducted by its composer, enchanted and tickled those who knew that it was a cellophane rose is a rose. *Figaro's* critic compared its Negro voices to savory, unctuous colonial fruits but remarked apologetically that Thomson's music reminded him of Erik Satie's, "from which nobody could tell whether he had renounced richness or resigned himself to poverty."

As for the writers' conferences on such hard knots as "Diversity and Universality" and "The Future of Culture," they proved that few writers talk well and most talk too long. Perhaps in consciousness of this, William Faulkner, who received an ovation from the French, merely muttered some incoherent phrases about how American muscles and French brains could form the coming cultural world and sat down, small, reserved, and inarticulate behind his little

Southern mustache. It was regrettable that creative Anglo-Saxon writers like Katherine Anne Porter, W. H. Auden, Glenway Wescott, Louis MacNeice, Allen Tate, and even James T. Farrell should have crossed waters to have, with one exception, merely journalists as their French colleagues on the platform. The single creative French writer to appear was General de Gaulle's man André Malraux. He made what was undoubtedly the most exciting, excitable speech of the conference, feverishly kneading his hands, as is his platform habit, extinguishing his voice with passion and reviving it with gulps of water, and presenting an astonishing exposition of politico-aesthetics that seemed like fireworks shot from the head of a statue. He never mentioned the General.

This has been a momentous fortnight for European history, which has been changed as much as it can be by statesmen's ink. Six statesmen signed up under the Quai d'Orsay's famous patient clock for an integrated European Defense Community. Their work can still be partially erased by non-ratification in any of their parliaments. Many French fear the whole business because it sounds like naïve New World idealism. The best thing about it may be that it operates on two of the least spiritual levels—that of pooled coal and steel and that of a pooled international army. General Eisenhower, who seemed to believe in the idealism, will be missed in France. He was the most loved and respected American citizen to function in Paris since Benjamin Franklin.

June 17

During the June *grande saison,* the quaintest and quietest event is the annual Concours International des Roses Nouvelles, of which the forty-fourth has just been held, like the others, in the ravishing topiary Parc de Bagatelle, where a jury chose the most beautiful new rose among fifty-five candidates, thirty-five of them French. The gold medal went to Flambée, officially described as "dark, brilliant red, with fiery reflections," which was grown by the French breeder Charles Mallerin. Even more impressive in the opinion of some was his Oradour, of a dramatic dark blood color, also with fiery reflections, which was named for the tragic town whose population was burned alive in the town church by some extra-sadistic Germans. Ominous dark roses seem to be this year's fashion. The only rose that was so new it looked positively peculiar was a fascinating little item frankly named Incendie, which had a center like pink gas-log asbestos and outside petals of burnt-out lavender. A pupil of Mallerin's, Francis Meilland, whose Mme. A. Meilland, named for his mother—yellowish with pink edges on an extraordinarily strong stem—was the rose sensation of recent years, has exported it to the United States under the name Peace, and over two million bushes have reportedly been sold there, making its breeder a fortune. This year, Meilland got no more than an honorable mention, for a handsome ochre rose called simply No. 29–31.

The roses are judged on six characteristics, with two points for *floribondité,* three points for vigor of vegetation, three for resistance to maladies plus beauty of foliage, four for qualities of newness, and four for general character—in which perfume figures only slightly. This year's winners were a delight to the eye, not the nose. None of them smelled much. According to gossiping rose men at Bagatelle, Louis XIV's gardener knew only fourteen varieties of roses; today there are fifteen thousand, and at least two hundred new ones are produced annually, some by "somatic accidents." Aside from the whistle-blowing of the park's spirited policemen whenever a visitor openly sniffed a blossom or caressed a bud, the Bagatelle rose competition was an exquisite performance and furnished an enchanting scene—prize-seeking multicolored roses as high as fountains on trellises or arranged like hedges or loading down bushes, and all these masses of carefully arranged color within an ancient garden of boxwood cut into cones and high embrasures, with, in the near distance, on a knoll at the edge of the blue-hazed forest trees, a Chinese-looking gazebo, serving countrified refreshments.

July 1

The most fastuous spectacle ever offered in the present Opéra house, and one superior in rich costuming, at least, to many staged at the Folies-Bergère, was the June-season revival of Jean-Philippe Rameau's "Les Indes Galantes," first given in 1735 at Louis XV's Académie Royale de Musique. Unfortunately, ultrarefined Parisians think the Folies-Bergère is just where the new Opéra show belongs. With the *polloi,* it has been a sellout. A royal *ballet héroïque,* "Les Indes Galantes" consists of plots, solo singing, choruses, verse declamations, choreographic *divertimenti,* a fable, and a moral. According to the fable, a European love feast, held in what looks like a bit of Versailles on Mount Olympus, is interrupted by a call to war. The moral is provided by a flock of cupids, danced by the *rats de ballet,* or the little girl ballet beginners, who take off, on an escalator rigged as a sunbeam in the Olympian sky, for climes where Venus is still supreme—specifically, Turkey, Peru, Persia, and an unnamed blackamoor isle. To these loving lands, the audience and practically the entire Opéra troupe go with them. This gives you the idea.

It is the overgenerosity of the production of "Les Indes Galantes" that makes it irresistible, with the Opéra's huge stage opened to its back wall for the ensembles, and crammed with ballets, marching choruses, star Opéra singers, a kaleidoscope of exotic costumes, and trick scenic effects that include a goddess floating on a cloud, ballet notables popping up through trapdoors behind disappearing gardens, perfume sprayed over the spectators to accompany a *divertimento* called "Les Fleurs," a shipwreck, a sweet-breathed Peruvian volcano erupting real fire, smoke, and incense, and an earthquake with falling temples. The Peruvian scene—which has a Lifar ballet of masked dancers costumed in clashing purples in a modernist abstract manner while preserving the Louis XV sartorial style that marks the whole show—is, artistically, the peak. There is also the sight of Mme. Geori Boué, usually seen as a seductive Thaïs, singing the Savage Queen in what looks like mammy blackface.

July 15

The schism in General de Gaulle's Rassemblement du Peuple Français is regarded as having been the most sensational event of this year's first Parliamentary term. It furnished the kind of intellectual political hubbub the French esteem and enjoy, for it ranged from mysticism to Olympianism and included rarefied theories of legitimism, pragmatism, and patriotism, plus the philosophic struggle between doctrine and action. In plain terms, it was really an old-fashioned bustup between the common sense of the Party militants and the purity complex of the statuesque Party leader. It was the sort of split that periodically splinters all intelligentsia-led European political groups. It really began in May, when so many R.P.F. deputies were upholding Premier Pinay in the Assembly, contrary to the General's strict orders, that he composed a stiff form letter of reproof, which began "*Mon Cher Député—*," with the names of the couple of dozen deputies typed in as needed. On being told last week, at the Party caucus in St.-Maur, that they must in future vote in Parliament the way the General, who is not a member of Parliament, orders from the sidelines, twenty-eight dissident deputies resigned from his Rassemblement and overnight organized themselves into a brand-new wilderness party of the Right, which they named Groupe Indépendant d'Action Républicaine et Sociale. In the suburb of Ivry, four R.P.F. municipal counsellors, including one woman, who was vice-president of the R.P.F. National Committee, also resigned, presumably to found a suburban wilderness party. Then a handful of R.P.F. senators resigned. Since French senators and deputies often double as mayors of their home towns, de Gaulle, in losing about forty of them, also lost some important mayoralties. The General's loss of face and Parliamentary followers is large, ironic, and probably not fatal. His R.P.F. deputation, which was the biggest in the Assembly, has merely shrunk itself out of first place.

According to Deputy Edmond Barrachin, chief of the de Gaulliste dissidents, the rebels are tired of voting no to everything, which has been the General's policy for his Rassemblement ever since 1946, when he resigned as chief of France. They are tired of being in opposition to every government and thus "voting more often than not with the Communists," the other perpetual Fourth Republic opposition. To serve France, the defrocked de Gaullistes are eager to go along with any party that shares some of their ideas, in the end hoping to dominate it from the inside. They are weary of the General's strange salvational conviction that only when everything else in France fails will the desperate country give him—him alone—a loud call. Barrachin said, "To wait in immobility for the national catastrophe, assuredly without wishing for it, so that General de Gaulle can be called to power seems to us an insufficient plan of action."

In the past week, the French and Europeans and their newspapers have been full of talk about de Gaulle. No two comments on him are alike. That he is still a magnetic crusading figure, able to attract men, whom he then puts to the exhausting task of waiting and doing nothing until history happens to him once again, is proved by the fact that his Rassemblement swelled to the biggest single party in France at the last elections. It was corroborated last week by the combined malice and satisfaction his hosts of enemies expressed at the news of his Party's schism, thinking that it weakens his chance of a coup d'état, which he says he disapproves of, too. Some of the things de Gaulle wants today are wanted by many other Frenchmen, who certainly do not want him also: a revised constitution, rechannelled patriotism, a centralized government carried on exclusively by men who were in the Resistance during the war and who would form a new aristocratic governing class, founded on bravery, and what he is always talking about, "the great social and national highroad that will lead to a regrouping" of France's welter of parties—a kind of upper-class Left of social reform, which still sounds like Fascism to the European working-class Left.

August 12

France is suffering from the worst epizootic of foot-and-mouth disease since 1939, and one of its most depressing aspects is that it is being blamed on the Americans, in an agricultural version of the Korean War microbe propaganda. The contagion has also increased Premier Pinay's unpopularity with the farmers, who think his government should have been ready with adequate vaccination virus. This is the first time that a French government was supposed to foresee an epizootic. Though the Pinay government had nothing to do with it, a vaccine that has been under study for the past five years at the Institut du Radium and at the Laboratoire Central de Recherches Vétérinaires was put in quantity production last week. It is dry, and cheaper and stronger than that previously imported from Switzerland for general use here; where one cow could provide only a few grams of the old vaccine, she can provide ten to fifteen kilos of the new stuff. If the new formula does its work, it will give French laboratories considerable honor and European farmers and cows great relief.

Since American farmers are thought by French Communist farmers to be the monsters who sent over the epizootic, it might interest our dairymen to know that this onslaught is produced by a new, stronger type of virus, never seen here or in America before;

that it started in Denmark last year; that the French farmers don't destroy their ill animals but merely report them to their mayor, stick up warning cards on their farm gates, and feed the sick animals grain mash or mashed potatoes or anything mushy that won't hurt their sore mouths; and that seventy-five to ninety-five per cent of the French cows recover. This must seem hardly cricket to the English, who are manfully destroying their sick animals during the present plague, which is also rampant in Belgium and Holland.

October 20

Until last week, it looked as if the Paris newspaper reports on the American Presidential campaign were going to consist of travelogues on the United States. For instance, there was the *Figaro* reporter's account of the fine time he had in the Eisenhower press plane, flying for two days around nothing but Texas, which he had never seen before and which he vastly enjoyed, taking particular pleasure in a mounted cowboy on some Republican greeting committee who told the Frenchman that he had never been on a horse before, being used to riding herd in a helicopter. At the end of the *Figaro* travel report, and well after the cowboy, General Eisenhower got a mention: "The crowds that came to hear Eisenhower were not large for this state of superlatives." Then, there was *France-Soir's* reporter, who had himself a splendid time at the New Orleans welcome to the General, which he wrote about as though it had been a Nice Mardi Gras carnival. Considering the offense taken here in France at Eisenhower's convention reference to the French as morally debilitated and half agnostic or atheistic, it is extraordinary how the French reporters allotted him the major publicity. Now they are also allotting him the major criticisms.

At first, the unknown Governor Stevenson was literally never mentioned in the leading Paris papers. Even his being *terre inconnue* was not treated as news. The opening pen portrait of him was given in *France-Soir* by its reporter, who saw him in Milwaukee: "He is a man of medium height, pink face, intelligent eyes, and Roman nose, possessed of elegance of manner and language, and yet capable of drolleries that make the people laugh. His speech here was on the academic side. It proved that he is a marvellous orator, far superior to Ike." Then the superior orator was dropped back into limbo. This past week, he has been brought forth again, with praise of a type which indicates that the visiting French reporters, at least, may have made their final personal selection. He is now suddenly hailed as "the great discovery from the West," the new midland American with *des éléments de grandeur dans sa nature.* A potpourri of their comment runs: "Stevenson's chances are augmenting"; "Stevenson appeals to the voter's mind, Eisenhower to the voter's emotions"; "Stevenson is a personality a hundred times more complex than his adversary" (high praise from a Frenchman); "Stevenson's speeches show his full stature as a statesman"; "If he wins the election, it will prove that the American voter has thought things over carefully, despite the organized theatricalities that are the *mise en scène* for the campaign, and maybe even despite television." The *Monde* reporter's latest comment on the possible outcome of the election is characteristically grave. He points out that it is not without irony that Negro leaders have said the next President may owe his victory to the colored people, "the so-called undesirable tenth [of the American population], who savor in silence this unexpected revenge after so many years of humiliation."

The French will certainly breathe easier when the election is over and they know whom they are going to get. They will be particularly relieved to have the campaign over, and an end to the candidates' competitive denunciations of Communists, Premier Stalin, and Soviet imperialism, which sound, some French think, too much like the Communist daily *Humanité's* denunciations of Wall Street varlets, President Truman, and Yankee imperialism, and make them nervous, placed as they are by history and geography as a way-station battlefield and occupation ground for whichever of the two twentieth-century giants should tire of being insulted.

Game birds now in season seem relatively cheap, considering how expensive even a pork chop is. Because game is extra-plentiful this year, fine pheasant and quail cost about the same as last autumn, which gives them the fallacious appetizing taste of a bargain. Even ortolans, those luscious, musical little mouthfuls, are available. They are seasonal here twice yearly, with a few in February—mostly lost last winter in high winds—and more in September and October. Ortolans are one of France's smallest birds of passage. They are brownish-grayish, gregarious buntings; but the peasants have always affectionately called them sparrows. The flocks, which mainly reside around Les Landes, in the southwest, fly off to summer in East Prussia and return in early fall to peck in the vineyards and glean in the grainfields, which is where they are hunted. The method of their capture and the subsequent stuffing of them to the limit of corpulence within their small measure has not changed since they figured as dainties on royal menus centuries ago. To catch them at this time of year, nets are set upright in the grainfield stubble, and live ortolan decoys are tied to them, to flutter invitingly. The hunters blow on little whistles devised to imitate the ortolan song, which is pretty. The birds, flying in dense coveys, must be entangled in the nets by the hundreds to make the hunt worth while. The hundreds are then packed into cages, are placed by the peasants in dark rooms, to keep them drowsy and inert, and are stuffed in the gloom for a fortnight with millet seed. Legend says that table ortolans meet their end by being strangled by the peasants with a horsehair. In reality, the peasants do it with thumb and forefinger. By that time, the ortolan is so plump that the back end of his little carcass is almost square with yellow fat. "He is so anemic—that is, bloodless—with fat as to be comatose and unconscious of death," a Paris chef classically said, and he added briskly that anyhow it was the natural destiny of ortolans to be eaten. Not many Paris restaurants specialize in them any more. This season, they cost two hundred fifty francs each, and two—or at most three—make a serving, for they are the richest bird in the gourmet's aviary. They are not supposed to be touched by knife or fork (though honestly they taste fine on a fork); the eater is supposed to seize them by the beak with the fingers of one hand and consume them, bones and all, beginning with the feet. The diner's free hand should be used like a cover over the ortolan to capture its fragrance, which is enticing; the bird's role is to please both the olfactory and the gustatory sense of man. It is ritually chewed slowly, to give it a chance to melt in the eater's mouth. Old engravings show ortolan-eaters with napkins hoisted like tents over their heads to enclose the perfume, and maybe also to hide their shame.

November 5

The Presidential election felt more local to the French than any other in American history. They were on the *qui vive* to the end, to know who was winning, who had won. By

Tuesday noon, Parisians had begun listening to their radios as if they could already hear the early-morning votes dropping into the ballot boxes across the Atlantic. And when the Wednesday news of Eisenhower's victory came in, they reacted to it, most of them, with chagrin. After all, Stevenson had, in a matter of weeks, become their man—their unspoken choice, who they had hoped would carry off the prize in a final sweep.

As the President still occupying our White House must be aware, there has been a lot of worry in Washington and Paris over something that the State Department and the Quai d'Orsay do not mention out loud officially but that the unofficial French have talked and written about incessantly for the past two years—French anti-Americanism. The main reasons for it have just been conveniently catalogued by the weekly *Paris-Match,* a French imitation of *Life,* which first, the week before, politely listed the reasons the Americans don't like the French. Americans living in France—provided they have ever met any French, that is—know both lists by heart.

A list of reasons for the French anti-Americanism that has now become so openly important runs about like this: Basically, the French, after seven years of peace, are tired of being occupied, even if for their own welfare, and especially of being occupied by Americans who, in their own phrase, "never had it so good." There are several thousand Americans in Paris alone, working in the intricate Washington services here, and thousands more, including the military, elsewhere in France. Since human beings are social animals, the first French anti-Americanism is cruelly social: The French think too many Americans talk and drink too much and too loudly in public. To jump to the more important economic realm, American high tariffs and high ideals, mixed, are a major anti-American canker. According to the French, what France wants now is trade, not aid, from America—business with America, not noble charity from it—no matter how much France has enjoyed or still needs aid. While deeply grateful for the Marshall Plan, the French say that the most intelligent thing about it was the Americans' original time limit on it, indicating a wise realization as to how much giver and receiver could psychologically stand. A commonly expressed opinion of many French and some West Europeans is that economic aid no longer provides the desired easy, early solution. The aid the French do want is military. Their six-year-old war in Indo-China has, according to

President Auriol, cost them nearly double the American aid they have received for it, is three times as old a war as the United Nations-American war in Korea, at the last accounting had killed several thousand more Frenchmen than the Korean war had killed Americans, and is even more unpopular, many times over, with French youths and their parents. (American contempt for France as a military ally is another sore source of anti-Americanism.)

The next reason for anti-Americanism here is certainly our high immigration walls, now guarded by a Gorgon Statue of Liberty, which the French say they are beginning to think they misnamed when they gave it to us. That a French student with a year's scholarship in America must, in obtaining his United States visa, not only furnish the American consular authorities here with his complete young life history but also subject himself to a medical examination of an embarrassingly inquisitive sort seems to the natives of France, which has for centuries been a haven to all, including sick geniuses in exile, a ludicrous example of our new, strangling red tape. Intrusive visa questionnaires and visa difficulties generally—especially for professors or any other kind of French brains—have soured our reputation for hospitality.

In international affairs, far and away the bitterest anti-Americanism still springs from our rigid anti-colonialism. The French respect our historical loyalty to the principle as decendants of a successfully rebellious colony in 1776, which quite properly possesses no colonies in 1952. But in our insistence that everybody else should be like us, the French say, we have helped ruin postwar Holland and England—countries we had fought to save—by encouraging the Dutch loss of Indonesia and by cheering on the breakup of the British Empire, which, over the years, controlled the very Mediterranean and Near and Far Eastern lands—even those unconnected with the Crown—that so worry us now: Egypt, Persia, India, and, of course, China. Wise to the delicate Dixiecrat issue in our Presidential election, anti-American Parisians ask how about our concentrating on our treatment of the colonials within our own home, i.e., our Negroes?

Next to the last of the major causes of anti-Americanism here is what the French jeer at as the irony of our hysterical hunts for a few hidden Communists, "like moths in an office carpet." Obviously, the final cause of anti-Americanism is the French fear that, after having liberated France in one war, in our clumsiness we might plunge her into another. *Paris-Match* summed up in part: "No country was worse prepared than America for the worldwide role that she brusquely had to play, and on so immense a scale. The Americans are leaders through the force of events, but without having the desirable first-rate qualities like sure judgment and a cool head. . . . They still lack almost completely the realism that the old imperial nations, like England, Holland, and France, learned from their own animated histories."

November 19

France has just lost two once important public figures, who could not have been more unlike—the harsh old royalist Charles Maurras, aged eighty-four, and the limpid Surrealist Leftist poet Paul Eluard, still in middle life. In January, 1945, a handful of us journalists managed to travel to Lyon, where Maurras was being tried for collaboration and was convicted of treason against the Third Republic. The trial was held in a bombed-out courtroom with snow filtering through its broken windows, near which Maurras sat in the prisoner's box, holding his walking stick (though he was going nowhere except to prison for life) and with a huge muffler, twisted like a fatal noose, below his large, useless ears. He was doubly deaf; physically he could not hear, and mentally, through habit, he was unable to listen to reality. Born in Provence and later, in Paris, a young protégé of Anatole France, he was by profession a self-constructed paradox. He began as an anti-Dreyfusard (who thought Dreyfus's final shame was his innocence), became a royalist (because he did not like republics) and then a holy monarchist (whom the Vatican put on the Index and the French royal pretender disavowed as a nuisance), was anti-British, anti-Semitic, anti-German (though he collaborated with Herr Abetz and was pro-Pétain), pro-Fascist, and forever pro-French. He founded the royalist Ligue d'Action Française, inspired Les Camelots du Roi, or King's Peddlers, who used to riot in St.-Germain-des-Prés, and, though by literary gift a purist, turned out, with Léon Daudet, daily virulent, scabrous editorials in their royalist gazette, *L'Action Française*. Both went to prison briefly for provoking a murderous Camelot attack on Léon Blum, who Maurras had written "deserved a carving knife." Even before this last war, Maurras' historical paradoxes began falling apart. At his Lyon trial, he already looked like a captured malicious, intelligent mouse—all beady eyes, swollen nose, vast ears, and diminished body. In prison these last years, he still scribbled royalist propaganda. He reportedly died lucid, writing up to the end.

Paul Eluard, whose real name was Eugène Grindel, was born in the Paris suburbs but early fled to the climate of the poetry of Rimbaud, Lautréamont, and Apollinaire, and then, after being hideously gassed in the First World War, to the new insurgent poets, and to the Dada movement, in the company of Tristan Tzara, Louis Aragon, and the painter Picabia, who later became the renovating, influential Surrealists. Eluard was a familiar figure at the Deux Magots, their café headquarters, and, unlike them, was a serene man, with a gentle, handsome, medieval face. In 1924, he disappeared and was thought dead, but he had merely quietly embarked on a tour around the world. On his return, his book of poems "Capitale de la Douleur" and the lyric phrase in one of them, *"Je chante pour chanter,"* became famous. During the last war, despite fragile health, he joined the Resistance, and emerged formally engaged with its Communist groups. His poetical material remained always private and poetic—love of love, of visionary liberty. In one of his vers libres, "Liberté," appeared his famous lines:

Sur toutes les pages lues
Sur toutes les pages blanches
Pierre sang ou cendre
J'écris ton nom.

As even the conservative *Figaro* has just said, "Communist or not, Eluard's lines on liberty should be known by every child in France."

December 2

France's war in Indo-China has been going badly, even tragically, with the ever-stronger Vietminh forces encircling French military outposts. The fighting is now so clouded by Army censorship that soldiers' parents here can only fear the worst. General Eisenhower's projected visit to the United Nations war in Korea, with its recent horrible bloody seesawing, has filled the French with the hope that first one, then another truce, on whatever terms, will bring a cease-fire for the New Year.

As for Pinay's government in France, it has been touch and go. For days it has looked in the evening as if it would fall, but it is always still there in the morning, like the not very radiant winter sun.

December 30

In one way, anyhow, French politics stuck to a pattern in 1952. In the first week of the year France lost her government, and in the last week of the year France lacked a government once more. It has lately looked as if France would have no government for New Year's Day of 1953, either. The new government, when it does turn up, will be the eighteenth—a dozen and a half of them—since the postwar Fourth Republic was founded, in 1945. The present hiatus is regarded by the French as the most profoundly serious of all, if only because it proves for the seventeenth time that something is wrong with the system, which it is now admitted must be fixed. Until recently, the demand for constitutional revision was suspiciously considered exclusively the product of the ideological mysticism of General Charles de Gaulle and his followers in the Rassemblement du Peuple Français. Today, few politicians would disagree with the General—not even those who wrote the Fourth Republic's constitution. The main trouble with the document is that it makes better provision for the fall of governments than it does for the coördination of their limited postwar powers.

It is significant and astonishing that after Premier Antoine Pinay's fall last week, de Gaulle's Rassemblement was given—if only in vain—its first chance to form a government. It was too much to expect that the "Trojan Horse" (which is what jeering anti-Gaullists, in disapprobation and fear, call the General's Party) would be able to take the preliminary jumps, let alone stay the course, loaded as it is with the weight of his remarkable personality and the personalities of those devoted to him. But that the Gaullists were asked at all showed a new Parliamentary attitude toward Gaullism, and certainly showed a new attitude on the part of the Gaullists toward themselves. Previously, their General had declared that his group should not even aim at taking power unless he could be the governmental chief, preferably President of the Republic; today he is not even a deputy—is, indeed, nobody but the fantastic head of his own Party, living in secluded campestral concentration in his country house southeast of Paris. He also instructed his deputies to vote nothing but no in Parliament, where they sat like monuments of obstruction until recently, when thirty-one of them revolted and were thrown out of the Party as rebels. In accepting an offer to try to form a government last week, the Gaullists, on the General's orders, emerged at last from their mysterious isolation, really with the object of reviving the faith of their voters, who were tired of the General's dignified policy of patiently waiting for France to collapse and then summon him as savior. What the other politicians hope they have gained from letting the Gaullists have a nibble at reality and power is that the Rassemblement will now permanently abandon its position of negation and help form a more stable coalition majority, without which no party is strong enough to found and hold a government in France today.

Jacques Soustelle, the Gaullist deputy who failed to become the new premier, is one of the group's several noted intellectuals, having been a distinguished ethnologist and the assistant director of the Musée de l'Homme before he took up a political career. As one accustomed to dealing with various species of man, he expertly interviewed ten former French premiers, of ten party mixtures, all of whose short-lived governments had fallen like houses of cards. Premier Pinay, in his bitterness over his recent fall, angrily described the French Parliament as a "bear garden" and declared that he would take part in no more governments. Experts opine that before long he will probably be called to take part in a government of his own again. The Banque de France warned last March that the state was in danger of bankruptcy, and it was the theretofore unknown Pinay who came in as a little businessman to save the franc. In the one week since he left, the franc has fallen and the dollar has risen. Financially as well as politically, Pinay may be the only premier France can now afford.

The Bibliothèque Nationale is holding a superb exhibition to commemorate the fiftieth anniversary of Emile Zola's death. It is the kind of amalgam of scholarship, literary odds and ends, leftover household objects, and revived atmosphere of an epoch that the French project so well, especially out of the nineteenth century, where they have such sure literary wealth to draw from. With characteristic thoroughness, the show starts with Zola's grandfather's birth certificate, issued in Venice, where the Zolas originated, and ends with a cast of the writer's hand in death and a copy of the discourse delivered at his tomb by his friend Anatole France. To set the background of Zola's greatest sociological novels—the series about those degenerating families, the rich Rougons and the impoverished Macquarts—a hideous, opulent Victorian parlor, suitable for the rich branch, has been assembled, as a sort of illustration. Then comes Zola's hand-written manuscript of "La Fortune des Rougon," with the solemn opening lines of its preface—"I want to explain how a family, a little group of beings, moves through society . . . giving birth to ten, to twenty individuals. . . . Heredity has its laws like those of gravity"—which laid the basis for this first naturalistic French novel on social evils. The rarest items are early paintings by Cézanne, friend of Zola's youth at Aix, which include a self-portrait of 1858 that looks like a Greco, and some fumbling young landscapes of the Aix countryside, then newly transformed by the famous dam built by Zola senior, an engineer. There is also shown a wealth of pictures of and by, and letters to and from, the great painters who made up the later Paris epoch Zola plunged into—Manet, Monet, Daumier, Toulouse-Lautrec, and van Gogh (with a still life of two books, one Zola's best-seller "La Joie de Vivre," the other the Bible). There is correspondence of the literary gods Sainte-Beuve, Flaubert, and de Maupassant (with a letter to George Sand complaining that she had written no puff articles on Zola's newest book), and there are stately communications from the Goncourt brothers. However, the dramatic, vital part of the show is the documentation on Zola's participation in the Dreyfus case. Here is shown his hastily scribbled, bold manuscript of "J'Accuse" and his printed copy of it—laconically marked by him in pencil *"A Garder"* ("To be saved")—as it appeared in Clemenceau's newspaper *L'Aurore,* where it shook Paris and Europe. There is also the French *état-major's* original photograph of the crux of the Dreyfus case, the notorious Esterhazy *bordereau.* The exposition catalogue states that the *bordereau* itself was, ironically, lost in 1940 during the exodus from Paris, after which the anti-Dreyfusard Marshal Pétain assumed anti-democratic power in France. The exposition is a thrilling historical treat.

There are not many living major French poets today—really barely enough for the literary circles to squabble about. Least contested as France's dominant poet of philosophy is René Char. He is a forty-five-year-old country giant, brought up among peasants in the Vaucluse, beside the river Sorgue, which wanders liquidly through his strophes; earns his living by manufacturing concrete building bricks; and was a redoubtable military chief of the Maquis in the war, when he kept a now famous militant diary, "Feuillets d'Hypnos," which, in exalted prose, records death, hope, and reality as the French knew them in the *forêts*. He is a man of limited schooling and vast reading; the main influences on him were the pre-Socratic Heraclitus, and Nietzsche and Hölderlin. His poetry, stemming from Dadaism and briefly Surrealist, is, for one thing, the opposite of T. S. Eliot's, being a sort of triumphant cry from classic individual man on the rack of the modern machine age, which his voice rises above. Char was recognized as early as 1930. His major postwar works are the volumes called "Fureur et Mystère" and "Les Matinaux," and his most recent one, "A une Sérénité Crispée." In his occasional love poems, he seems to French ears to achieve again the sonority of the senses that they heard in Mallarmé. Most of Char's poetry is in prose, consisting of aphorisms that link nature—his river, the sky, and harvests—to an aspirational philosophy so condensed as to read like an inscription on stone.

Char's influence on the non-Existentialist young French is enormous, though he is little known to Americans and English. There has been considerable animation in poetry circles here on seeing the first big selection of Char's work for foreign consumption—thirty-five pages, half in French, half in spirited English translation by Professor Jackson Mathews, of Washington State University, which are featured in the autumn issue of *Botteghe Oscure,* published in Rome, which has just arrived here. It is still the leading European literary review and probably the only important one in four languages—Italian, French, English, and American—addressed to the literati of Rome, Paris, London, and New York. In the present number, there are fewer Italian contributions than usual. There is a lot of English poetry, since the American-born Princess Marguerite Caetani, of Massachusetts, who is editor-publisher, is an optimistic believer in a renaissance right now of fine lyric English poets, led principally by Dylan Thomas. To the Old Guard French literary people who recall the Princess Caetani's Paris-published literary magazine *Commerce,* back in the days of her publishing association with Paul Valéry and André Gide in their earlier glories, her Rome production seems a distinguished lineal descendant.

1953

January 14

The incoming French government has taken on three faces, though one is usually all that can be managed. There is the regular face presented by the Fourth Republic's eighteenth government, just set up by Premier René Mayer—a Left and Right of Center compilation, whose principal local tasks are to revise the Constitution and to keep the franc, and itself, from falling. There is also the new governmental face presented by the Gaullists, hitherto hidden by their mystic veil of parliamentary nonparticipation but now openly and unexpectedly influential as the dominant coalition support. Behind them loom General de Gaulle's strict, proud views favoring French sovereignty; his ideas against the European defense community in its present aspect and against the international European Army as now planned; and his warm convictions against a Federated Europe, which he wishes to see only as an unfederated political Western union. As insurance against these last three policies, he and his party demanded, and received on a platter, the head of Foreign Minister Robert Schuman, the old Lorrainer who, like a kind of borderland godfather, was officially responsible for them. Yet it is precisely the idea of Federated Europe, the vastest idea of the three, that has just been amazingly accelerated in the final votes of the *ad-hoc* meeting of the European Constitutional Assembly, in Strasbourg. There, on a historic occasion, representatives of the six member countries' parliaments—with, from France, sharp Independent Republican Paul Reynaud, the Socialist Guy Mollet, and the Gaullist senator Michel Debré—met to take a decisive, if argumentative, step forward toward a functioning European assembly for "a political community, supernational and indissoluble, founded on the union of the people." And it is specifically as the creative intelligence behind these modern ideas that France shows its third face—the face of Europe's leader in political thought, of the revived France, whose imagination produced the only new European concepts offered since the war.

The confusing irony behind this portrait—an irony to which the French are highly sensitive—lies in the fact that quantities of French citizens, including members of Parliament, are increasingly dead set against these ideas (though not against the more materialistic one that produced the Schuman coal-and-steel pool, already functioning at a great rate), and especially against the ideas of a Federated Europe and a European Army, with its inclusion of a rearmed Germany, France's traditional enemy. Regarded as attractive theories left over from the postwar past, when men's imaginative energies were freer, they are now deemed, with growing conservatism, impracticable for the present and better reserved for some undated tomorrow.

It looks as if Premier Mayer were already being squeezed between two generals—the French one and the American one who is about to be President of the United States. It was to General de Gaulle that Mayer made his pre-Premier promise of so-called annexes, or changes, in the European Army setup, in return for help in forming a government. It is on Eisenhower that, as head of our government, Mayer plans to call soon, supposedly in regard to aid for France in her military commitments in the Indo-Chinese war.

Last year was a difficult time for getting down to brass tacks on Franco-American understandings, because the United States was having its elections, and this year may not be much better, because now it is France's turn at the polls. It is having municipal elections in the spring, which often cause governments to fall, and in the early winter it has the election of the President of the Republic, when, traditionally, the Cabinet resigns, taking the government with it. So whatever Premier Mayer is up against, he may not be up against it long.

January 27

For the past three weeks, a prolonged fog has transformed Paris into a phantom capital of gray beauty, of which everybody is growing extremely tired. The anticyclone has covered all France, and so has *la grippe,* in one of the greatest epidemics since the plague of Spanish influenza in 1918. Although the current visitation is fortunately only a mild form of the virus, it has laid the inhabitants low, especially in the cities and countrysides of Clermont-Ferrand, Bordeaux, Rennes, Strasbourg, Amiens, and Paris. A thousand Paris telephone girls are reported sick and off the job, along with thirteen per cent of the saleswomen in the big stores and thirty-five per cent of the Palais de Justice judges (but only twenty-five per cent of the lawyers, who seem tougher).

The persistent fog has acted like a melancholy condenser of people's present apprehensions. The French are startled and worried by the news—coming so soon after the war's deadly ambitions and racist horrors—of the Nazi revival and the arrest of its presumed leaders in the new, republican heart of their traditional despoiler, Germany; by the revival of anti-Semitism, with its arrests and fear, in so many places; and, not least, by their own republic's governmental instability. And, to make it all worse, there are France's deteriorating, tit-for-tat relations with the United States. After what Parisians have so far viewed of 1953, they will be glad when the opening winter segment is passed and the fog has lifted and they can see the spring, with the world still in place.

A sharp modern genre novel, "Au Bon Beurre," by Jean Dutourd, which last month was awarded the Prix Interallié, is now a best-seller. Enough time has elapsed since the war to allow Dutourd's characters and their cruel, comical avarice to arouse laughter, in retrospect. The family he features—a M. and Mme. Poissonard and their mealy little son and delectable daughter—are already classics, personifying those Paris shopkeepers in the butter, egg, and cheese trade during the Nazi Occupation who were known as *bofs,* the initials of the *beurre, œufs,* and *fromages* on which their dishonest fortunes battened while their customers grew thin. It is a matter of history that the *bofs* emerged as the *nouveau-riche* phenomenon of Paris, where they still climb. In "Au Bon Beurre," the Poissonards begin their climb by watering their milk and praising Marshal Pétain's doctrine of suffering. Their prosperity eventually leads them to Vichy to present duck eggs to the Marshal, which furnishes one of the driest, funniest tableaux in the book. Climbing ever higher on black-market produce, on hypocrisy, on cruelty, and on clichés that nearly prevent even them from knowing what monsters they have become, they step from Nazism into Resistance Communism; into democracy, as the Americans help liberate Paris; and then into prison as collaborationists, until they buy their way out. In corroboration of their *bof* belief that a big enough fortune always justifies the means, their daughter is then sought in marriage by a sensible poor young nobleman, who truly loves her, her parents' money, and his hope for a new democratic postwar France. Dutourd's scenes are scraped right out of real life, and his dialogues furnish the wonderfully accurate accompaniment.

As a secondary accomplishment, Dutourd has done the French translation of Hemingway's "Le Vieil Homme et La Mer." It is one of the greatest successes Hemingway has ever had in France. Even a costly de-luxe edition on fine paper is already out of print. In an amazing appreciation, the writer Jean Guéhenno stated that he was putting it on his library shelf beside "Feuilles d'Herbe," by Whitman; "Un Cœur Simple," by Flaubert; "Des Souris et des Hommes," by Steinbeck; and "La Mort d'Ivan Ilitch," by Tolstoy.

To honor the eightieth birthday of France's writing genius Mme. Sidonie Gabrielle Colette, born in St.-Sauveur-en-Puisaye, Yonne, on January 28, 1873, and still writing today in her apartment in the Palais Royal, literary weeklies here all fêted her with photographs of herself and with the compliments of others that have accrued over her lifetime. Facsimiles of letters addressed to her were printed, among them a typical one from André Gide presenting "praise you certainly did not expect. I, too, am astonished at my writing to you, and at the great pleasure I had in reading you. I devoured 'Chéri' in one swallow. Already I wish to read it again, but I am afraid. What if on rereading I find it less good?" Marcel Proust confided, in his wavering, evasive handwriting, "I wept a little this evening on reading 'Mitsou.' Humbly I compare your restaurant scene with those of my Swann, whom you do not yet know." Claudel, Valéry, Francis Carco, Jacques de Lacretelle, André Dunoyer de Segonzac, and Pierre Fresnay, along with Rebecca West, Katherine Anne Porter, and Rosamond Lehmann, contributed praise from near and far. Intimate letters of fifty years ago from Colette's provincial, earth-loving mother, the terrestrial Sido of "La Naissance du Jour," have been published by the literary weeklies for the first time, and also, like a third link in the female line of family sensibility, a paragraph from Colette's daughter, which terminates by quoting Saint Louis, the King: *"Merci, Mon Dieu, de m'avoir prêté Madame Ma Mère."*

February 17

It is too well-known a fact that governments in France fall too often. Everyone is also fully aware that there is a connection between government falls and the plethora of French political parties, of which right now there are eleven, six of them being major. To Americans, with their old-fashioned system of two parties, and even to the British, with their three parties, there seems to be something comic in France's having nearly a dozen. Obviously, the fact that there are eleven parties here is a tragedy. Since 1953 is bound to be filled with the acute argumentative decisions looming on both sides of the Atlantic, the prestige of France as West Europe's leader can ill support the strain of crumbling governments. Some sort of reform—under Premier René Mayer, if he doesn't fall before or during the attempt, or under whoever comes next—is regarded as inevitable, for to remain in power now is like trying to walk on marbles. The Fourth Republic's constitution, in memory of Marshal Pétain and in terror of General de Gaulle's position of solitary eminence just after the liberation, was expressly created weak, to prevent dictatorship. It was carefully written to give too much power to Parliament and not enough to the executive government. In Mayer's inaugural speech, he said he would single out for revision Article 13, which, if reformed, would permit a premier, under exceptional circumstances, to pass unpopular, needed laws (such as a law to tackle the French citizenry's tax evasions) by himself, thus relieving the deputies from having to answer for them to their angry electors; and Article 51, which, if reformed, would make it easier for a premier to dissolve Parliament. Then if a government fell, Parliament could fall with it, which, of course, would put the fear of God into deputies, and into political parties, too. But while these reforms may increase stability, they will not reduce the number of parties.

The Rassemblement du Peuple Français, General Charles de Gaulle's party, now has eighty-five deputies. In the 1951 elections, the R.P.F. became the largest Parliamentary party of France, by a margin of fourteen deputies. Recently it lost thirty-two members (and three affiliates), who bolted, or were ousted as heretics, after they had voted for Pinay's financial measures in defiance of de Gaulle's orders that his deputies sit like monuments, voting no to all government proposals. In 1946, General de Gaulle dramatically abandoned the Presidency of the Provisional Government in order to keep "the spiritual national investment," which he said the French Resistance and Liberation symbolized in him, from being sullied by party politics. The part of the French public and French politicians that has feared his later aims as being toward a *coup d'état* are still unable to explain why, if he desired dictatorial power, he did not seize it at the war's end, when France was at his feet. His R.P.F. political party was founded in 1947 not by him but by admirers, who gave it to him and the public like an extraordinary gift. What draws his followers is his conviction that France has rotted, socially, financially, and politically, and needs a drastic upheaval. Formerly, the General seemed to believe that a low-grade Parliament would bring about national collapse, which would thus allow what he calls *le pays réel* to vote him in as a savior. But since last month everything has changed. His party, originally "above party politics" and thus sitting in Parliament in a dignified vacuum, is now tentatively playing the parliamentary game. De Gaulle's aspiration is to be President of France, but a sort of idealized American President, with strong powers, a firm executive hand, and a Parliament reduced to a purely legislative role. As President, de Gaulle would treat the Communists, who obey Moscow, as treasonable criminals. He has consistently declared that the Fourth Republic's constitution demands a reform, which nearly everybody now admits. De Gaulle, as the incarnation of French patriotism, says that NATO has turned France into an American protectorate without adequate American protection; he wants France's defense run by Frenchmen, not by the United States. He is against a Federated Europe as being the death-blow to the sacred French nationality; what he does want is a Confederated Europe. General de Gaulle has lately been sending the Paris press frequent, lengthy communiqués on his newest political formulas. Even in addressing the newspapers, his language remains that of Bossuet, Bishop of Meaux nearly three hundred years ago. If the international situation deteriorates greatly, it is always possible that de Gaulle will make history again.

The French say that all their eleven parties and differing ideas—when they do differ—spring from the characteristic individualism of the French mind; that this double-edged genius for variety is the basis for the overdevelopment of the democratic principle of choice, now swelled through logic to the point of functional weakness. Even French deputies of the same party vote individualistically, as do some American congressmen. There is no party discipline, as in England, of obeying the whips. It is impossible to prophesy, for instance, how the French deputies and parties—except for the Communists, who will vote no, and the M.R.P.s, who will probably vote yes—will ballot when the European Army project comes up. French citizens who are disheartened by French politics think their politicians have become professionals, who deal in power as a business, like trading in eggs or real estate, as if their responsibilities were not the whole fabric of people's lives.

It is curious that the Third Republic, of which the Fourth is the descendant, started out in 1871 with hardly any party system at all.

March 10

Mournful singing by a Russian male choir preceded each of Friday morning's repeated Russian-language broadcasts, over the French National Radio, of Radio Moscow's announcement that had given people here the first news of Marshal Stalin's death. Then came Radio Moscow's French translation, accompanied by Tchaikovsky's "Pathétique" Symphony. Of the satellite capitals behind the Iron Curtain, Prague came in clearest over the air, playing the funeral march from Beethoven's Third. The French had listened to the same music with the announcement, from Germany, of Hitler's death and, from Washington, of Franklin Roosevelt's death. With anxious curiosity, the listeners wondered then, as they are wondering even more now, what would happen next in world affairs as a result.

L'Humanité—the only Communist daily paper left in Paris since *Ce Soir* was forced to cease publication last week, because of a dwindled circulation—perforce shouldered the Party burden of grief, propaganda, and official pronouncements attendant on the Marshal's demise. *L'Humanité's* Friday issue was a special edition of ten pages, with the front page bordered in black and a gigantic smiling photo of a Stalin of many years ago dominating the single column of text, which opened with "DREADFUL NEWS. STALIN IS DEAD. THE WORKERS

OF THE WHOLE WORLD, THE PEOPLE ALL OVER THE EARTH, ARE IN MOURNING." Thereafter, ironically enough, the Communist paper used, and credited, an American capitalist news agency, the United Press, for the death communiqué issued by the Soviet Union's Central Committee of the Communist Party, the Council of Ministers, and the Presidium of the Supreme Soviet—a communiqué that ended, as is customary when a European ruler dies, with cheers for the succession, in this case threefold and carefully impersonal: *"Vive notre puissante patrie socialiste! Vive notre héroïque peuple soviétique! Vive le grand Parti Communiste de l'Union Soviétique!"*

In its special-edition ten pages—along with a glorifying Stalin biography and an album of Stalin photographs, including the well-known happy one with Lenin, on a garden bench—*L'Humanité* reprinted, from the day before, as if insistent on getting the Soviet doctors' records quite straight, for once, the surprisingly detailed medical report on all Stalin's organs and the treatments used.

Samuel Beckett is an Irishman who came to Paris in the early nineteen-thirties in order to fall more completely under the sway of James Joyce, whom he already admired, and to whom he attached himself here. Since then Beckett has been best known for being a recluse who refused to meet people, and for his two novels, apparently written in French—"Molloy" and "Malone Meurt," which are in the Joycean "Finnegans Wake" manner and would be quite difficult to read even if they were in English. Now Beckett has written a curious and interesting two-act play that is being given at the Théâtre de Babylone, which is a typical little theatre hidden in a court behind an apartment house on the Boulevard Raspail. The play is called "En Attendant Godot." Godot is God, as nearly as anyone can make out. Those who are waiting for Godot are exactly two: a couple of tramps—one, named Wladimir, who is the spirit of wisdom, and the other, called Estragon, who is a weaker, coarser vessel. Across the heath where the tramps wait comes what looks like a decayed Irish squire, who may be the Devil or even might be Godot, whom the tramps don't recognize even when they see him. The squire drives and whips his old liveried servant like a horse. There is one minute when the servant, who may represent humanity, and who usually is dumb, suddenly starts talking at his master's order, spouting an insane hysterical muddle of erudition, formulas, and mental confusion that is one of the harshest, funniest satires on bogus learning since the satires of Swift. In Act II, the squire, who by now is blind, drives over the heath again but forgets he had met the tramps, and so drives off with his lunatic lackey, and the two tramps settle down again to wait for Godot, but far less sure he will ever come. Lucien Raimbourg, who plays the philosopher tramp, is a cabaret *chansonnier*. He is also a fine, simple, sensitive actor.

"En Attendant Godot" is written with an extraordinary sense of theatre, by which a drama with nearly no action and presented on an improverished small stage maintains acute interest in mere talk between people who do nothing but hope and get defrauded. Several of the critics have hailed it as one of the few truly intelligent plays in town. Certainly it combines many things. In its intelligence, it feels Russian, though done in the Irish manner and spoken in French.

May 6

If some of the French nowadays feel helplessly cut off from what goes on in the national government—in Parliament and inside their deputies' heads—most of the citizenry still feel close indeed to their local functionaries, the city or village mayor and councillors who do the neighborhood governing right under the citizens' noses. Accordingly, seventy-eight per cent of the voters actually voted the other day in the municipal elections in France's thirty-eight thousand communes. At least eleven councillors are elected in every municipality—even in villages with a population of a few hundred—which meant that all over France something like one voter in twenty-five was running for office. In small towns, mayors are paid merely a token salary, but they get to drape themselves in the official tricolor sash, which is worth a fortune in dignity; the councillors receive nothing at all. In a Hérault hamlet called Pégairolles-de-l'Escalette, all eleven councillors refused at the last minute to run again, because they had had too much trouble governing the one hundred and eighty inhabitants (and each other), so since Election Day the place has had no councillors at all, and heaven knows what may happen. At Montagnard-Dieu, in the Ardennes, all nine voters, who were using the mayor's cooking pot for the ballot urn, voted early so his wife could cook lunch on time. The daughter of Nancy's mayor was fined for nocturnally pasting posters around town that libelled her father's political rival. At Bessuéjouls, the mayor, who was up for reëlection, his wife, and one of his sons were all murdered during election week, and the addled local politicians failed to present a new candidate to take his place. More Balzacian incidents and characters are connected with France's municipal elections than with the voting for the national job of deputy, a big plum and sterner stuff. Among the special figures recently elected to office in their home towns were one member of the Académie Française; two actors, including one from the Comédie-Française; the president of the French Rugby Federation; American Ambassador C. Douglas Dillon's cousin Weller Seymour, of the village of Neaufles-St.-Martin; two Communists in prison, including Comrade Henri Martin of *"Libérez Henri Martin"* slogan fame; and the former noted Cabinet minister Georges Bonnet, who was not even a candidate.

The outstanding political result of the elections was the destructive defeat of General de Gaulle's party, Le Rassemblement du Peuple Français. Ever an unpredictable, Cartesian leader, in an amazing statement just printed in his party paper, *Le Rassemblement,* he dissolved the party itself. The old R.P.F. deputies and the few newly elected ones may no longer call themselves R.P.F.s. He does not disavow them as his *compagnons,* but as politicos they are now nameless, and on their own. (About thirty rebellious deputies of his achieved this personal liberty for themselves last year by backsliding out of the party.) The original salvational Gaullist movement, conceived to rescue France from the corruption of too many political parties, was itself transformed in 1947, by successful elections, into one more political party—against the General's wish. It is this party that, after these disastrous 1953 elections, he has just dissolved. The Gaullist Rassemblement movement itself he has by metamorphosis just restored to its exalted, unpractical form—a kind of patriotic political cult. Disdainful, as ever, of politics per se and interested only in the art of governing, the General scathingly said in his R.P.F. dissolution statement that in France "neither the Left nor the Right can govern alone. Acting together, they neutralize each other. The world sees this as it watches our sad political circus parade. The French regime is sterile and for the moment cannot change—a series of combines, bargains, majority votes, and office investitures that make up the games, the poisons, and the joys of the system." But he foresees, as he has been foreseeing for the past seven years, that France is facing a serious shakeup, and that with it will come what he bitterly called "the bankruptcy illusions." "The safety of France," he continued, "and the state will be at stake. *Il faut préparer le recours.*" And who will furnish the means that will save? Le Rassemblement, whose ex-R.P.F. candidates just lost the municipal elections.

"Le Salaire de la Peur" ("The Wages of Fear"), the French film that won the Grand Prix at the Cannes Film Festival, is now being hailed by Parisians as a truly great French film. It is certainly a great cinematic thriller. There are three hours of it, focussing on Georges Arnaud's brutal best-seller novel of the same name about international riffraff rotting, unemployed, in some Central American oil region until heroism becomes a paying proposition. A distant oil well has caught fire, and explosives are needed to blast out the flames. A tough American oil agent offers a fortune in cash to the four bravest barflies to drive two trucks of nitroglycerin over a dangerous mountain road to the conflagration.

The too long first half of the film is like a remarkably photographed novel, showing the barflies' sordid, greedy quarrels as a guide to what is coming. From there on the shocks begin, with a fearless, fat Italian and a disillusioned, heroic German in one truck and two Frenchmen, a lovable coward and his murderous, gay young friend, in the other. The mountain ride, which is what the film was made for, becomes the acme of anguish, a kind of motorist's nightmare, with a new twist of sadistic slowness, since the trucks dare not go fast. The decaying bridges, the precipices, a landslide, a near drowning in an oil pool, the deaths, and even the temporary victory are exploited in tension, inch by inch. Only the murdering young Frenchman arrives alive to claim his prize money. To the music of a remembered juke-box waltz, he then drunkenly waltzes his empty truck into a chasm on his return trip over the mountain road. The wages of fear have been paid.

The acting is excellent and the international principals—as well as the director, Henri-Georges Clouzot—deserve mention by name: Folco Lulli, as the Italian; handsome Peter Van Eyck, as the German; the late William Tubbs, as the American oil agent; Charles Vanel, as the white-feathered Frenchman, for which performance he won a Cannes acting award; and Yves Montand, ordinarily France's most popular tough-guy music-hall ballad singer, as the gay murderer. "Le Salaire de la Peur" is a superior character film with anguishing thrills.

* * *

The European antics of Senator McCarthy's youthful investigation team, Roy Cohn and David Schine, gave Parisians rare material to sharpen their wits on. Weary of hearing about American efficiency (and tired, too, of trying to find some comforting evidences of it in certain of the slapdash postwar American installations flourishing around France), the French went into stitches of laughter over a report that Cohn and Schine investigated the loyalty of twelve hundred employees of Radio Free Europe in Munich in thirty-five minutes. They thought it the greatest half hour of mass inquisition ever known in Europe's two thousand years of political practice. According to American diplomatic gossip from all over the Continent, the Cohn-Schine Katzenjammer Kids, which is what Americans here called them, have done more and funnier harm to the prestige of the United States in Europe than anything else that has come out of the astonishing McCarthy box of surprises.

What started three weeks ago as a small strike in the upholstery department of the nationalized Renault motorcar works in the suburb of Billancourt spread into a strike of ten thousand workers that has turned into a lockout with thirty-seven thousand men idle. The strikers demand twenty-five francs more an hour. There have been strikes in several of the big hotels—the Crillon, Meurice, Lotti, and Continental. The Continental's strikers marched over to the sunny Tuileries Gardens the other morning—the chefs in their tall caps, the waiters in their tailcoats, the bartenders in their white coats, the dishwashers in their dungarees, the *garçons d'étage* in their colored jackets, and the chambermaids in their billowing aprons—after kindly serving early-breakfast coffee to the guests, who thereupon proceeded to make their own beds. There is talk of strikes in the gas and electrical companies and in the railways, to tie up the coming businessmen's Foire de Paris. It is hardly a secret that most French labor is underpaid. Labor has apparently decided to let French business know, too.

May 20

For the past month, American visitors to Europe who are important enough to know important Europeans have been reporting that they are everywhere being asked the same anxious, two-headed question: "What are you going to do about McCarthy? What has happened to America?" In the past week in Paris, Senator McCarthy has suddenly become the main Franco-American topic of shrill conversation. The Paris newspapers, which at first were worried about McCarthyism, are now profoundly afraid of it and have been writing about it angrily. A recent typically complicated French headline was "MCCARTHYISM, FORERUNNER OF FASCISM IN THE USA; SENATOR IS LEADER OF PRO-FASCIST GROUP WHOSE CENTER IS IN CHICAGO (NEAR WISCONSIN)." A typical Paris editorial said, "In his indecent attacks on those he dislikes, insult is mixed with excommunication. Goebbels in his best days did not do it any better." *Franc-Tireur,* which has always been pro-Eisenhower, said in an apprehensive headline, "MCCARTHY IS COMPROMISING EISENHOWER'S FUTURE," and referred to the Senator as a scarecrow with a bloody mailed fist. The conservative *Monde,* the most influential newspaper in France, had as a headline "THE MANIAC OF THE WITCH HUNT; DAILY HE WEIGHS MORE HEAVILY ON THE LIFE OF THE AMERICAN PEOPLE."

Le Monde has given the most space, voice, and variety to the French concern over McCarthy. In an article called "The Two Troikas," it mentioned Moscow's three-horse government of Malenkov, Beria, and Molotov and asked, "Who reigns?" Then it took up the Washington triad of Eisenhower, Taft, and McCarthy, ending with the query, "Who governs?" *Le Monde* added, "The President of the United States should not forget that he is the leader of the free world, a title to which neither Taft nor McCarthy can pretend." And in an analysis of what it termed the danger to freedom of thought, which is what most alarms the individualistic French, the paper said, in part, "The drama of American liberals in their opposition to McCarthyism is that their counterattack aims at his methods rather than at the underlying issue in McCarthy's investigations. Nobody dares to raise the true question in the political and juridical fields: Can the Congressional investigations establish control over the political and religious ideas of private American individuals?" Of all the Paris press this last fortnight, the Communist *Humanité* alone has not lifted one stick of type against Senator McCarthy.

June 1

This is the time of year when French country cousins come up to Paris from the provinces and their estates to attend the June-season horse races, balls, family dinners, and matchmaking tea parties, and to take in the major painting exhibitions as their annual snack of art. The favorite exhibition right now is a luscious one of nudes at society's preferred gallery, La Galerie Charpentier. It will last all summer and is obviously an ideal hot-weather show. So much nudity on the walls presents an astonishing sight, with appetizing, rosy torsos and limbs from the days of the Ecole de Fontainebleau, a classic nude by Poussin, a goddess nude by Chassériau, and modern nudes by Renoir and Cézanne. It is a stimulating show, if only because it reveals how the human form has been bred during a four-hundred-year studio evolution, in which pretty, pink, round women have become thin, slab-sided, or even blue-breasted ones, with angles.

People here who have been worrying more than usual about the social unrest rising in France have just received an unusual, dispassinate analysis of it from an unexpected source. Monsignor Paul Richaud, Archbishop of Bordeaux, last year headed an inquiry into the possible causes, undertaken by the bishops of Catholic France. *La Voix Diocésaine de Besançon,* a religious review, recently gave an outline of the resulting report, which has provoked considerable amazement and comment on all sides. After the bishops had conducted a detailed examination of working and living conditions for the proletariat in all the dioceses of France, they concluded that though the bourgeoisie and the owner classes feel a certain desire to uphold human liberties, the dominant mainspring of their actions is the profit motive. According to the report, these classes show an unconsciousness of the disproportion between the way they live and the way their employees live, and they do not suspect that their comfort and riches prevent their lucid appreciation of the workers' problem. The idea of fair prices is losing ground, profit margins swell, and the sharing of profits with workers is almost nonexistent. As for the workers, the bishops went on, it is a fact that they always have to use force to improve their lot. Most are convinced that they are victims of organized injustice. Their salaries, even with social insurance and family allocations from the state, are proportionately less than before the war, though the national income has gone up. Workers, the bishops found, in many cases think that they have some rights in private business that today's society will not recognize. Though most of them—or so the churchmen thought—do not accept the Communist theory of class struggle, they recognize class struggle as a social fact, and their acute comprehension of the human rights denied them by the owner and bourgeois classes is back of their impatient desire for reforms in the social structure. For, the bishops concisely concluded, the French worker is more hopeful of changing structures than of changing the habits of the Frenchmen above him. French commentators are as impressed by the candor of the Archbishop's report as by the Church's obvious concern with France's present social malaise. Plenty of French also think that if the Church aims to use its vast influence for social betterment, it cannot start using it too soon.

The eighteenth French government since the Liberation having fallen last month, it was thought by many here that the political program demanded by the third of the premier-designates who failed to form a nineteenth government—little Paul Reynaud—was essential. He said that it was not worth while taking office unless the constitution was first reformed to assure a French government of eighteen months of governing, instead of the postwar average of five months, and that Parliament should bear the punishment and responsibility of dissolution. Until then, he said, France cannot be consecutively governed. Until then, as the French citizens helplessly see the tableau, each French government is merely another balloon that barely gets off the ground before it is snagged on the Parliament roof.

June 18

France has been four weeks without a government, although nine politicians have been offered a chance at the premiership by President Vincent Auriol. An acid newspaper cartoon by blasé old Sennep shows Auriol wondering whom to ask next and murmuring, "Maybe a well-known woman—Danielle Darrieux or Martine Carol . . ." Assembly President Edouard Herriot, aged eighty-one and sick in bed, received at his bedside his Radical Party leaders, whom he belatedly warned to stop playing party politics, saying, "At the close of my life, with all my soul I implore you to think now of nothing but France." The politicians had better think of their own skins, too. According to Article 51 of the Constitution, this Parliament can be dissolved and the deputies sent hunting for their jobs in general elections if they overthrow one more government on a question of confidence or censure between now and November, 1954. To the French public, the present crisis fundamentally shows just what the seventeen other crises since the Liberation have shown, but with a strange air of finality. It shows that if a French Premier is to govern with any continuity today, he must be given special powers. For the first time in a crisis, there is practically a sitdown strike among designate-Premiers, who will not lift a finger unless they are promised better Premier working conditions. Above all, this crisis, like a magnifying glass grown seventeen times stronger, makes ultravisible the fact that France's multi-party system and her disparate ways of looking at political matters—a disparity upheld by French logic and French republican liberty—have reached a point where, through habit and through shortsighted human psychology, political greed, and Gallic precedent, party-minded men, both in and out of politics, are concerned only with their differences in thinking, instead of with developing the ideas they have in common.

Considering all the pressures besieging France—the delayed Bermuda conference, the old unsettled business of the European Army, the new influential, softening Soviet policy that almost daily is seeping out from behind the Iron Curtain, and France's vital need for a revived diplomacy and some set foreign policy, even about its own war in Indo-China—considering all these exterior semi-crises, the ridiculous aspect of this present crisis is that it began in France's hip pocket over a question of money, although France is the richest country in Europe. There has always been the comforting theory that France's financial troubles come merely from the fact that her citizens don't pay their taxes. According to the last Finance Minister's Report on the Economic Budget of the Nation, the state revenue would admittedly be billions of francs higher if the citizens paid all the taxes they owe—that is, if French businessmen did not classically keep two sets of books and pay only on the lesser book. But the report says, nevertheless, that more than a third of the national income does wind up in the tax channels. Yet with all that money rolling in, Premier René Mayer had to borrow money from the Banque de France, which, in a way, is why he fell and why the crisis began. Then the Banque de France, dunning for a payment on the debt, knocked on the government's door and found nobody home.

June 30

If—as was certainly not the case—France had been able to afford her recent record-breaking five-week political crisis, during which she was without a government, the crisis would have done almost nothing but good because it so harmed the present kind of parliamentary regime in the estimation of the French people. Unbearably costly as the crisis was in lost prestige and even financially, it seems, at any rate, to have proved to France's citizens a fact they had to make sure of, once and for all—that the present constitution absolutely must be reformed, so Parliament will not have the power to do again what it has just been doing, and so the executive will be able to sit in the seat of state long enough to govern. According to experts, if anything is sure right now in French politics, after the incomprehensible choice of an obscurity like the Calvados deputy Joseph Laniel as Premier, it is that Parliament will undertake a revision of the constitution, if only to save itself from possible dissolution.

The outstanding salutary human element to emerge during the critical month was the bold, harsh intelligence and the uncompromising personality of the youngish politico Pierre Mendès-France, as revealed in his unaccepted program for saving the country through economic and social reforms. Plenty of French have got into the habit of thinking that their country cannot be saved. Mendès-France's program, outlined in the speech he delivered in Parliament when he was trying to get support for his bid for the Premiership, set a standard by which all other programs have since been judged. Though the parliamentary majority turned his program down, millions of French accepted it in their own minds and remember it as the one notable declaration among the millions of words of *blah-blah-blah* (French for "yackety-yack") spoken here. A lawyer and a banker trained by the Rothschilds, yet a representative of the younger-generation reform wing in the liberal, if money-conscious, old Radical Socialist Party, Mendès-France remains the dominant figure of the crisis and, with luck, he could be the new leading man of France, which certainly still needs one.

The crisis reminded one of Alice and the Red Queen when they started running, not to get anywhere but merely to stay on the same spot. With the crisis ended, France is just where she was before it began, though more winded. As ex-Premier Antoine Pinay, one of the unsuccessful candidates, remarked bitterly, there are two hundred and five Marxists on one side of the Assembly, and, on the other, four hundred and twenty-two anti-Marxist deputies, whom it is impossible to pull together into an unselfish, non-party national coalition that could put France back on her feet. And as the semi-Socialist afternoon paper *France-Soir* pointed out, still to be solved are France's interior and exterior financial deficits, the European Army problem, the Indo-China war, the Moroccan troubles, rising unemployment, inadequate salaries, a stagnant economy, investment difficulties, and insufficient housing. The height of Parisian editorial indignation at Parliament's feeble choice of the inexperienced new Premier—after its five weeks of lionlike roaring—was reached by the independent *Combat*. "The cowardly relief felt by the deputies in seating M. Laniel is not shared by the rest of the country," it fulminated. "They are making another grave mistake if they think it is."

During the five critical weeks, the Paris newspapers kept printing, if merely from habit, what the parliamentarians thought about politics. Only one paper extensively printed what the French citizens thought about Parliament. This was *L'Express,* the new Paris political weekly edited by Jean-Jacques Servan-Schreiber, who previously was one of the noted younger political experts writing for *Le Monde*. What he printed in *L'Express* was a culling from the famous regular reports on what the French feel and think about life and politics which are gathered (according to a shrewd system started by Napoleon Bonaparte) by the prefects' offices in each of the ninety departments of France; the reports are sent to Paris and boiled down into a synthesis, which is available to three officials—the President of France, the Premier, if there is one, and the Minister of the Interior. *L'Express's* own editorial analysis of its selection of nationwide prefectural reports was that the French are so sick of Parliament they might even accept some single leader to save France "if only he gives an impression of being honest, brutal, and courageous." Unquestionably most of the citizens' opinions, as represented in the prefects' reports, were scathing. In and around Rouen, people wrote three times the average budget of monthly letters to their prefect, all full of complaints. They charged that their deputies had shilly-shallied deceitfully in abstaining from voting on all the candidates for Premier put before Parliament, and in not stating clearly on the Assembly floor whether they were for or against Mendès-France's program, and why. They also said that Parliament ought to be dissolved, but only after passing an electoral reform, since "otherwise the same deputies would turn up again and the muddles would continue." In Compiègne, a leading citizen declared that "the deeply disgusted French people demand a dictator with a pitchfork and broom." In Boulogne, a businessmen's petition asked that "the nation choose new representatives, who would really work to restore France." In Lyon, home of Parliament's president, old Edouard Herriot, there was an increased wave of antiparliamentarianism. In the northern coal region, workers thought the high cost of living more important than politicians, "who never change anyhow." In the south, the major theme was again dissolution of Parliament, preceded by electoral reforms to prevent the reëlection of *"les incapables,"* along with prophecies of serious social troubles this autumn if there is not a new government atmosphere and crew. The prize reaction to the crisis came from a citizen of Marseille, who wrote to President Auriol (the President declared that his bulging private letter bag showed him how dangerous and profound is the malaise of the French people) demanding the dissolution of Parliament and of all eleven political parties in favor of a tricolor format of only three authorized groups: a blue party for the Republicans, or right; a white party for the center; and a red party for all the left. It was a sensible, if impossible, plan.

The major post-crisis worry now is just plain money. According to the caretaker government's report, the crisis cost France the equivalent of two hundred and eighty million dollars in unfloated loans and other losses. The state coffer is bare and is taking another massive loan from the Banque de France to pay state employees their end-of-June salaries. What the French people now want to know is by which of the two customary agonies will the deficit be met—by extra taxation or by printing more inflationary money.

Obviously, France has had so much history that it necessarily keeps repeating itself. Apropos of today's terrible deficit, there has been recalled, like an echo from the past, Louis XVI's financial dilemma, during which Marie Antoinette supposedly asked the Royal Finance Minister, "What will you do about the deficit, Monsieur le Ministre?" "Nothing, Madame," he replied. "It is too serious."

* * *

The Soviet violinist David Oïstrakh, officially described by his government as Russia's greatest, was enthusiastically accepted here, after his concert at the Palais de Chaillot, as one of the great performers from any land. A stranger to Paris musicians and an inaugural export in the new relaxed Malenkov policy toward the West, he packed the theatre, the largest in town, with political comrades, with music lovers, and with curiosity seekers. Oïstrakh is a nice-looking, big, blond, stocky Ukrainian with an undershot lower lip and extremely long, lithe fingers, which, as regards his left hand, may explain his impeccably accurate tone. He keeps his bow arm close to his side, produces a *gamme* of sounds that are beautiful—especially the soft ones, including unscratched pianissimi in alt—and displays no folderol mannerisms. Of the three concertos he played, the opening one, Mozart's No. 5, was unfortunately led like a cart horse by Jacques Thibaud, exceptionally directing the Conservatoire Orchestra, which was afterward vigorously managed by Manuel Rosenthal. The final work, a Khatchaturian concerto dedicated to the player, was a good-natured, folksy affair, with an amorous *valse lente* as its *andante sostenuto,* which, by giving merely entertainment, could offer no notion of Oïstrakh's important qualities. It was in between the two, in Brahms' Opus 77, that he presented his rich, complete musical report. Controlled and unified, his emotional interpretation seemed universal as well as particular; his musicianship serious, learned, and positive; and his technique a matter of almost luxurious ease, but used unobtrusively and without the counterfeit of tricks. At the concert's end, he received an ovation, the audience clapping without pause for a quarter hour, until he delicately played, with more courtesy to France than to musical taste, a violin arrangement of Debussy's "Clair de Lune." According to the program notes, Oïstrakh, who wore his Stalin Prize medal pinned to his evening clothes, was born in 1908 in Odessa, the son of an opera-chorus singer, and was a pupil of Pyotr Stoliarsky, who seems to have trained all the past generation of Soviet violinists. Since 1934, Oïstrakh has taught at the Moscow Conservatory. At his concert, he played a Stradivarius bestowed on him by the Soviet government.

August 18

Symbolic and descriptive of Paris on the fourteenth day of France's paralyzing national strikes was the long line of municipal refuse trucks driven by French soldiers and rattling past the empty, closed Parliament buildings—the Army en route to its matinal job of collecting city garbage while the deputies were off somewhere on Parliamentary vacation during the greatest civil-service crisis of the Fourth Republic. This is the biggest strike movement France has experienced since the violent Front Populaire days of 1936, and the only calm one of consequence in French history. So far, not one of the many sides involved—strikers, police, labor unions, political factions, the military, and the discommoded public—has lifted the theoretical or physical finger necessary to cause or incite bloody riots. No one—or nearly no one—on the Paris newspapers has raised his voice in the usual shrill, tantalizing editorial. As one ordinarily tendentious commentator wrote solemnly, "This is an enormous, majestic strike."

It began in the smallest, most careless way possible, according to two remarkable articles just printed in a couple of rival Paris weeklies. When the stories are put together, what they say is that the strike started because of two men and a typing omission of four words. These men were MM. Landy and Fossat, employed in the money-order section of the Bordeaux Central Post Office. At four-thirty on the afternoon of Tuesday, August 4th, there mysteriously came into their possession a mimeographed advance copy of one of Premier Laniel's economy projects, compiled by Edgar Faure, the Minister of Finance and Economic Affairs, which, among other things, listed the categories of civil-service employees whose retirement would be postponed for five years. Because four words, "*facteurs et facteurs-chefs* [postmen and chief postmen]," had been omitted, through a typist's error, from the stencil, postal employees were not on the list of *actifs;* that is, workers who, "because of fatigue in performance of service," were to be spared the delay in retirement. The postal workers thus appeared to be transferred to the list of *sédentaires*. This, to Landy and Fossat, seemed no place for foot-weary mailmen. At five o'clock, after consulting the local higher-ups in their union, these two men called the entire Bordeaux P.T.T. (Postes Télégraphes et Téléphones) service out on strike. At eleven the next morning, after the pair had talked by phone, which by now nobody else in Bordeaux could do, to the top leaders of the union in Paris, the national postal strike was called. When the Paris union leaders later sought the customary interview with the appropriate government Minister, they discovered that the Minister of the

P.T.T., Pierre Ferri, was in Lisbon to report to an International Postal Congress on France's fine postal service, and that the Minister of Reconstruction and Housing, Maurice Lemaire, who was assuming his functions in the interim, was completely ignorant of the Faure project's specifications. He also did not know how on earth Landy and Fossat could have come by a document that bore the stamp of the Minister of Finance and Economic Affairs. Investigation traced it to the Conseil Supérieure de la Fonction Publique, whose director, by law, must submit proposed decrees to the council members, twelve of whom, also by law, are labor-union representatives. One of these must have passed along the copy that somehow ended up in the Bordeaux Post Office. As soon as the project's original text had been checked at the Fonction Publique office, the omission of the four fatal words came to light, but it was too late. Twenty-four hours after the postmen struck, about two million other government employees began joining them in sympathy strikes, which by midnight on Thursday included transportation everywhere, and France was atrophied.

In Paris, the paralyzing effect of the strikes was increased by the lethargy of La Fête de l'Assomption, the big religious and bank holiday, which seemed bigger than ever because it fell on a Saturday this year, and on Monday the newspapers were also on strike. Boulevards are empty, hotels are stagnant, many restaurants are locked for their annual August closing, but enough are open for the reduced clientele, with fresh food brought in to town by country camions. The gas strike has merely made pressure low. As for electricity, Paris, being the Ville Lumière, still has it to burn, with the neon advertising blazing nightly, and this last weekend Notre-Dame and other sites were treated to nocturnal illumination. The Louvre, like all museums, is closed, the guards being civil servants, and thus on strike. The streets are cleaner than New York's usually are, because of the presence of soldiers equipped with trucks and brooms. On the Métro, now running more frequently, though still stopping at 6 P.M., we often ride several times on the same ticket, because ticket punchers are on strike. The trains don't stop at all stations, or even at all the stations they are supposed to stop at. You get out where you can and walk back, or go to the end of the line and hope for better luck at making your particular station on the return trip. Everybody walks a lot. The Army has saved many people's legs by substituting Army trucks for the striking city buses, but they stop at nine at night. An operational center has been set up on the Place de la Concorde, near the Strasbourg statue, with a map of Les Lignes Intra-Muros Exploitées par l'Armée leaning against a lamppost, and a two-way-radio truck run by an efficient, hard-boiled corporal of the Compagnie Républicaine de Sécurité, toughest of the French police shock troops. The Army trucks have a couple of boards, set lengthwise, to sit on and usually no top, so standees can be packed in more easily; are driven by a soldier; and have a soldier on the tail to hoist passengers on and off. Bus tickets are bought by the book at tobacco shops, for the soldiers are not supposed to handle cash. In front of the Grand Palais, a motley collection of privately owned buses, ordinarily used for tours, weddings, or funerals, are now operating to carry people at least in the cardinal directions away from Paris. Inside the Palais, the ticket sellers are flanked by blackboards with *"Nord," "Est," "Sud-Ouest"* written on them in chalk, as mere points of the compass for the travellers to head toward, with the specific town, like Caen or Cahors, that the bus is going to added almost as an afterthought. Waiting passengers—each day they are fewer, but they shrewdly come hours early to be on the safe side—sit on the Palais steps, tidily piling their bread crusts or chicken bones in the crevices of the façade sculpture. Mothers sprawl on the grass beneath the trees, nursing or changing their infants. Aside from the ticket sellers, the huge interior of the Palais is empty while the patient citizens sit outside in the sun or occasional rain.

The Palais bus schedules, and the street addresses and bus schedules of half a dozen private tourist agencies that are also providing transportation, are printed in the newspapers and announced during the news broadcasts of the national radio, which is operating again. The radio also announces personal tragic news, such as that the mother of Mme. Telle-et-Telle, of such-and-such a place, is dying, and agreeable collective news, such as the good health of children in the hundreds of vacation colonies all over France.

September 2

The strikes are over, nearly everybody is back at work, and nothing is settled. It is now figured that at the peak of the strikes four million French—or close to a tenth of the entire population, including infants in arms—were out. Yet the French themselves say that after this vast social upheaval it is not clear who won—or, indeed, whether anyone won. Only the losses are easy to see. The government lost twenty-five billion francs in revenue from its paralyzed railroads and bureau of Postes, Télégraphes, et Téléphones, which is reportedly just about what it had hoped to save on the economy projects that set the strikes going. Masses of workers lost three weeks' pay while they were striking against not getting enough pay in the first place. Now the government says it will allow certain categories of workers, such as the postal employees, who started it all, to make up part of their lost pay in overtime on undone work, which has collected all across the nation like unwashed dishes. Since most of us are now getting a dribble of letters mailed a month ago, there seems to be plenty of overtime cleaning up for the postmen to do.

Though *Figaro,* as the upper-class morning paper of Paris, was cautious in its editorials during the troubles, it has now printed an exceptionally frank warning to the government, and to private enterprise, too, which says, in part, "Let us not forget that the explosion of discontent was provoked principally because numberless workers once more arrived at the conviction that they would get no satisfaction unless social agitation brought about such a state of urgency that certain problems would have to be looked in the face, if not solved. What is the use of denouncing the very real harm the strikes did to the country if strikes still seem to workers to be the only way of getting anything done and if we wait to do anything until the strikes break?" *Le Monde,* the upper-class evening paper, has just published a statement made by the Action Catholique Ouvrière, the remarkable organization of worker-priests, which says, "For years the French working class's legitimate hopes (and they are not solely material) have been betrayed. Contracts to which it was a party have been torn up or ignored. Workers' living conditions are becoming increasingly precarious, while a small number of the rich and the pleasure-loving make a show of insolent luxury. It becomes less and less debatable that the present French social, economic, and political structures are largely responsible for social injustice, for an inhuman economic system, and for class politics that are contrary to the very spirit of the Gospel . . . and the city of justice and brotherly love." Very unusual words to read in the City of Paris today.

* * *

A flock of important events occurred during the strikes, when the scattered or immobilized Parisian public had neither sufficient concentration nor sufficiently ample news to take in the strangeness of some of the things that were happening. Among these was the unexpected absence of bloodshed in Morocco when the old pro-Moroccan Sultan, Sidi Mohammed ben Youssef, was deposed and virtually kidnapped, and the absence of shock at the installation of the new pro-French ruler, Sidi Mohammed ben Moulay Arafa. With the unpopular, insoluble Indo-Chinese war, with the recent one-day visit of Vietnam's Emperor Bao Dai to President Vincent Auriol in his summer quarters at the Château de Rambouillet, with the present sharp Cambodian independence demands, and now with the switch of sultans in Rabat, France's colonial troubles have certainly reached their apex. Over the last few years, much of liberal French opinion considers that the colonial tableau has been altered, willy-nilly, for all European nations, even France, by the change in England's former empire. An outstanding Parisian leader of this critical group is the novelist and Academician François Mauriac, who sees his connection with the Moroccan problem largely as an extension of his Christian conscience. He has boldly stood out against the government's colonial policies, and has been an ardent backer of the native reform movement. Mauriac bluntly termed the recent investiture of the new tame Sultan a plot in which, in his opinion, the present French government was one of the conspirators—strong stuff indeed. In the August number of *La Table Ronde,* the monthly magazine Mauriac edits and of which his column called "Bloc-Notes"—excerpts from his personal diary—is always a special feature, there is a painfully timely illustration of the violent bitterness a certain ill-educated, hard-bitten type of French colonial feels against any liberal French reform views. The August "Bloc-Notes" mentions threatening letters Mauriac has lately received—in particular, a brutal one from Casablanca, which the magazine quotes, including words unprintable in English. "You might as well know," the letter says, in a quotable part, "that if you continue to write such tripe [favoring the natives] you are going to have an accident one of these days. You're a dirty dog and a traitor to Marshal Pétain. Take care, because you are going to be beaten up. My fists are in fine shape, those of a colonial farmer who spews on you all his contempt. You call yourself a Catholic and Christian. Talent isn't everything. There is soul, too, and you haven't any, and your spinal column is as supple as a cobra's. In a few days, it's going to hurt you good. *A bientôt, salaud.*" It is on such conflicting points of view among the French that the new ben Moulay Arafa administration in Morocco has been founded—the most important French event that has taken place outside France this year.

October 1

The autumn symphony-concert season has opened with Beethoven's Ninth and the "Eroica," and with Debussy and Ravel as usual. Some more freshly and vigorously appreciated concerts of jazz music have also just been given. American jazz—when Parisians can obtain the real article—is still of concert-size significance here. Since the 1948 concerts in Paris of Dizzy Gillespie, fans of *le jazz-hot* have starved for the sound of a big-name jazz band. Now they are almost having a glut, with five jazz concerts in the last ten days, and with more, by Count Basie, soon to come. Stan Kenton and his band gave one sellout performance at the Alhambra, and Lionel Hampton's orchestra gave four concerts in two days at the Palais de Chaillot, the largest theatre in Paris, which he packed. French *jazz-hot* fans are as intellectual in talking of *swingue* as if they were discussing Schoenberg. They praised Kenton for—as one fan put it—"his meticulous orchestrations, the maximal efficacy of his howling trombones, and his whistling cornets, which bathed you, drowned you, stiffened you with sound, till they suddenly gave way to the soft languor of saxophones, which were like balm." Kenton was also thought to be too intelligent in his jazz, too rehearsed, and too ascetic.

There was no intellectualization at all at the Hampton concerts, especially after the intermissions, when some of the musicians came down into the aisles to play and some of the audience climbed up on the backs of their seats to cheer. Hampton was, however, critized as a formalist for his fidelity to elements of boogie-woogie. It was his tenor-saxophone soloists, his quintet made up of a flute, three trumpets, and a sax, his vibraphone solos punctuated by his odd, bleating voice, and, above all, a few melodic climaxes of wild octaves run up by the brass in shrill arpeggio that brought down the house. The costumes of the musicians were also much admired. They wore violet tuxedos, huge Byronic shirt collars, and bullfighters' string ties.

October 14

In 1927, the French poet and diplomat Paul Claudel wrote a spectacle called "Le Livre de Christophe Colomb" for Max Reinhardt, of Berlin. Knowing what the Germans like, Reinhardt stipulated that it should have orchestral music, a choir, a ballet, and two Christopher Columbuses—one the old, friendless navigator on his deathbed, the other the young discoverer in his prime, with the new, round world and glory just in sight. For various reasons, the opus has had to wait all these years for a production, now courageously undertaken by the theatrical company of Madeleine Renaud and Jean-Louis Barrault, who opened in it upon their recent return to the Théâtre de Marigny, after a year and a half of foreign triumphs. The only simple element of "Le Livre de Christophe Colomb" is the stage set—a vast sail, which sometimes represents a ship, at other times, when semi-furled, a white curtain at Queen Isabella's palace, and later a cloud in Heaven. Otherwise, the play is utterly complex. There is a prologist, in modern evening clothes, who reads history from Columbus's old notebook, and there is a supporting cast of thirty-two, who cluster on stairs leading to the orchestra pit, where they sing Darius Milhaud's exhilarating music or shout, as enunciators of public opinion, either for or against Columbus. Occasionally, after donning cloaks or mustachios, they swarm up onto the stage as Spanish courtiers or sailors. There is a ballet at the Spanish court, with dancers representing Envy, Ignorance, and Avarice, and later a ballet of natives of the Azores. Much is made of a pious pun on the name Colomb, which is supposed to mean "*colombe*"—French for "dove"—and thus identify Columbus with the Holy Spirit. Aside from a storm at sea and a sailors' mutiny, little dramatic action is furnished by the lines, which are full of atmospheric repetitions that approximate poetry. By means of brilliant stage direction, Barrault has supplied at least theatrical action, using his huge cast to catch the spectator's eye when the spoken lines fail to attract his ear. The play ends with Queen Isabella, the two Columbuses, and a pair of saints being hailed with hallelujahs in Paradise.

"Le Livre de Christophe Colomb" has been positively eulogized by the critics, only one of whom found anything to regret. He said that he thought some members of the audience didn't like it. Lots of members of the audience didn't.

October 27

A week ago, the French Parliament, for once, actually voted almost unanimously on something—to hold a full-dress, decisive debate on France's vitally pressing, two-headed Indo-Chinese problem. When the debate opened last Friday, two-thirds of the deputies failed to turn up, either to talk or to listen. Only the Communist members attended in full fig. The other parties' absentees were visiting their constituents to ask what they wanted them to say when the debate reaches its climax, as it will very soon. Certainly the answers to be given are extremely important not only to the French but to the rest of us. The two main questions are: What should France do in Indo-China about its French Union (formerly called the French Empire), which the Vietnam Congress in Saigon has just said it no longer wants to belong to—in its present form, it added hastily and too late. And what can or should France do about ending its unpopular Vietnam war? Already the Parliamentary group around Pierre Mendès-France, who is considered the new white hope of political realism, has asked that negotiations be opened with the Communist Vietminh leader, Ho Chi Minh. Expert civilian interpretation of the Army communiqués on the recent, much touted French-Vietnamese offensive south of Hanoi says that the military situation is actually no better than the political one, which is double poor news. Furthermore, from one end of France to the other the public is still extremely angered by what it considers the ingratitude of the Saigon Congress's recent demand for national independence (which, after all, France last promised in its note of July 3rd). The way the French see it, for seven years the cream of their country's manhood—its young volunteers and its Army officers, who are being killed at almost the same rate that new officers are being commissioned from St. Cyr—have been fighting and dying in Indo-China. Not only the popular indignation against the Vietnam Congress but also the possible opportunity for France to wash its hands of Vietnam in consequence were skillfully keynoted by the moderate-Left Paris newspaper *La Libération* when it said, "Those Vietnamese we have supposedly been fighting for now want the French to leave. In these conditions, what the devil are our soldiers doing out there? Why not bring them home immediately?" *Le Canard Enchaîné,* the satiric weekly, ran a cartoon that showed Marianne standing before a wall in Indo-China on which "Go Home" was scrawled, the way the French scrawled it on walls here for the Americans.

Inevitably, there has been more than the usual anti-Americanism in the press, provoked by the Washington administration's wish for France to continue bleeding against Asiatic Communism into the eighth year while we hold parleys for our political truce at Panmunjom. But some sensible observations have also been made. One concerned the common difficulty the French and the Americans, with their Western brains, have in dealing with the Eastern mentality. Both Emperor Bao Dai and his High Commissioner, Prince Buu Loc, have been right here in France during these recent important days, but for all the French officials could do with them, they might as well have been eating rice back home in Saigon. As ex-Premier René Mayer cynically remarked, "Probably the Vietnam Congress is no more slippery for the French to deal with than Syngman Rhee is for the Americans."

One of the few deputies who turned up for the Indo-China debate informed his handful of listeners that "the campaign of Maximilian in Mexico, which was one cause of the ruin of Napoleon III's army and the French defeat by the Germans in 1871, was a chef-d'œuvre of diplomacy and strategy compared to the absurd Indo-Chinese campaign, which swallows up all our Army cadres, prevents any straightening out of our domestic financial affairs, and annihilates our European defense program." Once more, the watchful French citizens are waiting to see how their Parliament, after its preliminary blowhard speeches, finally votes on the complex Indo-Chinese question.

November 10

One hears little any more of Les Six, except for the four who, since their chance union in 1918, have continued to write the major part of France's modern music. Les Six, if taken together, are Louis Durey, whose name is always frankly forgotten; Mme. Germaine Tailleferre, whose name is remembered; and Auric,

Poulenc, Milhaud, and Honegger, whose names and works are current and constant. Reassembled by Jean Cocteau, who made an almost paternal speech from among the Conservatoire orchestra's first violins on the stage of the Théâtre des Champs-Elysées, Les Six—with the exception of Honegger, too ill to be there, but including Milhaud, in a wheelchair—recently forgathered to hear some of their works played at a concert marking their thirty-fifth anniversary. None of the young Paris intellectuals attended. The enormous audience was composed of people who were young thirty-five years ago, when Les Six were *le dernier cri*. The major work played was a suite from Auric's ballet score "Phèdre," fresh and musicianly, rich, hearty, and delicious. Of all the program, it was most to the public's taste. Poulenc's cantata "Sécheresses," for choir and orchestra—written to a poem by the English poet Edward James, and supposed to trace a desert landscape by Salvador Dali—was magnificently melodic, and had, sure enough, an undulating musical line like a horizon. Milhaud's Second Symphony sounded important and scintillating but prolix. Architecturally, the big affair was Honegger's "Prélude, Fugue, et Postlude," from his "Amphion"—grandiose, savage, and melancholy. All in all, it was a melancholy concert. It recalled the wonderful first postwar Paris, when the Kaiser's Germans had just been defeated and Lenin's Russians worried no one yet.

November 24

The Parliament's present debates are only the semifinal. None of the various proposals for a united Europe are now up for ratification. They may be fought out in the new year and to judge by this past week, perhaps without there being enough of a majority either to kill the ideas forever or push them into effect. The debates have proved principally that to the French these proposals have become matters that concern the conscience (even in the case of politicians) or, at any rate, matters that arouse profoundly individual convictions, typical of the critical, individualistic French mind but, for once, all revolving about the same deep-seated belief—that it is necessary to fear a reviving Germany. The six most important veterans' associations are split exactly in two; three are resolutely hostile to the rearming of Germany in any form and three favor the proposed European Army.

Only one Parliamentary political party, the Communist Party, is of one mind about the E.D.C., and it is ready, on Moscow's orders, to vote against it en bloc. Every other party contains deputies who are for and deputies who are against the E.D.C., though the party itself may officially be against it, like the two Gaullist parties, or may officially be for it, like Bidault's M.R.P. Party. The Socialist Party is for the E.D.C. provided England comes in, too, the Socialists being fundamentally Europeanists from way back, long before the E.D.C. was ever thought of. It dominated the recent Parliamentary scene, yet it contains factions that, thanks to their characteristically severe consciences, have refused to accept the E.D.C. in its present form. As for the Radical Socialists, who include France's big businessmen, they have been so much for and so much against the E.D.C. that they have operated practically as two distinct parties. The pro-E.D.C. wing is headed by ex-Premier René Mayer, who has just said that he believed in the E.D.C. "as the indispensable pillar of the Atlantic community." The Radical Socialist anti side is led by rambunctious old Edouard Daladier, who as Premier signed the Munich pact with Hitler in 1938 and, as he grimly indicated in his recent Assembly speech, one year later lost his trust forever in any kind of Germany. In all these groups are men who belong to what should be called the Ostrich Party—usually chauvinistic or else earnest, unrealistic patriotic Frenchmen, who stick their heads in the sand so as not to see that once more a defeated and yet invincible Germany has sprung from its ashes, a Teutonic phoenix toward whom the tired Gallic cock, with his long, painful recollections of the previous fights, must now perforce take some sort of position. For the French as a whole, the E.D.C. problem is Germany—not Russia, as it is for the Americans.

Bankruptcy is something French financial experts have on their minds just now, being stoically convinced that France's démodé industry and old-fashioned agricultural system can run only another three or four years. Then, they believe, France will crack up, because of its low productivity, its high prices, and the fact that it faces modernized competition on all sides.

However—and maybe here is some good news—among both the pro- and the anti-E.D.C. French there is a distinct impression that Russia is now in no political or material position to desire anything but a continued cold war, since its European satellites, including East Germany, are in various states of unreliability and, as the Moscow newspapers themselves announced, after all these pinched postwar years the Russian people need the encouragement and reward of the higher standard of living and comfort recently offered by Malenkov.

The anti-E.D.C. French mostly think that the Americans have proved immature and often alarmingly indiscreet, and, jealous of old France's already tarnished sovereignty, rebel against any further bossing by us or lowering of France in the international hierarchy that is inherent in the E.D.C. Many pro-E.D.C. French agree with this unflattering notion of American leadership but think the world has now definitely shrunk, and that amalgamation across and around the Atlantic will be history's next instinctive step.

The French who are neutralists candidly want France and West Europe left out of Atlantic-defense treaties, so that in case there is an atomic war, Russia will not regard them as belligerents but will leave them alone, the fight for control of the world being, in the neutralists' eyes, only between the U.S.A. and the U.S.S.R. There are even some neutralist fantasists who envisage the possible future atomic war as taking place in the air between the United States and Russia, and entirely at long distance, with guided missiles being shot southwest at us by Russia and northeast by us toward the Soviet Union, both aimed in such a way as to give Europe a comfortable miss.

Both the pro- and the anti-E.D.C. French fear that Germany, out of habit, might provoke the next world war, or anyhow, once in it, would fall to conquering France, as usual, no matter what its treaties. The difference between the antis and the pros on this point is that the former believe, with all their hearts and souls, and all their hopes of France's and their own and their children's survival, that Germany can best be restrained by being kept out of any European Army, and the latter believe that Germany can best be contained in the European Army and the new European community that would go with it.

And there the two French views still stand, as they have been standing since February, 1952, the last time, up to this week of debate, that the problems were discussed in Parliament.

These may seem long-drawn-out thoughts to American readers, to many of whom the answer would appear to be "United you stand, divided you fall." But they are the thoughts that the deputies have been discussing this last week in Paris, that the newspapers have been printing, morning and night, and that the French citizens have been listening to on the radio and trying to understand in the papers, in spite of all the technical political jargon—thoughts that the French people, with an educated sense of national involvement, realize they, the Parliament, and their France as an entity must base a solemn decision on, probably in the first month of the new year. The French are aware that this decision can be a turning point in France's, Europe's, and even America's, England's, and Russia's modern history.

Victor Hugo was the first popular French modernist to talk of the practicability of a United States of Europe. It then seemed like a novelist's dream. To many French, it still does.

December 7

The Goncourt Prize, for the year's supposedly most talented novel, normally becomes the leading matter of pre-Christmas literary interest of France. This December, the interest has shifted to the discreetly unpublished leftovers of the Goncourt "Journal," the diary kept by the two famous brothers, of whom the survivor, Edmond, founded the annual fiction prize bearing the family name (except that the family name was really de Goncourt, they being aristocrats). The spotlight has centered on this part of the journal because the descendants of Alphonse and Léon Daudet—the father and son to whom Edmond willed the task of confiding it to the Bibliothèque Nationale, where it was to be kept under seal for twenty years, until 1916—recently filed a court action to prevent its publication even now. It consists of the more intimate pages of gossip written by the brothers, partly in hieroglyphics, as private comments on their literary friends. For this reason, and what with one delay and another, fifty-seven years of secrecy have shrouded it, until everyone mentioned could be presumed in his grave. Recently, these leftovers, become legendary in modern French literature, were announced for publication in 1954, to come out in an unspecified quantity of volumes, two volumes at a time, priced at fifty-three hundred francs, or fifteen dollars, a pair, in a numbered de-luxe edition sold sight unseen to subscribers only. The Daudet descendants haughtily demanded that publication be forbidden unless they were given the preposterous privilege of going through the manuscript and cutting any reference to Grandfather Alphonse that they disapproved of. Their lawyer claimed they had become alarmed when they heard that the diary described him as "hallucinated by flesh." In theory, nobody except the ten members of the Goncourt Academy, which bestows the annual prize, and their associates has seen the diary yet, but literary experts say with gratification that the phrase sounds perfectly like the malicious, refined de Goncourts, and just like lively old Alphonse, too, who wrote the novel "Sapho." What has made the Paris public laugh coldly at the Daudet family's priggishness is that the late Léon Daudet, who died in 1942, is still vividly remembered here as wielding the most scurrilous pen of all the editors of the prewar Royalist newspaper *L'Action Française,* notorious for its offensive vocabulary. Daudet's specialty was his abusive anti-Semitism, particularly against Premier Léon Blum.

The Daudets' protest also brought the terms of Edmond de Goncourt's testament into the newspapers, revealing its surprising proviso that the Goncourt Academy was annually to pay each of its members six thousand francs—twelve hundred dollars at the time—for reading and judging the novels. But the lucky winner of the Goncourt award received, and receives, only five thousand francs in prize money. To provide these sums, Edmond willed the academy the royalties on his books and those that would accrue "from the publication of my journal, which will be found after my death in my *boulle* [tortoise shell and brass] armoire . . . and this journal shall be sealed for twenty years." He had already published nine of the now classic fraternal volumes before his death in 1896. The Daudets' lawyer, in his plea, reportedly said that the excerpts were not worth printing, being inaccurate, indiscreet about several private lives, including Turgenev's, Balzac's, and Flaubert's, and full of braggadocio anecdotes of the sort that "even great literary men relate after a good dinner." Now that the Daudet court action has been dismissed and the long-sealed diary is sure to see the light of day in 1954, many Parisians—doubtless including the Daudets—can hardly wait to read it.

Today, the fiftieth of the Goncourt Academy awards—now, alas, worth the equivalent of fourteen dollars and twenty-nine cents—was given to Pierre Gascar for his novel "Le Temps des Morts." The latter is an autobiographical account of his experiences in a concentration camp, a form of life that the de Goncourts never heard of.

Though 1953 has been filled no more than any other year with conspicuous good will toward men, it has at least brought something like peace on earth to Korea, and the French hope that 1954 will bring it to Indo-China.

December 22

As the septennial Presidential election dragged on vainly through its fourth, fifth, and sixth day and night at Versailles, it began to resemble an accouchement in public, a long-drawn-out, agonizing strain, with Marianne lying in labor and everyone looking on, an indelicate spectacle of prolonged embarrassment. "PITIE POUR LA REPUBLIQUE" and "ASSEZ, MESSIEURS," newspaper headlines cried, as if the repeatedly balloting politicians, by their clumsy selfishness, were pitilessly inflicting real pain, more than could be borne, on the French body politic. It has been the worst, most weakening, and most disillusioning democratic experience France's Fourth Republic has suffered, and it has come, as usual, at the hands of the political men elected to strengthen and govern it. Only the French, with their unfortunate uninterrupted experience of little that is good from their Parliament, could have weathered it.

It all began so pleasantly. Thursday, Election Day, was the last warm, sunny day of the false spring that Paris has been enjoying at the year's end, and in Versailles's gardens finches were singing and primroses destined for April were mistakenly blooming. (That night it turned cold, and the next night it snowed slightly, as everything began to go from bad to worse.) For the Hôtel Trianon-Palace's famous septennial luncheon—traditionally served at high noon, since the voting begins at two—an impressive *tout-Paris* crowd of nearly a thousand had assembled. This is one of the few functions that carry on with the social energy of prewar days, probably because it occurs only once every seven years. The ladies were much less dressed up for the occasion than they used to be, but the crowd was as special as ever—Cabinet ministers, playwrights, scientists, big businessmen, actresses, duchesses, novelists, ambassadors, Quai d'Orsay people, wives generically, journalists, editors, and so on, plus leading French politicians, including Presidential candidates. For the three-thousand-franc *prix fixe,* the lobster was succulent, the champagne dry, the armagnac fragrant, the gossip unbridled. Some of the candidates and their wives had optimistically brought and stowed upstairs in bedrooms their top hats, tails, and evening gowns for the triumphal drive back to Paris, if they won, accompanied by the Garde Républicaine on horseback and in white breeches.

The Salle du Congrès, in the Versailles château's south wing, where the balloting takes place, is an uncharming place, rebuilt in 1875. None of us journalists had to look at it long. The press gallery, near the ceiling, consists of three steeply pitched little red velvet benches, which you clamber over at the risk of breaking your neck and which seat five spectators each. Here the several hundred assembled journalists took turns sitting for a few minutes. The sight below was monotonous, even with the President of the Congrès presiding in evening clothes in the afternoon, and, below his podium, the senators and deputies silently putting votes in the urn—the rule against harangues being so strict that when a priest deputy began to chivy the Communists, the President solemnly snapped, "Not even the voice of God can be lifted here." The only possible excitement can come when the winner is announced, which in the past was usually after the first ballot. At the present writing, the Congrès de Versailles has voted ten times in an unprecedented, scandalously selfish, ambitious, party-ridden dogfight to elect the President of the Republic—whose post symbolizes national unity and who himself is apolitical, since, once elected, he must resign from his party in order to be the arbiter of all—and still has elected nobody. In this last round, René Pleven's Union Démocratique et Socialiste de la Résistance refused to vote at all, in shocked protest at the awful way things are going. In the eighth round, fifty-three votes were listed by the ushers as *divers*—cast for diverse personalities who had nothing to do with the election, such as the Pasha of Marrakesh, Marshal Juin, novelist François Mauriac, General de Gaulle, and Marcel Boussac, the millionaire horse racer, along with twelve votes for René Laniel, brother of Premier Joseph Laniel. Had Premier Laniel received all fifty-three joker votes, he would have had a majority and been elected. Because he is an Indépendant and rich, it is natural that he should represent the Right in one of the two cleavages dominating the Versailles struggle. The European Army is the other, and even more violent, election dividing line, which was unexpectedly set up by Secretary Dulles's "agonizing reappraisal" speech, and it is less natural that Laniel, who is himself lukewarm on the European Defense Community, should now be loaded with it as the Premier who went to Bermuda, even though he was too sick there to count. It is just as ironic that Marcel-Edmond Naegelen, next-to-top candidate, who represents the Left, is a Right Wing Socialist and anti-E.D.C., although the Socialist Party favors E.D.C. (if England comes in). To Parisians, Naegelen is mostly familiar as the unlucky name signed to the pass-the-hat appeals in the Socialist newspaper *Le Populaire* to keep that staggering gazette running. Now *Le Populaire* limps behind by one lap in all the election returns, failed to announce Friday that Naegelen was then ahead, reported the ninth ballot when other papers were reporting the tenth, and remains forever one day behind the times, owing to its being printed somewhere in the provinces, where it saves money and loses the latest news. Also, the two and a half million postage stamps that so far have been imprinted with the special château cancellation "Congrès de Versailles"—always a philatelic feature of the election and particularly so this year, with a new stamp by Utrillo depicting the château gate—are still being dated December 17th, when the elections began. These two small phenomena, in which time is always a little out of whack, add to the peculiar air of destructive unreality that surrounds what is going on—and on—at Versailles, as if the Congrès out there had lost count, too.

This year's politicalization of the Presidential election may permanently change and corrupt it. In writing the Fourth Republic's constitution, the deputies made the President's powers so weak and theirs so strong that they have constantly overthrown the government, and have been forced to repair to President Vincent Auriol so often for counsel on a new Premier that he, given seven years' practice in negotiation, skillfully strengthened his office until he has become the most influential official in France. Suddenly seeing the value Auriol had created in France's only stable high office, hitherto rather ridiculed, each party last week stampeded forward to try to put its man in his shoes. Dulles's brutally candid warning to France to decide soon on E.D.C., or else, also increased the post's value in the eyes of politicians, who on each side of the fence are determined to elect as President a man who, merely by his former record, will be identified by Washington, London, and Berlin as a pro- or anti-European Army man. These are the reasons the politicians rushed in to politicalize the innocent Congrès de Versailles, which in one week of greedy maneuvering they have pulled down to the level of Parliament. At no other time in the history of this republic has public opinion expressed itself with such a vocabulary—in such words and phrases as "national catastrophe," "sinister farce," "parody," "sordid," "stupefying," "revolting," "unworthy," "indecent squatters," "lunar quarrels," "lunatics," "heartbreaking spectacle," "degradation of political spirit," and "dominating sense of humiliation."

There is an improbable rumor that Auriol himself, who is tired and old, and has had enough, will consent—if the indecent squatters pull out—to run for, and surely win, his high office again, in order to save its repute. "If he will do that for us," a young Frenchman said, "all we can say to him will be simply, *'Merci, Monsieur le Président.'*"

1954

June 18

Many people here think that if on June 4, 1953, when Pierre Mendès-France made his first bid to become Premier of France, Parliament had accepted him instead of choosing Joseph Laniel, the country would not have got into such dire straits. It was his program as would-be Premier last year that brought him forth as France's possible new political hope, the Left Wing chief of the powerful, middle-of-the-road Radical Party, the leader of the opposition against Laniel, and thus the natural politico to try to succeed him. Mendès-France's entrance into the Premiership was odd. In his speech to Parliament yesterday afternoon, he offered what he called a contract, valid for four weeks, to deliver his political promises like goods. While the Chamber sat astounded, he said, "Today is the seventeenth of June. I will meet you here before July 20th and give you an accounting. If no satisfactory solution has been found by that date, you are released from the contract, and my government and I will resign." The three priceless items he promised to deliver by then are: first, a cease-fire in the Indo-Chinese war; second, an economic-reform program for France (plus attention to a set of real political reforms for rioting Tunisia and Morocco, where, he thinks, old-hat French colonial policy is to blame); and, third, a proposal on European defense, on which a decision must be taken by the deputies before the Parliamentary vacation. Of Indo-China, he said, "If the conflict is not settled quickly, there is risk of war—of international, and even atomic, war." Before closing, he told the deputies, "I am asking for a clear answer. I am offering you a contract." In a vote held in desperation at 1 A.M. today, the contract was signed.

There is always a theatrical air in Parliament when a would-be

Premier—especially an inexperienced contender like Mendès-France—awaits his fate. On this occasion, the visitors' galleries were lively with women in summer frocks, dressed as if for a matinée; along with them were men from the embassies, French Army officers, and a solid listening bourgeoisie. At first, the would-be Premier sits alone on the Ministers' bench, since he has as yet no Ministers around to befriend him. The sense of theatre heightens when he mounts the tribune to speak his piece, like a soliloquy. Mendès-France is not a facile speaker; for a man with a big head and big shoulders, his voice is weak and uneasy. What makes his speeches is his ideas, which are hard and clear.

Mendès-France is of a Sephardic Portuguese-Jewish family. His father owns a prosperous *maison de confections pour dames* at Passy. His wife is Egyptian by birth, her family having become rich through their Egyptian chain stores, something like Woolworth's. She is handsome and a talented portrait painter. Mendès-France's career has been peculiar, distorted by the unpopularity of his strong ideas. Fresh from the University of Paris law school at the age of nineteen, he was the youngest lawyer in France; he was a deputy at twenty-five, a few months after passing the age limit required for the office; he had his first post, as Undersecretary of State for the Treasury, in Léon Blum's 1938 government. In the war, he flew a bomber and was a captain in de Gaulle's Free French forces until 1943, when the General asked him to get out of the air and become Commissaire de Finance in the Algiers provisional government. After the Liberation, he was the General's Minister of National Economy. But his ideas were too Draconian to be thought feasible, let alone to be popular, and he eventually became a sort of independent, brainy misfit in the Radical Party. He is considered to have the best head for economics of all the politicians. Since 1950, his ideas on the Indo-Chinese war have always been at least a year ahead of anybody else's, and therefore unacceptable. He has long demanded trained Vietnam officers and a firmer attitude toward conscription of native troops, and last year, as a would-be Premier, he demanded in his program a negotiated peace with Ho Chi Minh, which he will now try to obtain—"with fewer trumps than France held a year ago," he pointed out with spirit to the silent deputies.

There was a moment during the recent debates when it seemed as if he would be ruined by the Communists' insistence on giving him their hundred votes because he promised to stop what they call the dirty war. But then he insulted the whole Communist Party roundly by saying he did not want their votes counted in his possible majority. "What would our soldiers think if they learned tomorrow that their country is in part governed by men who refused to rise to their feet and honor their dead?" he asked. This reference to the Communists' recently having sullenly sat while the Assembly rose to honor those lost in Indo-China probably saved him.

Even though Mendès-France's Draconian ideas have never been popular, among the French citizens he is certainly the popular choice. They want to give his ideas a chance, at last, to function.

The outstanding result of their recent bitter experiences, the French now say, was that in the fall of Dienbienphu they discovered their loneliness. The main outcome of this belated knowledge of their isolation is that during the past six weeks, according to reports submitted to the government by prefects all over France, about sixty-five per cent of provincial opinion has come to favor E.D.C. in some form, apparently even including the European Army. Country parliamentarians grandly tend to become Parisians as soon as they are elected, and they, plus all the special political, nationalistic, and anti-German sentiments that are native to France's capital, have made Paris the center of the anti-E.D.C. movement over the past two years. But the hardheaded French countrypeople, more afraid of Moscow than of Bonn, now realistically accept the premise that West Germany, at present a powerful vacuum, will be armed eventually by the United States if it is not armed by E.D.C. Above all, they are convinced that in a world of mighty giants like the Union of Soviet Socialist Republics and the United States of America there must be something like a United States of Europe, so that Europeans, en bloc, can make themselves as big as possible in a new shape. Far behind the military crisis in Indo-China is still the real French historical crisis of what to do—and at once—about European defense. Georges Bidault's M.R.P. Party, the only one wholly sworn to E.D.C., abstained from voting on Mendès-France's Premiership, because he is distinctly not sworn to E.D.C. in its present form. Prior to the voting, it is said, the M.R.P. hoped to obtain new Parliamentary elections. The M.R.P. idea was that with a new set of deputies, truly representing the provinces (which really mean France, as Paris does not), a Parliamentary vote could be taken during the summer that would offer France her only chance of positive decision about her destiny—her chance of identifying herself as leader in a union of Europe, which was her pragmatic invention in the first place. To pro-E.D.C. Americans here in Paris, the whole project sounded inspired and impossible.

June 30

The victory of Pierre Mendès-France in becoming Premier, if only for the four weeks he gave himself to perform what are beginning to look like obtainable miracles, has had an extraordinary effect on the country. On all sides there exists "a more or less general hopefulness, even though it may be discolored by skepticism," as one newspaper phrased it. Informal polls have been hastily taken to find out what the citizens feel and think about their new leader, as if for once their reactions mattered. The findings are illuminating. The *populo,* or poorer class, and the topmost educated class are the most enthusiastic about him, the middle class the least. There is more incredulity among businessmen and industrialists about his chance of fulfilling his month's promises than there is among the intellectual and technical cadres; high-profit and low-output French business and industry have been screaming for reform, mostly on taxation, but they already suspect that in his economic-reform program he may try to reform them, too, and, naturally, believe that he cannot succeed. On the other hand, in a wave of curiosity, a recent conference of thirty highly educated technical experts in Paris industry took a vote on its feeling for the Premier, and the returns were twenty-seven for, only three against. And a recent reunion of *lycée* and university professors recorded a nearly unanimous outburst of confidence in the Premier. The students at the Ecole Normale Supérieure and at the Polytechnique, who are the cream of young French brains, are mostly for him, because they think he has an excellent mind, clear formulations, no tergiversations, and is honest, and because he is only forty-seven and full of sap, and has chosen six men under forty as Cabinet Ministers and State Secretaries. The Army brass tends to be for him, because he named as Minister of Defense General Pierre Koenig, who fought the Laniel Defense Ministry over the poor pay of combat officers in Indo-China and also over its conduct of the war. The support of Mendès-France that is closest to bedrock is probably that of the *fonctionnaires,* or civil-service employees, who keep France running for whatever government comes along—and even when there is no government at all—and who have a correspondingly poor view of politicians generally. Lower and middling *fonctionnaires* are out-and-out for him as the exceptional politician, and among the mature chiefs, men of importance in the state machinery, are many who might be kindled by him into hope for a renewed, cleansed France —a France they could more gladly serve.

Mendès-France's Parliamentary base is certainly shaky. The political parties represented by the men now in his Cabinet have a total of only about two hundred and seventy-five Assembly votes—and the parties involved would not, any more than his own Radical Party, necessarily support him generously. He even has two fence jumpers from Bidault's M.R.P. Party, which gave its members strict instructions against taking office with this newcomer, the first Premier since the war to put the M.R.P., as well as Bidault, after his long, faithful, uneasy seasons as Foreigh Minister, on the shelf of the opposition. The M.R.P.'s votes against him will be triply bitter.

Mendès-France's contract time is nearly half up. He has already created a Cabinet post new to French history—that of Minister for Moroccan and Tunisian Affairs—as the first step in carrying out his plan for new relations with those riotously inflamed protectorates. He has done what in his *Premier-désigné* speech in Parliament he warned the French Communists he would do whether his cease-fire offer ended the war or not—ordered reinforcements to be made ready for the Far East expeditionary force. He has called both on prior governments and on his own to present to the Assembly early in July definite proposals for reforming the constitution. His first fiscal-reform project, just announced, aims at strengthening and enforcing last year's halfhearted law taxing manufacturers' markups, which, if made to work, would enormously bolster the national economy. Though some of the French, especially the wealthy, feared unorthodox novelty reforms from him, he seems so far merely to be reforming the weak or inapplicable reforms other men passed as lip service to necessity or in order to keep previous reformers quiet.

The first, and most compelling, item on Mendès-France's program—to obtain a cease-fire—now looks closer, since, to everyone's surprise, Sir Winston and the President have announced that the United Kingdom and the United States will press forward with their security plans for Southeast Asia whether or not France negotiates an acceptable agreement in Geneva. This is probably the best incentive the Anglo-Saxons have yet given France in her efforts to get such an agreement at the peace conference. As France waits for the Indo-China project—physically the most vital issue to the French people, as war and truce issues always are—to be finished one way or the other, the great and almost philosophical French issue of the European Defense Community is close to boiling. It is the most nearly insurmountable problem in Mendès-France's program, because it will have to be settled by the French themselves, now and finally and at last. After twenty-five months of waiting, Belgium's Henri Spaak, speaking for the exasperated Benelux group, and Chancellor Adenauer, speaking for West Germany, this week began bringing pressure on the Premier, and the American Ambassador, C. Douglas Dillon, transmitted to him Washington's urgent demand that France ratify at least *a* European defense community. In an effort to get a compromise plan that French Parliamentary partisans of E.D.C. and those who are its enemies would both accept, the Premier had already set General Koenig, who is anti-E.D.C., and Maurice Bourgès-Maunoury, the Minister of Industry and Commerce, who is for it, to working on it together. Between this compromise E.D.C., which doubtless no one but the French would accept, and the old, original E.D.C., which other Atlantic nations have long since accepted, Parliament must finally make up its mind during the last week of the Premier's contract—and perhaps, of course, of his Premiership.

Mendès-France is nothing of an athlete in appearance, and nobody dreamed that he had the gift of drawing on himself the vast public eye as a politician. But as Premier he is like a runner running a unique, exciting political hurdle race while the citizens of France watch him closely, lap after lap. As far as real racing is concerned, this has been the high point of the horse-racing season in Paris, with well-dressed women, fine, sensitive animals, thin jockeys, and great crowds at Longchamp, Auteuil, Enghien, and St.-Cloud. But the Premier's race against time is the strangest historical contest anybody has ever seen run here, and France has her eyes on it.

July 14

The precipitate closing of the remarkable show of early (1900–14) Picasso paintings at the Communist Maison de la

Pensée Française, which occurred in the face of a writ for the recovery of stolen family property launched against the precious thirty-seven canvases from Moscow and Leningrad museums, has been relished here as one of the oddest happenings in all the eccentric, violent annals of modern French art. The writ was obtained by Mme. Irène Stchoukine de Keller, whose father, the Czarist industrialist Sergei Stchoukine, was the greatest Moscow collector of Picasso's young works. According to the Communist Party paper *Humanité,* which took a haughty tone, the Stchoukine collection "became nationalized property in 1918," and the writ was simply "*une prétention vexatoire et fantaisiste,* whose only result has been to deprive the French public of the sight of these works, sent for its enjoyment by the Soviet museums." *Humanité* pointed out that the lady—who indeed seemed to know little about her father's collection except that she naturally wanted to get her hands on it—even included in her list of stolen items in the exhibition the Cubist gem called "La Femme à la Guitare," which actually belongs to the late Gertrude Stein's collection. The paper also humorlessly quoted the celebrated Picasso art merchant Henry Kahnweiler as saying that Stchoukine, who died here in poverty in the middle nineteen-thirties, told him he had always intended to give his pictures to the Moscow museum, "only it happened a little too soon."

The court to which the claim of theft, or "seizure without indemnity," was presented immediately ordered that "everything should remain in place"—an order that the Soviet Embassy defied within the hour by whisking the pictures off to some safe, secret spot, just in case the judge should hold the claim valid and sequester them. The pictures were previously removed from sight in Russia, too, during the years when Picasso's art fell under the Stalinite cultural ban as cosmopolitan decadence; nobody here can say whether, under Malenkov's apparently less strict regime, the pictures had been declared healthy again and rehung in the Soviet museums. If, as the Paris correspondent of the Manchester *Guardian* succinctly commented, "they are in fact only shown when lent abroad, but cannot be lent abroad because of a doubt about legal ownership," these early Picassos are in a bad way. Picasso himself, who was attending a bullfight in Nîmes the day his canvases disappeared from the Paris show, said, "I am sorry. I would have loved to see my paintings again." He added that he did not think Stchoukine's daughter had a right to do what she did, remarking, "What if the Comte de Paris took it into his head someday to lay claim to Versailles?" Now that the court, as was historically inevitable, has thrown out the claim, there is no reason the Soviet Embassy should not bring the Picassos out of hiding and let the exhibition continue to be a major Paris summer art pleasure through September, as scheduled. However, nobody expects Russians to be reasonable.

A talented, short, and certainly unusual first novel by an eighteen-year-old authoress has become required vacation reading here, after having won last May's Prix des Critiques. The novel is called "Bonjour Tristesse" and is signed Françoise Sagan, a nom de plume devised in honor of Marcel Proust's Princesse de Sagan. The young writer's name is Françoise Quoirez. The daughter of well-off Paris parents, she was born in 1935, lived with her family in Lyon during the war, at seventeen entered the Sorbonne, failed to pass last July, and during the month of August—"having nothing to do," she says—wrote her first book. No matter how poor a student she may be, she is a born writer. Her style is being compared to Raymond Radiguet's. It has the same youthful, swift, unaffected manner of setting down characters and scenes clearly, as if written on glass, in the simple, permanent, eighteenth-century classic French vocabulary. Her story also has Radiguet's untroubled artistic amorality. It deals with a girl of her age, who is finally freed from boarding schools to live in unchecked enjoyment with her youngish widowed father, an affectionate, civilized lightweight immoralist whose life events are composed of rather commonplace passing mistresses, picked up in his easy Champs-Elysées business world. The crux of the story, which takes place in the Midi during the father's and daughter's summer holiday *à trois* with an especially blowzy mistress, is the arrival there of the dead mother's best friend—an intelligent, forceful Parisienne, who not only falls in love with the father and easily ousts the mistress but plans to marry him and save him, at forty, from his shapeless, tarnishing life and worse future, and to bring up the girl *comme il faut*. The resultant tragedy, in which the girl takes her first lover, is the struggle between two species—between the daughter, who instinctively fights to save her dronelike father and herself for the hedonism their natures intended them for, and *la femme forte*, whose superior, logical plan for salvation the girl intellectually recognizes but destroys. Defeated, the woman is killed, or kills herself, when her car plunges off the Corniche, leaving the girl and the father victorious and lost. Among the exceptional appreciations that "Bonjour Tristesse" has evoked is a moaning editorial by François Mauriac, who deplored the fact that a prize should have been given to "this cruel book, whose literary merit shines out from the first page and is indisputable," called the author "a charming little monster," and bewailed today's *"dévergondage de l'adolescence féminine."* Testy words on the subject of literary moral values followed this in some papers by critics who pitilessly analyzed Mauriac's new novel, "L'Agneau," as containing an extra helping of the sordid goings on, always without pleasure, which his provincial Christian characters are invariably involved in on their ultimate way to Heaven.

July 28

As a small proof of the finality of what has just been arranged in Indo-China, the aged King of Laos has arrived for an extended stay in France, where he will take the waters at Vittel, and Bao Dai, chief of state of Vietnam, is already taking the waters at Vichy.

There can be no doubt that Premier Mendès-France has become practically a national hero in the month it took him to fulfill his fantastic promise of an Indo-China cease-fire, which the French have generally called anguishing good news. He is now regarded as having done three major things concurrently in four weeks—ended a colonial war that might have become a Third World War; offered postwar France another chance, perhaps cheap at the price, at realistic political and financial salvation; and, along with Anthony Eden, revived the Entente Cordiale of that European-minded monarch Edward VII, substituting London across the narrow Channel for Washington across the vast Atlantic.

August 11

"Funérailles de Colette," her bare name printed in heavy black, with no other identification—only that of her fame—was the phrase used on the official invitation to her public outdoor funeral, accorded to her by the French state. It was held in the Cour d'Honneur du Palais-Royal, adjoining the palatial tree-filled and sculpture-filled Palais-Royal Garden, at the opposite end of which she had lived for many years, and where she had died suddenly, and painlessly, in the evening, after a small sip of champagne. It was appropriate that she died during a brief burst of magnificent rural weather here in Paris, on one of this summer's rare days of provincial heat, yet when autumnal colors were already on her garden trees, which themselves looked provincial rather than metropolitan; as a Burgundian-born countrywoman, she was sensitive to the point of genius in her pleasure in nature, and her written reports on it are unique in French literature, where she left that intimate record of her observant, penetrating love of creatures, blossoms, and foliage, of fields, woods, and seasons. She was aged eighty-one, had been immobilized in late years with arthritis, and had been a writer since 1900.

Colette's state obsequies were the only honor of their kind to be given a French woman writer in the history of all the four republics. She had experienced triumphs in her life, and now she lay in state on a great catafalque loosely covered with tricolor silk, which the wind billowed, and her glittering cross of a Grand Officer of the Legion of Honor and its scarlet ribbon were attached to a black velvet pillow that leaned against her coffin. Facing the catafalque sat her daughter, Mme. Colette de Jouvenel; Pauline, her faithful maid for a quarter century; and her last husband, Maurice Goudeket. Flanking them were members of the Goncourt Academy and other French notables. Across the court stretched a hedge of floral offerings, with pale-blue and dark-blue gladioli predominant. (Blue was her favorite color, and she always wrote on blue paper.) There was a wreath from the French Parliament; one from the city of Lyon and its Mayor, Edouard Herriot, an old friend of hers; a garland of roses with ribbons of the Belgian colors, marked "Elisabeth," from the King's grandmother; a huge sheaf of lilies from the Association des Music-Halls et Cirques, since in her difficult young days she was a music-hall dancer and mime; and a big country bouquet of dahlias from her "Compatriotes de St.-Sauveur-en-Puisaye," the Yonne village where she was born. Fenced off behind the catafalque and stretching toward Colette's corner of the garden, stood, very quietly, the great overflow Parisian crowd, her anonymous admirers.

As a writer and personality, Colette came with time to sum up for the French certain French essences, as in her love for excellent foods and wines, her perfect feeling for the written or spoken French phrase, and her literary sense *de l'époque,* whether the epoch was that of aging cocottes or of nubile provincial schoolgirls. In her writings, she even transferred to French readers her love for nature and for animals, domestic or roaming country hills. Tastes such as these had been absent—in an almost too civilized omission—from French literature until she brought her Burgundian girlhood to Paris and put her rural sensibilities on paper. She had a sensual harvest fullness in her writing and in her person, and a profound feeling for love springing up or being mowed down. She was indifferent to moral calculations, and composed her novels and stories with her informed instincts rather than by building any formal plot, and thus left behind her pages that are uniquely feminine and the work of a master, in which the perceptions of her five senses were made permanent through her genius for the exactitudes of the French language. She was indeed a writer who was "pagan, sensuous, Dionysiac," as the Ministre de l'Education Nationale, Jean Berthoin, loudly declaimed with admiration in his funeral address at her bier.

However extraordinary these words seemed, from such a source on such an occasion, there was much more just as extraordinary that was said, and also written, in the course of tributes and obituaries, for her death ranked as the greatest literary loss since that of André Gide. The director of *Le Figaro,* Pierre Brisson, wrote on the front page of that ultra-Catholic daily, "There was something androgynous in her; she was masculine in her initiative and authority, and a woman by her intuition and assent; she was both vigorous and a dreamer." Germaine Beaumont, the novelist, who had since childhood been intimately acquainted with Colette (who was Germaine Beaumont's mother's best friend), wrote in *Les Nouvelles Littéraires,* "How alive she was, to the degree of making others seem moribund! She had more sensitive tissues . . . and more aptitude than others for observing, seizing, holding. She who learned so well how to remain immobile, drawing repose over her like a coverlet, sometimes reminded one of those marine creatures that breathe, nourish themselves, and even circulate by means of their fringe of sensitivity." As his farewell, the poet Louis Aragon wrote her a fine, rousing poem of adieu based on a quotation from Tasso.

The two novels the critics cited most often this week as the quintessential Colette were "Claudine à l'Ecole," which was the first book she wrote, and which was published not under her own name at all but under that of her first husband (soon afterward divorced), the insouciant journalist Henry Gauthier-Villars, known as Willy; and "Chéri," regarded as her masterpiece, which tells the story of a tarnished, aging cocotte and her tragic, belated love for a young man. (Colette acted the role of the cocotte, Léa, in a stage version produced in Paris in the mid-nineteen-twenties.) "Le Blé en Herbe" was one of the great public favorites, and "Gigi," one of her last works, was popular as a novelette, as a film, and as a play on both sides of the Atlantic.

Colette's funeral, *aux frais de l'Etat*—the highest posthumous honor that can be granted to a citizen—viewed alongside the reaction of the Catholic Church to her death, illustrates in a remarkably clear modern fashion the still existing separation of Church and State. Colette's second marriage was to Henry de Jouvenel, editor-in-chief of *Le Matin,* from whom she was also divorced. She was thus a twice-divorced *libre penseur,* as well as a noncommunicant of the Church at the time of her death, although she had been born a Catholic. A request, made by friends of her family, that she be given a final burial service at the Eglise St. Roch was refused by Cardinal Feltin, the Archbishop of Paris, and this refusal set off a great deal of comment and argument here. In the weekly *Figaro Littéraire,* the English Catholic convert Graham Greene contributed a front-page open letter, in French, addressed to *"Son Eminence le Cardinal-Archevêque de Paris,"* in which he took him to task for his decision that no priest should offer public prayers at Colette's funeral. He wrote, in part, "Would you have invoked the same reasons if she had been less illustrious? . . . Are two civil marriages so unpardonable? The lives of certain of our saints offer worse examples . . . Your Eminence, without knowing it, has given the impression that the Church pursues an error even beyond the deathbed . . . To non-Catholics it could seem that the Church itself lacked charity . . . Of course, Catholics, upon reflection, can decide that the voice of an archbishop is not necessarily the voice of the Church." He ended the letter, *"avec mon humble respect pour la Pourpre Sacrée."* As literary circles noted, there was an analogy between Colette's burial and that of George Sand, over the past hundred years the other vastly popular French woman writer and public literary figure, who died three years after Colette was born, who was also a free-thinker and led her own life, and for whom the state also proposed a national funeral. George Sand's daughter, to the indignation of Flaubert and other friends, preferred a private religious service, which was permitted by the archdiocese. The Church took a stronger stand on Colette, perhaps using her fame to magnify its warning to other intellectuals of little or no faith.

Early this year, Colette spent a holiday at one of the Mediterranean resorts, where she was carried around in the sunshine in a sedan chair. At home in Paris, since she was practically bedridden the last several years, she sensibly had her bed placed on a platform by a window overlooking the Palais-Royal Garden, and there she continued to write—surrounded by her cats, her famous multicolored collection of glass paperweights, her books and mementos—and could look out on the active life of children and passersby under the trees below. A plaque is to be placed on the garden wall of her home, which will read, *"Ici vécut, ici mourut Colette, dont l'œuvre est une fenêtre grande ouverte sur la vie* [Here lived, here died Colette, whose work is a window wide-open on life]."

Mendès-France is still working up momentum. On the occasion of his meeting last Tuesday with Parliament, one of the few he has had since becoming Premier, he emerged from the Assembly's two sessions, morning and afternoon—which, in fact, dragged on until almost midnight—with the exceptional record of two votes of confidence won in one day. The morning vote, giving him special powers until next March 31st to carry out his sweeping economic reforms, followed the most applauded portion of his speech to the deputies, in which he declared, "France has been plunged into a deep sleep filled with nostalgic dreams and nightmares that have fed on the black future. We must wake her up."

The afternoon meeting, where the Premier's intention had been merely to ask that the scheduled debate on the grave North African problem be postponed until after the August 24th debate on the even graver problem of E.D.C., unexpectedly developed into a political duel on the Tunisian situation, and this swelled into the most tumultuous session of the Assembly in years. The fight was started by Deputy Léon Martinaud-Déplat, who, ironically, is chief of Mendès-France's own party, the Radicals. The deputy, long opposed to Mendès-France's ideas in general and to his project for Tunisian home rule in particular, accused the Premier of negotiating with enemy terrorists in giving the Neo-Destour nationalists representation in the government. The Premier's counterattack was adequately rich, since he had all the preceding governments' North African failures to draw on in defense of his own reform plans; he cited their repeated promises to Tunisians of autonomous rule, made every year since the Liberation and never kept—with the recent appalling North African violence and bloodshed as the dreadfully logical result, to his mind, of long years of French bad faith and Tunisian frustration. The Mediterranean colonial problem, and how to manage what is left in that area of France's shrinking and rioting empire after the loss of half of Indo-China, is a topic to inflame politicians, especially those who have become wise after the event, and as the two men argued and riposted, the hemicycle alternately was thrown into an uproar, when the deputies joined in pell-mell with their own exhortations, and was reduced to tense silence, while everybody tried hard to miss none of the two antagonists' finer political points. During the general outbursts, the Assembly President, André Le Troquer, high up on his private platform, made vain attempts to restore calm, whacking his desk with the schoolmaster's ruler that serves him as a gavel, and once even ringing his big bell, which is used only for moments of serious disorder. In the crammed visitors' gallery, people in the front rows were hanging over the railing in excitement, and those at the back were standing to see and hear.

At the start of the duel, there was a moment of trepidation for the whole Assembly, and particularly for Mendès-France's followers, when he broke in on his adversary's speech to say calmly that if he did not obtain a vote of confidence on his North African policies, he would resign. Parliament could not risk the onus of causing him to fall just now, if only because of his popularity with the people as the first man in a long while who has tried to get anything and everything done. So, with the second session's vote, he received his extra victory of the day. His audacity, his honesty, his skill at debate, and his drastic realism turned the duel into one more dramatic triumph for him—naturally, a far lesser event than the winning of his month's race on the Indo-China cease-fire, and a lesser one, too, than his surprise flight to Tunisia to call on and talk with the Bey, which was something no previous Premier had ever done during any of the many troubled times there. But all three incidents have a similar quality of vigor about them that catches French eyes and imaginations and that so far has made for a remarkable success with the citizens. For him, everything perhaps now hangs on the result of the Assembly's debate on E.D.C. during the next fortnight, and much that affects the whole world, too, will there finally become a matter of history.

September 1

The greatest tribute to the magnitude of the European Defense Community question is that the partisanship it aroused cut France in two—the people, as well as the Parliament. The three-day weekend discussion of it in the Assembly before it was symbolically voted down raised individual convictions and hopes, divergent patriotisms, angers, and passions, and divisions between men and men, rather than between parties only, to an altitude of tension reached by no other issue since the war. Reams of journalistic reporting appeared on the factual results of these feelings, but only *Le Monde* mentioned *la mystique* of E.D.C. as rational news. It said that this emotion for and against E.D.C. sliced across all accustomed separations, so that a pro-E.D.C. Frenchman felt closer to a German who was for the treaty than to a Frenchman who was against it; so that a Communist who was against it (as all the Communists were) felt closer to his boss or to an Army general, if his boss or the general was hostile to it, than to a fellow-workman who wanted E.D.C. ratified. What the French people *en masse* felt about E.D.C., history will unfortunately never know, since no plebiscite was ever taken. On general principles, Frenchmen have all along been against any rearming of Germany, because of their recent experiences in the war and the Occupation and because of the German wars that fell on their fathers and grandfathers. But it would seem that before the debate opened, slightly more than half the French citizens were in favor of German rearmament under E.D.C. if rearmament was inevitable, maybe because they could not comprehend the reputedly dangerous pitfalls for France in the complex treaty—pitfalls that gave the expert anti-E.D.C. parliamentarians their influential talking points before the other deputies and the public galleries. It is unfortunate, too, that history must record that, in a parliament lately so notorious for endless debates, everyone was not allowed to have his say on this dominantly affecting matter; that the vote was not a direct and dignified one on the specific question "Are you for E.D.C. or against it?," which, after two years of tergiversation, would have steadied France's reputation for clarifying a final decision, but was a tangential and procedural one, pushed through by the anti-E.D.C. forces as if in a quick panic. The Defense Community had the air of being hastily strangled, instead of being allowed, in accordance with proper democratic processes, to perish slowly—duly done to death by words from those who did not approve.

On Monday morning, by which time the Premier had already accepted the idea of returning to Brussels, the Cédistes, in an ill-advised maneuver against the Anticédistes, brought up their *motion préjudicielle* again, even though it was legally bound to be heard, if ever, only after the *préalable,* which had been introduced first. As an anti-E.D.C. riposte, and because a *préalable* can be spoken for only by its signer, old, infirm, Anticédiste Edouard Herriot, honorary President of the Assembly, where he actively reigned for a generation, was made a co-signer and was sent in alone to speak as the Anticédistes' trump card. Crippled by illness and his eighty-two years, and unable, with his swollen limbs, to mount the steps to the speaker's podium, above which he used to preside, he spoke seated, using a microphone installed for him on the Radical Socialist bench. His voice still boomed, but his facts had become weak; he muddled treaty clauses and figures and ignored shouted corrections. And at the end, for his great prestige of age and service, and for his flaming patriotism for a sovereign France, still intact, he was acclaimed with an ovation. He said, in part, "On the threshold of death, let me tell you that E.D.C. is the end of France, that it is a step forward for Germany and a step back for France, that when a people no longer runs its army, as France would not under E.D.C., it no longer runs its own diplomacy." Part of his task, he went on, was to explain to the Americans how wrong they were in thinking that E.D.C. was still good for France. *"La C.E.D. est une aventure, ne la faites pas!"* he ended, amid salvos of applause. He had been made the *vox humana* of the Anticédistes, and his speech was highly influential. By seven o'clock in the evening the European Defense Community was dead. While the Communists, who had won a victory with their ninety-five votes, rose and sang the "Marseillaise," joined by some Socialists and Anticédiste de Gaullistes, the defeated E.D.C. members shouted at them, in anguish and fury, "Back to Moscow!" The veteran Cédiste Paul Reynaud, his intelligent, small face drawn with emotion, ran up onto the speaker's podium and cried, "For the first time since there has been a French Parliament, a treaty has been voted down without its author or its signer being allowed to speak in its defense!" With this bitter obituary, the Communauté Européenne de Défense was buried in France.

The position of Mendès-France in all this remains obscure, even to his close friends (or so some of them say), as well as to his political backers, who risked much in their enthusiasm for him, and to his multitudes of French admirers. In his Indo-Chinese cease-fire transactions, he had been coolly successful in dealing at first hand with exigent foreign diplomats at Geneva, and his energetic *brio* had been deemed magnificent. Then, his negotiations with his own Assembly on the thorny, bloody question of reforms in Tunisia were a real political triumph, such as no other French postwar leader had ever expected, or even attempted, to achieve, and a brilliant example of his ability to manage and lead suspicious French politicians. But, as he told the Assembly in his recent foreign-policy speech, with the curious bold candor that is one of his appeals to French citizens, his Brussels experience was at times a humiliation. He was accused by the Cédistes of having been too hard with his confreres there to do E.D.C. any good. A French colleague of his at Brussels said, "He seems too intelligent a man to be an apt negotiator." One of his slogans, which he used as the title of a book of speeches, is *"Gouverner, C'est Choisir"*—"To Govern Is to Choose." A repeated caustic criticism in the Assembly last week was that while he urged everyone else to choose sides on E.D.C., he himself chose neither side. He also kept his government divorced from any responsibility for E.D.C., which meant that his government could not fall on a vote of confidence. Indeed, some of the bitterest criticism was provoked by this fact—that he took neither responsibility nor a side. He was perhaps too logical in thinking it his duty impersonally to force a decision on the treaty. Mendès-France's attitude was, of course, an oddly transcendental one for a French Premier. In his strict refusal to reveal his attitude toward E.D.C., lest he influence the Assembly in what the French called *cette question de conscience,* he acted with the detachment of a constitutional monarch—rather as Queen Elizabeth might conduct herself.

The tragedy of Mendès-France is that he wanted to settle the question of E.D.C. one way or the other, in order to release France from her immobility and start her on her liberated modern way. He wanted to inaugurate a French New Deal that would save French capitalism and satisfy French workers. He wanted a positive majority in the Assembly without the Communists, whom he wished to treat as if they were on an island; when he was invested, he scornfully told them that he would not count their votes in figuring his majority. In the recent E.D.C. vote, it was the Communists who supplied the majority that carried what was supposed to be his side. He had remained so enigmatic as to provide his own fatal dilemma. The intellectualism of Mendès-France and the gerontocracy spoken for by old Herriot, both so representative of France, seem to have set France floating loose and alone at last.

September 15

"The Alice B. Toklas Cookbook"—it seems that the "B" stands for Babette, which was the name of her French godmother—was, as Miss Toklas circumstantially states in her preface, lately written in Paris during a bout of jaundice, "when good foods hover in the invalid's memory," and will soon be published in New York. It constitutes delicious reading, in the opinion of Paris friends of hers who have seen the manuscript and who have, at her memorable lunches in the famous Rue Christine flat, eaten some of her gastronomic treats, for which she gives three hundred and fifty-eight recipes in the book. As might be expected, the Toklas opus is an unusual and often very droll cookbook, firm in its statement of essential eighteenth-century French cooking principles, and interlarded with comments, as dry as her favorite Chablis, on the kinds and classes of French who eat this or that, and in what type of bourgeois apartment or country château. It is also seasoned with pungent recollections of Miss Gertrude Stein, and contains as well a kind of palate history of war foods in France, which the two ladies knew in their two wars. In the first war, they munched luscious Alsatian cookies (the recipe for Alsatian cookies is given) while visiting the heroic ruins of Verdun, and they ate classic regional dishes (recipes also given) at local inns while driving their old Ford from Lorraine to the Spanish border to deliver medical supplies for the Red Cross. In the recent war, the degree of their extremity while living in their country house in Bilignin, near the Swiss border, is made clear in a chapter called "Murder in the Kitchen." Here Miss

Toklas practiced her first assassination when her fishman kindly gave her a live carp, to which she had to take the knife, feeling weak afterward (a recipe follows for carp and homemade noodles, plus her editorial assurance that "these noodles are very delicate"); later occurred the grimmer business of smothering pigeons, since the French think neck-wringing brutal, besides being a waste of the blood essential to the rich taste of the fowl. (A first-rate recipe follows for braised pigeon on croutons.) There is also the instance of the demise of the two ladies' Barbary duck, which was chased one day by a neighboring farm dog. The household's quondam peasant cook decided that it was about to die of heart failure, so she gave it three tablespoonfuls of brandy to swallow, "to add flavor," and then killed it—and how did Madame wish it to be cooked? "Surprised at the turn the affair had taken," Miss Toklas writes, "I answered feebly, 'With orange sauce.' " (Properly in sequence comes a recipe for duck and oranges.) Her Liberation fruitcake (recipe given) was concocted with the help of a few dried orange peels saved in a jar for over four years against the great day when, to everyone's astonishment, the American Army really did march into unimportant Bilignin.

As a sample of her domestic recollections of Miss Stein, Miss Toklas remarks, in connection with gooseberry-gathering and jelly-making at Bilignin, "Wasps, hornets, and bees rarely sting me, though my work with them has always been aggressive. Gertrude Stein did not care for any of them, nor for spiders, centipedes, and bats. She had no violent feeling for them out-of-doors, but in the house she would call for aid." The book also contains strict rules to be observed in good cooking, which "permits of no exaggerations," as well as thoughtful advice, such as that delicate sauces should be stirred with a wooden spoon and not a metal one, which can tinge the flavor, and that cream should be added to sauces only at the last moment, in time to heat but not to boil, and "should be tilted in the pan, not stirred." It is a book of character, fine food, and tasty human observation. Handsome decorative drawings by Sir Francis Rose head the chapters. Miss Toklas has a collection of nearly a hundred authoritative volumes on refined cooking. Her own volume can properly adorn her library.

The death of André Derain last week at the age of seventy-four, as the result of being ignobly run into by an automobile while riding his bicycle two months ago, was sad, because what he had been painting for the past twenty-five years made it difficult to recall how great he had started to be when young. In the 1905 Salon d'Automne, he showed with the Fauves, led by Matisse, and his wild-beast gorgeous colors—scarlet cabbage fields and a purple Seine—were second to none, not even those of Vlaminck, whom he had met in a railroad accident on a Paris suburban line, whereupon they both started painting in the new manner. Their paintings were like a paintpot thrown in your face, one critic said in shock. Derain later spent several summers with Picasso on the Mediterranean, became momentarily Cubist, and then went into a classical, rather noble formality of line, where he remained, by and large, until the end of his days. Recently, a court order was issued preventing him from working on or altering any of his recent paintings, since his wife, from whom he was separated, thought he might ruin them and thus diminish their sales value after his death. It was only what he painted forty or fifty years ago that today would fetch great, sincere high prices.

October 13

It is not only the size of the victory that Premier Mendès-France has just won—the Assembly's 350–113 vote of confidence in him and, by implication, in the London Conference formula, with which apparently only about a hundred and fifty deputies are actually satisfied—but the clarity, timing, and candor he constructed his victory on that still astonish the politicians who, perforce, gave it to him. It is true that he was aided by the frankness of Sir Winston's neighborly back-fence warning that there could be no question of further French fiddling with the London fundamentals, which made it clear to the deputies here that they would have to come up to scratch on the question of the fate of the Atlantic Alliance. Ironically, Molotov, in East Berlin, involuntarily aided Mendès-France by suggesting Big Four talks on disarmament, which gave the Premier, in the midst of fighting for controlled German rearmament, the chance to answer right back to him and to certain worried deputies. Yes, indeed, said the Premier, he would willingly take up such talks with the Russians, for which there was plenty of time, since the London accord—if and when finally ratified —could not operate for maybe four years anyhow.

As for Mendès-France's local difficulties, it was his raising of minimum wages a few francs an hour last week, with an April date set for further serious wage talks, that finally gave him the Socialist Party vote—absolutely essential to his majority. On the E.D.C. vote, the Socialists had bitterly split in half; at their weekend Party caucus to determine how they should vote on the London negotiations, they had labored up to their ears in argument over ideals, and the intellectual importance of remaining the Opposition party, until Mendès-France telephoned Socialist chief Guy Mollet (and let the press know about it) and realistically suggested that perhaps the Socialists might even take part in his government, which, after all, aims at being a sort of French New Deal. With French elections coming up next spring, and with Mendès-France's program of better wages, financial reforms, and action against the powerful alcohol lobby and its privileged subsidies already under way, it seems incredible that it took the Socialists another day of argument to decide to climb on the band wagon and to begin by voting en bloc for the Premier on Tuesday. Because of their dissatisfaction with the narrow social programs of previous governments, it has been the Socialists who have repeatedly overthrown them; if the Socialists should really enter the present government, they not only would look important to their working-class constituents but could act importantly by supplying this government with a regular majority, the usual lack of which is the curse of the splintered French Parliamentary system. As for the parties that still either love E.D.C. or loathe the idea of giving Germans a gun under any conditions, or that personally dislike Mendès-France and all his works, the Premier's skillful demand for a confidence vote only on the continuance of his London negotiations would clearly have loaded them—had they refused it—with the onus of having left France standing alone in history and, moreover, standing temporarily without even a government. That the hostile M.R.P. party of Georges Bidault largely abstained from voting at all, rather than vote against Mendès-France, and that the ex-Gaullist Social Republicans, who are also his enemies, largely voted for him, were unexpectedly meek replies.

In this recent victory, Mendès-France, who a few days before had been thought doomed to defeat, proved himself a master tactician. In the public mind, he took his risks openly, as part of his profession, but never gambled; he talked clearly, explained simply, promised nothing more than to do his best, and was in a hurry, as usual. Because of this, the French citizenry were able to understand for once what was going on in a vitally important Parliamentary decision, and unquestionably they comprehended the results. "He has created a political style which, if it pleases God, will survive him," piously commented François Mauriac, probably his most fervent literary admirer, in this week's *Express,* adding, "It would seem to me difficult for the successors of Pierre Mendès-France, even the mediocre and stupid ones, to go back to using the old political concoctions to govern by."

Amid the various uncertainties in France, one thing is sure: The French are seeing more flying saucers than have ever been seen around here since flying saucers were invented. They are also seeing new models of them, such as flying tops, orange-colored lozenges, flying mushrooms, and flying cigars, called *les Churchills*. Some of these phenomena are reported to be noisy, others to be as silent as the stars; some are said to fly faster than anything ever seen before, and some—the most alarming—are said to stand still in the night sky. Near Lille, a hundred people living over a broad countryside individually saw crescents dancing arabesques in the sky for twenty-five minutes, and announced the same to the country police. Near Briançon, a flying cigar was seen by a gendarme, a village mayor, and a respected hotelkeeper. West of Deauville, a taxi-driver saw an incandescent red-and-green disc with a phosphorescent tail, and so did some sailors close to shore. In the Nièvre, three citizens in different places saw flying cylinders, orange when they flew horizontally, dazzling white when they proceeded vertically. Not far from Paris—at Coulommiers, where the delicious cheese of that name is made—a member of the Société des Ingénieurs Civils de France, who is also a former aviator and an officer of the Aéro-Club de France, wrote a letter to the local paper anatomizing the object he watched for twenty minutes over his country house. It was something with "a thick circular wing, gyrating around through space with a noise like a jet plane," he wrote. "I am not the victim of hallucination." The second mate of a French cargo ship wrote his company's office in Brest that en route to Antwerp he and two sailors on watch with him saw "a kind of giant red star rising from the southwest, four times the size of any star we have ever seen, and at a point in the sky where no star was due," and set forth the phenomenon's date, its latitude and longitude, and its celestial movements during nearly two hours. The Governor of the French Ivory Coast received a communication from the Administrator of Danané, who declared that for half an hour on the night of September 19th he, his wife, many savages, the chief French doctor, and a missionary priest watched an unidentifiable oval flying machine equipped with a cupola and searchlights, which left two luminous halos behind when it disappeared. The Governor has demanded an investigation. A road mender in the Marne and a baker in Finistère have both met little men from Mars, wearing hairy suits—the baker's visitors also having "eyes the size of crows' eggs." In the last month, more than a hundred reports of strange flying machines seen nearly all over France, but never in Paris, have been printed in the Paris press, with the names of those who saw them, and often with the signed statements given to the local police by observers *"digne de foi,"* or worthy of belief. Among these worthy observers are men like a Conseiller Général des Alpes-Maritimes, a police inspector of the city of Nice, reputable mechanics, educated electricians, a schoolteacher on the Island of Oléron, rich butchers, a wealthy Normandy farmer and his wife, the father of a famous French bicycle racer, and the peasant father of a girl who would not believe what he saw until he dragged her from bed to look and then to the gendarmerie to report. A deputy in Parliament has just asked Mendès-France's State Secretary for Air what it is doing to explain all these phenomena.

November 9

The death in his eighty-fifth year of Monsieur Matisse, as he was always called, brought an end to his long, orderly, and individual reign of genius as *"le roi des Fauves,"* or the king of the artistic wild beasts. He and the young Fauve painters with him in the celebrated 1905 Salon d'Automne—Rouault, Derain, and Vlaminck—along with Braque, who joined them later, founded contemporary French art but no dynasty, because the others soon abandoned Fauvism for painting realms of their own, and although M. Matisse continued to be the emperor of Fauve color, he has left no heir. Early isolated, the revolutionary Matisse, born in Picardy, combined his precise Northern character with the sunny chromatics he discovered in Morocco, and developed into France's greatest modern classic painter. An indefatigable perfectionist, he once made (or so he said) three thousand sketches for one painting. Art became the unfaltering technique of his hand, variety a calculated part of his restricted, disciplined pattern, and only pure color remained free. He was a professorial and magical creator, whose improbable and dazzling Moroccan odalisques lacked all sensuous qualities except the voluptuous coloring he gave them. "If I met a woman on the street who looked like my paintings, I would faint," he once admitted in terse explanation of his theory of style. "I do not paint women, I paint pictures," he also said, summing up the artist's problem of composition. Just the same, his female figures have furnished much of the recognizably human art population of France over the past fifty years. His alternate title to fame came four years ago, when he completed his chapel for the Dominican nuns at Vence, with its modernist black-and-white Stations of the Cross.

M. Matisse was an explicit, logical talker. While painting, he enjoyed listening to gossip, which he did not repeat. He was a born organizer. Two years ago, on hearing that a M. Guillot, municipal councillor and pastry cook in Matisse's birthplace, Le Cateau, was planning a one-room museum of Matisse souvenirs in the town hall, M. Matisse took over. He sent color schemes for the walls, exact measurements for hanging his drawings precisely (one metre and three centimetres from the floor), and also seventy-five original art items, including his 1891 charcoal sketch of a male nude (which earned him a refusal at the Paris Beaux-Arts), some sculptures, some textiles and tapestries he had designed, and two paintings—a collection valuable principally for its intimacy. Though his pictures figure in all important modern collections, especially in the United States, two of the biggest agglomerations of his early works are temporarily invisible to the general public—seventy-five in the Barnes collection, in Pennsylvania, and fifty in Soviet Russia, including the panels "The Dance" and "Music," which he painted for the collection of his White Russian patron, Sergei Stchoukine. With the revolution, Stchoukine's collection was nationalized and put in the Moscow Museum of Modern Western Art, but after the Second World War, the museum's treasures were officially condemned as "artistic bourgeois servility." Their whereabouts was lost in mystery until last summer, when the magazine *Nouveau Femina* printed recent snapshots of the collection, and in particular of the Matisses, showing them unframed, hung by the dozen on portable racks, like washing, and kept locked from the public eye in the attic of the Hermitage Museum, in Leningrad, whose catalogue does not mention Matisse's name. However, the greatest unseen collection is the reported two thousand of his pictures that were owned by M. Matisse himself, many of them stored in a Nice bank. As he once said, *"Ce sont des valeurs."* Their value today is many millions of dollars.

There was difficulty at first in finding a French publisher for General Charles de Gaulle's "Mémoires de Guerre" (of which the opening volume has just appeared), owing to the astronomical price the General demanded for the manuscript and for various rights. There was also a feeling in publishing circles that the memoirs might not sell, because he has lost popularity through his retirement from politics, because his R.P.F. party is splintered, and so on. The highest—and, it now turns out, the luckiest—bidder was the firm of Plon, which is said to have paid him, for only this first volume, a twenty-million-franc advance (about fifty-seven thousand dollars) and, instead of retaining the usual half of the revenues from foreign and serial rights, ceded him forty per cent of the publisher's share. The first regular edition of the first volume, "L'Appel" ("The Call to Arms"), has sold out like lightning. And the limited and numbered de-luxe Holland-paper edition, at twenty-five thousand francs (or more than seventy dollars) a copy, as well as all the other numbered editions on alfa or pure-linen paper, priced at from twenty-one hundred to forty-five hundred francs a copy and reserved for "Les Anciens de la France Libre" and for "Les Membres de Touts les Associations Combattantes et Résistantes de la Guerre 1939–45," were heavily over-subscribed a month before publication. De Gaulle's memorialist style is nothing like Sir Winston's. At its best, his writing has the elegance and precision of fine eighteenth-century French literary style, which is a kind of patriotism in itself. He has a rich vocabulary of simile, recruited into the service of his critical mind by years of cultural reading. The aristocratic detachment of his recollections of his many enemies has been much commented on here, especially this brilliant word portrait of Marshal Pétain: "What a current swept him away, and toward what a fatal destiny! The entire career of this exceptional man consisted of his long effort toward self-repression. Too proud for intrigue, too strong for mediocrity, too ambitious to be froward, he nourished in his solitude a passion for domination, hardened over in time by his consciousness of his own worth, by the setbacks that had waylaid him, and by the contempt he had for others. Formerly, the bittersweets of military glory had been lavished on him. But glory had failed to gratify him fully, because she had not given herself to him alone. Then, suddenly, in the extreme winter of his life, events offered to his gifts and to his pride the opportunity, so long awaited, to burgeon to the full, though on one condition—that he accept disaster as the banner to decorate his fame. . . . But old age betrayed him to the uses of dishonest people, hiding behind his majestic weariness. Old age is a shipwreck. So that nothing might be spared us, the old age of Marshal Pétain was to be identified with the shipwreck of France." Up to the week of publication here, the English-language rights to the memoirs had not been sold, saving some translator a bad time, since the General's French defies easy translation.

Many of Mendès-France's well-wishers wish, for his sake and theirs, that he would stay at home right now, rather than distribute his energies visiting Canada, Washington, and New York. He has been demonstrating in his speeches, activities, weekly fireside radio talks, journeys, and projects on the home front the same talent for programmed momentum that distinguished him in his early, dramatic dealings with vital foreign affairs at Geneva and London, when he molded a new diplomacy for France. He has so much under way that those who believe in the possibility of his renewed France, uprooted from its immobility, feel that he should not drop his hold even for ten days in America, for fear that something may start slipping into reverse behind his back now that his political ill-wishers are recovering their wits and organization. During his five months of power, he has governed in a new kind of political space that he created for himself—above the political parties—and what has upheld him has been public opinion. His popularity with the dominant majority of the French people and with the younger element of Parliament—for he is the leader of the young-generation postwar politicos who are daring to try to do what the old politicos have only talked about—is what has given him the elevation he needed in order to operate in his new political style. But to set in motion the economic, social, and administrative reforms that undoubtedly are his greatest aims, and that Parliament has voted him special powers to tackle, he will have to come closer to earth and will have to rally support in the parties and give pledges somewhere—always the fatal danger of French parliamentarianism on the lower level. Mendès-France is now passing from his first stage, the phenomenal, into his second stage, the actual.

The French say that in addition to having Bidault's M.R.P. party, which has now become Right Wing, and the Communists bitterly opposed to him, Mendès-France has two elements in society against him. First are the all too numerous small manufacturers, whose poor organization, low production, and abnormally high profits make them a losing proposition for the national economy, and whom his reforms would first wipe out and then relocate more usefully. Second are certain high-tariff, power-lobby, and monopoly groups, some of which have been receiving enormous government subsidies; he has already collided with the beet-sugar-alcohol group and a number of big textile interests. He may soon have against him the *bistro* owners and barkeepers, to judge by his strong feelings about the disaster of France's rising alcoholism. A recent graph in *Le Figaro* shows that the French annually consume more than three times as much alcohol as Americans, with all their dry Martinis, do. Mendès-France is the first French Premier ever to drink milk in public, which his wife says he learned to do in the United States in the course of his short stay during the war. His announcement that, beginning with the New Year, France's surplus milk will be distributed to schoolchildren and to the boys in the French Army has caused consternation among French mothers, for the French think that no drink is as bad for the liver as milk. The *Mendésistes,* as his supporters are called, believe that the next three months will tell the story of how far his courage, lucidity, and exceptional intellectual grasp of economic affairs will be permitted to go in making the up-to-date France that everybody has been telling the French they ought to have.

December 8

In its weather, this has been a strange year indeed. It is ending with warmish air in December after a cold June. For Thanksgiving dinner, some Americans living near Paris plucked basketfuls of ripe red raspberries from their walled garden. For Christmas, if the genial late warmth holds, the French living on the Loire will have baskets of roses to put on their table with the

Christmas goose. There have been unusually vicious windstorms —nothing like the American hurricanes named after girls but nevertheless blowing sixty miles an hour. The wheat harvest was larger even than last year's, and bread has just gone up in price. All Western Europe is more prosperous than at any holiday season since the war.

December 23

At the year's end, the Musée du Louvre has received what could rank in art circles as the finest gift of the festive season—five van Gogh paintings, four Cézannes, and one Pissarro. The Cézannes and the Pissarro have never been seen before by the public, and only two of the van Goghs were ever shown—fifty years ago, at the 1905 van Gogh retrospective exhibition here in Paris, when they were little liked. This munificent gift has been bestowed by the elderly recluse Paul Gachet, and it comes, as did two others he made in 1949 and 1951, from the collection of paintings that the painters themselves gave to his father, the notable and eccentric Dr. Paul Ferdinand Gachet, whose inland portrait, painted in his garden at Auvers-sur-Oise and showing him in his fantasy commodore's white cap, was van Gogh's most popular work done in those last fertile weeks just before his suicide. To render justice to that Ile-de-France village, in its day only less famous than Barbizon as an artists' haunt, and to honor both of the Gachets' devotion to the art fostered there, the national Musée de l'Orangerie is holding a show called "Van Gogh et les Peintres d'Auvers-sur-Oise," a touching and, in parts, exciting exhibition of all the Gachet gifts, plus paintings (some lent by American museums and collectors) by all their artist friends who worked or visited there. The simplest of the hitherto unseen van Goghs is a bouquet of "Roses and Anemones," perhaps unfinished, since it lacks any typically anguished striations of color, but an unbeatably beautiful small composition. It was given in gratitude by van Gogh's brother Theo to the then seventeen-year-old Paul Gachet for having kept watch all night by Vincent's bedside as he lay dying. Next in gentle strength is an exquisite, creamy painting of "Mlle. Gachet in the Garden," blooming with white roses. The biggest and most violent picture, still vibrating with van Gogh's insane Midi style, is "Dr.

Gachet's Garden," the first painting van Gogh did on the family premises, showing a giant yucca plant and cypresses against the background of a fiery-red rooftop. These last two pictures have been kept so private since the summer of 1890, when they were painted, that they had never even been photographed until plates were made for the Orangerie catalogue; art experts had known of them only by Vincent's letter of June 4th to Theo, in which he wrote, "I painted two studies at the Doctor's, which I gave him last week," and then described the cypresses and rose vines *"et une figure blanche là-dedans."* The two other new van Goghs, both exhibited in 1905, are "Thatched Houses at Cordeville," a grand example of his ascending, hillside equilibrium in design, and "Two Little Girls," a serious-faced version of those two ugly, small peasants who are already famous in their smiling version. Among the four hitherto unseen Cézannes, all painted at Auvers in 1873, his backward-looking, so-called "baroque," manner is visible in "Bouquet of Yellow Dahlias" and, especially, in the fascinating jumble of table objects—including a medallion, an inkpot, a roll of paper tied with ribbon, and some of the inevitable fruit—which old Gachet humorously entitled "Cézanne's Accessories," the name the painting is now known by. The two other new Cézannes show his future style, in the boldly geometric houses of "A Corner on Rue Rémy in Auvers" and in "Green Apples," a small, truly great painting. Among the other painters in the Orangerie show—all of them the Doctor's friends—are Daubigny, Corot, and Daumier, as well as Pissarro, whose hitherto unseen Gachet canvas is a snow scene called "Chestnut Trees at Louveciennes."

The three Gachets were peculiarly lucky. None of the Auvers painters (all then still struggling either for fame or money) meant to give the garrulous, pushing, art-loving Doctor any important paintings—except van Gogh, who always shed his masterpieces wherever he was, like a fruit tree dropping ripe fruit. The unique charm of the Gachet collection today is its homely, connecting intimacy—its pictures by painters painting each other or the Auvers houses or the Gachets' house or the Gachets themselves or the Gachets' endless bric-a-brac, so useful for still-lifes, such as the Doctor's tasteless gray Japanese vase. It was used by both Cézanne, in "Bouquet of Yellow Dahlias," and van Gogh, in "Roses and Anemones," and, like the Doctor's white commodore's cap, it is on view today in an Orangerie showcase. The Gachet collection cost the

Gachets nothing except the Sunday dinners they offered to their artist friends. But in donating their twenty-nine pictures to the Louvre, son Paul and—until she recently died—daughter Marguerite, of the white rose garden, were generously giving away a large fortune. Though Cézanne was careful not to offer the Doctor his Auvers masterpiece "The Hanged Man's House," he did hand over to him seven paintings inescapably marked by genius and ultimate value. And in the total of eight Gachet van Goghs now the property of the French state there are three almost priceless masterpieces—the Auvers church, the pensive portrait of the Doctor in his seafaring cap, and Vincent's last self-portrait, with his tormented face surrounded by what look like blue flames. Paul Gachet, now eighty-two, has apparently come to the bottom of the family bin and has nothing left to give away. Austere, black-browed, looking like a gaunt Daumier drawing (the Doctor was red-headed, roly-poly, and oversociable), he is frugally finishing his days in the emptied Auvers house.

1955

January 5

Twice in four months the French Parliament rejected the idea of West German rearmament—once at the end of August, when it voted down the European Defense Community, and once at dawn of the day before Christmas. And then (one can hardly say suddenly after four years of shilly-shally), two days before New Year's, Parliament voted for it and for a Bonn army of half a million men. The changing vote did not reflect any change of mind. Because of history and memory, almost to a man the people of France, like their deputies, have been—and still are—opposed to giving any German any kind of gun. Premier Mendès-France was indeed accurate when, in the course of persuading Parliament to ballot his way, he said that it was "despite the repugnance of the French people" that French participation in West German rearmament had to be ratified, "as the sole means of preserving the Western alliance." He also told Parliament that Washington had come "within a millimetre" of organizing this rearmament of Germany on its own while the deputies were still needlessly arguing—many of them with intelligence and French logic—as if they could prevent it.

When Assembly President André Le Troquer, in the evening clothes that are his garb of office day and night, read the figures of the final vote—two hundred and eighty-seven for German rearmament, and two hundred and sixty against—there was a long moment of expressionless silence. Nobody applauded, nobody moved, no deputies inclined their heads together for a quick private comment; there was not the sound of a whisper. There was nothing but silence, maintained for a suspended instant in the presence of a vital act of history. Then Le Troquer quietly added that the session was closed, and the Communists, on their left benches, safely raised their first protesting shouts. Excessively disorderly acts or comments while Parliament is still officially sitting can result in the offending deputies' being fined as much as a day's pay, but now the Communists could vent their fury freely. They jumped to their feet as a group, the male deputies shouting and the female deputies screaming in a jumbled clamor, from which at first only single words came clear—"Assassins," "Traitors," "Shame." Then one woman shrilled a whole audible phrase—"Ten years ago, French women were being tortured to death at Ravensbrück!"—and a man behind her bellowed, "Mendès, you'll have a chance now to know what German crematories are like!" The Premier's pale, calm Jewish face did not alter; it remained masked, attentive, motionless. The uniformed ushers now rushed into the public galleries, calling loudly, *"Evacuez la salle! Sortez d'ici!,"* and even pulled some startled visitors from their seats, so that they might not witness any further disorders. When news of the ratification spread to the Quai d'Orsay sidewalk, in the early-evening darkness, the policed and barricaded lines of Communist delegations and sympathizers began singing "La Marseillaise," as if a Russian had written it. As they had done during the preceding ten days of debate, many men and women in the propaganda line held up banners inscribed with slogans like "The French Resistance Veterans Say No to German Rearmament" and "Don't Forget Auschwitz." Some displayed enlarged photographs of piled-up bodies at Buchenwald, of dead French faces bloodied by Gestapo tortures during the Occupation, or of emaciated, shaven-headed concentration-camp survivors, variously identified by those holding the photos as "My brother," "Papa," and, occasionally, "Me." For once, Communist propaganda merely coincided with French public opinion; its slogans and pictures only revived French memories of what the Nazi Germans had done, and solidified the angry fear of the French that such a race would do the same thing again if it were given guns.

On the other hand, what the Russian Communists have done habitually to the map of the world in their postwar program of occupations was, strangely, little mentioned in the ten days of debate, even by the five hundred or more anti-Communist deputies—an odd omission, considering the increasing Vietminh encroachment right now on the so-called democratic Vietnamese, whom France fought for in Indo-China for seven years. There was one exception—the militant speech by Socialist Deputy Guy Mollet, almost the only deputy who truly favored German arms. "We have to have them," he declared loudly, "because since the war Russia has kept millions of men under arms, because in the last ten years Russia has destroyed the liberties of so many people, and because all the troubles today come from Russian expansionism." (For this attack, the Communists denounced him as "a dog of a Socialist" during their post-ballot uproar.) In the minds of many American observers here, Washington officials typically gabbled out of turn once more when, in the midst of Mendès-France's desperate efforts to persuade the deputies to accept the American view of the urgent necessity for bringing in Germans, and thus swelling the ranks of the soldiery defending Western Europe, Washington suddenly made the bland announcement that the United States was reducing its own army, since the use of atomic weapons could substitute in a defensive action for great numbers of men.

It is a matter of history that the rearmament of West Germany—it was to have been accomplished with ten divisions of Germans—was first proposed, in 1950, by Secretary of State Dean Acheson, alarmed by North Korean aggression. The French countered with what became known as E.D.C., a European army that would have had some Germans in it, and even with vague supranational notions of forming a United States of Europe. However, although the French had created E.D.C., they were still alarmed at the thought of giving any arms to any Germans under any circumstances, and eventually voted against it last summer. Now, for the new year of 1955, they have resignedly ratified just about what Acheson outlined in the first place, except that the new agreement gives the Germans twelve divisions and provides sovereignty for Bonn. Thus the French lost what might have been their chance to form the mold for modern European history, and, moreover, were forced to take on the familiar old setup that they had most feared from the start. On December 31st, several Paris newspapers ran immediately beneath their final report on the Assembly's ratification the news that sixteen big German firms of the Ruhr, where the German armament crowd has always had its headquarters, are ready to start West Germany's first atomic pile, at Düsseldorf, just as soon as the Paris treaty starts functioning.

January 19

The Seine is in flood. The *quais* are under water, so that the river looks almost half again as wide as it is, and the bridges are black-edged with citizens hanging over the parapets to stare their fill at the dramatic swirling, yellowish stream beneath, the favorite bridge being the Pont de l'Alma, where the water is already halfway up the thighs of the famous Zouave statue between the arches. It came to his neck and almost drowned him, as the saying goes, in the great floods of 1910, when rowboats replaced carriages on the Place de la Concorde, and it is now climbing up him at the rate of about an inch an hour. All traffic on the Seine has been stopped, and boats have been ordered to tie up and register their positions with the Prefecture of Police, in case some have to be called to evacuate riverside dwellers in low-lying Paris neighborhoods. All the rivers in France are alarmingly high. The Marne, whose rain- and snow-swollen headwaters take eight days to flow into the Seine, is already above its 1910 high mark, and next Monday it and the Yonne, whose water, even now overflowing, takes only four days to reach the Seine, are together expected to make an accumulated high tide in Paris that will be six metres, or about nineteen feet, above normal level. The Paris skies over the waters are clear and sunny. The recent wind and rain storms at sea and on Channel lands were so fierce that numbers of sea gulls were blown into town; some now follow around on foot after the Louvre pigeons, hoping to pick up some of the crusts occasionally tossed their way by children, and even fly down into Parisians' back yards and gardens in the hope of charity. This has been an abnormally tempestuous new year, blowing first hot and then cold in no reasonable rhythm.

February 2

The floods in the cities and the countryside are now subsiding. A lot of France's arable land was under water. The winter wheat and oats are largely drowned. Paris itself was mostly spared. On the Ile de la Cité, there was some awkward flooding of the underground cells in the Palais de Justice, where prisoners are kept until they are brought upstairs for trial. At the Institut, thousands of books were rescued from seepage in the basement stacks; fortunately, the famous Mazarine Library was not affected. Along the Quai de Passy, anchored boats rode higher than the parapeted street level, and from there to the west nothing could save the low-lying suburbs and towns, where, for nearly thirty miles—from the motorcar factories at Billancourt, through Le Pecq, and on to Poissy and Mantes—the risen river simply flowed into people's lives via their shops, parlors, bedrooms, and factories. In the towns on the periphery of Paris, two hundred factories were closed, and to the fifty thousand workers the government has now promised out-of-work pay amounting to seventy-five per cent of the hourly minimum wage for single workers and eighty-five per cent for family men. In and around Paris, the organization of an estimated seventy-five hundred professionals and volunteers for rescue work and flood fighting was astonishingly efficient. On the job were six companies of French Army engineers; Paris police; highway police; every fireman and ladder within reach; municipal masons and ditchdiggers; L'Union des Femmes Françaises, which persuaded people in dry homes to take in the castaways; La Fédération Française de Canoë-Kayak, which operated its fragile pleasure craft for delivering medicines to the sick; Boy Scouts; local American Army units, which gave raincoats and invaluable rubber boots; the Pope, who gave a million francs to the refugees; and the city of Warsaw, which topped him with ten million. Thousands of student volunteers sandbagged river parapets, working under the scholarly and apropos group title of Fluctuat, taken from the old Paris coat-of-arms motto, "*Fluctuat nec Mergitur.*" Others worked in a group called Zouave, in honor of the Pont de l'Alma statue that always serves as a floodmark and on whom the river this time rose to the elbow. In the present unseemly spring weather, France is cleaning up her mud and trying to dry out.

Floods were also unkind to Pierre Poujade, the bookseller from the little town of St.-Céré, in the Lot, who is the leader and national stump speaker of a nineteen-month-old revolt of more than half a million shopkeepers and artisans against what they claim are the iniquitously high and unjust taxes the government imposes on them. He advertised that two hundred thousand delegates of his Union de Défense des Commerçants et Artisans would meet in Paris last week to air their grievances, but the inundations made transport irregular, the state railroads refused to issue the cut-rate tickets customary for pilgrims or mass delegations, and the Department of Bridges and Roads refused to permit fleets of hired buses on the waterlogged highways. The fifty thousand delegates who eventually turned up in the Parc des Expositions at the Porte de Versailles looked to be unusually pleasant, uncynical, modest French. There was a Paris rumor afterward that Poujade had ranted like a coming dictator while his men followers roared and his women followers screamed, threw kisses to him, and swooned with emotion. Actually, the women at the meeting seemed to be mostly married shopkeepers, used to keeping their eye on the money till; as Balzac made clear, *maman la caissière* is not given to fainting spells. Poujade himself, aged thirty-four, is a chubby, handsome, curly-haired brunet and an earnest and perspiring talker, whose statistics are usually wrong but who makes sense to his followers because they agree with him. In his speech, he claimed that recent government tax reductions merely martyrized the little fellow and favored big business, and that "Mendès-Lolo" (French baby talk for milk-drinking Mendès-France, whose name was booed, probably by the many café owners who are Poujade followers) wants to wipe out small tradesmen and artisans—"though for centuries we have been the backbone of France"—in favor of mass production and massive sales. He said that those of his followers who had chased nosy tax collectors out of their shops when they came to inspect the ledgers were only fighting for their liberties. "We do not want the moon," he said, and merely asked an annual tax exemption for *les petits commerçants* on their first three hundred and sixty thousand francs (about a thousand dollars); amnesty for all delinquents who have committed tax frauds; and a strike by his followers against paying any further taxes (these last two projects were enthusiastically cheered) until tax-code reforms should be established. Government tax collectors say that fiscal frauds among such small businesses are indeed widespread; that, at latest reports, four-fifths of the nation's tradesmen—including butchers, grocerymen, plumbers, masons, and *bistro* keepers, the groups that unquestionably skim off the cream—declared monthly earnings equivalent to eighty-nine dollars, only twelve dollars more than a factory worker's wage. However, financial experts say that Poujade's proposed tax revisions have some justification. In any case, his organization's threat that it can influence coming elections is already worrying some deputies. Meanwhile, the authorities have asked the Directeurs Généraux des Impôts et de la Comptabilité Publique, two high officials in the Finance Ministry, to prepare a report on whether they can sue Poujade for "inciting the public to refuse or delay payment of taxes."

February 15

Right now, the bourgeois politicians here are straining their capacities in an effort to scratch together a government to replace that of Mendès-France, which they overthrew. During that violent, deafening half hour of shouting and banging desk tops at four in the morning, when a majority of the deputies tried to prevent Mendès-France, just voted out of office, from speaking from the tribune, one of the oddest figures on the scene was the Assembly's Secretary-General, the only official who was perfectly calm. A familiar slender silhouette on the rostrum, with a distinguished shock of blue-gray hair, he is known to few Assembly visitors by his name, which is Emile Blamont. His duties demand discretion and a strong spine. He is the nonpolitical permanent authority on parliamentary procedure. During decisive debates, he sits with his back to the deputies, uncomfortably perched on a red velvet postilion seat that is attached to the rostrum beside the chair of the Assembly President, or speaker, so that he can lean down to talk confidentially into that official's ear if he is consulted or if he thinks that procedure or questions of order are being misinterpreted. In his replies or advice, Blamont must be quick-witted, explicit, and accurate, with an infallible memory for parliamentary and constitutional affairs, and must by his demeanor display great tact (as he did during the hubbub over Mendès-France), since he does not represent the authority of the people, as the deputies do—a responsibility they are very jealous of—but only the authority of the Civil Service, which has appointed him as its functionary, making him a nonpolitical and constant outsider. In his administrative capacity, he has all the other parliamentary nonpolitical functionaries under him, such as the relays of stenographers who take down the debates, and the silver-chained *huissiers* in their long tailcoats. After passing his civil-service examination in 1930, Blamont entered the Assembly organization in a junior role, was in London during the war until General de Gaulle founded his Algiers Assembly, and then became its Secretary-General, there being plenty of new politicians down in North Africa but he being the only functionary who represented continuity with the Paris Parliament. After the Liberation, he took up his present post. He has great admiration for the British House of Commons, and knows his opposite number there, Sir Edward Fellowes, who certainly has never had to remain impersonally calm in the face of any such hurly-burly as attended Mendès-France's fall.

March 2

"The prophetic oak has been brought low. He was one of the grandeurs of our time." "After Valéry, after Gide, now, with Claudel, disappears the last of the *grands maîtres* from the end of the nineteenth century." With such threnodies was the passing of the poet and dramatist Paul Claudel, aged eighty-six, recently mourned by Paris newspapers. They carried their appreciation of Claudel's literary gifts, and their expressions of national loss, on their front pages, along with the announcement of the Ministerial makeup of the new government. Claudel's phenomenal gifts made him an awe-inspiring figure. He was a noted dramatist; a profound mystic and religious poet; an almost lifelong diplomat, having been Ambassador to Tokyo from 1921 to 1926, during the earthquake, and to Washington from 1927 to 1933, during the depression; a passionate revivalist of the Roman Catholic faith; an authority on Franco-American finances, having served with the French Economic Mission at the end of the First World War; author of some half-hundred volumes, which he said he wrote in daily half-hour stretches; and a director of the rich Gnome & Rhône, France's big airplane-engine factory.

The general public knew Claudel only through his theatre pieces, which have lately been fashionably popular, and thus impressive to most people, if, in accordance with the inevitable dual reaction to him, very tedious to some, who found his "Le Soulier de Satin" merely the longest play they ever sat through. "L'Annonce Faite à Marie," a medieval mystery play, written in 1912, that was given by the New York Theatre Guild as "The Tidings Brought to Mary," now functions as a French classic in the state theatre. It has just been given a revival at the Comédie-Française, badly acted but with a glorious gala opening, which Claudel attended. After the opening, the powerful old Christian, with his own words about the glory of God still fresh in his ears, suddenly died, on Ash Wednesday.

Some Parisians have remarked that the nineteen days when they were without a government created a dangerous euphoria. France's various grave problems—North Africa, a new tax scale, a reformed constitution—were temporarily forgotten, because nobody in Parliament was talking about them, or even talking about doing something about them. The French citizens, thrown back on their own devices, lived and functioned as usual, except that they developed a vague feeling of national solidarity, of being the people, as against those six hundred and twenty-seven deputies who had been elected to serve them and, as a sign of their customary quarrelsome inefficiency, had left forty-three million citizens in the lurch, and thereby convinced of their own superiority.

Pierre Mendès-France is now called the Phantom in the Corridor, the ghost who haunts the Parliamentary halls with the memory of his regime. It is not easy to see how his successor, Premier Edgar Faure, will be able to settle the important problems that now, after the delay, face the country more immediately than ever. For Faure, holding his present Assembly majority together is like balancing a pyramid of eggs. If he so much as makes a move to do anything positive, or if one of his supporting Ministers so much as lifts a disapproving finger, the eggs, safe only while immobile, can well come breaking to bits around his head.

March 17

In a press conference held late yesterday afternoon, Premier Edgar Faure wryly said that if he and his government fell Friday night, the fall would hit him hard, because it would occur on his twenty-sixth day in office, whereas when he was Premier in 1952, he managed to stay in power forty days. If Faure falls this weekend, it will be because of Pierre Poujade, the pugnacious thirty-four-year-old provincial shopkeeper from St.-Céré, in the Lot, who slammed the door of his little stationery shop in a tax collector's face in July, 1953, and last year founded his Union de Défense des Commerçants et Artisans, an organization, designed to thwart tax collectors, that

Paris had never even heard of six weeks ago. The U.D.C.A.'s expansion in the past six weeks has been a social phenomenon. In January, at Poujade's first Paris meeting, which was made up largely of his devoted provincials and snubbed by Paris shopkeepers, he claimed four hundred thousand followers; this week, he claims eight hundred thousand. His organization is now nationwide, except for a few *départements* in the northeast, which is Gaullist, and a couple in the southwest, which is Basque. February 15th is the date when the French should pay the first third of their year's taxes. In eighteen *départements* of central France—the region where Poujade started, and where he is still strongest—thirty to eighty per cent of the little businessmen and artisans failed to pay their February taxes and closed their modest savings accounts, so that government authorities could not block their funds until that tax money starts rolling in.

This week, Poujade turned to direct action and political pressure in the capital of France. First, he sent Président du Conseil Faure an open letter—described as threatening—that accused him of having caused his Assembly majority to break faith with the U.D.C.A. on rapid tax reforms, which were put to one side in last week's preliminary debate on finances. "The responsibility for the rupture is yours, and you will bear the consequences," he warned Faure. In the same mail, he sent three hundred deputies a letter listing U.D.C.A.'s demands. In it, he said he wants amnesty for tax frauds, which he considers the consequences of injustice; suppression of the tax collectors' right to snoop in taxpayers' account books; abrogation of the Ulver-Dorey law of last summer, which provides harsh punishment for anybody who discourages tax collection; and the appointment of a Parliamentary commission to study tax reforms—with the U.D.C.A. itself, no less.

Poujade bypasses the Ulver-Dorey law, which imposes fines of up to a half-million francs, as well as prison terms, upon people who incite the public to refuse or delay its tax payments, by merely saying humorously to his followers, "Turn off the faucet. Don't turn it on again till victory is ours." There is no French law against tap-turning. He ridicules what is called the *polyvalent* system of tax collection by nicknaming all tax collectors *polyvoleurs* (multiple thieves). In central France, the U.D.C.A. is highly organized, with the result that when a tax collector makes a date with a U.D.C.A. shopkeeper to inspect his books, the shopkeeper calls two U.D.C.A. members, who each call two more, and so on, and within half an hour they have collected a crowd, which either keeps the taxman from getting near the shop door or chases him out of town. This system has been harder to work under the noses of the hardboiled Paris police, but a fortnight ago the newly organized U.D.C.A. branch in Paris temporarily broke up the bidding at the Hôtel Drouot's state auction rooms on some wretched bankrupt shopkeepers' worldly goods. To everyone's surprise, the marketmen of Paris, the fourteen prosperous syndicates of food sellers, and even the rich Butchers' Association have climbed aboard the Poujade bandwagon in the poor man's tax revolt.

Yesterday, Poujade's direct action brought in a small tidal wave of results. Combined-political-party groups like the Independents, the Independent Peasants, and the A.R.S., an ex-Gaullist splinter faction, sent delegations to Faure demanding "profound tax reforms" if they were to back his Friday demand for a vote of confidence. Yesterday, too, some deputies spoke up in Parliament about the pickle they were in, caught between the need for defending him and the risk of offending their aroused U.D.C.A. voters. And the Federation of Finance Officials, which includes tax collectors, all of them furious, held a wonderful press conference, fulminating against Poujade and declaring that some shopkeepers had threatened to nab tax collectors as hostages, had refused to sell goods to tax collectors' wives, and had instructed their own children to put tax collectors' children in Coventry, neither talking to them nor playing with them at recess. "We can no longer tolerate this situation!" the Federation's president cried. "If the government persists in refusing us police protection, we will set up our own defense and launch reprisals. We will refuse to buy from shopkeepers who don't pay their taxes," he added weakly. In addition, yesterday the Parliament's Finance Commission suddenly voted—thirty-five to seven—to make abrogation of the Ulver-Dorey law the price of its support of Faure's special powers on Friday. Last night, *Le Monde,* which spoke with contempt of the Finance Commission's cowardice, carried on its political page seven articles and news items that dealt with *l'affaire Poujade*. This morning, *Combat* ran five front-page stories on it and an editorial entitled *"Un Précédent Dangereux,"* in which it said sadly, "Poujade has proved the merits of direct action against a decadent democracy."

Whether Faure falls or gives in and stays in so-called power, if Poujade has anything like the number of followers he claims, right now he controls the biggest single-idea social-reform group in France.

March 30

Considering the constant political hot water most French politicians live in, it is a relief to know that a few of them occasionally take time off to practice an avocation. It was not admitted until recently that Premier Edgar Faure has written three detective stories, under the nom de plume of Edgar Sanday. "Sanday" is a kind of phonetic joke, meaning *"sans d"* and referring to the fact that his first name is spelled the English way, instead of being spelled "Edgard," *à la francaise.* "M. Langlois N'Est Pas Toujours Egal à Lui-même" ("M. Langlois Is Not Always at His Best"), which is Sanday's last detective story, was printed in 1950 and is still selling. (His first two, written as pastimes during the Occupation, when the Germans were hunting for him, are out of print, and little is generally known of them now except their titles—"Pour Rencontrer M. Marshes" and "L'Installation du Président Fitz-Mole.") The Langlois yarn starts as a highly entertaining suspense story of character, focussed on a mysterious, dull foreigner of that name who suddenly arrives in an elegant provincial town and undertakes the odd business of settling money quarrels out of court, and the odder use of drugged tobacco to paralyze the resistance of his clients, the hapless local rich. After bankruptcies and subtle murders, and some shenanigans by his accomplice, an exotic actress, Sanday weakly lets the pair of them disappear in an equivocal finale. It seems that his family, to whom he read his story by chapters, were indignant at this evasive ending. Premier Faure is a habitual reader of other people's detective stories, especially when travelling, his last favorite being everybody's—Albert Simonin's classic in argot, "Touchez Pas au Grisbi."

April 13

You can tell it is spring here mainly because the tourists have burst into bloom. Nature herself is belated. While a million and a half Parisians headed out of town for Easter, half a million visitors, the foreigners among them mostly English, German, Danish, or American, flowed in for the chilly fête as part of the largest weekend holiday migration that West Europe has yet recorded, with citizens travelling in all directions—an inspiring parade of prosperous pocketbooks.

Spring being the proper season for major art, "Salut à la France, Hommage Culturel Américain," the biggest presentation of American culture ever brought here, has opened its first exhibit, "Cinquante Ans d'Art aux Etats-Unis," at the Musée d'Art Moderne. It is no secret that this salute is an expensive propaganda project, launched in the hope that it will counteract part of the ill will that some of the Americans over here and some of Washington's foreign policies have gained for us since the war. It is also no secret that the whole scheme was viewed as dubious by certain State Department and Congressional figures.

Doubtless to everyone's surprise, this modern-art show has attracted some of the largest crowds the Musée has ever had, and has received mostly thoughtful critiques, often praising the very artists the same critic condemned two years ago. New York's Museum of Modern Art, which assembled the show from its own collection of paintings and sculptures, has put on display a group of photographs, some advertisements, samples of typography, and blown-up pictures of such examples of American architecture as Frank Lloyd Wright's glass tower in Racine and the Chicago glass apartment house of Mies van der Rohe, which the French consider miraculous. The entire Parisian press has given the show attention. The artists most frequently cited have been the elders—Lyonel Feininger and Maurice Prendergast, who were previously scarcely known here, and were immediately traced to Cézanne and Bonnard and rated as important. Everyone, rightly or wrongly, has been identified with a school: Marsden Hartley and Arthur Dove with the Blaue Reiter; Jackson Pollock and Arshile Gorky with Expressionism; Morris Graves and Hedda Sterne with the romanticists; Mark Rothko with the constructivists; Mark Tobey with the Orientalist Intra-Subjectivists; and the Ecole de la Poubelle, or ashcan painters, with the Zola realists. John Marin was unanimously selected as the only painters' painter. In general, the critics said that American figurative painting is socially ironic, never imaginative, and that American abstract works tend to be young and dry. Some of the criticisms were unconsciously funny, such as that in *L'Express,* which kindly explained American artists by saying, "Cut off from Europe in 1940 by the war, or in contact only with European émigrés, the young Americans had to follow their own path almost without guidance." All the French critics showed an almost morbid interest in pointing out how many of the artists have Continental names, but only the weekly *Carrefour's* critic went so far as to say, "I perceived in the exposition no American art, no American style. . . . Nothing but foreigners."

Parliament is on vacation, so that it can keep a finger on the country's pulse during this week's cantonal elections, but the deputies' absence does not mean that political life in Paris has ceased. The government is straining to settle its bloody North African colonial-reform questions before April 23rd, the start of the great Moslem festival of Ramadan, which is always a period of high tension, owing to the people's prolonged fasting and then the final, explosive celebrations and feasts. In the meantime, the native leaders of the Comité Maghrebien, representing the Istiqlal, the Neo-Destour, and the Liberation Front of Algeria, have all gone off to the conference at Bandung, in Indonesia—until recently a Dutch settlement, the French keep reminding each other while wondering about the future of their own colonial possessions—to meet other non-Europeans, including sixteen prime ministers, among them Chou En-lai, Ngo Dinh Diem, Nasser, and Nehru.

The destructive squabbling between France and America over the Indo-China imbroglio has made for renewed worry about French and American foreign policies while the Communists seep farther southward into Vietnam, giving French parents who vainly lost their sons there a doubly sad anniversary, for the fall of Dienbienphu occurred almost a year ago.

April 27

The long shadow cast by the Bandung meeting of Afro-Asiatic premiers and delegates of color, speaking their minds for the first time in modern history without the white man's domination while they deliberated as racial authorities on colonialism (which they condemned), may possibly have aided the French government this last week, since there were Tunisian delegates at the conference, criticizing the do-nothingness of the French in settling the Franco-Tunisian crisis. With the eyes of the world thus focussed on colonial problems, the Faure government was able to reach an accord with the Protectorate of Tunisia, by which, for the first time, France gave the Tunisian natives limited home rule. It was not too soon, after thirty years of reform talk and broken French promises, punctuated lately by the Tunisian natives' murdering of white French colonials as a sign of their impatience. Although the protocol was signed by Edgar Faure, as the French Premier, and Tahar Ben Ammar, as the Tunisian Premier, Faure was signing, in a way, for Mendès-France, who, as Premier, last July solemnly engaged France to grant this long-promised autonomy, and the Tunisian official, in another way, was signing for Habib Bourguiba, chief of the Neo-Destour Independence Party, whose consultation with Faure two days before established him as the real intermediary in arranging this new Franco-Tunisian step forward. Bourguiba's suddenly admitted importance in Paris was an extraordinary story in itself, even for this cultivated rebel against French rule, who, through his education at the Sorbonne, is more familiar today with the libertarian Voltaire than with the Koran. Arrested three years ago for his activities by the Resident General of the Pleven government, he was later exiled from the Tunisian mainland to some unnamed island off the coast, which his son, in his turn a student at the Sorbonne, identified to friends here as the island of La Galite, adding that it was uninhabited except for his father and the three soldiers guarding him, and that his father had been forbidden to take books or any other reading matter with him, thus being exiled even from the companionship of print. Removed from his island in one of Mendès-France's first steps toward relieving dangerous Tunisian tension, he was brought to France and settled comfortably outside Paris in *résidence surveillée,* which roused against Mendès-France the fury of Tunisia's politically powerful, colonial conservatives. These white diehards were affronted anew last week at seeing the native they most resent consulting freely with the head of the French government on this matter of limited home rule, which liberal colonials and most Paris politicians realize is the minimum that could be belatedly offered to the Protectorate in 1955.

May 11

Historically, this has seemed to most of the French the strangest week since the end of the war, because all that was postwar ended, too; Western Germany is now not only sovereign but an ally. It was also the most important week since the end of the war for anniversaries, memories, and ironies; for hopes and plans for one more new Europe; for vitally important international diplomatic talks and sharp disagreements. The highest British, American, and French figures in foreign affairs have had their first meetings here in their new relation with Western Germany as friend and equal, and if, of the original Allied quartet, Russia was absent, she was certainly present in the conferees' thoughts one way or another. It must have been due to the haste with which history is fabricated today by supersonic flying diplomats that although Saturday, May 7th, was the tenth anniversary of Nazi Germany's unconditional surrender, Monday, May 9th, was the day chosen to welcome federal Germany as a sovereign nation, fit to be rearmed, into the bosom of the Atlantic Pact ministerial meeting at the Palais de Chaillot. The French were not the only ones in Paris to have their memories harried by this indelicate lumping together of contrary feelings and events into a bargain weekend in history. The Norwegian NATO delegate, who, like the fourteen other delegates, spoke optimistic words of welcome to the incoming fifteenth power, represented by Chancellor Adenauer, had the greatest reason of all present to hope the moment was indeed "a decisive turning point toward European peace," since he spent two years in the Sachsenhausen concentration camp.

Some French papers stoically printed photos of the Kaiser's old red, gold, and black flag hoisted in the Allied flag circle at SHAPE, but none printed a photo of West Germany's military representative there, General Hans Speidel, who was tactfully dressed in civilian clothes. Only the Communist paper *Humanité,* pursuing the Soviet line against German rearmament even after the event, ran any information about him. In a column entitled "Qui Est Speidel?" it stated that as Rommel's chief of staff, commanding the German forces north of the Loire in the spring of 1944, he, like Rommel, had been intelligent enough to realize that Hitler was headed for disaster, and that he and Rommel had received at their headquarters at La Roche-Guyon the well-known German writer Captain Ernst Junger, who was already preparing a peace treaty for submission to the Western Allies. According to its paragraph headings, this treaty, later published here in book form under the title "L'Appel," was based on the idea of "Europe unified on the base of Christianity and German predominance, destined to avert Bolshevism."

Germany as an entirety is the European hinge on which either the Eastern Russian Communist influence or the Western democratic and American influence must eventually swing, it has been thought here. Adenauer's request for Allied aid in unifying the two Germanys, and Russia's proposal at the London disarmament conference for the suppression of atomic arms and the withdrawal of all Big Four troops from the two Germanys, were like psychological and diplomatic bombs in themselves as they fell on Paris. There will be plenty to talk about at the coming Big Four conference, which looked so unlikely a month ago and which it is taken for granted here was pushed by President Eisenhower, rather than by his Secretary of State. The French now feel that at least one good thing has come from the rearmament of West Germany by the Paris accords, and that is a concentration of full attention on the ultimate European problems. It is worth repeating that this past week in Paris has been the most important week since the war ended in that memorable month of May ten years ago, when there existed so much simple hope and confidence in what was to come.

May 25

The musical contribution to the American propaganda program called "Salute to France" has consisted of three concerts by Eugene Ormandy and the Philadelphia Orchestra, which made a brilliant impression on Paris music critics. That is to say, its violins were appreciated as wonderfully silky; "I wager there are some Stradivariuses, Guarneriuses, and Amatis among them," one critic bet in print. It was praised for its youthful ardor and disciplined virtuosity but criticized for lacking nuance and for playing almost the whole time as loud as all outdoors. The programs, which it is rumored were imposed on Ormandy by an influential impresario who guaranteed the State Department that he knew what the French liked, supplied nearly everything sure not to please them, except one Beethoven symphony. The French, who still care relatively little for Brahms and less for Tchaikovsky, got both, as well as arias from Handel's "Samson" and Verdi's "Otello," a Bloch symphony, and such French standbys—of which the French are weary—as Debussy's "La Mer" and Ravel's "Daphnis et Chloé," and "La Valse." They also got Brailowsky, at the last concert, in impressive Chopin, but to the critics these were *programmes déséquilibrés,* without enough *vraie musique*—meaning serious classics—and, of course, with nearly no pianissimi. Thus, this part of the Salute to France, for which so much praise was expected, backfired. And a great pity.

June 15

The Peking Opera's fine clowning and acrobatics, the last pleasures on earth Paris was expecting from the mysterious Communist East, proved to be such a hit in the Festival International d'Art Dramatique, at the Théâtre Sarah-Bernhardt, that the troupe has been scheduled for additional performances at the Palais de Chaillot. Practically everything connected with the Chinese show was contrary to what had been anticipated. The performers wore no splendid old robes, weighty with hand embroidery, but colorful, gaudy costumes of factory shoddy that looked as if it had never seen a silkworm—easy for the actors to turn somersaults in, as a means of crossing the stage between speeches, in the comic legend-plays that are part of the Opera's surprising repertory. Because of Parisians' familiarity nowadays with dodecaphonic and "concrete" music, even the old pentatonic-scale melodies in the Chinese orchestra sounded quite comprehensible here. Only the high-falsetto operatic singing of both soprano and tenor in Act VIII of the Ming Dynasty opus "The White Serpent" (no other acts from it, or from any other opera, were given, perhaps through instinctive tact) was still painful to Western ears—unfortunately, since this was probably the summit of the company's elegant Chinese classicism of unreality. The lowest point was a dainty Sino-Soviet work ballet featuring maiden tea pickers, pretty as pictures with their rouged eyelids, their smiles, their fans, and their exquisitely idle-looking hands.

The most highly refined clowning was performed by Chang Chun-hua, the Peking Opera's most celebrated acrobatic comedian. His role was that of an innkeeper hunting for an enemy wayfarer in a supposedly unlighted bedroom. The deft game of hide-and-seek, which lasted nearly an hour—the Chinese are more patient than we are, and all their acts were very long—actually took place under bright theatre lights, so that nobody could miss the fun as the two men, silently somersaulting, leaping, and groping, worked side by side as a team, perfectly missing each other. The joke was seven hundred years old, being taken from a Sung Dynasty play, and certainly seemed the ancestor of many of our circus-clown gags. Both actors were clearly in their thirties and were expert gymnasts—fifteen years of physical training reportedly being part of the Peking troupe's apprenticeship, even for falsetto singers. The big production number, with chorus, was "Troubles in the Heavenly Realm," starring Wang Ming-choun, the Opera's greatest satiric mime, as king of the monkeys in revolt against the stupid gods—a role he played like a Chinese Till Eulenspiegel, with the addition of fabulous tumbling and brilliant fencing. "The Yentang Shan Fortress" was a modernized version of a medieval battle scene, with the opposing troops fighting in ranks of somersaulters—they looked like martial pinwheels—until the victors finally took the castle by double-somersaulting over its wall. At this, the French audience cheered, it being the finale of the program.

The Chinese People's Republic's Peking troupe was bound to arouse the greatest curiosity this year of all the national productions sent to the International Theatre Festival, since Paris had never seen any Chinese Communist actors before, and their country is a crux in the political news. The troupe's shabby, colorful gaiety and exotic high-style circus entertainment seem to have made the most fetching propaganda of any company so far.

A hundred and thirty paintings by Picasso, constituting the most significant group of his works exhibited here since the famous Galerie Georges Petit show of 1932, has opened at the Pavillon de Marsan, in the Musée du Louvre, and will be on view through October. A parallel exhibit of his etchings, drawings, book illustrations, and lithographs will open this week at the Bibliothèque Nationale for the same period, so that people, and especially tourist visitors, can see all that is to be seen of him in Paris at one fell swoop. This is the highest honor possible for the French state to render to a living artist—the privileged invitation to have his works on view concurrently in the nation's two greatest treasure buildings. Everyone important in the Atlantic world as a Picasso connoisseur, collector, or museum expert, or as an authoritative Picasso writer has been involved in putting his show together. The names listed for thanks in the catalogue compose an international modern-art *Who's Who*—people in Paris and elsewhere in France, in England, Sweden, Switzerland, Italy, and the United States. This, with the omission of

Moscow and Prague, is just about the itinerary the collecting instinct for his art originally took, after a few men and a woman in Paris, mostly foreigners and certainly not rich, appreciatively sighted his genius here about fifty years ago and bought some of it at what they could afford to pay, which was not much but which he was glad to get then. Today he is the highest-priced living painter, for both his current works and his old works fetch the highest modern-art prices on earth. An early owner of a fine Picasso portrait lately sold it for the equivalent of twenty-two thousand dollars to a dealer, who shortly resold it for double that.

Among other intelligent, unusual, and sensible bits of personal information about the painter in the Pavillon de Marsan catalogue is the statement that Picasso's *point* today is a hundred thousand francs, a *point* being a unit of measure in the artist-dealer milieu, according to which, for instance, a thirty-*point* Picasso canvas, or one measuring nearly thirty-six inches on its long axis, would have a minimal asking price of three million francs—something in the neighborhood of $8,570. However, the selling price, if Picasso chose to sell, would naturally be much higher. According to his art dealer and old friend, Henry Kahnweiler, who was one of the earliest Cubist authorities, Picasso never sells this year's pictures, because he is developing what is in them, and usually keeps last year's pictures, too, as points of reference until he is sure he is through with what they represented in his work. He also never sells personal pictures, of his children or of his mistresses, and is shocked if they sell a portrait he has painted of them and given them, for, being punctiliously Spanish, he does not regard such art as publicly vendible. The most recent sale, M. Kahnweiler says, was to the Swiss Kunstmuseum, of Basel, which bought "Le Bord de la Seine, d'Après Courbet," painted in 1953, for a little over ten million francs, or around thirty thousand dollars. This is one of the amazing series of experiments Picasso has been making in reworking the composition of a previous great painter in his own style of invention.

Though the Pavillon de Marsan show furnishes a magnificent retrospective of Picasso works from 1898 through 1953, many the property of the artist and never exhibited before, they represent a long promenade over fairly familiar rich ground. The *clou* of the show is the fourteen Picassos called "Les Femmes d'Alger," which are variations, in this new manner, on a Delacroix picture of that name, painted in 1834 and now in the Louvre. Picasso started his series on December 13, 1954, and finished it on February 14, 1955. The theme began with two Oriental women, one smoking a narghile, and a servant holding aside a curtain, in a haremlike room with a latticed window. It is impossible to describe the alterations he has made in it, for they are like the slight shifts a kaleidoscope makes when it is turned slowly, its colored fragments evolving new patterns before one's eyes. Fourteen of these new patterns Picasso has halted and fixed in his fourteen pictures, occasionally adding one more woman and then subtracting her again as a radical change, or making one figure recumbent, as if drooped in slumber, and then elevating her limbs into the air, with a few of the pictures in low gray colors and the others resonant in scarlets and whites. What these fourteen variants amount to are fourteen different Picassos, in a new form of multiplication of his own art and style, with similarities separated by his genius. Already appreciations—and, with them, prices—are beginning to form in the air around "Les Femmes d'Alger" as an extraordinary multiple unit that illustrates his styles—a unit that, it is supposed, must go to a museum intact. Probably only a museum, as a multiple unit itself, could afford it.

June 22

This is the end of the 1955 Grande Saison, passed in a mixture of soft sunshine and chilly storms amid a climate of French prosperity, discernible in Parisians' being able to afford their own high prices. There have been elegant dinners, soirées, and entertainments, and the elaborate weddings proper to this annual high social season. On the Paris Bourse, the overbid stock market took a natural slump, but the French class that has money seems to have a lot of it, and to be spending it. France's Armée de l'Air and airplane industry enjoyed the luxury of a great satisfaction this week, just ten years after they started with nothing, at the end of the war—their impressive participation, along with nine other nations, including the United States and England, in their own XXIe Salon International de l'Aéronautique at Le Bourget Airfield. Last Saturday and Sunday, a weekend crowd of half a million saw France's leading trio among its many new planes—the jet bolide called the Trident; the jet transport called the Caravelle, capable of carrying nearly a hundred passengers at a speed of close to five hundred miles an hour; and a helicopter nicely named the Alouette, or lark, which has risen higher in the air than any other of its genus. Luxury hotels are so crowded with tourists, mostly Germans and Americans, come to see the June goings on, that families are sleeping three to a room. Among the myriad attractions was the reopening of Florence's, the famous Montmartre champagne night club; the Grand Palais international horse show; racing at five tracks; Bois de Boulogne polo; Basque pelota; and a rose growers' competition at Bagatelle, won by an American rose fancier. The suburban Casino d'Enghien offered, along with its gambling tables, Verdi's "Le Bal Masqué," with La Scala singers, including Tagliavini. At a televised concert of sacred music at the Ste.-Chapelle, with floodlighting on the thirteenth-century stained-glass windows, an American Negro troupe assembled and led by that folk-song artist from the Left Bank, Gordon Heath, sang spirituals. The Brazilian composer Heitor Villa-Lobos, increasingly popular here, directed the Orchestre National in a program of his own works, among them a first performance of his new piano concerto. In a welter of art shows, there have been such items as an exhibition of Hiroshige prints and drawings, an exhibition of seventy Rembrandt drawings at the Louvre, and the Galerie Louis Carré's highly appreciated show of twenty-seven paintings, dated from 1913 through last year, by the seventy-nine-year-old Jacques Villon, still semi-Cubist, still as gifted in his belated fame as he was before the First World War, and even before the Second, when no one paid any attention to him. The Grande Saison ends this week in the Grande Semaine and the Grand Prix de Paris at Longchamp, run as always on the last Sunday of June, the most fashionable sporting Sabbatical race of the year.

It should be added that, on top of everything else going on in Paris, the city is unfortunately being improved, so that automobiles can have an easier time. Part of the Boulevard Raspail's fine central allée of trees is being deforested to make a shadeless, ugly single-track traffic artery. The magnificent chestnuts by the Place de l'Alma are gone, victims of a riverside traffic tunnel under the square, which looks as though a bomb had hit it. The Avenue de l'Opéra's sidewalks are being sliced away a metre and a half on each side—or about ten feet in all—so that cars may have more room and pedestrians may walk all over each other. Now the energetic Prefect of Police, André Dubois, who at least made Paris automobiles silent by forbidding horn tooting, which everyone said would be impossible, has a plan for garaging them underground, which sounds all too believable. The Municipal Council is about to ask for bids for his *urbanisme-souterrain* project of building a three-story parking garage for eighteen hundred and thirty cars under the Tuileries gardens; eight others at various points, including the Champs-Elysées; and a five-story garage for six hundred cars beneath the Square Louvois, practically in the cellar of the Bibliothèque Nationale. Altogether, these would shelter an estimated eleven thousand cars. The Municipal Council also intends to build thirty-eight hundred small Paris apartments for families of three, or shelter for about eleven thousand four hundred citizens. It is nice to see that in the modern housing struggle here between people and automobiles, the human beings are a little more than holding their own.

The Salon International de la Police has put on a policemen's show called "Le Faux dans l'Art et dans l'Histoire," devoted to the topic of counterfeiting in art and history, which deserves special mention because it is so odd and interesting. Nearly everything on display is false by wicked intent to defraud, which is why it fell into the police net—often from the hands of collectors who got fooled and complained. To begin with, it shows half a dozen patently counterfeit smirking Mona Lisas. To add to the fascination of this show, ranged upstairs in the Grand Palais, original, true works are occasionally included with the black-hearted counterfeit jobs to educate the visitors—most of us being unable to tell the difference even when it is demonstrated right under our noses. The disparity of the things falsifiers have falsified is incredible, for they are connected only by their unifying logic as deceptions concocted to get money. For instance, there are false laces—old Chantilly, Valenciennes, and so forth—that must have been as much trouble to fabricate as the originals. There is a whole library of false handwritten manuscripts and letters collected by a simple-headed French Academician—a letter from Christopher Columbus to Rabelais, one from Napoleon's little son, and even one from Sappho. There are cases of false money, which the police at first hesitated to put on view for fear of giving encouragement; false stamps; false German food-ration cards from the war; bogus antique Greek drachmas; and examples of the handiwork of the master forger named Becker, of the last century, whose spurious coins of Plautus's time, in the second pre-Christian century, are beautiful copies of the hand-struck originals. False pewter objects abound—an industry cooked up under the Second Empire, when Renaissance goblets and plates became a fad among the *nouveaux riches*. The faked pictures are, naturally, among the most interesting exhibits, especially when accompanied by museum laboratories' radiographic photos showing the deceits, increasingly difficult to practice today. The two greatest art fakes shown are famous false Vermeers made by that Dutch genius van Meegeren, who sold his works for fortunes during the war to a Dutch museum, as well as to the far less expert Hermann Göring. Yet "Christ with Martha and Mary" looks faked even to a layman, and its explanatory radiograph shows up a battle scene painted earlier behind the two sisters. But a second, smaller van Meegeren—of Vermeer's model in that familiar yellow jacket—is a slick, lovely job. Also displayed are a fake Rembrandt and a fake del Sarto, fake Italian primitives, dozens of fake late Renoirs, when his brush had grown loose and greasy, and fake Courbets, Corots, Degas, and Toulouse-Lautrecs. Historically, the greatest item offered is the Esterhazy *bordereau* of military secrets that led to Captain Dreyfus's arrest and started *l'affaire*. There is also a photostatic copy of Colonel Henry's infamous forged letter inculpating Dreyfus, the original of the Colonel's shameful confession, the letter from poor, honest Picquart that helped unravel the mystery, and many other engrossing period documents assembled from this counterfeiting of guilt that cut France in two fifty years ago. What the international police have put together in "Le Faux" is a highly interesting, cynical exhibition of human credulity and beguiling deception.

July 6

The most acclaimed theatre item in the Festival International d'Art Dramatique, at the Théâtre Sarah-Bernhardt, was unquestionably Bertolt Brecht's Berliner Ensemble, from Communist East Berlin, in his piece called "Der Kaukasische Kreidekreis," or "The Caucasian Chalk Circle." Its peculiar title refers to a chalked circle supposedly scrawled in a market place somewhere in the Caucasus, around which two women struggle before a judge for legal possession of a child in the center, each trying to pull him out of the circle to her own side. The honest Georgian peasant woman who nurtured the boy after his wicked, rich, noble Persian mother deserted him is judged the truer mother, and wins him because she chooses to cede him rather than pull at his arms as if pulling at the wings of a fly. The final morality song that accompanies the curious play gives the dialectic key to this Sovietized version of King Solomon's judgment: "Each thing belongs to the one who does it the most good." The rest of the play is far more complicated, being set during a medieval war between honest, bare-faced, ragged Georgian peasants and evil, wealthy, masked and costumed Persian nobles, and involving a dozen-odd characters, the passage of several years, many journeys, and some entirely independent folk stories full of gusty, lusty repartee—all this overrich content for the ear made coherent through its presentation as a kind of vision that gives its news direct to the spectators' astonished eyes. Brecht's play was indeed something to see—a stylized, *maniériste,* modernist stage production, *echt deutsch,* yet certainly derived from the early Moscow experimental theatre of Taïrov. The big, bare, white-hung stage was decorated on the left side only, by a severe backdrop—a succession of pendent strips of white silk painted with Chinese-looking black landscapes, constantly renewed to indicate change of scene. The peasant woman, with the boy in her arms, sometimes plodded on a treadmill to indicate her journeys, and sometimes little gray huts rolled toward her on its track to offer shelter. As for Brecht's noted theory of *Verfremdungseffekt* in acting, according to which his actors are supposed to be physically detached from their roles, so as to leave the audience's precious critical faculties free, it seemed merely to boil down to excellent stage directing, which permitted no emotional ranting and featured cold realism almost to the point of symbolism, and thereby stirred Parisian critical faculties to appreciation, if not comprehension. Accompanying the stage performance were three singers, seated on the proscenium, whose songs, to music by Paul Dessau, insufficiently recalled the famous topical manner of Brecht and Kurt Weill in their "Dreigroschenoper," the work that first made both of them internationally known, almost thirty years ago. Brecht and his wife, Helene Weigel, have organized what seems the most stimulating experimental theatre of Europe today. He appears to be the playwright most intimately troubled by the events of our epoch, and he has projected his disillusioned imagination onto the German stage as his form of relief.

It should be kept in mind that the works presented here in the Paris drama festival by almost every free nation in Western Europe, plus Fascist Spain and Red China and Iron Curtain Poland and Communist Berlin, all functioned as artistic propaganda vehicles, like the more elaborate contributions in the American "Salute to France."

July 20

For the first time since the Liberation, July 14th seemed a real *fête nationale*—a day for public pride, merrymaking, and the parading of soldiers. During the past ten years, the old July victory of the Bastille has been superseded by the June defeat of 1940 as an annual recollection, and simulated martial pomp marching down the Champs-Elysées has been a spectacle of humiliation for French eyes to look upon while French memories were helplessly remembering. Maybe a decade and a half is a span of time in which agonizing history can fade. Anyhow, throughout this present year the French seem to have been turning some invisible psychological corner and to have rediscovered themselves. At the start of the Bastille Day parade last week, cheery applause rose from the perspiring, shirtsleeved sidewalk crowds for the President of the Republic, René Coty, standing upright in his open car, and wearing evening clothes at nine-thirty in the morning, with his scarlet *grand cordon* of the Légion d'Honneur flashing in the heat wave's early hot sun, and there was also vigorous hand-clapping for the St.-Cyr cadets, in their ancient tricolor uniform—white cassowary plumes, blue pinchback frock coats, ballooning red pantaloons.

Painful present-day history also had a new treatment. France's relations with her North African possessions still being at the point of bloody insurrection, some carefully chosen colorful native troops and black majesties from the further reaches of the French Union had been summoned to appear on Bastille Day as honored participants and guests, the parade's spectacular novelty being the Garde Rouge from Dakar, riding small Arab stallions. These handsome brown men made a barbaric picture, like a group by Delacroix, transported to canter down the metropolitan avenue in their tall red *chéchias,* flowing red capes, and blue Oriental trousers, with drawn scimitar-shaped swords. There were also marching youths from military preparatory schools in the Sudan and on the Ivory Coast—the educated young generation, solemn and unpicturesque in

European white gaiters and khaki uniforms. Sitting among the diplomats in the President's reviewing stand were amazingly garbed dark visitors, the cynosure of all eyes—especially His Majesty Alohinto, King of Dahomey, wearing an incongruous gold-embroidered French Army kepi above his draped bright silk robe (but without his fancy fringed umbrella, which had been held over him when he was being presented to Mme. Coty in the Elysée Palace). The young Sultan Youssouf, of Massénya, in Chad, wrapped in white wool, wore a dignified little white cap, but the African hinterland chiefs were more savage in fancy headgear, with floral embroidery, and festooned, multicolored gowns.

The other novelties in the Champs-Elysées celebration were strictly modern—the new, top-grade French military equipment, including powerful, fast tanks, to show France's recent recovery, and, for the first time, public formation flights of the latest French jets, led by forty-eight Ouragans, screeching high in the air as they disappeared over the Louvre and followed by twelve big Mystères. The traditional night dancing in the streets seemed newfangled, too, with few *bistro* accordions breathing sentimental waltzes. Generally, they had been replaced by phonographs playing mambos. One of the grander *bals du quartier* centered around the firemen's *caserne,* a stone's throw from the Ritz, in the Place du Marché-St.-Honoré. The unusually artistic firefighters who occupy the building had draped their emptied apparatus room with painted curtains representing the old walls of Paris, had hung the ceiling with highly inflammable tissue-paper decorations, and had set up their bar in the doorway from which the hook and ladder usually emerges. The dancers were mostly the neighborhood marketmen and their families, professionally indifferent to occasional whiffs of fish rising from their adjacent stalls. It was a very animated ball.

The day the Dakar Garde Rouge was galloping as a guest in Paris was Casablanca's worst day of anti-French riots. The festering Moroccan and Algerian problems are still to be settled. Though plenty of anti-home-rule deputies had previously said the fate of France, or at least of Tunisia, was at stake, only about a fifth of the six hundred and twenty-seven deputies bothered to turn up for the opening Assembly debate on ratification of the Franco-Tunisian home-rule pact. The surprisingly large majority that finally ratified it was created by the Communists' last-minute switch, when they gave their ninety-eight votes to what they cheerfully called "the first step in liberation of an oppressed people" (though the liberation of the Communist-satellite oppressed peoples is an item the Russians have wanted to hear nothing about at Geneva). In the debate, the anti-home-rule Gaullist splinter party, the Action Républicaine et Sociale, accused Premier Faure of holding somebody else's baby, meaning that Mendès-France fathered the pact last year when he declared at Carthage that France would really start living up to her promises of reform—made years ago, and always side-stepped till now. Clever, elderly Paul Reynaud begged the deputies to be "men of 1955," meaning that colonialism is over, as, indeed, Premier Faure also stated, adding that if the Tunisians hoped for eventual independence, who could "deny this ideal," ironically learned from French libertarianism? Experts see the ratification of the Franco-Tunisian pact as a turning point in the history of the French Union—France's first surrender of power in her African territories. Since 1951, Parliament had refused to cede an inch to Tunisian nationalist aspirations. The recent change of mind may have been pushed by French public opinion, weary of bolstering French authority by force and risking another Indo-China.

Eleven large and lovely gouaches by Juan Gris, painted in 1917, then put away, and until now unknown to the public, have finally achieved the book form for which Gris intended them, as Cubist lithographs illustrating Cubist poems written in 1917 by Pierre Reverdy, who today is regarded as one of the half-dozen great living French poets. The volume has just been published, under the title "Au Soleil du Plafond," as a bibliophilic item by Tériade, editor of *Verve* and probably the only Paris editor who would lovingly risk such a refined enterprise. It took three years to prepare the volume. There are two hundred and five copies, priced at forty-five thousand francs—or about a hundred and thirty dollars—each, and worth it to collectors. The story behind the book is an odd one. According to Reverdy, in 1917 Gris and he conceived the idea of this doubly Cubist book, to contain twenty poems, which Reverdy duly wrote, and as many gouaches, of which Gris painted only eleven. The volume was accepted for publication by the art merchant Léonce Rosenberg, but the project fell through for various reasons—maybe partly because Gris was not appreciated until long after he was dead. Picasso and Braque were the Cubists who were then bought by intelligentsia collectors—when any Cubists were bought at all. Gris was lost in their shadow; his pictures started to sell only just before this last war, and then sometimes for as little as a few hundred dollars. He was, Reverdy says, a melancholy Spaniard who loved to drink coffee and dance at the artists' balls at the Bal Bullier. He was also an exile, unable to go home because he had refused to perform his military service, so when, in the mid-twenties, he felt his health was failing, he had to send to Spain for his son, Georges González Gris, who had been brought up there, to come and say farewell. Gris died in 1927. The son kept the eleven gouaches as his father had left them—in an old cardboard box. Today, the son is a chemist in a French factory that makes paint for automobiles, and is not interested in art. Three years ago, he suddenly wrote to Reverdy, asking if he knew anything about those gouaches. The present book is the result.

The eleven original gouaches are not for sale. In the book, their pure Cubism of the *belle époque* seems intact, as if exhumed in a perfect state of preservation. They bring to life once more the severe iconography of the period—the violin, the sheet music, the lamp, the bottle, the pipe, the fruit dish, and the coffeepot, related by the imagination of Gris in browns and grays, sometimes with a core of purple or blue, and occasionally with dapples of white. Reverdy saw with the same eyes, achieving in words the same strict, methodical sobriety and the same emotional essence, wrought deliberately from the commonplace. His poems appear in the book in his handwriting, lithographed, like the Gris *estampes,* by Mourlot Frères, master lithographers of Paris. In its union of poetry and painting—especially coming more than a third of a century after its native epoch—it makes a rare and interesting volume.

August 3

It is a blessing right now that France's North African holdings are not as vast as French imperialist visions used to be, because the bloody troubles in Algeria, Tunisia, and Morocco are more than the government in Paris can control, or the more moderate North African Nationalist leaders can calm, or the roused Moslem mobs can resist expanding into further bloodshed. The state of emergency in Algeria, which is in its tenth month of armed rebellion, has just been prolonged, on general principles, to next spring by Parliament. This week, Tunisia is to enter into the uncertainties of its limited home rule after more than three years of sporadic bloodletting. For the past fortnight, Morocco's events have daily filled the Paris newspapers with awful reports and awful photographs from former favorite tourist and residential cities like Marrakech, Casablanca, and Rabat, where there has been death and destruction in cafés, cinemas, and streets, with white counter-terrorists killing both whites and natives, and natives killing whites and one another—especially those favoring the whites—in what seem outbreaks of savage incoherence. The French government's only sustainers of phlegm and order appear to be the Foreign Legion, with its helicopters and tommy guns, and M. Gilbert Grandval, the new liberal French Resident-General for Morocco, imperturbably shouldering his way through rioting mobs, both brown and white, on his tour to discover what is going on down there and why.

The most prodigious summer exhibition is in the Château de Versailles. Entitled "Marie-Antoinette—Archiduchesse, Dauphine, et Reine," it is the richest evocation of her life ever assembled, and will be on view until November 2nd, the bicentenary date of her birth. This unsurpassable exhibition was largely brought about by the initiative of two amateurs (the Baronne Elie de Rothschild and the Duc de Mouchy) and one scholarly professional (Gérald van der Kemp, the curator of Versailles). It contains nearly a thousand contributions lent by the few royal families still functioning, by princes, nobles, and courtiers' descendants, by palaces, museums, and private collectors everywhere. All these items bear the burden of history, the stamp of Marie Antoinette's person or her family, her fatal follies and final tragedy. The numerous portraits are of extreme interest, starting with those depicting her on her arrival in France from Austria, when her pleasure-loving blue eyes and maidenly fresh coloring were gratefully seized upon by court artists as compensations for her lack of beauty. Then, after the decade that it took for her to lose the French nation's affection, even the temperate portraitist Mme. Vigée-Lebrun began realistically portraying her heavy, obstinate Austrian jaw. And finally (as the exhibition also shows) came the Revolutionist David's triumphant and terrible little sketch of her, riding backward in the tumbril a fortnight before her thirty-eighth birthday.

Of the exhibition's hundreds of intimate objects connected with

Marie Antoinette, and miraculously saved from the Revolution's fury, a special few frivolous or tragic items seem perfectly to sum up her life and time. Among them is the early warning letter from her mother, Maria Theresa, scolding her for her dangerously silly conduct—"more like that of the Du Barry" than the behavior proper to a young archduchess. Another illuminating sight is the Sèvres *bol-sein,* or breast cup, modelled from her bosom when she was Queen. From it, guests supped milk while she played at being a dairymaid at the Petit-Trianon. But the pièces de résistance are her court jeweller's copy, in crystal, of the famous *collier de la reine*—the mysterious, fabulous diamond necklace that, involved in a public scandal, helped overthrow the extravagant monarchy. Twenty-two of the original huge white diamonds, which were smuggled to London, have been lent by their present owner, the Duchess of Sutherland, and are on view in a simple setting. Also shown are Marie Antoinette's sapphire-and-diamond jewelry set, which was purchased after the Revolution by Napoleon for Joséphine, and has been lent now by the Comte de Paris, heir to the theoretical French throne.

Among the enriching background contributions are two unroyal portraits—one of the Queen's rather untalented dressmaker, Rose Bertin, and the other of the writer Beumarchais—and Her Majesty's copy of Beaumarchais' "Le Mariage de Figaro," which she had attendants read aloud to her at the very time when it was fomenting uprisings in Paris. On loan from the present Queen of England is the French Queen's wonderful trick clock, La Négresse—an automaton that gave the time by rolling its eyes, and also could play tunes in its black head—and there is a letter from a watchmaker named Gide (of the family to which André Gide later belonged) about repairing the Queen's so-called perpetual-motion watch, which she had dropped. The last folly displayed is the silver-fitted travelling case that was specially made for her to carry on that vain, clumsy Varennes flight from the mob. From her days as prisoner in the Temple, there is shown a small waistcoat that she embroidered for the little Dauphin—pale flowers on mourning-mauve silk—during her dreadfully idle hours there, and also the wooden spoon furnished for her meals. The final exhibit is part of a black silk stocking that she wore to her execution. It was exhumed, with her remains, in 1815.

Far more than her lethargic Bourbon husband, Louis XVI, the Austrian Marie Antoinette still represents to the French the last of

France's *ancien régime,* and her fall the beginning of modern times. The impressive Versailles exhibition being the first of its kind, Paris papers have run serious articles asking whether it will make today's Fourth Republic children love or hate her. Nancy Mitford, who is a resident of Paris, reported on the exhibition for the London *Sunday Times* and stirred up a hornets' nest by writing, "To me, Marie Antoinette is one of the most irritating characters in history. She was frivolous without being funny, extravagant without being elegant; her stupidity was monumental." Though she duly added, "When all hope was gone, she became an exemplary figure," not only were there protesting letters to the *Sunday Times* but she herself received hundreds from the French (from indignant vicomtes, from pious, elderly provincial royalists, and also from obviously unreconstructed Vichyites), oddly deploring "the fate of our dear Queen"—small, if significant, leftover contributions to France's confused political tableau of today. According to history, Marie Antoinette's last remark was to her executioner, on the scaffold, when she accidentally trod on his foot and said, *"Monsieur, je vous demande excuse. Je ne l'ai pas fait exprès."* ("Excuse me, sir. It was not intentional.") As *Le Figaro Littéraire's* critique on the Versailles exhibition concluded, it was an apology that she might well have made to the entire French nation.

August 17

The Bibliothèque Nationale's exhibitions built around great French writers from the past are noted for their exhausting effect on the visitor, the material being so complete, stimulating, and irresistible that it takes hours to see it. The present exhibition, honoring the bicentenary of the death of the Duc de Saint-Simon, France's amplest secret memorialist and most illuminating historical gossip, is even more special. On view for the first time in a century are the eleven elegant calf-bound portfolios of his original "Mémoires," written in his swift, legible script and adding up to forty-three volumes of print in their complete modern edition, which true Saint-Simonites, by skipping the dull patches, still read like a serial whose satisfying end they already know. Among the rich memorabilia, the Bibliothèque features his famous portrait, showing his wide, observing eyes and doglike short nose, tilted to catch the scent of news, along with portraits of those whose news he secretly wrote about, such as old Louis XIV and his frigid Mme. de Maintenon. A small, frail nineteen-year-old ducal officer off at the wars, he hurried in from a Rhineland post one evening, sat down in his tent, and suddenly began writing. From then on, he kept notes on everything and everybody, and at forty-eight he started refining them into his memoirs ("I was born in the night of the fifteenth and sixteenth of January, 1675, of Claude, Duc de Saint-Simon, peer of France, and of his second wife, Charlotte de l'Aubépine, only child of this bed.") He died at eighty in his rundown house in Paris, in debt for the candles used for his night-and-day writing, disgraced, and dismissed from the court at Versailles, where he had lived for thirty years, summing up its intrigues, its history, and its dominant personages; covering the elderly Louis XIV, the Regency, and the child King Louis XV; and mentioning seventy-three hundred and fifty people by name, often devastatingly. He had a fetishist's worship for court etiquette—such as the precise angle for a noble's bow—revered chastity, unpopular at the time, and genealogy; organized and wrote about his dangerous campaign against the King's legitimatized bastards; was against the King's persecution of Protestants and against his Ministers' bankrupting taxation of peasants (and dukes); and was received only three times in royal private audience. The King told him he talked too much, having no idea that what he was writing would be far worse.

Chateaubriand, Stendhal, and Sainte-Beuve were the first modern writers to appreciate the "Mémoires," which eventually influenced Proust, who applied the Duc's passion for etiquette and genealogy to the Guermantes, and took something of his overloaded syntax and style. Today, the "Mémoires" are still appealing, because, along with events, grave or gossipy, Saint-Simon supplied realistic, scintillating word portraits, the first in French literature. Of Mme. de Castries he wrote, in part, "She was a quarter of a woman, a kind of unfinished biscuit, very small . . . with no backside, bosom or chin; very ugly. . . . She knew everything—history, philosophy, mathematics, and dead languages . . . was cruelly malicious and polite." And of the Prince de Conti, he wrote, "This highly agreeable man loved nothing. He had and wished to have friends as one has and wishes to have furniture." Illness and deformities fascinated him, and he reported on all aspects of them—on Pontchartrain's glass eye, on the Duc de Bourgogne's crooked shoulder, on the Duc de Vendôme's syphilis, on the Chancellor's dropsy, on one royal bastard's indigestion and another's apoplexy, on the royal mistresses' miscarriages, and on the King's fatal gangrene.

Some new books on Saint-Simon have just appeared in connection with his bicentenary, but the best seems still to be "Saint-Simon par Lui-Même," by François-Régis Bastide, which appeared year before last. It is one in a satisfying cheap series of generously illustrated pocket books on great French writers. They are written half *"par lui-même"*—that is, by the great writer himself, through quotations from his works—and half by the modern critical commentator, who in this case is lively, amusing, and expert. The little Duc having been the first gossip columnist, it seems strange that Bastide's volume has not been put into English for Anglo-Saxon gossip-column lovers of today.

August 30

Last week, after years of French inattention to swelling Moroccan political demands, French bullets furnished the first rapid reply Moroccans have ever received from a French government. In repressive measures carried out by the military governor of Casablanca, a thousand natives, more or less, were shot around Oued Zem, in classic punishment of roughly ten to one for the eighty-eight white French colonials barbarously massacred in and around that settlement during the horrible uprisings that started on August 20th. *"Au Maroc, Messieurs, le temps c'est du sang"* ("In Morocco, sirs, time means blood") was the warning earlier given the French by Gilbert Grandval, Premier Faure's liberal Resident-General there. To his forceful mind, haste was finally vital for the French if they were to work out a rational accord with Moroccan Nationalists that could both protect French interests and forestall the sanguinary, fanatic violence otherwise due on August 20th. August 20th was the anniversary of the day two years ago when the then Foreign Minister, Georges Bidault, let the pro-native Sultan Sidi Mohammed ben Youssef be deposed and bundled off to exile in Madagascar with a small selection of wives. There ben Youssef became for the Moroccans what Habib Bourguiba, exiled in France, had become for the Tunisians. The ex-Sultan, a fairly worldly Moslem, was transformed into an anti-French martyr and national symbol—something the Moroccan independence movement had lacked until the French ironically supplied one, to be used as a wild rallying cry for this year's significant August 20th anniversary. After the installation of his successor—an obscure, elderly pro-French puppet, Sultan Sidi Mohammed ben Moulay Arafa, regarded as illegitimate by most Moroccans and especially by the Istiqlal, or Independence, Party and its followers—Moroccan affairs worsened to the point where Faure, who shared Mendès-France's North African reform ideas (for which Mendès-France was thrown from power by Parliament, whose majority deputies then paradoxically chose Faure to succeed him), sent Grandval to Morocco to make a first-hand report, complete with advice. Grandval's proposals practically duplicated Mendès-France's. And the powerful anti-reform colonial diehard interests and their lobby of conservative deputies, who had defeated Mendès-France and his projects, duplicated their success by defeating Grandval and his plan. Even after the fatal August 20th that he had prophesied, his reform policies were still unacceptable last week to the section of Faure's Cabinet that misnames itself the Moderates. (No French political group today ever calls itself conservative, let alone reactionary.) To save his government from falling in defeat in its turn, though its usefulness and reputation are already much weakened, Faure has just offered to trade a couple of heads—the head of Grandval, who had already offered to resign as Resident-General, to placate *les Modérés,* in exchange for the turbaned head of Sultan ben Moulay Arafa, supposedly ready to oblige by abdicating, to placate Moroccan Nationalists, who demand the return of Sultan ben Youssef. But old ben Moulay Arafa, chosen because he was presumably so malleable, has twice declared that he will not give up his "divine mission" as head of the Moslem faith. This has been a shock to the conference of French and Nationalist leaders now going on at Aix-les-Bains, since the throne, as the French have discovered too late, is the spiritual and temporal keystone of Moroccan unity. There may be another shock, and possibly another bloody upheaval in Morocco, when the liquidation of Grandval is formally proclaimed to the natives. He is the Frenchman they have learned to trust.

In the interim, whatever happens this week in the way of a Franco-Moroccan accord will be too little and too belated. As *Le Monde* severely stated, the Moroccan problem, "at the rate it has been allowed to rot away," can result now only in some sort of compromise, which will be "neither glorious nor sufficient." Parisian journalists and cameramen sent down to cover the sudden Moroccan campaign (a reporter and a photographer for *France-Soir* and an N.B.C. television-movie photographer were murdered in the uprisings) furnished descriptions and photographs of the anomalies of Moroccan life that were news to many French. In text and pictures they showed the modernity of the French cities and towns, with their up-to-date whitewashed concrete, and, outside them, the anachronistic native Moslem rural tents, made of tree branches and shaped like wigwams. Barrett McGurn, covering the uprisings for the Paris edition of the New York *Herald Tribune,* gave Americans here the most effective picture of those brush habitations from Morocco's nomad past. It is, he said, "as if the Indians had stayed on in New York, still maintaining their ancient tribal ways, still brooding about scalping parties, never merging into the modern world of subways and automobiles."

The famous creators of modern painting in the Ecole de Paris, having grown old—as, indeed, modern painting has itself grown old—are disappearing. First Derain, then Matisse last fall, and now Fernand Léger are gone, leaving behind only Braque, Rouault, and Picasso. Léger, always an active, resolute man, died quickly of a heart attack, aged seventy-four, in his country studio outside Paris, in the valley of Chevreuse. As a young man, he early came under the influence of Cubism, which he turned into a version irresistibly called Tubism. In the First World War, he served with the artillery, designing breechblocks for guns, and he was thereafter obsessed with the cylindrical shape of gun barrels. Fascinated by the constructive aesthetics of machinery, he not only applied the patterns of mechanics to his compositions, which frequently featured bicycles, but mechanized the human figure to match. He was the one major French artist who was influenced by, and found himself perfectly at home in, the United States, and during the last war he lived in New York, where he found "the glorification of the machine." (As early as 1924 he had made a curious, interesting movie called "Le Ballet Mécanique," which starred the movements of pistons and other pieces of machinery.) Back in France after his American period, he contributed a huge gay mosaic, interpreting the Litany of the Virgin, to the famous modernist village church of Assy, in Haute-Savoie, and he recently designed a brilliant series of stained-glass windows for the church at Audincourt. Léger's beautification of these churches, which were also decorated by other leading modern masters, was part of the aesthetic scheme originated by the late Père Couturier, the intellectual Dominican who wished to use the greatest living artists for the Church's glory—regardless of what some worshippers called their unholy style—just as the great Italian churches used artist geniuses in the Renaissance.

An extraordinarily sober evaluation of Léger by the Paris art critic André Chastel has just appeared here as an obituary—one that might well make the artist turn in his grave. Chastel said, in part, "From 1910 on, his views of cities with smoke like zinc, his country scenes incised as if by a wood chopper, his still-lifes made as if of metal, clearly showed what always remained his inspiration: the maximum hardening of a world of objects, which he made firmer and more articulated than they are in reality. Sacrifice of color and nuance was total, and line was defined with severity and a well-meaning aggressiveness, reflecting his violent, cold, Norman temperament. This revolution he consecrated himself to seemed rather simple—the exaltation of the machine age, which, after 1920, dominated the Western world. . . . To some huge canvases of perfected articulation, painted between 1925 and 1930, Léger brought a tonic richness that summed up the century. . . . Any definition of his art, whose energy and tension were based entirely upon the decision to be modern, makes clear his art's limitations." Léger's funeral, held in his village studio, where a half dozen of his Tubist pictures, on easels, were placed like mourners behind the flowers around his bier, was held under the auspices of the Communist Party, of which he was a member. The funeral oration was given by Etienne Fajon, secretary of the Party, which, Fajon said, Léger had "loved with all his heart and served with all his might."

There seemed no special rush about reading the now completed first two volumes of Paul Léautaud's "Journal Littéraire"—it may eventually cover fifty years of his diary notes—since the first volume starts with 1893 and the second, published a few months ago, ends with 1909. The author, now eighty-three years old, was born the illegitimate son of a prompter at the Comédie-Française; as a little boy, he sat in the prompter's box, soaking up the French classics, and at thirty-five he became what he remained for many years—the ill-paid, rather obscure drama critic of the well-known Paris magazine *Mercure de France*. He burst out as a public figure five years ago, when someone had the bright, dangerous idea of putting him on the radio for weekly reminiscences about the homeless cats he has loved and collected in his life. His interpolated reminiscences about his former mistress of twenty years, whom he called *"le fléau"* ("the scourge"), were so pertinent that he was cut off the air, and censored records were made in advance for the rest of his causeries. Piquant selections from his diary, describing amorous quarrels, and especially reconciliations, as late as his sixtieth year, all related with the egotism and candor that he chose as his literary standards, were then suddenly featured in such leading Paris monthlies as *La Table Ronde, La Parisienne,* and *La Nouvelle Revue Française.* His démodé libertinage, his sharp, intelligent pen and tongue, his poverty, cats, steel-rimmed glasses, pixie face, and crowning antique tweed hat belatedly made him a temporarily popular, cross-grained old star in the drawing rooms of Paris intelligentsia, and Cartier-Bresson photographed him, articles featured him, and an issue of *Le Point,* a provincial intellectual magazine, devoted an entire number to him. Not long ago, when an old friend of his was finally being received into the Institut, Léautaud, who had no invitation, turned up for the fashionable ceremony in that hat and a pair of carpet slippers, and carrying a string bag filled with raw meat for his cats. He was refused entrance, and, to the delight of the journalists assembled for the Institut event, gave his uncensored opinion of academic honors generally, some of which could even be printed in the next day's newspapers. For years he has lived, for his cats' sake, in an old house with a garden, now his animal cemetery, in the suburban town of Fontenay-aux-Roses.

Unwittingly, he gave a key to the interest his journal has today for the literary French by early noting in it "the slavery of writing down one's daily ideas and happenings." The result is a serialization of a life and a period that both ensnares and alarms present-day readers. His close friends, if he really had any—his long poverty made him gauche and timid—were Rémy de Gourmont and Marcel Schwob. His acquaintances included Pierre Louÿs, Catulle Mendès, Jarry, Péguy, Mirbeau, Redon, and François Coppée. His chief enemy was Huysmans. In 1903, Léautaud published a little masterpiece of a novel, "Le Petit Ami." It went on sale the same day as Zola's book "Vérité," which by night had sold forty-one thousand copies. "Le Petit Ami" sold less than three hundred in two years, and today is worth a hundred dollars a copy, if you can find it. He loathed Flaubert, calling him "a day laborer of style," and saying that anyone could have written "Madame Bovary" if he worked hard enough. He despised Anatole France as a vulgarian, and adored Stendhal, whose tomb in the Montmartre cemetery he visited to thank him for having written "Lucien Leuwen." Léautaud's own writings scandalize by their candid verbal accuracy only when dealing with his many mistresses, his physical passions, his parents, and anybody's deathbed. A lonely egotist, he wrote in his journal, "My egotism is so natural that I am all that interests me. If I had to write about a table, I would still find the means to speak of me."

November 9

In the past week, Paris has experienced the warmest, sunniest, most beautiful November days since 1899. The only familiar climate has been that of French political storms. Yet even the constantly shifting, bloody insurrectional tempests that swept over Morocco during the last three months, threatening the unity of the North African empire, on which France still sets such store and pride, have now subsided in a peculiar calm, thanks to the return to the Sherifian throne of Sultan Sidi Mohammed ben Youssef, who is right back where he started from when he was exiled two years ago, but with all this summer's burned villages and savage assassinations, bitter mutual recriminations on the part of natives and whites, and incalculable loss of French prestige lying vainly in between, like events that might as well not have happened, since they only circled back to their own beginnings.

The death of Maurice Utrillo from pneumonia, at the age of seventy-one, finally ended his lifelong practice of what could be called automatic painting, a manual reflex of genius that first made its way to canvas through a vinous cerebral haze. He was an alcoholic at the age of ten, and the illegitimate son of a remarkable woman, Suzanne Valadon, a circus acrobat who turned artists' model for Toulouse-Lautrec, Renoir, Degas, and even Puvis de Chavannes. They, recognizing her talent, encouraged her to paint. Maurice was charitably adopted by a chance passerby in her life, Don Miguel Utrillo, who was reputedly a Spanish expert on El Greco. By the time Maurice was eighteen, alienists were advising his mother to lock him up with a paintbox in order to avoid having him shut up in an asylum. Under her home teaching (though her forte was female nudes), in 1902, at the age of nineteen, he began an amazing series of fine paintings in grays, blues, and browns—the visionary pictures of Paris, falsely seen as a provincial town, that were his peculiar invention. These still fetch high prices, as do the paintings of his famous white period, dating from 1908, in which the dark cobblestone streets of Montmartre look purified by snow. In 1921, mother and son held a joint exhibition. By 1924, in spite of almost two decades of intermittent confinement in jails, prison hospitals, and the Asile Ste.-Anne, he had made his name far more famous than hers. There was just enough coarsening of his subtle palette by this time to give him a vital success. His prices rocketed. Over the years, he became the Paris tourists' favorite painter. He painted Paris churches and streets that he had never seen, drawn from postcards, carrying bogus realism into a flight of the imagination. Fake Utrillos appeared on the market, some supposedly painted by the second husband of his devoted mother; his café quarrels were alarming. Sober, he was docile, and said nothing of consequence but painted on order, with an obedient, if lessening, genius. Before his marriage to Mme. Lucie Pauwels, widow of a Belgian banker, his mother and her young second husband became his managers and provided him with fine cars, a country château, and a splendid Paris studio, to keep him out of bars. Since he was valuable and helpless, everyone's effort was to save him. Final salvation and sobriety were arranged for him by his wife, but too late. Only a few months ago, he was still repainting, as if in a daze, his most popular Montmartre scene, the Sacré-Cœur. A unique movie sequence of him at this work was made for Sacha Guitry's forthcoming film, "Si Paris M'Etait Conté." Art critics here rated him, at his apogee of delicate color and nostalgia, as one of France's great city *paysagistes*. Even after he had outlived himself, he was cherished as a mysterious artistic automaton and the last real bacchic bohemian of Montmartre.

Henri Cartier-Bresson is the only photographer who has ever been honored by a one-man exhibition in a national museum here. At the Pavillon de Marsan, in the Louvre, four hundred of his most notable pictures, many of which make up his two new volumes, "Moscou" and "Les Européens," are now on view. They are the first of his works to be published in bound form in France since his famous volume on China in transition, "D'Une Chine à l'Autre," which had a preface by Jean-Paul Sartre. Cartier-Bresson's unfailing historical intuition—which has led him to keep dates, prophetically sensed in advance, with world events and changes, so that he was able to be present to take their pictures—makes his current exhibition a great general contemporary record of our time, sensitively seized by one man's eye and his camera lens. In it, his snapshots, magnified to the size of paintings, become amazing modern portraits of humanity and its background scenes, both private and public, over the past few years, showing what people have done to each other in war, or what has luckily escaped history and remained a perfectly patterned agricultural landscape, such as a Korean rice field or a Greek olive grove; showing continuous proofs of the rebuilding of existence, if only through the presence of Spanish children playing in architectural ruins, or French wine-growers laying down their vintage for the years to come, or Parisian lovers, hand in hand, smiling at the future, or old Russian women praying in church, still planning as far forward as Heaven itself. It is the intimate Moscow pictures, taken last year, before the official affability between East and West set in, that visibly satisfy Parisians' most acute curiosity. The French are not born travellers; Cartier-Bresson has travelled for them, bringing back to the walls of the Louvre what he calls "the decisive moment" of varied national existences, when thousands of people, singly or grouped, unconsciously furnished him, if only for an instant, with those perfect physical compositions which make great pictorial art, and which, with an artist's eye, he seized, and in that instant made permanent.

The battle now going on between ex-Premier Mendès-France and Premier Faure for the leadership of their Radical Socialist Party, which they started splitting in two, each with astonishingly fine speeches, at the Party's Salle Wagram National caucus last week, is really a fight for the leadership of France next year, after the new elections. If effective electoral laws are not passed first, the ungovernable kind of Parliament that sits right now will be sitting then, and, as usual, nobody will lead France except in fits and starts.

December 7

Till now, post-war French governments have collapsed with such ease that their twenty falls in ten years constituted the major connecting parliamentary history of the Fourth Republic. Last Tuesday's twenty-first fall became a harsh crash, through the consequent dissolution of Parliament itself—for the first time since May 16, 1877, a date made memorable by the unpleasant, autocratic Marshal de MacMahon, then President of the Third Republic. After Premier Edgar Faure's government was overemphatically voted from power the other night, there was a long moment of fatigued silence, and no emotion, no hate, no grief—Faure being a chilly sort of leader—such as made the impressive climax to the fall of Pierre Mendès-France and his government last February. That was the occasion on which Faure started his astonishing rise to fame. As the Mendèsist junior Premier, he set up his government to carry on the policies of his fallen chief, and ended it trying to drive him into the wilderness.

In this struggle, Faure has won. Mendès-France—and maybe France herself—has lost. Instead of winning by overthrowing Faure that final Tuesday, the Mendèsists lost through somebody's overshooting—*une erreur de tir,* as it was sportingly called here. Somebody arranged that seven more anti-Faure votes should be cast than were needed for a simple defeat, and thus made the anti-government majority—by six votes—greater than half the total roll of the Assembly. (Ironically, a similar too heavy parliamentary majority overthrew Mendès-France himself ten months back.) Mendès-France is the only anti-Marxist who has ever bothered with youth, the future of France. He calls his new movement the Front Républicain, to distinguish it from the Front Populaire idea, which would include Communists.

After the terrific sensation caused by Faure's dissolution of Parliament, Mendès-France achieved a second-best sensational riposte by having Faure expelled from the Radical Socialist Party. In France, party expulsion leaves a politician as disgraced and homeless as an Englishman who has been pitched out of his club. With all these melodramatic surprises erupting here, the front pages of the Paris newspapers have looked like chapters from serialized thrillers. The episode the Parisians liked best was the Assembly's being booted out, for Parliament is mostly a despised institution today. Among the excitements have been the violent denunciations of Faure's dissolution order as a reactionary plot, an anti-democratic *coup de force,* and a piece of political chicanery that served him rather than the nation for whose aid it should have been intended.

Mendès-France has also been painfully criticized—at least in private—by some of his too exalted followers of last year. He has been reproached by them for the disillusioning, irascible demagogy he has displayed in *L'Express,* the Mendèsists' weekly paper, where, in his brief signed editorials, he has fulminated about "tricked elections," "guilty men," and "a plot against La Patrie." Perhaps the worst of the many ill results of his and Faure's destructive struggle is that the toga of Mendès-France seems to have slipped, or at least to be showing discouraging signs of wear and tear.

December 20

This must be the funniest election campaign—unfortunately reflecting the dire gravity of the whole parliamentary situation—that either of the two modern Republics of France ever saw. It is as if the nation's former genius for old-fashioned farce were finally taking over the nation's politics, which have too long invited it. The fact that the campaigning to elect an entire new Assembly on January 2nd is restricted to a single month makes for a ludicrous situation in itself, and it is complicated by the uproarious confusion of five thousand-odd candidates struggling for five hundred and forty-four deputies' seats on nearly a thousand electoral lists presented by twenty-eight national political parties and scores of minor local groups. It is this overcrowding and hustling that gives the comic touch—this frantic haste of mobs of politicos, all on the run after being caught short, all spouting speeches and promises as they hurry in and out of the public view in a helter-skelter of cross-directions and cross-purposes. Invectives are being hurled, and even objects. While being televised at a country political meeting the other night, ex-Minister and present candidate François Mitterrand was hit on the nose by a pear, and bled freely before the camera. Already eleven of the national political parties have dropped from sight, as if they had fallen through a trapdoor. Even the names of the fantasy midget parties that only Frenchmen could father seem unusually odd this year. One outside Paris that has half a dozen candidates running is called the Witness of Christ Party, and is politically opposed to people's taking medicine. Another party calls itself the League of Consumers in Favor of Lowering the Cost of Living and Stabilizing the Franc. Still another, more vengeful, is named Social Solidarity

Against Former Deputies. The most optimistic little party is simply called the Fifth Republic.

It was well known in advance that Mendès-France would lead a new Left—his Republican Front—in a try for a majority to effect the vitally needed reforms in whatever sort of Parliament is hatched out in 1956. Nobody realized that a new extreme Right was also about to burst into the campaign—the Poujadistes. Pierre Poujade will be recalled as the husky, belligerent, thirty-five-year-old shopkeeper from St.-Céré, in southwestern France, who last winter roused a popular revolt among other little businessmen against paying what they call unfairly high taxes. Since then, his followers have cut their political eyeteeth pretty well all over France by getting into the Chambers of Commerce, which are elected bodies here. This month, exactly like Hitler when he was still a Fascist débutant, Poujade is shouting that his party is neither Left nor Right but only national. It is also anti-Semitic, anti-Communist, anti-democratic, anti-parliamentary, and pro-violence. A week or so ago, at a hysterical mass meeting, Poujade thundered, "When we come to power, if the deputies don't do their job right, we will hang them!" At Mendès-France's Salle de la Mutualité meeting for women voters, the well-organized Poujadiste strong-arm squad of hecklers yelled, "Mendès to the scaffold, Mauriac to the jackals [because of his democratic Moroccan sympathies], and Herriot to the Panthéon!," this last meaning that the octogenarian Radical Socialist leader is so old and dead that he should be entombed. At Poujade's Salle Wagram meeting, on mounting the platform he immediately did his regular striptease act, pulling off his windbreaker, scarf, and sweater and then rolling up his shirtsleeves, before firing his hearers with the declaration that "Our ancestors cut off the head of a king for doing far less than the men who govern us today!" As enthusiasm mounted, a woman devotee screamed, "Poujade is Jeanne d'Arc and Henri Quatre both!" In the tough style he affects, he finally called not only on his shopkeepers but on underpaid workmen and the ever dissatisfied peasantry to vote the Poujade ticket, "to save their guts and France." It is now expected that the Poujadistes will elect about ten deputies to the new Parliament—not bad for a beginning.

Registration has been the heaviest in the history of the two modern Republics, and the voting should be, too. Once more, it is Mendès-France who has galvanized the whole political scene. His speeches are dramatic and damning against the late government leaders. He is still attacking the curse of drink in France, and "the kingdom of alcohol" ruled by the industrial-alcohol trust. Though middle-class Left liberals are always saying that what France needs is a leader, some now say that they are afraid to vote for leader Mendès because he may be too autocratic. Others, being anti-Semitic, say that they are afraid to vote for him because voting for him, a Jew, will increase anti-Semitism here—a fine case of upside-down logic. The best anti-Communist political wisecrack of the campaign was made by Socialist chief Guy Mollet, who said disdainfully, "French Communists are not Left, they are East." Conservative Antoine Pinay, addressing a small, refined group of youths in a salon at the Hotel Lutétia, opened by remarking, "Someone has said that politics is the art of making possible that which is necessary." "Valéry—Paul Valéry, the poet—said it!" one listening youth shouted impatiently. Pinay, who was pinch-hitting for his more important and now ultraconservative running mate Edgar Faure, also told the young men, "Military service is out-of-date—just a few months of it will be enough." As further flattering planks in the Faure youth program, he promised them scholarships and organized part-time jobs, poverty among university students and the need to earn while studying being a terrible education problem here. He also promised government loans so that youth could get married while still young enough to enjoy marriage, with the loans being repaid in part, on a sort of installment plan, by the birth of each child. Oh, this is undoubtedly an extraordinarily entertaining French election campaign!

1956

January 5

The Tour Eiffel caught fire the day after the elections. It was something that no one in France expected and that could hardly be believed when it happened—and it was a perfect symbol of the election results. Nobody had been able to imagine anything worse than that the new Assembly should turn out to resemble the old one. Neither politicians nor voters had any advance notion of the curious monster they were creating between them, with its body paralyzed in the middle and with swollen, extraneous wings on its left and right. It was the wild success of the Poujadists that upset all predictions and calculations and has left in its destructive wake nothing but explanations as strange as the victory itself. According to *Figaro,* it is now clear—too late—that the Poujadists are the myriads of little forgotten and discontented men, anti-parliamentarian and leaderless, who rose with a shout in 1951 to follow the nobilities of General de Gaulle and this year settled for the fisticuffs of the stationery-shop keeper of St.-Céré, who thus inherited de Gaulle's leadership in an illegitimacy of descent such as no previous political campaign has ever seen. There was certainly nothing secretive or hidden in the Poujadists' campaign, animated as it was by shouting hecklers at rival meetings, yells, fights, threats, and a violence of language and sentiment that echoed in every corner of France. Maybe all this deafened the Institut Français d'Opinion Publique, the French Gallup Poll, which heard nothing at all to indicate that Poujade's men would come out of their fights with fifty-one Assembly seats. It was predicted that the Communists would win a couple of dozen additional seats, but no one dreamed they would win fifty-two new ones, which makes them the dominant party, with a hundred and forty-five deputies, and, furthermore, the only established party in all France to win new seats, every other party having lost in strength. Never before in the electoral history of the four Republics have all the parliamentary parties slid downhill together this way, in a crumbling decline set going by a kick from the discontented voters, and never before have the only parties to pick up new seats been two anti-parliamentary parties.

On Tuesday night, with the returns mostly in, *Le Monde* went straight to the heart of the matter. "The problem of tomorrow" it stated, "is to ascertain whether, outside of the Communists and Poujadists, a government majority can be located." On Wednesday, two days after the election, the Communist paper *Humanité* suddenly ran an enormous headline: "VIVE LE FRONT POPULAIRE!" *Huma's* idea of the Popular Front today is a kind of Communist houseparty where everyone is welcome to stop in and make common cause against the reactionaries, and since both the Socialists and Mendès-France's adherents have refused the invitation, it now appears that the guests for whom *Humanité* is hanging out the latchstring must be the reactionary Poujadists themselves, though they are considered by everybody else the fiercest and most ignorant reactionaries now going. Nobody in the center is blind to the fact that the two parties, rigged up in an unnatural plurality, would be a terrible combination. The Faurist majority no longer exists, and the strict Mendèsists, too, are a minority. The number of Mendèsist deputies elected is probably around a hundred and fifty, and of Faurists perhaps two hundred; nobody can tell exactly, because a baker's dozen or so on each side are affiliates who defy positive categorizing until tried and proved. The only optimistic prophecy given out so far on the future of this new Parliament is that it cannot last more than six months before being dissolved.

The thing that is clearest now is the picture of the voters—of their energy and determination to express themselves, and their definite frame of mind, which is largely discontent with what they have been receiving from the government as it has been set up recently, and also over the past ten years. This is considered the only reading possible for the dwindling number of seats they gave the old-line, established French parties. It is the key reading for the big gain they gave the Communists and for the landslide sendoff they proffered the Poujadists—votes representing, to an unidentifiable degree, social protest, dissatisfaction, and hopes for change, rather than any recent flood of dialectical conversions or any great historical conviction as to Poujade's odd notion of reviving the Etats Généraux of 1789 (which, he would have discovered if he had read a little farther in Larousse, resulted in a governmental paralysis that led to the creation of a National Assembly, which is what France has now and which has long been paralyzed in its turn). This time, the voters were voting for what they thought they and France ought to have now, not someday, and for the politicians or groups most likely to be able to provide at least part of it—and, above all, for men who would get something, amost anything, done.

In an expectedly heavy turnout, over eighty per cent of the voting population went to the polls—a figure that makes American election intensities look puny. There has not been a winter national election in France since 1876, winter being considered a poor time to get people out to vote. And the day after New Year's, the biggest annual family holiday, is the worst day for an election in the whole year. Parisians who had gone off on the traditional holiday cut their pleasures short in the civic resolve, rare in any democracy, to get back and do their duty. The state railways assisted, with more than a hundred extra so-called voters' trains coming into the Gare de Lyon alone on Sunday and Monday mornings from the South—especially from the Riviera. Beginning on Monday, motor routes leading to Paris were reported thick with family cars of all grades, bringing the adults—generally accompanied by country baskets of Brussels sprouts and pale winter butter, about the only farm produce available just now—to the *urnes*. The importance of this big turnout was that it constituted a grave warning. One of the most bitterly popular slogans was *"Sortez les sortants!"* ("Throw out the outgoing deputies!"), and a hundred and forty-six of them were so thrown into political oblivion. The Gaullist Social Republican Party was almost wiped out, Bidault's M.R.P.s took a bad drubbing, and the theory and functioning of Parliament itself once more suffered a hard beating. However, according to Wednesday night's *Le Monde,* Parliament will have its new chance in the hands of the Socialists and of Mendès-France, on both of whom the majority and the government of tomorrow will depend. That can well be a lot better luck than Parliament and a great many voters deserve.

January 17

The immortal Mistinguett has finally died, at the age of eighty-two. Her obituaries were as spectacular as the finales of her prewar Folies-Bergère revues. Academician Jean Cocteau contributed one that scintillated with melancholy, like paillettes shining on her dramatic black stage gowns. "Her small face," he declared, "seemed like that of a little girl, sculptured as if by the blows of childhood. Her voice, slightly off-key, was that of the Parisian street hawkers—the husky, trailing voice of the Paris people. She was of the animal race that owes nothing to intellectualism. She incarnated herself. She flattered a French patriotism that was not shameful. It is normal that now she should crumble, like the other caryatids of that great and marvellous epoch that was ours."

Known to all France as "Miss"—pronounced "Mees"—she was familiarly tutoied by her affectionate audiences, who would shout from the back of the Casino, *"T'es belle, toi!"* It was glory. She started her career in 1890, and for forty-nine years her Parisian genius was her figure, her optimistic *brio,* her penetrating, touching voice, her thirty-two white indestructible teeth (she had them all till the end), and her million-dollar legs (always prudently covered with wool fleshings, against drafts, beneath her silk tights). In 1911, she entered the Folies-Bergère and there met young Maurice Chevalier, whose talent she perceived with her heart—as one of her obituaries stated—as well as with her acute theatre sense, and they became the great paired stars. In such songs as "C'est Mon Homme" and "J'en Ai Marre," she carried the torch of the *filles de Paris*—of the *gigolette* in the Rue de Lappe, of the sidewalk *gonzesse* and the apache *gommeuse* of Montmartre. She was not held to have advanced French culture, but between the wars she helped make Paris famous again. She was a flower seller as a little girl. Her parents were mattress makers. She was born Jeanne Bourgeois. Around 1897, she concocted her stage name of Mistinguett in imitation of a popular song called "La Vertinguette." Mistinguett loved her fame, the footlights, and her money—she earned a fortune—and was never tempted by marriage. By a liaison with a Brazilian admirer, she had a son, Leopoldo de Lima et Silva, who is now a well-known Paris doctor and was her physician on her deathbed. Colette once said of Mistinguett, "She is a national property."

February 1

The investiture of Parliament yesterday was marked by an extreme lack of enthusiasm and applause. All that anybody really knows about it and its Front Républicain government (Socialist Premier Guy Mollet and Radical Pierre Mendès-France, Minister without Portfolio, are the two men who count) is that either it may or may not last long. Nobody expects a party's programs and promises to be taken as seriously as marriage vows once an election is over, but the ten programs on which the ten political groups got their deputies elected last month contain the seeds of the kind of squabble and disagreement that has produced chaos in Parliament over the long yesterdays, and can do the same tomorrow.

February 16

For Paris, this has been the longest, coldest stretch of septentrional weather known since the first winter of the Occupation, in 1940, and for Europe in general, the temperatures have been the lowest so far endured in this century. A mosiac of ice blocks covers the Seine, and the Tuileries gardens are dazzling with snow and sunshine. One of the dangerous freaks of the cold snap everywhere in France has been the blizzard drop in temperature at night and the warmish rise in the sun the next day, often with a swing of forty degrees in twelve hours. This sort of weather has made thaws, refreezes, burst water pipes, icy streets, motor accidents, broken legs, and pneumonia the regular news.

In Paris, braziers have been set up for customers on the café terraces along the Champs-Elysées and for the city's *clochards,* or tramps, on the Place Maubert, the ragpickers' mart. A fourth of the street traffic lights froze last week, but fortunately there was nearly no traffic, even the Place de la Concorde being almost bare of cars. Shipping is paralyzed on rivers and in ports. The Seine is blocked from Rouen to the sea; coal barges are stuck fast in the upcountry canals; even at Marseille one of the port basins is frozen shut, under brilliant sunshine and the fiercest mistral gale in years. The wind has been blowing at eighty miles an hour down the Rhône Valley, and the River Saône is frozen for twenty miles around Lyon. Over last weekend, the two coldest cities in France were Strasbourg, in the north, and Limoges, toward the south, both registering only eight degrees warmer than Moscow; yesterday we heard that Mulhouse had just beaten the Moscow temperature by six degrees, having dropped to ten degrees below zero. Another weather oddity is that it has been colder on the Riviera than here in the Ile-de-France. There is skiing on three feet of snow in the streets of St.-Tropez; snowplows have cleared the roads around Cannes; after its Battle of Flowers, Nice turned into a Christmas card overnight, with the worst snowfall since 1887. Along the rest of the Côte d'Azur, the fields of carnations are so badly damaged that prices have sextupled on the wholesale flower market in Nice. Around Pau, the famous crop of early artichokes for the Paris trade has suffered, and at Arcachon thousands of dozens of the succulent *claires* oysters have been literally frozen to death in their beds. Paris vegetable prices for last Sunday's dinner leaped sky-high. Potatoes jumped from sixteen to twenty-seven francs per kilo and soup leeks from a hundred and twelve to three hundred and fifty; lettuces soared from two hundred francs to four hundred and twenty, which meant that few families could afford a salad with the weekly roast; and truckloads of fish, poultry, and meat are stalled on icy roads all over France. Mounting food prices are an added irritant that French citizens and their government could well do without right now.

Socialist politicians here are generally regarded as too intellectual, too humanitarian dialectically, sometimes too truthful, and usually too inexperienced to be practical as government leaders in a crisis—almost the only time they are ever called on. It was humanitarian and intellectual of Socialist Premier Guy Mollet, in his radio speech in Algiers, to say to the eight million native Moslems, nine-tenths of them illiterate, "I recognize your material misery, the injustices you have known, your impression of being second-class citizens, your suffering in your dignity as men." And it was certainly not practical, no matter how true, to tell the French white settlers that some of them were "an egotistical small minority" bent on selfishly preserving its financial and political superiority over the natives. The mob violence with which the white French greeted Mollet's arrival in Algiers—pelting him with eggs, stones, rotten tomatoes, and dung—was a scandalous indignity that no French

Premier apparently has ever before experienced. But his failure to make a strong speech, for all France to hear, denouncing such dangerous anti-Republican mob pressure, and his even seeming to turn the other check by declaring that the "dolorous demonstrations" had informed him of the white settlers' attachment to France and their fear of being abandoned in appeasement of the natives—these things shocked many elements in Paris, including certain members of his own government. One Paris newspaper editorial jeeringly said that French politics is not a game for choirboys. François Mauriac contributed a denunciation in *L'Express* by quoting a scholarly line from Malherbe's "Ode to Louis XIII"—"Take thy thunderbolt and advance like a lion"—and then adding, in contemptuous slang, "Alas, M. Guy Mollet did not take his thunderbolt. He took it on the nose, in the shape of rotten tomatoes."

It was known in advance of Premier Mollet's presentation of his Algerian program to Parliament, which has just begun, that his main reform for the natives—an eight-to-one majority of the population—is a promise of equality in every way with the French whites, who up to the present, for many reasons and for all the privileges, have kept the natives as a depressed minority. What the Algerian native leaders reportedly want now is no longer equality but an independent Algerian nation, in which the French white settlers will be free to live as a minority.

The price has gone up during the last few months in all the French Arab lands, and this is the week of the triple climax in France's relations with her North African holdings. The restored Sultan of Morocco, Sidi Mohammed ben Youssef, in Paris on a state visit, has already clarified for President Coty his desire for a Sherifian Empire and eventual Moroccan independence. Habib Bourguiba, leader of the Tunisian Neo-Destour independence movement, has just held talks in Paris with the French government, and now the French High Commissioner for Tunisia has arrived here to report to his government that His Majesty the Bey desires new talks with the French, which means new Tunisian libertarian demands. Bloodshed, terrorism, and a state of small, awful civil war that involves the terrorist natives and the better part of the French Army continue in all three Moslem lands. This week is of the greatest importance in statesmanship for the future of Republican France and of an importance only slightly less for her democratic allies.

* * *

Everybody—even the French, in between times—always seems to forget the terrifying indigenous French capacity for violence in language and in physical scrimmages in the melodramas of ordinary political life. The new Poujade Party, in inspiring a revival of the cry "Down with Fascism!," has rekindled all over France those fiery partisanships of Left against Right inherited from the Revolution, and the Poujadists' filibusters, arguments, and losing struggle (so far) against the invalidation of some of their deputies, because of incorrect use of the election lists, have brought a new intensity into Parliament. In the quarrels that have developed, the parliamentary language exchanged between the Poujadists and the Communists—the moderate Center kept a more civil tongue in its head—has been appalling. Deputies have called each other Hitlerite, Muscovite, gangster, stool pigeon, bandit, whore, carrion, rotter, thug, and denunciator. This week's fist fight, which broke out between the extreme Right and the extreme Left, and then involved almost the whole Assembly in a struggle either to calm the others or to manhandle them, featured bloody noses and the throwing of chairs, with peace restored only by surprise, when an overexcited madman in the visitors' gallery fired four blank pistol shots. In the four weeks this new Parliament has been sitting, this fight was probably the most important session yet held.

February 29

This has recently been a stimulating theatre season for its extreme and interesting oddities—like Little Theatre experiments—probably staged because of the success, three years back, of Samuel Beckett's "En Attendant Godot," which set a style in the peculiar. Outstanding is "Le Personnage Combattant," by Jean Vauthier, the newest avant-garde playwright, at the Petit Marigny, an upstairs theatre and workshop. It is in two fifty-minute acts, with Jean-Louis Barrault alone on the stage and talking full tilt for forty minutes of each, in what is, for once, a tour de force of brilliant, egotistical, intellectual acting. He plays a disillusioned, unsuccessful writer, come back like a soiled homing pigeon to a cheap hotel room over a railroad station—the play's elaborate sound track of whistling locomotives furnishes a kind of mechanized Greek chorus—where, years ago, he wrote his only fine pages. These he reads aloud, and in starting to expand them, as if rewriting, audibly composes his sordid history, with its noble aspirations and admitted failure—his true short story as the would-be artist of words who cannot now write his life tragedy but can only talk it, in a lonely monologue. It is the most interesting play and acting in Paris.

The other popular unorthodox playwright is Eugène Ionesco, whose use of logic—first as a vehicle of folly, then as an agent of destruction—in his playlets has given him an admirable reputation (one is never quite sure just why) among intellectual theatregoers. His present playlet, a revival from three years ago, when few seem to have seen it, is at the upstairs Studio des Champs-Elysées and is called "Les Chaises." It shows an old married couple living in some remote tower by the water. The husband still has a message of salvation to give to a world that has never listened to him, and they invite a numerous imaginary company as listeners, for whom the chairs of the title are brought onstage. The invisible guests culminate with the Emperor himself, plus an orator who is supposed to read the great message but turns out to be deaf and dumb. As part of their triumphant farewell to the also deaf world, the old couple throw themselves into the water below. Well, there you are.

March 20

One of France's many worries in connection with the rising tide of the Arabs in North Africa has been Washington's silence as to which foot it is standing on—our historic anti-colonialism or our modern anti-Soviet policy that ties us to our allies and our North African military airfields. The decisive speech just made at this week's diplomatic-press luncheon by our Ambassador, Mr. C. Douglas Dillon, has been headlined in the Paris papers for his statement that France's search for liberal solutions to insure the continuance of the French presence in North Africa "has the wholehearted support of the United States government." In thanking him for "this remarkable intervention," *Le Monde* added, "One can imagine the resistance he must have overcome in Washington"—a reference to the rumor here that the Ambassador had to fight his way up through the State Department to the President himself for permission to make any positive declaration.

This week, the independence of Tunisia has been recognized by

France, as the independence of Morocco was two weeks ago. As French colonies, they have ironically and suddenly won where Algeria, regarded as an integral physical part of France located across the Mediterranean, is in the position of our South in the Civil War in rebelling to obtain the same independence; its *fellaghas* are fighting for secession, which is illegal. The Mollet government has now reached the peak of its effort in the dual consignments it is sending to Algeria, either to enforce peace or to negotiate it. It is transporting an enormous French army to fight the rebels, and it is repeating to the natives its promises of a better new life, of more government jobs, of agrarian reform, of higher wages, of more employment, and of fair elections. Had previous French governments offered the reforms two years ago, many French parents of sons being sent to kill or be killed in Algeria feel, the present government would not now be involved in this Moslem-Christian civil war.

March 27

The Communist daily, *L'Humanité,* is now running one of those circulation-boosting competitions (first prize is a three-week trip for two to the Soviet Union) based—unfortunately, at this moment in Communist history—on the old game of questions and answers, the competition being called *"Vrai ou Faux?"* Last week, *Figaro* pulled *L'Humanité's* leg by sarcastically listing questions of its own that *Huma* might well ask, such as "Stalin was wrong for twenty-five years. True or false?" and "Stalin was tyrannical, maniacal, and sanguinary. True or false?" It is certainly true that the February attack on the Stalin myth by Moscow's Twentieth Communist Party Congress, falling on the utterly unprepared and rigorously pro-Stalin French Communist Party, was the most destructive blow the Party here has suffered since its foundation in 1920—a blow from which it staggered into a recovery, at least officially, only last week. Another obvious truth is that the French Party delegates to the Congress—Maurice Thorez and Jacques Duclos—were not warned on their arrival in Moscow of the imminent anti-Stalin coup de grâce. Consequently, the wretched Thorez made a rousing pro-Stalin Congress speech so contrary to the coming new Soviet policy that if he had made such a *gaffe* (on a quite different line, of course) during Stalin's lifetime, the genial Georgian would doubtless have had him purged the next morning. With the temporary crackup of Party discipline here over the last month, many intellectual Communists are speaking with more bitter candor than ever before. They say that the French Party has for several years been ignored by Moscow in favor of the Italian Communist Party, which is more militant, more useful, and bigger than theirs and has a more intelligent, finer-brained leader in the highly educated, intellectual Palmiro Togliatti, who comes of a university family (his brother is Dean of the Sciences Department at Genoa University) than the French Party has in the former pastry cook Jacques Duclos, who is its dominating secretary. It is thought here that because Togliatti never once mentioned Stalin's name in his Congress speech, the Italian Party had surely been warned, as too valuable to Moscow, not to let its leader make a fool of himself there and so increase the difficulties of de-Stalinizing the Italian Comrades, who, having been accustomed over long centuries to saints, were inclined to especially easy credulity where the Georgian was concerned. In canonizing Stalin, the task of the French Party propagandists, dealing with the more cynical and more agnostic-minded French workmen over the last twenty-five years, had been harder. Yet they had succeeded in instilling in them a kind of glamorous, historical, deep devotion to Stalin as a remaker of the world—a devotion like the one their grandfathers felt for the myth of Napoleon. All that is gone now.

It took the erstwhile pro-Stalin French Communist Party leaders five weeks to make up their minds to eat crow. They swallowed it whole last Thursday. In *L'Humanité's* March 23rd front-page headline, the French Central Committee hailed "LE VINGTIEME CONGRES DU PARTI COMMUNISTE DE L'UNION SOVIETIQUE" as "UNE AIDE INESTIMABLE POUR NOTRE PARTI." On an inner page was given the French Party's resolution, arrived at by the chiefs during a twelve-hour closed meeting the day before. *Huma* printed the resolution in three scant columns (in Rome, chief Togliatti, possibly better prepared, had earlier given twenty-seven columns to his crow-eating in *L'Unità*), of which seven-eighths was given over entirely to "the superiority of Communism" and its amazing recent advances in technology and production, as reported at the Twentieth Congress. Only the last fraction of the resolution mentioned Stalin. There the French Party's humiliating capitulation was printed, in what sounded like fragmentary heretical *mea culpas*—"Stalin's erroneous theories . . . harmful consequences . . . violation of Leninist principles"—with the final solemn ending "Let us fight against the cult of personality." Not only had the French Party made a cult of Stalin but it had made an even stronger cult of its own Maurice Thorez as a *fils du peuple*—handsome, strong, a miner who was a miner's son, the ideal Communist proletarian who became the French Comrades' real idol and who led them deeper into the Stalin error at the Congress of Moscow.

This has been the first Paris sight of a Slav holy man's being ruled off the international Marxist saints' calendar—the first time people here have ever seen what would have been heresy in January become revealed doctrine in March to five million French workers, supposedly the best educated and most intelligent in Europe. It has been an extraordinarily unholy spectacle to watch.

Les Concerts du Domaine Musical, a series dedicated to contemporary and often brand-new music, have filled a real want here and lately have overfilled the Petit Théâtre Marigny, the Renaud-Barrault little-theatre workshop over the Théâtre Marigny, where listeners have been packing the hard benches and sitting on the floor with a lack of old-fashioned comfort suitable to such modern, angular compositions. These are the only concerts in Paris devoted mainly to twelve-tone music, which is considered a trifle démodé by other Europeans, since they have known it since Schoenberg's early days, but which has only recently struck French youth and, indeed, many French adults. The Domaine's final concert of the season, given last week, featured in its first half the 1928 symphony of the late Austrian composer Anton Webern and six of his songs (two of them written to poems by Rilke), and demonstrated once again his amazing endowments—his conciseness, his subtlety of musical language, and his originalities, which could actually be followed even by the musical layman. Webern's music and the more satisfying romantic works of Alban Berg—his "Wozzeck," given here by the Vienna State Opera four years ago, still ranks as a memorable event—make these two dodecaphonists seem to the French today more highly gifted composers than their master, Schoenberg. Born an aristocrat and a *von,* Herr Webern, as he called himself after he turned Communist, was *chef d'orchestre* of the Vienna Workers' Symphony Orchestra for many years. (He died just after the Second World War.) In accordance with his political decision, he was dutifully styled without his *"von"* on the Domaine program. The second half of the evening was given over to "Le Marteau sans Maître," which has poems by René Char as a text. It was a mixture of occasional soprano singing and continued instrumental comment by a flute, a guitar, a vibraphone, a xylophone, and little drums like flowerpots, the music having been recently written by Pierre Boulez, the Domaine's director and the leading French twelve-tone composer. His music is purely Gallic, purely stylistic, and purely brilliant in its invention and syncopation, and it was flawlessly executed, like everything by everybody that is played at these concerts. Other composers featured this month have been the important young Italian Luigi Nono, the German Hans Henze, and the irrepressible French experimenter Olivier Messiaen, in an opus composed of birds' songs transcribed into ancient musical modes to avoid commonplace majors and minors, with diverting scholarly results. Parisians ceaselessly criticize what they call a general letdown now in the performances, audiences, and programs of their once famous big classic orchestras. The Domaine concerts appeal exclusively to lovers of extremely modern music; no one else could bear to listen to them. Their dodecaphony is so popular and the Petit Marigny so small that the same program is always given two nights in succession. The concerts receive fine critical notices and discriminatingly enthusiastic applause. These make them doubly rare in the Paris concert field today.

May 20

The violence and horrors of the war in Algeria and the divisions of opinion on it here in Paris have been profoundly worrying the French. There has even been talk of reforms that have no bearing on anything right now but represent the general malaise, the restlessness of hopes, the onset of self-criticism. There is talk of copying the American Presidential form of government, so as to have a strong elected head, instead of unstable, helpless Premiers. There is some talk of a return to the highest office of General de Gaulle, sure sign of the temporary idealism that comes with deep national anxiety—the phantom of the incorruptible strong man, who would now consent to govern only if he could start from strength, not from the weakness of the present form of government. The drab Champs-Elysées military parade that recently celebrated the eleventh anniversary of the ending of the war gave a picture of France's deprivations these last months in North Africa. There were no colonial troops in the parade. General de Lattre de Tassigny's famous Atlas Mountain *goums,* in turbans and on galloping stallions, have been enrolled in the Sultan's army in Morocco, now an independent Sherifian state, where natives have been burning each other alive. There were no regiments in red fezzes from Tunisia, also newly "independent in interdependence," where massacres have been continuing and where Premier Habib Bourguiba has just demanded the right to send Tunisian diplomats to Washington and London and to establish a Tunisian Army. There were no white-capped, bearded Foreign Legionnaires, now fighting in Algeria, where all forms of horrible death are part of the war. Men have been mutilated, children have been stabbed, throats have been cut, farmhouses and farm crops, and their owners, have been fired by torches and gasoline, with natives fighting the whites, whites fighting the natives, and some natives fighting other natives. Because, after hundreds of years, history has come to a sudden head on the south side of the Mediterranean, Premier Mollet, Socialist and pacifist by training, has been forced to do in Algeria what previous, reactionary French governments neither dared nor wanted to do. He has been making a war of pacification with one hand and, with the other, offering drastic reforms to eight and a half million roused Moslem natives, all the while also trying to preserve the existence there of the one million colonial whites—French, Italian, and numerous Maltese—for whom he and France are responsible today. Many French here in France, recalling Indo-China, think that nobody can prophesy how this racial war between two peoples at such different stages of civilization will turn out. Millions of the French in France passionately, patriotically believe in the righteousness of the war and in its victorious outcome. Other millions believe that history in the past ten years finished the colonial cycle of all Western liberal peoples (thus excluding the Russians). And still other millions are Communists, to whom the Algerian war is *une sale guerre*. Though the Communist deputies in Parliament supported Mollet's demand for special powers to fight it, they are now agitating for negotiations to stop it with a cease-fire. The forceful Robert Lacoste, Resident Minister in Algeria, has just stated that "though I promise no miracles, I have a reasonable hope that by the end of summer law and order will reign in Algeria."

What discourages so many French is that law and order have not yet started to reign in independent Morocco and Tunisia.

May 29

Eleven Frenchmen and one Frenchwoman had their throats slit last Friday by Algerian rebels a few kilometres south of Biskra, in the Sahara, the desert once featured in "The Garden of Allah," that ancient best-seller that touched on tender relations between natives and whites. Earlier in the week, outside Philippeville, two Moslem families—among them seven women and seven children, one three months old—suspected of loyalty to the French also had their throats cut by rebels, who, furthermore, decapitated their victims' chickens. Most of the Moslem students at the University of Algiers have abandoned their classes, well before their June exams, in response to a rebel slogan declaring, "Examinations make no sense today! Join the Maquis against the French!" Ten days ago, in the gorges near Palestro, seventeen out of twenty-two green French soldiers, in their third week of war, were ambushed and massacred by the rebels they were hunting. After certain Paris newspapers printed not only the names of the boys—eleven came from small towns near Paris—but the horrifying particulars of the mutilations and tortures that killed them, a wartime censorship was set up, forbidding the publication of "morbid details." Premier Guy Mollet is awaiting the results of a three-day Parliamentary debate about the Algerian situation. Grave as that situation is, he is not expected to fall, for though his Rightist political enemies think the war is going badly, no opposition party wants to be nationally responsible, as the Socialists are now, for trying to make it go better—even if any opposition party were sure it knew how. Finance Minister Paul Ramadier has just warned the public that the Algerian campaign will necessitate immediate new temporary taxes, the last adjective being the only part of the statement that sounds optimistic.

This is a cruel, fanatical, démodé Arab holy war, an intimate, hand-to-hand war of native knives and barbaric tortures, in which French helicopters supply the outstanding modern touch, a war of *petits paquets,* with the communiqués mentioning such small parcels of men as to sound ludicrous—except that they are descriptive of the endless, frittering kind of hide-and-seek, hill-and-desert war it really is. One day's communiqué last week featured engagements at Lourmel (rebel band surrounded, fourteen prisoners), Gambetta (three rebels killed), El-Kseur (nineteen rebels killed), and Aurès-Nemencha (skirmish with rebel bands, eleven wounded, two French military killed)—a total of twenty-two dead Algerians and two dead Frenchmen, at a cost of millions of francs, for that day.

The resignation of Pierre Mendès-France from Mollet's Cabinet—where, unfortunately, he had been doing nothing anyhow—brought to light again his "seven significant measures," which he announced in April, and which he still thinks can alone "save the French presence in Algeria." Practically all the French colonials there, and many Frenchmen here, think that if these measures were applied, there would be nearly no Algeria worth saving, as far as French interests go, so why shed blood for such remnants? (An increased war effort is part of the Mendès-France program.) As an economic expert, Mendès proposed the expropriation of all sizable agricultural properties, in order to turn them into small family holdings, and a fundamental reform of agricultural credit that would "extract it from the selfish hands of big owners, who have always profited at the expense of little producers." He wants raised wages, recognition of Moslem labor unions, freedom of opinion for native Arabic newspapers, and the removal of those anti-native French functionaries who from the start have kept everything in their own white hands and out of Arab reach—all this to "promote native confidence and hope in France, without which, sooner or later, we French will be evicted from Algeria and from all of North Africa." Most scandalized French politicians look upon this as a program so bold that only the daring Mendès would risk trying it out, if he should become Premier—an event they are determined not to let happen to France.

Apropos of Mendès' resignation, *Le Monde* dryly remarked that he "is not an accommodating man or at his best except as first fiddle." For the nine years between 1945 and 1954, he played no solo part in Parliament except as a constant, ruthless—and by the outside world unknown—critic of all the French governments. Upon his sudden emergence, two years ago, as France's strong man, he roused the greatest hopes and the greatest devotion—and also the greatest personal hatred on the part of many—of any new French leader of modern times. Now both the former strong men who rose to save France after the war are off the stage—de Gaulle and Mendès-France, two most complex characters, and two incalculable losses for France in her present troubled hour.

July 5

The new novel, if it can be so called, by Albert Camus—"La Chute" ("The Fall")—is fascinating, strange, and brief. It consists of two hundred and sixty-nine pages of monologue by the only character in it; is the single consequential work of fiction so far this year by any of the French intellectuals, new or old; has already achieved magnetic popularity among general readers; and ranks as an imaginative creation on the same high and unhappy level of human inquiry as "La Peste" and "L'Etranger." Called a *récit,* it is a one-voiced confessional report on the character of a former Paris lawyer named Jean-Baptiste Clamence, who, in a moral shipwreck, has come to land in Amsterdam, in a sailors' bar. A chance French visitor "of the same race"—that is, also a lawyer—runs into him there and hears the *récit.* Clamence's story contains one sole anecdote: Having always defended only noble causes in the Paris courts, where he ranked as a moral dandy in the legal profession, he is promenading alone by the Seine one night when he hears the sound of a body striking the water and then a woman's voice crying for help—a repentant suicide, whom he indifferently lets drown. From then on, choosing his helpless clientele in this low seafarers' bar, he practices his new combined professions—those of a godless priest and father confessor, a judge, and a prosecutor, who prosecutes himself ceaselessly for his crime of omission, wrings confessions from the sailors of their crimes, and judges everybody on the theory that a judge must be guilty himself to understand and assay guilt. Obviously, what Clamence has arrived at is his own version of the fall of man, of what he considers to be God (in whom he does not believe), and of man's destiny, which cannot be pure and which makes both the Deity and mankind eternally guilty. Camus's fictional monologue is thus really a philosophical dialogue with life itself—different from Malraux's heroic inquiry, yet also based on proof by noble action; different from Sartre's Existentialist answer, yet also based on man's helpless absurdity. "When we are all guilty," Clamence says, finally, with mad and subtle lucidity, "that will be democracy."

July 11

The second volume of General Charles de Gaulle's "Mémoires de Guerre," covering the years 1942–44, has now been published. It is selling less well than the first volume, which became a best-seller largely through public curiosity, but its high literary style, matching de Gaulle's exalted patriotism—and, indeed, his physical stature, as if the latter permitted him a superior, lonely view—allows this second record to become a classic, indifferent to popularity. His historical position was strange and unique, like his Gothic nature and vision, and what he records is as individual as his experiences. "As for human relations," he writes poignantly, "my lot has been that of solitude." The memoirs are, signally, his story of his and France's history. They lack the universality and humanity that could perhaps be characterized as the genial reek of cigars—part of the smoke of the democratic battle—which hangs over Sir Winston Churchill's books on the same war. De Gaulle's aim as leader of the Resistance is summed up for himself and for his comrades of that time in the sentence "We bring back to France independence, the Empire, and the sword." A few days ago, when asked by a French journalist to make a statement on the present situation in the French Empire, de Gaulle said merely that he had made so many statements over recent years that a new one would add nothing and have no effect. This is tragically true, and the sadder for being stated by him.

September 5

The gravity of the Suez Canal situation was not lightened here by the Compagnie Universelle du Canal Maritime de Suez's making a fool of itself. Ten days ago, the company's main office, which is in Paris, mailed a check for a hundred thousand francs (about two hundred and eighty dollars), accompanied by a mealymouthed but indiscreet letter, to the Progressiste morning newspaper *La Libération,* which promptly printed photostats of both on its front page and ran a biting, jocular editorial that should have made the faces of the French stockholders in the Canal Company turn scarlet. The letter, which was written in the first person and bore the rubber-stamped signature of the *secrétaire général* of the Paris office, said, in effect, that ever since the Egyptian government nationalized the Canal, the company had had to issue press communiqués and hold press conferences aimed at "reëstablishing the truth and enlightening public opinion about the company's point of view" and went on, "I have not failed to realize that in some cases the publication of this information may have entailed expenses that I consider it legitimate for us to bear in part. In consequence, please find enclosed a check for one hundred thousand francs, as a contribution toward your August expenses. It is understood that our part in meeting them can be continued if the eventuality arises." The letter closed with the optimistic phrase "Hoping you will agree with us," as if it were a perfectly ordinary office communication, and not dynamite.

Paris was scandalized and disgusted. For the first time, the Canal Company lost face with some of its bourgeois and conservative admirers. The next morning, *La Libération* ran an editorial that righteously fulminated against this "attempt to bribe the press" and demanded to know why the rest of the Paris papers—which, the editorial writer said, must also have received checks—had remained mum, and it also printed on its front page what the editor called "the Suez Canal Company's confession," which did not amount to much. In it, the *secrétaire général* simply said that the whole thing was a regrettable mistake—that the company had thought it had to pay for news in newspapers, just as it did for its financial announcements on the stock-market pages, because it was "inexperienced in dealing with the press." This was a breathtaking admission of incompetence at a moment when the company's fate and that of the Suez Canal, which it has administered for nearly a hundred years, were making front-page news all over the world.

The most unexpected feature of the Suez crisis has been the continuing lack of nuance in the way the French react to it. Uncharacteristically, all the French seem to have managed a real union, for once—all militant, aroused, convinced, and all behind the government in its taking of what it openly calls its "extremely firm stand" of being prepared for military action, if necessary. All the French, that is, except that pro-Communist quarter of them that has been cheering for Colonel Nasser. Aside from the small Communist press, all the papers you read, which ordinarily feature dissenting convictions, and all the French people you see, whom you formerly listened to for their differing opinions, have been printing or saying essentially the same thing, in an impressive sincere chorus of extreme national sentiment. There has been no moderate note, no voice of opposition. For the past three weeks, those members of the American colony here who have wanted to know at least what opposition sounds like—and who have also realized that the Suez struggle concerns England no less than it concerns France—have been reading the London *Economist* and the Manchester *Guardian*. On Monday of this week, as the Cairo Conference opened, these publications were finally given major French recognition, in a *Figaro* editorial, as "two of the principal organs of the British press, the most notable weekly and the most respected daily of Great Britain," but both of them, unfortunately, "partisans of resignation"—that is to say, against immediate shooting and in favor of trying to end with nothing louder than words the sudden Mediterranean dilemma that history has appallingly brought to pass.

Paris is united principally by what it calls "the Munich complex." It is haunted by its twenty-year-old memories of the Führer and the nationalized Rhineland, which recently led to Foreign Minister Pineau's anguished inquiry "Is it not our duty to stop Nasser immediately?" Nasser is considered a Fascist here, and is automatically treated as a psychotic, rather than a politician. His Fascistic paranoia seemed proved to the French when, like the Führer after the Rhineland annexation, he turned toward Russia as his next move. It is to prevent his Pan-Arabianism from igniting the world the way Hitler's Pan-Germanism did and starting a great war that France appears willing to risk a small war. That usually reserved evening journal *Le Monde* declared in its Monday-night editorial, "The idea is firmly held here that stepping back now could constitute a more fearful menace for peace [than forward action]. To this is added the belief that the risk of the conflict's spreading would be graver in a few months, when the United States (its Presidential election over with) would have fewer motives for staying out."

While the talking at the Cairo Conference was getting started, the French began to figure out what they would have to face if, owing to the Suez crisis, gasoline should be rationed, or even cease to exist altogether—imaginatively suffering in advance that nightmare in which one tries to run but cannot move. France has a three-month supply of gasoline on hand, two-thirds of it in reserve tanks. The National Printing Press has denied that it has received a government order to print gas-ration coupons, adding that even if it had been so instructed, it has no watermarked official paper to print them on. The only good gasoline news is the recent announcement by the Compagnie de Recherches et d'Exploitation Pétrolières au Sahara that oil has been found in the Sahara Desert, at Edjellé and Tiguentourine. As late as a few years ago, when France still had a free hand in that desert waste, nothing much was heard of what is now called "the Sahara's hidden wealth of minerals and oils." Even today nobody knows the exact boundary line between Algeria and Morocco in the lower Sahara region, for the desert sands, roamed over only by wild tribes, were never considered important enough to survey.

September 18

Summer has finally come to Paris, in the early autumn. There are lovely cool nights that seem to be in communion with the calendar, and then sunny, warm July days, with the trees already carrying the colored foliage of October—a mixture of weather and seasons that passes everybody's comprehension and most Parisians' recollections but that serves well indeed for pleasure, for a feeling of holiday here at home at last. The farmers, who did not cut their wheat when they should have normally, in mid-July, are now making their harvest in mid-September, mowing and threshing and bringing in a fine retarded, rich, ripe, dry crop. No one has ever seen the seasons so turned about and around, but never has a St. Martin's summer been more welcome than this, which should by rights come in November.

The shoe is on the other foot now. When the dangerous Suez Canal crisis began, Paris loudly complained that Washington was manifesting too little concern over the vital matter, and today Washington is showing so much concern that the French wish it would let up somewhat. A plaintive editorial in *Combat* this week opened by saying, "As on most of the days that God grants us, M. Foster Dulles had something to say yesterday."

October 9

After a fifty-nine-day vacation, the French Parliament has opened again, with France on exactly the same two spots it was on when Parliament adjourned in August—the unsettled, grave Suez crisis and the worrying, unfinished Algerian war. As the influential evening paper *Le Monde* pointed out, "The Parliamentary reopening took place in a singular atmosphere. There was a contradiction between the public declarations and the private comments, and a contradiction, moreover, between the serenity and optimism of some and the reality of certain events these last weeks." The serene optimists are those who agree with Robert Lacoste, Resident Minister of Algeria, who stated on opening day that the twenty-three-month-old war in Algeria is surely being won, that the French Army only hit its stride in September, that October might be the bloodiest terrorist month of all, but that in November things should look brighter. One of the recent troubling realities was the latest Suez divagation, uttered at last Tuesday's press conference, by Secretary of State Dulles, who, *Le Monde* sharply said, "overstepped himself by airing the differences between the United States and its allies," and who also struck irritated sparks in Paris and London governmental, diplomatic, and editorial circles by his reference to colonialism. Secretary Dulles's further, semi-idealistic press remark that good might even come of the Suez difficulties if they stimulated European federation brought a grim smile from French politicians. It is true that lately there has been revived talk on the Continent about a United Europe, but the feeling of union unfortunately seems to be founded largely on a common dislike of Mr. Dulles.

The major Lacoste news was his announcement that two hundred thousand acres of private Algerian property—farm lands belonging to the Compagnie Algérienne and to a Swiss company—have just been handed over to the Algerian agrarian-reform bureau as the first gesture toward dividing up certain nineteenth-century domains larger than twenty-five hundred acres into small farm parcels for land-poor natives, a French pacification effort. Another top announcement on Parliament's opening day was that the entire issue of government bonds to fight the Algerian war has been subscribed, and that the sale is now closed. A hundred and fifty billion francs had to be raised if income taxes were not to be boosted; actually, three hundred and twenty billion francs' worth of bonds were sold, though the issue was on the market only three and a half weeks. Bankers say that this was the quickest—and thus the most successful—national war loan ever undertaken, even including the one with which the French spiritedly paid their War of 1870 ransom to the disappointed Bismarck before it was due. Bankers have also pointed out that this recent loan was the most tempting investment and convenience any French government has ever dreamed up. (Its lures actually frightened off some people, who suspected a tempting trap.) The loan bonds pay five-per-cent interest, their redemption price is tied to an index of selected leading stocks on the Bourse, to prevent their devaluation, and the income from them is tax free for five years. After Nasser's nationalization of the Suez Canal, there was a heavy flight of French capital to Switzerland and New York, in an effort to recoup losses on the freezing of the Suez shares—a disaster for investors here, since they paid eight per cent, now only a golden memory. Since mid-September, many really rich French have sold their American shares and put the money in the French war loan—an ideal mixture of patriotism and attractive investment. This has certainly been a surprising Socialist government in most people's eyes. Socialists are supposed to be fuzzy about finance, and are theoretically pacifists. Socialist Premier Guy Mollet has just raised the fastest state loan in modern French history to help pay for a still unfinished rebel war that the preceding conservative governments did not have the courage to tackle.

Though Jean Dutourd's "Les Taxis de la Marne" has been out only a month, it is the book that is the most talked of, for and against, in Paris now. Dutourd, in its final lines, says that he gave it its title to recall the engagement with history that was "the most glorious—and least miraculous—of the twentieth century." This provocative essay of close to three hundred pages is a critique of France today and yesterday—an angry inquiry into what happened to the fibre of the nation and that of its Frenchmen. In part, it is a comparison between the France of September, 1914, which had the spunk and imagination to taxi its reinforcements of *poilus* to the Marne battlefield to save the country's life, and the France of June, 1940, when "the Generals were stupid, the soldiers did not want to die," and France was lost. Himself aged twenty in 1940, Dutourd says that, like most young men of his generation, he was a soldier without patriotism and without fight in him—or even the need for it—during his military career, which lasted fourteen days exactly, while France took time to fall. "It was not the hour for courage. France had forgotten the word," he says. His callow indifference to victory and to *La Patrie* he blames on the people who made the climate in which his generation grew up: the pacifist generals, the anti-war bourgeois men of the Left, the government men who wanted anything they could get except responsibility, the mediocre men like the lachrymose President of France, Albert Lebrun—"the man of destiny of the century." With heavy irony, he says that they robbed him of possibly being a hero and of maybe being a youthful captain with a Legion of Honor rosette for his bravery—"Ah, those bandits!"

François Mauriac, in his column "Bloc-Notes," in *L'Express*—the most carefully followed column of Paris—has said that Dutourd's is "an important book, perhaps less for what it clearly tells us than for what it represents," adding, "It is an outcry, at least. Someone has raised his voice." Dutourd says that he confined himself to inscribing "a phenomenon of which I myself was the source"—that is, his slow development into the patriot he is today, "unrecognizable in my own eyes, incarnating in the extreme everything I had despised eighteen years ago." The value of his confession, his critique, his anger, and his grief is that his book reads like a man talking out loud to himself; it is an account made up of little remembered things from his history or France's, from his mind, from Voltaire's mind, from the mind of his sergeant in the war—a book that is confidential and emotional, an analysis of remorse, memories, hope, and late-born love of his country. Searching to find out why patriotism was early killed in his generation and why it is still being murdered today, he lists what seem to him to be the French people's favorite weaknesses—their narcissism, their lack of faith, their egotism, their frivolous anarchy, their individualism that constantly drives them to nonconformism, their false myth of their "glorious defeat" (since defeat without an adjective would be unbearable to their pride), and their concurrent rival myth of French panache. His frame of reference is mostly the week that he and four soldier comrades, led by their sergeant, spent tramping around Brittany on a comfortable promenade of inglorious defeat after France fell. It was then, listening to a middle-aged barmaid, that he first heard the name of General de Gaulle—to Dutourd today the only man of honor, who brought back from England the little that was left of honor for France, and has taken the even smaller quantity remaining today into retreat with him, almost as if it were his personal property. Literary and intellectual French circles have been able to disdain Dutourd's book as too popular. Because he brings up no political problems of today, other circles have accused him of trading on the nonpolitical tricolor. But nobody accuses him of not having written something that the French of all classes, and even American residents here, can understand—a handbook of patriotism. This is why it has been the most talked-of book of the month.

November 4

October, with its violent historical surprises, has partly altered the Western world. Even those things that may turn out to be only temporary—the successful liberalization won by the Warsaw Communists; the wild, inspiring revolt for freedom in Budapest, now drowned in its own blood; the crumbling of Cairo's troops before the soldiers of Jerusalem; and the Paris and London unilateral move for independence from Washington—already have their own form of permanence in the new memories of European men and European governments, being a private file of parts of a new pattern for this hemisphere. It is widely considered here that October brought rebellions, of obviously different types, against the two rival power leaders of the West—the Soviet Union and the United States—now both gravely weakened in their influence. Neither of them, it is said, had been giving enough leeway to its captive or allied associates, who have now made a bolt for freedom in order to manage their steadily worsening affairs more profitably—they hope—and, most important, according to their own national necessities and lights. These last months can be called, in all historical gravity, the period of the worms that turned—Gomulka, Nagy (now in prison), the Sultan of Morocco, Premier Bourguiba of Tunis, Ben-Gurion of Israel, the amateur, intransigent dictator Nasser, Premier Guy Mollet, Sir Anthony Eden, and, finally, Sir Winston Churchill, in his intimate backing of the British Government's necessity for doing what it has done.

A vital cross-Channel footnote to this week's events is contained in the fundamental difference between the British Parliament, with a

Government acting for Her Majesty, and the French Chamber, representing utter republicanism with nearly a dozen negotiable parties, in their debates on the ultimatum to Egypt and the prospective invasion. Whereas the verbal, intellectual conflict between Opposition and Government in the British Parliament resounded worldwide, the Paris Chamber reacted with a laconic, if favorable, monotony that was its only distinction. On Tuesday night, its visitors' galleries were packed and tense and its hemicycle was richly filled with former Premiers and other officials, all come to hear what the French Assembly's reaction might be to the big event—Mollet's earlier declaration of the ultimatum to Egypt. A hundred and forty-nine Communist deputies voted against Mollet, as well as twenty-eight Poujadists—Poujade himself (who runs his party from outside) having phoned in for them "not to vote for a war to help the Queen of England," which offered the only rewarding moment of the evening. As for the Opposition, Mendès-France, who leads it, abstained from speaking, abstained from voting, and even abstained from applauding Mollet—"to mark his anxiety and disapproval," one newspaper sententiously remarked. There was literally no dissent raised against this critical, this possibly dangerous, government decision ("a throw of the dice," *Le Monde* called it, accepting the gamble and underlining its necessity) except the purely formal "speech of response," which Chamber law imposes after a government declaration. This response speech was astutely allotted to a Communist deputy, as a lightning rod on whom any Parliamentary distemper would naturally strike. His untimely Muscovite references to "colonial tyranny" naturally aroused heckling deputies, and shouts of "And Budapest?" and "Tell that to Stalin!" were the evening's only protests. Shortly afterward, Mollet, in asking for a vote of approval, said, "I have confidence in the patriotism and wisdom of the Assembly"—which showed it by voting three hundred and sixty-eight in his favor—and the strangely muted great Parliamentary debate was finished.

The two important explanations for its muteness are, first, that ever since Nasser nationalized the Canal, the French have been united as never before in wishing both to punish him and to save themselves from an Arab Hitler, as they did not save themselves from the Austrian original in 1938, and, second, that with the Socialists as the government, though unsocialistically acting according to their own ideology, there remains not one French party to speak as grouped oppositional liberals—a viewpoint that was lost the other night in a chasm of silence, without even an echo from the tempestuous events in England. However, the result was as the French truly wished it—an ultimatum not only to Egypt but to their own loss of pride, leadership, and energy, and to their discouragement and, indeed, bitter disillusion with Washington, Dulles, and the United Nations.

Owing to the air-raid arrest of the five leaders of the Algerian National Front, now imprisoned in Paris, the Sultan of Morocco has declared that the humiliation to his sovereignty can be appeased only by an explanation from his French equal, President René Coty, who, since he disapproved heartily of the air piracy, could say little. Premier Bourguiba has declared that he and the Bey of Tunis have now taken a public position against French military action in Egypt. "The hatred of the Moroccans and Tunisians will be redoubled against us, because of Algeria," François Mauriac, the great Arab sympathizer, justly wrote in his column "Bloc-Notes," in *L'Express*.

But more consequential this weekend than the fight against Nasser, or than sympathy for ill-used Israel, or than anxiety about their own troubling North African problems, has been the French emotion over the anguish in Budapest. There are no newspapers here on Sunday—nothing but the radio. In its noon announcement today, the Budapest rebel station broke off, saying, "We are now going off the air. *Vive l'Europe! Vive la Hongrie!* We are dying for Hungary." Then silence.

November 8

The French and British so-called armed police action in Egypt lasted only from six-thirty Wednesday evening until midnight Tuesday—the shortest, gravest, and most unsettled (and still the most unsettling) military campaign in the immediate history of our time. The French people and the French government, intrepidly united six days before by the Suez action, were indescribably relieved—like the world at large—by the cease-fire. During the six-day Egyptian war, as it was called, the French, who, because their Army is largely engaged in Algeria, were able to supply only a third of the Anglo-French armed forces, were disproportionately satisfied with the communiqué by their Secretary of State for Air that between Thursday and Sunday their fliers had "carried out more than five hundred assault and reconnaissance missions, without a single loss." And, after the official blackout of news that began in the first minutes of Wednesday morning, they were semi-satisfied with Premier Guy Mollet's announcement that the Anglo-French forces were installed "temporarily in key positions on the canal at Port Said, Ismailia, and Suez." Only belatedly have they discovered that the troops are nowhere near that far but are, in truth, only about thirty miles down the Canal, now blocked with the ships and dredges that Colonel Nasser triumphantly sank—his big naval victory. Mollet has just gravely declared, in totting up the final six-day account, that "there has been more gain than loss" in the explosive, startling, and short Egyptian campaign, which turned out to be too short for success by a few days—maybe by a few hours—while the world held its breath. "France and Great Britain had swallowed an impressive number of slaps in the face and kicks before taking steps in Egypt," *Le Monde* sombrely remarked. As for the United Nations' moral censure, the paper said, with cruel realism, "The nations sitting in judgment there apply to others principles they would not follow if they were in a similar situation. The Soviet Union condemns France and Great Britain for what they have done in the Near East, but it has done worse in Hungary. The United States has clean hands and a pure heart in both cases, because the United States is not involved, but has it forgotten what it did in Guatemala?"

As seen here, the single and tremendous result of the Egyptian campaign—one that can possibly have an immediate effect on the world and history—is that the United Nations will now have its own international armed force, its own mixed army, to fight against fighting, whose first contingents are expected to be assembled this very weekend with haste and realism, stimulated first by fear and now by hope.

The French flag on the Paris Hôtel de Ville has been flying at half mast to honor the Hungarian dead. In the sudden, unexpected glut of bloody history, with two unofficial wars on hand, one of them embroiling the French, the reaction of Parisians has never swerved. Regardless of what their Army was doing in Egypt, their emotions were fixed on Hungary's fight for liberty. All available news of it overflowed the newspapers and filled the air on radios and on television, where hanged patriots were seen, pendent from a Budapest bridge. The latest boulevard newsreel shows parts of the shattered city itself; it looks like the ruins of Cologne or Berlin at the end of the Second World War.

As one of the odd coincidences that have added to the tension here, a Budapest circus (as well as a dainty circus from Peiping) was playing in Paris when the revolution broke. At a gala charity evening, it raised two million francs for the Hungarian Red Cross while the lions roared, some of the acrobats visibly wept in mid-air, and the clowns vainly tried to be gay. The Municipal Council of Paris has given ten million francs to the French Red Cross for transfer, which includes four million it had intended to spend on a coming visit here of Russian officials, now cancelled. At the reception held Wednesday in the Russian Embassy, on the Rue de Grenelle, to commemorate the thirty-ninth anniversary of the 1917 October Revolution—the old-style Czarist calendar making the difference in the dates—the French diplomatic corps, French officials, and all but definitely pro-Communist French guests failed to appear.

The French feel that, in crushing Hungary, Soviet Russia has destroyed not only Budapest but its own tentative place in civilized European history. "The Soviets' brutal, bloody repression of Hungary"—the customary phrase in shocked press clippings from around the world—also shocked certain Communists here, as important a happening as the first leak in a dike. A few talented literary Party members, like Louis Aragon and his novelist wife, Elsa Triolet, "though deeply divided in interpreting recent Hungarian events," as they declared in a manifesto, were united enough to ask Hungary's new Muscovite Premier Kadar not to kill or imprison the rebellious patriot Hungarian writers and intellectuals—"carriers of a part of human culture." Some former Communist-inclined *progressistes,* including Simone de Beauvoir and Jean-Paul Sartre, protested to the Soviet government against using "cannons and tanks to break the Hungarian people's revolt," adding that nobody could join their protest who had been "silent when the United States snuffed out the Guatemalans' liberty in blood, or who had applauded the *coup de Suez.*" However, the major single revolt was by Sartre himself, in a ten-thousand-word analysis in this week's *Express* of why, after Budapest, he is no longer pro-Communist—an amazingly calm, quiet, clear document. Among other things, he says that the Budapest crime lay not only in the tanks but in the fact that, from the Soviet viewpoint, they were necessary "after twelve years of terror and imbecility." He says that what the Hungarians have taught with their blood is that Marxist Socialism, as "merchandise exported by the U.S.S.R.," is a failure; that he thinks the de-Stalinization plan was sincere and courageous, though Khrushchev's anti-Stalin speech was in itself folly; that friendship can no longer be felt for the Soviet leaders, who now predominantly inspire horror; but that the path of mankind to the Left, although uncomfortable to tread, and maybe impractical, is the only way. He ends by saying that if the French Party calls him a jackal and a hyena (as it already has), this is "a matter of total indifference to me, considering what they called the events in Budapest," which was "a Fascist uprising." What he has written is a great modern corrective pamphlet.

December 7

After two years of remarkable prosperity, this season should be bringing a rich Christmas here. Instead, the French will be fortunate if they receive a few tankers of high-priced American oil. It is already urgently needed to keep men and industry at work in this part of the world until the Suez Canal flows freely again, perhaps in the spring. Politically, this oil has already cost dear in terms of weakening the Western alliance. The French feel that President Eisenhower has been doggedly using oil as if it were a kind of club held over his Franco-British allies—either they withdraw their troops from Egypt as a sign of wrongdoing or they will be punished by having no oil to keep business alive—and that this was only one of the many moralistic American attitudes during the Suez confusion that have jeopardized the Western ties. The possible loss of America's friendship was something that a multitude of French and British citizens—at the height of the recent anti-American bitterness—wished their countries could afford. For the past fortnight, everybody here except the Mollet government has known that in this Allied sector of the oil struggle the Franco-British pair would be beaten—that the moral General Ike and the amoral Colonel Nasser would win. Because of these two men's separate geographic strangleholds—as a result of which no oil from the old friend would come across the Atlantic, and none from Arab enemies could pass through the clogged Suez Canal—the troops are being hurried out of Port Said this week. Perhaps there will be some American oil for Western Europe and the British Isles by at least New Year's Day.

Thus comes to an end that earnest flight from reality which was the brief Franco-British invasion of Egypt, a lunatic, destructive slice of history hopefully set going by two sensible, highly patriotic men—Sir Anthony Eden, political pupil of old Sir Winston Churchill himself, and the humbler, Socialist Premier Guy Mollet, anti-Socialistically waging his second African punitive war. As the French clearly see now, the consequences have been catastrophic. Not only has Britain been hard hit financially but they themselves must face up to war costs, probably having to foot the bill for cleaning up Nasser's damage to the Canal, and losing the dollar credits they need for Texas oil, so much dearer than the Mohammedan pipeline variety. In addition to all this are the facts that the Franco-British soldiers who marched victoriously into Egypt and are now marching out again in defeat had only a toehold on the ruined Canal; that the oil is stopped; that every Arab has been turned into an enemy; that Russia is now firmly in the Middle East; and that the United States and the United Nations are so angry that, with brisk Soviet help, they have sanctified Nasser in the eyes of the world as the injured party after (in the eyes of the French and British, at least) he burgled their Suez Canal Company, which ably served the whole globe (Israel excepted). The cynical French being more realistic than the English, no bones were ever made here about what the French hoped was the Egyptian campaign's real aim—to throw out the Fascistic Nasser and imperiously seize the Canal for the democracies.

The French, having supposed that Sir Anthony Eden would disappear from power as a result of Suez, were agreeably astonished by the Conservative Party's victory last night in the House of Commons, but there has been no serious notion here that Premier Guy Mollet, though involved in the same Egyptian enterprise, would not continue as head of the French government. Incredibly enough, not until the week after next will there be a full-dress Parliamentary debate on his foreign policy, Suez included. Though England and France were militarily united in action, what happened in their countries and Parliaments from the beginning of the affair to the end of its aftermath yesterday was as different as day and night. It must be realized that during the six-day Egyptian war, and ever since, the biggest news on the Suez affair printed in the French papers has always been the British battle of public opinion over it, splitting the House of Commons and the British press and people—that already historic fight against Eden's pragmatic Conservatives and their war, waged, according to various shadings of conscience, by the British Labour Party, which is precisely the opposite number of the French Socialist Party, led by Eden's war partner. In addition to the irony of an alliance between France's supposedly Left government and the aristocratic English party, what must also be recognized is that the French, as a people and as a Parliament (Communists and Poujadists naturally excepted), were united behind Mollet's Egyptian campaign with a unanimity literally never seen before in modern France—as behind a kind of energetic Crusader's dream of righteousness in arms and of pursuing the treacherous infidel. The only violent public opinion aroused here that was comparable to the reaction in England was the unified, bitter conviction that America and the United Nations—with Russia—stopped the crusade in disapproval of its imminent victory, since that victory would have proved the garrulous inefficacy of the U.N. in bringing Nasser to terms, the unreliability of Mr. Dulles's multiple views, and Washington's lack of leadership in the Near East. Dulles's arrival here this weekend for consultation is awaited with grim interest.

As for the French foreign-affairs debate, those deputies who abstained from opposing Mollet's Suez project will, of course, belatedly voice their criticisms, and he will certainly be once more berated for his conduct of the ever-present Algerian war. To many of the French, that war and its possible localized military victory seem almost meaningless now, with the whole Arab world, including Morocco and Tunisia, fervently united against France since the Suez campaign. If Mollet remains in power, it will be because no other French political party is yet willing to relieve him of his accumulated burdens.

1957

June 18

Anyone who has been absent from Paris for six months and has just returned finds France in practically the same situations she was in last December (except that, unfortunately, they seem worsened by solidification or repetition)—finds the same draining of blood, morale, and especially money into the continuing Algerian war, which last year's government prophesied would be won by last autumn, and finds, indeed, practically the same government, since the new one set up last week by Radical Socialist Maurice Bourgès-Maunoury is regarded by all as a hand-me-down copy of Socialist Guy Mollet's preceding government, the only difference being that this one is so feeble it cannot possibly live as long and will doubtless die by summer's end, maybe sooner. To make the verisimilitude painfully perfect, the incoming American traveller, in full tourist season, will also find the French Line ships, such as the elegant, elderly Ile-de-France and the giant Liberté, tied up like houseboats at the docks of Le Havre because of a strike, just the way the line's boats were tied up before Christmas in the same kind of strike. Paris newspapers, perhaps through mixed embarrassment and national pride, have relegated this news to their back pages. Yet it is the most important, if unwelcome, news of the week for French shop- and hotelkeepers, and even for the new Minister of Finance. Any interruption in the incoming crop of American tourists obviously means a cut in that richest financial harvest of all just at a moment when the French state, facing an extremely acute monetary crisis, is already borrowing against the Banque de France's gold reserve; has been forced to restore import quotas on goods bought from the member nations of the Organization for European Economic Coöperation, in order to help close the foreign-exchange leak that has been sapping France's economy; possesses the biggest dollar deficit of any member of the European Payments Union; and is literally in need of every red Indian cent she can garner. The Havre strike is of the new type, in that it is not a strike of the common seamen but of the marine gentry—the engineer officers, who are demanding a pay increase of from ten to fifteen per cent, which would make their chief's salary equal to that of the ship's captain himself, in an imbalance of authority, privilege, and reward never before heard of since men first took to the sea in ships. As may be recalled by passengers immobilized aboard the Flandre at Le Havre in last December's strike, the striking engineers then described their demand as "a new philosophy of the modern sea," according to which the highly educated technicians necessary for the operation of the complex machines that nowadays make boats go appear to have taken over the arcane mystique of Aeolus and his winds, as masters of power. They explained that they regard seagoing today as a responsibility divided in two—half to their chief below deck, seeing to the boat's mechanized innards, and the other half to the captain above deck. This would seem to leave a French marine commandant merely the captain of his soul, rather than of his ship.

Though Bourgès-Maunoury's government is called a stand-in for Mollet's government, both could properly be called Robert Lacoste's government, he figuring in each as the all-powerful Resident Minister in Algeria, the dominating chief of the Algerian war policy. Amid France's present high industrial prosperity and unprecedented commercial expansion, the war, which is costing a billion francs a day, has been the plague bleeding the French economy white. To pump up new financial blood, Bourgès-Maunoury will immediately ask Parliament for, and doubtless obtain, the high new emergency taxes that, when Mollet asked for them, led to his downfall. These will feature a ten-per-cent increase in corporation taxes, a jump in postal, telephone, and telegraph rates, an increase to twenty-five per cent in the sales tax on luxury goods, and an alarming boost in the price of gasoline. French gas at the present seventy-six francs a litre is already dearer than the gas of any other European country. The proposed new price of ninety francs would make it equivalent to almost a dollar a gallon. Bourgès-

Maunoury will also free gas from ticket rationing, which France alone has maintained ever since the French and English invasion of Suez. The first French ship since that fiasco and France's subsequent boycott of the Canal is about to pass through the waterway, her toll to be paid in sterling directly to Nasser's Canal administration, which refuses francs—a double, bitter piece of humble pie for France. Ironically enough, Bourgès-Maunoury, as Minister of National Defense in the Mollet Cabinet, was *l'homme de Suez* last autumn, the political leader of that ill-fated adventure. The only novelty in his new Cabinet is a Minister of the Sahara (also a Mollet idea), who is considered necessary because of France's belated recent discovery of rich Saharan oil deposits at Edjelé, Hassi Messaoud, and Ouargla. They are all in Algeria, which only intensifies the dominance of the Algerian question politically, economically, psychologically, ethnically, and morally.

Unfortunately, Lacoste has taken such a harshly repressive Ministerial stand against certain journalists and their writings—among them Jean-Jacques Servan-Schreiber, of *L'Express,* whom he caused to be prosecuted as a demoralizer of the French war aim—that few clear reports, criticisms, or analyses of the realities of the Algerian problem have been printed until this week, when a small brochure called "La Tragédie Algérienne" appeared. It is from the pen of Raymond Aron, the brilliant, nonpolitical staff writer for the conservative *Figaro*—which immediately expressed its disagreement with his booklet. He opens by quoting Montesquieu's austere words: "Every citizen is obliged to die for his country but not to lie for it." He then tells what many Frenchmen either fear or hope has long been the truth—that it is to France's interest to give up Algeria and recognize what he calls "Algeria's vocation for independence," and that it is better to deal now with the rebels of the National Liberation Front than to try to exterminate its men by the hundreds of thousands in a so-called war of pacification and then deal amiably with the remains of the population. Recognizing that France feels she is also fighting for her national honor, he points out that "the maintenance of unconditional French sovereignty is impossible," because it is seeking to break the will of another people. He concedes that the examples given by Tunisia and Morocco since their independence "are not encouraging," but maintains that "to send an army of four hundred thousand into Algeria is senseless" after freedom has been accorded to the two other North African French holdings, and that there should be a logical policy to cover all three. Since Saharan oil offers the first bright economic prospect Algeria has ever had, though it can hardly offset the country's "barren underdevelopment by the French," he says, "the richer the Sahara, the more necessary it is to come to an understanding with the Algerians." He adds, "The best way for France to lose the Saharan oil is to want to keep it for herself." His solemn final lines are "The nationalist demands, with their mélange of religious and racial fanaticism, of Western ideology of self-government, and of the aspiration of humanity toward equality, are a fact that cannot be ignored without a catastrophe. The grandeur of power is something that France no longer possesses, can no longer possess."

July 11

By a generous majority, the French National Assembly, after a debating session that lasted all day and all night, has just recommended the ratification of a plan new in Europe's history—the European common market, aimed at uniting the six democratic nations of France, Italy, West Germany, the Netherlands, Belgium, and Luxembourg in a nondiscriminatory trade community.

What is clear is that three years after the French parliament and people rejected the European Defense Community (France's own invention), which dealt federally with armies levied against possible war—always the first thing European men think of—the common market repeats the federated idea but applies it to business and money-making, civilized mankind's second preoccupation. Whatever idealism there may be in the common market is, fortunately, worldly and hardheaded. In the Assembly debate, the government's State Secretary for European Affairs put his finger like a compass needle on Western Europe's necessary direction for survival by saying, "We are still living on the fiction of the four great powers [of which France was one]. In reality, there are only two—America and Russia. Tomorrow there will be a third—China. It depends upon you," he warned the deputies, "whether there is a fourth—Europe. If you fail to make this choice, you condemn yourselves to walking backward toward the future."

Among the ways the common market will affect the common

man is by letting a citizen from any of the six countries go into any of the five others to hunt work, to shop, to found a business, or to set himself up in his trade—all things that are close to impossible now. This freewheeling of men was the most difficult aspect for the French to swallow, knowing that no Frenchman would set up anything in Germany but that hard-working Germans might successfully set up all kinds of things in France. As one deputy said, "Better a dialogue with Germany than a monologue"—that is, letting Germany listen only to her own voice, as in the fatal past.

In the Assembly vote, the three so-called Old Fathers of the United Europe idea—Schuman, Reynaud, and Pleven—spoke in its favor with passion, hope, and experience. The remnant of the Gaullist party voted against, their diehards and General de Gaulle himself still believing that France should stand on her own, on glory, with no surrender of her nationalism. Mendès-France and his handful of followers (from whose leadership he has just resigned) also voted against, probably for the same reasons that led him to help defeat the E.D.C. when he was Premier—his conviction that England should do her duty and join in to make Little Europe valid and larger. One of France's particular tragedies today is that both these men—the transcendental, Gothic general and the brilliant, Oriental-faced politician, the only new leaders and doers since the Liberation toward whom, for a time, the French people have instinctively turned with belief, aspiration, and a stirring of the sense of security—should now, when they are most needed again, each in his separate way, both be absentees in retirement, though still part of the vital furnishings of France, like the largest, most important portraits hanging on her walls.

The trouble with most new operas today is that it is the melodic old operas that go on being popular. The Paris musical event of this year was the recent first night, at the Opéra, of Francis Poulenc's "Dialogues des Carmélites." It was ordered as an original opus by La Scala, which gave it its world première, in Italian, last January, when the notoriously difficult Milanese critics and gallery gods received it enthusiastically, and when it impressed the major French critics, who all went down, as something long desired and new—a popular success in the field of contemporary opera. Reportedly, the Italians gave it the works—overelaborate scenery for the Carmelite nunnery, and singers with gorgeous voices singing in their great open, emotional, lyric style. Since Poulenc, who was present, felt that the Italian treatment was too worldly and operatic for his pious intentions, the recent Paris presentation became, instead, practically a miracle of impressionistic, controlled musical nuances, echoing in correct gray stone Gothic décors. The French critics who saw and heard both versions found them different, almost opposed, works. Poulenc dedicated his score to Debussy, who "gave me the taste for writing music," and to Monteverdi, Verdi, and Moussorgsky, "who have served me here as models"—which is occasionally true, especially of two or three touches of "Boris." His opera score is marked by his characteristic ecstasy of expression and subtlety of harmony; by lofty reaches of mounting melodic grace; by the rich polyphony of his chorals, such as the "Salve Regina" and "Ave Maria"; and by an all too brief last-act overture of really passionate loveliness. The opera is too long. This lets Poulenc's talent seem to *manquer de souffle*—to run out of breath. Nor were the Paris Opéra voices all gorgeous, by a long shot.

Most operas feature trouble between the sexes. This opera, about chaste nuns and with almost no male characters, is taken textually from the play "Dialogues des Carmélites," presented here five years ago—a tremendous dramatic success written by the late, highly intelligent Georges Bernanos, who, in turn, took it from a German novel, "Last on the Scaffold," which is indeed its *Hauptsache*. Its heroine, Blanche de la Force, is a purely fictional aristocrat who has sought the cloister because she is morbidly afraid of the violence of life, yet, in imitation of Christ's agony, finally mounts the French Revolutionary scaffold as a volunteer, the last to die among her condemned Carmelite sisters (real historical characters these, beatified by the Church in 1906 and now also part of the opera). Its final scene shows the sanguinary mob before the offstage scaffold, as a bloodcurdling offstage mechanical noise imitates the repeated falling sound of the guillotine's knife. Poulenc's opera has already been given in Germany, where it opened in Cologne last week, and is listed for production in San Francisco.

The ten-day European heat wave, with the Paris thermometers standing officially at ninety-seven degrees in the afternoon and actually at a hundred and twenty on midtown sunny balconies, seems now broken by storms. Exceptionally, the Paris police were allowed to shed their woollen dolmans, or jackets, and direct traffic in their pale-blue shirts—very smart with their white revolver holsters and white clubs. Wedding photos of the Comte de Clermont, dauphin pretender to the Bourbon throne of France, showed him mopping the sweat from his royal brow during the church service at Dreux. More than a fourth of the tough professional bicycle riders in the annual international Tour de France simply gave up by the third day. Those who stuck it out wore fresh cabbage leaves under their caps for insulation. When they pedalled through the big cities, the local firemen doused them with fire hoses. All last week, the Paris sidewalk cafés were running out of ice, beer, vanilla ice cream, and unsqueezed lemons by evening. The apéritif favored by the French was Pernod, which, because it is based on aniseed, they benevolently regard as a fortifier of the intestines during heat, and thus a classic thirst quencher. On July 4th, the sun set some tar paper on fire on the roof of the unfinished new UNESCO building, near the Eiffel Tower. Parisians, who by no means stand heat well and who incline to see international politics in everything, called the hot spell "atomic weather," forgetting, until their own weather bureau reminded them of the fact, that it was even hotter here, and for a longer stretch, just ten summers ago, when those terrifying weapons were infants.

August 17

American tourists are giving Paris the go-by because of high prices, and two million Parisian workers and employees are off on paid holiday, so the city is delightfully empty—ideal for a resident on vacation. Owing to the crisis in the falling franc that preceded its devaluation and the fact that paper pulp for newspapers is imported, the Secrétariat d'Etat à l'Information limited the number of Paris newspaper pages to eight during the rest of August, so we are also isolated from all except the most signal news. One such item that just received full space in all the dailies is that five neighborhoods of the city are suffering an invasion of termites—in Passy, around the Gare d'Austerlitz, around the Sorbonne, in Ternes, and in St.-Germain-des-Prés. Apparently, this is the worst invasion since the time of François I (1494–1547)—a pretty clean record.

September 10

M. Georges Salles is leaving the Louvre, where for thirteen years he has been the Directeur des Musées de France and a distinguished, energetic, creative-minded figure in modern European museology. He came to the Louvre in October, 1944, when it was still emptied of most of its treasures—an unheated, desolate, non-functioning edifice—and his gigantic task over the first year was to bring back its great belongings. This writer recalls standing below the Escalier Daru on the day when that enormous antique fragment, the Winged Victory of Samothrace, was being restored, inch by inch, to her former position at the top of the steps—was being slowly slid upstairs on primitive greased wooden runners, the power being supplied by a series of ropes, pulled with appropriate strength, and yet with the right watchful delicacy, by the Louvre workmen's arms—an impressive, old-fashioned demonstration of pulleys, hemp, and expert judgment. Under Salles' aegis, some significant experiments and changes were made in hanging the Louvre's special wealth of European paintings, the aim in each case being aesthetic elegance but also the educational and psychological effect on the public, for whose edification, after all, the art is on view. In 1948, for instance, the school system of picture hanging was reorganized, the Italian school being hung in the Grande Galerie, the Spanish in the Salon Carré, and so on. Then, in 1953, the orientation was completely altered to the satisfying presentation still used today, which is according to the relationship of styles, so that you can see mingled, rather than separate, the chefs-d'œuvre of all the European national schools during the great stylistic periods, and also their regional differences. M. Salles also influenced the Musée d'Art Moderne here by encouraging the postwar Conseil des Musées to buy for it modern masterpieces of the kind that the French state, in its shortsightedness, lacked—seven Matisses, four Braques, three Bonnards, and a Laurens sculpture being purchased in 1945 alone. In 1955, the first exhibition of pre-1850 French art ever seen in Japan was shown in Tokyo. It was organized by Salles and proved to be the greatest stroke for French prestige achieved in the East in recent times—an epoch-making aesthetic event for the Japanese, more than a million of whom attended the show. Modern French art they knew; it was what came before that so excited them, such as medieval stained glass and the pictures of Chardin and the growth of French art in the seventeenth and eighteenth centuries.

September 25

Wednesday morning, the Communist paper *Humanité* front-paged a drawing called "School Opens in Little Rock." It showed Father, Mother, and little son at home enjoying their televised news, which was showing them a lynched Negro boy hanging from a tree. The conservative *Figaro's* special French correspondent in the United States referred in his long Wednesday dispatch to "the ignobilities" of the previous day that had "provoked President Eisenhower to a spectacular dramatic action"—duly announced in a mid-page *Figaro* headline as "DES TROUPES AEROPORTEES ENVOYEES A LITTLE ROCK"—to protect nine young Negroes who were merely trying to go to school. The liberal *Combat* ran a Wednesday editorial called "Eisenhower with His Back to the Wall." It said, in part, that "in an epoch when people of color everywhere are trying to emerge with their own entities, the United States is fortunate," since its Negroes "aspire to nothing more than to have the standing, rights, and dignity of the average American." It added that not only was President Eisenhower's prestige being diminished "by the whites' brutality" but there was risk of injury to America's prestige. "In Washington's bitter struggle with Moscow for the friendship of the Afro-Asian bloc," it went on, clever use of the Arkansas events could "show America to be a land of race hatreds and hypocrisy. The rioters in Little Rock have just rendered a major service to Soviet propaganda."

President Eisenhower's proclamation this week, ordering the Little Rock fomenters of trouble and illegality to "cease and desist," plus his radio speech and his decision to employ the Army to restore calm and enforce the law, has naturally intensified French interest in the Little Rock rebellion. Already its daily developments had been passionately followed here. The photos of the white high-school boys' faces stretched in a rictus of hate, the bowed head of Elizabeth Eckford, the strange, démodé visage of Governor Orval Faubus had all become perfectly familiar to the French by name, identity, and meaning, our bad news having become an international affair to which everybody has paid close attention. Besides, the French have an exceptional knowledge of our Southern scene—in most cases without ever having visited it in the flesh. French children are taught a great deal more about our Civil War than American children are taught about the French Revolution. French intellectuals have a larger knowledge of Southern character, through reading Faulkner, than our American intellectuals have of any French regional class except the *faubourg* group of ducal Guermantes and friends in Marcel Proust. In a character sketch of Faubus, the independent *France-Soir* disparagingly described him as *"un hillbilly, qui sont les plus pauvres et les plus arriérés des Américains de race blanche."*

October 9

The first reactions here to the Soviet Union's launching of its artificial satellite were almost poetic in their felicitously phrased astonishment. Parisian papers called it "a myth become reality" and "the first proved possibility of an effective evasion from our planet," said of it that "the road to the moon has been opened" and "a giant step in the sky has now been taken," and wrote that "for the first time, an object fashioned by the hand of man is promoted to the condition of a celestial body, endowed with an independent existence in cosmic space." Phrasing it more simply for history, one Parisian paper commented, "Friday, October 4, 1957, was the first day of the Year 1 in the interplanetary era." Yet it was not until Saturday morning that the Communist Party paper *Humanité,* like every capitalist journal in Paris, came out with the world-shaking news. You might have thought that for propaganda or prestige value the faithful Comrade paper here would be given a scoop on this astounding, victorious Soviet event of the century. But, as usual, the French Communist Party was treated by Moscow like a poor country cousin. The Tass Agency must have given out its satellite news so late that *Huma's* front page could not be changed beyond squeezing in a last-minute headline above its title, saying "PREMIER SATELLITE ARTIFICIEL LANCÉ HIER PAR L'UNION SOVIETIQUE." On page 2, usually the theatre, movie, and book page, it ran the Tass Radio Moscow story, plus a triumphant little paragraph about the *"vive sensation"* in Washington.

There are no French Sunday papers, so it was not until Monday that *Humanité* swelled into its limited propaganda stride. The Tory *Figaro* of Monday morning carried four pages on the Soviet satellite, plus a huge front-page announcement: "SENSATION THROUGHOUT THE WORLD." But if you think that *Huma* made the Russian savants' achievement its main front-page news, you are dead wrong. Its major headline was about Mollet and Pleven and the French government crisis; football and sports got a big front-page play, and so did the steelworkers' strike. Then came a satellite feature story for the lower-brow echelons, which have already nicknamed it *"le bébé-lune"*; this story was called, believe it or not, "A Baby That Jumps from Bordeaux to Barcelona in One Minute." And, finally, tucked away among this front-page rubbish was a short, official, pure-propaganda editorial, called *"Le Spoutnik"*—a word that it never once translated for its French readers. Its theme, of course, was that this new mastery of celestial nature is owing to Soviet science, and that Communism alone created the social conditions in which Russian science brought to flower the world's first satellite, as well as the world's first intercontinental ballistic missile, whereas "in lands still subjected to capitalism," like the United States, "scientists complain of the insufficient means put at their disposal for research." Then came the sombre warning: "The launching of *le spoutnik* should riddle those Western propaganda lies that seek to make people believe that when the Soviet Union talked about its intercontinental missiles it was only bluffing." This was followed by the carefully baited illogical question "Does not the launching of this satellite prove that science today has reached a stage where a happy life for all mankind can be assured only if it is relieved of the burden of armaments?" And "Mankind is now prepared to conquer the heavens" was the editorial's conclusive, high answering thought, which is probably the truth, too.

There has naturally been some shrill French laughter at the poor astronautic position that the United States finds itself in—especially in this International Geophysical Year—with the Russian-manufactured baby moon beep-beeping over Paris, Washington, and New York as it hurries around the world fifteen times a day, just after our Atlas rockets, supposed to hold up the defense framework of the Western world, fizzled out and fell flat. It is constantly being remarked by Parisians that America talked about—indeed, is still talking about—its satellite, but that the Russians built and launched theirs, which is the one being talked about right now. There is a folkloric phrase being much cited here—"selling the bear's skin"—which the French find especially suited to the American satellite situation. The phrase comes from a fable about a braggart who sold a bear's skin before he killed the bear.

France still has no government. This makes everything seem nice and quiet. M. Guy Mollet, who was Premier last year, was asked last week if he wouldn't be Premier again, and he said yes, but the deputies said no, and refused to have him. Then M. Pleven was asked, and he said yes, but the deputies said no once more. Now M. Mollet has been asked a second time, and has said no. Pretty soon, somebody will say yes, and the deputies will say yes, too. Then France will have another government and the dissensions and rigmaroles can start all over again. It is something to look forward to.

October 24

This has been a worrying, busy week—the week of France's most overdue engagements with her immediate 1957 history; the week of unavoidable dates with her people, her politicians, and her bank account; the week of finally facing up to recent reality, on which her Fourth Republic must try to survive. On Monday, the twenty-first day that France was without a government, the week's vital opening date was with the experienced seventy-one-year-old M. Robert Schuman, of the Catholic Mouvement Républicain Populaire, who, it was hoped, might be allowed to become the new Premier, three previous candidates having failed, but before he considered trying to head a new regime, he called on M. Wilfrid Baumgartner, governor of the Banque de France, from which the state has already borrowed billions. A former Ministre des Finances himself, Schuman reported succinctly to President Coty that "France's financial situation is tragic." His second information for Coty was that until the left of center, which is Socialist, and the right of center, which is moderate, pulled closer together in their notion of what might save France, nobody could found a government at all, though clearly one of some sort is initially necessary for her salvation. Even possible national bankruptcy is apparently a pleasanter prospect for most deputies than the one vainly proposed a few days ago by the conservative Premier-candidate Pinay, who dared demand, as one basis of his program, that for an entire year he be allowed to govern without their interference.

This present difficult week, openly called *une semaine d'agitation sociale,* began with what was also called extreme tension. After the general public's disgust on Monday that there was still no government (which, once in, it always regards with aversion), labor troubles became intensified. The unexpected amplitude and success of the previous week's strike of the men in the nationalized gas and electrical companies, which practically paralyzed Paris and France for twelve hours, were naturally heartening, surprising, and inspiring to French workers and employees, cruelly squeezed of late between constantly spiralling costs of living and, in most cases, the same old immutable pay, and further harassed by the deputies' inability to get their own work done, which was to set up the next regime. On Monday, plans were announced to make Friday of this week "a great day of action, pay demands, and protests," most notably by a major, crippling twenty-four-hour strike of the French railways, beginning at 4 A.M., accompanied by a strike of the same duration by the postal and telegraph services. Other strikes scheduled for Friday are of the building trades, the metalworkers and the synthetic-textile workers, the Métro and Paris bus workers, and, above all, the vast personnel of the state civil service and the governmental offices, including that legion of scribblers in the tax bureaus—plus a partial strike among schoolteachers, who are to refuse to teach classes of more than forty children in their overcrowded schools. Latching on to the band wagon, even the policemen's union urged its members to avail themselves of the big day "with the only legal means at their disposal"; i.e., a mere request that their monthly salary be raised by seven thousand francs, it being legal for them to ask for it but not to strike for it. During the week, the unrest has been manifested in big, practiced proletarian demonstrations, such as walkouts by the steelworkers in the Loire Valley, and in Nantes and St.-Nazaire on the Atlantic coast, and in smaller gestures by the most refined artisans, such as the tailors at Lanvin and Creed, reported to be laying down their needles for a fifteen-minute strike every hour.

Though the Communist-dominated Confédération Générale du Travail, the biggest and toughest union, has naturally been bossing the Friday plans (which the Socialist Force Ouvrière has rather snobbishly declined to participate in on equal terms), it is the reaction of usually the mildest of the three unions—the Catholic Confédération Française des Travailleurs Chrétiens—that has furnished the most astonishing new labor element. Not only has it backed the C.G.T.'s Friday plans but it has boldly invited its followers "to give the day of October 25th the general character of a warning to the state and to the employer class," and, further, "to give an expression of the determination of the working class to say no to the rising prices, to the lowering of living standards, and to social regression."

The financial experts have been talking gravely during the week of the effect that the important increase in wages being demanded by the strikers will have on France's perilous inflation. Yet none of the major labor groups or unions so far is asking for wages that match the increase in the price of turnips, which cost forty per cent more than they did last year at this time, or string beans, which are sixty per cent higher, or tomatoes, which have gone up sixty-six per cent. Now Socialist Guy Mollet is again going to try to be Premier of a government—of limited life, he says. Since the war, France has only too frequently lived in the limbo of a protracted political crisis without a government. But this is an extra-grave political crisis, currently in its fourth week, with barely a mirage of a government in sight, with victuals dangerously expensive, with massive labor troubles about pay accumulating amid an alarming financial situation and amid the persistence of an insoluble, continuous, and costly colonial war.

There has been general, but nothing like complete, satisfaction here over the fact that a French writer was awarded the Prix Nobel de Littérature and that this Frenchman was Albert Camus. For there are a great many readers and writers who agreed with Camus himself when he said, with his insistent truthfulness, "Had I been on the Swedish jury, I would have voted for Malraux." In making the award in the office of Camus' publisher, Gallimard, the Swedish Ambassador compared him to the resistant seventeenth-century heroes of Corneille. In thanking him, Camus significantly mentioned his appreciation that such a prize had come to "a Frenchman of Algeria"—a mere colonial. Young for the honor, though twice married and with adolescent boy and girl twins, he was born in November, 1913, near Bône, of humble farm laborers, his father being killed the next year in the Battle of the Marne. Poverty and the maladive beginnings of what finally became tuberculosis interrupted his studies in philosophy (partly on St. Augustine), and he had to earn his living at odd jobs—in a garage, as a shipping clerk, as a schoolteacher, and, finally, as a journalist, first in Algiers and then in Paris. During the war, he joined the Resistance group called Combat, whose little clandestine newspaper became the postwar intelligentsia Paris daily *Combat,* and after the Liberation he worked on it as an editor, along with Sartre and Simone de Beauvoir. His literary career had started during the Occupation with the publication, in 1942, of "L'Etranger," the first of his novels, which, in retrospect, the French oddly see as American in their sparse, unheroic style but utterly Mediterranean in thought, with the antique, abstract qualities indigenous to that early, educated, civilizing region. In "L'Etranger," the man Meursault becomes the figure of truth, as a form of nihilism. In his philosophical essay "Le Mythe de Sisyphe," man's vain, constant push toward the summits becomes not punishment but stoicism, a repeated form of moral courage. "La Peste," published in 1947, is his most famous, influential novel on the theme of good and evil, which nobly obsesses him, and to the French its two most illuminating statements are still "What is neutral is the microbe" (of the mysterious plague), and the lofty, agnostic query of one of the men fighting it—"Can one be a saint without God? This is the only concrete problem that I know of today." Camus became and remains for the French what Mauriac has called "the conscience of his generation"—the spokesman for the outsider in today's moral crisis of alarm, anger, and despair, and for that rather young war-raddled European generation, freed from religion but still the captive of its ceaseless, puzzling questions about man on earth, to which Christian faith formerly supplied all the answers. In 1951, his essay "L'Homme Révolté," the most controversial of his writings and the hardest to read, analyzed man's instinct for revolution, a subject dear to French hearts, and concluded that revolutions always create their own tyranny. This and his ideas on Soviet labor camps led the following year to a break between Camus, on the one hand, and Sartre and pro-Communism and Existentialism, on the other—a public quarrel much enjoyed in Paris because the men fought it out in Sartre's magazine, *Les Temps Modernes*. "La Chute," or "The Fall," his latest novelette, which is a fascinating study of justice gone mad, will be followed by one called "Le Premier Homme," which he is now writing. Since youth, Camus has worked around the theatre—has run his own troupe, has written and adapted plays, and has just finished an adaptation of Dostoevski's "The Possessed," which takes four hours to perform and will unquestionably be played here even so. Camus is certainly the only obsessed moralist the Swedes could have found among the French today to receive a literary prize for "earnest study of the problems of the human conscience in our times."

November 5

This crisis of thirty-seven days without a government has left its mark. Not since the wave of anti-parliamentarianism that culminated in the bloody riot of 1934 on the Place de la Concorde has there been such openly expressed disgust among the French for their National Assembly as a weak, selfish, do-nothing institution. During the crisis, the French did not even want to talk politics, as if politics were a sort of incurable malady raising a stench over the land. At the movies, whenever deputies were shown in the newsreels the audiences, including many of the women, booed and jeered, and the younger men usually shouted a few insults. But that was all. After the four-year occupation by the Nazis and the French people's bitter disillusion with their Fourth Republic since then, there is no climate for rioting. Even the faint rumor of a Fifth Republic, under the magic banner of de Gaulle, has aroused nothing but derision and disbelief. This last week, the French deputies refused (for the moment, anyhow) to accept an increase in salary, now being offered to senior civil servants generally, which would have given them an additional seventeen hundred dollars annually. Prudently enough, they thought parliamentary prestige was so low that their higher pay would only disgust their electors further.

November 20

The Allies' intergovernmental relations are usually on such a talkative high level that the ordinary citizen here makes little effort to follow their ins and outs, but this certainly was not the case with the British and American delivery of arms last week to President Habib Bourguiba, of Tunisia. Since, for once, this was a matter of acts, not words (until France's new Premier and her ambassadors, politicians, radio commentators, and newspaper editorial writers let loose a thesaurus of indignant phrases), the French people felt that they understood it perfectly—that it was a treacherous, inimical gift to France's ex-rebels of guns that would be easy to pass over the border to her present rebels in Algeria. Parisians, in their talk on the subject, are roused and galled, and forgetful of Premier Gaillard's levelheaded parliamentary statement on Friday that London and Washington had warned Paris they would have to send the requested arms, since France had refused to and Moscow and Cairo would be delighted to oblige. Parisians, however, remembered his other statement: "If the Atlantic Pact should fall to dust one day, we will know the artisans of its failure"—John Bull and Uncle Sam, not La Belle Insouciante Marianne. So acute was the tension that on Friday and Saturday nights, five hundred police from the riot squad, wearing steel helmets, lined up before the American Embassy, just off the Place de la Concorde—unnecessarily, it turned out—and similar unneeded protection was given to Her Britannic Majesty's Embassy, and the Embassies of Tunisia and Morocco. The American Embassy says that by Monday morning it had received an "avalanche" of letters from parents of French soldiers in Algeria asking that they no longer be sent *Information et Documents,* a free and till now popular biweekly magazine about America published in French by the United States Information Service. The parents also expressed their anger, shock, and horror at the thought that the United States should have sent arms to North Africa, where they could be handed over to Algerian rebels to kill their boys.

America's already well-established unpopularity here progressed over the weekend by leaps and bounds. The arms-for-Tunisia incident, coming, as it did, after the recent discovery of rich oil fields in the Sahara, led to a belief that this time the Americans had become disloyal to their ally in order to satisfy their cupidity. The always excitedly nationalist paper *L'Aurore,* strongly Rightist in its views, said editorially, "The oily explanation [*l'explication pétrolière*] of the Tunis maneuver is only too obvious." The conservative *Figaro* called the arms shipment "an odious blow by our allies." The august *Monde* referred to "the entente without cordiality." Ex-Premier Georges Bidault protested, "We cannot be the ally in Europe and the scapegoat in Africa." Raymond Aron, a noted non-Leftist political writer (who is, notwithstanding, anathema to the Right Wing, because of his belief that Algerian independence is practically inevitable), voiced his distress that London and Washington should have "chosen such a deplorably clumsy method of expressing no confidence in France's Algerian policy." Ex-Ambassador André François-Poncet, who until recently was stationed in Bonn, was unique in publicly expressing a mixture of Gallic indignation and diplomatic wisdom. He said that the arms shipment was "not only inimical but also shocking and humiliating, and marked by the brutality that, it seems, M. Foster Dulles has an increasing tendency to utilize." The Tunisian incident, he continued, "without doubt expressed our partners' impatience with and disapprobation of our country's politics, our quarrels, our interminable Ministerial crises. The lesson they intended to give us is not absolutely unmerited; it would be unmanly not to admit this. But the Anglo-Saxons made a bad calculation. They dealt the Atlantic Alliance a disastrous blow."

November has been a month of anniversaries for the French, nearly all of them disagreeable. On November 1st, three years ago, the Algerian war began, as a supposedly unimportant native uprising. On November 5th of last year, the French and British vainly sent off paratroopers to blast Colonel Nasser out of the Suez Canal. On November 7th of this year, Moscow celebrated the Bolshevik Revolution of forty years ago, which began the era of Soviet Russia, whose theories a fourth of the French Republic's voters supported in the last election. And this November 5th was the thirty-eighth birthday of Félix Gaillard, and the day on which he took office as the seventeenth and youngest Premier of the Fourth Republic. He became Premier not because, being young and brilliant, which he undoubtedly is, he stood for a rising, intelligent, new generation of leaders in stale French affairs but because, as the French said only too clearly, the old parliamentary hands' selfish disunion was more precious to them, as a major part of politics, than getting together and governing France. It is thought here that possibly the one ameliorating result of the Tunisia-arms incident is that Premier Gaillard will not be allowed to fall for a while. There will, of course, be plenty of time for that later.

As a natural result of social unrest, government financial troubles, inflationary prices of consumer goods, food, and *vin ordin-*

aire (they have just gone up for the third time since early autumn) and the greatest industrial prosperity and bourgeois spending boom that modern France has known, there has been a rain of strikes by undersalaried employees, especially those who have the honor of working for the City of Paris and the French state. The latest strike of *petits fonctionnaires* took place on Tuesday. The strikers' demand was for an increase in the basic wage on which all salaries in the lower level of government services are calculated. The clinics for diagnosis and treatment in the city hospitals were closed, garbage was uncollected, gravedigging was suspended, and penitentiary guards quit their jobs. During the one-thirty radio news broadcast, the speaker announced that the station would be off the air until eight that evening. The zoo and the public libraries, including the Bibliothèque Nationale, were closed; water and gas pressure was low. The meteorological services struck, and so did the customs officers; the Paris airfields were shut down; Air France cancelled all its European flights; long-distance phone calls to points outside France were nonexistent. However, letters were mostly delivered, and in the general confusion telegrams were usually distributed twice.

This has been a great month for one pleasure, at least—the splendid art shows customary at this time of year. Finest and rarest in content of them all is the exhibition called "L'Atelier de Juan Gris," in the elegant new Rue de Monceau gallery of that early Cubist-art connoisseur Daniel-Henry Kahnweiler and his sister-in-law, Mme. Louise Leiris. Gris died in 1927, only forty years old. The twenty-two canvases now displayed were painted in the last year, and even the last few months, of his life, and were found after his death in his studio in Boulogne-sur-Seine, a suburb of Paris. They had never been seen by the public.

When Gris died, his small pictures were selling, if he was lucky enough to find a buyer, for a few hundred francs apiece—perhaps no more than twenty dollars in those days. Their sale price in the present show is six million francs, or around fourteen thousand dollars, and the big ones get more than twice that. During his brief lifetime, Gris was appreciated only by a very few, and their number did not include his compatriot Pablo Picasso, whom Miss Gertrude Stein bluntly reproached for his phrases of what she said was false grief after Gris's funeral. These twenty-two canvases, the product of his last burst of genius, have the pristine freshness, in color, of paintings that look new because they have been hidden away, have never been handled or exposed to light and public opinion. There is in their limpid yet austere composition a reflection of the certitude of Gris, which here has a meditative quality that came perhaps from his sense of approaching death and his final sureness in his art. The largest still-life, "Guitare et Papier et Musique," offers as a startling surprise, considering how low his palette usually was, a patterned blaze of vermilion, as red as blood. Two paintings, each showing a large seated female figure of neoclassic dignity, are also rarities. One of the figures holds a harvest basket of fruit, the other (one of three pictures in the exhibit that are signed) has empty, folded arms and a strange, graceful, gray lunar face. Of his small final *natures mortes,* one depicts a carafe and lemon, another a wineglass and egg, and there is one with bananas. The small, perfectly produced catalogue that M. Kahnweiler had printed, surely at considerable expense, is a collector's item. Its cover, which bears a stunning colored lithograph of the canvas called "Fruits et Bol," was prepared by Mourlot Frères, the great lithographers of Paris.

The *clou* of the Salon d'Automne—in the gloomy, clammy Grand Palais, which is probably the worst place on earth to show art, but which in its time has shown the beginnings of the great Ecole de Paris, and the last, in posthumous retrospectives, of Cézanne and Gauguin—is a retrospective show of about fifty canvases, dated from 1900 to today, by that belatedly appreciated master Jacques Villon, now aged eighty-two. He is still painting with the purity of research that he pursued during those long, too quiet years when he was unjustly ignored. The exhibit traces his aesthetic history from his early, almost banal period of youthful realism, through his Cubist stylizations, to the refined geometric patterns of color, like shards of rainbows, that have become the style of his present apotheosis.

The chill of November has finally arrived, after half a month of Indian-summer sunshine and a full complement of yellow leaves—comforts left over from October. Not for years has the autumn season been so extended, mild, and handsome in the city gardens and in the forests around Paris. The wild-mushroom harvest in the woods was particularly plentiful. Morning mists, so heavy that they dripped moisture onto the leaves and from there to the ground, and then warm afternoons, as the sun burned the mists away, gave all the fungi their ideal climate. In certain woods in the Ile-de-France, the crop of *les trompettes de la mort,* or *Craterellus cornucopioides*—the so-called trumpets of death, though no mushroom hereabouts is safer and tastier—was especially heavy and succulent. *Les trompettes* usually grow beneath young oak trees, in clean glades devoid of underbrush, rising from cushions of green moss, where they congregate in clusters, looking like purple, black-shaded crocuses. Floral-shaped, tubular, decorative, mysterious, they are difficult to find, half hidden by last year's fallen leaves. In taste similar to the dark morels of spring, they are autumn's richest gift of all such spored growths here. If they are to be tender, they should be cooked until they turn as black as dead flowers. They are then served with rice *al dente* and a little olive oil, and consumed with a gourmet's appreciation, and no fear, since for once nature has not created any deadly duplicate. Ten days ago, there were still a few handfuls of red raspberries in the gardens, and the small wild strawberries planted by the garden paths were again in bloom, uselessly. Now winter has started to settle down, and with a rather special melancholy, owing to turbulent human events.

December 4

The present overinflated art prices, demonstrating the cheapness of today's money and the exaggerated social or investment value placed on modern canvases, have naturally resulted in a lively wave of counterfeits of contemporary French masters. The French police recently nipped in the bud a plan to sell a bundle of fake Picassos, Braques, and Utrillos, among other counterfeits, in Texas. The situation has led to an investigation here of the experiences that have befallen the descendants of some of the dead great French painters, which are both interesting and alarming. Mme. Cachin-Signac, daughter of the Pointillist, says that anything styled in little dots tends to become a Seurat or a Signac, but that occasionally, with permission from the owner, and in the presence of a bailiff, she has been permitted her right—that of scratching her father's signature from a false canvas. Isabelle Rouault, the painter's daughter, says that with the permission of the owner she has sometimes been able to deposit a fake Rouault with the Syndicat de la Propriété Artistique, which prevents its being circulated, and has even succeeded in destroying some bogus canvases. Pierre Cézanne, himself a painter in Montparnasse, says that he has seen hundreds of false pictures attributed to his grandfather; that the owner of an exposed fake is always furious with him; that lately he twice saw the same false Cézanne, which the second time contained a couple of little houses newly painted into one corner of the canvas; and that most of the fake Cézannes are copies of works done between 1870 and 1880, and are invariably signed—often the real evidence of their falsity, "since the signature of my grandfather during those years was rare."

1958

January 8

The publication shortly before the year's end of André Malraux's latest illuminating illustrated book on art, "La Métamorphose des Dieux," put it in a correct position to be the most notable art volume both of 1957, when it came out, and of 1958, when people can take the necessary time to read and ingest its four hundred pages. They are less difficult to read than his six hundred and fifty pages of "Les Voix du Silence," of 1951, provided the reader has actually read that preceding crucible work and is therefore familiar with Malraux's molten ideas, with his glowing memory for the light of art all over the world, and with his fiery literary style. The compliment to him as the accepted remaining genius of French letters since the death of Valéry and Gide was manifested by the really majestic treatment that Paris gave "The Metamorphosis of the Gods"—a treatment of such grandeur and amplitude as no one recalls ever seeing accorded an author before, including Malraux for his earlier books. The first edition of "La Métamorphose," which consisted of ten thousand numbered copies, priced at six thousand francs a copy (more than fourteen dollars, and considered costly here), was immediately sold out—a rare occurrence for so de-luxe and hermetic a work.

As the title of the new book indicates (a second volume will follow), it is a special amplification of the aesthetic theory that Malraux has already stated and has held since youth, when he began his intellectual concentration on art as the earthly immortality of man. This is that "metamorphosis . . . is a law governing the life of every work of art," meaning simply that art takes successive forms in remaining itself over the passage of time—a rationalistic modern notion of universality, which was not shared, Malraux points out, by the nineteenth-century artist Delacroix, to whom Egyptian tombs were not art "but high-class curiosities," and whose ignorance of Romanesque art (regarded for five centuries by the French as barbaric) was "equal to that of Baudelaire, and even Cézanne." Today, however, Malraux declares in a clarion phrase, "From the history of dead civilizations, as from the ethnography of peoples who are dying, we expect to be informed of what man was when he did not look like us."

The body of the book is divided into two main considerations of art—that of the divine and that of faith, or, in other words, the pagan and the Christian. Fortunately for the reviewer, Malraux has provided, in trenchant phrases at the book's end, an analytical table of his ideas, which, since one travels at vertiginous speed in company with his mind, serves in the manner of a railway timetable (as one French critic has gratefully pointed out), so the reader can know which way on earth Malraux is headed. He starts by declaring that the Western world might have known more about the profound questions posed by art's existence if it had not erred for centuries in thinking that the origin of all art was the Greek conquest of the human likeness, and, moreover, in thinking that "Greek sculptors wished the gods to look like men," when their aim was the other way around. Beauty was a matter of divinity, "which set the goddesses apart from mortal women." The statues of the prize athletes—for, as Malraux points out, Greece also invented glory—were "not portraits but ex-votos in the grand style," given by the crowned athletes to the temples, as, later, the Christian princes gave statues of saints to the churches. And when the Greek heritage passed to Rome, in that city, "for the first time, a major art recognized the system of resemblances as the system of the world; for the first time, resemblance became *the real.*"

Malraux's chapters on the art of faith, which was Christian, open with his statement that to replace the former pagan art peopled by statues, Byzantium created a population of immobile apparitions—the holy figures of the mosaics. Then follow chapters illustrated with reproductions of extreme interest to any travellers familiar with the carved Romanesque and Gothic figures of the great churches. As the Gothic style and the veneration of the Virgin flowered, and love, pity, and charity became the new ideal of human faith, the carved life of the Virgin came to settle at home in the cathedrals—Queen of the feudal hierarchy of peasants, seigneurs, emperors, and popes who made up the medieval civilization of faith. In its wake, as an extension, came the art of painting—first in two dimensions, flatly stating the world of God, then (with Giotto) in three dimensions, in loving imitation of man and nature. And far to the north, in Flanders, where painting was also strong, came portraiture and the world of Flemish art. There this volume ends, almost abruptly, with the art of van Eyck, who painted Eve, the saints, and the Virgin as people in a living world, enriched by the reality before the painter's eyes, the reality that he saw existed, whereas in the south Italy was getting ready "to paint Venus because she did not exist."

February 5

President Eisenhower's post-midnight announcement of Friday's successful launching—at last—of our first heavenly satellite, Explorer, came too late for the Saturday-morning newspapers in France, so the Paris *Herald Tribune,* in order to spread the good news through the American colony over the weekend, brought out its Monday paper on Sunday morning (a day when no papers are normally published here by anybody), calling it, rightly, a special edition and dating it Sunday–Monday, February 2–3. It carried the New York Sunday edition's eagle-cry editorial about how quickly America can overtake a lead "once the nation rolls up its sleeves and tackles the job," and it also gave the complete, astonishing details (many already published in the Saturday-afternoon French papers) concerning the former German, Dr. Wernher von Braun, and his ex-German Army group of rocket specialists from Peenemünde, and how it was these captured brains with the rolled-up sleeves who had sent Explorer into its orbit on advanced versions of the V-2 rockets that they had earlier devised and launched for Hitler. These facts, with their full significance of German, rather than American, know-how, cut the enthusiastic edge off the French people's suddenly revived belief in Yankee technical leadership—at least, if one can judge from the disappointed way many Parisians talked, as if they had been sold a false bill of goods. The fact that the Russians also had their parcel of captured Nazi technicians was sufficiently appreciated here a full month ago to make popular a joke about the Russian sputnik and the American satellite talking German to each other in the sky—provided the American satellite ever got up.

March 4

For the first time in history, the little-known opera house in the Palais de Versailles is today open for ordinary people to go in and look at, though few seem to know this, since there are neither descriptive catalogues nor even postcards of it at the Palace stationer's counter to publicize the new privilege, and since only a scant announcement has ever been made in the Paris press about the reopening of this hitherto dilapidated architectural treasure. In the time of the aging Louis XV, when it was finally finished, it was loyally and royally called the most beautiful theatre in Europe. It is still unsurpassed, no other old theatre being comparable in allure, extravagance, and elegance, except perhaps those two classics—the Fenice, in Venice, and the Margraves' private rococo theatre in Bayreuth, both of which benefit in delicacy of effect from the refined fading of their original décors. The Versailles Opéra, which has just cost the Fourth Republic nine hundred million francs and five years to restore, is now as brilliant and as magnificent as it was in the King's day, so that we see it fresh, as if with his protuberant, carnal royal eyes. Its opening performance, in 1770, of Lully's opera "Persée," was in celebration of the marriage of his fatally unfortunate grandson, who was to become Louis XVI, to the unlucky, unpopular Austrian bride, Marie Antoinette.

Apparently, the court architect Jacques Ange Gabriel (he who designed those great pillared Place de la Concorde façades) had a hard time of it after his first plans for the theatre were submitted in 1748, with work and funds typically interrupted by the Seven Years' War and the King's continuing shortage of money for the next twenty years. However, from Gabriel's long, often discouraged concentration came a novelty of technique, and even of orderly ornate beauty. Theretofore, theatres had customarily been rectangular. He conceived and built the Versailles Opéra as an oval of fine wood, with the accurate acoustics of a violin for the ears and, for the eyes, an opulent mélange of green-painted false-marble panels, white fluted pillars, intervening golden statues of goddesses, small golden zodiac signs, and golden balustrades around the lower balconies, topped with bull's-eye windows covered with golden grilles, like elegant prison windows. Rows of benches (now in place again with their blue cut-velvet cushions) served as orchestra seats. The Royal Family sat in state on front-row chairs in the raised dress circle to the theatre's rear, and over their heads was a series of loges, with square golden grilles, behind which they could retire to look at the performance without being stared at themselves. In the King's time, the floor was covered with Canadian bearskins against the cold—replaced today by a modest animal-brown wool carpet. It seems that during the wedding celebration to honor Marie Antoinette, the Opéra was used on three successive evenings to serve three different social pleasures, which became the ritual for all later marriage fêtes given there, often enough for the royal bastards. On the first night, by the use of remarkable machinery operated by ropes, the orchestra floor was raised to the level of the enormous stage and a gala dinner was served; on the second night, with the floor lowered, the Lully opera was performed; and on the third night, the floor having been hoisted up again, the theatre functioned as a ballroom for minuets. Closed after the Revolution and left to molder, the theatre was opened a few times by Louis Philippe in the nineteenth century to fête visiting minor royalty, and once by Napoleon III, for a dinner for Queen Victoria. After its recent renovation, it was reopened with the great Rameau divertissement "Les Indes Galantes," which was offered to Queen Elizabeth of England on her visit to Paris last spring. It seems worth noting that the troubles from which the Paris operas are now suffering to extinction began at the Versailles opera house last October, when the state sceneshifters sent from Paris first struck, causing to be cancelled the fashionable première of a new Cocteau ballet, "La Dame à la Licorne," since which no performance has even been attempted. In 1875, the Constitution of the Third Republic was proclaimed in the theatre, and no visitor to France's Fourth Republic should miss it, now that it has finally been made democratically visible.

Once again an intellectual, independent Left Wing—though anti-Communist—periodical has been suppressed by the police, on order of the French government, because it put into print certain seemingly incontestable unpleasant reports on exceptional phases of the conduct of the Algerian war. This week's *France-Observateur,* edited by Claude Bourdet (son of the noted author of social comedies), has been seized, in the fifth suppression in twenty months, for its publication of, and horrified comments on, the tortures, mostly by electricity, that were inflicted by French parachutist officers in Algiers on Henri Alleg, the French former editor of the *Alger Républicain,* which was politically against the Algerian war. The next day, Bourdet brought out an edition with the offending Alleg passages omitted but containing Bourdet's protest at the seizure and also at the loss of revenue—around twenty million francs—that the various seizures had caused. The Alleg torture case has become so widely discussed and so troubling an issue in France that Les Editions de Minuit, the little Resistance publishing group of the Nazi Occupation, recently published the whole book of Alleg's horrifying experiences, written in secret by him in prison and called "La Question"—the question being: Should the French torture political prisoners? From this book, which is still freely circulating, Bourdet's *Observateur* reprinted what it claims is nothing like the worst part of Alleg's gruesome story. An earlier issue of Jean-Jacques Servan-Schreiber's weekly *L'Express* was suppressed for giving similar information on the parachutists, who, as Alleg discovered, are the French Army's specially privileged, tough combat units. François Mauriac, the Catholic Academician, in his back-page *Express* column called "Bloc-Notes," has also written with Christian horror of the tortures. Nor has this French government action against the freedom of the press—a freedom basic in civilizing French concepts since the time of Voltaire—been confined to independent French papers only. Two January, 1958, numbers of our conformist *Saturday Evening Post* were temporarily impounded by the French police because they contained articles written for the *Post* by a former New York *Times* man who had easily gone behind the Algerian battle line to visit with the Front de Libération Nationale troops. He merely described their highly organized setup for supplies, weapons, food, and so on, but the French government apparently did not wish to have this presented to American or bilingual French readers here as having any reality, since Robert Lacoste, the French government's Minister in Algeria, has for months been saying that the war is "in its last quarter of an hour." International journalists here have also been scandalized that Miss Nora Beloff, Paris correspondent of the respected old British weekly *Observer,* was recently given, in private, a spirited, well-informed governmental calling down for her critical articles on the conduct of the Algerian war, the complaint against her having passed from the French Embassy in London to the British Embassy in Paris—all very polite and formal and menacing to the freedom of the responsible international press.

An understandable exception to this government censorship was made in the case of *Le Monde's* courageous publication in December of the extremely important report on French—and also Algerian—excesses in Algeria, as compiled on a tour of investigation by a distinguished French civilian Commission for the Safeguarding of Individual Rights and Liberties. This was indeed a public-spirited *Monde* service, since the paper printed this report, already much rumored about, without government authorization three months after it had been presented to the government, which had promised to publish it and then had done nothing. Nor did the government risk doing anything to the sternly reputable, influential *Monde*. Especially impressive in the text was a December, 1955, quotation—made long before the safeguarding commission had seemed necessary—by the then director of the French Sûreté Nationale, reporting on Algeria to his superior in Paris. He said he found it intolerable and embittering to human relations between the French and the natives that "French policemen can recall by their behavior the methods of the Gestapo," adding, "As a reserve officer, I cannot bear to see any French soldiers compared to the sinister S.S. of the Wehrmacht."

France-Observateur, in both issues of this week, reports that for the third consecutive time delegations from the British Labour Party have demonstrated on Saturday morning in front of the office of the French military attaché in London, to denounce "the parody of French justice" at the recent trial of the well-educated Algerian woman Mlle. Djamila Bouhired. Accused of complicity in terrorist bombings, she was legally condemned to death by a French court in Algiers, where—most illegally, it is claimed—her counsel was not permitted to plead for her. The British Labourites have been demanding that President Coty reprieve her from her approaching execution, and in Oslo the president of the Norwegian High Court of Justice, along with many judges, two prefects, one Army general, and a pleiades of professors, writers, poets, and so on, has demanded a revision of the Bouhired trial, if only for the sake of France.

Since the French Army's deplorable bombing of Sakiet, which was a real and great shock to most French—except the majority of the French deputies, to judge from their lack of bold, angered comment in Parliament—the war in Algeria has significantly increased in activity, on both the rebel and the French sides. Typical is one of this week's front-page communiqués in *Le Figaro,* announcing "very violent fighting and ambushes in Algérois and the Constantinois," with a hundred and sixteen rebels laid low, and forty-five French military men killed and eleven missing, which, *Figaro* adds, is "the worst fate of all, perhaps, considering the more savage natives' mutilating form of revenge against the Western white man who still defends the remnant of France's North African empire." Never in modern times, fortunately, have so few men on both sides been killed in a war, but this war has been costing the French the gigantic outlay of a billion francs per diem, thus practically bankrupting the state without the war's being won. The present so-called "good offices" of our Mr. Robert Murphy in trying to settle the differences between the French government and President Bourguiba of Tunisia seemed to be progressing usefully until the French Foreign Affairs Ministry announced that good offices from foreigners could not include stopping this forty-month-old persistent, envenomed, and perhaps final white and Arab war.

May 25

For the past fortnight, the French Fourth Republic has functioned in what has seemed a state of unrealities that have become facts, upon which it still survives, with difficulty. Wednesday evening, the pro-Gaullist newspaper *Paris-Presse* said, with irony, "To sum it all up, the situation is now clear. Parliament has confidence in Pflimlin, who has confidence in General Salan, who has confidence in General de Gaulle, who has no confidence in Parliament but is waiting for it to show confidence in him." *Paris-Presse* then undermined its concise gibe by adding that things here in France "are obviously less simple, less tragic, and less absurd" than that. Actually, the tragedy, the lack of logic to the point of farce and fantasy, and the intricate complexities have all been major, dominant, equal, and probably unavoidable since May 13th, just twelve days ago. That was when the contagious Algiers insurrection broke out against the Paris government, soon coming under the command of a military and civilian junta to which General Raoul Salan, chief of the

French forces in Algeria, gave his blessing—a troubling double performance in which the General is still starring, rather like a trick cavalryman aloft, riding with one foot on the back of each of two dangerous, plunging horses. The strain on parliamentarianism and the Fourth Republic was increased by General Charles de Gaulle's stately offer, repeated at his press conference last Monday, to take over power in France—an offer that, as the days go by, makes him seem the inevitable, unique, and perfectly non-Republican solution to the Fourth Republic's present political drama of paralyzation.

In the accumulated confusions, one thing alone now looks clear. For the first time in peace, Paris is not the political capital of France. Temporarily, at least, the colonial city of Algiers is the French political epicenter, is making the violent, dominating political news, is claiming to be the revolutionary leader "of the renewal of the French spirit," and has been making the active decisions, to which Paris is helplessly susceptible. Even if in the next few days, or possibly weeks, President Coty, equipped with all due legality squeezed from the Paris parliament, should offer de Gaulle the leadership of France, Algiers would still triumph, because its citizens—by the hundreds of thousands—lawlessly shouted for him first, crying, "De Gaulle to power! *Vive de Gaulle!*" This is a call for the savior that has not yet been massively heard here on the Paris streets.

The two weeks' growth and emerging aim of the Algerian uprising constitute the most peculiar colonial rebellion of modern times. The dissidents' goal—since it was a movement from the Right, drawn from Algeria's million French *colons,* or white settlers, who are the country's prosperous racial minority—was not to obtain independence from France but to attach themselves indissolubly to it, in order to make sure that they would not be abandoned by it through the unsuccessful ending of the three-and-a-half-year-old, ill-fated French war against the liberty-loving *fellagha* rebels, who are the activists among the nine million Moslem majority. In case you have not been able to unravel the tangled Algiers events since May 13th, it seems that on that afternoon there was a solemn, angry memorial service at the city's Monument for the Dead to honor three French Army soldiers killed by the Algerian nationalist forces in reprisal for the execution of native soldiers by the French. After this patriotic service and the chanting of the "Marseillaise," a gigantic riot occurred, in which thousands of the French citizenry, instead of assaulting the Moslem quarters, as usual when enraged, sacked the French Government Building, aided by anti-*fellagha* Moslems. According to the latest newspaper reports here, the riot was the opening battering ram of a well-laid plot by a group of hard-core *colons,* who had distributed tracts all morning to both the white and the Moslem populations. The tract urged an uprising against "the worn-out system," meaning the weak Paris governments of splintered political parties, and especially the Pflimlin government. Pflimlin, the tract said, was scheming to hand over Algeria to the *fellaghas* in a negotiated peace, stranding the *colons* in costly independence from France—a money-losing, undesired liberty indeed. There was also, perhaps, a less well-laid plot for May 13th among certain professional French Army officers, long bitter against what they have called the inefficient, ignorant, unpatriotic Paris politicians, who, they claim, engineered their defeat in Indo-China and, peace being more popular with most French voters, have been hamstringing the Algerian war. Friday, the independent Paris paper *Le Monde* printed a May 13th letter that the youngish Brigadier General Jacques Massu, of the crack, brutal 10th Paratroop Division, sent to his whole division, officers and men, which at one point said, classically, "The hour is grave." Then it assailed the Paris stabs in the Army's back, "aimed at dishonoring us and weakening our accomplishments," and asked that the letter be sent to the soldiers' families in France. "You, our parents, and our friends in Metropolitan France have an obligation to help us in denouncing the campaigns against the Algerian war by so-called intellectuals, lay or Christian, and those who have lost their national sentiment and now play the game of the foreigners, whether of the East or West," it said—meaning Russia and the French Communists, who call it "the dirty war," and the United States, with its anti-colonial and supposedly pro-Algerian foreign policy. That May afternoon, Massu, with his red beret, his Cyrano de Bergerac nose, his brown-and-green camouflage battle dress, and his jumping boots, was reportedly a noticeable stalwart in the frenetic Algiers crowds, which, as the excitement, violence, and rioting continued, became host to a new phenomenon—fraternization between *colons* and Moslems in a sudden brotherly unity that, after a hundred and thirty years of French occupation, is already being called "the miracle of Algeria" and that, to common cries of "Long live French Algeria!," is still going on all over the land.

To restore order among the delirious mobs, General Salan took command of the uprising, and just before midnight issued a communiqué saying, "Having the mission to protect you, I have provisionally taken in hand the destinies of Algeria." By May 15th, the General was himself shouting with the crowds for de Gaulle. Since then, Salan has been nightly addressing throngs of about fifteen thousand and invoking the installation of de Gaulle from a rostrum that now flies the tricolor of France barred with de Gaulle's Cross of Lorraine. Three nights ago, on Thursday, when the still wild and enthusiastic crowds shouted their newest slogan, "The Army to power!," he thanked them for *"cette bonne parole"* (for "these good words"), adding, "We shall all march up the Champs-Elysées together and be covered with flowers."

Two days ago, a newly enlarged Comité du Salut Public de l'Algérie et du Sahara held its first meeting in the Algiers Summer Palace, with a red carpet, an honor guard of spahis holding sabres aloft, and General Salan in the chair, surrounded by delegates from the Departments of Oran, the Sahara, and Constantine (some of them natives who had been flown in), and by about three times as many French *colons* as Moslems. General Massu and Mohammed Sid Cara, former Paris deputy from Oran, were elected joint presidents. The official report of the meeting declared that the Salut Public movement had done more work in three days than any Paris government had done in three years, and added that it was its firm resolution to set up in France "a public-safety government, headed by General de Gaulle, to demand a profound reform of the Republic's institutions."

Yesterday afternoon, according to a prepared speech by Pflimlin that, inexplicably, was first broadcast on the national French radio at two-fifteen this morning, when the French were asleep, the Prefecture of Ajaccio, in Corsica, was captured by force by Pascal Arrighi, Corsican Radical Socialist deputy to Parliament here, on his return from a visit to Algiers, an action in which he was aided by some local Ajaccio citizens and a hundred and fifty French Army paratroopers stationed there. Premier Pflimlin came almost out in the open in his speech when he said that "despite the culpable conduct of certain men," the fraternization between French Europeans and Moslems had "given hope for the birth of a new Algeria"; but that there was no such pregnant excuse for illegality in Corsica. "I have not the right to hide from you the fact that the same danger exists in

France," he went on. "It is my duty to warn all those French who are attached to their liberties as guaranteed by the Republic's laws that sedition-mongers here are attempting to drag us to the brink of civil war."

As seemed natural and heartening, Pierre Mendès-France made the major diehard liberal speeches recently in the Assembly. He not only denounced the Algerian generals but declared that the more important general, Charles de Gaulle, had "aggravated a dramatic situation" in his press-conference speech last week. Mendès said that during the war he had been a follower of de Gaulle, in which he took some pride, and had always thought that someday—Mendès himself being a critical pessimist in political affairs—de Gaulle would once more become the artisan of a national reconciliation, fatally due in France. "However," Mendès said, "sedition has just broken loose in Algiers. Civilians and military men took a weighty decision in invoking the name of de Gaulle. In the face of insolent sedition," Mendès said boldly to Pflimlin, "your strength is your legitimacy," as representing Republican law. "It is the Republic that entrusted these military chiefs with soldiers to command," he went on, "and it is time that these chiefs were recalled to a sense of their duty and honor. . . . General de Gaulle should resuscitate the emotion that he arouses in the people in order to strengthen the Republic, for which he now reserves his severities—after, admittedly, having restored it to life following the Liberation."

Half a million men of the French Army are in Algeria, and a handful are in Germany; Paris not only is without protection but, were it not for the military men who now operate as the official bridge across the Mediterranean, would be without communication with Algiers, its alarming godchild. Pflimlin is calling a special Assembly session tomorrow, to be followed by his bill for constitutional reforms, which comes up Tuesday. It may not pass, since, with desperate intelligence, it cuts the deputies' Parliament-sitting to only five months of talk, sets the limit of a government's life at two years, and prohibits the overthrow of any government unless a new Premier and new government are all ready to replace the old one. This constitutional reform has been talked of for twelve years, was cooked up in committee in four days, and is slated to be passed in one week—thus being twelve years one week and four days late in contemporary history. It is supposed that Pflimlin will be followed by General de Gaulle.

De Gaulle's enemies will automatically be the Communists. There are well-informed Parisians who think that Moscow, with its telescopic long view of the world, will not order French Communists into street riots against him. The Muscovite vision, they say, sees any republic as a rotting fruit that will sooner or later be soft enough to drop into their hands—a process that de Gaulle, by his personal flame, might only hasten. Militant Communist Party members declare, however, that if he comes to power they will fight against him in the streets—"our skin against his"—despite his having been a war leader whom the Communist Resistance greatly served and admired. If the Communists choose to fight, they will paralyze France by strikes. The Socialists, though they have hardened in the last few days against de Gaulle, will doubtless accept him, since the choice for them now is de Gaulle or a revived Front Populaire with the Communists, in which the minority Socialists would be eaten alive, as if by political cannibals. The hour is indeed grave for the Republic. Much depends on General de Gaulle.

To judge by his recent statements, he still has no sense of human relations and no personal ambitions—nothing but his sense of sacred destiny, which has seemed to be an intermittent one. He is, as a political poet recently said, like a stained-glass Chartres window—an awkward, colorful, large male figure seen against heavenly light, a glassy symbol of devotion that, because of its optical distance from human observers, prompts them to reverence. A giant of a Frenchman in outer and also in hidden ways, he has just been critically described by Jean-Paul Sartre as "the interminable man." Loving nothing but France, he is the Frenchman of sacrifice.

June 1

Never since the time of Mme. de Sévigné have so many high-styled, personal, historic letters about vitally important public events been written and rapidly sent off in France, to become the talk of the nation, as have been written here this past week. On Thursday afternoon, beginning promptly at three o'clock, the reading aloud of one of them by the Speaker of the Assembly, addressed to him and *MM. et Mmes. les Membres du Parlement* by M. René Coty, President of the French Republic, at a moment of national destiny, was rewarded by a scene of such fury, tumult, and party passions as will leave a deep scar on the annals of that institution. Speaker André Le Troquer, standing narrow-shouldered in his evening clothes—which are the Speaker's prescribed attire, night or day—and addressing the Assembly in his fast, experienced, smooth voice, first invited the tense deputies filling the hemicycle to rise to listen to the message from the highest official of France. As everyone now knows, the Coty letter was a despairing appeal to the Assembly to call upon General Charles de Gaulle to form a legal, exceptional government to save the crumbling Fourth Republic. "Now we are on the edge of civil war," read Le Troquer in his quick, skimming tones. "On one side and on the other, people seem to be preparing for fratricidal strife. What will become of our France?" Then he went on to this passage: "In the moment of danger for the country and the Republic, I have turned toward the most illustrious of Frenchmen, toward him who, in the darkest years of our history, was our leader for the reconquest of liberty . . . one whose incomparable moral authority would ensure the salvation of the country and the Republic. I ask General de Gaulle to confer with the head of the State. I shall then, in my soul and conscience—" At a sign from the Communist leader Jacques Duclos, on the front bench of his party's seats, the entire Communist group of about a hundred and forty men and women deputies sat down, in one obedient, interrupting action, on hearing the phrase "soul and conscience," as if the utterance of such words in connection with de Gaulle and power had sent them a little underground, in company with many neighboring Socialists, who seated themselves in belligerent accord. At such gross manners, a deputy from the Center contemptuously shrilled *"Goujat!"* ("Scum!") at the Left.

The Coty letter came to an end after his promise, *"en mon âme et conscience"* to resign from the Republic's Presidency if his attempt failed. Instantly, pandemonium broke loose. The Communists beat their desks with their hands, bellowing insults and threats, shouting "Fascism shall not pass!," and shaking their clenched fists at the other deputies in what looked like genuine human hate and destructive rage. At a further signal from Duclos, they suddenly jumped to their feet and burst into "La Marseillaise," while the other deputies (except for those sympathizing Socialists) remained seated, as a mark of indignation, but gesticulated and twisted around to scream epithets at the Left. Somebody in the topmost visitors' gallery let fall a cascade of tracts onto the heads of the Christian M.R.P.s sitting directly beneath. The Communists had already started another song, "Le Chant du Départ"—the celebrated Revolutionary hymn written to honor the fifth anniversary of the fall of the Bastille and sung even under Napoleon's early rule. At its most famous line—*"Tremblez, ennemis de la France!"*—the Communists lifted their arms, like a choir trained in elocutionary gestures of hatred, to point to the deputies on the Right, and at the end of the song they rapidly walked out of the Assembly in a body, the session having been declared at an end by Speaker Le Troquer. Then the members of the Pflimlin government walked out; the Poujadists, of the extreme Right, marched out, also chorusing the "Marseillaise"; and the rest of the hemicycle emptied itself quickly. The whole scene, from the Coty letter on through to the last note of the last song, had taken exactly fifteen minutes by the big Assembly clock.

De Gaulle's most important and characteristic letter of the week was dated Wednesday, an hour before midnight, and was written in answer to one of harsh criticism sent to him by the Socialist former President, old Vincent Auriol. The General said, in part, that "the Algerian events were provoked, as you well know, by the chronic impotence of French governments," and that in his desire to serve the country he had struck "determined opposition" in the Assembly. "As I could not consent to receive power from any other source but the people, or at least from their representatives," he wrote, "I fear that we are moving toward anarchy and civil war. In this case, those who, moved by a sectarianism incomprehensible to me, will have prevented me once more from saving the Republic will bear a heavy responsibility." Then emerged his great, tragic final phrase, in the style of the seventeenth-century French classic dramatist Corneille. "As for me," the General wrote, "there will be nothing more until I die, except to dwell in my sorrow."

If this vitally influential trio of letters, each written on its own altitude of character and of patriotic love, best clarify the week's events when read chronologically backward, the rest of what was said, secretly or overtly, during the week was entirely confusing. To put the main and opening fact simply, the Socialist Party members not only were aroused by Auriol's letter to intransigence against de Gaulle's coming to power but were also partly in rebellion against their own Party chief, Guy Mollet. In early 1956, Mollet was elected Premier on his Party's regular platform of pacifism and anti-colonialism, but once he had been hit by tomatoes and dung thrown by Algiers *colons* on his first visit there in February of that year, he speeded up the Algerian war against the native rebels with a military severity that even Rightist deputies had not dared demand or hope for. Furthermore, Mollet this week favored de Gaulle's candidacy after a secret, pleasant exchange of letters with the General, which he hid from his followers until Pflimlin let the cat out of the bag in Parliament. However, behind his back, his Socialist Party members had organized their mutiny against de Gaulle without telling him, either.

The week's events soon turned into the regular farces, dramas, and nocturnal Assembly sittings of an exceptionally desperate French political crisis, plus fatiguing late nights of conference for the elderly important men like Coty and Auriol, and even de Gaulle, who made four three-hour motor trips between his country house in Colombey-les-Deux-Eglises and Paris in his old black Citroën—a total of more than a thousand miles, partly done in the dead of night at great speed—accompanied by motorcycle outriders and pursued by exhausted reporters and photographers. One day, there were three tiring sessions in the Assembly, which meant nine flights of stairs to be climbed by those of us faithful listeners who sat in the modest topmost visitors' gallery. At the Tuesday session, Communist Duclos made the most able, if hypocritical, speech for the defense of the Republic, and old Socialist former Premier Ramadier mumbled in his gray beard about the perennial piety of Socialist actions. On Thursday, when Paris became alarmed at the long delays and, through the English papers and the B.B.C. (never more popular here, what with the censoring of the French press and radio), learned of the Algiers threats of a showdown and of Algiers planes being poised for flight to France, one of the earlier days of inaction was called "Chloroform Day" by the Communists, since the de Gaulle push in Paris seemed anesthetized. At one point during the week, Mollet and a fellow-Socialist named Deixonne actually took a private plane, on de Gaulle's summons, to fly out to Colombey-les-Deux-Eglises and talk with the General, whom Deixonne, obviously surprised, later described as "nothing like Louis XIV." Motoring back to the airstrip, they were held up on the road by a herd of cows.

On Thursday, the false rumor was bruited about—two days too soon—that Coty had accepted the resignation of Pflimlin's government, which indicated (also too soon, it turned out) that through last-minute Socialist aid de Gaulle would have a comfortable parliamentary voting majority for his Assembly investiture and could come to power. From about ten that night until the early morning, well-to-do young French, in good and sometimes spectacular cars, drove in an endless carrousel up and down the Champ-Elysées and around the Place de la Concorde and other districts, tooting their horns (forbidden for several years), either because they enjoyed tooting them again or because they were in favor of de Gaulle. In any case, they always produced the same three short, two long squawks, which supposedly could be decoded to mean *"De Gaule au pouvoir"*—a gay but silly and provocative performance. The next night, when they were giving a sonorous encore, Communist militants armed with shovels—an odd nocturnal weapon for the Champs—smashed some cars and faces. Result: seven injured, no one killed, many of both factions arrested.

The most significant demonstration of mere people—as distinguished from Assembly activities—against de Gaulle was Wednesday's gigantic late-afternoon march of probably a quarter of a million men, women, and students, mostly bearing signs that said only *"Vive la République!,"* from the Place de la Nation to the Place de la République. It was organized by a suddenly collected group of resistants to de Gaulle, called the Comité d'Action et de Défense Républicaine; the Communists were not invited to take part, but they forced their way in. Beneath the majestic carved columns on the Avenue du Trône, set up in the time of Louis XVI, tracts were distributed by professors and their students, the demands being dignified and restrained. They said, in part, "General de Gaulle's last declaration leaves no doubt; it is a defiance to the workers and the people of all France. The question is not now one of either government or a constitution but of our most elemental liberties. Freedom of speech, of public assembly, of unions and their right to strike is today menaced by military power." The demonstrators marched by professions, by trades, by tragic experiences they had shared in the war. One old ex-schoolmaster carried a homemade wooden sign with bits of bread tied to its top, illustrating the ancient French cry "I am defending my bread." French Negroes from the lower African territories marched in affiliation with all groups. The most attractive section was the women lawyers, mostly nice-looking, who got heavy applause from the sidewalks. There were workers from the Renault automobile factory, some still in their dungarees and pushing the bicycles they had been about to ride home. Among the professors marched Francis Perrin, France's most distinguished physicist. Among the intellectuals were Jean-Paul Sartre and Simone de Beauvoir (frequently cheered) and the movie and stage star Gérard Philipe (whom the sidewalk girls screamed for). The most dramatic group was the former inmates of German concentration camps in their blue-and-white-striped uniforms, like pajamas for a last fatal sleep. As the marchers turned into the Boulevard Voltaire toward the Place de la République, the Communist elements filtered in with their slogans and signs, and the strictly republican character of the march changed. There were signs and shouts of "Down with de Gaulle!," "Down with Fascism!," "Put de Gaulle in a museum!," and, referring to his long neck, "Put the giraffe in the zoo!" Wisely, the police had been given orders not to interfere. It was the biggest, most orderly assembly of street demonstrators in Paris since the war.

Last night, it seemed almost—but not quite—sure that de Gaulle would go before the Assembly today to be invested. His appearance was announced for ten o'clock this morning, and then for eleven, and then it was said that he might not go at all if he failed of the majority of four hundred that he demanded in advance. The ceremony was finally set for three this afternoon. The afternoon started out as a fine, dulcet sunny one for this tense national event, so anxiously desired by millions of French, so angrily impeded by other millions. By two this afternoon, it took at least a press card even to stand on the quais across from the Assembly. Armed police in vans had assembled without sounding their sirens and were lined in silence everywhere around the Parliament. Behind it, in the Place du Palais-Bourbon, front rooms in the Hôtel de Bourgogne et Montana had been taken by a few French ladies and some photographers who wanted to see the General emerge from his car. He had said earlier this week that he had "a phobia about the Assembly," but he was persuaded that his presentation for investiture might be counted illegal—and also that he might be thought lacking in courage—if he failed to mount the tribune to state his elementary program. For the ceremony, he was dressed in gray, and he looked waxen and weary as he made his brief, succinct, intelligent speech. He said, in part, that "the government I shall form—granted your confidence—will immediately set to work on constitutional reform." Such a reform, if he gets it, will doubtless give him the powers of an American President, which he has always insisted were needed by a Premier of France. He defined the three basic principles of republicanism in France: One, that universal suffrage is the source of all power; two, that the legislative and executive elements must be separate; and, three, that the government must be responsible to Parliament—which (as in Pflimlin's earlier proposed reform) he said he would send on a six-month vacation, to leave him free to govern without its constant gabble and interference.

During de Gaulle's short speech, the Communists sat completely quiet. There had been a top-drawer rumor that Moscow, through its Paris Ambassador, would tell the Communist Party to do just that and then make a few forceful street demonstrations, though not forceful enough to have their own men killed. Shortly after three, the General finished his speech and retired from the chamber to await the Assembly's vote. In the Tuileries, shock troops of the Compagnie Républicaine de Sécurité, in blue uniforms, gently cleared the gardens of people, starting from the Place de la Concorde. The guards, with their carbines on their shoulders, pushed the few lingering adults along toward the Louvre exit in a leisurely manner and corralled the last straggling children who had paused for a final kick at their footballs. By six o'clock, the Tuileries was empty beneath its trees, even of the armed guards. The voting for or against de Gaulle was still going on. A thunderstorm suddenly broke the good weather. The sirens of police cars were audible along the Seine, but there was no sign of any anti-de Gaulle manifestants—perhaps too dampened to push on to their goal, the French Parliament. Finally, at eight o'clock, the news came that the General had been elected by a pitifully small majority of 329 to 224. The evening ended in a vigorous dark storm.

June 8

In the almost unbelievable public changes that have taken place during the past two weeks, General de Gaulle, who is victoriously responsible for them, has himself been changed in the process into M. de Gaulle. Properly speaking, that is. In becoming Président du Conseil (in the Third Republic more classically called Premier), de Gaulle as governing head of the Fourth Republic automatically outranks himself as General, and must take the superior title of M. le Président. The result, so far, is that he is simply referred to as both, eighteen years of his fame as *le Général* being too strongly associated with his militant, patriotic personality for the public and the newspapers to drop it easily.

The newly formed Cabinet of M. de Gaulle, as everybody expected from his contemptuous opinion of most parliamentarians during these last, fatal years of their disservice to the Republic, furnishes—in part, at any rate—a welcome, important novelty for France. A fourth of his Ministers are men who have done many things but at least have never been deputies. His Minister of Foreign Affairs, M. Maurice Couve de Murville, was, until last week, French Ambassador in Bonn, and before that in Washington, and thus knows American and German policies inside out—highly useful experience for this unusual new French government. He is, furthermore, a strong United Nations and NATO man, and this may quiet Washington's fears that de Gaulle will be intransigently nationalist. Another de Gaulle Minister with Quai d'Orsay ties is M. B. Cornut-Gentille, former Ambassador to the Argentine, who as yet has no fixed portfolio. The new government's Minister of Defense, M. Pierre Guillaumat, has been a topflight functionary in national bureaus dealing with atomic energy, mines, and, above all, oil, the last being of greatest importance to France since the recent Sahara oil discoveries. De Gaulle's forty-six-year-old *chef de Cabinet,* M. Georges Pompidou, after a precociously successful bureaucratic career, has for two years been director of the Rothschild Bank.

The Minister who is inevitably arousing the most public interest and curiosity is André Malraux, so-called Minister of Information. The information services are indeed under him, but actually he is something rarer, called Minister Delegated to the Presidency of the

Council and meaning de Gaulle's Special Minister. Informally and characteristically, he has just referred to himself, according to one Paris newspaper, as Minister of Urgent Affairs. The most renowned literary figure in France today, an *homme engagé* since youth, a legendary romantic adventurer in the early days of the Chinese revolution and in the Spanish civil war, a Resistance hero, the Goncourt Prize author of the great revolutionary novel "Man's Fate," and the most brilliant intimate admirer of de Gaulle, whom he served briefly as Information Minister in the post-Liberation provisional government and later as a phenomenal rally speaker for his ill-fated R.P.F. political party, Malraux is, to boot, the most compulsive, stimulating conversationalist in French intellectual circles, offering the widest panorama of political and social ideas. It is therefore not surprising that, since he is always extremely quotable, fragments of some of his conversations apropos of the "urgent affairs" of de Gaulle—and of the nation—over the past two weeks should, through the reports of friends, be frequently heard in Paris.

Three days ago, Malraux is known to have said to a friend, speaking of de Gaulle's aim, "It is capital that this revolution of French institutions—because, let's face it, 'revolution' is the correct word—should be accomplished without the shedding of a drop of blood. You understand, if the price of what he is trying to do were to be even a thousand dead in Algeria, for the General that would be too much." When the friend asked "And what if this bloodless revolution fails?," Malraux reportedly replied, "Then the forces that only he can hold in check will set to work within fifteen days." It will not be possible, in that event, to escape civil war, he went on to say, and France will be lost. It will be the way it was in Spain; civil war will not be localized but will break out regionally, and, weakened as the country already is, it will be ravelled away—and North Africa, too—until nothing is left. It will last three years; there will be a million dead. There will be no more France as a great nation; it will be finished.

The outstanding general criticisms of de Gaulle's Cabinet were against his choice of the recent Christian M.R.P. Premier Pierre Pflimlin and of the former Socialist Premier Guy Mollet, but in Algiers there is acute and dangerous resentment against all the Cabinet members who represent what the Algiers insurgents call *Le Système,* meaning all the familiar political faces from a now discredited Parliament—all, of course, except Deputy Jacques Soustelle, himself a member of the Algerian junta. This week, Malraux reportedly said, speaking of de Gaulle's struggle with the Assembly, "Though the parliamentary spirit is fairly foreign to me, I must say that Ministres d'Etat Pflimlin and Mollet showed from the first day an admirable civic spirit." It is known that they and President Coty, who has been described as "even more Gaullist than Malraux," having all been profoundly alarmed by the French state's collapse of authority and deeply convinced that only de Gaulle could save Algeria, and perhaps the country, from anarchy and bloodshed, acted as good-will bargainers between the Assembly and the General. Day by day, they ascertained what the recalcitrant deputies demanded. When the Assembly agreed to grant the General special powers to govern by decree, it ceded them for France but balked at letting him have them for Algeria, where he considered them an absolute necessity. When Mollet carried to him the message to that effect, the General is reported to have said *"Bon,"* stating that if he was invested Sunday, he was supposed to go to Algeria within a few days, and if a vital decision arose there, was he supposed to hurry back to Paris and convoke the deputies so as to meet the emergency? *"Eh bien,"* he added, it would not be he who would come to Paris to convoke them, it would be the parachutists. For he would be dead.

According to men around Malraux, the General with difficulty determined on patience in dealing with Parliament's reckless, talkative dawdling, even though he considered that every day's delay helped the junta forces in Algeria that were organizing against him, which, if the Assembly would hasten to face up to the inevitable, he could check. His patience with the Assembly, like his determination to avoid anyone's shedding a drop of blood in his name, was, in his mind, to serve as proof, which the whole country could see, that those who called him a dictator, or a Fascist, pursuing power, had either lied or erred.

As for the General's aims in Algeria, Malraux has reportedly said that "even if this recent new Franco-Moslem fraternity was in the beginning more or less organized"—even *truqué,* some French declared—"it is clearly apparent now that it is an extraordinarily popular and powerful movement, with a historic sweep." To make a new Algeria, two elements are already available, he thinks—the French Army and the Arabs. Astonishingly, according to him, the Arabs fraternize with the soldiers, who are all young, and call them "the Frenchmen from France," in distinction to the *colons,* or

Algerian French settlers. And the soldiers fraternize with the Arabs as a way of dissociating themselves from the *ancien régime* in Algeria, with its fifty or more dominant wealthy families, who practically own whole *départements,* such as the winegrowing Département de Bône, and are now considered a diminishing part of the Algerian political picture. For an important new social pattern is supposedly being formed. What de Gaulle will try if peace is established, Malraux is said to have declared, is to launch a really big fraternal operation between the Arabs and the young soldiers.

As for the French Communists, who will be de Gaulle's most tenacious local enemies, it is said to be Malraux's opinion that the Gaullists think they can considerably enfeeble the Communists' already rather weak attacks (the Party never having recovered its full popularity in Paris since the Hungarian suppression) by taking a series of real measures, or doing things, as he expressed it, the way they're done by the Anglo-Saxons, who believe more in realities than in words—and who are right, too. In a nutshell, by fighting Communist ideology with facts. Apparently, de Gaulle does not think it useful to fight against Communism in the name of any ideology, even a denunciation of capitalism, since mere capitalism is no longer the acute question. It is, instead, necessary to fight by setting forth objectives for the working class that have hitherto not been possible under French capitalism. Furthermore, on June 18th, the eighteenth anniversary of de Gaulle's historic broadcast from London to France, in which, to however few listeners, he announced that France would fight on, and thus founded the Resistance, Malraux, evidently counting on bringing to bear what is in theory a brilliant psychological coup, plans to have the General hold a parade not on the Champs-Elysées, where the official parades of Paris are traditionally held, for the bourgeoisie and what is left of the old carriage trade, but in the Place de la République, for the populace that arrives by Métro; that is, he will hold the parade for the working class in its neighborhood stronghold, thus perhaps changing the geography of public feeling and partisanship.

Who or what is really responsible for the horrifying crisis of fallen republican authority in France? To this question, which one hears on all sides in Paris, Malraux has a curious answer, according to friends' reports. In large part, he says, the accumulated collapse has been due to the taste of the French deputies for mere talk. When the General appeared before the Assembly, he spoke simple truths and was impressive: Certain things are going to have to be done to get the country out of the trouble it is in; if you don't want to do them, we won't get out of the trouble; in that case, I'll simply go back home to my village of Colombey. In the Assembly, at the end, even Duclos, who is ordinarily a precise speaker, spoke, says Malraux, for a half hour without saying anything. His speech had no reality; it was an abstract discourse on Communism which was not Communist, against a dictator who was not a dictator. It is this garrulousness that has made a farce of the republican parliamentary form.

Just before the General flew to Algiers, he is said to have remarked to Malraux that he was an old man, to which Malraux replied that he did not seem to be one. The General reportedly then said he would have energy till the day he died, like Clemenceau, but he had the feeling within him that he was old. He said he had done what he could—once. The result of what he was doing now would be only to give a certain glow to France. If he succeeded this time—which at the moment appeared possible—and if for French youth his *patrie* could before he died become a reality, then, despite all, he would have brought about the real Liberation. General de Gaulle was, Malraux is said to have declared, in vivid description of that moment, in a state of both hope and despair that was not far from true grandeur.

September 24

During General Charles de Gaulle's weekend of speechmaking in four key provincial cities—Strasbourg, Rennes, Bordeaux, and Lille (his birthplace)—on behalf of his new constitution, which is to be voted on in a referendum this Sunday, he realistically told the immense crowds, in his toneless but trumpetlike voice, that his aim was "for France to keep her place in the hard world of today" with modernized governing institutions. As one innovation, his constitution could prevent Parliament from making French governments fall like autumn leaves (but several times a year). In his speeches, he mentioned France's need for greatness but did not refer, as he used to, to her old habits of glory. With further realism, he begged his listeners for "a massive number of yes votes, a crushing majority of yes votes, which would be a proof of faith in him who now speaks to you—faith that he needs," he added loudly, in that stately, confidential manner with which he refers to himself in the third person, as if he were his own public witness. For this referendum, each of the possibly twenty-eight million voters (who have had to register specially for the exceptional balloting event) is being sent a four-page copy of the new constitution, so that its ninety-two clauses can be perused. Though the referendum has only acceptance or rejection of the constitution as its immediate goal, the mere monosyllables of "yes" and "no" will, in an inferential way, have a three-way spread. The yes votes will mean that de Gaulle should be kept in power as Premier until November, when, it would seem logical, he himself can be voted on as a new kind of powerful, executive President of the Republic. The Sunday yes votes will also be an affirmation for a legitimatized Fifth Republic, which de Gaulle represents in advance—as, indeed, he seems to represent everything salvational now in sight.

A sharp-witted old Paris charwoman recently said to a foreign acquaintance, "*Bien sûr,* my husband and I will vote for de Gaulle, but without enthusiasm." A youngish Paris businessman voiced the same prevalent feeling by saying, "I shall vote yes and think no." A millionaire industrialist more candidly said, "Certainly we don't want him, but we will vote for him. Better vote for him than for a revolution." Three weeks ago, Parisians already were saying that everybody would vote for de Gaulle, though nobody was a Gaullist, and that he would get a landslide eighty per cent of the votes. This figure has now been more temperately estimated at around sixty-five per cent. Not even his bitterest political enemies think that he can lose. The French will vote for him in masses because in this catastrophically troubled year for France he is the unique, untarnished great figure on their horizon to turn toward; they will vote for him by the attraction of historical gravity, with none of the magic delirium of adulation that gilded his majestic popularity after the Liberation, when France was at his feet.

De Gaulle's weekend provincial crowds were the first to be enthusiastic. The main reason the French have mostly lacked open enthusiasm for him seems to be that he worryingly reminds them of themselves and of their ancestors, and of those special figures in history to whom their ancestors rallied, with increasingly diminishing returns—Napoleon Bonaparte and then Louis Napoleon, who, at his own request, was transformed by the French citizens' vote from a President into the shape of an Emperor. This Second Empire recollection has inspired de Gaulle's political opponents—who consider his republicanism suspect and his constitution's strengthening of the President's powers dangerously Bonapartesque—to nickname him the Imperial President, the Prince President, and the Monarchical President. Last Sunday in Lille, on a wall of the house where his father, a professor of philosophy and literature, lived, and where, sixty-seven years ago, Charles de Gaulle was born, the local Communists derisively scrawled "Charles XI born here," putting him in direct succession to Charles X, France's last Bourbon king, who believed in absolute monarchy. Something from all these characters to whom the French at times have mistakenly rallied has been rubbed off, by a kind of cruel decalcomania, onto the electoral picture of de Gaulle, including a supposed likeness to General Boulanger on his black horse and, obviously, to de Gaulle's arch-enemy, the anti-republican, autocratic Marshal Pétain. Today, in the confused light of all these historic warnings, pressures, and hopes, mixed with many Frenchmen's latent shame for their veneration of Vichy and the instinctive French suspicion, ever since the Dreyfus case, of all high-up Army men in political life, General de Gaulle alarms people's imaginations as their prospective Fifth Republic political leader, just as his unquestioned probity, lofty intelligence, and Gothic character rouse their faith in him as a man and as the only figure—or so they believe—who can morally hold France together.

The greatest deterrent to de Gaulle is that he was brought back onto today's scene by the bulk and cream of the French Army in their Algiers *coup d'état* which successfully invoked his name as its borrowed banner. "At the present moment," comments a brilliant British correspondent, writing with a detachment that the French now lack, "liberals and diehards in France are waiting to see which way the General will turn after the referendum. He has left the diehards an almost free hand in Algeria for four months. He could have done little else without revealing the limitations of his own power. . . . He has nonetheless kept alive the hope that the policy of Algiers is not his." The danger of civil war that de Gaulle faced four months ago, with the prospect of insurrectional French paratroopers dropping on undefended France, is the same civil-war danger, with the same *paras,* that is being conjured up now—plus Communists fighting against them from behind Paris street barricades if de Gaulle loses and if, as is his habit at dead-end moments in his personal history, he simply goes back home to Colombey-les-Deux-

Eglises and leaves France flat. What the liberals here profoundly fear, on the other hand, as do the French politicians, is that if de Gaulle wins with too massive a vote he will be a presidential prisoner of this extreme Right, with no sizable liberal or Left Wing parliamentary opposition to help maintain his liberty. Pierre Mendès-France denounces the civil-war threat as pro-de Gaulle political blackmail. But (or so many French believe) he says this without taking account of a very real possibility of civil war—the civil war that might come if he, with all his remarkable political intelligence, but with his special unpopularity, were now faced with the task of holding Catholic France together.

Obviously de Gaulle's most potent enemy and the leader of the vote against him is the Communist Party, with its morning paper *Humanité's* scurrilous cartoons of him and its latest hypocritical chicanery—its slogan that the Communists are "the defenders of the Republic," which they have successfully helped to scuttle. The rich industrialists and the big businessmen, who will vote yes, are against de Gaulle as a man who wants to change things, which alarms them, so *Le Figaro,* which represents the conservative bourgeoisie, has been straddling the fence. Only today, four days before the referendum, it came out with a melodramatic editorial urging a vote of yes—less for de Gaulle than against the Front Populaire and a possible civil war. The General's most effective opponents are the left-of-center intelligent liberals, whose daily spokesman is *Le Monde,* the best-written analytical newspaper in France, and the sharp, courageous weekly *L'Express.* Little *Combat* is the only hysterically pro-de Gaulle paper.

Naturally, "yes or no" has become the new phrase of France—in talk, in night-club songs, in advertising. Thousands of the big and little organizations that are basic to Frenchmen's instinctive centralization of life and to their appetite for controversy in groups are now busy declaring how they will vote on the referendum. Newspapers print their decisions in adjoining columns, headed "Yes" and "No," as a means of showing which way the election wind is blowing. Thus, you can read in your daily papers that the Primary Schoolteachers Union and the University Committee for Republican Defense will both vote no. But the National Association of Parents of Public-School Pupils and the National Committee of the Middle Class will vote yes. The Friendly Society of Former Deported Jews of

France will vote no, along with the National Federation of Former Deportees, Internees, Resistants, and Patriots and the Communist Friendly Society of Widows, Orphans, Descendants, and Victims of War. The Comte de Paris, official pretender to the throne of France but personally a Socialist, has published his monthly public communication as a stately little essay entitled "Oui." There is even a Civic Action Front Against Abstention, which hands out free publicity for window displays from its office on a boat, tied to the *quai* below the Pont de l'Alma. Guy Mollet's Socialist Party decided in caucus, with a certain ambivalence, to vote yes, except for a little splinter group that pulled loose so it could vote no. With similar ambiguities, the Radical Socialist caucus also registered a majority decision to vote yes, though its most important member, Mendès-France, will, naturally, vote no. Higher up, five Cardinals of France have declared that the absence in the constitution of "all reference to God, obviously painful to a Catholic," is no reason to neglect the imperious "duty to vote" in these moments of supreme decision for the nation. The constitution's second article merely says, "France is a republic, indivisible, secular, democratic, and social," without adding that it is Christian. One prelate had earlier said that good Catholics should not vote on such a godless document. The Cardinals' decision, with its urgent tone, implies that the invaluable Catholic vote will be yes.

To date, the most searing denunciation of de Gaulle, and of the events leading up to and now surrounding his present position, is that of Jean-Paul Sartre, called "The Constitution of Contempt," of which the first installment was printed recently in *L'Express*. Nothing so far has equalled its talented vitriol, nor is anything likely to, unless Sartre surpasses himself in the promised second article. He opens with sarcastic *brio* by saying, "To begin with, who suggested this plebiscite? Nobody. It has been imposed on the sovereign nation. . . . Our referendum enjoys the doubtful charm of being impromptu. . . . They began by trampling our old institutions underfoot; now they propose this elderly frippery, a royal charter"—his synonym for, and opinion of, the General's new constitution. "The voter lost in the no man's land that separates the dead republic from the future monarchy has to make up his mind all alone; it is all or nothing, 'all' being King Charles XI and 'nothing' being the return to the Fourth Republic, which nobody wants any more." Speaking with disdain of the General's characteristic pride, Sartre adds, with mordant humor, "I do not believe in God, but if in this plebiscite I had the duty of choosing between Him and the present incumbent, I would vote for God; He is more modest." After tracing the events of the French Army's May *coup d'état* against the Paris government as foundation for de Gaulle's present position, Sartre says that nothing and nobody "can make us forget that General de Gaulle was carried to power by the colonels of Algiers," and continues, "We are promised a return to calm, to discipline, and to tradition, provided that we give our votes to the rioters of Algiers. Let us not fool ourselves; all the plebiscites in the world cannot prevent a *coup de force* from being, and from remaining, a form of disorder. The barrel will always smell of herring; the Gaullist regime will always smell—to the end of its days and in all that it does—of the arbitrary violence from which it sprang." He ends with a call to vote no and a final warning to the General, saying, "On one point we are in accord with you: the Fourth Republic is dead, and we have no notion of resuscitating it. But it is not for you to make the Fifth Republic. That is for the French people themselves, in their full and entire sovereignty."

If further proof were needed of the weighty importance and extraordinary inclusiveness of Sunday's vote, it should be added that this simple yes or no, when in the hands of the millions of dark-skinned inhabitants of France's thousands of square miles of deep African territories, will mean for them a vote of "Yes, we wish to remain attached to the new de Gaulle French commonwealth" or "No, we prefer our independence from France." In a really astounding application of logic to the premise of self-determination of peoples, de Gaulle has given all these territories the right to have independence merely by asking for it—provided they can afford such freedom, for they will, if free, automatically cut themselves off from all French financial aid and administrative guidance. One old Dahoman tribesman is reported by a traveller to have said sagely, "The white General does not understand. We do not wish freedom as a donation, we wish to wrest it from him." It is amazing that the French and their politicians have accepted almost without demur this fabulous invention of de Gaulle's for avoiding further ruinous and unsuccessful wars against men wanting independence. True, Deputy Jacques Isorni, the diehard nationalist lawyer who defended Pétain in his trial, wrote an indignant piece in *Le Monde* complaining about the General's giving away pieces of France as if it were his personal property. And Pierre Poujade, chief of the shopkeepers' political party that bears his name, expressed himself in simpler commercial terms, saying, "He is disposing of the empire as though at a bargain sale." Nigeria and French Guinea have already stated in advance that they will vote no to any suggestion that they "lack responsibility to run their own affairs," meaning that they choose independence.

In Algeria, of course, a heavy yes vote will be cast by the white French *colons* in support of Algeria's integration with France. But Algeria, being considered part of metropolitan France, is the one overseas region where a no vote does not constitute a vote for independence. So the rebels' National Liberation Front, which has been fighting for nearly four years for the country's independence, is aiming at preventing the Moslem population from voting at all, to judge by a report of their terrifying orders for voting day in the rural sections. These say, "It is forbidden to go to the market place. In forest regions, the population is to go to the woods. The roads will be mined and road traps set up, and corpses [presumably of those who headed for the market-place polls instead of the woods] will be placed where they can be seen. Ambushes will be laid for vehicles sent for voters far from the towns. Through our control system in the villages, we can know who has disobeyed these instructions. They will be punished one way or another."

The acts of Algerian terrorists, increasing in violence as their desperate protest against the coming election, are like a fanatical fringe of the Algerian war that has been carried all over France and into all sections of Paris. Two Sundays ago, a stabbed Algerian lay dying in a pool of blood on the sidewalk before Lipp's *brasserie* in St.-Germain-des-Prés, with a crazy old flower vender shuffling in the gore and offering his faded bouquets for sale, as if it were all a scene from a Surrealist picture. Minister Jacques Soustelle was almost murdered at the Arc de Triomphe, and now a dynamite bomb has just been found in a ladies' *lavabo* at the top of the Tour Eiffel.

What lies behind de Gaulle's revolutionary change in French republican history is the problem of the Algerian war, which brought the Fourth Republic to its knees, as the French know and say. On the Algerian problem, the General has so far said not a word—not even the word "integration." What the French are waiting to see, they declare, is what he must inevitably say and how soon he will say it, to save France.

October 1

The towering majority of referendum yes votes given this past weekend to General Charles de Gaulle—almost eighty per cent in France and a fraction more than ninety-six per cent in Algeria—is so impressive that it has changed France's relations not only with herself but with the rest of the world. Certainly the Western democratic peoples now eye France with real hope for the first time since November, 1945, when the General initially took power for what turned out to be merely three months. And the time before that—the final opportunity in a regular Republican France—was Sepember, 1939, or nearly twenty years ago, at the start of the war, which is a long, long time for doubts. Even the General, with his oracular, intellectual truthfulness, says that his new constitution is not perfect but "corresponds to the necessities." *Le Figaro* has just remarked, "Even an excellent constitution, which no country has, cannot suffice to reconcile different political points of view." Deputy Pierre Poujade, with his vulgar knack of sometimes hitting the nail on the head, has just said, "With the help of God, who is certainly also a Gaulliste, [the General] is now going to try to reconcile the irreconcilable and give satisfaction to Christians and Marxists, to liberals and collectivists—in short, to all sections of his new majority, or to nobody."

What all these power dissensions produce is the scandalous, bigamous accumulation of France's sixteen political Parliamentary parties, which the French continually deplore and vote for. Though often bastard fractionizations, they are based on six political conceptions that represent profound, legitimate differences of contemporary Gallic opinion on man's relation with government, and are the real, separate, and specific essences of French political thinking—essences and conceptions so ineradicably opposed that already many French are saying that they must deadlock, if not strangle, the Fifth Republic, even under the exceptional authority of de Gaulle. As the public and the politicians admit, only panic fright and helplessness to do anything else temporarily led four of these divergent political forces to unite long enough to vote the Fifth Republic in over the weekend—that quartet being the old anti-clerical republican force, the political spine that divides the French body politic toward the Left and the Right; the pro-clerical Catholic force; the forces of the

Right; and the Socialists, a mildly Leftish, respectable brand here. The two recalcitrant forces that refused to take cover and, as a consequence, voted no were the intellectual Left liberals and, of course, the undeviating Communists. It would seem that the French—the most logical, literary-minded nation, made up of the most individualistic citizens, whose brains and fertile political imaginations invented the eighteenth-century French Revolution, thus influencing and redating all the Western world—are today, in the twentieth century, bringing their own republicanism to impotence not only through breeding too many theories but through the overuse of logic. To all this, their inherited medieval taste for schism has added the final weakening touches. In June, *Le Monde* announced, with its customary authority, that "the Fourth Republic died of widening splits, which separated the boundaries of the political parties from the real frontiers of public opinion." As far back as three years ago, M. Edgar Faure, then Premier of France for the second time and one of the nation's shrewdest younger political brains, said publicly, "I want to speak my conviction, resulting from personal experience, that in the present [multiple-party] condition of the regime, government of France is not scientifically possible. The problem is not, as is often said, one of governmental instability. It is one of governmental impossibility. The governments here are unstable because they are impossible." This is the fractioned French political state that very likely even de Gaulle's constitution and new electoral laws cannot greatly stick together. In any event, that will be his second difficult task. He is now working on his first and even more important difficult task in Algeria, which voted its almost unbelievable ninety-six-per-cent-plus for integration with France in the face of the bankrupting Algerian war for independence.

The new Paris UNESCO headquarters, in the curious Y-shaped building on the Place de Fontenoy, behind the Tour Eiffel, has long been counted on to show, when completed, the most spectacular manifestation yet of modern art as decoration, produced by a galaxy of the most famed international artists. Well, practically the whole set-up, including the creations of the Spaniards Picasso and Miró, was opened last week, and the public, the professional art critics, and even modern-art lovers do not like it, by a loud majority. In Picasso's eighty-square-metre fresco—slapped onto plasterboard panels and put up crooked (so the panel figures don't jibe perfectly)—there is one white disc-faced female with triangular breasts, of his war-period style; one recumbent, foreshortened male figure (who, through economy of outline, is shaped like a pretzel) baking himself in the sun; and one half-female, seen only from her ballooning hips on up—the implication being that the rest of her is hidden underwater, as she is apparently wading. In the center is a characteristic postwar-Picasso bouquet of what looks like four white skeleton arms and fingers on black. What is sure is that when the afternoon sun brightens the fresco's plain blue and green-blue lower panels, they look as if they had been painted slap-dash by Picasso's children, with brush strokes going every which way. Miró's contribution of a short, thick ceramic-brick wall that separates nothing from nothing in an empty garden space is decorated with red spots, ticktacktoe stars, black rings, and a blue moon. "Why so much art that looks like playthings?" an irritated Paris critic asked, including in his disgruntlement the American Alexander Calder's gigantic two-ton black mobile near the Avenue Suffren, which passing children do indeed pause to admire. Yet if you get a beeline perspective on the building and the Tour Eiffel beyond, a kind of artistic metal aerial brotherhood is established between the two—the single connection that UNESCO has with the neighborhood. The English sculptor Henry Moore's garden figure, with holes, and the French sculptor Jean Arp's abstraction are not yet placed—perhaps luckily. The Italian Afro's painting outside the seventh-floor restaurant was called "a discolored daub"; the Chilean Matta's canvas in the bar was said to look like "unidentifiable machines."

The uncontestedly admired aesthetic contribution is the large Japanese garden, planned by Isamu Noguchi, on the Avenue de Ségur side, with its upright green and gray stones worn to contemplative shapes of beauty by time at work on nature, and with its dwarf conifers—both stones and trees having been presented to UNESCO by the Japanese government. There are panels of running water atop walls, and an arched stone bridge leading nowhere except into the imagination. In the apogee of criticism of the whole UNESCO building and its contents, one art critic finally said sharply, "This new aggrandizement of UNESCO demanded the destruction of eighty-three trees on the Place de Fontenoy. The future will decide the worth of this functional architecture, denuded of aesthetics and sensitivity." This seems to bring us back to the old-fashioned criterion that only God can make a tree.

October 15

For any connoisseurs of curious brief periods of French history, this present one should indeed be memorable—an important, fascinating hiatus to be living through, to watch and listen to, in which the larger, shaping events are only now beginning to show and be heard from. Since the referendum, the French public, usually volatile during exceptional political scenes, has seemed to be struck almost dumb by a mixture of relief, shock, and hope. The main definite new fact is that the Fifth Republic now legally exists, without a cheer's having hailed its birth, since it was merely born twice on paper, in two different editions. The first birth was on Sunday a week ago, when General de Gaulle's constitution was published, for anyone to buy, in the state's inexpensive brochure of records, *Le Journal Officiel,* its appearance there having the automatic effect of making it the supreme law of the land. On Monday afternoon, it had its more elegant second birth in the Empire dining room of the Ministry of Justice, in the Place Vendôme. There, as tradition demands, the seal of state and the legalizing Ministerial signatures—though Premier de Gaulle himself was too busy to come and sign at that moment—were affixed to the single, historical, deluxe copy of his constitution, to be saved for posterity in a glass case along with the dozen or more French constitutions created since 1791. This special copy, bound in gold-embossed scarlet leather, was splendidly printed by the *Journal Officiel* printers in Jaugeon type on vellum. Neither on the red cover nor in the text does this newest constitution indicate that it is for a Fifth Republic. However, the succinct few words spoken after the signing by the Minister of Justice dated it tragically and accurately. He said that the constitution's aim was "to create a great communal association, above races and religions . . . in a century . . . of violence and acute racial struggle"—an unmistakable reference to today's Arab Moslem and French white-Catholic Algerian war. He narrowed down his time sense even more when he spoke, as though in warning, about the glass box full of opposed French constitutions: "The ordeals and quarrels of France lie written there. We must admire the permanence of the nation despite its lacerations. We must admire the permanence of the state despite the unparalleled shocks to its power.

But let us make clear that nobody should, as a continuing practice, stake all on a miracle, because one has always to pay high for a miracle, and it is possible that one day a miracle could fail to happen."

De Gaulle is now the fully functioning miracle in France, and it is merely the defunct and abused Fourth Republic that is paying history's high price for him. Veiled by his own legends but unobscured by any power politics of Parliament (closed until January), he temporarily holds all the viable power in his own hands, free of the melees of deputies still back in their constituencies but busy preparing themselves for recrudescence in November's reduced elections—all of which makes this probably the last time to see fairly clearly what kind of wonder-working qualities he has brought to France's shabby political scene. According to many Parisians, what he has really brought is the result of his long life—his repeated tragic experiences, as a high patriot, with French history, when he seemed to be the only one who knew which way French history was going and could not stop it. To this past is added the psychology he has drawn from his classic military education. In his final chance now to fix up modern France for survival—or so he must hope—his precise contributions to his government from this double past have been his elderly sense of dynamic realism, his impatient haste to get important things started before it was too late, and his infallible instinct for strategy. Notably in Algerian affairs, he has realistically been pushing France, in his constant loud-voiced speeches, toward humane reforms and generosities, which he thinks can alone accomplish her reconstruction and salvation in North Africa. But the problem of ending the Algerian war, which has bled France's finances white, he has treated only strategically—that is, with his typical complete silence, no one having maneuvered a single word out of him, in public, on that subject. For his strategy in important affairs is to ignore what is not ripe enough to talk about. What he will say to this last weekend's humbled but tremendously important offer from M. Ferhat Abbas, the leader of the Algerian government-in-exile, he is still being strategically silent about. But Parisians are discussing Ferhat Abbas' proposal with relief and hopefulness. It is the rebels' first offer to negotiate a cease-fire without demanding, as a precondition of negotiation, recognition of their people's independence, for which, to date, they have been fighting three years and fifty weeks—a *cessez-le-feu,* Ferhat Abbas said, "to bring to an end the indescribable sufferings that this war has already caused." The N.L.F. rebels consist of—at the outside—perhaps a hundred thousand Algerian fighting men, whom the French Army's four hundred thousand soldiers have not been able to defeat. If the Algerian war ceases, it will be one more bitter end to a little war fought in minor history.

Algerian affairs being once again more important in France than French affairs, the other major strategic silence de Gaulle has been maintaining is on the word *"intégration,"* which he has refused to pronounce in his speeches here in metropolitan France as well as in Algeria, where it was considered an insulting omission. Its particular meaning, especially important to them down there, is that sandy North African Algeria is actually a geographical extension and physical part of France. *L'intégration,* the main idea that the Algerian rebels have been fighting, is, of course, the belief of Algeria's million French *colons,* who believe in white-man supremacy, and it is also the key dogma of the Algiers colonels' junta. Their chief, General Raoul Salan, recently avowed that General de Gaulle had said to him, "Algeria is and will always remain French soil." General Salan further observed, in order to make clear his belief in the complete geographical naturalness of integration, "The Mediterranean traverses France the way the Seine traverses Paris." One of the Paris papers immediately published a wonderful cartoon map of Paris, showing it traversed by the Mediterranean instead of the Seine, with the Place Pigalle located in the north of France, the Opéra in France's middle, the Place de la Concorde down in North Africa, the Gare de Lyon somewhere east of Suez, and Montparnasse deep in Africa's jungles.

Ever since May 13th, when the junta took power, liberal Gaullists here and all over France have been waiting for their General to speak up, to dissociate himself from what seemed neo-Fascist French military men, who, by shouting his name, brought him to power. They have been waiting for him to prove he was not the Algiers colonels' property as a dictator—or, indeed, a dictator at all—and, by denying the colonels their intimacy with him and by throwing them from power, to raise himself aloft alone, the elderly liberal leader in an old general's uniform. In his new instructions to Algiers, he put them in their place—beyond the pale. Tuesday morning, when these sensational communications were read on the breakfast radio news program and appeared on the front pages of the daily papers, lots of French began telephoning each other about *"ces bonnes nouvelles."* Many French who had voted for him but were against him in fear of his becoming their autocrat seemed almost glad to be proved wrong. Among liberals and pro-Gaullists, the General's liberation of himself—doubtless finally made possible on the strength of his showing in the referendum—has aroused admiration and the first complete satisfaction as to his republicanism since his equivocal entry into power. In his brief but astonishing personal letter to General Salan, he wrote that the government felt that the best interests of Algeria required the November Algerian elections for Parliament to take place "in conditions of liberty and absolute sincerity," and added, "Candidates representing all the political tendencies [meaning the rebel N.L.F. candidates, as well as any others] should be allowed to solicit the votes of the electorate competitively and on an equal footing. You will, in consequence, conform to the directions here enclosed. *Croyez, mon cher général, à mes sentiments cordiaux,* Charles de Gaulle"—a very cool ending.

In the enclosed instructions to the Army leaders came the retribution for the Algiers French military men in the peremptory order to put an end to their powerful regime: "Furthermore, the moment has come when members of the Army must cease taking part in any organization of a political character, whatever the reasons that may have furnished exceptional motives for joining. . . . Nothing from now on can justify their belonging to such organizations. A report shall be made to me on the measures taken to execute these instructions."

In the referendum, de Gaulle won the most smashing victory over the Communist Party ever registered and admitted by the Party since it became the biggest voting bloc in France. The Central Committee has finally published in *L'Humanité* a remarkably frank analysis of why the Communists lost a million and a half of their voters ("and we did not even feel it coming"), who were supposed to vote no against the General but voted yes instead. "One voter out of five did not listen to us," the report said bravely. "This is the first time since the Liberation that such a phenomenon has occurred." Among the reasons listed was "the real desire of the French people for a change," which is putting it mildly. Another was the Algerian terrorist activities in France. Still another reason that the French Party cited as perhaps influential was, after all, "the vestiges of anti-Communism after the events in Hungary." Then came what sounded like an almost confessional explanation: "To millions of French, humiliated in their pride by the servility of previous governments, de Gaulle seemed the guarantee of national grandeur and independence . . . the negotiator who would make peace. There reigned great illusions about de Gaulle in our working class." It appears that a million and a half of them had faith in him.

Seen historically, de Gaulle now seems to constitute the sole dynasty of modern France; for the third time, he has succeeded himself, after a due interval, as the country's leader. He has the ability to be automatically reborn to power through France's dire needs or tragedies—as in last May, as in August of 1944, as in June of 1940. Over the dozen years since early 1946, when he angrily walked out of his last leadership, he has gradually turned into the portrait of an entirely different man. The rural seasons at Colombey-les-Deux-Eglises have added weight that minimizes his impressive height; an operation on his studious eyes has cost them their former haughty glance; in the hollow toning down of his voice, it no longer leaps sometimes to falsetto, like a trumpet played out of tune, as it used to do. With his waxen features and lengthy nose, his face is treated by French caricaturists to look like a melted candle. But when he speaks, that candle still burns fiercely. In this, his third functioning as France's savior, he seems to the public to have taken over France's identity—he at the age of sixty-seven, and she, owing to her recent batterings, nothing like as young as she appeared after the Liberation. In his speeches during these past months, he has perhaps more often than usual referred to himself in the third person, as if absent-mindedly throwing aside the disguise of being anything except the voice of France herself. The purity of his patriotism, this mystic feeling of his that France is his mission, was what the eighty per cent of the people voted yes for, not being sure of much else at the moment. His exalted, romantic passion for France, which he used to treat almost like his private concern—fervently defended, like any man's personal passions, against all intruders or sharers—he now presents differently. It is something that he actually seems to share with, not just define to, the French people today. An austere, superior rationalist and eccentric, descended from long generations of privileged, educated minds, he never used to be at ease with gregarious democracy or with the idea of sharing his elevated sentiments with forty million other citizens. A reasonable misanthrope, he did not love people by the million. Now, in this peculiar hiatus that separates the two republics, it is the millions who have really helped him save his *belle France* and start her on her way again. After his lonely, thoughtful years at Colombey, humanity appears to have become his broadened concern. In his recent speech in Constantine, which the French feel marked the new de Gaulle as humanitarian and statesman, he offered a magnanimous five-year plan for Algeria's uneducated, impoverished citizens—provided, of course, that the French can afford to pay for it. Above all, where he was once obsessed by the idea of reëstablishing the glory of France, he is now merely aiming at its unity.

In this last fortnight, he has gone a long way toward achieving it. He has set up a true voting democracy for Algerians, for the first time in the two races' common experience. By his now famous brief communications to General Salan and his military, he has overthrown the Army's power politics in Algiers and the supporting *colons'* white-supremacy ideal, which together in May sacrificed the Fourth Republic, rather than face the long-due Algerian peace negotiations that de Gaulle is now free to consider. By this republicanism, he has restored Paris as the political capital of France, has freed himself from strategic ambiguities, has thus aroused a unifying approbation from the major political parties and the men who were still waiting to see and believe, and has himself suddenly become the greatly popular leader of France. In the first two weeks of his Fifth Republic, General de Gaulle has taken his biggest active place to date in the procession of history.

October 29

The sex of the automobile in France—where sex is of the highest importance, especially verbally—has been officially settled. As of the last fortnight, the automobile here is a he instead of a she. This change of gender was proposed a couple of weeks ago by Academician Jean Cocteau to the Académie Française, and accepted, without public explanation of what must have been the valid etymological reasons, in one of its scholarly lexicographic séances, such as led to its great first dictionary, in 1694, and now aim, through slow studiousness, at bringing one out on twentieth-century French, too—possibly around the year 1999, to judge by the rate at which it is creeping through the alphabet. Whatever the Académie decides, however, immediately becomes correct usage. Right after the First World War, the French automobile was already tending to be slightly androgynous, with the 1923 edition of the big, two-volume Larousse dictionary defining it as a feminine noun but adding, "Some make it masculine." These few, if still alive, would have been right in style again talking about *un bel auto* at the Forty-fifth Salon de l'Automobile, which has just closed at the Grand Palais, and where, for two weeks, ordinary Frenchmen tried to pick out *une belle auto* as usual, she having become completely female and increasingly desirable over those intervening years. As one gazes today around Paris—until a few seasons ago a city of open vistas and spacious beauty, now a night-and-day necropolis of inert parked cars on every historic square and nearly every street—it is tragic to ponder the fact that the Salon's natural function is to stimulate the sale of the thousand French cars a day that are being turned off the assembly lines and that absolutely must be sold for the economic good of France and the expanding aesthetic ruination of her loveliest old cities and towns.

The winter literary season is now under way. As the publishers recently announced, in what sounds like a warning, one out of every three novels that will be printed in it is by a woman. So far, only one remarkable new volume by either sex has come off the presses—"Mémoires d'une Jeune Fille Rangée," by Mme. Simone de Beauvoir, which reads like a novel but is an autobiography, based on her private diary, of the conformist first twenty-one years of her life, in her polite Parisian prison of social and Christian obedience to her parents, from which only her precocious young brain and senses at first escaped, via the window of her mind, to soar with grave juvenile questions about God, love, and death. This was the primary compartment of her life—from her birth, on January 9, 1908, among the white-lacquered furnishings of her parents' bedchamber in their superior apartment on the old Boulevard Raspail, to her first meetings with Jean-Paul Sartre in the Sorbonne student cafés twenty-one years later, when her adult life abruptly began. One reason her autobiography is as emotional as a novel is that its basic theme is an individual's struggle for physical and intellectual liberty—the double imprisonment due to her being a well-brought-up upper-class young French female, of a "good but obscure name," with its ennobling particle. It was still that period of the French *culte de la famille* in which nice young girls were reared in the salon, in innocence and stupidity. Her family was halfway between the bourgeoisie and the aristocracy, toward which her lawyer father, as long as his money lasted, leaned by pretension and preference. Thus, what imprisoned Simone and her less fractious younger sister, Hélène, was really the leftover nineteenth-century ideas that ruled the upper-class French until long after the First World War, when the twentieth century finally overcame them. In certain fascinating pages of Mme. de Beauvoir's book, her childhood seems as far back as Marcel Proust's, though not so rich, and never unhealthy. She had high-spirited vitality, was violent, and was prone to what she calls *extrémisme*. Her father, who dominated her by his charm, despised the Republic, liberalism, Zola, and Anatole France, but read aloud to her Victor Hugo poems and Rostand, and also de Gobineau, that pre-Fascist French authority on the inequality of the human races. An anti-Semite, M. de Beauvoir was as convinced of the guilt of Dreyfus as her mother was of the existence of God. It was the disequilibrium between her father's worldly male skepticism and her mother's female piety that early drove the daughter to search for the proofs of ideas and that "largely explains why I became an intellectual." Indeed, at the age of thirteen, leaning one night out of the window of her grandfather's château in the Limousin, and already in love with love and nature, she painlessly lost her faith in God. Even then disillusioned by the lies, hypocrisy, and folly of adults and by the horrors of the war, she reports, "It was easier for me to think of the world without a creator than of a creator guilty of the world's contradictions"—certainly adult philosophical reasoning for the age of puberty. The void left by religion she filled with literature, reading, among other works, George Eliot's "The Mill on the Floss," in English, because it also dealt with a case of conscience, and wading through parts of her grandfather's library, including a seven-volume history of the Bourbon Restoration, which turned her into a democrat. At the age of fifteen, she knew that she wanted to be a celebrated writer.

Now that she has become one, it is her professional writer's talent that makes her autobiography read like a novel, through her elaborate portraits of her family and friends, who seem to become sad minor characters as the fiction of their lives trails along. The *belle-époque* summers at her paternal grandfather's modern château, with peacocks on the lawn and four horses hitched to *le break* for family drives, ended with his death. Her mother's father, a pious banker from Verdun, lost his fortune through crazy investments. Zaza, the girl for whom she had had a passionate friendship since their first schooldays together, died, mad of brain fever, when her bourgeois family opposed her marriage to the man she loved—another female victim of lack of freedom. Cousin Jacques, whom Mlle. Simone had loved and wept over for years, though with no desire for marriage—with her instinct for liberty and feminism, she scorned the position accorded to the French wife—at least enriched her life before eventually ruining his own and dying a penniless sot. That is, he gave her the new, modern France in books that, in her lonely family life, she had missed—Gide, Montherlant, Claudel, Alain-Fournier, Barrès, Mauriac, Cocteau, Jacob, and even Dostoevski, all of which her father loathed at a glance. M. de Beauvoir had long since lost his practice as a lawyer, vaguely going into insurance instead, and as the family finances slid downhill, he warned his daughters that they could expect no dowries and therefore could not marry but would have to earn their livelihoods, after which he regarded them as already *déclassées,* with Mlle. Simone headed for the Sorbonne to become a teacher, and Mlle. Hélène headed for art school. Studying ten hours a day a pell-mell mélange of Greek, Latin, English, Italian, mathematics, philosophy, and logic, and by sheer brilliance cramming four years of university work into three, Mme. de Beauvoir still had the energy for fits of *extrémisme* in Montparnasse night clubs—Le Jockey, Stryx, La Jungle—with mixed drinks, jazz, wild antics, and the first tastes of liberty, still hidden from her family's ears and eyes. In her last year at the Sorbonne, the three student ornaments in philosophy were Paul Nizan, André Herbaud, and Jean-Paul Sartre—a haughty, hermetic trio, followers of the famous Professor Alain, of the Lycée Henri-Quatre. The course of her friendship with Herbaud changed her life, for when he failed in his final exams and disappeared—and she passed—she came under Sartre's wing. He was, she reports, a man who thought every minute of his waking time, knew women as well as he knew books, had no intention of marrying, and had planned his life for travel and writing, for exploring the world and truth. Again as in a novel, this made the unmistakable happy ending to her youthful years of struggle, romanticism, and isolation, and to her longing to be equal, appreciated, and free. This first volume of her memoirs, which she will surely continue, is at once the changing history of modern social and intellectual France and the personal, preliminary history of a brainy woman who has helped change it.

General de Gaulle's impressive offer last week to the rebel Algerian Army of a *paix des braves*—a peace for brave fighters—united around him literally every shade of French political opinion, all filled with high hope that at last this dangerous, bloody, bankrupting racial and political small war was coming to an end. The rebels' unexpected sharp refusal—after the previous offer of a cease-fire by Ferhat Abbas, chief of the Provisional Government of the Algerian Republic, or shadow government-in-exile—killed the hope. It also constituted Premier de Gaulle's first setback in his miraculously successful opening month of Fifth Republic leadership. The double disappointment has been acute.

The war, which in French official semantics is called "the pacification," will enter its fourth year on Saturday.

November 13

Owing to the out-and-out novelties and the unparalleled confusions facing the French in their Parliamentary elections ten days from now, on November 23rd, the Paris political reporters can write only in a state of more or less complete muddle. There will now be seventy-nine fewer deputies for metropolitan France than there were under the Fourth Republic—merely four hundred and sixty-five seats, which de Gaulle hopes will make for a more manageable Chamber. For these seats—and a five-year term of office—there are 2,784 candidates now preparing for the scramble, from half a dozen major parties and about a dozen minor parties or splinter combines. In de Gaulle's arbitrary new slicing up of France into four hundred and sixty-five voting districts, each entitled to elect exactly one candidate, the winner will be the one with the majority on November 23rd, or with the plurality in a runoff election one week later. With an average of twelve candidates now running for every seat, it looks as if nobody could obtain a majority in such a panting crowd. By his single-constituency voting system, de Gaulle, of course, hopes to break up the feudality of the big parties' localized power and to favor the election of individual, responsible deputies, instead of the party-machine hacks or the intransigent party devotees, who, between them, brought the helpless Fourth Republic to its knees.

Certainly Premier de Gaulle, in a late-October press conference, warned the public and whoever was aiming to compose this new Parliament of what was facing them in the Fifth Republic. "After a certain number of months' suspension, the Parliamentary institution will reappear," he declared. (It is now thought that its reappearance will be in a special, brief session in January.) "But [Parliament] will no longer be omnipotent. . . . The future Assemblies will have precise limits and powerful brakes. . . . If it should unhappily come to pass that tomorrow's Parliament does not wish to accommodate itself to the role assigned it, there is no doubt but that the Republic will be thrown into a new crisis, from which no one can know how it might emerge—except that, in any case, the Parliamentary institution would be swept aside for a long time."

As further warning and advice to all the political parties that are trying to sail into power in the new Parliament on his coattails and under his name—their own party nomenclatures under the Fourth Republic being now so weakened in appeal as to need a timely refresher—de Gaulle said, "Everybody understands that I neither desire nor am able to lend myself in a direct manner to this competition. The mission that the country has confided to me excludes my taking part. Therefore I shall not favor anybody, not even those who have offered me friendly devotion through all the vicissitudes. *Bien entendu,* I shall not disapprove of those political groups that publicize their adherence to what de Gaulle has done," he interjected, in one of his most historic third-person references to himself. "But impartiality obliges me to insist that my name, even in adjectival form, be not used as a title for any group or any candidate." This prohibition has added the final confusion to the election campaign. This will be as strange an election as any French Republic has ever known.

The obscurities surrounding the elections in Algeria (in many ways far more important for France than those in France itself), where nearly no candidates for deputy turned up until just before the lists were closed, have produced in Paris almost a paralysis of interpretation and hope. In a belated rush, almost two hundred candidates finally appeared—either Europeans of the May 13th persuasion or Moslem Right Wingers, both in favor of Algeria's remaining French—to run for the sixty-seven seats in the Paris Parliament. Parisians can only suppose that the rebel Moslems' fear of identifying themselves publicly as candidates for the French Chamber, which might bring death by having their throats slit in reprisal, shows to what extent the ninety-six-per-cent yes vote that the native population gave to de Gaulle last month was false, owing to the vote's being steamrollered by the French Army there. It may be that, in having already offered them "a peace for brave men" and now Parliamentary rights—both refused—de Gaulle, remarkably experienced as he is in modern French history, has been too civilized to be immediately useful.

November 26

What the French people voted in favor of last Sunday was a single issue—the miracle-making quality of General Charles de Gaulle. He had his sixty-eighth birthday on Saturday, and from his Fifth Republic, which held its first Parliamentary elections the next day, he received the duly expected political gift of a strong swing to the Right—much more of it than he probably wanted.

Considering the peculiar confusions and circumstances of Sunday's election—only about four-fifths as many seats to run for as before; old political boundary lines broken down; new parties set up, with multiple hedgehopping in between; old faces searching to be rechosen; new, unidentifiable faces pushing forward to squeeze in; all the candidates whipped by more than the customary ambition and by a feeling that a new, last-ditch legislative period in France was taking shape, in which they had to participate or perish—considering all these factors, the results of the election have been illuminating, yet rather comic. A turnout of about seventy-five per cent of the nation's voters managed to elect exactly one deputy in Paris and only thirty-nine deputies in all France, since an absolute majority of the votes was necessary in order to win. So four hundred and twenty-six seats will have to be disputed again in the second-round runoff this Sunday, when a mere plurality will suffice.

It must be understood that this election, in which twenty and a half million votes were cast, really had no issue but de Gaulle. It was an election held utterly and entirely in terms of him, of this one Frenchman who was not even running for office. During the campaign, people turned up literally in twos or threes in the villages to hear the candidates speak; even in the cities, the bigger crowds cared little what was said, nobody really wanting to know one more professional politician's opinions on the vital topics for France today—such as the quarrel with England over the common market and with the French Minister of Finance for shortening the Sorbonne's educational budget—let alone wanting to hear any politician's notions on how to end the Algerian war. What the voters wanted to know was how the candidates stood on de Gaulle—whether they would back him, and whether they were running for an annual privilege of a very few months in Parliament on the truthful understanding that Parliament had failed to know how to govern and that only de Gaulle, by fiat and miracles, could now be trusted to direct the destinies and problems of France.

The only major party to campaign on a platform that decried de Gaulle and his constitution, the Communists got a million and a half fewer votes, all over France, than they did in the 1956 Fourth Republic elections. Their vote last Sunday was not quite nineteen per cent, which, by a tiny margin, still gives them the biggest cut of the nation's ballot. The Poujadists, also anti-de Gaulle, were practically extinguished on Sunday; they received less than one per cent of the nation's vote, enough maybe to elect half a deputy. Even ex-Premier Pierre Mendès-France, the single great political figure who, ever since last May, had been conducting an intellectual counter-offensive against the General, was defeated spectacularly on Sunday in his normal fief of Louviers, in the Eure, held by him since 1932. (Oddly enough—or so it is said—de Gaulle had hoped that he would be elected, so there would be one excellent intelligence in the parliamentary opposition.)

The winning mixture was the Union pour la Nouvelle République, or U.N.R.—initials that it might be well to learn now, since the party won close to eighteen per cent of the national vote and will figure predominantly in the coming Parliament, although nobody yet knows exactly how.

The new Chamber will add up to an absolute Rightist majority and a possible perplexity for de Gaulle in solving France's most vital unsolved problem, which is the Moslem rebellion for Algerian independence, just now entered into its fifth year. Much of the French Right—and, precisely, the U.N.R. leadership—stands for what is called the *intégration* policy in Algeria, which regards the country as a province of France and part of France's soil, without autonomy. The General has made it known that he favors a more moderate evolution, which could develop internal self-government for Algeria within the new French community.

Paris has just emerged from a five-week deluge of thirty-five concerts by fifteen nations, called Les Semaines Musicales de Paris and created by the UNESCO-sponsored International Music Council to honor the opening of the controversial new modernist UNESCO building behind the Tour Eiffel. The music lover's only problem was to figure out which dozen or more concerts he had the taste, the time, and the ticket money for. The city has probably never known such a daily variety of star players, orchestras, and conductors, of foreign musicians and foreign music, or such combinations of all of these. On one Salle Pleyel program, Ravi Shankar played the sitar, Shinichi Yuize played the Japanese koto, and then Menuhin and Oïstrakh played their Strads in Bach's D-Minor Concerto for Two Violins, but did not hit it off well together. The other outstanding disappointment was Stravinsky's new opus "Thréni," inspired by the Biblical prophet Jeremiah, which Stravinsky conducted. It was like a stony labyrinth, through which the listener wandered, pathless, without echoes, without pleasure. Before the performance, Stravinsky confided to an American musician that it was *"très ennuyeux et très savant"*—"very boring and very scholarly." True. At the Salle Gaveau concert by the excellent small orchestra that Queen Elizabeth of Belgium founded for its leader, Franz André—it was vainly hoped that Her Majesty would attend—the virtuosities of the violinist Arthur Grumiaux were a revelation in a Mozart concerto. Von Karajan, with the Berlin Philharmonic, packed the vast Salle de Chaillot, where he had played during the Nazi Occupation as junior replacement for Wilhelm Furtwängler, who refused to conduct in Paris because he had loved the city. However, the great old Hans Knappertsbusch, conducting the Vienna Philharmonic in Brahms' Third, displayed a discretion, coming from complete authority, that united his poetry and the instruments' sounds so that they all became one with Brahms himself. There were concerts by the Frankfurter Singakademie; a miners' chorus from Ostricourt; the Juilliard Quartet; an organ recital at St.-Sulpice by Marcel Dupré; the Czech Philharmonic; at least one piece of modern music included in each concert, so there was enough Webern and Berg; and one concert featuring "micro-interval music on sixteenth tones"—absolute bedlam.

The American Leonard Bernstein was the comet among all the stars. Heard of as a prodigy but not yet heard as a conductor, he accomplished the impossible at the second of his three concerts here when he played and directed the Lamoureux Orchestra in four piano concertos—a Bach "Brandenburg," a Mozart, a Ravel, and Gershwin's "Rhapsody in Blue." The appreciation that Bernstein aroused among music lovers and critics here was astonishing. Even Clarendon, the most trenchant of Paris critics, said, in *Figaro,* "Bernstein triumphed with an incredible ease over the multiple difficulties presented. To my mind, this session offered, like a mountain, two slopes. With the Bach and Mozart we were elevated to the summit of precision and poetry. With the Ravel we lost a little altitude, but with the Gershwin we were stabilized on a reassuring level. *Ne persiflons pas*—a success of this quality goes far beyond being a merely *sportive* performance. I regard Leonard Bernstein as a prodigiously gifted musician." At Bernstein's third concert, his deep and instinctive reading of Mahler's Second—without a score, and conducting an orchestra, vocal soloists, and a choir he had barely met—gave his listeners the impression of having heard an extraordinary local event in musicianship and pleasure. To his compatriots here, it oddly seemed that Bernstein, by his youthful generosity of gifts, momentarily restored among Parisians the popularity of certain American qualities.

December 11

In the last of the string of sabbatical elections here, on Sunday, December 21st, General de Gaulle will unquestionably be elected President of France—the personal, apostolic solution he has proposed ever since 1946 for bringing a strong single-headed government to this country. Even for the Fifth Republic, it seems really fantastic that only one candidate will be running against him—the Communist Party's token sacrificial goat, M. Georges Marrane, Red mayor of the suburb of Ivry, who will thus assure an election almost, but not quite, as limited as would be run off by the Communists in Soviet Russia, an ironic fact unappreciated by the French Muscovites here.

The new Parliament will not start functioning legislatively until the last Saturday in April, a good long time from now—an interval that its members, the French citizens think, can well use in figuring out how to act and survive better than their predecessors. However, this Parliament enjoyed its first temporary sitting on Tuesday, to elect its Speaker. The visitors' galleries were jammed to view this quiet, confusing, historic scene of gathering deputies (including one Algerian chieftain in gold-and-white turban and flowing robes). The moment awaited by all was the entrance of Premier de Gaulle, white-faced, dressed in dark gray. The deputies rose with a burst of applause as he took his seat on the front-row government bench and then mounted the little staircase to the tribune to shake hands with the eighty-two-year-old deputy and priest Canon Kir, the Assembly's senior deputy, who was to make the address of welcome. Only after the General sat down again, the cynosure of all eyes, did the Parliament cease politely standing. In his address, the old canon—cassock mussed, hair awry, spectacles perched crooked on his nose, an eccentric figure long known in the Chamber for his humor and ineptitudes—said that he "piously saluted the memory of those no longer with us" (meaning all the deputies who had failed of reëlection); that all candidates, like himself, had suffered from the public's violent criticism during the campaign; and that this new Parliament would have to fight such public opinion, since it could rapidly lead to "a dictatorship, which the great majority of the French do not desire." Somewhere, from some deputy, there arose a faint whistle.

For the spectator, this was a nebulous experience, this first sitting of a new Parliament of predominantly new men, of whom the nearly two hundred U.N.R. deputies "hardly know each other by sight," as *Le Monde* commented, with its customary trenchancy. The paper added, "Among them all, they have only one tie—Gaullism, a state of mind much more than a doctrine. As for a program, there is none. There is nothing but an unlimited adherence to the acts and even the intentions" of one man—de Gaulle himself.

December 29

In General-President de Gaulle's nationally televised Sunday-night broadcast concerning his government's dramatic financial measures, he looked to be much more vigorous than on the recent afternoon when he appeared at the temporary session of Parliament. His voice, the characteristically awkward, sudden gestures of his hands—as if discarding something—his whole mien, and his mental and physical presentation were energetic, authoritative, and certain. There were perhaps one or two occasions when he seemed to ad-lib, as if to make his lofty statements clearer on rapid second thought, in a speech that lasted precisely fifteen minutes and that he had written himself, as is his custom, and then committed to memory—this last an amazing feat of brain and concentration for a man of his age. It must be understood that if President Eisenhower's state of health was at one moment of sufficient emotional concern to the United States to affect the stock market, de Gaulle's condition of body and mind is of far vaster importance to France, because, on his own terms, he is literally all that the country now possesses for the state to rest on. In the opening portion of his Sunday speech, he said that the repeated recent elections and the referendum had confirmed him in his task, and added, "As the guide of France and chief of the republican state, I shall exercise the supreme power." He spoke pungently, being gifted with French literary talent and with a style formed by rich and extensive classical reading. Among other notable sentences was his statement that if the country "has charged me with leading it, this is because it wishes to go forward, certainly not toward what is facile but toward effort and renovation." He also said, with a touch of his dry humor, that of late France had been vacillating "between drama and mediocrity." Of the devaluation, he said, "Furthermore, for the old French franc, so often mutilated by our vicissitudes, our wish is that it regain the substance conformable to the respect due to it." The key of his speech was that his financial measures could base the French nation on what he called, in a near pun, *"vérité et sévérité"*—thus reuniting for his listeners these two grave, intimately related words, which "alone can permit France to rebuild its prosperity." He ended by apostrophizing, in a loud voice of conviction, *"Peuple français, grand peuple! Fierté, courage, espérance! Vive la République! Vive la France!"*

1959

January 14

No French chief of state has ever been voted for so much or so often as Charles de Gaulle—first in the September referendum, second in the general presidential election, and then, for the third time, in the presidential election by the special electors—the newly invented founding formula of his Fifth Republic being triply tested to make sure it will stand. On Thursday's Eurovision, or European television hookup, covering the procedure in the sumptuous chandeliered ballroom of the Palais de l'Elysée by which the supreme office of the state was transferred from the shoulders of the outgoing President Coty to those of the incoming President de Gaulle (seen for the first, and probably only, time dressed in a civilian cutaway coat), it was to be noted that once more the vote played a role—its last one. It came when an unfamiliar little white-bearded old Frenchman, who looked like a figure left over from the early Third Republic of a lifetime ago but who turned out to be M. René Cassin, head of the provisional Constitutional Committee that created last September's new constitution, advanced to the microphone. In a voice trembling with a sense of history, he read aloud the number of ballots cast for the victor and the two losers in the special electors' voting (when, until almost the last minute, it had been supposed that de Gaulle would be the unique candidate). The votes for the General, M. Cassin said, were 62,394; those for the Communist candidate, M. Georges Marane, were 10,355; and those for the Radical Socialist candidate, M. Albert Chatelet, were 6,721. In consequence, he then declared, the provisional Constitutional Committee—and here his old voice rose—"proclaims General de

Gaulle President of the Republic." With that phrase and at that precise moment—twelve minutes past noon of a sunny, cold Paris January day—in the eyes of the law and of French history Charles de Gaulle became the first Chief Magistrate of the Fifth Republic, which he created. Also at that moment began the twenty-one-gun salute fired by cannons placed beside the Seine to honor the arrival of a new head of state.

After General Georges Catroux, Grand Chancellor of the Legion of Honor, standing on tiptoe, hung around the giant de Gaulle's throat the great golden collar of the Grand Master of the Legion of Honor, founded by Napoleon—the badge of office with which all the French presidents are invested, and which they wear only at this ceremony—Coty recited his brief speech of welcome and adieu to the new incumbent of the palace. For this, he gracefully used Pascal's famous conjunction of "the grandeur of the establishment" and "the grandeur of the person." De Gaulle's speech of thanks was grave, impassioned. At first, he looked close to manly tears. He said that it was his duty to represent the interests of the nation and the *Communauté,* and even to impose them, since "these are my obligations." He added, in clear warning, "In this I shall not weaken—I bear witness to that in advance." After calling for the same aid that was given him last spring during national danger and is needed again "as the horizon brightens with our great hopes," he ended by crying, *"Vive la Communauté! Vive la République! Vive la France!"*—the new *vivat* of the Fifth Republic. De Gaulle's final shout of *"Vive la France!"* seemed to come from the very depths of his lungs, closest to his heart.

And now what? De Gaulle's government supporters, exclusively Right and Center, add up to a parliamentary majority of 88.8 per cent. Parliament will have its first brief sitting tomorrow, to hear, debate, and certainly accept the government's program—the first debate it has had since early last June—after which it will go home again until the last week of April. It is not clear what it will do when it does return, except mostly continue to say yes, which it was largely elected to say by the French people. (Were it to prove fractious and start saying no or perhaps, de Gaulle, by his constitution, has the power simply to dissolve it after one year.)

As the French intellectual Left analyzes it, the entire Left lost its strength and meaning by its démodé class-war ideology over the past two or three years, falling out of step with the Fourth Republic's surface prosperity, rising living standards, rising wages, and social-service handouts paid for almost entirely by the owner class, behind all of which were menacing state financial problems that were too much for mere dialectic to solve in a democracy. As for the Communists, the intellectuals think that Khrushchev, as much as anyone, cut them down from the biggest to the littlest French party, first costing them their belief in Moscow's infallibility by the revelations on Stalin, then undermining them with the bloody purges, followed by Budapest and, finally, even by Boris Pasternak, whose "Le Docteur Jivago" (as it is called here) was the best-seller of 1958—and not only among the bourgeoisie. Since the Socialist and the Communist Parties, which were sworn enemies in Parliament, have lost their influential major-party seats, it is now feared that they will make their real opposition to de Gaulle outside Parliament, and together—in strikes.

January 28

"At last we have a retrospective exhibition, at the Galerie Charpentier, of a hundred and thirteen pictures worthy of the highly original scenic art that was Maurice Utrillo's—at least up to about 1925," wrote one candid critic of this newly opened and biggest art attraction of the midwinter Paris season. For once in a modern French art show, the pictures have almost all been lent by French collectors, Utrillo being the sole famed School of Paris artist whom the French immediately appreciated and purchased, leaving the pictures of the half-dozen others who in various ways shook the art world to be admired, bought, and taken home by foreigners. As if to give a sharp educational correction to the public's sentimental affection for any Utrillo picture at all that is of Montmartre, is smooth, and is white, the opening fifty Utrillo canvases featured by the Charpentier are his early blue-and-green gems, as roughly faceted as if by Sisley himself, whom Utrillo then greatly admired, and painted in country towns or back gardens, like the Montmagny series. Furthermore, two-thirds of the pictures in the show fall strictly within the brief twenty-year period, from 1905 to 1925, when, as the catalogue preface makes clear, the tender genius of his painting was at full strength, with the apogee, the infinitely appreciated White

Period, coming between 1908 and 1914. Then, after 1925, began the decline, which led him first into honorably mediocre and finally into merely naïve painting. In 1923, his devoted mother, Suzanne Valadon, the painter, former Renoir model, and ex-circus performer, who had vainly been trying to keep her son off drink since he was a boy of ten (his father, if he was the man she supposed he was, had himself been a hereditary alcoholic), actually bought a lonely feudal château in the Ain for Maurice—with his money, of course, for by now he was a big success, who had exhibited at Paul Guillaume's. Here she lived with him for two years as one of his guardians. He was given a bottle or so of red wine, like good-conduct pay, only after he had finished his day's painting stint for his art merchant. Even in that rural spot, his work consisted of transforming and illumining scenes shown on the local postcards—a technique that had become basic to him. Maybe in that half-furnished nightmare medieval castle he became permanently disoriented by nostalgia for his cardboard vistas of Montmartre streets, leading around corners to nowhere, or perhaps luxury had become his most destructive imprisonment, whereas misery and poverty had, earlier, left his vision free. In any case, his rare emotional essence as an artist, always haunted by walls (which he put on canvas perhaps in memory of his many captivities), began deserting him, leaving only his manual talent, which his years of inebriation had never blurred. Between his teens and the age of forty-one, he had been, as a dipsomaniac, confined ten times—once for three years—in private clinics or Paris lunatic asylums, and always he had painted as well inside them as outside them. Until about 1946, when he was sixty-three, he continued painting with some coherence—mostly inept flower pictures, in which dahlias look like carnations—working under luxurious surveillance in a Paris mansion with barred windows. He had become a rich man who could buy anything for himself except liberty, for, as a famous national figure, he could not be allowed freedom. The government made him an Officer of the Legion of Honor, he was allotted an entire room for his paintings at a Venice Biennale exhibition, his white pictures of Sacré-Cœur—and even the counterfeit ones—were loved over the Western world as the essence of Paris. But he himself was like a guttering white candle, kept indoors. He died only in 1955, aged seventy-one, in a rich villa in suburban Vésinet (equipped with a private chapel for his inchoate prayers to Jeanne d'Arc), where he was watched over by his bossy wife, a Belgian banker's widow to whom his dying mother had married him.

The catalogue gives Utrillo's formula for his famous white paint—white of zinc, ground plaster, and glue, applied with a palette knife. But it gives no explanation of the hallucinatory snowfalls with which he later covered Montmartre's streets—snow, after all, being a great Paris rarity, except, perhaps, to a painter with his own favorite recipe for white paint. Among the pathetic memorabilia in the exhibition are illustrated poems, scribbled on brown paper in Utrillo's schoolboy hand, denouncing the Montmartre children and housewives who tormented him in his public drunkenness until they drove him off the streets, where he painted from real life, and into his lonely room and his enforced practice of painting from postcards—*"Une population profane,"* he fulminated, *"une voyoucratie,"* or government by hooligans. This enormous Charpentier retrospective implies that for the next years in Paris there will be no sizable Utrillo exhibitions. The art critics, as if in farewell, gave Utrillo a garland of their talented praise, such as "The painter of poverty and abandon, he transfigured the most wretched scenes by the tenderness that lighted and colored his heart." And "Tender and conscientious, with delectable diversity, he evoked the pathos of Paris and the anonymous soul of the suburbs."

The production, at Charles Dullin's picturesque old Théâtre de l'Atelier, on its tree-decked square behind Pigalle, of "La Punaise" ("The Bedbug"), by the noted Soviet poet Vladimir Mayakovsky, has given intellectual disappointment but childish ocular pleasure since its opening last week. Anticipatory interest had been aroused here by the fact that this would be the first time such a specimen of Soviet humor had been played in Paris, and also by the fact that the play is being currently presented at the Satire Theatre, in Moscow. Probably too much was expected of it because so much was already known about Mayakovsky. Paris has an active Communist press-and-book center, which, willy-nilly, keeps us abreast of some Moscow cultural news. Mayakovsky's poems, in beautiful translations, have become well known here, as has, recently, his youthful friendship with Boris Pasternak. Also familiar was Mayakovsky's early, stimulating Moscow career as a so-called Futurist, or avant-garde leader in art, poetry, and ideas; then as an ad writer and a designer of striking posters for various Soviet state enterprises; and, just prior to 1930, as a leading journalist on the *Komsomolskaya Pravda.* Indeed, almost everything was known here about Mayakovsky except why he put a bullet through his heart in April, 1930. However, this followed the 1929 production of "The Bedbug," in Stalin's time, at the Meyerhold Theatre, where it was a failure, plus violent attacks, in March, 1930, on the Meyerhold production of his play "The Baths," which was such an assault on Soviet bureaucracy that it had to be withdrawn, as Mayakovsky himself withdrew from life the next month. Both plays were successfully revived in Moscow a few years ago, and, in the Khrushchev thaw, they have been in the Satire Theatre repertory ever since. As far as is known here, the Atelier's is the first production of "The Bedbug" in Western Europe.

The idea—at least as many of us had imagined it in advance—is extremely funny, capable of being cruelly comic and loaded with the deadly satire that can come from anachronism. It concerns a post-revolutionary lout named Prisypkin, who deserts his laboring-class comrades and milieu to marry a fat manicurist. In the wedding party's drunken revelry, the house burns down. All but one of the revellers are pulled out, and after the firemen have flooded the site with water, it turns into a block of ice. Fifty years later, Soviet scientists vote to thaw out their latest great scientific discovery—a subhuman in ice—who turns out to be Prisypkin himself, not dead but frozen, and who is soon restored to life with everything intact, including a bedbug that had been on the wedding party with him. By now, both he and it are sociobiological forms unknown in advanced Soviet culture, he being classified as a *Petit-bourgeoisus vulgaris* and the insect as a *Punaispa normalis*. The bug is seized for observation by the zoo. The thawed lout, reeking of vodka fumes in a Soviet Union so pure that his breath makes the Comrades sick, infects all society, which breaks out with a passion for drink, for dancing the Charleston, and for acting so contrary to Marxism in general that even the dogs start walking the streets on their hind legs (which a couple of them obligingly do on the stage). The finale shows Prisypkin in a cage at the zoo, where he has been put to furnish food for the bug; suddenly he sees the theatre audience, whereupon he shouts happily at it, recognizing the audience to be like himself—made up of unfrozen human beings—and the play is over.

Even in such bald outline, one can see how good the play sounds and ought to be. Well, it is not much good as played here, and no good at all as a slashing satire. There are thirty leading characters in it, and about fifty extras, who play double walk-on roles in what looks like a jolly Chauve-Souris-style production, with treadmills onstage to imitate the passing of crowds, scenery that moves, and so forth. The wedding party's drunken revelry is the drunkest-looking and longest-lasting drunken scene in the memory of Paris theatre-goers—a banging, falling-down affair of nothing but naturalness and pantomime, without a word spoken, which goes on for perhaps twenty solid minutes. Many of the spectators laugh uproariously; many yawn in silence. The *Figaro* critic said of "La Punaise" that it had bored him to the point of anesthesia. One has the feeling that Mayakovsky's script has disappeared from the Atelier production under a muscular mass of interpretive pantomime, though the Atelier producer, André Barsacq, is himself a Russian, it turns out, who translated the Mayakovsky opus and thus should have known what he was doing. It is strange that this so-called satire on a new modern society by a brilliant, idealistic mind so acute in its powers that it could not bear living in that society any more should seem a less penetrating comment on the Russians' perpetual search for personal liberty than that given us years ago by the fairy-tale ballet "Petrouchka," where the struggling characters had only the tragedy of being dancing puppets, and their dictator merely the tyranny of a magician.

March 11

The retrospective exhibition called "The Twenties: American Writers in Paris and Their Friends," which has just opened in the St.-Germain-des-Prés quarter where they lived, is an act of recrudescence. It restores to life that memorable, far-back decade when talent and faces were fresh, when the young expatriates came here in numbers and in a united coincidence and founded what became the new contemporary school of American literature. The exhibition is under the aegis of the cultural wing of the American Embassy and is being held in the new United States Information Service Cultural Center on the Rue du Dragon, the narrow, short street just beyond the Brasserie Lipp and across and down from the Café des Deux Magots, those focal points in the old days. The exhibition's six hundred items, many rare, owe their presence almost entirely to the fact that Miss Sylvia Beach, of the Shakespeare and Company bookshop, on the Rue de l'Odéon, has never lost anything or thrown anything away. So now here it all is, gathered together with a few memorabilia from others of the epoch—the scribbled, jocose notes, the corrected page proofs, the photographs, the snapshots, the first editions dedicated "to Sylvia, with love" from Hem, Dos, Djuna, E.E., Ezra, Thornton, Gertrude, Scott, and others. As source material of literary and documentary importance, it is a miraculously complete show, with the first editions of the expatriates (often printed here in France on private presses by other expatriates, because no New York commercial editors had the faith to print them), and with examples of all the vital, struggling literary magazines from everywhere—splendid silken ragbags, sometimes backed by the rich—for which, in the early days, the poor-of-purse writers gladly wrote without remuneration, just to see their wonderful words in print. It is also a clearly, handsomely, and imaginatively arranged exhibition, using glass cases set upright against the walls, so that what is in them is easily visible and legible, with entire cases devoted to an outstanding writer—including his letters, manuscripts, photographs, snapshots of family increases, bullfights, fishing trips, and so on—so he can be studied all at once.

The expatriates' literary clubroom, the Shakespeare shop not only sold books in the English language but also rented them out as a lending library. Miss Gertrude Stein was Sylvia Beach's first subscriber, and early wrote a poem called "Rich and Poor in English to Subscribers in French and Other Latin Tongues," which Miss Alice B. Toklas typed off—there is a typescript copy in the show—and mailed to friends to encourage them to subscribe also. Robert McAlmon, who ran Contact Editions, a private press, published Miss Stein's enormous "Making of Americans" (shown along with one of her corrected page proofs), because Hemingway wanted him to and because no publisher in America would print it, and also printed Hemingway's first book, a small blue paperback called "Three Stories & Ten Poems." William Bird, who had the Three Mountains Press, published Hemingway's "In Our Time," a tall yellow book whose cover was ornamented with disjointed cuttings from newspapers, printed in red—phrases including "two billion dollars," "guidance from God," and "learn French." In the Hemingway showcase is a jovial note to "Madame Shakespeare," meaning Miss Beach, in which he remarked, "To hell with the book." In Scott Fitzgerald's showcase is a copy of "The Great Gatsby" dedicated to "Dear Sylvia, from Harold Bell Wright," which he crossed out, signing his own name. Bird also published "XVI Cantos," by Ezra Pound, who had brought Joyce and his "Ulysses" from Trieste to Paris in that almost willful concentration here of talented outlanders who were having trouble being published. Because English typesetters refused to set type for the bawdy parts of "Ulysses," Miss Beach and her Shakespeare shop became its publisher, the printing being done in Dijon by Frenchmen, ignorant of what the English words meant. In the Joyce showcase are order forms for the 1922 first edition of "Ulysses" sent in by Lawrence of Arabia, who ordered two copies of the most expensive edition—on Dutch paper, at three hundred and fifty francs—and by Yeats and Gide, who each ordered a copy of the cheapest edition, at a hundred and fifty francs. Also shown are some of Joyce's corrected page proofs. As the publisher of "Ulysses," Miss Beach became both martyr and heroine when its detractors and admirers began congregating, over the years, in her shop. Near the Joyce material, flanked by dashing photos of Margaret Anderson and Jane Heap, is the famous 1920 autumn number of the revolutionary *Little Review* in which they announced "our arrest" for having published sections of "Ulysses" in New York.

In the exhibition's photograph section, entitled "Portraits of a Generation," and mostly taken by Man Ray and Berenice Abbott, everyone is present who was attached, in one way or another, to the Shakespeare shop: T. S. Eliot; Eugene and Maria Jolas, of the intransigent magazine called *transition;* Archibald MacLeish; Katherine Anne Porter; Allen Tate; Virgil Thompson; Djuna Barnes, in profile in a cape; Kay Boyle, front-face in a beret; Dos Passos; Bryher; Arthur Moss, of *Gargoyle;* Louis Bromfield; Cummings; Sherwood Anderson; Wilder; Nathanael West; Caresse and Harry Crosby, of the Black Sun Press; Nancy Cunard, of the Hours Press; Alexander Calder; George Antheil; Edmund Wilson; Mary Reynolds; and others—plus the French writers and artists drawn to this new fire of foreign talent blazing in their own city, among them Gide, Valéry, Larbaud, Schlumberger, Chamson, and Marcel Duchamp.

In one corner of the exhibition room, the walls are covered with a photo-montage of the façade of the old Dingo café, in Montparnasse, where the St.-Germain talent spent many of its nights over the years. Real café chairs and tables are placed in front of the montage, and there, late in the afternoon of the exhibition's opening, sat Miss Alice B. Toklas and Thornton Wilder in literary reminiscence, while behind them a pianola beat out the rhythms of Antheil's "Ballet Mécanique," the shock music of that decade.

March 25

The highest skyscraper in all Europe—fifty-five stories—whose work-in-progress name, if you can believe it, is Antigone (daughter of Oedipus, who became his guide after he put out his own eyes), will figure as the towering center of the controversial complex of ultramodern buildings that are to replace the shabby old Gare Montparnasse and incorporate the new one. The project, which comprises four separate sections, is to start this June, it has just been announced, and will be finished, *Deo volente,* in 1964. This will constitute the greatest Paris urban project since that of Baron Haussmann, back in the eighteen-fifties and sixties. The skyscraper is to be the railroad station's hotel, with a night club on top. It will rise to more than half the height of that Paris landmark and trademark the Tour Eiffel—also, in its work-in-progress state, resented by the populace, who then, as now, wanted nothing ultramodern. It will be visible from the Place de la Concorde, the Place St.-Germain-des-Prés, the Esplanade of the Invalides, and the terrace of the Palais de Chaillot, and thus will change the familiar, loved silhouette of Paris. The hotel, approached by a *parvis* facing the Place de Rennes, will contain a shopping center, a cinema, a press club, a swimming pool (maybe), and a hall for public meetings. Beside it will lie the railway-station section, its entrance flush with the sidewalk, but with the tracks unfortunately nested nearly twenty-five feet below, which means stairs and suitcases, mixed, for the travellers. The outgoing tracks may have to be covered with a garden as far as the Boulevard Pasteur, for the sake of the nineteen-story buildings on either side of them—one for offices, one for apartments, with artists' studios on top. The triangle remaining on the Boulevard de Vaugirard is to be a green park, with a subterranean parking lot for fifteen hundred cars. Part of the project's cost will be borne by the Ville de Paris and by the S.N.C.F., the nationalized association of French railways, but most of it will be met by private investment. To those Parisians who outspokenly regard the fifty-five-story skyscraper as aesthetically unappealing, non-native, unnecessary, and bound to throw the architectural equilibrium of the famous Paris skyline out of plumb, the Council of Buildings of France gave a tacit rebuff last week by voting final approval of the entire project, thus officially accepting a new architectural future. The Council's opinion was: "Paris cannot afford to lose herself in her past. In the years to come, Paris must undergo imposing metamorphoses." *C'est bien triste.*

April 7

For the English-speaking colony here—provided it could follow the Irish accents—the treat of the current Théâtre des Nations festival has been the London Workshop's uproarious performance of Brendan Behan's hit "The Hostage." On Monday, its last night, Behan, who had been on public view drinking Pernods in the theatre bar, unexpectedly joined the company as it was taking its final bow onstage, and burst into a long, ponderous Irish jig, stamping his huge feet in inebriated rhythm, while the audience clapped to help him keep time. As symbol, explanation, and integral proof of his play—a talented, showoff Irishman, gay and belligerent in his drink, slovenly and confidential in his shirtsleeves and suspenders, the Gael himself, unique, theatrical, spirited, his national essence a form of patriotism unconnected with the rest of the world—he was as good as his play, and just like it. "The Hostage" takes place in a shabby semi-brothel and I.R.A. headquarters in Dublin, and is animated by motley characters—including one lunatic, dressed in kilts like Brian Boru—who burst into bawdy or anti-British songs, and drink and quarrel constantly, all with a rich gift of the gab that is their only wealth. The hostage himself is an English soldier boy, held against the life of an Irish soldier who is due to be hanged at dawn in Belfast Castle. The Tommy is shot anyhow, by accident, in a midnight brothel raid; comes to life again; and joins the others in singing "The Bells of Hell Go Ting-a-Ling-a-Ling," the finale. It is all mad—a superb, violent, civilized evening's entertainment.

Spring has finally come to Paris, but this year in a different style, almost with a new method. In the Tuileries gardens it came cautiously, tree by tree. On Friday, there was a tree or so that sprouted green leaves; another scattered dozen burgeoned in Saturday's heat; and on Sunday the pattern was set by verdure everywhere, with the giant blue Paris pigeons bolting above it, two by two.

April 22

The floral treat of the spring, of the year, and maybe of all time in Paris will be offered this Friday (for ten days only), with the opening of the first, and perhaps the last, of the Floralies Internationales ever to be held in the French capital. The greatest flower-and-shrub show in the city's history, it will be displayed in the city's newest, most imaginative twentieth-century construction, Le Palais de la Défense, only recently completed as one of the loveliest exhibition halls of our time. It rises just outside the city limits, at Puteaux, on the Rond-Point de la Défense, where Paris vainly made its last stand in the war of 1870 against the invading Germans, and is the pilot building of the new Paris that, in accordance with the city's modern urbanization plan, is starting to stretch west with skyscrapers and vertical communities that will soon lead to and connect with St.-Germain-en-Laye, the royal town where Louis XIV was born. In appearance, the Palais de la Défense is a pure and also a practical fantasy. It consists of a ribbed roof of pre-stressed concrete that looks like a billowing white parachute slit below into three parts, with each part coming to rest on its pointed tip upon the earth, making a three-faced building, walled in on its arched sides by glass only—the largest and the airiest-looking exhibition hall in all Europe, now filled with Europe's greatest potted garden of flowers and bushes in bloom. Even as seen in preview, the combination of the floral gifts of nature and the architectural gift of contemporary man makes this an exhibition to endure for long seasons in one's eyes and memory.

It is becoming increasingly clear that France's Fifth Republic is like no other she has ever had—in many ways a blessing—and that in one respect, despite the now unquestioned integrity of General de Gaulle's republican sentiments, it strangely resembles a monarchy. Among the French, at least, when a man, whether as President of the Fifth Republic or as a sovereign, holds power of a certain exceptional sort, from which nothing except death or revolution can remove him within a given period of time, his national popularity (or the contrary) becomes the pulse of his governing. About de Gaulle's popularity there is constant public and political curiosity (Is it going up again? Has it gone down? Feverish? Cool?), as though it were a kind of emotional temperature registered on some mostly invisible thermometer of public opinion that the public itself and the newspaper editors are constantly trying to calculate. This was not true, of course, of France's normal political leaders of the Third Republic—the historically notable Premiers like Clemenceau, for example, or Briand or Blum, or even Daladier—for whom the important thing was their popularity with the other politicians in Parliament, and who were not constantly engaged in a nationwide popularity contest, as de Gaulle is now.

Because de Gaulle is today's sovereign personality, his stately visits to the provinces, such as the one he has just made, in the pouring rain, to Burgundy, to the industrial center of France, and to the agricultural southwest, are of great informative importance. On the whole, he was unpopular everywhere with the war veterans, who failed to turn out with their battle flags to receive him, because he had cut their pensions. He was unpopular with the little winegrowers around Mâcon and through all that region, because his government has doubled the tax on inferior wines, continued its anti-alcoholism campaign, and followed the previous government's policy of ordering vines of inferior grapes to be torn up in order to make way for edible crops, in a modern agricultural plan. He was, however, extremely popular with the winegrowing farmers in the Burgundy regions of *les grands crus,* which still sell splendidly from the hills of Chambertin, Vosne-Romanée, Clos de Vougeot, and Beaune. He was unexpectedly popular with the majority of the thirteen thousand workmen at the great Creusot steel works (formerly the old Schneider works, which used to manufacture cannon and are now making machinery for Russia and Communist China), where the men who cheered him drowned out the few who whistled against him. At the Dunlop tire factory in Montluçon, which is a fief of the C.G.T. labor union, dominated by the Communists, the Party had ordered the men to lay down their tools and fold their arms as a sign of displeasure during the General's visit. The men stopped work, all right, but for the most part to shake hands with him. In the ancient village of Cuisery, near the cathedral town of Tournus, he made an extra-popular brief visit to the Cuisery chapel to see the tomb of a 1704 ancestor of his—the de Gaulles having originally been a Burgundian family, starting with a certain Captain Gaspard de Gaulle, given special privileges by the King in 1581. This was an extra-popular part of his tour simply because the French respect lineage. In one town, he sneezed into the microphone, trumpeted into his handkerchief, and confided hoarsely to thousands, "I've had the grippe. But it's much better." Twice, he was too hoarse to add his loud, off-pitch voice to the singing of the "Marseillaise." He repeatedly spoke outdoors in the rain, was hatless, coatless, drenched, good-natured, optimistic, and humanitarian. The theme of his speeches everywhere was the same, and could be summed up as "Not for the good of France alone but for the good of all men, let France go forward!" To the Montluçon workmen he said, "The world is round. There is only one world. All the men of the world are men like you and me. [Applause.] I have confidence that this year will see the beginning of that fraternal [world] organization for which France will set the example." Deliberately, he chose to stop off at Vichy, former government seat of Maréchal Pétain, whose name he did not mention. Instead, with great dignity, he said in a downpour to the thousands of umbrellas of the Vichyssois surrounding him, "It is, I will say to you in confidence, rather moving for me to find myself here officially. History makes its links. Whatever the changes, we remain one people, we are the real, the unique French people." Throughout the trip, his private car flew his private flag—the French tricolor pennant struck with the cross of Lorraine—and throughout the trip his popularity as the great, patriotic, highly educated, eccentric, and powerful President of the Fifth Republic was on the whole undeniable, and at times even touching.

May 20

The great surprise that has contributed to the de Gaulle Republic's quasi success, so far heavily qualified by many losses of invisible values, is the altered psychology of Charles de Gaulle himself. It seems thrice altered, actually—from his original rigid, patriotic tactlessness with President Roosevelt and Prime Minister Churchill to his sudden flight from responsibility when he was head of the provisional postwar government, and from there to his present metamorphosis, after his isolated years at Colombey, reading and writing history but not living it, except by his sibylline prophecy that France in real disaster could call only on him for salvation, a combination of unlikely and alarming eventualities no one had dreamed of till they came true. This time, he came to power a changed man, an obstinately responsible, superorganized elderly chief and educated patrician, so superior a French figure that even his dreams for a revived French *mystique* of mission and glory seemed merely gentlemanly visions. With all these, he brought new wisdom and grace—his Machiavellian ambiguity giving him the magic ability to function with Frenchmen of opposed views, which he amalgamates.

It may be recalled that millions voted for the General out of sheer fear of nothingness. Thus, at least once—and it may be that this was his only miracle—he united the untouchables of French politics: those extremists in a French republic's left and right who over the decades have regarded each other as doctrinally impure, and in their quarrels have cut France to pieces. There is already far more worry about who will take over the power inherent in the Fifth Republic's strong Constitution once de Gaulle is retired—or dies, he being no longer young—than there was about the dying Fourth Republic and its Constitution's anemia. How this Fifth Republic can democratically function with a bobtailed parliament that rarely meets—it is almost unnoticeably meeting now, with little power to debate and almost less to legislate—nobody yet knows. France, as plenty of its citizens now realize, is living in a new kind of republican world, with new and fundamental dangers to match.

June 3

For a month, Paris movie fans and critics have been debating the problem posed by Ingmar Bergman, the Swedish film director who is now ranked by those who reverently admire his works—and, perforce, even by those who don't—as the dominant world cinematographer today. Technically, he is an imagist who practices *Expressionismus,* and he has made twenty movies since 1945. Most leading film critics (far more important to Paris entertainment than mere theatre critics) have lauded him with eulogies of a fervor never heard of here before—at least not in relation to a row of painful movies, in an incomprehensible foreign tongue and with inadequate French captions, made by a man who has "a Swedish preoccupation with loneliness, death, and eroticism." The films shown here, at select neighborhood houses, have included "Smiles of a Summer Night," the glacially gay one about a middle-aged man who has a new young wife the same age as his son by a first wife; "The Prison," about prostitutes in one, and infanticide; "The Seventh Seal," about a medieval knight amorous of death; "Summer Games," about swimming in the fiords, and a young lover who dives headfirst onto a rock and dies; "Threshold of Life," which is set in a maternity hospital; and his latest, "Wild Strawberries," which is being called his masterpiece. The leading role is wonderfully acted by the elderly Victor Sjöström, an old star from the Malmö Stadsteater (which Bergman has also directed). He plays a venerable doctor who, at a ceremony honoring him as his city's finest citizen, realizes, in dream sequences and memory flashbacks, that he has killed love throughout his life. The "Strawberries" review by Claude Mauriac, the sincere, perspicacious movie critic of the weekly *Figaro Littéraire,* was an illuminating example of the Paris fervor. Among his phrases were "Bergman, a great, a very great artist . . . cinematographic miracle . . . the cruelty equals the poetry . . . humanism as well as harmony . . . cinema on a level with the great modes of noble creation." He touchingly added, in a personal address to his readers, "If you see only one film in six months, this is the one to see."

Bergman's direction of the Malmö Stadsteater production of the homonymous Hjalmar Bergman's play "A Saga" was considered harsh and cold when it was recently given here, in Swedish, at the International Theatre Festival. Since the theatre is Ingmar Bergman's real vocation, with moviemaking only his hobby, each May, when the theatre season ends, he enters a hospital in a state of collapse and stays six weeks, writing his next film, which, during Sweden's long summer days, he shoots in a furious two months of concentration. He hates critics; when he was here for "A Saga" and the Paris movie critics admiringly asked him why he made his films the way he did, he coolly said, "To mystify." According to a non-French report, he "is a character straight out of Strindberg, neurotic, insomniac, hypochondriac . . . neither smokes nor drinks; rarely shaves; goes about in corduroys and an old brown sweater . . . and once threw a chair through the control-booth window at a sound mixer who had bungled a recording." He is the son of the old King of Sweden's chaplain.

July 2

In this June season, the most talk and critical interest have, for once, centered on entertainment that everybody can afford—the three French films that, one way or another, were top winners in this spring's international Cannes Film Festival, all three having peculiar qualities, and peculiar men and histories behind them. The Golden Palm winner is a French film that was made in Rio de Janeiro, and in Portuguese (there is also a dubbed French-language version), during last year's carnival down there. It is called "Orfeu Negro," and it is an emotional shantytown, samba version of the antique legend of Orpheus and Eurydice, acted by Negro natives of Rio. Its hitherto unknown director—in all three cases, it is new directors, and not the actors, who have become the stars—is Marcel Camus (no relation to the novelist), aged forty-six, who had directed one film before in his life, and that one not noteworthy. He was so short of funds that he could buy only a one-way ticket to Rio to make this film, which he had determined upon, and was so heavily in debt by the time he started his return trip to France that he almost missed being allowed to take his unpaid-for sound track back with him. The seduction of his film is its naïve quality, emanting from its untrained Negro actors, who are like local shadows repeating the motions of a great civilized myth. The main site of its drama—the high mountain plateau above the sea and the city—affords magnificent scenic views from the ramshackle cabins where the protagonists dwell. The Eurydice is a pretty, light-colored girl named Marpessa Dawn, reportedly a Puerto Rican who has lived in both Philadelphia and Rio—but this is not a film in which civil identities count. During the day, Orpheus, a big, handsome black man, is a streetcar motorman down in Rio, but at night he takes on his humble musical role by strumming his guitar in his plateau hut; Eurydice, who becomes his beloved, is a visitor in her cousin's cabin, next door. The big scene of the film, for which it was obviously made, is the first carnival night, with what looks like miles of Rio streets covered by garishly costumed natives doing the samba with hypnotic fervor to the insistent pulse of multiple brass bands. Among the crowds is a mysterious male figure, disguised in a carnival costume of death, who pursues Eurydice into an electric powerhouse, where Orpheus, seeing her frightened face, and intent on saving her, accidentally touches a switch and she is electrocuted—certainly the most innocent, mechanized metamorphosis of the old legend yet contrived. Technically, the film is often rickety, but of the three great Cannes triumphs it is the one the French love most and argue about least.

The dominant Cannes film, which actually won nothing there except a general agreement that it is a passionate, troubling chef-d'œuvre, is "Hiroshima, Mon Amour," which was made in Japan and is the second long film directed by the almost unknown thirty-seven-year-old Alain Resnais. It opens on the embracing nude torsos of a Japanese man and a Frenchwoman in Hiroshima, after the couple's first, and only, night of love. He is, it turns out, an educated bourgeois; she is a French actress who has just made what one gathers is a pacifist film about Hiroshima. However, details are left submerged in the actual movie; the complex pattern of its emotions and ideas forms its substance. To judge by what has been written about it here—and it is the most written-about, talked-about European film since the war—every movie critic has had difficulty giving an adequate description of what happens in it, because attempting a verbal translation of its multiple photographic facets would be like trying to summarize the lyric speed and complex structure of some new piece of sensuous, emotional poetry. The film's main theme is what the French, in a passing fit of revivalist enthusiasm for a perfect tragic love, like that of Tristan and Isolde, now call *l'amour passion*—an ideal, doomed love that, because of its magic brevity and the forces working against it, marks the lovers' lives and is romantically preserved in memory across the earthly distance that ever after separates them. It is this kind of love that unites the Japanese man and the European woman, condemned to be separated that very day by her return to her own land. Like the film within it, "Hiroshima, Mon Amour" is a film of pacifism—a pacifism that stems, basically, from the two politically experienced brains that produced it, turning it into artistry. Whatever director Resnais's precise political attachments may be, he is clearly angry in a world of constantly increasing atomic bombs. The well-known novelist Mlle. Marguerite Duras, who wrote the film's scenario and dialogue, was, she declared in a recent interview, a Communist Party member until she was thrown out for the heresy of her views on Budapest, and she is certainly anti-bomb where the American devastation of Hiroshima is concerned.

The theme of the last of the three Cannes films is international only in that it concerns a delinquent boy. A hard, clear, excellently created movie about a thirteen-year-old Place Pigalle lad, it is called "Les Quatre Cents Coups"—a French idiom for what we would call "a bad lot"—and was directed by twenty-seven-year-old François Truffaut, who is anything but unknown in Paris moviemaking and movie-fan circles. As a precocious, authoritative critic, writing of late mostly in the weekly *Arts,* he has for several years been brilliantly insulting about some of the most successful and popular French moviemakers. A member of what the French call *"la nouvelle vague,"* or "the new wave," which means any young French people who are sick of old methods and ideas and are trying to utilize their own new conceptions, he has been the leader in disseminating the revolutionary notion that French films can be intelligent, even truthful to life, and still make money, citing as proof such directors, of varied nationalities, as Renoir, Hitchcock, Rossellini, Bresson, and Ophuls. He so impertinently, and justifiably, attacked the boredom that recent obsequious Cannes Festival decisions on prizes have begotten that for the past two years the Festival directors shut him out as a critic. This year, not only did the French selection committee choose his film to represent France but he saw it win the second important prize at Cannes—that for the best direction. In speaking of this film on juvenile delinquency, Truffaut, who is an explosively candid fellow, told the press that he himself had been a delinquent and had been put in a reform school, so he knew that his film represented real life, and he added that he thought it intelligent, and had every reason to expect that it would make money, which it undoubtedly is already doing in France. His boy actor is, in private life, merely a schoolboy named Jean-Pierre Léaud. In the film, he is plunged into a Parisian situation that is both sinister and commonplace. His parents quarrel in bed every night, and one day he sees his mother kissing a strange man in the shelter of the steps of a Métro station; he then discovers that his mother's husband is not his father, that she has been tart, and that he himself is illegitimate. The rest is classic: the boy runs away; steals, because he now has an obsession to go see the sea and needs money for the trip; is arrested, at his bewildered parents' request; is taken to jail, along with prostitutes, in the police wagon (the glitter of his tears and the corresponding twinkle of Pigalle's hedonistic night lights in the rain are a brilliant invention); and is sent to a normally brutal country reform school somewhere in western France. (The school psychiatrist's only questioning of the boy—exclusively on sex—is a stunningly good scene.) The boy escapes. Then follows a remarkable sequence that shows him running through the countryside, from one kind of France into another, from fields into hills into marshy plains, always breathless, as if escape took forever. The picture finishes when he sights the sea, runs into the water up to his ankles, turns, gazes at the landscape as if he were now insulated against pursuit, and, lifting his expressionless black young eyes, gives a long, a very long, motionless look beyond, which falls on those who are looking at him—on the spectators in the theatre, on them as humanity, on the society they represent.

July 15

For superior vacation reading, two novels of exceptional quality have attracted unusual attention at the tag end of the publishing season, one of them, "Le Planétarium," by Nathalie Sarraute, having been cited as a chef d'œuvre of the subconscious—a rarity indeed in contemporary French writing. Mme. Sarraute was born in Russia, where her mother was a writer, her father a chemist, and his brother a terrorist who, after attempting to assassinate a grand duke, fled to Sweden disguised as a woman. Long a resident of Paris, married to a French lawyer, and mother of three grown daughters (one also a writer), she is today still foreign-looking in her way, with her black hair combed back, in the classic Russian style, above extraordinary eyes, as black as black cherries—an impressively quiet, observant, international-looking intellectual. She has always written slowly, she says, and has produced only five books in twenty years. The "anti-novel" has been her aim as part of the experimental literary movement here known as Le Roman Nouveau, or New Novel, of which you may at least have heard, since it has been talked about a great deal more than it has produced. Its only two notable public successes have been Michel Butor's strangely phrased, effective novel about a train journey, "La Modification" (called "A Change of Heart" in its American edition), which won the Renaudot literary prize last year, and now Mme. Sarraute's latest novel, already in its third edition. Perhaps it should be explained that the Roman Nouveau writers' general aim has been to break the classic fiction mold maintained by French genius over the past hundred and fifty years, in order to accommodate more properly the broken shapes and new psychologies of modern life. While these experiments have been eagerly followed by the Paris literary cliques, much of the intelligent Paris public has found them, on the whole, mystifying, and even downright bizarre—or, at any rate, hard to read. The young leader of the Roman Nouveau, Alain Robbe-Grillet, as his experiment, has developed an avant-garde neo-realism actually based on listing objects or things, which his British admirers have called his *chosisme,* or thingishness. His latest example of it—a plantation novel called "La Jalousie"—is certainly astonishing. In the space of four pages, he lists the exact number of local banana trees—"the middle row, which should have had eighteen . . . had only sixteen," and so on. It seems worth citing the Robbe-Grillet formula for a New Novel if only because Mme. Sarraute's "Le Planétarium" is not in the least like it.

As Mme. Sarraute's title indicates, her novel involves the traceries of a set of people circling in their own orbits and gravitations of character like the spheres and planets, with their mutual attractions patterned against fatal collisions—an enlightening symbol of the complex mechanics of close human relationships today. The novel opens on an elderly aunt in her overlarge Paris flat; turns to the spoiled, ambitious, semi-intellectual nephew she has brought up, and to his wife, both of whom are living on the wife's affluent parents; and then to a passée famous woman novelist (a wonderful satiric, gaseous figure, as true and swollen with pride as a balloon), to whose literary salon the snobbish nephew craves entry, just as she, in her waning glory, craves to have recherché new young male faces ornamenting it. In progressive encircling relations between the old and young generations, the young couple obtain the old aunt's big flat through intrigue, and the nephew, moving into a higher stratum, is able to despise the pretentious old novelist as a distinguished bore—two accelerated new movements through social space that seem like a promise of his final airy freedom. "Le Planétarium" is really a novel about the avarice of the emotions at a particular level of bourgeois French hearts, to which Mme. Sarraute has added a modern sonority by using, in parts, the interior monologue, that terrible, echoing second voice of the present century. She seems the only one among the New Novel experimenters who appears finally to have struck her own style—intense, observational, and personal. Her book is to be translated into English by Mrs. Maria Jolas, one of the founders of *transition,* the famous prewar Franco-American experimental literary magazine here.

* * *

Another publication, which must be mentioned because of the grave shock it has produced, is a hundred-page booklet called "La Gangrène," composed of seven signed statements by Algerian students here—members of a government-banned rebel intellectual group—in which they describe their alleged torture by the Sûreté Nationale's notorious secret-police unit known as the D.S.T., against which the seven lodged useless formal complaints with French legal authorities last winter, after the events so cited. The booklet first came to public notice here just after its publication, in the last part of June, when a rousing article about it appeared in the independent afternoon paper *Le Monde;* within two hours police confiscated the remaining unsold copies of "La Gangrène" at the Editions de Minuit, the internationally known Resistance publishing office of the Second World War. A few days later, Premier Debré declared before the Senate that "La Gangrène" was "mendacious and dishonorable," and was written for pay by two Communists (an authorship that the Minuit office formally denied); and the Minister of the Interior actually filed with a Seine court a complaint against the publishers, charging "libel against the police." All these items, including accounts of the seizure and the contents of "La Gangrène," were published by all the Paris newspapers, but only *Le Monde* carried on a campaign for the booklet, declaring, "To call it infamous is not a substitute for the firm denial one would have liked to hear of the essential point: were the men tortured or not?" The tortures described by the seven Algerians (one of them the brother of the so-called Minister of Finance in the so-called Algerian rebel government-in-exile) allegedly took place partly in the cells of the D.S.T. in the Rue des Saussaies, about three hundred yards from the Palais de l'Elysée, the official residence of General de Gaulle. The booklet's seven signed statements are written in a matter-of-fact style, unhysterical though detailed, and are mostly similar. Stripped nude and flogged, the men were then laid over a bar, like fowls on a spit, and electrodes were applied to exposed parts of their bodies; two had to do knee bends while balancing the big Paris telephone book in their hands, and were beaten insensible when they failed. On page 97 of "La Gangrène," one Algerian describes the appearance of another after repeated beatings: "Only his protuberant eyes indicated that it was the face of a human being."

Perhaps the greatest shock produced by "La Gangrène" for millions of French comes from the realization that both the opposing prophecies about General de Gaulle before the referendum calling him to power fatally continue to be proved true—that he was France's only signal chance for recovery, and that though he is a man of the highest honor, always a patriot and now a liberal, he would to some extent be the captive of his Fascist followers. In the case of "La Gangrène," on which he has not said a word, he has also become the prisoner of his own silence. The French are now beginning to believe that while his painful, sacrificial silence at certain times is what is literally holding the straining Fifth Republic together, it is also dissipating part of its democratic citizens' hope and faith.

July 28

The only perceptible development in Montparnasse since the war is that, from the viewpoint of Paris history, hedonism, literature, and painting, it has slid downhill into quietude, losing its importance and crowds to the new night clubs and writers' cafés of St.-Germain-des-Prés. The latest proof is the razing of the notable old Café Rotonde, across from the Dôme, and the substitution on the same site of the newly opened La Rotonde Cinéma—a transformation performed with such an intelligent sense of nostalgia as to make the theatre the most extraordinary neighborhood movie house in Paris and a monument well worth visiting. Above the screen, an inscription by the poet Jacques Prévert greets the spectator—and if the spectator is left over from the old Montparnasse days and nights, it is enough to bring a tear of affection to the eye: "The names on these walls are those of persons of all sorts who haunted this place long ago. May they still be at home here as they used to be. This theatre belongs to their dreams and serves as their remembrance." Then, while the lights are still on and one sinks back into one's elegant rose velvet seat, one can read the names of a hundred and three Montparnos—some of whom one used to eat and drink with, laugh and quarrel with—cut like a decorative frieze on the stone-colored walls, in an alphabetical listing, beginning with Apollinaire and Aragon and ending with Vlaminck and some mysterious unknown whose name begins with "Z." On the list of those who frequented the Café Rotonde and have since known fame are Cocteau, Radiguet, Modigliani, Max Jacob, Foujita, Picasso, Braque, Honegger, Hemingway, Henry Miller, Bromfield, Utrillo, and, in a class by themselves, Lenin and Trotsky, who used to sip their *cafés-crèmes* there in 1915, when in exile. The lights go down, and a Russian version of Dostoevski's "The Idiot" comes on the screen. One can smoke in La Rotonde—the only small Paris movie that permits this—and while you hold a cigarette in your left hand, with the other hand you adjust a simultaneous-translation speaker beside your right ear. It is a metal disc mounted on a flexible stem, and in the present case it gives you Joseph Kessel's French translation of the Russian screenplay, recited by a French cast and so precisely correlated to the lip movements of the Russian actors on the screen that if you have finished your cigarette and clap your left hand over your left ear, shutting out the Slav sounds, you believe, wide-eyed, that the Russians are speaking French. Ocularly, the film looks more like Dumas than Dostoevski. Directed by Ivan Pyriev and covering only the first half of the novel, it is a big spectacle in color, with snowy Moscow street scenes as beautiful as if done in Hollywood. Its importance is that it inaugurates the Rotonde's policy of showing intellectual foreign fare worthy of the international intelligentsia that made the café famous.

August 12

The French Assembly probably deserves a word of mention right now, if only to remark that it has recessed for the summer, with its departure arousing even less public interest here than its presence did. It had been sitting since late spring, for three of the five months it is allowed to sit under the Fifth Republic—which is "only faintly parliamentarian," as a political wit recently said, in disapproval. The Senate has closed, too. Made up of older, tougher politicians, many of them reëlected as popular leftovers from the Fourth Republic, and with nothing like the Assembly's majority of débutants and members of the neo-Gaullist party (which seems increasingly to mean Gaullists who do not agree with General de Gaulle), the Senate in its recent Luxembourg Palace session at least showed signs of life by occasionally kicking with old republican vigor against the present government's traces.

More than a word must be said about the latest state of affairs surrounding the Algerian war, which never stops. General de Gaulle reportedly described it a fortnight ago as "this senseless war," adding, "Peace is a necessity. This absurd war concerns us all, and you must help me to end it." He is supposed to have said this off the record to the colored officers—largely Negro ex-colonials, mostly from Africa—newly elected to the Senate of the French *Communauté,* de Gaulle's Fifth Republic extension of France's vision of the future. His summing up of the war as *"insensée"* and *"absurde"* is simply a new reflection of the dichotomy of opinion on how to halt the struggle in Algeria and settle the country's future political status that has existed from the first between the General and his hand-picked Premier, Michel Debré. In Debré's most recent statement about the war, made before the largely white French Parliament here, he seemed to speak of France as being personified by himself, rather than by President de Gaulle, when he declared, "France would do anything—anything at all—to keep Algeria French." While the biggest French military effort of the entire five-year Algerian war, called Operation Binoculars, has been going on for the last two weeks in the mountains of Kabylia, de Gaulle has been exploring tentative solutions with Algeria's neighboring Arab countries, as his own way of discovering a means of ending the bloodshed. It is known that the King of Morocco, in the interests of peace, is willing to undertake a mission for the exchange of information between the Arabs and the French, though if he is to furnish his French interlocutor (General de Gaulle) with information on the state of mind of the Algerian rebel army chiefs and of the leading Ministers of Le Gouvernement Provisoire de la République Algérienne in exile, whom he recently received at Rabat, he will presumably have to know the real intentions of General de Gaulle in regard to Algeria, which the General's ambivalent statements have so far not made clear to His Majesty (or to millions of French). For this purpose, a confidential meeting with de Gaulle was arranged on the King's recent arrival here for what was elegantly called "an ablation of his tonsils." But before the two could meet, the King had to return hastily to Rabat to mend Morocco's political and financial fences; the tonsillectomy was performed there, too, and he has been recuperating in the Royal Palace ever since.

Added propaganda tension among the non-white races came last week from the Pan-African Conference in Monrovia, Liberia, where the nine independent African states, instead of concentrating exclusively on their own troubles, unanimously voted that "France should recognize the Algerian people's right to independence, should withdraw the French Army, and should start negotiations," which was admitted here to be a diplomatic victory for the Algerian rebel cause. But there was also a big diplomatic victory for de Gaulle reported from Monrovia in the conferees' statement that "his prestige has remained intact among all the delegations." However, a real international crisis on the Algerian question is now considered possible in New York at the mid-September session of the United Nations General Assembly, when the necessary two-thirds majority of the delegates may vote that France should give Algeria her independence.

The one bright aspect of the Algerian problem is that during this past fortnight Premier Debré, who at least sees eye to eye with his President on the industrialization needed to raise Algeria from the status of an undeveloped area, visited there and brought back to his Paris press conference an extremely impressive report on the opening and hitherto unmentioned results of de Gaulle's Constantine Plan—the economic new deal for Algeria that in the General's view is the costly but unavoidable evolutionary accompaniment to France's "military pacification," as the Algerian war is officially still called here. Since May, the Fifth Republic's new Société Algérienne de Développement et Expansion has approved seventy-two applications from firms willing to invest about thirty million dollars in the country (with preferential tax relief), thus creating six thousand Algerian jobs at the outset; a big steel plant is going up in Bône; and the pipeline from the rich Hassi Messaoud Sahara oil wells to the coast is almost completed. It is this fabulous oil deposit on which the French state is gambling to pay for the Constantine Plan. Sixty-two thousand new jobs for Algerians are expected to be available by this time next year. Also by this year's end, private industry will probably have furnished seventy-eight million dollars more in investment money—which takes spunk, pioneering spirit, and no doubt patriotism, too, considering the political risks that even optimistic believers in L'Algérie Française cannot close their eyes to. Peace in Algeria is still the acme of the hopes of millions of French people under de Gaulle. But in the meantime it is de Gaulle's Constantine Plan that has apparently begun the real, secondary miracle.

August 25

This year, Paris has visibly built itself into the middle of the twentieth century at last. Whether you like it or not, you can see the proofs in the suburban ring of new apartment houses, containing three hundred thousand new flats, that now circles Paris where there were bosky vacant lots, or even green fields, a year ago. These *cité-parcs*—new inventions springing up all over France and given this new name—are architecturally identical and look monotonously like dominoes or dice, being of white cement spotted by rows of fenestration. Some have small, slab-fronted balconies (for parking the baby carriage) that are invariably painted red, blue, green, or yellow—a single color to a floor. One development, which claims to be the longest block of flats in all France, is just outside the northern Paris suburb of Pantin. It is a novelty in that it is built in the form of a wriggling snake; is nearly a half mile long, containing four hundred and fifty flats to house fifteen hundred tenants; has four acres of playground and lawn for children and baby-sitting mothers; and, by its pleasing serpentine pattern, gives light and air to all. Huge square fifteen-story towers are going up at Boulogne-Billancourt, near the Renault auto works; new five-story apartment houses have appeared in the forests near the Seine at Vernouillet, Rueil, Argenteuil, and dozens of other suburbs; and in Paris itself the Marché aux Puces, the old flea fair at the Porte de Clignancourt, is, alas, going to be more decently lodged nearby to make room for domino-flat buildings. Three miles outside the suburban town of Poissy, seat of the Simca auto works, in what has been for thirty years beautiful blue-green fields of cauliflowers, there now rises, like a strange urban excrescence, a *cité-parc* of forty-five apartment buildings, with twenty-two hundred flats housing eight thousand people, and featuring three twelve-story skyscrapers alien to such an empty sky.

Yet even at this rate of construction, France's housing shortage could continue for another century, according to statistics. The rent for a modest flat in these new buildings around Paris—three rooms plus kitchen, a *salle d'eaux,* with hand basin and shower, and a separate lavatory—runs to about fourteen thousand francs (twenty-eight dollars) a month; if a workman wants to buy a flat in a new coöperative building, he must figure about a million and a quarter francs (twenty-five hundred dollars) per room. Previously, the economical French used to figure on spending from four to eight per cent of their budgets on rent—living without modern comforts but saving money. (Even today, forty per cent of French *logements* lack running water, the water being down in the court; seventy per cent lack private lavatories and ninety per cent lack private showers or baths.) Only the desperate postwar housing shortage could have driven today's families to spend what amounts to twenty per cent of their budgets on rents that include modern conveniences whether they want them or not. Over the centuries, French fastidiousness has always leaned toward good food, on which a third of what a family earns is still spent. Nobody saves money any more; it is eaten instead.

This eruption of new housing is entirely owing to de Gaulle, who ordered the 1959 government building credits jumped by thirty-five billion francs, to a total of a hundred and ninety billion; created six new building societies under government control; and has favored what is called the Habitation à Loyer Modéré, or H.L.M., plan for the working class. There comes a moment in the modern life of a magnificent, previously regal, highly stylized, great old city, whose architecture has made and been part of civilized history, when breaking one's heart over the jerry-built monotonous ugliness of H.L.M. flats turns into a cardiac form of aesthetic hypochondria.

Another modern manifestation hereabouts has been France's first experience (which came only this month, showing how lucky it has been) with juvenile-delinquent gangs. Apparently, they call themselves Les Gadjos, though nobody knows the etymological derivation of the word, or has dared to ask. The peaceful citizens they attack with bicycle chains on the streets after dark have given them the name of Les Blousons Noirs, since black imitation-leather jackets are their tribal regalia. They are the French version of London's Teddy boys, of Germany's so-called "half-salted ones," and of Russia's hooligans—all based on the genuine, original New York "West Side Story" article. Les Blousons Noirs are also devotees of the late James Dean. In the Paris suburb of Drancy, where Paris Jews were first put in concentration camps under the Nazi Occupation, a hundred and seventy Black Jackets, under the orders of a fourteen-year-old chief, were arrested a fortnight ago; near Arras, a seventeen-year-old neophyte vainly tried to blackmail an obstinate old farmer out of half a million francs by threatening to set his wheat fields on fire; up in Finistère, that pious Breton land, sub-adolescent Black Jackets, aged only ten to thirteen, sacked their local school, about to open; on the beach at Les Sables d'Olonne, little Black Jacketeers almost disarmingly attacked a beach shop to steal money, balloons, and candy; near the Pas-de-Calais, a thirteen-year-old beat up an old gentleman in an odd attempt to force him into adopting him legally. In the Parisian Thirteenth Arrondissement, forty Black Jacket boys staged a real coup in the Rue Brillat-Savarin—first in warfare against another gang, then against the local post office, then against all passersby. ("If we didn't like their faces, we smashed them in.") Their parents, called to the police station, could not believe their eyes when they saw their sons there. The Black Jackets made their first national appearance in Cannes early in August, when forty of them fought it out with the local police, terrifying holidaymakers in décolletage. They act as they do, or so they say, *"parce que nous nous ennuyons"*—"because we are bored." It is France's latest *mal de siècle.*

1960

March 23

It is now painfully evident that de Gaulle's troubles, accumulating increasingly in the past month, throughout the last fortnight, and even over the weekend just gone by, have seriously affected the temper of the French nation and how it feels toward him. His once radiant popularity has begun to fade, and the docile obedience of Parliament has dangerously diminished. For nearly two years, he has been the extraordinary, salvational leader, who came to power as a symbol of new hopes and faiths for the French and for France, and who even appeared to be saving French republicanism by using his high hand to perform the labors that Parliament had demonstrably and repeatedly failed to be equal to, or even to have time for, because of its constant, preoccupying power quarrels, its rivalries, and its tattered patriotism, which left a vast rent in the fabric of the state, through which successive governments fell to the ground, like lost valuables. The drama of this change in attitude toward him is dated precisely, like a historical event. It began on January 24th—naturally, in the purlieus of Algiers—when the French Army clique of *ultras* again defied him, and were punished by him for mutiny against what seemed his hope of soon ending their war with the rebel Algerian forces by means of a negotiated cease-fire, to be backed by some far-future vote on Algeria's self-determination or, at worst, its independence. At least, this had seemed de Gaulle's hope from what he had previously said, even when he did not say it clearly. Unfortunately, the French people's overstimulated devotion to him and to peace began expiring under the sudden illogical contradictions that inexplicably came flowing from the General's highly educated mind. He declared, in a *volte-face,* that the war must go on until the Algerian supporters of independence were utterly destroyed—and with that the French Army again triumphed in an old-style colonial military victory, climbing back into the saddle of political power from which he had just thrown it. The most painfully popular cartoon in Paris was one by Vicky, reprinted from the London *Evening Standard.* It showed de Gaulle standing on his head in war-torn Algeria while stating, "As I was saying last week . . ." De Gaulle came to power two years ago largely on his implicit promise that he would end the war, now proceeding apace through its fifth year. Opinion here seems to be that he only recently found out that he could not stop it—his tragedy and France's. Until he made this discovery, his hopes led him to speak ambivalently, the hopes and facts in the case diverging importantly. To the French now, the only clear fact is that there is to be no peace. Another opinion, more special, is that General de Gaulle, because of his mystique, his professional career at arms, and his intimacy with French history, still believes that only the Army symbolizes the unity of France, and is psychologically unable now to separate Army and country. This, at any rate, is the bare, condensed scenario of the suspense drama currently going on here, of which the last act is not yet written, and perhaps not even imagined.

General de Gaulle's civilian troubles with the parliamentary deputies started only a fortnight ago with a demand by a legal majority of them—as fixed by his own constitution—that he convoke the Chamber in a special session before its normal April term in order to talk over the financial crisis of the French farmers, out on a limb and left behind by the country's economic recovery. This, some newspapers think, was parliamentary Machiavellism to flatter the peasants and at the same time to use the poor price of Brittany potatoes as a political cover for the unbearable national cost of French blood and money being spent in Algeria, the deputies' real aim being to weaken him by adding to his unpopularity on any pretext. In this the General helped them by refusing to grant their demand, quoting multiple reasons that he said were also contained in his constitution. This refusal has, in turn, raised the graver question of whether de Gaulle, the man of acknowledged probity, the leader with a fetish for *la légalité* such as French kings claimed for ruling, has used his constitution in a constitutionally illegal way. In any case, his categorical, courteous refusal to give the deputies what most citizens thought they had a right to demand has had a spirited and bad national reaction—quarrels among jurists, millions of words of argument and criticism in the press, increased public bewilderment, and even hostility. In a magazine article, Guy Mollet, the Socialist chief who helped put de Gaulle in power and has supported his regime, has warned him, "No further mistakes can be permitted, *mon général!*" The phrase "the Sixth Republic" has been spoken and printed (so far sparingly), as if the Fifth Republic might be brought down by the exceptional Frenchman who founded it.

April 12

It is too bad that President de Gaulle's welcome home included grave trouble with the French farmers. They are now a changed lot, know it, and are at the end of their patience. Even just after the war they were still picturesque, were stilled called *les paysans,* were still supposed to be rich enough to stuff their straw mattresses with bank notes, still plowed their fields with Norman stallions or oxen, and were the politicians' pets, constituting twenty per cent of the population and a huge vote. Now they call themselves *les cultivateurs,* wear yellow gum boots *à l'américaine,* are backwardly trying to industrialize their production, are a dwindling class because their sons go to work in town for real money (and for plumbing and movies), plow with tractors, use chemical fertilizers, are in debt, and are unpampered by the politicians, who, they have just said, treat them like "poor relations." In France's contemporary social family, this they certainly are. They have now pushed their financial crisis over the last two years to the front, where it belongs as the nation's leading domestic problem. A week ago, close to half a million *cultivateurs* held mass protest meetings in seventeen of France's biggest market towns. The farmers' union—La Fédération Nationale des Syndicats d'Exploitants Agricoles—ordered them not to take along their pitchforks, the age-old weapon and symbol here of peasants in revolt for their rights. The union's preliminary mass meeting in Amiens in February had ended in a riot with the state police, in which tear-gas bombs, pitchforks, and paving stones were used, and hundreds were injured. At last week's monster meetings there was less violence but more organized indignation, with slogans on placards that showed which way the wind is blowing. At Nancy, the slogan was "Better Be Rebellious Than Resigned"; at Tours, "We Don't Want to Be Slaves of the Fifth Republic"; at Nantes, "The Peasants Are Certainly Worth As Much As One Atomic Bomb, *Mon Général.*" Considering the French farmers' addiction to *"la goutte"*—the "drop" of hard liquor, like Calvados or *marc,* that they lace their coffee with and swig by the glassful whenever they get together in the *bistros*—the meetings were pretty orderly, instructive, and constructive. The main farmer speaker at the Laval town meeting spoke for all ordinary small French farmers (big farmers with two-hundred-acre farms being rich and rare) when he said, "This is our last warning to the government. It knows our situation. We hold it responsible."

Eh bien, so far the government's proposed reform bills offer too little too late, in long-term plans for 1961–63, which are of no earthly help to the peasants' tight budgets right now. The deputies will certainly try to speed things up when Parliament opens in two weeks. The projects are for rural equipment, more agricultural schools, livestock inoculations, water supplies, and sick benefits for all farm workers (something they don't get now), but there is no project for the farmers' principal demand, which has been ducked by the government for fear of renewed inflation—guaranteed adequate farm prices tied to rising living costs, as they used to be. It is the French cities that have created and enjoyed the recent big prosperity boom, the advancing technology of France, and the high wages of workers, who can pay for and eat like the bourgeois, with the same Sunday *filet de bœuf* and daily *bifteck*. French farmers, who are nature's conservatives—the perfect producers of perfect rich-tasting produce by nineteenth-century methods, on farms still as lovely-looking as landscape gardens—are way behind the times in living standards and are outraged that factory workers can buy the best they raise when they themselves cannot afford to buy even the average of whatever the factory workers manufacture. What drives farmers really mad is to read in the local-newspaper produce quotations that the Paris housewife pays three hundred francs for a kilo of leeks when the farmer has sold four kilos for half that—the difference going largely to the Halles' great central-market middlemen, France's most hated locusts. Farmers here want land mortgages at three per cent interest, like their neighbors in other countries, instead of at the twelve per cent the French pay, and want government money loans at one per cent, instead of three and four per cent, which is unheard of beyond their borders. Briefly, they want to get out of debt; want to modernize, because government technocrats assure them that it pays; and, most of all, simply want to make money again. France cooks and passionately enjoys eating the best food in the world. Maybe she had better help her fine food raisers to prosper.

April 29

On Tuesday, the first regular 1960 session of the French Parliament, in recess since last December, opened with the expected lukewarm Socialist and Radical threat to try to overthrow the government of President de Gaulle's Premier, M. Michel Debré, by a motion of censure. The censure motion against the government (for, by President de Gaulle's Constitution, de Gaulle is not responsible to Parliament, may not himself be censured, and, indeed, may be charged only with treason) is largely a political gesture for the record, to show that the Socialists and the Radicals, leaders of the Left Opposition, now definitely existing, deeply disapprove of the General's refusal to call a special session of Parliament last month to discuss the agricultural crisis, even though the Opposition had obtained the legal right to demand a session by assembling a constitutional majority of deputies—a double brushing aside that both Parliament and the farmers are still smarting under. Naturally, Debré's opening speech to Parliament on Tuesday was on the agricultural problem. In it he first recalled the classic agrarian formula that the two breasts of France are her tilled land and her pastures—the bread and milk to feed her people—and then went on, less bucolically, to matters of hard cash, calling the farmers' demand that their prices be automatically hitched to rising living costs "a one-way infernal machine" that would inevitably make all prices run uphill.

This being the first significant anti-government political maneuver against the Fifth Republic, comparisons with the Fourth Republic, which used to mow governments down like weeds, are now being freely made, if only as a means of estimating the Fifth's strength. Everyone agrees that any government under the Fourth would have fallen flat by now but that it would have been too smart to let the farmers' predicament fester. Another difficulty for the government will come from this week's ousting of M. Jacques Soustelle from the Gaullist political party, the Union for the New Republic, or U.N.R., which, ironically, Soustelle founded and is now splitting. As a champion of Algeria's integration with France and of war to the finish to exterminate the rebels, he will now be able to raise an uncontrollably loud Opposition voice among the *ultras* on what still remains the vital emotional and political touchstone of France—the Algerian problem and lack of peace.

June 22

Monday's news of the sudden acceptance by Le Gouvernement Provisoire de la République Algérienne of President de Gaulle's offer, in his last Tuesday-night radio speech (today's decibel-laden substitute for former secret diplomacy), of plans for a talk here in Paris "to find an honorable end to the war that still drags on" roused only a mixed measure of hope and dubiety in the French people. It was as if the over-familiar alloy of doubt had dulled the shining radiance of hope, and its value. Four years ago, the Resident Minister of Algeria, M. Robert Lacoste, had assured the French that the war was in its "last quarter of an hour"—that idiotic, ill-computed phrase being his only memorable contribution to the war. The Socialist Mollet government, brought to power on its pacifist intentions, merely waged the war all the harder after M. Mollet himself was pelted by the natives with tomatoes, in season at the time of his friendly opening visit to Algiers. Even General de Gaulle, from whose exalted superiority something as high as a miracle was expected, founded his Fifth Republic on his belief, shared by the majority of the French people, that he could bring an end to the war. Now, two years later, he seems to have brought it within sight. There is still a large gap in vision, however, as was mentioned in the blunt communiqué of acceptance issued by President Ferhat Abbas, of the so-called Algerian Republican Government. In it, Ferhat Abbas said forthrightly that it is his government's belief that if a "sincerely free" referendum on self-determination were actually offered by the French to the Algerian people, "their choice, without doubt, would be for independence." This probability has been met head-on only by the serious, independent paper *Le Monde,* in an editorial of the kind that is written exclusively at grave moments in French affairs by its austere editor, M. Hubert Beuve-Méry, under the mystifying nom de plume of Sirius, as if the Dog Star were suddenly shedding needed extra light. In the Monday-night front-page Sirius editorial, entitled "Hope," M. Beuve-Méry boldly said, as did no other editorialist, "It is alleged that any accord made with the Army of the Algerian National Liberation Front will open the way to independence sooner or later. This is true. But when all of Africa is shaking off its European tutelage, can it be believed that Algeria alone will be able to remain outside this gigantic revolution, and that a million French can impose their law indefinitely on nine million Moslems in full demographic upsurge?"

The answer is "yes"—at least, as given that same Monday afternoon by what was pedantically called "Le Colloque de Vincennes," a symposium of ultra-Right Wing politicians (mostly mavericks who were once in more moderate parties) held in the suburb of Vincennes, where they declared themselves a possible new political party against de Gaulle, and certainly against Algeria's being regarded as anything but French forever. Their basic fear—and they are not alone in feeling it—is that an independent Algeria might all too easily change from a formerly rebellious French colony into an obedient Kremlin colony, to judge by Moscow's and Peking's recent violent propaganda for Algeria's liberation. The Vincennes colloquy had long been planned, but the sudden news of the impending de Gaulle-Ferhat Abbas talk so increased its timeliness that it was attended by thirty-five deputies, some senators, some former Premiers, and two hundred important figures from universities, big business, labor unions, and government administration, along with a crowd of political experts on the *qui vive*. The principal speakers were M. Jacques Soustelle, former Gaullist leader and now the most dangerous, brainy anti-Gaullist leader, and M. Georges Bidault, once the sanctified chief of the liberal Catholic M.R.P. party, who, after de Gaulle's Tuesday radio speech, declared that de Gaulle's proposal to Algeria was "sombre folly" and possibly tantamount to treason—which, even in France, was an almost incredible attempt at verbal political assassination. How violent may be the reaction to de Gaulle's peace policy by the French Army *ultras* in Algeria itself nobody here is yet sure of, except to recall the bloody example given on January 24th, when they barricaded the center of Algiers in their mutinous maneuver against the Paris government—a mutiny that President de Gaulle, suddenly becoming General de

Gaulle, broke by his military orders. It is hoped here, and fervently, that French political civil war does not break out again in France's Army.

Among the scars suffered by the French social fabric through the five and a half years of this peculiar war have been the public's enforced awareness that torture has reportedly been practiced by elements of the French forces in Algeria, on both French and native sympathizers to the Algerian rebel cause, and that reputable French papers carrying carefully authenticated reports of such shocking things have been seized by the police, apparently on what amounted to Army orders. These practices have constituted a double offense to French republicanism in the Fifth Republic—first in the disgraceful, anguishing abuse of human bodies, and second in the violation of the freedom of the press. On June 3rd, *Le Monde* reported that its June 2nd edition had been seized in Algiers for having published an article by Mme. Simone de Beauvoir about an Algerian girl, Djamila Boupacha, who, as the examining prison gynecologist attested, was indeed suffering acutely, just as she maintained, and who claimed that she had been vilely tortured into making a false statement about participation in a bomb-throwing incident in a café—the Army's only counter-claim being that she had made her admission. Her awful story, which was first talked of in March, drew a great deal of shocked comment here. Last week, she came up for trial in Algiers before an Army tribunal, whose judge ordered the proceedings postponed, "pending further information," until July, when she can be condemned to death. These strange violations of civilized republicanism are considered by the French to be the humiliating mysteries of General de Gaulle's Fifth Republic and of his portion of the five and a half years of the demoralizing Algerian war—*la sale guerre,* the dirty war, as the younger French generation calls it—which he now may be bringing to an end, without victory.

Last Saturday, June 18th, was the twentieth anniversary of de Gaulle's first intimate and influential historical relationship with his *belle France,* which he has, on his heights, continued whenever possible. His first words to her were those he spoke from the B.B.C. in London, dressed in the uniform of a defeated army but wearing white gloves. This was not that prophetic, legendary appeal that we have all come to think it was—the one beginning "France has lost a battle; but France has not lost the war!," which was printed on posters and pasted on London's walls a few weeks later. The appeal he made that June day began, characteristically, with identification —"I, General de Gaulle"—invited the remains of the French Army in England to get in touch with him, and ended, "Whatever happens, the flame of French resistance will not, must not, be extinguished." Last Friday evening, he lit the first vigil flame before the enormous new Resistance Memorial that has been constructed below the old suburban fortress of Mont-Valérien. It is the only monument to the heroic dead of this last war that France, in all conscience, could erect—honoring the dead Resistance fighters, the dead voluntary patriots who fell for Free France, and, in particular, the forty-five hundred Resistance fighters whom the Germans captured and imprisoned in Mont-Valérien, where they were shot by Nazi firing squads, many of them just before the Liberation. For this reason, Mont-Valérien has become the sacred site of the French Resistance. Before a huge crowd of fifteen thousand French, drawn by memory, sorrow, or national and personal pride, and composed of former Resistance members, men and women from all over France, and of the families of those who failed to survive, there was a military torchlight procession that accompanied the placing within the crypt of sixteen coffins, containing nameless dead, which have been sepulchred in the fort ever since the Liberation. The Versailles Cathedral choir sang "Le Chant des Partisans," that melancholy Resistance song, and at midnight twelve cannons sounded in salute for the dead. The next day, the public came by the thousands again, to view the memorial by daylight. It is handsome and dramatic, with noble, solemn proportions. Below an old wall of the fort on its hill has been built an immense lower wall, three hundred feet long, of a reddish, almost flesh-colored, stone, dominated in the center by a gigantic stone Croix de Lorraine, nearly forty feet high. On either side, ornamenting the wall, are eight bronze *haut-reliefs,* each by a different French artist and each depicting some phase of the Free French struggle. One, of twisted hands and barbed wire, symbolizes the concentration camps; another is a huge human heart in an opened breast, symbolizing torture; another is a crane flying with wings drooping, like a parachute; a wounded lion struggling with a Hydra-headed beast stands for the desert fighting; and for the seamen there is a youth fighting with an octopus whose twisted tentacles vaguely suggest the Nazi swastika. The memorial is officially called Le Mémorial National de la France Combatante.

Those who fought these battles were members of de Gaulle's private army, and the new touching and magnificent structure is their memorial. But, in its way, it is de Gaulle's monument.

July 6

Until Monday afternoon, when the announcement was made of the Algerian rebels' spirited and profoundly disappointing refusal to send another cease-fire delegation to France, because it would not be "opportune in the circumstances," millions of French had thought that the Algerians' earlier acceptance of President de Gaulle's June 14th offer to discuss "an honorable end to the war" looked like the best chance for peace in the sixty-eight months since the fighting began. For five days last week, these optimists were able to let their hopes play freely while the first fact-finding Algerian delegation, to its surprise, sat housebound, invisible and incommunicado, in the handsome old Prefecture building at Melun, forty-five kilometres outside Paris. Thus, the opening difficult motions for honorably ending the war got off to an awkward start, at least in the view of the influential chief Algerian emissary, Maître Ahmed Boumendjel, a genial, popular former Paris lawyer who speaks French better than Arabic (doubtless one of the reasons he was chosen), who only lately joined the rebels in exile, and who, with his aide, M. Mohammed Ben Yahia, *chef de cabinet* of President Ferhat Abbas, found himself confined in Melun for strictly secret conversations with the two French delegates to the cease-fire conference—one the General Secretary of Algerian Affairs and the other an elderly high Army officer. Nor was any information as to what the four were really talking about given to the press to hand on to the impatient and deeply interested French public. The journalists who went to Melun were kept outside the grilled fence that shuts off the Prefecture's courtyard just as strictly as the Algerians were kept invisible, day and night, inside it—the last thing they had expected or desired in a meeting of such vital Franco-Arab importance, from which they wanted their libertarian point of view to be heard around the globe.

As French citizens themselves have repeatedly noted with exasperation, official public relations are peculiarly unbalanced in this present republic, whose chief not infrequently communicates with his compatriots and the world in extensive, splendid literary addresses that are ornaments to the French language. But his government, supposedly on his say-so, is a great one for keeping mum, especially in dispensing information that might do it or the public some good. Of the brief Melun meetings (at which the two French representatives never shook hands with the Algerians—strange protocol indeed), a disgruntled foreign observer noted, with obvious restraint, "The past week has shown French diplomacy and treatment of public opinion at its most baffling. The Frenchman in the street, on whom the regime must count to resist political extremists, and whose own fate is closely involved, has had to go through an incredible game of trying to guess what half-hints, contradictory statements, and leaks from Tunis meant or did not mean." Even the government's all-important communiqué at the end of the five restricted days at Melun merely said that conditions for negotiations on the honorable end of the war had been laid down, without giving any reader, Christian or Moslem, the slightest idea of what those conditions were. The last curt line of the communiqué was, however, only too comprehensible. It said, "These preliminary conversations having been concluded, the emissaries are now to return immediately to Tunis" (where the Algerian rebel government sits out its exile)—a phrase that sounded to some alert-eared Parisians like a sharp dismissal indeed of the emissaries, and perhaps also of any immediate possibility of Algerian peace.

It is probably unique, even in ultra-modern state documents, for a complaint about not being allowed to use the telephone to figure in an official paper issued by a people at war, with peace at stake. Yet in the Algerian Provisional Government's Monday list of protests against the remarkably protocolar restrictions laid down by the French for the conduct of any future Algerian emissaries (one of whom might be Ferhat Abbas himself), there is mention of the fact that such emissaries would be forbidden even "to communicate indirectly, by telephone," with certain captured Algerian Ministers held here either in prison or in military fortresses. Indeed, they would not be able to telephone anybody, since no one of the Algerian delegation would be permitted to make contact with "anyone, in any manner, either in France or outside France, except in Tunis." They would also be forbidden to have any communication with the press; would be obliged to live in total isolation; and so on and so on. However, in all that list, it is the unexpected, intrusive image of the telephone in relation to that savage, primitive, empty North African countryside where the Algerians have been fighting their war of rebellion that sticks like a Dali landscape in one's mind. Both the Algerians and the French must now face the fact that the entry of peace in their relations has been proposed, that both their peoples desperately want peace to come in, and that neither the rebels nor the French can afford to risk being criticized by world opinion, or even by their own nation, for having been the ones responsible for slamming the door against peace, which, logically, would mean going on with the useless war.

The sudden pressure of French public opinion on the welcome possibility that peace will indeed come to pass has been building up here for a month, and reached a climax this last week. In what way, or on whom, this organized energy will now expend itself after the Melun Algerian impasse remains to be seen, and might prove to be a public problem, as some of the French already fear. On Thursday of last week, a remarkable declaration was signed jointly by four powerful French unions. These were the Communist-dominated Confédération Générale du Travail; the Confédération des Travailleurs Chrétiens, which is the Catholic workers' union; the Fédération de l'Education Nationale, the teachers' union; and the Union Nationale des Etudiants de France, composed of ninety thousand university students—the most influential aggregation of well-educated youth in all France. The declaration said, in part, that "at this moment, when the Algerian drama is entering a decisive phase . . . the above organizations affirm in unison their desire to see negotiations really opened and carried through to their normal conclusion—a cease-fire and an agreement, with indispensable guarantees, on putting self-determination [of the Algerian people] into motion. These organizations have together renewed their resolution to use all the means at their disposal, including that of the general strike, as an answer to any insurrection or *coup d'état* that might tend to impede the Algerian peace, or even tear down further the essential democratic liberties [of France]." This is, of course, a double warning—to the de Gaulle government to get on with ending the war, and to the *ultras* not to repeat their bloody *coup d'état* of January 24th in Algiers, raised in protest against de Gaulle's increasingly liberal Algerian policies.

To get back to the students' union, which is extremely important, it has already paid dearly for its energetic stand on peace. On June 6th, its officers resumed the union's old relations with the Union

Générale des Etudiants Musulmans Algériens, which in 1958 had been declared officially dissolved, and therefore illegal, by the last government of the Fourth Republic, because of the Moslem students' loyalty to their home cause. Upon this renewal of relations, the two student groups, French and native, signed a communiqué setting forth their conviction that "discussion between the French and Algerian nationals is possible, and the only competent means of bringing the colonial war to a close." On June 16th, in punishment for its association with the Moslem student union, the French government's Minister of National Education cut off the French student union's annual subsidy, which it had been receiving along with other educational or cultural youth movements, and which would have amounted this year to eighty thousand New Francs, in part payment for its services in organizing student housing, distributing scholarship monies, and doing other university jobs. On Sunday, June 19th, the student union held a Paris meeting to which a hundred and fifty or more regional delegates came from all over France to declare whether they still backed the peace stand, earlier voted in a Lyon meeting by a massive majority. The delegate of the Ecole des Langues Orientales, founded in Paris by Louis XIV, thought the *rapprochement* with the Algerian students questionable. The delegate from Paris-Science also thought that the student union was on the wrong track. But Paris-Pharmacie and Paris-Médecine delegates thought that the Minister of National Education's removal of their subsidy was an attack on students' rights and liberty of thought. Motions criticizing the union's officers for their realliance with the Moslem students and demanding that the union return to its previous non-political stand on current national events were both heavily defeated. As the union's president—twenty years old and a Sorbonne man—is reported to have said, "Apoliticism is impossible today. The Algerian war is too present all around us. We don't want any more of this war. Our increased political substance is what will unite us against it."

Tuesday of last week had been chosen as the day for demonstrations all over France in favor of negotiating the peace—demonstrations that the government forbade, fearing public disorders while it was itself supposedly negotiating at Melun for the opening of peace. In the provinces, at St.-Etienne, an industrial center of machine-making and ribbon-weaving, a crowd sang the "Marseillaise," hung a floral wreath on the statue of Liberty, and shouted

"Vive le succès de la négotiation!" before being dispersed by the police. At Roanne, another important manufacturing center, the crowd shouted not only for peace but against the government's ruling against their shouting for it. At Grenoble, from among a large crowd of demonstrators, eight citizens calling for peace were arrested, including a priest and a lawyer. At Poitiers, the police used their clubs against the crowd, and at Nantes they used tear gas. At Châlons-sur-Marne, the state police were called in from nearby Reims to deal with the peace manifestation. At Lille, Brest, Le Havre, Nîmes, Dijon—some of the best-known tourist towns—the police were also forced to break up the congregations of peace demonstrators.

For the past twenty years, June has been a month of painful historical recollections for the French. And over that fifth of a century they have suffered almost continuous small, troubling wars. But the endless Algerian war, which the young French angrily call the "Hundred Years' War," has been the most destructive of the essence of France itself. Certainly it had been hoped that by this June's end the seemingly century-long war might at last be coming to its close. Not in years has there been such active peace sentiment in France as in this deceptive past month of June.

July 19

"Stevenson, the eternal 'possible' candidate for President if the other candidates first eat each other up . . ." This was the astonishing manifestation of pro-Stevenson sentiment carried in a Paris headline just before the Los Angeles convention opened, Mr. Stevenson having been the French favorite for President on three occasions now, whether running or not, and even after he has lost. There was not a crack Paris journalist sent to the California Sports Arena who failed to star the prodigious emotional acclaim that greeted Stevenson's entry there—"slender, elegant, aristocratically bald, his eyes bluer than ever under the camera flashes and spotlights," *Le Monde's* special reporter cabled back home, which was accurate, surely, but dreamy. The convention's immediate choice of the youthful Senator Kennedy has led to long French analyses of him and of the recent acute dissatisfaction here with the "fatigued" President Ike's administration, which has automatically helped popularize Kennedy in France as "fresh and dynamic," with a "rather worrying virtuosity." Brought up to the practice of gerontocracy, the French earlier had a filial respect and affection for Eisenhower, which has given way this year to a list of criticisms of his Republican administration that clearly show the French hope of a change for the better in a Democratic victory, with, if must be, a very young President. "For eight years, the Americans chose 'the father' in politics," one expert has just pointed out. "Today, the American public sees the perils of it. The country's traditions—even its security—are at stake. The dramatic, dangerous events in Cuba, the aerial incidents over Russia, have added to the American public's confusion, giving them the indisputably mounting impression that they have been outclassed in the power struggle and in diplomacy, as well as in spying and sputniks." "Right now, it may be that youth has to be trusted," one Parisian was heard cautiously saying in a discussion of the coming election struggle. The strongly liberal Left Wing weekly *Express,* most influential journal of all among intellectuals and the young French, last week used a photograph of Kennedy on its cover, with the famous quotation on old men's wisdom from Hemingway's "A Farewell to Arms," translated into French: "No, that is the great fallacy; the wisdom of old men. They do not grow wise. They grow careful." Inside, *L'Express* used the recent pro-Kennedy piece by Mr. Joseph Alsop—also in French, of course. Kennedy's Harvard education, his ability to read important books, and his brain trust (quoted here as being composed of "M. Kenneth Galbraith, economics expert; M. Arthur Schlesinger, Jr., as specialist in social history; and Dr. Zbigniew Brzezinski, young chief of the Harvard group") make the French think that a Democratic White House could be a stimulating change. To the French, naturally, the most personally interesting facts about Kennedy are that he may be the first Catholic President of the United States and that he has already declared his intention of adhering to what the French liberals and the Left have for two hundred years called anticlericalism and, at the beginning of this century, obtained—noninterference in politics by the Church. But the greatest French hope in Kennedy is on the mundane side. They hope that with his youth, his sharp, educated brain, and his realistic eye he will institute a State Department that will look at modern geography as it really is, from Cuba to South America to Peking to Moscow and, above all, to Europe, with its intimate susceptibility nowadays to what Washington says, does, and thinks. Furthermore, most of the French certainly seem to hope that his Secretary of State will be M. Adlai Stevenson.

August 2

The so-called *"nouvelle-vague,"* or "new-wave," French films have increasingly aroused moral concern at high governmental levels, their libertinage having become a visible public fact in four of them that are still being shown here in Paris month after month. Since the de Gaulle regime's style is one of dignity and *bon ton,* its Ministers have been gravely embarrassed by the severe criticism these movies have received from the Church, family organizations, parents, and displeased adult spectators, and by such denunciations as that of the ultra-conservative Professor Pasteur Vallery-Radot, a well-known explosive member of the Académie Française, who said their aim was *"gangsterisme ou érotisme."* Questioned recently in Parliament about French films' immorality, the Minister of Information could only say that he planned more effective censorship. This is a government measure that French liberals have distrusted on principle ever since the notorious censoring of Baudelaire's "Les Fleurs du Mal" and Flaubert's "Madame Bovary," which survived to become classics, and which, of course, none of these movies, with their gifted or meretricious sensuality, faintly resemble. The Minister of Justice is working on a bill for pre-censorship, or censoring the scenario before the film can be made, with the logical idea of preventing very young adolescents from working as actors in any film—as two did in "Les Régates de San Francisco," one of the four new-wave pictures still showing here—that the censor will later mark "Forbidden to Anyone Under Eighteen." The ticket sellers for these *nouvelle-vague* films are strict about their job. They demand that every young film fan show his *carte scolaire,* which lists his birth date. The movie that gave the *nouvelles vagues* such a bad name (many have been absolutely excellent) was "Les Liaisons Dangereuses 1960," directed by Roger Vadim, first husband and discoverer of Brigitte Bardot. It was the last film, unfortunately, that Gérard Philipe made before his death, and it still serves as an unpleasant obituary to his fame. It is running here, full tilt, as the single new-wave film that the French government has refused to grant an export license to, because it would give France such a black eye. You are missing nothing—a shoddy, queasy modernization of the classic novel that was ironically written against licentious corruption in high society by one of Napoleon's officers, Choderlos de Laclos. In the Vadim version, which ludicrously takes place at the ski resort of Mégève, the famous wicked lovers, the Vicomte de Valmont and the Marquise de Merteuil, and merely a rich, fast married couple, as if to make more respectable their demoralization of innocent little Cécile, who already looks like a pretty sophisticated young starlet. To its credit, the Société des Gens de Lettres, indignant at what Vadim had done with the old book, forced the addition of the date "1960" to the title. Since to the public this seems to imply modern orgies, the change has made it super-popular.

Considering the long-drawn-out hullabaloo over the *nouvelle-vague* films and the French government's recent involvement, this might be a good moment to set down some facts. Started two years ago, they were at first called *"les films des jeunes,"* and their fundamental quality was that they were created by a new school of very young, unknown directors, who saw things with brand-new camera eyes, had to make their movies on a shoestring, and so developed a fresh, realistic, compact, and stimulating technique, using décors that cost nothing and were true backgrounds to young life—sidewalks, cheap cafés, and beds. Several of these young men had been sharp-penned movie critics on the influential *Cahiers du Cinéma;* all were sick of the costly, ripe films made by their elders. Their new-wave movies ("Les Tricheurs," about the young immoralists at the Sorbonne, was a typical early example), like all those that have followed, are part of today's intimate fight between the mature and the young on both sides of the Atlantic. What these young directors have shown best is what they know best—the anarchic, spasmodic, lawless, and rebellious lives of certain modern young French, intensely lived within their own cycle. In these films, the short cut to romance is sex, the stencil for beauty is the nudity of lovers. The roster—by name, age, rank, and major film—of the most important of these young directors runs like this: Alain Resnais, thirty-eight, considered the master of the new generation, "Hiroshima, Mon Amour"; François Truffaut, twenty-eight, leader of the *Cahiers du Cinéma* wing, "Les Quatre Cents Coups"; Louis Malle, twenty-eight, "Les Amants"; Claude Chabrol, twenty-nine, "Le Beau Serge" and "Les Bonnes Femmes," his latest, which shows the best of him and also the worst; Jean-Luc Godard, thirty, also from the

Cahiers du Cinéma, "À Bout de Souffle" ("Breathless"), which is called the chef-d'œuvre of the new school, is now the big hit in Paris, and is the best French film of any kind this year.

"Breathless" is a Champs-Elysées-sidewalk and bed film, perfectly directed, that features a Paris *type* who has killed a policeman while stealing a car, his regular profession. He is in love with one of those pretty American girls in slacks and sweaters whom you now see on the Champs selling the Paris *Herald Tribune,* with the name of the paper writ large across their bosoms (a role well played by the American Jean Seberg). A tart, and tired of him, she tips off the police, who shoot him down in the street as he is making a getaway. The big bed scene, when she comes home and finds him in it, as he has often been before, is a comedy passage at first, in which, while he keeps talking, he drapes the sheet over his head and nude torso until he talks her under the sheet, too—the sheet remaining like a tent over them in a very daring yet utterly discreet dénouement. The film's terrific drawing card is Jean-Paul Belmondo, whose ugly attractiveness is the latest emotional rage—a tiptop young actor who was thrown out by the Conservatoire d'Art Dramatique because he was so remarkably ugly, they said, that he could never appear on their stage with a woman in his arms, since the audience would laugh. This turns out to be utterly untrue.

November 2

For several reasons, none of them agreeable, this present week is being called *la semaine algérienne*—in Paris, at least. In the recent sudden stampeding of French public opinion toward its old, impatient vision of peace, the seven-year-old Algerian war problem has now become the dominant national concern for France; for the survival, possibly, of the Fifth Republic; and certainly for the verbal genius of President de Gaulle to solve and finally give his clear answer to. Tomorrow, Thursday, there opens at the Palais de Justice the trial that has already been dubbed the *procès des barricades,* which will intensify the emotions of the diminishing group of the extreme Rightists, who demand that Algeria must remain unindependent, unautonomous, and purely French. Chief among the sixteen civilian insurgents who will appear in the prisoner's box is M. Pierre Lagaillarde, deputy from Algiers and mainspring of the bloody insurrection of last January 24th, when the *ultras* set up their barricades in the center of that city in rebellion against the distant authority of the French government and, more locally, against General de Gaulle's then recent declaration for Algerian self-determination. In the melee, twenty-four French people were killed. Also on Thursday, M. Jacques Soustelle, leader of a brand-new anti-Gaullist Right Wing integrationist party, which he candidly calls the National Front for French Algeria, will be holding a surburban caucus with his best-known followers, mostly former high Fourth Republic politicians like Georges Bidault, Maurice Bourgès-Maunoury, and Robert Lacoste. In order to appreciate all these incredible confusions now going on here, it must be recalled that Soustelle was the leading brainy figure behind the other Algiers insurrection—the one of May 13, 1958—which put de Gaulle into power in the first place; was chief of the Gaullist Parliamentary party, the Union of the New Republic; and was also de Gaulle's appointee as Minister of Information. Then, last February, de Gaulle dropped him from his government as a malcontent, after which the U.N.R. ejected him into limbo, where he has found other anti-Gaullist companions.

To all intents, the week will end on Friday night, when President de Gaulle will address his uneasy country in a televised allocution. France is waiting to listen to him with critically acute hope and a certain preliminary sense of alarm, anxious to see how well, at this perhaps crucial moment, he will be able to do for himself in his accustomed literary outflow of echoing, magnificent, though not always communicative, language. Now, according to the French, is the time for the General to communicate—now, when pragmatic faith in him has started falling, even though he is still master of France, with its citizens, and even history, once again waiting to hear him speak. It is true that he has been talking briefly, off and on for the past few months, in the conscientious majestic appearances that he has made in the countryside and in towns all over the land—a bareheaded, aged patriot still offering the more intelligent glories of France to provincial, often humbly chauvinist crowds, who have cherished his words and his appeals for national greatness and strength as they listened under their umbrellas in the rain. *"Aidez-moi, Français!"* he demanded in an appeal he made in one Alpine town, and was loudly reassured by cheers—as, indeed, he was almost everywhere. Talking in the Midi city of Menton, and again pursuing the topic of how France should be run and by whom, he declared, "The control of France belongs to those who have been made responsible for it, and it thus belongs, *par excellence,* to me. I say this without any beating about the bush." Not since Louis XIV's declaration *"L'Etat, c'est moi,"* at which no one in those times dared smile, have the French as a nation smiled so broadly as at de Gaulle's paraphrase. He has now been nicknamed Général Moi in the weekly satiric papers. Since the Menton speech, *Le Canard Enchaîné,* which is always against any government, and especially de Gaulle's, has been running a political gossip column entitled "La Cour," written in an uproarious take-off on the grand style of the court memoirs of the Duc de Saint-Simon, which the *Canard* has illustrated with a wonderful caricature of de Gaulle dressed up like the King, with a nose the size of a Versailles chandelier.

De Gaulle was called to power two and a half years ago by what seemed destiny—plus an enormous majority in a referendum—as the one man in France who might perform the miracle of bringing his country back to something like its old portrait. He has made France once again rich, sound, prosperous, handsome. Only in one major way, as the French deplore, has the miracle failed to come off—in Moslem Algeria. Part of the loyalty and hope still felt for de Gaulle lies in the fact that now, as then, there is nobody else of his patriotic height visible on the French landscape. In fact, there is no one in sight at all, of any experienced quality, who has not already failed at what de Gaulle has not yet succeeded in completing. The only real fear here among the general public and the Parliament is that he might abandon them under criticism and disappointment, and retire again to Colombey-les-Deux-Eglises and his solitary study of history, leaving them with no one fit to command—the replica of their situation when he came into it.

Of M. Jules Roy's much discussed brief book "La Guerre d'Algérie," published a fortnight ago, one literary critic here said, in grave appreciation, "It has taken six years of the Algerian war's death and tears for such a voice to be heard." Actually, two fraternal voices—one French, one Algerian—rise from its author, Roy being, like his friend Albert Camus (to whose memory he dedicates the book), a *pied noir,* or blackfoot, which is colonial slang for those white French born in North Africa. It is this dual identity, like a double slice of racial knowledge and human emotions, and this

French brain, familiar since childhood with the Arab mind, that give Roy's book its impact as the most moving condemnation to date of the war and the most authoritative simple explanation of its cause; together, these qualities have already brought it an enormous reading public at this moment of high tension in the Algerian problem. It was partly in memory of Camus that Roy felt forced to visit the Algeria of his youth this summer, where he crossed the damaged countryside "escorted by ruins and spectres"—the burned native villages and the roadside encampments of homeless, hungry Arabs. "I had to go to see it all in order to explain where it seemed to me the truth lay, provided I could find it," he writes.

His book's simple account, in the first person, is enriched by his feelings, mostly sadness and anger, at what he sees, is told, or remembers. A third-generation *pied noir* on his mother's side, he was brought up south of Algiers on her family's modest farm, where the men-folk had died, mostly of overwork or malaria, in clearing the marshland to plant their grapevines. They were helped to prosperity by the ill-paid Arabs, whom they called *les ratons,* the rats—a filthy, inferior, stupid, animal-like race (he was taught), whom, as he recently heard in Algeria from today's embittered, alarmed French whites, including his own sister-in-law, "our error has been to treat with too much humanity." Roy's first, and indeed final, conclusion about the truth, backed by pages of anecdotes and painful conversations with both races, is that simple "social injustice"—the white men's contempt, tyranny, psychological cruelty, and greed—"opened the road to the Algerians' rebellion."

The last part of the book could be called "Dialogue with a Captain," who is a French officer of harsh, high intelligence, a man of arms devoted to his cause with the passion of a crusader because he believes it noble and just—"the defense of the Occident," the great, civilized West. This dialogue is the crux of the book, a vivid, multiple-paged analysis by two military men of opposing political and social minds (for Roy served in the French Air Force for twenty-six years and fought as a colonel over Germany and in Indo-China). It is a basic dialogue between an Army *ultra,* or patriotic French Fascist, and a French intellectual liberal. It takes place dramatically in the captain's nocturnal fighting post, a control tower overlooking part of the electrified barbed-wire barricade that seals off Algeria at the Tunisian border so as to intercept and electrocute any Algerian night fighters slipping in from their camps in Tunis, though often enough it captures only wild boars or hares—"roasted, the captain said." In his finale, Roy declares, "The only way to stop this war is to negotiate—on condition that each of the adversaries abandon part of his pretensions." He ends his labors on the Algerian truths with a tender, reproachful invocation of his close friend Camus, who he thinks could have handled the matter better, saying, "You could have saved me all this by returning [to Paris from the country] by train on January 5th, as you wrote me you would, instead of leaving by car a day earlier." It will be recalled that Camus and Michel Gallimard, the son of his publisher, lost their lives in a motor accident on January 4th, en route to town.

November 15

Because of world tension, France's unrest, and the unclassic youthfulness of both the Democratic and the Republican candidates, our Presidential election last week aroused exceptional interest and worry among the French. The spectacular athletic-endurance quality of the last days of the campaign, the dramatic narrow margin of the victory, and, above all, the corporeal image that the contest set up in the active imagination of the French (themselves accustomed only to seated, elderly politicians), of two young men running a foot race for votes through the vast geography of the United States and ending, in a sweat, close to equal—all this stirred up almost as much spectator interest as political excitement among Parisians. What some of the French were worried about was money, of course—fear for their boom and prosperity, and fear of the effect that President-elect Kennedy's projected spending program could have on the dollar and the franc. In general, the well-to-do Parisians were the ones who spoke nostalgically of Vice-President Nixon; the modest-pursed ones seemed glad that Kennedy had won. Elderly Parisians—rich or poor, male or female—spoke as if they were convinced the United States had gone crazy in trusting its fate to a pair of such youthful politicos, with Kennedy, because he is four years the younger, regarded as exactly four years the less trustworthy of the two.

Until the Presidential election is over and won, Paris newspapers, as is their prudent quadrennial custom, print little that is personal about the two contestants except biographical material.

Then all the papers, each representing and influenced by its own special national and political inclination, produce their editorial analyses and portraits of the new incumbent. Of all the papers, last Thursday morning's *Figaro* gave the heartiest, most unexpected editorial welcome to Kennedy. As the leading morning guide of the *haute bourgeoisie,* it is ultra-conservative, old-fashioned, and pious—though supercritical, it is true, of the second Eisenhower regime. "Audacity and intelligence greatly aided John Fitzgerald Kennedy during the electoral campaign," it wrote, in part. "These are precisely the qualities that the thirty-fifth President of the United States most needs in facing up to the major problems that confront his country and all the West. The man is young, dynamic." Then it added, with an anti-Ike flourish, "The White House will find again the all-powerful quality it knew in the time of F. D. Roosevelt," and noted how easily Kennedy had "swept aside the old religious prejudices," without mentioning that the newspaper itself and the bases of those old religious prejudices are all Catholic. The liberals', the artists', and the intellectuals' modest morning paper, *Combat,* wrote, "Good luck to you, M. John Kennedy!" It then said, "The first ambition of this young chief of the American Democrats seems to be to cut loose from the geopolitical ignorance that in the past dictated to the Washington State Department its many awkward and unfortunate efforts"—a reference to the ghost of the unpopular Mr. Dulles. Then it criticized Kennedy, too, for thinking that America could help settle France's Algerian impasse. The extreme Rightist *Aurore,* fiery leader of the Algérie Française Army coterie and the colonial hotheads, ran its election editorial on Wednesday morning, addressed to "Monsieur le Président des Etats-Unis, whoever you may be, Nixon or Kennedy, Richard or John." It warned him that "your compatriots know little about Algerian affairs and are more susceptible than most to slogans, of which the latest is anti-colonialism," and advised him strongly to revise his opinions. What France was fighting for in Algeria, it said, was "a bastion against Communism," which could otherwise overrun the West "and you Americans, too." At the other political extreme, the Communist *Humanité* also addressed itself to both candidates, in an Election Day cartoon that showed each of them stuffing bundles of dollar bills into the ballot box. Its later editorial italicized its opinion that the United States had "voted not *for* Kennedy but *against* Nixon."

As for *Le Monde,* the dean of postwar French and international analytical political thinking, in the very first sentence of its Friday editorial it went straight to what it clearly considered the only real major point of the American election. It said, "The entire world is asking itself what consequences M. Kennedy's election may have on foreign policy." It stated that, at forty-three years of age, his ambition was not only to be elected this time but to be elected again in 1964. "The fragility of his Tuesday victory will thus force him to raise his own prestige, which the voters clearly let him know had not dazzled them."

The most personal French appreciation of Senator Kennedy's victory was addressed not to him but to his wife, née Jacqueline Bouvier, from the southern village of Pont-St.-Esprit, down in the Gard, where her French ancestors lived in the seventeenth century. It consisted of a long and surely costly cablegram sent to her by the village mayor and the municipal council, which offered "to the President and to yourself our warm felicitations and our ardent and respectful good wishes," adding, "The unanimous population of this little French town, the cradle of your family, salutes with enthusiasm and pride your entry into the White House."

The spectacular *procès des barricades,* or trial of the leaders of the January 24th Algiers insurrection, is now in its second week in the grandiose Cour d'Assises in the Palais de Justice by the Seine. The military tribunal on the bench is an imposing sight, with three red-robed civilian judges, and four generals and two colonels in medals and uniform. Their combined duty is to ascertain whether the sixteen accused men—four more are absent in flight—who crowd each afternoon into the prisoner's box, below a gigantic wall tapestry portraying some boy king of France on his throne, are guilty, as charged, of attempting to overthrow the French government and inciting to rebellion and involuntary homicide when they took up arms behind their Algiers barricades. Twenty-four people were killed, including fourteen gendarmes, and more than a hundred people were injured in their bloody riot against President de Gaulle's then new policy of self-determination for Algeria. Algeria is, of course, the complete essence of the trial—in the fact that these prisoners, in their way, represent all those other French who still violently believe or have believed that Algeria must remain a possession of France; in the fact that the courtroom houses the climax, at last and at law, of the dangerous division between de

Gaulle's progressing Algerian policies and those of the Algérie Française *ultras,* civil or military, and their repeatedly rumored coups d'état; and, finally, in the fact that, with three hundred witnesses to be called and a brigade of forty defense lawyers, all *ultras* (among them Maître Isorni, who was the defense lawyer for Marshal Pétain at his trial), the trial is bound to become a forum for anti-de Gaulle, pro-Algérie Française propaganda, and an attempt to expose the government to embarrassments, which have, indeed, already begun.

The trial opened with a Gallic bit of *opéra bouffe,* when one of the prisoners, against military orders, insisted on appearing in court in his insurrectional commando parachutist's uniform and was sent back to prison to change. Socially, the prisoners are a mixed lot of colonial Frenchmen, including a bank director, a *bistro* owner, several doctors, some insurance and real-estate agents, a professor (Comte Le Moyne de Sérigny, who was the editor of the *ultras'* newspaper, *L'Écho d'Alger*), and one lone Army officer. Wearing twenty-eight decorations on his pale-blue dolman, the intelligent, monk-faced Colonel Gardes, former chief of the Army's Algerian Fifth Bureau of Psychological Warfare, talked for a total of nearly thirteen hours during two afternoon court sessions, before crowds of lawyers who had nothing to do with the case but had come in from all over the Palais just to hear such a good talker. Among other strange items, he explained how he had been ordered by his Army chiefs to present de Gaulle's Algerian self-determination policy to pro-French Moslems and French *ultras* as "merely a maneuver to get around the United Nations debate on Algeria." The most important prisoner, the bearded, hawk-featured young lawyer-deputy Pierre Lagaillarde, regarded as the leader and hero of the barricades, where he stuck it out for eight days, was unexpectedly released on parole Wednesday, on a technicality concerning his Parliamentary immunity. Coming after two days of his brilliant, arrogant self-defense under cross-examination, the judges' sudden announcement of his release created pandemonium and one of the most melodramatic scenes ever witnessed in Palais history, with the defense lawyers and the *ultras* among the spectators screaming "Algérie Française!" in victory, and then singing the "Marseillaise" while the prisoners in the box stood patriotically at attention, after which armed guards rushed through the crowd, clearing the court. The government, even before Lagaillarde's release, which was considered a slap in the face for it, had already been badly embarrassed by the lawyer defending Dr. Bernard Lefèvre, who declared that the Doctor's part in the insurrection had been inspired by some May, 1958, writings of de Gaulle's Prime Minister Debré in the political review *Courrier de la Colère*. There he had written, "When the government violates the people's rights, insurrection becomes the most imperious duty—naturally meaning the Fourth Republic government, and naturally meaning the May 13th insurrection that brought de Gaulle to power. Under cross-examination, Lagaillarde had also greatly damaged the government's position on legitimacy by stating, "I took part in the attack against the government on May 13th, in uniform and armed"—naturally meaning the Fourth Republic government. "I am informing you that no punishment was ever prescribed. If you want to judge me for what happened on January 24, 1960, I demand that I be indicted for my activities on May 13th, which were of a much more highly insurrectional character."

On Wednesday, General de Gaulle also made his expected announcement of his proposal for a national referendum early in January on the new Algerian state, which he describes as an Algerian Republic, related to or independent of France, whichever the Algerians wish. In the incredibly aggravated present tension, many French now wonder whether planning anything in 1961 is not looking dangerously far into the future.

December 14

After the awful, bloody events in Algeria over last weekend, it would seem that the mere physical presence in that land of General de Gaulle as the symbol of France had, by its emotional power, tragically caused an explosion in each of the two races, the European settlers and the Arab natives—a freed combustion of their opposite reactions to France itself and of their hatred of each other. On Friday, the blood set flowing by the French *ultras* on the streets of Algiers and Oran, where de Gaulle did not even set foot, provoked no surprise, such rioting and killing of Moslems being one more of the *ultras'* customary dreadful messages to the chief of state—this time miles away across the sand in the little Arab village of Aïn Témouchent—that Algeria must remain French territory, in their masterful hands. It was the violent answer of the Arabs on Saturday, when they first swarmed out of their casbahs—the clamor of their voices by the thousands screaming "Independence! Ferhat Abbas to power! Free Algeria!" and the waving of their green-white-and-red Algerian rebel flags, these being actions and sounds never heard from them before—that furnished the terrified and total astonishment of what has been called in Paris "the day of truth." Until that day, through intimidation or understandable timidity (caught, as they have been, between the occupying French soldiers and their own *fellagha* army), the urban Arabs had never before demonstrated en masse what now seems to be their real national truth—their consuming desire for independence—for which their Saturday riot was their act of war. In Paris, it is considered that three myths died in Algeria over the weekend, these being the selfish myth of the white *ultras* that Algeria is French; the mendacious myth of the French Army that only a fistful of fighting rebels in Algeria wanted independence in all those years of war; and the major, miracle myth that de Gaulle could make peace—though no one here, or probably anywhere, thinks that anyone else could make it. He still stands alone, the unique dedicated figure of elderly courage and hope, as he appeared in Monday's photographs amid those pushing crowds in Algerian towns where assassination could have come in a gesture as easy as his handshake with those pressing around him—the burnoused Arabs trying merely to touch him, as if he were an amulet, while angry white French settlers brutally shouted across to him, "De Gaulle to the gallows!" Today, it is likely that only the Arabs still think that he can give them peace, as they also believe that he will give them independence—and, with it, new Algerian problems.

So far, only one criticism has been directed at de Gaulle, most respectfully made by *Figaro* in its Wednesday-morning editorial, entitled "The Return." He had come back to Paris the night before, and it was then impatiently hoped that he would at once speak to the nation on the radio, weary as he must have been—that he would say something, anything, because people wanted to hear his voice—and *Figaro* first criticized him for "not having uttered a word." Then it came to the heart of the matter, on which much of Paris public opinion agrees. "Too great an indifference to warnings and to the need for caution made de Gaulle's Algerian visit a tactical error," it said succinctly. "An enormous psychological drive had preceded Saturday's outbreak into action. A campaign of rumors and false alarms had been shrewdly spread by the partisans of one-way integration—that is, integration without equality or real fraternity between the Arab and the white communities. The overtones of it all announced that a maneuver was under way and predicted the coming of the tempest," timed to break upon his arrival. In conclusion, the editorial said, "In three days, the Europeans' rebellion against de Gaulle gave more aid to Ferhat Abbas than he had received in three years from the subversive rebel war." As you may recall, *Figaro* is the ultra-Catholic-bourgeois morning paper for the powerful, conservative middle class and the big industrialists, many of whom have heavy financial interests in North Africa. Until now, they have quietly backed the hope of a French Algeria, and this was the reason for their initial support of de Gaulle, in whom they then placed their faith. Such a *Figaro* editorial, including harsh criticism of the Algerian Europeans (whom it further called *"les comploteurs"*), has been regarded here as a strong patriotic and Christian warning to the *grande bourgeoisie,* and, coupled with the fact that certain Sahara oil shares fell heavily on the Monday stock exchange, has already caused a great deal of talk. Tuesday night's *Le Monde* printed—in a special box to attract the reader's attention, though without comment—the official report of the French government's Director of Information in Algiers, who stated that autopsies on fifty-six Arab corpses showed that of the twenty-nine killed by shots only five were killed by bullets of the sort used by the French Army or security forces, the others having been killed by pistol shots, which, according to multiple witnesses, including journalists, were fired by terrified French civilians on their balconies into the Arab mob below.

There is something cynically farcical in nearly all sudden French tragedies. This time, it was the government's Tuesday-night announcement that those responsible for the weekend riots and for the hundred and twenty-two dead (a hundred and fourteen of them Moslems, leaving only eight white Europeans) would be prosecuted. No moment could be less appropriate for such a project, since the continuing trial here of more than a dozen Frenchmen who took some part in the Algiers insurrectional riots of last January, in which a mere twenty-four people were killed, has so far resulted in a courtroom triumph for the accused. Pierre Lagaillarde, the barricade leader in those riots, and three other defendants fled to Spain upon their temporary release from the Santé Prison, as you no doubt know, and are at present safely out of the reach of French jurisdiction and justice. In fact, Lagaillarde's flight was openly considered here to be one of the disregarded warnings that accompanied de Gaulle on his recent journey to Algeria—although at least Lagaillarde was unable to arrive there for participation in the bloody weekend events.

Friday, the Parliament's current brief session—the second of the two sessions now permitted it in the year—will end. It is logical to suppose that the next few weeks will be decisive in Algerian affairs—and, indeed, in those of the Fifth Republic—though in what way nobody knows. Whatever occurs, the Parliamentary deputies can read about it in the newspapers, like the rest of the French, and with no more say-so or power. Tomorrow, Thursday, the Senate, which sits in the Palais de Luxembourg, was to have discussed general Algerian topics in a debate that had been scheduled before the riots. It is now thought that the government will decide that it is too soon after those tragic events to bring forth any official arguments—if only because of the lack, so far, of definite information for the senators, and of time for their mature pondering. Such a postponement would also enable the Debré government to avoid the imbalance caused by the absence from the discussion of the several Algerian senators, some of them Moslem, who have, with melancholy dignity, already refused to take part in any such talk. It is likely that the government will now merely read a statement to both the Parliament and the Senate—though here again no one yet knows what Premier Debré, recognized as an *ultra,* and one who writes his own speeches, may say. Too often before in this period of power, his sentiments have failed to resemble those declared by de Gaulle, and sometimes they have even been the diametrical opposite. Nor does anyone know whether the national referendum on Algeria that is scheduled for January 8th will actually be held then. Many citizens hope that it will not. It would, they think, be like reading the last will and testament too soon after the deceased has drawn his last breath. The Communist Party, which controls nearly a fourth of the French voters, announced a few days ago that it was conducting an extensive campaign among the working class generally—of any or all political affiliations—to bring in a massive vote of no against the de Gaulle referendum. In this, the Communists would be joined—or so it is thought—by the reactionary political parties that represent the Algérie Française *ultra* view. Some Paris commentators think that the *ultras'* position has been greatly strengthened by the Arab attack on Saturday, since it demonstrated the suddenly dangerous helplessness of the outnumbered French settlers there, whom France has always declared she would not abandon. The ultimate possible plan, which de Gaulle earlier proposed as a settlement of the Algerian problem—consisting of partition of Algeria, with the French, Italian, Spanish, Maltese, Jewish, and other foreign elements, lumped as Europeans, probably given the northern coastal ring of the country and the predominantly Europeanized cities, and the Arabs given some special territory, where they would be cared for and supplied with work and housing—is now considered, in the back of many French minds, as the worst that could happen. Separating the two races would be like separating capital and labor, Paris commentators think, or like cutting up the map of Algeria with a pair of scissors as a way of making history.

In the town of Blida, addressing a large contingent of young officers in training there, de Gaulle last weekend made his most informative, concise speech of the past half year, unfortunately little mentioned or quoted in the French press. Only the small intellectual morning paper *Combat* printed it here in full. In it he said, in part, "Because of this insurrection, the population of Algeria, which is Moslem by a great majority, has developed a consciousness that it did not have before. Nothing will prevent that. It must also be realized that this insurrection of the Arabs, with all that attaches to it, is taking place in a new world—in a world that in no way resembles the world I knew when I was young. There is, as you are well aware, a process of liberation now going on from one end of the world to the other that has affected our black Africa, that has affected all the former empires, without exception, and that cannot but have important consequences here. . . . It is thus necessary that the efforts of France in relation to Algeria continue, and it is very evident that they cannot be carried on in the conditions of yesterday. You can well imagine how a man of my age and my training has dreamed with regret of what could have been done earlier, and what was not done." It is to be supposed that the General, with his long historical memory, was thinking of the middle thirties in Algeria, when the only rebellion imagined by the Arabs was to ask for integration on what would now seem modest, loyal, republican terms. They asked to be integrated into the French nation with the privileges of the vote and representation accorded to all French citizens—the privileges enjoyed by the white settlers there, who refused them.

It is said that President de Gaulle will probably address the nation tomorrow night, though this has already been denied by a semi-official rumor that he will not speak until next Tuesday, or even sometime in Christmas Week. The nation is waiting—with patience, if necessary—to hear that unique, broken, trumpeting voice, and to listen to his thoughts.

December 28

For many years now, monthly bulletins on economic and social problems have been sent out to the press here (which for various reasons has rarely used them) by the Bourbon pretender to the throne of France—Henri, Comte de Paris—who is reputed to be Socialistic and is known to be pro-de Gaulle. His bulletin of December 14th has exceptional news value, because in it he announces that he is suspending these studious, rather solemn communications, in what he calls the troubled times France is going through, and says why. It is, he states, because "I trust General de Gaulle." With close to royal dignity, he declares that "rather than uselessly mingle my voice in the frantic clamor, I, whose vocation is to unite and pacify, choose to keep silent while waiting for the day when the French will comprehend" that they must unite "in understanding of and respect for the realities of our time and the world we are living in." To the *colons* of French blood in Algeria, he sternly adds, "Follow General de Gaulle. He is the only chance France has, your only safeguard." With this he stirred up a hornets' nest among what is left today of the old ultra-reactionary, anti-republican, onetime pro-Pétain, Action Française royalists. In their weekly paper, *Aspects de la France,* they declared with anger, "We have a right to be consternated by the Prince's terms, which constitute unconditional approbation of General de Gaulle" and a deplorable acquiescence in "the error of modern times" by the "inheritor of the Capets" (his earliest dynastic ancestors, who rose to power around the year 987). After describing Algeria as "the last land tied to the crown by our kings" (meaning the unlucky Louis Philippe), they end up by saying frankly that "it is as much for the heritage of the present pretender himself as for France's immediate interests" that the Action Française "refuses to follow M. de Gaulle into Algerian Algeria." All these anachronistic references to kings, addressed to those monarchs' final, symbolic, Socialist relic, the Comte de Paris, and coming to him, as they do, after the machine guns and Molotov cocktails on the streets of Algiers a fortnight ago, make it clear that President de Gaulle's problem of the mixed races in Algeria is also a problem of the persistent admixture of certain kinds of strange French people living in France today.

1961

January 12

It is easy now, after the success of the event, to say that President de Gaulle was bound to win his majority in metropolitan France in the referendum last weekend, though actually those were three of the most confusing days, involving conscience, dialectics, and muddled opinions and hopes, that French voters have gone through in all the cloudy political years since the peace in 1945 began. It is easy to say that he won by staking his reputation on the outcome and by even raising his ante with a faint threat to resign if he was not given the "frank and massive 'yes'" that he said he must have in order to carry on his Fifth Republic, with no one in France suited to fill his shoes were he to abdicate. Yet there was certainly an incalculable but important number of bourgeois citizens who, though they forced themselves to vote yes, are politically tired of the abnormalities of personal power essential to his regime and who openly look forward to the end of the war in Algeria as also the end of de Gaulle, that extraordinary leader of an interlude, after which France can get down to the necessary, more vulgar reality of trying to run itself again. It is also easy to say that he won his unexpected 69.09-per-cent affirmation in Algeria because the French Army of Occupation was ordered to tell the Moslems to vote yes. Yet the French Army itself largely voted no. Just before the referendum, sixteen generals signed a public round robin of protest against their chief's Algerian Republic policy, declaring their devotion to the French Algeria that they had all fought for and still believe in. France's only living marshal, Maréchal Alphonse Juin, who was born in Algeria, even wrote a rebellious, insolent letter to General de

Gaulle and gave it to the French newspapers to print. De Gaulle's sole answer was to remove Maréchal Juin from the Supreme Defense Council and forbid him to go home to Algeria to propagandize for a vote of no. He also sacked General Salan from his high-council functions, so Salan is now sulking idly in Spain. The more important of two secondary de Gaulle victories in the referendum is its proof that though he may well have broken the hearts of the Army's élite, he has also broken the Army's political power. His third referendum triumph lies in the ludicrous collapse at the polls of the previously self-important Right Wing Algérie Française diehards here in France. They voted no, in a political paradox, with the Communists, the other brash talkers, yet even together the two parties polled a no vote of only 24.74 per cent. Of all the political parties, the Communists had laid down the heaviest barrage of propaganda; in the Paris working-class districts daily bundles of tracts from *L'Humanité* in favor of no were stuffed into voters' mailboxes.

De Gaulle's final television appeal to the voters to let him "know what is in your minds and hearts" had some unexpected and funny reactions. In the wine regions of the southwest, certain groups let him know they had their minds made up against his recent viticultural policy. In Corsica, where there was talk of the Paris government's suppressing a small railroad, the peasants let him know that in their hearts they were certainly against his stand on the railroad question.

As a result of the referendum, de Gaulle's policy in Algeria—his plans to create a provisional Algerian government of Moslem Algerians even before peace is obtained or the Moslems' vote on self-determination has been held—is now law. In this week's meeting with his Ministers, he has already approved the creation of Algerian administrative and deliberative institutions, so that the Moslems will have had some practice in doing things for themselves when the great day of freedom finally comes. What the referendum did not mention, but what surely lies behind all the yes votes, is everybody's desire for a negotiated peace. The sooner General de Gaulle arranges for it, the broader his historical fame will lie, on both sides of the Mediterranean.

Edith Piaf's triumphant and pathetic recent opening night at the Olympia Music Hall was regarded as a resurrection. For two years she has been in a kind of limbo of mortal bad luck and danger, beset by illness and motor accidents, her money prodigally wasted, her apartment stripped to pay her debts, all this followed by a collapse on a provincial stage when, of necessity, she started to sing too soon, and, finally, the fear that her voice was gone, like everything else. Since she is the best loved and most significant of the *populo Paris chanteuses* (her mother reportedly gave birth to her on a sidewalk in Belleville), she and her melodramas were followed with that special sympathy the Parisian public gives to its aging theatre favorites. Her first night at the Olympia was a gala benefit performance for the First Free French Division, which helped liberate France. Old General Georges Catroux was present, as well as some Cabinet members, various stage and movie stars, and the Garde Républicaine, in their helmets and white breeches. Her triumph has continued nightly, with the crowd shouting its appreciation and battering her fragility with its unrestrained applause. What makes her performance touching—and, in a way, terrifying—is that her tiny, stiff-moving body and her lunar, modest face, with its faint nimbus of sparse hair, belong to an unfamiliar, ravaged woman inhabited by that familiar voice, which suddenly bursts forth without age or change and with its rolling, throaty "r"s, singing about disappointed love like a city-park nightingale. She walks with difficulty, her heavy feet shapeless in sandals, and her poor-looking black dress (her trademark since her young days, when she sang and begged on the streets) stretches tight over her thin arms and chest. On legs spread wide to give her balance, she fixes herself before the microphone, and then comes her soaring, intact sound, carrying her ballads—every banal word and the full drama of their meaning perfectly articulated—without a single physical gesture, not even that of lifting her hands. When the thunderous applause strikes her, she mostly acts as if she did not hear it, or else vaguely smiles, being in haste to announce the next song and get on with her heavy program. It consists of ten new songs and, as final encores, seven or eight of the old favorites—a champion performance.

Her contract at the Olympia is for a month. People queue up all day, every day, on the boulevard in front of the ticket office. Nightly, she brings down the house with her confessional new song about her own life, "Je ne Regrette Rien," with its plucky refrain, *"Balayés les amours, avec leurs trémolos, Balayés pour toujours, je repars à zéro!"* In one song, called simply "Mon Dieu," she asks God to give her a few more days of happiness with her false love. In "Boulevard du

Crime," a Guignolesque ballad, she essays a few mocking dance steps. "Les Blouses Blanches" is about the white-jacketed nurses in a madhouse. Her new sentimental successes are "Les Mots d'Amour" and "L'Homme Qu'Il Me Faut"—typical nostalgic Paris *bistro* waltzes. Artistically, her dramatic projection of her songs is still unequalled. Starting again at zero, she is making a new fortune for her new self. Her real name has long been forgotten—Edith Giovanna Gassion. Since her teens, when she first began chirping her songs, she has been known as Piaf, which is Paris slang for "sparrow."

January 24

President Kennedy's Inaugural Address stirred rare interest and praise here. It was talked about with satisfaction by Paris citizens and was written about with serious appreciation by the Paris papers (one of them called it "an exception in the Western political literature of today"), and the laudatory reaction to it was the same whether the people or the newspapers were right, left, or merely middle in their own local politics—a unanimous frame of mind extraordinary in France. *Figaro* devoted a special editorial, entitled "A New Tone and Style," to what the President said and how he said it, pointing out that "his formulas were constantly direct and his figures of speech always striking, making no mystery of the dynamism, which youth alone cannot explain. . . . It was virile language, aimed at arousing the energies of a great nation that is menaced today by the very excesses of its own prosperity." *Le Monde's* Washington correspondent, a Frenchman, cabled that "all the American and foreign confreres agreed in thinking that his speech was of an exceptional richness of thought for a discourse of this sort," adding, "It was written in beautiful language, in which certain phrases resounded like poetry."

February 9

All France is once more waiting for the decencies of peace. The French had hoped that de Gaulle's referendum majority last month would lead to a negotiated peace as directly as might be possible for the stately de Gaulle and the Oriental-minded Moslems, neither side being likely to proceed by nature in a straight line toward any important settlement. Now we hear that each side says the other has got to start first on the humble pie of opening the negotiations. On Monday, everybody was hailing the Paris headline news, taken from a Tunisian weekly, *Afrique-Action,* that President de Gaulle, of France, would like to see President Bourguiba, of Tunisia, in Paris, at the latter's convenience—the eager interpretation being that Bourguiba, who needs some extra French good will on the question of the port of Bizerte, might serve as the honest broker between Algiers and Paris in peace talks. He has been quoted by *Afrique-Action* as saying that General de Gaulle is understandably feeling his way, is looking around, is taking precautions that may seem superfluous. "But it would be to nobody's interest to have him run too many risks or have him fail," Bourguiba is reported to have said. "That would be a catastrophe. And if three or four weeks from now the peace negotiation has not got under way, that will be an equal catastrophe." On Wednesday, M. Mohamed Masmoudi, Tunisian Minister of Information from Rabat, was received at the Elysée Palace by President de Gaulle in "a cordial conversation," though what about was not said. It is deduced that M. Masmoudi will next get in touch with President Bourguiba, now on holiday in Switzerland, who will get in touch with Ferhat Abbas, now in Cairo, who, as president of the provisional Algerian government, is the rebel in exile with whom the peace must be eventually made. Then M. Masmoudi will arrange for Bourguiba to have "a cordial conversation" in Paris with de Gaulle on how the land lies. But nothing so far has been said to the French public on any of these vital matters by General de Gaulle. It is a curious experience to be living under what is so often and for so long a silent government, led by a man who is the greatest speaker now in power in our hemisphere.

February 24

Napoleon III, though he has never been considered a very farseeing monarch, had an early, precise metaphor for Algeria, which around 1863 he called *"un boulet attaché aux pieds de la France"*—a ball and chain attached to France's feet. "Algeria is not a colony, properly speaking, but an Arab kingdom," he added, in a testy spirit. With the French government's sudden announcement yesterday that President Bourguiba of Tunisia, expected here last week, will positively appear on Monday to talk with President de Gaulle about de Gaulle's coming talks with Ferhat Abbas, President of the Algerian Provisional Government, on peace in Algeria, it looks as if the colonial ball and chain were going to be soon removed. The protocol of this Monday visit is worrisome, since Arabs are touchy. However, the visitor's safety from death has to be taken into account as part of the courtesy he is entitled to. Personal violence against him from embittered French *ultras* here is naturally to be feared. Where to house him safely and how to treat him socially so that he will not have a bomb thrown at him are matters that have apparently not yet been settled. He is a visiting chief of state, so he must be received as such, but he must not be entirely treated as such, with a parade and parties, which could be mortal. The French government had thought to house him in the magnificent Château de Champs, only twenty kilometres from Paris, which was built in early 1700, was occupied eventually by Mme. de Pompadour in tremendous style, and during the nineteen-thirties, when it was owned privately, was the scene of some of the grandest balls of that giddy period, after which the state got it back as a gift. But already the Tunisians have politely let it be known they prefer not to be quartered in country quiet but wish to be handier to things in Paris. The memory of how the Algerian peace delegation at last summer's fiasco meeting in Melun was cut off, as if in exile, from all social intercourse, and even from telephone communication with Paris, still rankles in all Arabs. In addition, the North African Arabs have not only the embittering long recollection of colonialism but right now the political hypersensitivity of the dark-skinned, brought into focus by the various kinds of explosions between white and colored all over the globe, from New Orleans to the Congo. The most difficult diplomatic, policing, and housing problem will be that of where to put Ferhat Abbas when he comes, for he is known in advance to be a morbidly sensitive, patriotic Arab and a high symbol of the French *ultras'* hatred. And will President de Gaulle, with his genius for French glory and Gallic formality, actually consent, after all, to "have direct contact with the chief of the Algerian rebellion"—even to make peace? Once again this question is being raised here with fear. Along with Thursday's brightening news about Bourguiba came the bad news from Algeria that suddenly the rebels had picked up the war again and were fighting, at exactly the wrong historical moment. Yet the war, of course, is really over, except for occasional terrorist murders or bombings here and there—and except for talking about, making, and signing the peace.

The largest, most illuminating collection of Henri Rousseau's paintings ever shown in Europe is now on view at the Galerie Charpentier. Consisting of eighty canvases, it is the first major Douanier exhibition in Paris since the two retrospectives given him shortly after his death, from gangrene, in the Hôpital Necker, at the age of sixty-six—the one at the Salon des Indépendants in 1911, and the big commercial retrospective put together in 1912 by the art merchants Bernheim-Jeune, who had collected a valuable lot of Rousseaus in the two years after the old man was buried in a pauper's grave. Among the notable items at the Charpentier are nine jungle scenes, three of which, owned by Paris collectors, the Paris public had apparently never laid eyes on before, any more than it had on the privately owned gray-colored lion's face and the two full-length owls (these three look like miniature animal portraits), making six brand-new aesthetic pleasures in all. But even more talked about is the new, serious, appreciative attitude that is being manifested by Paris art critics and art lovers toward the Douanier as an artist, and the completely new inquiry that is being made into his character. Formerly, he was viewed as a lovable simpleton who was arrested two or three times for minor thefts, probably a mythomaniac but possibly an actual ex-soldier who had accompanied an expedition to the jungles of Mexico, and the admired innocent painter of the popular wedding-party picture "La Noce" and of the monstrous barelegged child with her doll. In last week's *Arts,* which devoted three full-size newspaper pages compiled by four Rousseau experts, and accompanied by fifteen photographs to reveal the new justice being done him and to present the now available truths about him, a statement by that weekly's M. Yann Le Pichon was the most astonishing (including its failure to explain why the revelation has come so late). Le Pichon says that just after Rousseau died, his daughter, Mme. Julia Bernard-Rousseau (the only one of his nine offspring to live to maturity), found in her father's Rue Perrel studio a battered children's book on animals, which she took for her own child Jeannette—a cheap, dog-eared volume she later showed Le Pichon. The cover of this book, a publication of the well-known department store Aux Galeries Lafayette, was reproduced in *Arts,* and showed an appealing design of lizards, snakes, and tropical birds surrounding the title: "Bêtes Sauvages: Environ 200 Illustrations Amusantes de la Vie des Animaux, avec Texte Instructif." Inside were good realistic drawings of monkeys, whose exact poses on the trees Rousseau zealously copied in such paintings as "Jongle" and "Paysage des Tropiques," though he managed to have it appear that the monkeys were fancifully playing ball, like little boys, with oranges. The album's serpents and duck-billed birds served as models for his magical "Charmeuse de Serpents," also present in the Charpentier exhibition. The department-store album's lions and tigers Rousseau set loose in his imagination amid the Paris Jardin des Plantes's exotic botanical exhibits, whose salad-green or elephant-black foliage he tenderly, laboriously copied, leaf by leaf, for he was an uneducated classicist. Le Pichon's disclosure about the animal book, together with certain references from an Army report on Rousseau, now proves beyond a doubt that there never was any adventurous journey to Mexico with Maréchal Bazaine's troops, which Rousseau fondly pretended was the source of his jungle paintings. He voyaged only on his pictures, as on magic carpets.

In the new evaluation, which changes Rousseau's aesthetic ranking, he is hailed as having created his own clear, logical painting line in a reaction against the spongy softness of Impressionism. He is credited with being the first important French exponent of *l'art brut,* now much admired here for its oneiric, providential creativeness, and he is also called the forefather of Surrealism. As for his most naïve, puerile canvases, which the public has so affectionately appreciated, they are now said to contain, aside from their coloration, "nothing admirable." Quite rightly, the revelation of the Charpentier exhibition has been his hitherto little-known Paris water-and-land paintings, as examples of calm, minor French painting genius, such as the 1888 "Evening View of the Ile Saint-Louis and Bridge," the 1909 suburban "Fisherman Among Trees," and the 1893 "Sawmill Outside Paris," with its humble but superb composition of pallid logs on a curved forest road, along which a mother walks with one child in her arms and another at her side—a great and human small painting.

In the matter of the mind of the Douanier, a man until recently regarded as the helpless butt of everybody's practical jokes—proof of both his naïve nature and his naïve art—the new criticism has a tougher problem of reappraisal. The painter Gauguin and the writer Alfred Jarry, author of that unrefined satiric play "Ubu Roi," were his liveliest, most inventive tormentors. They privately presented him with the Legion of Honor, which he blissfully wore; hired a tramp to dress up as Puvis de Chavannes and call on him with words of praise; sent to visit him the real painter Degas, of whom he mildly inquired, "And how is your painting coming along?" Rousseau told Cézanne, apropos of the latter's Salon des Indépendants paintings, "I could finish those for you"—for, after all, Rousseau had been showing at the Salon for years before Cézanne was accepted. One night, Gauguin told Rousseau that he, the Douanier, was expected by the President of the Republic at the Elysée Palace, and Rousseau washed and hurried over. When he returned, he said that the President had received him most kindly but had explained that everyone else was in evening clothes, so would he please come back another night. True? Or was he, in turn, pulling the malicious Gauguin's leg? The shrewd, hard Vollard, his art dealer, at times suspected that Rousseau was really as sharp as a tack. Many people regarded him as an enigma, but some thought that he imaginatively played the fool to fool others—his complacent form of fun. Yet he referred to all foreign painters as Americans, which was surely irrational, and he shouted over the telephone because the people he was talking to were "so far away." It is now supposed that the famous Montmartre banquet of honor given him by Picasso and Apollinaire at the Bateau-Lavoir was only an elaborate, vinous farce. Since they so wonderfully built up his painting reputation as a joke, it is further deduced that once he was dead and they had the legend of his innocent genius laid at their door, like an exotic funeral wreath, they had to revivify it, out of shame and loyalty. Three years after his death, his painting "The Virgin Forest," which he himself had vainly tried to sell for two hundred francs (then forty dollars), fetched ten thousand gold francs. The legend had become truth.

March 8

It is to be noted that much too little has been said overtly by anybody about the Sahara oil. Ten days ago, Premier Debré, on a Sahara tour, said, as if to the desert air, "Take note that France is present here and that she will stay." At once, the Algerian rebel government reaffirmed its earlier stand that the Sahara "forms an integral part of Algeria" and that "sovereignty must be exercised over the desert as over the rest of the national territory." To that western part of North Africa, the Sahara oil is almost what the Katanga mines have been to the Congo.

April 5

No one now knows where the peace negotiations between the French and the Algerians are headed for, or have gone to. Surely never in modern European history has the comic fiddle-faddle of squabbling officials, supposedly with olive branches in their briefcases, seemed more melancholy, more sad. Plastic bombs believed to have been planted by white Algérie Française *ultras,* who are against the peace ever coming at all, killed six people in France and Algeria over the Easter weekend and wounded fifty, with thirty more wounded this week by a plastic bomb in the men's room of the Paris Bourse. The Hôtel Lutétia received a letter of menace because M. Mendès-France was scheduled to speak there on Wednesday afternoon to the press, but nothing untoward occurred, nor did he say as much as was hoped, except that "the little diplomatic guerrilla war must cease, since it is making the war itself last longer."

April 27

What we have had here has been the alarms, fears, and repercussions of a longish-weekend Algerian military insurrection, fomented on the other side of the Mediterranean by four retired French generals, which began as a total surprise to the French government shortly past midnight on last Friday night and ended as a completed failure, amid the surprise and intense relief of the French people, a little past midnight on Tuesday night. The whole restless, ill-focussed adventure had a crazed, nightmarish, nocturnal quality for all of us here—especially, of course, for the French, because all of the few events that connected them with it took place at night, with one major, miraculous exception, which took place on Monday afternoon. In it, the entire French nation woke up to a spirit of rare, refreshed unanimity against the folly of what was going on—millions of French all over France, clear-eyed for once, as if coming out of an insanely grotesque dream, joined in the greatest general strike of protest of all classes, political beliefs, and social levels that France has ever known in all its agitated modern history. It simply consisted of everybody's stopping work early, at five on Monday afternoon, thus forming what seemed like a vast human blockade in the path of the far-off Army plot—a block of French republicanism loyal to its government and its leader, whether or not it ordinarily likes it or him, in a sudden period of danger and stress. Here in Paris, the Métro, the buses, and the commuter trains stopped running, movies stopped showing their films, shops closed, the post-office clerks laid down their stamps, everything came to a standstill. It was a handsome sunny spring afternoon, and everybody, armed with the latest newspapers, took to the midtown boulevards to stroll, almost with insouciance. Only the cafés remained open for work, but too crammed to do business. The Place de l'Opéra was a mass of human beings, gay in the open air, as if having a fête. It is now known that this gigantic inhospitable demonstration against the idea of parachutists' dropping in from Algeria to dismantle France's Fifth Republic by a military coup added to the confusion of the four seditious generals in Algiers, whose *Putsch,* whether they had sense enough to realize it or not, had already failed. It was these four traitors who were leading this new *Putsch.*

The opening evening event had occured Friday, after President de Gaulle had been characteristically attending a performance of Racine's "Britannicus" at the Comédie-Française with a suite of his Ministers, including M. Louis Joxe, his Minister for Algeria—thus proving that the French President's Secret Service for Algerian affairs was as far off the track on insurrection matters as President Kennedy's C.I.A. had been on Cuba. At two o'clock in the morning of Saturday, de Gaulle was awakened in his palace to be given vitally important and alarming information: four of his former comrades and admirers were now leading the third Algerian insurrection to force the hand of Paris. The first insurrection on May 13, 1958, had pulled down the Fourth Republic and brought de Gaulle himself to power, and at that time General Raoul Salan had actually raised the first voice to call for de Gaulle, who later named him Commander-in-Chief of Algeria. General Maurice Challe, a notable fighter and organizer in de Gaulle's wartime Resistance, was later also named Algeria's Commander-in-Chief, but was replaced after the Algerian-barricades insurrection in January, 1960. Algerian-born General Edmond Jouhaud had also been a great Resistance fighter, and was made de Gaulle's Chief of Staff of the Air Forces in Algeria, but later declared that he would vote no in the January, 1961, referendum on de Gaulle's Algerian policy. The fourth and least consequential, General André Zeller, an up-from-the-ranks volunteer from the First World War, was chiefly distinguished for being the most loquacious rebel of all the Algerian Army brass against de Gaulle's policy.

Sunday night at eight, General de Gaulle finally addressed his nation, on television and in uniform. It was the greatest speaking performance of his career, being the words and voice of an aged patriot, ripe in civilization, wounded in heart and mind, angered by the treachery of former friends, emptying the classic phials of his disdain upon the evil "usurpers—partisan, ambitious, and fanatical—who see and comprehend the nation and the world only through the distortion of their frenzy," in an outburst of scorn as old as the antiquity of power itself. When he cried three times *"Hélas! Hélas! Hélas!"* it was the male voice of French tragedy, more moving, because anguished by reality, than any stage voice in "Britannicus." "The state is flouted, the nation defied," he said. "In the name of France, I order that all means—I say all means—be employed on all sides to bar the route to these men until they be subjugated. I forbid all Frenchmen, and first of all any French soldier, to execute any orders of theirs. . . . *Françaises, Français,* look where France risks falling, compared to what she was once more about to become! *Françaises, Français, aidez-moi!"* Then came the "Marseillaise," trumpeting at the call *"Aux armes, citoyens!"*

Just before midnight, when the state radio is always turned off, a voice announced that it would function all night, because there might be grave news to impart. A little later came the bourgeois voice of Premier Debré, speaking jerkily and in detached phrases, to make them plain, and declaring that "a surprise action, particularly in the Paris region," was shortly expected—"a mad attempt" by aircraft "that are ready to drop or land paratroopers on various airdromes to prepare for a seizure of power"—and that, as of midnight, all French fields were closed to airplane traffic. Then he added, as one of the queerest of all the nocturnal experiences, "As soon as the [air-raid] sirens sound, go there on foot or by car to convince the misled soldiers of their grave error. Good sense must spring from the people's soul, and each must feel himself a part of the nation." This speech was still alternating on the radio with de Gaulle's at 3 A.M., when many of us millions of worried, worn-out listeners went to bed. At least one of us (your correspondent) was possessed by an imaginary *tableau vivant* in which we saw crowds of hastily dressed French citizens on foot at some airport convincing misled, tough Foreign Legion paratroopers—eighty per cent of whom are Germans—of their erroneous conduct.

Next morning, Monday, there was a cynical, superior tendency on the part of a few—which soon became the day's vogue—to say that Debré's speech was a bluff, that there had been no airplanes ready to take off, that the bluff was a cracking good piece of psychology that someone must have thought up for him in order to arouse and unify with terror the usually apathetic French. At the present writing, no one knows whether this is true or not. All over town, people say, but no officials have admitted, that the insurrection's planes were indeed ready to fly up toward France on Sunday night but that some pilots refused to fly against the homeland and some French parachutists refused to go aboard. Other Parisians say that there was a bad Mediterranean storm that held up flying; that some planes were sabotaged; that they had a flying radius of only a thousand kilometres, or not enough to make Paris and return. And so on. What is definitely known is that France was naked of protection on that Sunday night, when four small tanks were clustered as defense before the President's Elysée Palace, plus policemen and Gardes Républicaines on foot—a chief of state in complete vulnerability had his palace been invaded. Thereafter, big tanks were nightly shuffled into position before the Parliament, with a soldier or two, their heads in the green leaves of the Quai d'Orsay trees, asleep on top in the steady night rains. Empty prewar autobuses were lined up nightly in the Rue de la Paix, on the bridges, in the side streets near de Gaulle's palace, to serve as impediments in case the paratroopers came to town. And in the rain, all of us in Paris went to stare at them. Each morning, they were all cleared away, both tanks and buses, at breakfast time, in a gesture like emptying dustbins that during the night have accumulated unsightly social debris. All this time, everybody knew that France had half a million men, including the Foreign Legion mercenaries, under arms, more or less, in

Algeria, but that she had no men worth speaking of here on the home ground, and could not be sure even of their loyalty or that of the special shock police. The insurrectionists had a wealth of equipment in their favor, but they lost the chance of their greatest imponderable—that of surprise—when they failed to descend from the rainy skies on Paris Saturday night.

Throughout the painful long weekend, before the insurrection suddenly collapsed and the generals fled in ignominy, the question constantly asked, in various phrasings, was "How can educated, more than middle-aged, highly trained Army men have launched themselves on such a crazed adventure today, in the face of the world's risen tide of liberties for all?" One possible answer is that, forgetful of loyalty to de Gaulle and duty (for which derelictions all four generals had been earlier reprimanded or removed from their Algerian high posts), they had imbued themselves with the white Frenchman's sense of possession of Algeria, like those old-fashioned figures in Delacroix canvases, galloping in proud ownership across its exotic scene and sands.

May 2

Last Friday afternoon, five days after the insurrection plot against President de Gaulle and his Fifth Republic by the four ringleader French ex-generals, *France-Soir,* which is the biggest popular paper in all France, presented a front page that looked like a bankruptcy report on the morality of the French Army and the French civil and public services. The facts and figures, printed in round numbers and adding up to hundreds of Frenchmen in high or trusted or secret places who had been accused of complicity in the mutiny, were more frightening to most of the French public than anything in the four days of the rebellion crisis itself. For nothing really happened here during those four days, so that fear became vague and empty of reality and was replaced by confusion, deep worry, and a kind of angry curiosity as to what was really going on. *France-Soir's* front page was something positive and informing, which the eye could take in at a glance—something enormous, only a fraction of which we had supposed or suspected. It was a printed opening total, to date, of the top Frenchmen, often listing their names as well as their posts, who had been involved in what still seems to have been an insane *Putsch* to overthrow de Gaulle's government, take power, and rule the next Republic of France by military junta. The front-page announcements were mere headlines, big and little. They stated that General Marie-Michel Gouraud, former commander of the Constantine Army Corps, had been imprisoned, along with four other generals and five colonels; that two hundred officers in the French Army had been arrested; that four French Army regiments had been dissolved, including the famous, overpopular 1st Regiment of Foreign Legion parachutists, whose acting commander, Major Elie de Saint-Marc, had also been arrested; that the 14th and 18th Foreign Legion Regiments and a commando regiment of French paratroopers had likewise been dissolved. They said that the second most important officer in Algeria—General Héritier, chief of staff of the combined Army, Navy, and Air Forces in Algeria—had been removed from his post, and also Colonel Cousteau, chief of the Troisième Bureau, which plans military operations. In Paris, three officers from the Ministère des Anciens Combattants had been arrested, the paper said, and so had a hundred functionaries and four hundred members of L'Organization de l'Armée Secrète in Algeria—where the chief magistrate of Algiers, the Président de la Cour d'Appel, had himself been suspended. General Jacques Faure and the ten officers who were among the first arrested down there have now been questioned here by inspectors of the Criminal Brigade of the Quai des Orfèvres—an office and a police force made famous by Georges Simenon's Detective-Inspector Maigret, who, in the ordinary way, would never have met eleven high Army officers unless they had all become murderers or bank robbers. It is to be noted, too, that ex-General Maurice Challe, official leader of the ex-generals' quartet, who gave himself up and will shortly stand trial for his life, has been lodged in the common-criminal division of La Santé prison, not in the more select cells for political rebels.

On the other hand, amid all this appalling news, there is word that General Guy Grout de Beaufort, who held the critically important high post of Attaché de l'Institut des Hautes Etudes de la Défense Nationale, here in Paris, and who had earlier been chief of de Gaulle's own staff, has been released from arrest and is now only under surveillance. However, General André Petit, formerly Premier Debré's military adviser, has just been imprisoned, and his successor, General Jean Nicot, of the Army of the Air, who was the officer responsible to Debré for France's air defense, has just been put under fortress arrest. He is accused of having enabled, possibly with forged passports, two of the plotting generals—Challe and Zeller—to secretly leave France (where they had been restricted by government order, because of their stated disagreement with de Gaulle's Algerian-independence policy) and to regain Algeria and there lead their crazed, inefficient mutiny. In all, fifty more arrests were made in Paris over the weekend, bringing the total to about three hundred and fifty for all France since these stern repressions began—a few weeks and several years too late. In damage to France's morale and international standing, this has been the most disastrous plot of Army disobedience to state authority and the most enfeebling split in French Army unity—in theory still a sacred *mystique* here—since the notorious Dreyfus case.

There is embarrassment and real grief among many Parisians over the disloyalty and dissolution of the famous 1st Regiment of the French Foreign Legion. In military parades on the Champs-Elysées in the old days, before they were paratroopers and took to the sky—when they still carried their earthy pickaxes or shovels tilted over their shoulders, like weapons for their peculiar combat with the desert sand—they always received the greatest storm of applause from the Paris sidewalk crowds of any unit except France's own élite sons, the cadets from Saint-Cyr. The Legionnaires' snow-white kepis, their long, slow stride for desert walking, the fringe of beard that most of the *sous-off'* wore on their stony bronze faces, their unified air of perfected masculine combative discipline, like homeless fighting cocks, endowed them with a spectacular attraction that magnetized the domesticated French bourgeoisie. The Legionnaires' melodramatic departure last week, when they blew up their quarters at Zéralda, so no other soldiery could be sheltered behind what had been their own walls; the civilian crowd from Algiers, for whom they were the supreme favorites, tossing red roses and bottles of cognac as forms of farewell into their trucks; and the Legionnaires pulling out while singing insolently, *"Je ne regrette rien, je repars à zéro,"* the Piaf hit *chanson* this winter at the Olympia Music Hall—all this was part of their bold and inspiring theatricalism.

Nearly nothing has been told here in Paris about how the insurrection got under way in Algiers on that Friday, April 21st. Information has just been gathered by a couple of frequent visitors to

Algiers, now returned, who flew down there from Paris a few days after the insurrection's collapse to listen to their many Algiers acquaintances and friends—Army, civilian, political—and also to French settlers, both pro- and anti-Algérie Française. Some of the facts they returned with seemed absolutely incredible and were merely perfectly true. According to these informants, events started on Friday afternoon when a soldier in the Kabylia district told his captain, "I have been ordered to go to Algiers tonight to take part in a *Putsch*." The captain told his major, who told his colonel, who told his chief, General Simon, who hurried off in a helicopter to tell the Army corps commander, General Vézinet, in Algiers, where the news, still going up the ladder of command, was passed to the top echelons of the Air Force and the Navy, and then to General Fernand Gambiez, the Commander-in-Chief in Algeria of the combined Army, Navy, and Air Forces. The first reaction on a high level was that this was merely another case of *l'intoxication* (usually called simply *l'intox*), the maladive hysteria of rumors common in the always tense situation in Algiers and caused by the close quarters of the different races and the military forces. At eight that night, a meeting was held in the office of Jean Morin, Delegate-General of Algeria, attended by all the brass—General Gambiez, the directors of the military and civilian cabinet, the head of security forces, the prefect of police. Somebody produced *une lettre confidentielle*—one of those extreme-right-wing newsletters (its author has now been arrested) that can be subscribed to for a fee in Paris—which said, "At 2 A.M. Saturday morning, the loyalty of the Army can no longer be counted on." This sounded to the brass like sheer bosh; it was unbelievable that any insurgents would let out semi-public news of their D Day and H Hour in advance. But patrols were ordered doubled and the 14th Squadron of the Gendarmerie was alerted. Then the brass played some bridge and went home to bed. Before midnight, somebody reported by phone to the general staff that a transport truck company had been seen en route to Zéralda. General Gambiez, who was alerted, phoned General Saint-Hillier, the paratroopers' division commander, telling him to phone Major de Saint-Marc, commander of the 1st Foreign Legion Regiment, and ask what in the devil was going on. Mme. de Saint-Marc at first said that her husband was sick with a headache, which Saint-Hillier knew was not true, since the two men had messed together, and then said that he was not at home anyhow. Saint-Hillier then recklessly put the question to her direct: "*Dites-moi,* Madame, is your husband up to some dirty trick tonight?" Feebly she answered, "I fear so." Saint-Hillier and Gambiez started off at breakneck speed in their cars toward Zéralda, about twenty-five kilometres distant. En route, they saw the trucks coming toward them, pulled to one side, leaped out, stood in the middle of the road, wigwagged their arms for the first truck to stop—and jumped for their lives to keep from being run over, as some Legionnaire shouted down, "Squash the old fools!" The two generals turned their cars around, caught up with the trucks, and passed them. None of the *paras* fired on them; what the two generals did not yet know was that this was a military coup planned so as not to have a shot fired. They beat the trucks to the General Delegation Building—the seat of the city's civilian and military government—which in any struggle is the goal to capture at once. The building's forecourt has an iron grille fence around it, with two gates, both locked at night. One general stood before each gate as the parachutists arrived. Gambiez is a short-statured general; a couple of big paratroopers picked him up—their commander-in-chief—as if he were a little boy, and set him down out of the way, and officers arrested him. Other *paras* climbed over the iron fence like monkeys in leopard-spotted uniforms and unlocked the gates, and they all swarmed inside. A little later, General Gambiez was taken to General Challe, and so found out who was running the insurrection. Challe politely asked his commander-in-chief to come over to the insurgents' side and take charge, which Gambiez indignantly refused to do, so he was taken to prison—the second time that night he had been put out of the way. Some Algérois in nightclothes stuck their heads out of their windows to see what was going on. But nothing was going on, according to their standards, for not a shot was being fired, so they went back to bed. "It was a textbook *coup d'état,* a model of how to take over a city," one officer said later, adding, "The insurrection show was run by about fifty Army men"—out of four hundred thousand Army men in all Algeria.

The insurrection failed because General Challe erred in thinking that a big slice of the armed forces would defect to him. He did not get the Navy or even the Armée de l'Air; all he had was perhaps eight thousand *paras,* and he had to use them like messenger boys, sending them on first one job, then another, trying either to persuade or to bully. Challe captured and controlled buildings in Algiers,

Oran, and Constantine, but he never won whole cities, let alone all of Algeria. He never really had a base of operations. For another thing, he had not informed any of the Algerian activist civilians of the insurrection, saying that he wanted no politicians and townspeople underfoot to make another failure, as they had with their barricades insurrection of January, 1960, when they held out nearly a week in the center of the city and then let their insurrection be broken up at long distance by de Gaulle's threats and arguments. In his mutiny, Challe did not even aim at the quick overthrow of de Gaulle's government, it is said, for he had no political substitutes, or even candidates.

One young French paratrooper said, "I would not have dared to fly over Paris. My mother lives there, and if she had laid eyes on me, she certainly would have slapped my face, *bon Dieu.*" Actually, it is now believed that Challe probably had no plan to drop *paras* on Paris. This will no doubt be his defense when he stands trial. The objective of the insurrection was to take over Algeria completely and at once, to liquidate utterly the F.L.N., or rebel native army, and then to turn to France and say, "Here is your liberated Algeria—liberated from the F.L.N. Here is French Algeria, for France. Put Evian and the peace negotiations out of your mind; they are already forgotten." If this sounds mad to the point of dementia, it can be better comprehended (or so the pair of visitors to Algeria intelligently explained) by taking account of the mental decadence in the diehard officer class—isolated by their six-and-a-half-year war in Algeria, cut off from contemporary, fast-moving colonial history all over the world by their morbid patriotism and their hypnotic obsession with the cult of triumph after France's long list of defeats, beginning in June, 1940. That the insurrection was to thwart the menace of Communism in a liberated Algeria that had no association with France was apparently a very secondary consideration in Challe's notion for the insurrection—though it was certainly of primary importance to the right-wing, often rich civilian accomplices that the mutiny clearly had in Paris and Metropolitan France.

It is said that Challe knew he had lost on Monday night. De Gaulle's Sunday speech had been picked up by lots of the soldiery on their transistors, as well as Debré's Sunday-night warning that the parachutists were coming. Yet Challe gave no orders for the planes to fly to Paris. It is also said in Algiers insurgent Army circles that the insurrection failed because it was an old man's revolution—because it was led by four old generals, three retired because of age. Actually, it was really a colonels' insurrection, it is now known, originated by them and then passed over to the protection of the generals, whose rank and prestige might give it the high hierarchical authority felt necessary to rally the rest of the Army. It is claimed that the idea was first conceived by Colonel Jean Gardes, former chief of the Algiers Army's Fifth Bureau of Psychological Warfare, while he was sitting in the prisoners' box in court in Paris at the trial of the barricades rebels, of whom he was one.

May 15

L'Institut Français d'Opinion Publique has taken a poll of how French citizens feel about various facets of the April French Army insurrection in Algeria, now that it is apparently over and people here in Metropolitan France can steady their thoughts. The poll presented perspicacious questions that covered a great deal of ground, and brought forth some unexpected and illuminating answers. This sampling of public opinion, printed in *France-Soir,* seems especially informative when set against the mixed confusion and flat relief that immediately followed the events. To the opening question—What elements caused the check of the Algerian revolt?—the action and influence of President de Gaulle rated top among the answers, though at only thirty-nine per cent; the determined hostile attitude of the French people against the insurgents was next, with sixteen per cent; the firm attitude against the rebellion of the French Army conscripts in Algeria drew fourteen per cent; and the attitude of the American government got one per cent. This last was an agreeable and surprising antidote to the current rumor—denied here by Ambassador Gavin—that agents of our C.I.A. had tried not to check but to cheer on the insurrection as a laudable effort to prevent an eventually liberated Algeria from possibly going Communist. To the question as to what fate should be meted out to the insurgent ex-generals, thirty per cent were for the death penalty; twenty-five per cent proposed prison, presumably for life; twenty-one per cent judiciously favored leaving them to the "extreme rigors of the law," as de Gaulle promised; one per cent thought that they should be exiled; six per cent thought that they should be shown clemency; and one per cent thought that the generals were right in what they did, and within their rights to do it, too. It is taken for granted that the last three opinions, totalling eight per cent, came from activist sympathizers, of whom only one per cent still had the spunk to speak up openly. As for the French government's immediate prosecution of those who rebelled against it, forty-nine per cent thought that it should prosecute very rigorously, twenty-nine per cent thought that mere rigorous prosecution was enough, and twelve per cent thought that the government should be clement—again that soft, sympathetic note. The answers to a question about the possibility of another Algerian uprising were in part fatalistic and alarming, with twenty-four per cent—almost a fourth of those polled—frankly saying yes, they did think one possible; forty per cent saying no; and thirty-three per cent still so troubled by the uprising itself and by the sullen, angry, anti-France reaction of the Algérois white French settlers that they said they did not know what to think. Even more tragic were the answers to the question of whether the French felt they could now trust the loyalty of their regular French Army, with which since Napoleon's time the French nation has carried on a kind of love affair. Only twenty-four per cent declared that they were very confident they could trust it; forty-three per cent felt rather confident; eleven per cent had no confidence in it whatever; and twenty-two per cent, or more than a fifth, were unable to make up their minds—signs of tepid faith in the worthiness of France's Army, which is also now gravely worrying NATO and France's allies. As for Algeria's future—which is, after all, what the insurrection was about—fifty per cent thought Algeria would ultimately be independent and would follow de Gaulle's warning and his hope that it would maintain an association with France thereafter, and nineteen per cent thought it would be independent but would try to have the remotest possible relations with France (in other words, almost three-quarters of these French think that Algerian independence is a sure thing), while only three per cent said they believed Algeria to be French property. Whether so small a proportion with the courage of its convictions covertly represents a much bigger French faction, numbed by discretion or real fear right now, when the government's dragnet is spread to pull in activist sympathizers, nobody knows, of course. Unfortunately, it is fairly easy to suppose that many of those queried on Algérie Française were simply lying in their answers. Certainly the complicity with the insurrection in high military and government circles and the sympathy for it among the rich industrial section of French society have been amply notorious. However, it is thought possible that the rapid collapse and the unpopularity of the insurrection may have brought many of France's diehards up to date at last on the futility of their fetish belief in the continuation of Algerian colonialism. On this point, de Gaulle a few nights ago, in his latest speech to the nation, specifically begged them to give up "their outdated myths."

The next-to-last question in the poll obtained the expected proportion in its major response, but also some odd by-products. It asked, "What do you think is the most important problem for France right now?" "Peace in Algeria," seventy-eight per cent said, with two per cent particularizing, "Peace negotiations with the rebel Algerian F.L.N. Army," which now seem actually set for Evian later this week. However, five per cent said that the most important problem in France now was its low salaries and standard of living. A more patriotic four per cent thought that "the stability of the regime and its institutions" was dominant. Three per cent—a low fraction of idealists—gave "world peace" as their answer. And only two per cent of the French who were questioned thought that the ex-generals' Algerian insurrection was still of paramount importance, even though it shook the French nation and them and the Western world only three weeks ago. For another two per cent, "a variety of things"—none specified—were of supreme importance to France in this still quasi-troubled hour of its history. One wonders what on earth they were. The final question was a natural: "Are you confident that General de Gaulle can settle the Algerian problem?" "Very confident," said forty-six per cent; "Rather confident," said thirty-eight per cent; "Rather unconfident," five per cent reported; and four per cent bluntly declared, "No confidence at all." It is felt that peace absolutely must come now, or the unsuccessful, crazed insurrection of military hotheads will, after all, have been victorious. In any case, the answers to the poll's final question sum up a decimal portrait of a France in a remarkably high state of unity after such a grave disturbance—indeed, in a high state of unity for any time. For the essential French tragedy is that Frenchmen always think with greater disparity than men in any other country. Yet after three years of him, General de Gaulle is still all they have—the sole great figure, with a voice, on the landscape.

As the London *Sunday Times* succinctly said in its position of a worried neighbor of France, "It is more than ever a sobering thought that the destinies of a great nation at the center of the world should depend upon the heartbeat of a single man."

November 16

During the last fortnight, if you were reading in bed around midnight in the midtown section of Paris, with the window already open and the wind in the right direction, you could have plainly heard at least some of the recent nocturnal bombs exploded by the O.A.S. terrorists. Eight were set off a week ago last Wednesday. The night before that, this writer heard, shortly after eleven o'clock, a bomb in the Rue de Ponthieu, next to the Champs-Elysées, and another up in the Avenue Franklin Roosevelt, which splintered the porte-cochere and all the windows in an apartment house inhabited by M. de Beaumarchais, an assistant to de Gaulle's Foreign Minister. If the bombings are properly planned, they are aimed at somebody the O.A.S. regards as its enemy. (Actually, many of the Paris bombings have been aimless, as if they were committed only for the sake of the noise, and to scare the wits out of the public generally.) On Monday afternoon of this week, an apartment house near the Sorbonne, inhabited by, among others, a distinguished mathematics professor who is Jewish and who had denounced racism, was so badly wrecked by a *plastic* that his library and the keys of his piano were blown into the street, along with the staircase, and firemen had to take everybody out on ladders. That same afternoon, the bombers struck the apartment building where the nationally known radio court reporter Frédéric Pottecher lives, after sending him a letter that warned him to choose either "the coffin or the valise," meaning "Leave town." Earlier, they had bombed the quarters of the *doyenne* of court journalists, Mme. Madeleine Jacob, of the morning paper *Libération*. Both of these victims had reported unflatteringly on the prisoners in the Barricade Trial. Even the suburban Château de Louveciennes, which belongs to the Comte de Paris—pretender to the French throne, and a good Gaullist—had its bomb. So far this year, a hundred and ninety-one plastic bombs have been set off in Paris and a hundred and sixty-one in the provinces.

The heaviest plastic charge yet exploded wrecked the super-popular establishment called Drugstore, at the top of the Champs-

Elysées, shortly before five o'clock this morning. The scent of perfume rising from its smashed stocks still dominated the sidewalk outside at noon, when an enormous crowd of young French gathered to mourn. The Drugstore had been the most vital center of Americanization for them, for it was a complete replica of what an American drugstore is and means in the American way of life, and had more influence on Paris youth than any American book translated into French, or any Hollywood film ever shown here.

Sixty cadavers of Algerians have been fished from the Seine or gathered from nearby wasteland since October 17th, when, at dusk, thousands of Algerians living here surged out of the Métro stations into central Paris in protest against and in defiance of an eight-thirty curfew. On Tuesday of this week, there was a painful discussion in Parliament about the bloody brutality of the Paris police, who were held responsible for these deaths, though it was admitted that gang warfare between rival Algerian groups might account for a few corpses. The new appropriations for the Department of Justice were also up for a vote on Tuesday, which was awkward. Furthermore, three deputies who had been officially sent to inspect the Vincennes reception barracks, where thousands of the anti-curfew Algerians are still detained—many with medically unattended head wounds, alleged to have been caused by police clubbings—had reported that the conditions there were "scandalous." The Parliamentary discussion about the police and the Department of Justice was thus enlivened by passion and political venom, which added to the logical difficulties of Prime Minister Debré, who was presiding. The Paris Prefect of Police has declared he will sue any newspaper that criticizes his policemen—the only funny item so far connected with his gendarmerie's October 17th mayhem and slaughter.

The tortures practiced in Algeria by the Fifth Republic's Army—so horrifying at first to civilians—at the time when the French were still fighting to keep Algeria a French province have disappeared from the news now, and the increasing Fifth Republic noise of exploding plastic bombs in Paris seems neither to distress nor to impress Parisians—unless, of course, their apartment is one of those wrecked—for a certain degree of violence, of terrorism, and of cruelty appears to be a normal part of present-day French life. Both the torturing and the bombings were from the beginning repeatedly deplored in printed manifestoes by certain intellectuals, but their energy has gradually faded away, like ink. It is an accepted fact that the O.A.S. and its bombs represent the sentiments of—and are paid for by—the French Rightists, which means, socially, some of the nicest people in town, well educated, well-to-do, and *comme il faut.* The bang of their bombs going off furnishes a peculiar, brutal sonority in Paris, once considered the most civilized and cultured spot on earth.

December 5

There was a unique domestic quality about Miss Gertrude Stein's wonderful collection of modern French pictures, because they were a major part of her household. Over the years, they kept company with Miss Stein and her friend, Miss Alice B. Toklas, and the ladies, on their side, maintained a close companionship with the canvases, in the civilized intimacy that relates certain human beings and objects when they have long lived together. It was a collection with its own kind of private life. It was the oldest permanent collection of modern French art in Paris, because it was formed in appreciation of what no one else then wanted, and certainly it was the only one that, while illustrating new forms of Ecole de Paris art on the Stein walls, was also a literary witness to the creation of the new school of American writing in the Paris twenties, which first took shape in endless, important talk—often animated by young Hemingway's strong voice—in the ladies' salon. When Miss Stein suddenly died, in 1946, and her collection was willed to Miss Toklas, "to her use for her life," the inventory listed twenty-eight Picasso pictures, one Picasso sculpture of a head, twenty-eight Picasso drawings, and seven Juan Gris canvases. In late April, 1961, the collection was removed from the Stein-Toklas apartment, in the Rue Christine, on the order of the Tribunal de Grande Instance de la Seine, and it is at present in the vault of a bank in Paris under the trusteeship of a court-appointed administrator. Today, the only trace of these masterpieces in the apartment is the faint, empty outlines left by the picture frames on the white walls. Miss Toklas—now eighty-four and fragile, though spirited—was fortunately not present for the shock of seeing Miss Stein's pictures borne away. She had been absent in Rome—precisely the opening basis for the Tribunal's act—ever since the previous autumn, so as to avoid the chill of the French winter and late spring. ("My first infidelity to Paris, and a big mistake," she says succinctly.) Only her close friends have known of the immolation of the Stein paintings, though not what lay behind it—of which even Miss Toklas, alas, at first had no inkling.

It seems that, on sound tax counsel, Miss Stein described herself in her will as an American who was resident in Paris but legally domiciled in Baltimore (a sort of vague second home for her, where she had attended Johns Hopkins as a student and still had relatives), because American death duties start only on a net estate exceeding sixty thousand dollars, whereas the French taxation starts with the first franc if the inheritors are not in direct family line. In the case of a collection that had become as valuable as hers, the high French duties could have meant the enforced selling of some of the contents so that Miss Toklas might inherit the rest. The will named only two reasons for which any pictures might be "reduced to cash." The first was to permit the publication of any remaining unprinted Gertrude Stein manuscripts—all willed to the library of Yale University, which subsequently published eight volumes of them. The second was to provide for Miss Toklas's "proper maintenance and support," if necessary. However, any sale had to be authorized in Baltimore by a court-appointed estate administrator (who, early on, was an elderly lawyer named Edgar Allan Poe, the poet's great-nephew, who died last week). This authorization Miss Toklas seems to have had in 1958, when she sold a Picasso "Paysage Vert" to M. Daniel-Henry Kahnweiler, the venerable Cubist dealer and a friend from Cubist days, for $18,750. In 1953—without Baltimore authorization but for one or both of the reasons stipulated by Miss Stein's will—she had sold Kahnweiler, for about $6,000, half of the twenty-eight Picasso drawings, later exhibited and put on sale at the Galerie Berggruen, in the Rue de l'Université. The prices were modestly set by Picasso himself, Miss Toklas says, whom she had asked for advice. Fairly recently, one of these Picasso drawings was resold at Sotheby's, in London, for three thousand pounds.

Late last year, the British news came to the knowledge of the widowed Mrs. Allan Stein, here in Paris, and the recent drama started, Mrs. Stein's interest in art being strictly that of a mother. Her late husband, Allan, the son of Gertrude's brother Michael, will be known to art experts through an early Picasso portrait of a little boy holding a tennis racket, though his adult sports preference was reportedly race horses until his early death a few years ago. It was to nephew Allan that Miss Stein arranged for her art to go after Miss Toklas's lifetime, and now, with his death, the new heirs will be his eldest son by a first marriage—today in his thirties and living in California, where Miss Stein grew up—and another son, Michael, and a daughter, Gabrielle, both in their young twenties, who are resident in Paris with their mother, who regards herself as their art guardian. As such, Mrs. Stein early this year demanded a new inventory of the collection they will ultimately inherit, and this revealed the absence of the twenty-eight Picasso drawings, which, though they had been sold for reasons that Miss Stein's will approved of—half were sold to pay for publishing the last of Miss Stein's manuscripts—put Miss Toklas technically in the wrong with both French and American law. The action brought by Mrs. Stein opened with a complaint against Miss Toklas's protracted absence in Rome, which left no one living in the apartment with the pictures, and went on to complain that even when she was in residence here she was alone and defenseless at night amid such great art, that there were no bars on the apartment's windows against burglars, and a few other items. All the complaints were concentrated in a demand to the Tribunal that, for the good, the protection, and the preservation of Gertrude Stein's collection—today worth more than a million dollars, with an estimated value of $150,000 alone for the great rose nude on a gold background, unlike any other Rose Period picture Picasso ever painted, which used to hang in the Stein salon—all the pictures be immediately put in a safe, dry, guarded place, thus landing them in the Chase bank in Paris.

Miss Toklas's eyesight is, naturally, not what it once was. Of the disappearance of Miss Stein's familiar pictures from her salon and foyer, she only says, "I am not unhappy about it. I remember them better than I could see them now."

December 13

In many ways, this has been a troubling, disputatious, and disillusioning year for the citizens of France, and also for plenty of others—white, black, and yellow—scattered around the world, worried or hungry or blood-stained in villages or jungles, or cut off from their neighbors by a new city wall, or harried by arguments and democratic perplexities in the high seats of government, or buffeted by harsh international debates in a certain glass skyscraper, with a fifty-megaton explosion in the East and plastic bombs in French doorways having become more vivid to most people than the Star of Bethlehem at this season. No matter what paper you pick up in Paris, it contains its budget of painful news of some sort. One paper declares that France is living on the edge of chaos. One editor says that the civil war that has ravaged Algeria for seven years has, by terrorism and counter-terrorism, spread to the mainland of France itself. One evening journal's analysis concludes that an ever-widening section of the French population is "ceasing, little by little, to live within the law." Straight news consists of reports on the thirty or more inhabitants of Oran or Algiers who were bombed to fragments in cafés over the weekend, or on the more or less daily plastic explosions, so far luckily without deaths, in Paris, or on the leftist protest marches against these rightist bombers all over France—in Toulouse, Rouen, and Lyon—with fracases and broken heads in the struggles between the marchers and the police. Tuesday night, thirty bombs were set off in Paris, of which eleven, with good luck, failed to explode. All were accompanied by tracts of the Organisation de l'Armée Secrète, which the explosion was supposed to scatter. Of those that went off properly, two were on the Champs-Elysées (where five were duds), and single ones were in the Place de la Sorbonne, the Mairie of the Sixième Arrondissement, not far from Place St.-Germain-des-Prés, in a church, and in the Gare du Nord; two bombs were in the Gare Montparnasse, and four in the Gare de l'Est.

It may seem astonishing (though, after all, it is only logical) that there is a whole section of the Paris press—on public sale, like any other papers and periodicals—that serves the many readers sympathetic to the extremists of the O.A.S., without, of course, openly cheering their plastic explosions, which it usually refers to as "of unknown origin" or as the work of Algerian terrorists, or simply does not report. The two dailies of this section of the press are *L'Aurore* and—much more powerful—*Le Parisien Libéré,* with a circulation of eight hundred and fifty thousand. The latter also prints the weekly *Carrefour,* with its tendentious editorials and gossip—a journal that recently described itself as "in no way a Fascist enterprise but a force of resistance to oppression," meaning chiefly the government's policy of Algerian self-determination, which the *ultras* still resist as a plan to rob France of part of herself. The weekly *Aspects de la France* is also pro-*ultra* and anti-Fifth Republic. All are anti-Communist in a defamatory manner, rather like our John Birch Society. The weekly *Rivarol* is the boldest and most insolently anti-de Gaulle. Lately, it declared, "De Gaulle can puff himself up all over France, but it is only the ignorant or the imbecilic who believe that he is qualified to preach about obedience."

The biggest recent press event was a large plastic bomb set off last week in the editorial offices of *France-Soir,* which fortunately hurt no one seriously and did an incalculable amount of good, because this popular apolitical afternoon *journal d'information* has a circulation of well over a million and a readership of five million—the largest in France—and is sold daily by its own special venders on town streets literally all over the country. News of the attack came like a personal outrage to its myriad readers everywhere, to judge by the fantastic volume of letters that began pouring in to the editors, proving a sense of personal identification or of shock, at last, instead of the curious apathy to violence that has spread like a miasma over much of France. In a special political editorial, *France-Soir* declared, "The French population has a right to be protected. It has equally the right to be informed about the measures taken against the *plastiqueurs* and those who animate them, as well as about the results of accusations brought against them. [This was a polite way of pointing out that, despite repeated demands from the public, the government had taken no such measures at all.] Public order must be maintained by those who are in charge. Justice must be rendered by those whose mission it is. The authority of the state must be imposed by those who have received its mandate. It is for the press to clarify public opinion." And it ended firmly, "Nothing will prevent it from doing its duty." This indignant professional determination was, of course, natural, and, indeed, it had already been manifested. *France Observateur, L'Humanité,* and *Le Monde* had already been bombed once each, and the apartment of the editor-in-chief of *Figaro* had been bombed twice, without any subsequent soft-pedalling of their anti-O.A.S. reporting or their criticism of the government's inexplicable inertia in taking legal steps against these crimes. The inertia was finally dispelled last Friday, when the *Journal Officiel* printed the government decree pronouncing the dissolution of the Organisation de l'Armée Secrète, with heavy fines and fairly light prison sentences for those found guilty of membership, of serving as accomplices, or of giving funds to it. This last will make trouble for many banks, oil companies, and big business, which have been blackmailed into O.A.S. financial contributions so as to be left in peace by the bombing squad. The decree was accompanied by orders for the arrest, on a charge of plotting against the authority of the state, of ex-General Salan and ten of his O.A.S. chiefs—provided anyone can lay hands on them, since they have all been successfully in flight or in hiding since July, when the Paris military court sentenced most of them to death for their part in the spring Algiers insurrection against the French Army. On Friday afternoon, shortly after the dissolution order was made known here, the O.A.S. impudently hoisted its black-and-yellow commando flag—and not once but thrice—on the roof of the Hôtel de Ville, right over the heads of the City Councillors, who were meeting there.

Yesterday, the enfeebled Socialist Party (which has just announced the suspension, at the end of this year, of its pitiful one-page party newspaper, *Le Populaire,* an influential, brilliant daily back in Léon Blum's day) brought a motion of censure in Parliament against the Debré government, which "by its maladdress, weakness, and inner divisions has lost the authority necessary to meet the threats accumulating against the Republic." Naturally, the Socialists do not expect to obtain anything like the majority of votes needed to make Debré fall, for the Chamber is not of the brilliance or the unity required even to imagine any premature uprising against what is really the personal government of General de Gaulle, who is still France's single necessity and only hope for eventual peace in Algeria. The censure motion, which will be debated Friday, appears to have been merely a straw in the wind for the deputies to let blow by before Parliament closes down for Christmas, not to open again until the spring of 1962.

The widest dissemination of personal glory for an old great artist who is still alive must be to have one of his paintings become a postage stamp—to have the vast postal system of his country become, in part, his art gallery, to have an envelope with a mere dull business letter inside, or even an airmail postcard, serve as a small, inexpensive travelling exhibit of his genius. This is the glory that has come to Georges Braque, now in his eightieth year, who was honored this last week by the French postal authorities with the issuance of a very large, very pretty fifty-centime stamp showing the long-necked white bird that has rather become his trademark in his old age silhouetted in flight against some dark-gray foliage on a pale-blue background. Braque was the literal creator of Cubism, the most famous, influential, arbitrary invention of the early *école de Paris*. So why, art lovers here are wondering, could the Braque stamp not have reproduced, for instance, his "Still-Life with Musical Instruments" of 1908, which any village postmistress today could easily identify as a Cubist horn, concertina, and lute? Or, best of all, why not have made the Braque stamp a full-blown 1910 example of his arcane analytic Cubism, such as "Woman with a Mandolin," showing music visibly recumbent upon geometry—an art work that would have perfectly signalled his greatest period and established a bold aesthetic exception even for French modern philately? France is now the first country to start using its twentieth-century artists' paintings for postage designs, and has, for beauty's sake, installed new presses that print six colors in a process believed to be superior to anybody else's.

In the fifteenth Paris Salon de Philatélie last week were shown two other notable new stamps honoring modern masters, though now dead—a stunning sixty-five-centime Matisse, bearing two of his cut-out blue female nudes (all these art stamps are so big—two inches by an inch and a half—that the Matisse heirs decided that a nude pair was aesthetically necessary), and an eighty-five-centime Cézanne, of "The Card Players." This is the painting that was lately stolen from the exhibition in Aix-en-Provence. Of the three stamps, the Cézanne is obviously the public's favorite—two provincial Frenchmen swigging wine and playing *belote* in a *bistro*. Its dark background makes it a less satisfactory example of graphic coloring, the stamp collectors say—probably an opinion of minimum consequence, for it is the picture itself that counts, the lost Cézanne masterpiece with the two men familiarly playing their card game on a postage stamp.

December 27

The sporadic feverishness in the history of the Fifth Republic seemed well diagnosed last week by an official spokesman when he said that the government refused to choose between "the plague and cholera," meaning that France is menaced by Communism as well as by Fascism, those opposite political maladies, and that one is no better than the other for the health of the nation. He was referring specifically to the enormous unified protest marches held all over France at six o'clock on the Tuesday afternoon before Christmas, which were organized by the Communist-led Left against the Rightist Organisation de l'Armée Secrète and its planters of plastic bombs. By the time he spoke, which was on Wednesday, the march here in Paris had already resulted in about thirty hospitalizations from among the hundred or more injured participants—half of them marchers, half police—in a bloody two-hour struggle on the streets between the Place de la Bastille and the Hôtel de Ville. Since the marchers had been, for once, glad to demonstrate support of de Gaulle's government, because of its belatedly declared fight against the O.A.S., they seemed to suppose that the government would—or anyhow should—back them up in their demonstration, and so did the editor of *Le Monde,* who rarely makes so optimistic an error. Why, he asked, in a short, disillusioned editorial entitled "Contre un Néo-Nazisme Français," had not all the authorities (civil, military, spiritual) planned to direct and utilize Tuesday's popular demonstration in defense of the Republic, since the Republic had itself—through the mouth of Premier Michel Debré, speaking over the radio—appealed to the public for help in those dark, frantic midnight hours of the April *Putsch,* when Debré thought the insurgent French parachutists were about to drop onto France? "Must we go through another such nocturnal tragedy, with the alarmed French people suddenly summoned to rush forth without arms or support, in the middle of the night, on foot, in their cars, or on horseback?" *Le Monde* gibed bitingly. What is generally regarded here as the government's lack of political psychology was further demonstrated by its disdaining to recognize that the major police unions had earlier sent letters to President de Gaulle, to Debré, to the Ministry of the Interior, which controls all the police forces, and to the prefect of the Paris police, protesting against the government's ban on the anti-O.A.S. demonstration—a ban that raised a "question of conscience" for those of the *gendarmerie* who were also against the Rightists but would have to fight the Tuesday marchers instead. This they did, once they got started on the job, with exceptional professional brutality—as, apparently, the prefect had ordered them to "draw blood."

The newspaper photographs the next day were appalling, showing a melee, at close range, of hatless civilians trying to hold one hand in protection over their skulls—smashed hands and cracked heads were the commonest hospitalized injuries—while the police flailed, as if during a harvest, with their extra-long white riot sticks and the helmeted special security troops used their rifle butts as truncheons, pounding with them, like pile drivers, into the massed marchers, or into the backs of men who had fallen to the sidewalk. Four marching municipal councillors, three of them Socialist and one Communist, wearing their tricolor sashes of office, were beaten, like anybody else, and injured—one on a hand, two on the head, and one in an eye. A third of the marchers hospitalized were women, knocked down and trampled on in their incredibly determined participation in the hurly-burly. Among the uninjured female marchers were Mme. Simone de Beauvoir, who walked with Jean-Paul Sartre; Mme. Jeannette Vermeersch, wife of the Communist Party leader Maurice Thorez; and the Communist woman mayor of Bobigny, a Red suburb.

The banners the marchers carried mostly bore the slogan *"Contre l'O.A.S., Pour la Paix en Algérie par la Négociation,"* but what the marchers mostly shouted was *"L'O.A.S., assassins!"* In the circumstances, it was natural that on Wednesday morning the Communist *Humanité's* front page should be a mixture of falsehood and jubilation. An enormous headline declared, *"Plus de Cent Mille Manifestants dans les Rues de Paris."* The police figures—also probably false—put the crowd not at a hundred thousand but only at fifteen thousand, and most newspaper reporters settled for about twenty-five thousand. But thanks to the marchers' resolute facing up to their inevitable beating by the police, the Communists emerged with an invaluable new front-page slogan, which at this moment in the history of the Fifth Republic seems to many non-Communist ears to ring true: "The people of France can count only on their own force to defeat Fascism." On Wednesday, the Fifth Republic was also inevitably accused, by the organizers of the march, of *"de-facto* complicity with the Rightist activists." In the lead among the organizers had been France's most powerful labor union, the pro-Communist Confédération Générale du Travail, supported by the Leftist teachers' and students' national unions, and also by the non-Communist Confédération Française des Travailleurs Chrétiens. The Socialist labor union, Force Ouvrière, had refused to take part, because it won't touch anything the Communists have a finger in, but the new Socialist splinter party, the Parti Socialiste Unifié, to which M. Pierre Mendès-France belongs, furnished some marchers on Tuesday and, on Wednesday, a piece of its mind. It said that the de Gaulle government had mobilized more police in one evening against the anti-O.A.S. defenders of the Republic than it had "in months against the Fascist killers themselves."

President de Gaulle is to address the nation on television this Friday. It is a nation in which Left and Right are once more openly and dangerously at loggerheads, because, in a way, the French Revolution of 1789 has never been finished.

The winter art season opened late, coming to its full growth only close to the holidays. The major one-man show of the season was the retrospective exhibition of more than three hundred paintings by Mark Tobey at the Musée des Arts Décoratifs—the first time an American artist has been so honored there. It is the greatest honor Tobey, who has just passed his seventy-first birthday, has ever been given, and greater by far than any he has been shown in the land of his birth. The fact that this museum is physically a part of the Louvre and spiritually a semi-official focussing point for contemporary artists of the highest rank—Picasso was the first to be given a retrospective there, and last year Chagall had one—adds to the kudos that Tobey has won here. He first became significantly known in Paris only a few years ago, when, as he says, he and his paintings were generously hailed by Georges Mathieu, head of the so-called French Tachiste school, whose followers regarded Tobey not only as an exponent of their style but as a forerunner—in fact, a kind of unconscious founder—of it. This seemed to Tobey not to be true, without diminishing his pleasure in so friendly a brotherhood. The appreciation he has aroused among the French public and critics is like a blossoming in winter. As one critic said, he is "one of the most singular artists of our time, but little recognized in his own land." The critic went on to declare that Tobey "could be provisionally described as the painter who introduced the Oriental spirit into non-figurative contemporary art." Because of his invention of his "astonishing white writing," he was further credited by this critic with having left behind "the forms of expression that founded modern painting," and with having, by his "fundamental originality, invented a new space, completely abolishing volume, to the benefit of modulation and rhythm." The critic of *France Observateur* said of

Tobey's white-writing style that it was "a discovery on the highest plane of present-day art; a momentous entry into sensibility and silence," as opposed to the clamorous quality of much of the painting done now. The magazine *Preuves* called him "perhaps the most important painter of our epoch," and went on to say, "In Picasso and Tobey, who is only ten years younger, the future lies prefigured. Tobey's labyrinths, trellises of color, nebulae, and eruptions of atoms are, in their true signification, the measureless universe."

Tobey at present is back in his seventeenth-century house in Basel, where, as if his paintings were enamels, he is once again slowly drying them in the vast cooking oven of his kitchen.

1962

January 9

It takes at least a week to get a couple of tickets to the little Montmartre Théâtre de Dix-Heures, owing to the popularity of Henri Tisot in his now nationally famous and uproariously funny parody of "qui vous savez"—as the French regularly identify his subject, their not openly mentioning General de Gaulle's name somehow adding to their irreverent glee. What Tisot has created and gives is a brilliant vocal and intellectual takeoff of de Gaulle the speechmaker—a total mimicry of the august voice, with its sometimes uncontrollable comic falsetto and its solemn nasal trumpeting of sacred syllables like *"la Fraaaance,"* coupled with bull's-eye precision in pinning down the *démodé* verbal elegances of his vocabulary. Most astute of all is the imitation of the General's style of special thinking—of his complicatedly pointing out or splendidly obscuring his ideas, which has become his individual rhetorical pattern in historic oratory. The takeoff is based on those de Gaulle speeches to his nation that referred to auto-determination for Algeria, which Tisot has turned into *"autocirculation,"* or the terrible traffic problem in Paris. A recent Pathé record of the parody, made live at the Dix-Heures with the audience's roars of laughter, has in the last month sold almost a quarter of a million copies—a hit not equalled in France since the "Third Man" zither tune. Tisot, who is thirty-one, has something of the heavy facial structure of the President himself; can purse his lips like the Chief of State for similar labial effects; uses his hands, thumbs up, exactly as the General does; had his training at the Comédie-Française, where he was rarely given a chance to act; and is now nightly doing his *"autocirculation"* parody in a special early turn at the big Olympia Music Hall, where, to add realism for the large, non-intellectual audience, he stands on a speaker's platform draped in official tricolor bunting, which is rather daring.

As a fact of de Gaulle's Fifth Republic's oratorical history, his New Year's radio speech was the most unpopular he has yet made to the nation, with its lithographic, optimistic portrait of France as an island of stability, self-confidence, and prosperity amid a world in tumult. His speech to listening millions sounded as if he were uninformed about the opposite present truths, and is still provoking caustic references. In a recent *Figaro Littéraire,* to whose back page François Mauriac has transferred his trenchant "Bloc-Notes," he comes forth as de Gaulle's sole apologist. He explains his belief that the reason de Gaulle said nothing consequential to the French people at New Year's was that he knew too much to be able to say anything with safety. Mauriac states, in part, "Never has assassination that has become endemic in a country coincided with such languor. We hate and we kill meanly and apathetically. It was not for de Gaulle to tell us what we have become. It was not for him to hold the mirror up to us. As always at the bedside of someone very ill, nothing was left for him to do but to voice words of hope. He could not cry out to us '*Eh bien, oui,* Frenchmen, you are in a bad way and no pleasant sight to see.' This he could not say." Unfortunately, many Frenchmen still think that this is exactly what he should have said, and loudly, too.

The incredible price of fresh black truffles over the holiday season—the highest ever recorded in modern French gastronomy, and coming, of course, just when they were most needed for slipping under the skin of the turkey's breast or into the goose's liver—seems to have aroused truffle raisers to an almost confessional frame of mind. An authoritative article on trufficulture, compiled by government mycologists, biologists, truffle growers, and barren-soil experts, has, as a rarity, just appeared in a weekly farm newspaper, *La France Agricole.* It makes confused, fascinating, and mysterious reading. Truffles, which for years had been selling quietly at the equivalent of seven or eight dollars a pound, in December suddenly leaped to twenty-one dollars, or about two dollars and thirty-five cents for one warty, thick-skinned, coal-black, high-scented, delicious *Tuber melanosporum* the size of a Congo baby's fist. This peak price both delighted and alarmed *trufficulteurs,* whose present drama it indicated—"the penury of growing truffles, which are extremely capricious in their reproduction" and "have an evolutionary cycle of which little is known." What is very well known is that Italian and Hungarian black truffles are now competing in the international market to fill the shortage (lately amounting to two-thirds of the former crop) of the famed Périgord type of truffle, which has long furnished its erratic troves of subsoil riches from among the thousands of acres of otherwise unredeemable stony land in the southwest, especially in Dordogne, Lot, and the Corrèze. (The country inns down there serve you sliced truffles on everything but a boiled egg.) Apparently, only one simple fact is known about a truffle, and it used to be denied. It is definitely an underground mushroom. According to the official Truffle Committee of Périgord, truffle growers perforce know little about growing them, except that if they grow at all, they mostly do it under pubescent (or hairy) oaks—though they won't do it even there except maybe under ten trees that have "a special truffle vocation," out of a hundred saplings that the wretched farmer may have planted, in clay above fissured limestone. He plants them not upright in a hole but lying sidewise in a trench running north and south, with a supporting stick to lift the branch end, so that the leaves can later give their miserable shade to the roots near which the truffles perhaps will grow. It takes the trees about eight years to reach their stunted and scrofulous-looking maturity, when they should manifest their vocation, if any. In that case, the ground around the tree "burns," as the peasants say—the lichen or sparse moss becomes mysteriously scorched. This, "we think," the Périgord Committee opines hesitantly, "proves that the parasite truffle is living in a state of symbiosis with its tree"—from then on honorably called a truffle tree, or *un chêne truffier*. "It is certain," the Committee says more firmly, "that the tree combines the unknown conditions that give the determining cause for truffles. It may be a secretion from an injured root. Truffle-making is the particular characteristic of a certain tree, not the normal function of the species." The great plantations of 1900, now dead and creating the present shortage, flourished in old vineyards that had been killed by Phylloxera (accidentally imported from California). Since the isolation of the truffle mycelium in the early nineteen-forties by a Clermont-Ferrand botany professor, it has been used to inoculate young oaks, and even their acorns, for starting new plantations. But no one seems to know if it really works. There was recently a celebrated truffle tree near Meyssac, in the Corréze, which had a truffigenous radius of a hundred and twenty square feet, and between 1954 and 1958 produced twelve hundred dollars' worth of truffles. This is why truffle growers and government agriculturists wish they knew more about the truffle's private life. Brillat-Savarin called the truffle "the black diamond of the kitchen." It is possibly a delicious, edible underground mycological malady.

January 25

The heaviest, so far, of all the plastic bombs set off in Paris exploded Monday afternoon in a courtyard of the Quai d'Orsay, and its hollow boom could be heard as far away as the Place de la République, about three kilometres distant. It was a lovely, clear-skied late afternoon, and many of us living high up in the hotels along the Rue de Rivoli had a window half open, so the alarming sound, bigger than any we had yet heard but familiar, came to us direct, across the river and the Tuileries Gardens. From our little balconies, we could see a column of smoke starting to rise from the part of the Foreign Ministry across from the Invalides air terminal, and in a few minutes we could lean down to see and hear the fire engines and ambulances plowing through the Rivoli traffic, their sirens raising a bedlam and their big red lights winking as they hurried toward the Concorde bridge. This outrage committed against this major government edifice—at first, people thought it was Parliament, next door, that had been bombed—has shaken, angered, and horrified Paris at last. On all sides one hears the French saying that things can't go on like this, why isn't someone doing something to stop it, where is the government? On Tuesday, *France-Soir* published a front-page photograph of the body of a man who looked made of charcoal, with a caption explaining that "this atrocious document" showed "the cadaver of the modest Quai d'Orsay employee" carbonized by the O.A.S. Monday bomb (miraculously, the only death from plastic bombs that Paris has had), and that although the policy of the paper was against pandering to morbid curiosity, it was high time for "public opinion to be a judge of these terrorist practices." Monday morning, a Gaullist deputy had been kidnapped by men with machine guns—"Chicago-style," as one Paris paper put it—and that night, in the new Paris style, the police searched the domiciles of four hundred people for incriminating documents and arrested twenty-nine suspects, many of them teen-agers from the best of the city's *lycées*. The activity of the police, so long inert, and the entry of decent people's young sons into the nasty arena of events have been the week's unexpected big political elements. In the Sorbonne's law-school classrooms, right-wing student sympathizers recently painted enormous "O.A.S."s on the ceilings and "Algérie Française"s on the walls. This pro-Fascist youth movement is opposed by the biggest student union, which is pro-left, their dual political precocity being a natural microcosm of the warring split among adult partisans in France.

Monday night, the homes of half a dozen Communist deputies or officials were plastiquéd; yesterday it was the liberal journalists' turn. In less than half an hour, after lunch, seven bombs partially wrecked, among other homes, the apartments of M. Beuve-Méry, the editor of *Le Monde* (it was his second plastic); of M. Maurice Duverger, a Sorbonne law professor and a frequent *Monde* political writer; of Mme. Françoise Giroud, co-editor of the leftist weekly *Express* and of Michel Droit, the editor of the weekly *Figaro Littéraire*.

Since the Quai d'Orsay Monday bombing, there has been a new, urgent, angry tone to what most of the Paris papers have to say about the Fifth Republic government and its chief. *Figaro,* which until now has been carefully courteous in expressing its dissatisfactions, lost all decorum in its editorial yesterday, and in being truthful became tough. "Yes, General de Gaulle disappoints us," *Figaro* said, in part. "Yes, the ignorance amid which he has installed himself at the top of his ivory tower, and the obstinacy of his disdain, seem in defiance of current events. Yes, the sense of attachment to him is no longer present in most hearts. But he has at least the immovable sentiment of fidelity to his duty. We have no choice, and neither has he." On this subject the satiric weekly *Le Canard Enchaîné* also had its say, in a cartoon that showed President de Gaulle in his nightshirt sleepwalking on top of a Paris building. Inside, Prime Minister Debré is leaning from a window above a crowd waving banners marked "Stop the O.A.S." and "O.A.S. Assassins," to whom he whispers, "Quiet! You will wake him."

The cleaning of that splendid row of Place de la Concorde palaces built by Louis XV for the reception of ambassadors and potentates, which in our tourist epoch have been mostly identified with the Automobile Club, the Hôtel Crillon, and, until lately, the Guaranty Trust Company, is now finished, after months of detergents, and the transfiguration is complete. You can hardly believe your eyes. The formerly dramatic blackened porticoes and pillars have become elegant cream-colored façades of delicate nuance, of carved intricacies behind faintly runnelled classic columns, all restored to their original, shallower perspectives. These buildings are the pilot portion of a grandiose clean-up program for certain notable *monuments historiques* lately undertaken by M. André Malraux, Ministre des Affaires Culturelles, who, with characteristic aesthetic flair, chose to launch it on the Concorde as "the most spectacular site." As pendent extensions of the Concorde's view, the Madeleine and Parliament will also be scrubbed this summer. The cleaning up of the Chamber of Deputies, even on the outside, will indubitably be reflected in the press by harsh political cartoons and jokes on the scandals that have too frequently stained republican history there. Also to be cleaned by autumn are the three long, richly pilastered, and fastuous garden façades of the Palais-Royal (where Louis XIV lived as a boy, and which still contains the most secluded, coveted walkup ex-royal apartments in all Paris). With its rehabilitation, the Palais-Royal will look like an enormous restored painting, its sepia-tinted stone emerging as a pale, rich chrome. This is already the color revealed in the garden's Cour d'Honneur, where Malraux has his Ministry offices, and which he ordered cleaned first, as a sample. His 1963 program will include the red brick Place des Vosges (built for Henri IV) and the opulent Place Vendôme (known to Louis XIV only when he was an old, unpopular monarch). Malraux's extraordinary effort to freshen certain great elements of the French architectural past, to redate beauty by bringing back, as far as possible, the complexion and coloration they had when their period was young and royal—or at least to repeal half a century of recent time and the black crust deposited on this beauty by modern prosperity, by industry's and motor traffic's fumes, and by today's atmospheric filth—has naturally divided Paris opinion into two camps, this being a long season of unflagging, nerve-racked French dissension and dispute about everything, about anything. Those against say that making the old buildings appear younger has robbed them of their weight of reality, that the Concorde palaces now look like Hollywood movie sets of the Concorde palaces. Among the owners of these sites, only the Hôtel Crillon was reportedly opposed to being cleaned up, on the ground that its clientele, especially the Americans, had faith in the dirt on the façade as a guarantee that they were living in a genuinely historic old place.

Apparently there have been many cleaning methods used on old stone here in France, several of which have been dropped because they were injurious either to the stone or to the men working on it. Sandblasting is now forbidden here as perilous to the workmen. Steam jets have proved too brutal for antique façades, but jets of water at high pressure are still permitted. Eighty years ago, the Germans undertook to wash the Cologne Cathedral. The English washed Buckingham Palace with water and sponges. Nowadays, the atmospheric filth of big cities is so adhesively gummed onto the old stone that detergents are necessary. According to experts, the great danger in cleaning old stone is the destruction of its *calcin,* or epidermis, whose removal "kills the stone," in the masons' phrase; to renew the stone's resistance to weather, it has to be treated with fluosilicate. A stone virus, or sickness, has also recently been discovered. The cleaning in the Malraux program is done with a detergent powder of secret and antiseptic formula, invented in Germany, which is mixed with water to the consistency of paste, is applied to the stone with a mason's trowel and left to act a few minutes, and is removed by a stiff scrubbing brush, the stone then being rinsed off with water—rather the same general process as brushing one's teeth. By a law of 1852, French property owners must clean the front of their buildings every ten years. In the case of the state's *monuments historiques,* M. Malraux has decided that the state should itself submit to the excellent law it imposes on its citizens.

February 7

This being so palpably a moment of near-final crisis in France's Algerian ordeal, de Gaulle's Monday-night speech was considered of major importance throughout the Western world as well as here. The London *Times* at once signalled it as "one of his most persuasive discourses." On the whole, the ordinary French people seemed satisfied with it, and with the last part especially, because there, for once, he was speaking factually—an exception they were hungry to hear. The Paris press is distinctly less critical and hostile than after his December 29th address, in which his ill-starred soothing phrase that "all is simple, all is clear," along with a few other paternalisms, combined to give him for the new year what could be fairly called a unanimous opposition press. But since Tuesday it is more pro-de Gaulle than it has been for a very long time indeed. It is through his words—far more than through his deeds—that he rules again. For itself, *Le Monde* rallied to him fraternally with its own special gift of language in its front-page editorial, saying, in part, "Yes, for the first time perhaps in seven years, these days we are close to our goal and, before that, to an end of the fighting. There was something moving, tragic, in seeing, in hearing this lone man"—without naming him—"intrepid, immovable, sure of himself, seeking to communicate here and elsewhere the certainties at which he has arrived across the eddies that for three years carried him so far in the opposite direction from what he had hoped, planned, declared, and to which events cruelly gave the lie at a time when he believed himself powerful enough to command them. These certainties, which he gained at the cost of his own disavowals, are that there is a determinism to history, that Continental France retains its potential as a great power, with an eminent role to play in the 'union of organized states' that will be Europe, and that no alternative exists to the phenomenon, soon to be universal, of decolonization."

As for the extreme-Right newspaper reaction to de Gaulle's speech, the full folly of it is spread in the news of the Algerian response to the speech as detailed here in Tuesday's *Aurore,* the Paris Rightists' morning paper. It said that, in obedience to O.A.S. orders, the streets of Algiers became deserted just before the broadcast; that when the speech began, a deafening tumult broke out, with the anti-de Gaulle *colons* blowing trumpets or beating drums or saucepans from their windows; that in the harbor the tugboats blew their whistles throughout the twenty minutes of the speech; that, hidden inside their parked cars at the curb, other anti-de Gaulle Europeans played "ta-ta-ta-ti-ti" on their horns, which scans "Al-gé-rie Française." In Oran, most violent of the cities, the long-wave radio transmitter had been plastiquéd in the afternoon and its director and technical assistants temporarily kidnapped. In the city of Bône there was a *"concert de casseroles,"* or frying pans, plus sixteen plastic bombs, including one that exploded in the police prefecture during the General's address; at Mostaganem, one plastic bomb per minute was set off during the speech's twenty minutes. "And that is how the discourse of the Chief of State was welcomed in the Algerian cities," *Aurore* commented. About twenty people in Oran and a half dozen in Algiers were murdered on Monday.

February 20

The only words that will satisfy the French people will be brief and printed ones, headlined on the front page of every newspaper, declaring that the cease-fire has been signed. It won't actually be peace, but it will feel like peace, because it will mean the end of the two armies' shooting at each other in Algeria, as they have been doing for seven and a half years. Maybe it will come this weekend, or the one after. It is the only event that could follow suitably on two earlier events that people here will long remember and talk of, and that will become modern legends of Paris. The first event, of course, whose importance lay in its horror, was the Thursday killing, just the week before last, of five men and three women in the shambles and bloodletting around the Bastille quarter between the gendarmerie and about twenty thousand anti-O.A.S. marchers, largely Communists, whose march had been forbidden by the government—some of the dead dying of suffocation or from internal injuries inflicted by the pressure of the crowds when they panicked before the gendarmes' clubs, one or two dying of head wounds, and the youngest, a boy of sixteen, being trampled to death. It was an evening of shameful and historic savagery in the capital of France, comparable to the night of February 6, 1934, when on the Place de la Concorde the Third Republic, faced with a collapse of the government and threatened by both Right and Left, ordered its soldiers to fire, killing eighteen in the dense, excited crowd around the statues and fountains.

On the Tuesday morning following the Thursday deaths came the gigantic funeral march for them, of a million marchers, or a half million, or a quarter million—nobody seems to know exactly how many, nor could we who were there count ourselves, knowing only that on the Boulevard du Temple we packed the streets and sidewalks solid all the way from the Place de la République, which was also overfilled, to the black-draped Bourse du Travail, where the coffins lay, and which was turned into a *chapelle ardente*. The street was almost gay with men carrying official *couronnes mortuaires* and set pieces of flowers bearing red ribbons with the names of the donors in gold, such as the Railwaymen's Union of Vitry, a Paris suburb, or a local printers' syndicate. It had rained during the night, and the air was moist, making the flowers glisten freshly in the big floral constructions—flower beds of lilacs, arum lilies, and scarlet carnations, which two men usually carried between them. There were little humble bouquets in the hands of the women and girls, mostly of multicolored anemones and yellow mimosa, still fluffy in the chill atmosphere. Other girls were selling small black-bordered cards bearing the words *"En Hommage aux Victimes du 8 Février, 1962,"* which marchers pinned to their coats, paying whatever they chose, the money going to the victims' families. Seven of the eight dead, including the three women, had been Communist Party members. The husband of one, Mme. Fanny Dewerpe, had been killed in the Communist riot organized against the 1952 Paris visit of General Matthew Ridgway, then being accused by the Left of having exploded bacterial bombs in Korea. In the European processional manner, an enlarged photograph of each of the dead was carried on a pole by a member of the family, who headed the procession as it finally started for Père-Lachaise Cemetery (which those marchers at the end of the procession reportedly did not reach until four rainy hours later). The photograph of the adolescent, Daniel Féry, who had been a handsome lad, was carried apart and alone by a boy who had been his best friend. Daniel was an apprentice of some sort working for *Humanité,* the Party paper. His father told one of its reporters, "Whenever there was a street demonstration, he always attended. He liked to exteriorize [*sic*] himself. I suppose I should have been firmer with him. I would have been if I had known it was going to kill him."

By the end of 1961, six hundred plastic-bomb explosions all over France, many of them here, had damaged a lot of property. A list of three thousand addresses to be plastiquéd in 1962 was recently found on an O.A.S. agent when arrested. So far, there is no official count of the January and February thousands of bombings throughout the country, or of the hundreds in Paris. The big French question now is: Who is going to pay for the damage? French fire-insurance policies, which are apparently what bombs normally come under, do not cover acts of civil war, which are apparently what the O.A.S. explosions come under. (The insurance companies have already prepared a clause refusing responsibility for atomic bombs, too.) By now, there have been so many explosions in Paris that one is bound to know people or apartment houses or shops that have had their bomb. The destruction is freakish, and can be utterly shattering. In the elderly apartment house that was bombed early in January because Jean-Paul Sartre had a flat there, the staircase and stair well were blown to smithereens halfway up, the whole central open spine of the old building was damaged, and doors were splintered and walls cracked. Repairs are estimated at twenty thousand New Francs. It is coöperatively owned, and probably Sartre is the sole tenant who is well enough off to pay his share of the damage. (He has just lodged a complaint at the Palais de Justice against "X" for an attempt on his life.) For the other literary tenants, such as Mme. Béatrix Beck, a former Goncourt Prize winner but no best-seller, such financial participation is out of the question. She and the other upper-floor tenants now go up and down by the service staircase. Just behind your correspondent's hotel, last week at dusk, a bomb went off in the Rue du Mont-Thabor on an apartment building's inner-court staircase—always the favorite spot, with a greater chance of material destruction but a lesser chance of costing life. Every window in the house was shattered. The blast, illogically, also blew out the glass street front of a dry-cleaning shop, leaving the clients' garments hanging in perfect order on their racks; the young concierge was cut about the throat, and her baby injured. Anyone walking by on the sidewalk in front of the cleaner's would have been pierced like a colander. The shattered glass was ankle-deep all over the street. By the next noon, a glazier had most of the new court windows in place. Glazing has become an active revived profession here. Some journalists especially distinguished for their anti-O.A.S. sentiments have been bombed twice over, with private libraries or bookshelves ruined, the books' spines blown off, the glue blown loose, and volumes sometimes blown clean out of the windows.

The carelessness and inefficiency of the O.A.S. bombers in some cases have added to the angry contempt in which they are held. They mix up addresses. Recently, they bombed an apartment house at No. 13 on a certain avenue near the Invalides when they meant to bomb No. 15, where two Gaullist deputies lived. Nice young married couples used to try to rent flats in apartment houses where a deputy lived, since his presence gave tone, and even security, to the whole establishment; now mothers and mothers-in-law warn them to stay out of such bomb traps. M. Sartre, who had early received menacing letters from the O.A.S., had actually left his flat two months before it was bombed, and, on top of that, the bombers got the wrong floor when they planted their plastic. The other day, the O.A.S. bombed the apartment of a Communist deputy who has been dead for two years.

March 8

In the course of the cease-fire talks that are finally going on at Evian-les-Bains, the leaders of the Algerian Nationalist Party have unexpectedly asked if the French government can control the murderous unofficial violence of the O.A.S. against the Algerian population, the O.A.S. now being where the gunfire comes from—usually casually, on the main streets of the cities. This question turns the original French thesis for peace upside down, since that thesis was based on the premise that the French whites would have to be protected from the liberated Algerians. In Monday's pre-dawn shower of a hundred and seventeen O.A.S. plastic bombs in Algiers, twenty-seven of the thirty-five people killed were native Algerians, such as, over the months, have supplied from three-fourths to four-fifths of the daily dead. If the embittered Moslems, overprovoked by the O.A.S.'s small, unrelenting day-and-night massacres, burst from the Casbah with their knives drawn, the peace will be lost before the dove ever becomes the bird in the hand.

At the moment, hope still centers on Evian. In the weekly *Express,* the mordant, phantasmagorical artist who signs his cartoons Tim lately had a picture illustrating the cease-fire, after seven and a half years of war. It showed a one-legged, one-armed French soldier leaning on a crutch and holding a bugle to the mouth of a bugler who has both legs but no arms.

March 23

The curé of a small village near the Channel coast is reported to have rung his church bells at dusk on Sunday to announce the good news of the cease-fire in Algeria to his little countryside—apparently the only tintinnabulation of the sort noted anywhere in France. Here in Paris, the expected seven-o'clock Sunday-evening official radio announcement of the truce in the Algerian war seemed to give people a sense of profound relief but elicited no signs of animation, as if it had been awaited so long—and, lately, so often—that it was already too familiar as a hope to need the panoply of sudden flags on balconies or cheering street crowds, of which there were none, or the sound of the great Bourdon bell in the belfry of Notre-Dame, also silent. Obviously, the emotional satisfaction at the truce was troubled even in advance by doubts about how it can or will work at first. Also, this satisfaction was greatly debilitated by the fact that, with enormous difficulty and endless litigious arguments, the truce finally bound over only the two original belligerents in the war, the French and the Algerians, whereas behind them, for more than a year now, has been the constantly increasing third force, the uncontrolled enemy of them both and of the future peace as well—the random, deadly, implacable power of ex-General Salan's Organisation de l'Armée Secrète, at least as it operates in Algeria. President de Gaulle, in his television speech to the nation at eight o'clock Sunday night, referred with supreme and angry disdain to certain former Army elements as "misguided chiefs and criminal adventurers" (with a stately kind of linguistic purity, he never permits the name of the O.A.S. to cross his lips), but his millions of listeners all over the country knew only too clearly whom he meant, and may well have wished that he had gone on to say what he planned to do about them at this eleventh pacific hour, and about those who favor them. *Le Monde,* in its front-page Monday-night editorial, titled "Au-delà de la Guerre" and signed "Sirius," nom de plume of its editor, Hubert Beuve-Méry, who takes to his pen only on dangerous or vital occasions, stated drastically, "What above all must finally cease are the evident complicities [these men enjoy]. When these 'misguided chiefs and criminal adventurers' make themselves masters of the streets and of the commissariat with ease [as they have done in Algiers and Oran], receiving food, supplies, and arms by train and by truck, there is ground for declaring that they benefit from alarming collusion and, without doubt, from powerful aid. If this does not change, the worst fears are justified. Citizens of a weak state that is more and more powerless, the French will indeed find themselves plunged into a civil war."

Half an hour after de Gaulle spoke on the air, Premier Benyoussef Ben Khedda, of the Gouvernement Provisoire de la République Algérienne, spoke from Tunis to the Algerians in Arabic to announce the successful conclusion of the Evian conference ("It is a great victory for Algeria"), and to order the cease-fire. In closing his speech, he bluntly warned, "The period of transition will demand the greatest vigilance. The cease-fire is not the peace. The danger is great. The Fascist hordes and the racist-minded O.A.S., despairing of maintaining their French Algeria, will try once more to cover the land with blood. Up to now, the French civil and military authorities have been more or less accomplices of the O.A.S. In the superior interests of peace and of coöperation between the two countries, this complicity must come to an end." This final item of official bold comment and advice from the newly former enemy was omitted by certain Paris newspapers—even by papers that had themselves earlier expressed the same worried criticism of the de Gaulle government, if more tactfully.

On Monday, each of the papers gave a full page to the detailed and lengthy contents of the Franco-F.L.N. Evian accord, in which the elaborate chapters concerning the statutory position of Europeans in Algeria were, of course, of major interest to French readers. In Paragraph 1, titled "Dispositions Communes à Tous les Algériens"—which includes white Algerians of European stock—the opening clause, on "Personal Security," declared, "No one shall be disturbed, hunted, pursued, or condemned, or made the object of penal judgment, of disciplinary punishment, or of any discrimination whatsoever because of acts committed in relation to events that occurred in Algeria between November 1, 1954 [when the war began], and the day of the cease-fire." The second clause read, "None may be disturbed, hunted, pursued . . . because of words or opinions uttered in relation to Algerian events between November 1, 1954, and the day when the Algerians will vote on their self-determination." It is thought that this vote will be in July, until which time the Algerian settlers can say anything reckless or vilifying that comes into their heads—for instance, about General de Gaulle, whom they hated before for having promised to end the war, and now hate boundlessly for having patiently preserved his word of honor. In clarification, the next paragraph, entitled "Protection of Persons and Goods," states that "French nationals"—i.e., the white settlers, or *pieds-noirs* of European stock—who "exercise Algerian civil rights" as residents "will benefit by the same measures and under the same conditions as in Paragraph 1." This would seem to mean that there is to be an amnesty (though that word is nowhere used in the text) for the raging, murderous participation in the O.A.S. terrorist campaign of formerly ordinary, normal adult white citizens who have run amuck under the recent pressure of events and become lawless, bloodthirsty monomaniacs in their hope of keeping their Algeria French forever, and for the blood-drunk *ratonades,* or rat hunts, on the Algerian city sidewalks, in which rich bourgeois *colons'* sons shot down passing *ratons* (the old settlers' name for the poorer Algerians) in the sadism of youthful bravado—an amnesty, in short, for all these human degradations and horrors, commonplace or spectacular, and many dating from only last week. The realistic, historical wisdom behind this implicit amnesty—or so some French feel—is that there is no difference between soldiers and civilians in a bitter civil war; both kill.

However, the French government's first act since the cease-fire has been to create courts-martial in Oran and Algiers, empowered to judge, by the most rapid procedure, any adult French citizens who murder or throw bombs and are caught in the act. So far, no one seems to have been caught *in flagrante delicto,* doubtless owing to the extremities of confusion, hope, bloodshed, and violence and the unaccustomed attempt to set up order down there on two levels—that of the Moslems, whose disciplined conduct is now officially in the hands only of the Algerian F.L.N. authorities, and that of the French and European whites, whose conduct so far constitutes the bigger danger to peace. By yesterday morning, about fifty dead and nearly two hundred wounded—mostly Moslems, as usual, and all struck down since Monday noon's declared cease-fire—had already been reported here in Paris from still anguished Algeria, in its first bloody peace throes.

A multitude of secret documents detailing ex-General Salan's plan of action after the cease-fire were seized only last week—just in the nick of time—at the Résidence de St.-Raphaël, in El Biar, in the hills above Algiers. In order to have these papers boomerang against the surprise on which the O.A.S. was clearly counting, the French authorities have intelligently broadcast them in Algeria, in Arabic and in French, and have given them out for publication on both sides of the Mediterranean.

His secret papers reportedly said, "I want a general offensive, an extension of the revolutionary war that we are waging. The aim is not to attempt a definite *Putsch*." What Salan did want was to multiply the O.A.S. subversive action everywhere, and "by favor of this chaos" to replace little by little the legal authorities with O.A.S. power, and he added, "In brief, we must rot conditions to the maximum, so that Algeria will at the end fall into our hands like a ripe fruit." As for his precise elements of action, he said that the O.A.S. should play on the city dwellers' emotional reflexes. One of the first objectives would be "to asphyxiate, to stifle, the urban centers by strikes." The *bled,* or countryside, he considered unimportant; it has not shown itself to be "valuable ground for revolutionary action." He added, "A *maquis* does not do much good." His dominant principle, as revealed in his secret papers, was to develop the subversive war in every way, to institute massive shutdowns of all kinds of work and other normal activities. On the purely tactical side, he said that his commandos had to multiply "their harassing of the forces of law and order, so as to wear down their nerves—to weaken them, if breaking them proves impossible." Also, the commandos were to fire on the gendarmes and the C.R.S. (the French shock police), burn their vehicles and gasoline stations, and pour oil on the streets, so the C.R.S. trucks and tanks would skid; "that way, our men can more easily attack them." At its end, the Salan plan got around to the native Algerians as a final human domain for the O.A.S. psychology. According to *Figaro's* transcript of the Salan secret papers, "All the Moslem cadres must be attacked with increasing vigor—doctors, lawyers, druggists, civil servants, technicians, and so forth. The object is to destroy the best Moslem elements in the liberal professions, so as to oblige the Moslem population to turn to us."

On Thursday afternoon in Algiers, the O.A.S. pasted on walls warnings addressed to the French C.R.S., the gendarmes, and the French Army soldiers on patrol duty, saying, "You have until midnight tonight, Thursday, March 22nd, to withdraw from the Bab-el-Oued quarter. After that, you will be considered troops serving a foreign country. The cease-fire of Monsieur de Gaulle is not that of the O.A.S. For us the fight begins." It actually began a few hours earlier, in the first all-out O.A.S. attack, with heavy weapons, on Algiers and its Bab-el-Oued district. Apparently, the civil war down there has truly started.

On Tuesday, the French Parliament opened for three days, in a tense atmosphere, to listen to President de Gaulle's special message to them, read standing by the Chamber speaker and heard standing by all the deputies except the Socialists and the Communists, who remained seated on their benches as a sign of disrespect. No vote on the message was allowed. Though this Chamber is a remarkably biddable one, de Gaulle will doubtless soon dissolve it, and call for new elections after his April 8th referendum, on which he should win a ninety-per-cent "Yes" vote. The opening speech in response to the message was by Pierre Portolano, deputy from Bône, in Algeria, and chief of the Unité de la République political group, which is pro-Algérie Française but anti-O.A.S. and anti-de Gaulle, and some hundred deputies rose to hear him—an impressive array. His was an intelligent, unhysterical, strong speech by an Algeria-born right-wing diehard. He deplored the handing over of an undeveloped Algeria, to become, in its independence, a pro-Communist popular republic (he feared), and he deplored the lost rights of Parliament, "baffled by General de Gaulle." To Premier Debré, on the Government bench, he delivered a telling shot by saying, "Your former words still remain in our spirit: 'The abandonment of Algeria is an illegitimate act' "—which, of course, Debré, who had early been pro-Algérie Française himself, had indeed said. At the end of the morning session, the one-time Poujadist deputy Jean-Marie Le Pen, a former paratroop officer and still a hotheaded bully, said to the Minister of Overseas Departments and Territories, Louis Jacquinot, a former lawyer, "You'll all be hanged," to which His Excellency replied, "You might need me someday to save your own head." In the night session, Le Pen accused the absent de Gaulle of using Algeria to "strangle the Republic and set up a dictatorial empire."

"The mere fact, M. Le Pen, that you can speak so intolerably proves the liberties of this government," the Chamber speaker replied.

They were rather sad farewell sessions.

Parisians, familiar with the unabating, witty, insulting anti-Gaullism of France's only fearless Leftist satiric weekly, *Le Canard Enchaîné,* were astounded to see its sturdy *amende honorable* in the present number, headed boldly, "To de Gaulle, from His Grateful Country: Once and for All, MERCI!" The impertinent, intelligent little editorial that followed said, in part, "It is extraordinary how many times we have had to shout *'Vive de Gaulle!'* or *'A bas de Gaulle!'* We admit it, it's crazy. Yet when a gentleman says one day to his nation, 'Algeria is a French land today and forever' (June 6,

1958), and another day proclaims 'Algeria will be a sovereign independent state' (October 2, 1961), that is rather crazy, too. Well, let's pass over all that. To the man who would bring us on a silver platter the end of the Algerian war, whoever that man was, we were ready to take off our hat. You could say that we've been waiting for that man. It could have been Guy Mollet, but it wasn't. It could have been de Gaulle in 1958, de Gaulle in 1959, de Gaulle in 1960, de Gaulle in 1961. But it wasn't any of those de Gaulles. It could only have been Salan in 1964, if he had staged a successful insurrection in 1961. However, at the end of it all, it was de Gaulle just the same. *Alors, 'Vive de Gaulle!'*" With the same grateful spirit, if not the same gaiety, millions of French citizens feel the same way: *Vive de Gaulle!*

April 3

Paris will now go back to politics, or as close to politics as the French ever get under President de Gaulle. The French are invited to vote next Sunday in a referendum, which will be like voting under a blanket. In his own recent words on television, de Gaulle asked them to give him "a massive affirmative response," declaring their adhesion to him "in my capacity as chief of state"—a strange but not unaccustomed request on his part for direct homage to that double identity in his eyes, France and himself.

April 18

According to the latest political French joke from London (no such quips are native to Paris these days), President de Gaulle fixed himself up with such extraordinary added powers in his last referendum that if he wanted to he could change a man into a woman. Actually, the only thing he has changed is his government. Over the weekend, it was changed for the first time since he came to power, in 1958. It was so long-lived a government that it lasted three years and ninety-eight days—the most durable republican government known to French history. With it went Premier Michel Debré, its head, also a historical record-breaker in that he was the most unpopular Premier of modern times. Speaker Jacques Chaban-

Delmas of the Assemblée Nationale compared Debré to St. Sebastian, martyred by the arrows of fate, which were continually being shot by his enemies into his small, pugnosed person, many of them symbolically aimed at President de Gaulle himself, against whom few have dared really draw the bow, Debré being a more vulnerable and convenient target. His disappearance and that of his veteran government, after these three constructive, vital early Fifth Republic years, took place quietly within a mere half hour, just before noon on Monday, in the Hôtel Matignon, where Debré shook hands with, and gave way to, the equally quiet incoming Premier, Georges Pompidou, at whom the extreme French Left, consisting of the Communists and the Socialists, have already dutifully started taking pot shots because he is director-general of the Rothschild bank. In this rapid, civilized change of governments, there were none of the customary preliminary offstage political noises—the crash of the falling regime or the panting of the newcomers scrambling toward brief Parliamentary leadership—and no sign of the regulation chaotic, anarchistic rumpus devoted to the carrying on of republicanism which the French people became so familiar with in the cynical, elderly Third Republic following the First World War, and which the younger French had to learn by heart as their main political lesson in the ill-starred Fourth Republic after the silence of the Nazi Occupation. Although this new Pompidou regime is only the second government that the Fifth Republic has installed, it is the twenty-seventh since the Liberation, which gives one an idea of the turmoil and turnover that de Gaulle's high and autocratic governing hand has spared his *belle France*.

The new government is, by chance, the most literary that modern France has known—another odd contemporary record. Son of a schoolteacher in the Cantal region, which is known for its delicious large, pale, solid cheese, M. Pompidou was educated at the Ecole Normale Supérieure, where the élite of the French teaching profession is recruited; took his degree in literature; was a professor in his subject in Marseille and also at the famed Paris Lycée Henry IV; has published studies on Britannicus, Taine, and the works of Malraux; and recently brought out a pleasant anthology of poetry, Baudelaire being his favorite poet. He also gave some respectful editorial advice to de Gaulle in the compiling of his official memoirs. Pompidou has been an associate and a devoted counsellor of de Gaulle's, off and on, ever since 1944, when the General became head of the Provisional Government, part of his constant value being that he has never been in politics, as either deputy or senator. He was secretly used early last year in undercover meetings in Switzerland with the rebel F.L.N. leaders, and prepared the basis for the truce negotiations, for which others got the credit. In all these various activities, de Gaulle has, in complimentary fashion, referred to Pompidou as "my signature," and he is already being called "the master's voice." With this non-political Premier, the Fifth Republic's executive power will be centered in Parliament even less than it was under Debré and more than ever in the Elysée Palace. Pompidou's apolitical career may make him more sympathetic than was Debré (a former senator and thus legislative-minded) to de Gaulle's announced faith in referendums as "the most frank and democratic method" for the ordinary citizen to use in discharging his political responsibilities—or so de Gaulle told his citizenry on television just before he held his last referendum, ten days ago. This was a statement which to the intensely partisan-minded French politicians was sheer historical heresy on the General's part. They would have fought against it in the new elections that it was thought de Gaulle would call this spring but that he has, with far-sighted statesmanship, postponed to the spring of next year.

Maurice Schumann, who was *porte-parole* for de Gaulle's Free French on the British radio during the war and is now the new Minister for Regional Planning, has recently written his first novel—"Le Rendez-vous Avec Quel-qu'un," which purports to be the confessions of a German S.S. man—so he is second on the new Ministerial literary list. The writings of Pierre Pflimlin, the Minister for a new post called Coöperation with the African States, have been more technical, since he comes from the northern textile city of Roubaix; one of his books is "L'Industrie Textile Alsacienne." Alain Peyrefitte, the new Secretary of State for Information, dropped his first name of Roger so as not to be confused with his cousin Roger Peyrefitte, who is the author of "Les Ambassades" and other semi-scandalous books occasionally put on the Vatican Index; Alain Peyrefitte has himself written much less talked-about novels.

Many of the ten new Ministers are professional politicians, and some were early professional Gaullists, like Schumann and like Gaston Palewski, the new Minister for Scientific Research and Atomic and Space Affairs, and until lately the French Ambassador to Italy, who was an admirer of Captain de Gaulle and his new mechanized-army theory (which later meant tanks) as early as 1931, and who, in June, 1940, was one of the first to join General de Gaulle in London. These are men whose loyalty and lengthy political experience could go a long way toward making this new government a realistic body, to offset the Elysian relations in the Palace between today's President de Gaulle and Rothschild's Pompidou. The truce in Algeria marked the end of the principal effort to terminate the Algerian war, which brought de Gaulle's Fifth Republic into being and de Gaulle himself into his phenomenal power. His new government marks a second stage in his republic, and a new stage in the ripeness and in the coming struggles of the President himself.

May 1

When President de Gaulle's new Premier, M. Georges Pompidou, well-dressed in blue, with what looked like a white silk summer tie, presented himself last Thursday morning before the National Assembly, he was a French public figure without historical precedent. He was the first in France's five republics to be merely a civilian personality who had never belonged either to the Assembly or to the Senate and had now come before the deputies as head of a government. Architecturally as well as politically unfamiliar with the scene, he hesitated, as if unsure of his proper place, before seating himself on the government bench in the first row, that seat of power which so many backbenchers know so well from having vainly stared at it for years with envy. When he started reading his speech from atop the speaker's tribune, his voice sounded as if he felt moved at hearing it there; then, with steadiness, he began enumerating the new government's program of de Gaulle ideas, which, as a long-time confidant of the President's, he must have known by heart. Though his Premiership was a de Gaulle personal appointment, he tactfully requested of the deputies a vote of confidence, which, in a manner of speaking, he won the next day by 259 votes to 128, qualified by 119 abstentions—a result that many deputies interpreted as 247 votes against de Gaulle and only a few more than that in favor of his Premier. By that time, M. Pompidou had undergone a lengthy, heckling question period, lasting until late Thursday night, at the hands of thirty deputies who were dissatisfied with de Gaulle's policies, and had also endured two of those dramatic Gallic interpellations—part wit and part political anger—that often furnish Parliamentary *coups de théâtre.* One anti-Gaullist deputy of the extreme right, denouncing the "progressive abasement of Parliament," suddenly said to the new Premier, "Your predecessor, Debré, was an easy target to shoot at. You are less vulnerable. You have not expressed your opinions on anything, if it so happens that you have any. You are a new man. Profit by this advantage; it will not last. Virginity, like matches, can serve only once." Then came the most vigorous Chamber critique of de Gaulle's government of "benign personal power" yet heard in the Fifth Republic, made by one of the Chamber's oldest republican practitioners—eighty-three-year-old former Premier Paul Reynaud, still a dominant, tiny figure, hardly taller than a large dwarf, for over thirty years de Gaulle's most durable Parliamentary friend, and until Thursday still thought a staunch Gaullist. (It is rumored that he had loyally warned the General in advance that their political friendship was now over.) To Pompidou, Reynaud said, "The proof that we are not in a Parliamentary regime is that you are here, Monsieur le Premier Ministre. You have already been thrown from power under Louis-Philippe; at that time, you were called Count Molé." At the aptness of this Restoration fantasy, the deputies began to laugh. "He was a very distinguished man, like you. Completely unknown to the general public, like you. One whose political opinions nobody knew, like you. And who had the entire confidence of the King, like you." At this reference to de Gaulle as a monarch, the Chamber, except for the discomfited Gaullist U.N.R. Party, burst into applause and louder laughter. "His majority was so derisory that he could keep power only by dissolving the Chamber. But on facing the people's vote he was defeated, despite indecent official pressure"—this last being an angry reference to the new Premier's having been personally appointed, instead of selected in Parliament by politicians representing the people. Then Reynaud railed against the Fifth Republic practice of taking referendums, leading merely to a Yes or No, which short-circuits endless Parliamentary debate on vital matters, and he added, "Is not the proper essence of a Parliamentary regime the formation of statesmen? Take care! When the Constitution is not respected, there is no longer a Republic." At the end, he received a salvo of applause.

Reynaud had begun by asking, "What will happen when de Gaulle is no longer here?" What a majority, perhaps two-thirds, of the ordinary French people seem to fear is that there will be a Sixth Republic identical with the Third and Fourth Republics, in which governments will rise from and fall back into Parliament's hemicycle like boomerangs, and power will again be purely political and splintered. (There are seven political parties in the somnolent Chamber right now.) It will no longer be personal, benign, semi-autocratic, and ultra-patriotic—qualities that, with a new government in focus, anti-Gaullist sentiment has now openly spoken against.

After the sensational arrest in Algiers on Good Friday of ex-General Raoul Salan, the police photos of him rigged up for clandestinity with black hair and a cavalryman's mustache were a considerable shock to the Parisian public. They had had an image of him, in his infamy. In these police pictures, not only did he look unlike the way they had seen him pictured for an exact year, lacking five days, as the Algerian O.A.S. chief and the supreme enemy leader against the French state—smooth-shaven, with white hair above his odd, unsymmetrical eyes and inscrutable expression, like an elderly, pessimistic silver fox—but he did not even look alive. He looked as if the death sentence that he will certainly be given at his coming trial had already been carried out and here was the proof of it—the posthumous-looking, inanimate wax dummy of himself, readied for the Musée Grévin's chamber of horrors. The other immediate public reaction to his arrest was that it would probably save his subaltern, ex-General Jouhaud, recently condemned to the firing squad. At first, perhaps because both were housed in the Santé Prison here, there arose a feeling that the two of them were irresistibly united, and that both should be shot for all the lives and limbs they had ordered destroyed. Now, more reasonably, has come a realization of the appalling, typically French paradox and the dreadful delicacy of de Gaulle's problem in his coming decision on Salan. It was Salan's insurrectional cry against the Fourth Republic of "Vive de Gaulle!" four years ago, on May 13th in Algiers, that brought de Gaulle to supreme power as head of France today and gave him the right to reprieve Salan that he will use or fail to use before the end of this month.

The trial should open in three weeks and last for a week. It will be the most important and disturbing trial in modern France since that of Marshal Pétain, because once more it will involve the Army, which, though waning and much declined, is still the greatest emotional cult in France except for the Church. Because Pétain disdained his trial as illegal, he sat through it without speaking, as if he were not there. Salan may be silent at his trial, too, as he has already been in the presence of his *juge d'instruction,* who on Monday completed a last series of monologues with him, representing the more than two hundred questions he was required by law to ask in preparation for the trial. "If I do speak in court," he has let it be known, "it will not be for my own sake. My life is finished. It will be for the sake of history." His secret code name as O.A.S. chief was Soleil, the Sun, carrying with it an undertone reflection, like the false shimmer in Salan's *folie de grandeur,* of Louis XIV, the Roi Soleil.

The psychological portrait of Salan now current in Paris is elliptical but fascinating. A complex personality, he was considered throughout his career and until recently only a brilliant second-in-command. Protestant in religion, son of a poor tax collector, and brought up in Nîmes, he was a Meridional without warmth, devoid of magnetism but endowed with amazing sangfroid and with a lucidity sharpened by peril whenever at a dangerous turning, so that, when younger, he always pulled the right string to unravel a situation, political or military. In brain, style, and *panache,* he never held a candle to his long-time chief in Indo-China, the aristocratic little martinet General de Lattre de Tassigny, to whose command there he eventually succeeded. In the East, he was nicknamed Le Mandarin, partly because he was secretive and enigmatic, partly because, like many French officers there, he reportedly smoked opium. He was described as melancholic, somewhat majestic, using his hands in slow gestures, one finger ornamented with an elaborate ring. Most of his career was in the Far East—Tonkin, North Vietnam—with an earlier stretch in North Africa; in any case, he was always far from France, in the dust of outposts. He negotiated with the Vietnamese and with Chiang Kai-shek, held conversations with Ho Chi Minh, was considered an ace in the Deuxième Bureau secret service, was brave in combat, and became the most decorated officer in the French Army, with fifty-seven decorations indicated on the board of ribbons he wore on his breast. Apparently, the great alteration in his military and political vision came in 1954, when he was sent back to Indo-China to investigate the circumstances of the French catastrophe in the fall of Dienbienphu. There he became a prey to the *complexe de l'abandon*—the embittering belief that the modern French state invariably deserted its Army, thus forcing it into defeat and the empire of France into another humiliating loss. This morbid, romantic military idea spread like a contagion among the French officers and was basic to the organization of the Secret Army in Algeria, where the civilian white French population was already suffering from similar delirious symptoms. Shortly after this, the blood began to flow in the streets of Algiers and Oran, and the deadly plague of the O.A.S. civil war was started. Salan's arrest has come dangerously late in the Franco-Algerian peace plans.

May 17

The prisoner spoke only once on Tuesday afternoon at the opening of his trial in the Palais de Justice, when, as is customary in a French court, he gave his full identity and particulars at the judge's request: "Salan, Raoul Albin Louis, born June 10, 1899, in Roquecourbe, ex-general"—for the disqualifying prefix he raised his low voice to make it distinct—"of the Colonial Army, Grand Cross of the Legion of Honor, Military Medal, Cross of the Liberation, wounded in action." It was the only time he was to speak during the five hours of the proceedings, though his pessimistic mouth kept moving almost continuously, his thin lips active in silent nervousness. His pallid face had an emptied, impressive look of lost and dissipated energy, odd beneath his clownlike hair, grown freshly gray over his ears but still a mawkish henna color on top—a leftover from the dye he had been relying on as disguise when arrested in Algiers. Gradually, he began covertly looking around, reconnoitring, in a slanting glance taking in, to his right, the imposing High Military Tribunal, with the president of the court, the prosecutor, and the court clerk in their pseudo-ermine capes and scarlet robes; then he looked more vaguely at the French press box opposite, where the journalists sat staring at him and taking him down as a portrait in words. He appeared not to listen when the clerk rose and read aloud the pair of long reports to the President of the Republic—the special form in which the charges against him were contained. Like two connected scenarios of Salan's recent subversive private military life, which brought him to where he sat, inattentive and overfamiliar with their story, the first dealt with the action of the unsuccessful 1961 spring *Putsch,* and the second, like a sequel, with the ensuing

O.A.S.—the elaborate, irrational, and dangerous product of his imagination, sectarian patriotism, Army training, and egotism. Rapidly read aloud as a series of facts in an enormous, overcrowded courtroom, and listened to while their creator sat in the prisoner's box, smartly enough dressed in civilian slate gray with a diagonally striped black-and-blue tie, his O.A.S. projects, including their indubitable successes to date, seemed like nothing but incredibly well-planned, sanguinary lunacy. Salan was accused of leading an armed revolutionary force against the Republic's institutions and of inciting citizens to take arms against each other, which constitutes civil war, and for which the penalty is death.

Salan's power of disturbance continues. On the *quai* leading to the Boulevard du Palais and before the wings of the Palais itself, iron barricades have been set up to keep people and possible plastic bombers off the sidewalk. Military police with small machine guns are stationed every few feet, and all but one of the high, ornate grilled gates to the Palais outdoor courtyard have been closed. At this gate, identity papers must be shown to armed guards (even by outraged lawyers bent on private business); inside the courtyard, full of gendarmes and police cars, the Sainte Chapelle, that jewel of medieval glass, is closed to visitors throughout the trial (as are five minor Palais courtrooms near the trial room). Five hundred journalists from all over France and the Western world requested tickets for a courtroom that has press space for perhaps an uncomfortable two hundred. In a judgment of Solomon, the Presse Judiciaire bureau gave the newspaper people all the hard benches normally claimed by distinguished visitors. Inside the Palais, one must show a court ticket and a professional press card to military-police officers, who courteously ask permission to search lady journalists' handbags; the men are equally politely frisked. To avoid possible danger in driving Salan to and from the suburban Fresnes Prison every day, he was transferred to the Palais on Wednesday at dawn, to be lodged in a basement section for temporary prisoners, where he has been inexplicably put in the women's wing, under the care of the Sisters of St. Vincent de Paul. His is the small room in which Pierre Laval vainly tried to commit suicide after having been given the death sentence in the famous assize court above, where Salan is being tried—where Marshal Pétain was tried.

This being the most important political trial in France precisely since that of Pétain, it has been well understood in legal and political circles that Salan's lawyers could try to defend his life only by prosecuting the Fifth Republic, for which his team of three lawyers was perfectly chosen, all being rabidly pro-Algérie Française. It is the first historically important case to fall into the gesticulating, theatrical hands of the trio's chief, Maître Jean-Louis Tixier-Vignancour, wellborn, highly intelligent, with a Mephistophelean basso voice and a semi-infernal wit. At once on Tuesday, he began his delaying and destructive tactics by impugning the judicial competence of this High Military Tribunal, among other things complaining of an insufficient preparation of the prisoner by the *juge d'instruction*. He declared that Salan had been given only "three days, reduced from the three months accorded Marshal Ney"—Napoleon's "bravest of the brave"—"who was shot." He added, with an insolent glance at the bench, "But a Paris boulevard was named after him. The magistrate who handled the affair did not even have his name put on an alley."

Yesterday, Tixier-Vignancour demanded the presentation in court of more than forty of the witnesses he had already cited, as another annoying tactic of delay, and, with unexpected stage-managing, he had them brought into court by a back door and introduced to the judge by a *huissier,* who asked their names and repeated them to the judge like a butler at a fashionable reception, after which they were hustled off into a waiting room. It was a disruptive and astonishing scene. Among the witnesses were the still beautiful widowed Mme. la Maréchale de Lattre de Tassigny, dressed in her permanent, elegant melancholy black and a chic black hat; a parade of generals and colonels, some of whom bowed cordially to the prisoner on the way out; high civil servants; a former Fourth Republic Minister; some extreme-right-wing deputies; one witness whose name nobody in the press section caught and who was manacled to a police guard; and, suddenly, a debonair young Army captain, wearing his cap and immaculate white gloves, who, on being introduced, smartly saluted the judge (who bowed, dazed), pivoted on his heel, and equally smartly saluted Salan (who, for once, smiled, and could afford it), and then removed his cap and gave the judge his news. He declared that, newly on duty in Lille, he had been telephoned long distance by a commanding officer five minutes before he started for court and forbidden to appear as a witness. But since his subpoena had declared that his failure to appear was punishable by law, there he stood—*"et me voilà!"* This example, following that of an admiral and a reserve general who also declared that they had been warned by phone by the Chef de Cabinet du Ministre des Armées not to answer their summonses as witnesses, adding that the official had told them the court president concurred in this (which, in some confusion, the president denied)—all this gave Tixier-Vignancour his tremendous chance. His huge voice lifted in a cry of indignation, and he launched into a diatribe, declaring that the Chef de Cabinet must be called as a witness, too, and that within the hour a charge would be made against Pierre Messmer, Minister for the Armed Forces, accusing him of suppressing legal communications and of breaching Article No. 173 of the penal code. While this was going on, crescendo, Tixier-Vignancour received word, and passed it on to the bench, that the young captain in the waiting room had just been ordered by an Army messenger to report at once to the office of the Chief of Staff of the Armed Forces. All this produced an exceedingly unpleasant impression, especially on the many lawyers in their robes who had dropped in to listen to this important trial. It was felt that the Ministry of the Armed Forces had badly served the standing of the Fifth Republic, and might even have helped save Salan's head, were that possible, which no one believes it is.

It was deduced that the reason Tixier-Vignancour had dawdled on Tuesday afternoon, leaving Salan no time to make his personal declaration—the crux here of any great trial—was so as not to have his prisoner diminished by sharing the front pages of the French and world press with President de Gaulle, who, to the surprise of many of the French people, had chosen to dominate the news that particular afternoon by giving, in an Elysée press conference, his own personal declaration on Europe, the Common Market, German relations, President Kennedy's United States, and, of course, de Gaulle's France. So it was not until late Wednesday that Salan was heard from. In a dry voice, and wearing gold spectacles, he read for almost an hour a report on himself that certainly he never wrote but that, in its few personal statements, which he must have dictated with bitter emotions and memories, was impressive. *"Quand on a connu la France du courage, on n'accepte jamais la France de l'abandon,"* he declared, in part. "From the beginning, self-determination for Algeria was merely a lie destined to cover abandonment of that country." He said he was convinced that on May 13, 1958, when the rightist officers in Algeria first rebelled against the Paris government, he had been "the dupe of a frightful sacrilegious farce." Yet on May 15th, "I chose to bring de Gaulle back to power. If I misled the people of Algeria and the French Army, it was because I myself was misled. It is [today's] government that, denying its own origins, is responsible for the blood now flowing, and more responsible than anybody is the one I gave power to"—meaning, of course, de Gaulle. "I do not have to exonerate myself for not wanting to see Communism install itself an hour away from Marseille, and Paris within distance of its short-range rockets. I do not have to exonerate myself for having defended the wealth that young pioneers have given France in the Sahara, assuring its independence in oil. If the Allies had lost the war, the Germans . . . would have loudly demanded de Gaulle's head, just as the F.L.N. today demands mine. From now on, I shall keep silent." This was the final phrase of his declaration to the court, and for an instant nobody else spoke at all. Later, the prosecuting attorney requested and received the judge's permission to question Salan, of whom he first asked, "Are not your heart and spirit shaken by the facts that have been recalled and of which you stand accused?" The prosecutor waited, and then said, "No answer. Do you consider your crimes legitimized by your intentions, and by what claim do you find absolution and excuse? . . . You do not answer. Do you consider that, lacking excuses, these crimes could be extenuated by your reasons for committing them? . . . Obstinate silence. I do not wish to comment on it. There are no responses for us to comment on, so even less may we comment on these silences." This monologue of deep, earnest curiosity addressed to Salan by the official who will surely demand his death was the most dramatic incident of the trial's opening two days.

May 31

The eight-day trial in the Cour d'Assises of the terrorist leader, ex-General Raoul Salan, was peculiarly monotonous, considering who he was and what was at stake. But its last half hour, before midnight Thursday, rang a sudden change. The finale was grotesque, bringing such an unexpected somersaulting of values that it became horribly ludicrous, as if justice itself had been posed upside down. In that tense, silent, animal moment when the courtroom waited for the verdict of life or death, the presiding judge declared "in the name of the French people" that the Military High Tribunal had answered yes to Questions One, Two, Three, Four, and Five, which all affirmed the prisoner's guilt, and yes to Question Six, the most important, which—had he been heard to finish his phrase—conceded extenuating circumstances. His words were lost but their meaning was comprehended in the violent partisan uproar of surprise or joy over the fact that Salan's head had been saved. Those who felt only a sickening shock sat silent, as if stunned by disbelief, or robbed. French pandemonium filled the courtroom. It was led, like a personal triumph, by Salan's stentor-voiced chief lawyer, who bellowed to the bench *"Merci, ah, merci!"* and embraced the prisoner, who leaned down from the box white-faced, astonished. His frenzied devotees, standing at the back of the courtroom, screamed *"Algérie Française!"* and were joined by many black-robed Palais lawyers, filling the aisles as if for the last act in a theatre. Some voices rose in "Le Chant Africain," the O.A.S. song; then came, inevitably, an ensemble shouting of "La Marseillaise." During all this hurly-burly, the nine members of the bench sat blank-faced, as if themselves amazed at what their pondered decision had wrought. Only after their unceremonious departure was it learned that in substitution for death Salan had been sentenced to life in prison. In court, as in Algeria, he had provided the most chaotic scene ever known there.

The majority of French opinion has been shocked and disgusted by the weak Salan verdict, like a last straw after the Gaullist Republic's cautious evasion of forceful tactics against the renegade officers when there was still time—when these dangerous Army generals and mad colonels had not yet created their uncontrollable private Algerian civil war. Ironically, de Gaulle was also greatly displeased with his Military High Tribunal for not giving Salan the death sentence, and over the weekend simply dissolved it (though it had taken his Presidential decree to set it up). Being nonexistent, it could not fulfill its special Monday task—and this is brutal irony indeed—of trying the youths who, one night last September, had attempted to assassinate de Gaulle on his road home to Colombey. This would seem an unconscionably long wait before getting around to trying would-be assassins of the head of state.

The public's great unsatisfied curiosity following Salan's trial lay in wondering what in the name of God—a name more than once mentioned during the last of the proceedings—could have served the Tribunal as extenuating circumstances. Legal circles say that it may well have been the brilliant bombshell that Maître Tixier-Vignancour launched on the eighth afternoon, when he theatrically declared, "The Parliamentary commission considering the amnesty bill met yesterday. Think, Messieurs, of your drama of conscience if, a week after General Salan has fallen before a French firing squad, an amnesty law is passed. For the rest of your lives you could not wipe away your remorse!" It is also conceivable that Salan's silence during the trial oddly served to save him. By his speechlessness, he became somehow partly absent; his muteness protected him, in a curious way, from intimate identification with what was said against him, as if, being dumb, he was also deaf and beyond reach. In contrast to the Jouhaud trial, no prosecution witnesses were presented who were still crippled from the O.A.S. sidewalk murderers' guns. Among the pro-Salan witnesses in plenitude there was signally the influential Mme. la Maréchale de Lattre de Tassigny, with her loyal, meandering reminiscences of her husband fifteen years ago in Indo-China, which she somehow draped around Salan, then at de Tassigny's side—the mandarinlike, already untalkative youngish French general of top standing. A pair of big-brass witnesses also spoke endearingly of Salan's patriotic past, bringing it nicely to life. It was as if Salan's career had been arbitrarily cut in two, and only Part I, which was estimable, was used in court, whereas Part II, bloodied over in this past year alone by more than two thousand murders in Algeria, mostly of Moslems, committed under his command, was never featured. Another omission was that in neither the Jouhaud nor the Salan trial was it ever mentioned what the Algerian natives were fighting for—their independence. Both were modern political trials that willfully omitted contemporary history.

The most important witness was de Gaulle's former Prime Minister, Michel Debré, who in defending himself and de Gaulle even defended Salan, in a way. To the outlandish suggestion (nor was it new) that Debré shared a moral responsibility for Salan and the other insurgent generals by having written, in 1957, as a rather obscure opposition senator in the Fourth Republic, that insurrection for *Algérie Française* was legitimate—as, indeed, it then was—Debré said, nostalgically, candidly, "*Algérie Française!* Who has not hoped for it over the last twenty years?" That it had profoundly "troubled consciences" and caused "bitter difficulties" was self-evident, he said, looking over the court. "*Hélas,* the world has evolved," he went on, decolonization having achieved such force and value that nations resisting it found themselves outside the pale. With Morocco and Tunisia having been given independent status before de Gaulle "was charged with the national destiny in 1958," Debré said, he decided in 1959 that Algeria's self-determination was legitimate and necessary, and in 1961 the French people's massive referendum made it law. This mention of the referendum aroused such a protesting mutter among the pro-Salan standees that the presiding judge threatened to clear the court. "If only one could do that in Parliament," Debré was heard to comment. After the cease-fire, he said, only two paths in Algeria were possible—"the road to reason and the road to folly." Looking coldly at the prisoner, he concluded, "The latter has led to blind criminal terrorism." But Debré's admission that the preservation of *Algérie Française* had been a deep emotional desire and a bitter problem had benefited Salan. He benefited, too, from the testimony of a certain debonair young captain, seven years on combat duty in Algeria, who said explosively of the F.L.N. *fellagha,* "He is a man who cuts everything—trees, roads, a nose, ears, hands, heads." Toward the end of that last tense day in court, Salan's secondary defense lawyer said, in his final, ultra-emotional speech, "It would be impious to take your life. If you must perish, you will mount the cross. But it is we who will be crucified. I salute you, *mon général,* and I cry to you *'Merci, mon général! Adieu, mon général!'* " The prosecuting attorney (who was suffering from a bad bout of sciatica and remained seated during most of his nearly two-hour final address, formally rising only at the end) with refined euphemism did not mention the word "death" in demanding it but referred to it as "the only irreversible punishment." His last words to the prisoner were regarded by many listeners as dubious theology and also as clearly ineffectual legal oratory, since they failed of their aim. Having pleaded with Salan to speak, if only to express his repentance, the prosecutor ended thus: "Do you not fear that, when your hour comes, God Himself, before your unremitting obstinacy—that God Himself will not deign to wipe the tears from your eyes?"

June 13

This is the final fortnight before France's seven-and-a-half-year war with Algeria comes to its factual end and solution. What was so long going on in blood will now finish up on paper, in ballots. On July 1st, the great day, the Algerian electorate—both the dominant Arabs and the minority whites (continually diminished by the daily thousands fleeing in panic to France)—will vote in the self-determination referendum on what form their future Algeria is going to take. That is to say, they will give their answer, which is sure to be affirmative, to the single question of vital interest to President de Gaulle, which constitutes his referendum's entire program: "Do you wish Algeria to become an independent state, coöperating with France under the conditions defined in the declarations of March 19, 1962?"—meaning the Evian accords. The Moslem masses being mostly illiterate, few of them can have read the Evian agreement, but they all know about the desirability of becoming an independent state, which is what their men in the F.L.N. were fighting and dying for all that time, and the answer will be yes, we wish it—even with France tied like a tricolor tail to their high, politically ambitious kite. The public announcement last Sunday of the single question marked the official opening of the referendum campaign. Special itinerant voting bureaus are to be set up in the oasis *départements* in the Sahara, where the population is small and scattered—the only *départements* where women vote. By Saharan tradition, the Tuareg women are the tribe's militants and go unveiled, and now that there is a ballot, they will use it. The ballots come in two colors—white for "Yes" and rose for "No," which seems an odd psychological *gaffe* on the part of de Gaulle's election agents. The white ballots have *"oui"* printed on them, and also transliterations of *"Kab-el"* and *"Kag-lah,"* which are Arabic and Kabyle, respectively, for "Yes."

Half a dozen political parties—most of them exclusively Moslem and all of them favoring a "Yes" vote—are active in the referendum campaign, the dominant one being the Front de la Libération Nationale, whose F.L.N. army made the war. Then there is the Parti du Peuple Algérien, led by the picturesque old Messali Hadj, formerly a Communist, now a Trotskyite, and the revolutionary founder, years ago, of the Mouvement National Algérien, the first ever organized to demand liberty, for which he was eventually arrested by the French and until recently kept in *résidence surveillée* on the lonely Breton Ile d'Aix. He was politically eliminated during the Algerian war by the new young bourgeois leaders, Mohammed Ben Bella and Benyoussef Ben Khedda, and is now rather a sad elderly nostalgic figure but still of some influence. The French

Communists and Socialists have each installed a campaign party, so as to have a finger in the Arab pie. There is no all-European party, which de Gaulle has stated he regrets, because it leaves incomplete the total representation he so clings to as a fetish of democracy.

June 26

Rosamond and Georges Bernier, editors of *L'Œil,* most intelligent and beautifully edited monthly art review here, have opened under its name an elegant new picture gallery in a huge, romantic Left Bank mansion at 3 Rue Séguier, around the corner from Picasso's atelier in the Rue des Grands Augustins. *L'Œil's* initial exhibition is a tribute to another art magazine, the famous, influential *Minotaure,* of the Paris nineteen-thirties. It was unique as the avant-garde progenitor and purveyor of the ideas of the Surrealists, then in their second and matured period—that militant group which, as you may recall, for the two decades between the wars was the strongest, most stimulating power combine in the French artistic field of new painting and writing. *Minotaure* served as a luxurious illustrated almanac—as often as there was enough cash to print it, which meant irregularly; in its nearly seven years of existence (from 1933 into 1939) there were only eleven issues, all bibliophile items today. Its founders were André Breton, Surrealism's Pope; the poet Paul Eluard; and two leading art-book publishers of Paris—the Swiss Albert Skira and the Greek Tériade. *L'Œil's* exhibition is made up of twenty-nine paintings and some sculpture, all of which were either reproduced in *Minotaure* or created during its regime by artists who were working Surrealistically at the time—by Picasso, Max Ernst, Tanguy, Arp, Miró, Chirico, Dali, Duchamp, Man Ray, Magritte, Brancusi, Giacometti, Masson, and Matta. Seen all together, they make a rare, historic show. Dali, of course, was expelled from the group as he approached the level of department-store decoration; Chirico left it for his private medieval limbo; Picasso moved on to his production of monsters; and Duchamp ceased painting. Aragon, the group's literary chief and the bitter rival of Breton, departed from its discipline to become a Communist Party *éminence grise;* one or two Surrealist writers were suicides and those of its major disciples still alive today are either venerated authorities or aging artists of international repute. In the gallery's foyer is displayed a row of medallion photographs of their faces when they and Surrealism were young, in the early twenties—faces of vivid, youthful heretics, with the heavy-jowled Breton already looking like a pope in exile, Dali like a picaresque Spanish male beauty, Ernst like an early Dürer drawing.

There are four Picasso contributions to the exhibition, all un-Surrealistic in style—nor is it sure that he was ever a Surrealist at all. Miss Gertrude Stein once authoritatively said, "Surrealism was no help to him." There is a grandiose, virile pastel, from his mythological period of 1933, of a minotaur crouching over a nude goddess, and also his "Portrait de Lee Miller" (now in the London collection of her husband, Roland Penrose), with her features randomly scattered about her face and yet with her identifiable 1937 likeness as the Left Bank American beauty invincibly held captive by his genius. A Brancusi bronze "Bird in Space" is on view, lent by Baron Philippe de Rothschild, who had never heard of the sculptor when he bought it but, as a racing-car enthusiast, responded to its suggestion of speed. The three Max Ernst canvases—the gigantic "Paradis," "La Joie de Vivre," and "Les Jardins des Hespérides"—demonstrate his superior aptitude for Surrealist art: his power of painting like a poet; his mastery of enigma, of the debris of dreams; his modest eroticism (libertinage being one of Surrealism's tenets); and his deep attachment to nature and its mimeticism.

Surrealism is démodé now, but it has left visible marks on French culture and American advertising. It was *au fond* a literary movement that aimed at paralleling itself in art—a doubled intimacy unknown here before, even in the time of the Symbolists. Created around 1924 by Breton, it has been his fame and will be his epitaph. Under his guidance, it seized on elements of the new century, which it aggressively popularized among the intelligentsia, rich or poor, if only by the scandals of its brawls in favor of all that it chose to be interested in. This included the interpretation of Freud, whom Breton personally knew; the sociology of Trotsky, another friend; automatic writing; oneirology; the irrational, the unconscious, and the psychosomatic; hypnotism, hallucinations, and free association; and ethnology as almost an esoteric study. Most of these are conversation pieces everywhere today, but they were not then. The dead writers the Surrealists were closest to were the Marquis de Sade, Rimbaud, Gérard de Nerval (who hanged himself in his top hat), and the so-called Comte de Lautréamont, who was their fetish for his malefic, imaginative creation "Les Chants de Maldoror." An acute international art critic has just commented, "The chief tenet of Surrealism was that contemporary art must be subversive, menacing, and a shock." Though the Surrealists were regarded by the French bourgeoisie as anarchists, they operated as prophets, for prophecy is what most modern art over the past forty years has turned out to be, even when not Surrealistic.

Brittany is now going through its second artichoke war, Artichoke War No. 1 having taken place about this time last year. The plethora of artichokes around St.-Pol-de-Léon, in Finistère, where they are tenderer and have bigger hearts and less spiky leaves than those raised elsewhere, has once more led to surplus, bitterness, a *jacquerie* among the farmers, and strikes among packers at the railroad stations, with some peasants dumping their artichokes by the thousand on the village streets rather than sell them below the established price. What is worse, the discarded chokes have been used as vegetable grenades in the resulting street fights, producing bloody rural faces, calls for the riot police, and official appeals for calm by the Ministry of Agriculture. In nearby towns like Brest and in the regional cigarette factories, tons of the surplus vegetables were offered last week to workers and townspeople for nothing, but they aroused hostility rather than gratitude. One smart worker said to a Paris reporter, "The St.-Polliens have the air of offering us charity. In reality, the chokes they hand out don't cost them anything, because they are subsidized by the government. So it's only a way to unload their stuff, and we taxpayers are the ones who pay." Last year, some members of the Primeuristes Indépendants, or the Independent Growers of Early Vegetables, trucked their artichokes down to Paris and sold them at neighborhood street markets with the old hawker cry of *"Voilà mes artichauts, tendres et beaux!"* Last Wednesday, their more powerful rival, the Société d'Intérêt Collectif Agricole, cut down the telephone poles outside St.-Pol, Plouescat, Plouvorn, and other villages, and laid them across the roads to prevent anybody from bringing his glut of artichokes to town to sell at less than the minimum price of forty centimes a kilo—about four American pennies a pound. The Primeuristes Indépendants, who had apparently planned to do just that, then telegraphed President de Gaulle, declaring that they "placed themselves under his high authority" to preserve their safety, "imperilled by the collectif's reign of terror."

Continued bloodshed, the blowing sky-high of buildings that represent and house civilization in cities, the miscarriages of justice, and the second thoughts about where justice is even to be found in a great country like France, which has seen the dignity of ending its own war removed from its control and given in part to men in prison—all these confusions, whether going on here or in Oran or Algiers, are like an amateur script for some kind of coarse, comic charade in which even anger, hatred, and desperation are the qualities of buffoons. The letter that ex-General Salan wrote a few days ago from his solitary-confinement cell in Fresnes Prison, advising the O.A.S. terrorist army he created and led to befriend the new Algerian independence, and begging the Algerian whites to stay by their cities and their land, largely ruined at his orders, was an ironic sequel to the earlier one from the same prison by ex-General Jouhaud, who offered the same solemn good advice—but to Salan himself, and at a moment when such good advice seemed a comrade's treachery. These elements have almost made judges out of the two criminals and traitors in finally settling France's war. Though it was France that the Arab rebels fought for seven years in pursuit of their independence, it is with the army of France's new enemy—the white French O.A.S., formerly high in France's own army—that the F.L.N. Arab forces have lately been agreeing to negotiate the peace. There is no common sense in the vital seriousness of all that has been going on. That the vote in the referendum to be held in a few days in Algeria will be overwhelmingly in the affirmative is right now the only seemingly certain consequence of this long colonial war, so often referred to by General de Gaulle as "*cette guerre absurde*." The making of the peace has been permitted to be far more absurd.

July 10

The end at last of the Algerian war, on Sunday, July 1st, in the overwhelming self-determination vote in Algeria, and its transformation into official Algerian independence on Tuesday in Paris seemed almost a precipitation of history. It was the longest war that France has known in the West in modern times, and, during its last two or three years, the most generally despised by most of the French.

The only residents here who celebrated Tuesday with joy were the Algerian Arabs. After all, they had won—or, at any rate, had received what they had been fighting for. To honor their independence, they gave gigantic, orderly free feasts in their various Paris neighborhoods. In the poor Algerian quarter behind the Panthéon, in a humble Arab restaurant that normally serves a dozen *couscous* an evening, hundreds of plates were served free, like manna, from noon on, and any of us foreigners or French who had been the restaurant's clients were welcome. In the Rue de la Goutte-d'Or, the *médina* of Paris, just below Montmartre, the hospitality from noon on was more luxurious. This was the center for the gargantuan free victualling supplied by the Fédération de France du F.L.N. for its celebration—tons of semolina for the *couscous;* hundreds of sheep carcasses; hundreds of sacks of white and broad beans, of onions, tomatoes, and cucumbers for relishes, and of pastry flour for the *baklava* and fritters; and bales of mint for mint tea. Forty *médina* restaurants and cafés had been mobilized for the gratis hospitality (and the patriotic night of unpaid work in the kitchens and back courts that preceded the feasting), and for once the rather sorid Drop of Gold Street looked gay by night. There was no wildness of joy or shouting crowds on it—only the Arab men, dressed, if young, in their best French clothes, with all ages in a voluble state of disciplined excitement that was more impressive than noise. The tawdry Oriental arches over the café exteriors were hung with streamers and flags, and inside, behind the bars (serving free orangeade), among bouquets of greenery and more flags, patriotic mottoes were written on the fancy tiled walls in Arabic and sometimes in French, of which the most popular declared, "There is only one hero—the people," and a tragic one said, "Two million dead and an ocean of blood so Algeria might live free." Everywhere in the bars were amplifiers playing "La Marche des Moudjahidines" (the Arabic word for volunteers in the war), with its long, wavering musical phrases and flowery falsetto improvisations like garlands of Oriental melody. The most dramatic musical number—or so it was explained by a Kabyle acquaintance—was recorded in the Aurés Mountains when the men were about to go into battle. You hear them first called to prayer by the shrill voice of the mufti, because if they die as pious Moslems they will go straight to Mohammed's paradise; then comes a roll of machine-gun fire and, suddenly, the song itself—rhythmic, melancholy, and stirring, to a semi-French, Orientalized marching tune—which the Arabs in the bars each time joined in singing softly.

This was their new national anthem, composed in clandestinity.

The *pieds-noirs,* or white French Algerians, are still flowing in a panic tide across the Mediterranean to Marseille, in terror of possible retribution from the Algerian knives. It is this difference in the age of the two civilizations involved in the Algerian war that adds possible leftover horrors to the peace. When the war began, the majority of the impoverished, illiterate millions of Algerian natives were still at about the level of 1000 A.D., or the time of the Crusaders, with an inexpensive knife blade as their rational weapon, whereas the French Army's napalm fire bombs, bazookas, and high-powered guns achieved death at a distance, in the civilized twentieth-century manner. Actually, over the nearly eight years of fighting, the Arab peasants in the F.L.N. Army were understandably more modernized by their Czech guns and other Iron Curtain matériel than by the more than one hundred years of French occupation. More than a quarter million of the former million *colon* whites are now in France, and are being daily added to. They are a loss down there and not popular here.

September 12

The first major French film of the opening season stars Brigitte Bardot, directed, as in the beginning, by her inventor and first husband, Roger Vadim. It is called "Le Repos du Guerrier," or "Rest for the Warrior"—the title of a poignant, realistic first novel written a few years ago, apparently as a painful autobiography, by Christiane Rochefort. The book bore all the marks of tragic personal truth—the story of a young Parisian bourgeoise who goes to a provincial town to claim a modest inherited property; puts up at an inn, where by accident she opens the wrong bedroom door and discovers a young man dying as a suicide from an overdose of drugs; is responsible for saving his life, that of a sadist and drunkard; and is thereafter dragged down with him in the course of love. The arterial lifeblood of this novel Vadim has professionally set flowing on film in color. It displays Bardot as what she was born—a member of the well-off new Parisian bourgeoisie, though devoid of its official cliché of good manners—and no longer the exhibitionistic pretty rebel of her early film days. This new film does show her nude, though—three or four times—with beautiful, dignified photography.

In her new manner, Bardot is truculent, for in this film she is also very rich. There are brief moments in a series of bedroom scenes in which, in physical psychology and under excellent Vadim direction, she becomes the complete, competent little actress.

It was undeniably a shock last week for French radio listeners to hear the unmistakable Presidential baritone of General de Gaulle speaking to the massed citizens of Bonn during the first stage of his stately visit to Federal Germany, and saying, *"Wie sollte ich nicht bis in die tiefste Seele verspüren, wie bedeutungsvoll und ergreifend meine Anwesenheit . . ."* ("How should I not feel in the depths of my soul," *und so weiter*)—adding, for good measure, *"Es lebe die deutsch-französische Freundschaft!"* ("Long live German-French friendship!") Parisians seemed to have been unaware that he spoke German at all. His incredible mnemonic feat, at his age, of committing to memory his speeches *auf Deutsch* soon aroused a pride here in his excellently cultured and educated French brain that was as acute as the irritation aroused by much of what he said, when it was translated so his compatriots could understand it. His speech to the officers of the War College in Hamburg (and this one was in French) was considered outrageous here—that he should have said, with a high Army man's complacency (and, indeed, with a historian's accuracy), that the Germans "had never accomplished great things without something military having eminently participated in it." To the workmen at the vast Thyssen steelworks he said, again in German, "I wanted to come to you here where you work to give you friendly greetings from the French. For Charles de Gaulle to be here, and for you to give him so cordial and moving a welcome, is proof that confidence really exists between our two peoples." (The workers, it seems, unaccustomed to his protocolar language, were astonished to hear him refer to himself in the third person, as if he were absent, instead of standing there before them—so tall, one young workman said, that it was as if "the Eiffel Tower were visiting us.") The emotional, complimentary tone of all he said to and about the Germans, in his references to brotherhood and profound admiration, also offended many French. One Paris paper scathingly referred to his German trip as "Operation Seduction." An English correspondent in Paris said of his sentiments that "no other Frenchman would have dared employ such language." It must be added that at first the German population and press took him with a grain of salt;

the *Süddeutsche Zeitung* printed a delightful cartoon of old Adenauer in a top hat hanging an enormous welcoming wreath of laurel on the end of de Gaulle's enormous nose. At the last of his visit, however, the Germans were in a state of mob acclaim for him, reminding one cynical Bavarian of the response that Hitler formerly aroused.

What *Le Monde* had to say on de Gaulle's return to Paris was what French public opinion was waiting for, nor was it very generous. "Only the poor in spirit," it began, "could fail to rejoice in General de Gaulle's journey through Germany. That theatricality has played its part is not surprising. Weaned for years from spectacular political manifestations, the German crowds applauded a great and prodigious actor, and if they have to have a hero, even for a day, better a French general than a Bavarian corporal. In any case, through de Gaulle's person, it is the French people who, despite themselves, feel flattered and satisfied. All this is pleasant, sympathetic, and fragile," the paper went on with sharp disdain. The French people themselves, after three wars with the Germans in the past century, and two defeats, are immeasurably relieved that at last these two remarkable old men—or perhaps only their own astonishing septuagenarian—have tried to bury the hatchet for our time, which seems forever, the French people being convinced that though Europe cannot be constructed on two nations alone, it cannot be reconstructed without France and Germany in amity.

Owing to the second attempt on de Gaulle's life just before he went to Germany, and to the fact that nobody lifted a hand against him there (where he was discreetly accompanied, it was reported, by a German medical-corps unit carrying blood of his type, just in case), the French, on his return safe and sound, and after what he had accomplished, are saying, as they so repeatedly are driven to say, how difficult it would be to do without him—and, indeed, how hard it is to get along with him, too. This last new worry refers, naturally, to his announced project of assuring his successor, whoever he may be, to the governing of France by a vote of universal suffrage—preceded, of course, by the customary referendum to validate his project in the first place. Once again he plans to bypass Parliament, this time even to the point of reorganizing the government itself, and once again Parliament has declared that it will fight for its old rights, which none of its constituents fancy it will.

The immediate concentration of gratitude over the fact that de

Gaulle has not been assassinated as yet had a focus last week in the assizes court in the town of Troyes, where those would-be assassins who arranged to blow up his car at Pont-sur-Seine last September while he was passing on his way home to Colombey were being tried. There were many peculiarities about this trial, in which the leader of the murderous band—a certain Henri Manoury, former insurance salesman—had his head saved by Maître Jean-Louis Tixier-Vignancour, who also saved ex-General Salan's head, and who, being a rabid anti-Gaullist himself, makes a specialty of using his thespian gifts and Machiavellian legal talents as defense lawyer for such subversive criminals. He saved Manoury by insinuating that three members of de Gaulle's official Elysée family of functionaries had secretly been forewarned of the plot—if they were not a party to it. So susceptible are average French people now to suspicion of corruption and treachery in high places that the jury was influenced to the extent of leaving Manoury's head on his shoulders and giving him incarceration for only twenty years. And so great was the heat of the trial during its last days that when a witness happened to mention an outrage suffered at the same time by the French consul-general in Algiers, who, it seems, was undressed in public and beaten, Tixier-Vignancour insolently declared, "The posterior of a consul-general is never the symbol of France but is indeed the symbol of the present regime." He was not ordered from court or asked to apologize. During the Troyes trial, most of the would-be assassins who made the second attempt on the General's life, on August 22nd—this time by shooting machine guns at him (and Mme. de Gaulle) at Petit-Clamart while his car was once more en route to Colombey and home—were arrested, giving an extra, unneeded, shocking fillip to the melodramas of French justice and governing today.

September 26

Watching and listening to President de Gaulle on television last Thursday evening, as he instructed his nation on the special system by which he wishes his eventual successor to be elected and to function, one found it impossible, even three years in advance of that event, not to pity the incoming new President of the Republic in 1965, whoever he may be—floating out of his depth in the historic, turbulent wake that will be left behind by the unique, iconoclastic, enormous figure of *le grand Charles,* to whom the newcomer will be inevitably compared, if only as a form of intense relief to the anti-Gaullist minority and to practically all the politicians of France. For his TV speech, possibly his most important single selling talk since he took power, de Gaulle was in extra-good form, the mobile, elderly, unfatigued thespian face and the bold, inventive, ripe mind both seeming refreshed by his recent triumphal German outing. What he was pressing the French nation to accept was what he originally called (as you may remember) the American Presidential system of government, now become his own idea, to which he has just added our American system of electing our Presidents by universal suffrage instead of by an autonomous body—uninstructed by the voters—such as elected de Gaulle himself in 1958. These innovations, if made permanent, as he plans, would completely transform the entire political life of contemporary France. Both these American methods could be initiated, de Gaulle claims, by a referendum of the people, and without Parliament's assent, through the famous Article XI, on the organization of public powers, in de Gaulle's own made-to-measure, supposedly rigid and foolproof constitution, admittedly one of the best-drawn-up that modern France has had. In outrage, all the political parties (except, naturally, his own loyal, rather meek group, the U.N.R.) have unanimously declared that what he proposes would be a grave constitutional violation—one of the few acts that French politicians regard as heinous. Furthermore, de Gaulle's plan for an Americanized President would make the President so far superior in power to the Parliament that Parliament would perhaps be rated even lower in value in the future than it is now, under de Gaulle himself, whose high notions of the American President's supremacy over Congress seem in many ways to have little to do with the realities in our White House.

De Gaulle's harsh comments on Thursday against French politics and their politicians did nothing to soothe the latter. His optimistic determination to further rescue his beloved France by leaving it with something more solid in the way of a future government than the short-lived, dying-duck, Parliament-run governments of the past logically forced him (and how he relished it!) to enumerate the appalling situations they used to lead to—"the chronic confusion and perpetual crises" that periodically paralyzed the country, and "the abyss awaiting France if, unhappily, it were to fall anew into the sterile, ludicrous political antics of yesteryear." He also deplored France's curse of political divisionism, meaning the half-dozen or more political parties demanded by Frenchmen's fundamental inability to agree with each other on much of anything, to which de Gaulle himself has added three more divisions—those who revere him as a savior, those who do not trust him because of his autocratic Caesarism, and those, alas, who so hate him that they try to assassinate him.

The blast that his speech received from the major political parties, the political leaders, and the newspapers seemed the most united and hostile ever directed at him since he became President. Parliament's ancient, most authoritative deputy, the tiny Paul Reynaud, of the Indépendants, unexpectedly said of de Gaulle's projects, "Government by President works badly in the United States and would work much worse in France." Maurice Faure, leader of the Radicals, said, "No jurist in the world would swallow de Gaulle's interpretation of his own constitution." The Communist *Humanité* imaginatively declared that his scheme for a popularly elected Presidential government amounted to "a revival of the monarchic principle of divine right." The Socialist journal, *Le Populaire,* ironically jeered, "Long live personal power!" *Combat,* the morning paper of the intelligentsia, said that his election project laid the basis for a *"monocratique"* regime, and the ever-influential, stately *Le Monde* feared an excess of *"monocratie,"* neither of these words being listed in the new and remarkably up-to-date 1962 Petit Larousse dictionary, though at this point in de Gaulle's career, apparently, they should be.

October 4

Now that Parisians are home from their vacations, they can enjoy fine sights they never saw before in the middle of their own city. The *blanchissage,* or façade-washing, of the major elderly historic buildings radiating from the Louvre, which was begun in June, 1961, as a five-year program of aesthetics, by M. André Malraux, State Minister of Cultural Affairs, is now well along its course. The result is superb, at last popular even with the ordinary public, which feared that the sense of French history would be washed away with the dirt. Cleanliness has restored the architectural youth of these majestic piles, and one sees them in their original fresh, pale sixteenth- to eighteenth-century grandeur, as if one had the ocular privilege of being several hundred years old. This summer's really glorious revelation via soap and water was the intricate beauties, previously black and unintelligible through time, of the Cour Carrée, that huge square inner court of the Louvre, which few tourists—footsore from the picture galleries—ever have the strength to walk back over the cobblestones to view. It is the greatest art exhibition in Paris right now, and should be so advertised this winter and the next few springs and summers. (It will stay clean a longish time, being sheltered from the motor fumes of the streets outside and being prohibited to cars.) The chef-d'œuvre of the French Renaissance, it was in part carved by the great sculptor Jean Goujon himself, and its pristine complex incised beauties are now clearly legible on the three-story, almost blanched stone walls—a carved mixture of pagan gods, statuesque goddesses as caryatids, bearded Greek philosophers, fat cupids, and flower garlands, with the ciphers and initials of all the kings for whom the Louvre was built (from François I and Henri II through Louis XIV) visible amid rows of pilastered Corinthian columns. The famous, elegant Perrault outside portico, across from the church of St.-Germain-l'Auxerrois, has been cleaned, and so has the Madeleine. Its dirty dignity gone, it now looks attractive, even though cleaners in green oilskins are still scrubbing, with hoses and little rags, the last traces of soot embedded in the runnelled columns, and its distant companion piece, the Palais-Bourbon, or Parliament, is as spotless as if it had never known a political smudge. Other masterpiece buildings cleaned are Mazarin's curvaceous Institut and Louis XIV's Invalides, with its handsome carved ornaments of war and armory such as had crippled the invalids living inside it, and now Richelieu's Palais-Royal garden walls are undergoing the treatment, driving the ordinarily lucky inmates of the coveted apartments mad with flapping rubber curtains, scaffoldings, dripping water, and the omnipresent oilskinned men. Most of these great buildings belong to the state or to the Académie des Beaux-Arts, though there is some private ownership on the Place Vendôme (also being cleaned), where the Morgan Guaranty Trust Company has led the way. What the state, the Beaux-Arts, and the private owners have in common is the high price of the cleaning—nine New Francs, or a dollar-eighty, a square metre for plain soap, water, and scrubbing-brush treatment, and at least thirteen New Francs for cleaning by detergents, which kill the stone disease. Whether Notre-Dame can and will be cleaned—a rumor that has caused considerable excitement in Paris—remains for the ecclesiastics to decide, it being Church property. Laymen seem to think that the job needed for Gothic and gargoyle would take an infinity of time and would cost more than the Church would think it prudent to pay. After all, Notre-Dame has been famous, dirty, and inspiring, for nearly a thousand years.

October 10

It seemed characteristic—and certainly it was an old familiar act—that the first use the French Parliament made last week of its suddenly unloosed political energies after these four inert years under General de Gaulle's autocratic Fifth Republic was to overthrow a government—his government, headed by his Premier, Georges Pompidou. This opening and successful defiance of the all-powerful President de Gaulle took place in that dramatic, historic all-night Parliamentary session which ended shortly before dawn last Friday. Its damaging and, at the same time, liberating results will be spread over the next month and a half, until a French government is put together again, with a newly elected Parliament. But whatever comes now will be only like a postscript to the heroic Fifth Republic.

As harsh, realistic proof that de Gaulle was indeed the savior of France, his sacrosanct salvationist importance has ebbed in the few months of peace since he ended the Algerian war. His solo pattern of governing today's prosperous, revitalized France has seemed increasingly démodé to many of the French. This, combined with his age and the recent appalling and so nearly successful attempts to assassinate him, made imminent the French Parliament's return to the surface of national life, and, unfortunately, the inevitable restoration of some of the bellicose republican practices and politics normal to France—provided that Parliament could find an opening, some chink or hole, in de Gaulle's impervious personal armor for its reëntry. It was this that he supplied by a so-called violation of his own constitution—contemptuously bypassing Parliament and relying only on a coming popular referendum to validate his project for the election of his dynastic Presidential successors. These he proposed to have elected by popular suffrage, in order that they might not be selected by Parliament's politicians. De Gaulle's war against the French politicians has been like a religious war, in which the politicians a fortnight ago suddenly found him guilty of a kind of heresy—a violation of the Sacred Writ of Constitution. Here was their chance to attack him.

That de Gaulle had in truth violated his constitution was also the opinion of France's Council of State (which corresponds to our Supreme Court), of the majority of the Sorbonne law faculty, of leading jurists all over the country, of the powerful French trade unions, and of Paris and provincial newspaper editorialists. It was also the opinion of his two immediate predecessors, ex-Presidents Auriol and Coty, and of that high official who would follow him as a stopgap President if he should be murdered or should die in office—the notable French Guiana Negro M. Gaston Monnerville, long-time president of the French Senate.

All this disapprobation reverberated as cumulative news through the press from one end of France to the other. The only sign that de Gaulle had overheard it at his height was his astute decision to give his nationwide TV speech twice last Thursday—first at 1 P.M., before Parliament convened and started talking against him, and then at eight that night, his usual time. Relayed over the state-owned Radio-Télévision Française, it was one more demonstration of his unique privilege of communication, of personal propaganda, and of influence with his special little nation of eleven million radio owners and three million TV owners, to whom his gifted microphone voice and his dramatic, elderly face, now the visage of France herself, have become exclusive symbols of state leadership. One must understand that the power of his privilege is enhanced at all times by the R.-T.F.'s being a state monopoly and strictly censored, so that, in the ordinary way, no one and nothing subversive or antagonistic to or critical of the state—which means de Gaulle's government and himself—ever gets on the national French air. (However, this monopoly will be temporarily lifted on October 15th, the official opening of the referendum campaign, when his opposition can have its belated say.) De Gaulle's most important announcement in the one-o'clock broadcast, which certainly had some influence on the afternoon Chamber speeches, was his closing solemn threat to the French people that he would retire from their midst if they failed to support him adequately in his now truly vital

October 28th referendum on that Presidential-election project, as much a necessity for his plans for the future of France as it is a measure of his prestige.

All this was the agitating background of the extraordinary Thursday-into-Friday Parliamentary session that brought to the foreground this first organized political defiance of the monumental, solitary *chef d'état*—the first pandemonious, garrulous attack in what has openly become an intense power struggle between him and them, they being the long humiliated and now vengeful "men of politics," as he disdainfully calls them, as if somehow rather illegitimatizing them. The aim of the Thursday session was to pass a motion of censure against de Gaulle's violation of the constitution to carry out his Presidential project as an "opening breach through which, someday, an adventurer might pass"—a remarkably pretty and sinister phrase. He himself was, naturally, absent. At the session's beginning, the deputy-filled hemicycle hummed with revived animation. Once more, Parliament was the disputatious center of Paris, of France. A choice audience was also there assembled, almost as many women as men, drawn by a special appreciation of the unrehearsed, ad-lib drama, in which they could watch and listen to a government that may end in mortal agony among its final and futile political forms of speech—an audience that continuously packed the luxurious visitors' loges and crammed the public gallery's wooden benches beneath the roof during the twelve hours (from four o'clock Thursday afternoon until four-thirty the next morning) of intermittent speeches, debates, shouts, cheers, insults, interruptions, bangings of desk tops, and occasional long suspensions. Then the figures on the overwhelming vote of censure—more than three-quarters of the entire house being in favor—were read aloud, and de Gaulle's government was dead.

Another exceptional thing about this session was that the five traditional old big parties, all quarrelsomely opposed to each other in Parliament in the past, had this time united as an opposition. As their opposition leader they had chosen the Chamber's most brilliant, vivid, quick-tongued orator—the diminutive, sturdy octogenarian Paul Reynaud. Chief of the attack against de Gaulle on Thursday, thirty years ago he had been the first in political circles to discover and admire the then unknown Colonel de Gaulle, with his vain dream of a modern, mechanized French Army. As Premier of France in the early, desperate days of the last war, Reynaud had made de Gaulle Deputy Minister of War; in 1958 he had helped bring him back to power; and recently he had broken with him over republican principles when the General chose as his Premier the estimable Rothschild banker Pompidou, who had never even been in politics, let alone been elected a deputy. Reynaud's Thursday speech glittered with emotion and intelligent substance. Standing at his full brief height on the speaker's rostrum, and as if musing in disillusion over his illustrious former friend who had gradually seized all the functions of government in his own two large hands, he said, "How could we have fallen into such intellectual disorder? It is because General de Gaulle wanted to combine the honors of the Chief of State with the powers of a Premier—to be both Winston Churchill and George VI. . . . To those who say with fright, 'But what if he should leave us?' "—the threat contained in that noon's TV speech—"I say that this fright is not justified unless you doubt France. It is not very deeply patriotic to lose faith in all the French except one. To use this argument does not make one man bigger, it makes one's own country smaller. . . . In all civilized lands, the Parliament represents the nation, with its qualities and defects, its diversities, and even its contradictions. If the Assembly represents the nation, then France is here"—in the hemicycle itself—"and not elsewhere." His final, rather gallant sally was addressed to de Gaulle's Premier Pompidou, listening as if mesmerized on the government's front bench. To him little Reynaud ordered loudly, "*Monsieur le Premier Ministre,* go tell the Elysée that our admiration for the past is intact"—a noble compliment to de Gaulle's earlier days—"but that this Assembly is not degenerate enough to renounce the Republic!" There was then a burst of what the French papers called "*vifs applaudissements prolongés sur les nombreux bancs.*"

A very noticeably high proportion of the thirty-eight speakers listed were from de Gaulle's own party, the U.N.R. These were mostly self-important, inexperienced young men with nothing consequential to say. However, the charge of favoritism was not made until fairly late in the night, when an angry deputy suddenly announced from the floor that the regular nine-thirty TV news—broadcast, of course, by the government and shown all over Paris—had given exactly one and a half minutes of its afternoon Chamber news to Reynaud and his dominant speech; the same to Socialist leader Guy Mollet, his colleague in opposition, who followed him; and a full thirty minutes to Premier Pompidou's exegesis of de Gaulle policies. At this, the Chamber broke into an uproar of boos, shouts, desk thumpings, and angry voices crying *"Voilà le fair play français!"* Pompidou himself seemed both surprised and embarrassed by the discrimination. The Speaker of the Chamber ordered a long suspension to consider what to do, then reported later, to repeated booing, that no TV news at all would be recorded of the evening session's proceedings, which increasingly looked like a defeat for the de Gaulle forces. The session being resumed at midnight, the passage of time was carefully indicated by a change in the attire of the Speaker, young Chaban-Delmas, of the U.N.R., who, sitting aloft in his great chair on the tribune, with his gavel ready to rap to restore order and a bell to clang if the noisy deputies started to get really out of hand, looked as he always does—rather like an expressionless, handsome tailor's dummy. For the afternoon opening, he had worn a very smart black cutaway coat and striped trousers. For the night session, he reappeared, as he invariably does, in full evening rig of tailcoat and a somewhat flamboyant big white butterfly tie. Just before dawn, when he announced the final news, he was probably the only man in the Chamber still immaculate and unwrinkled.

That portion of Pompidou's speech which was devoted to de Gaulle as a man, and was not a defense of his fashion of governing, was bold and touching. In part, he said, "This President of the Republic, General de Gaulle, is not a general in the popular sense that General Bonaparte or General Boulanger must have been. But it is he to whom you all, *Messieurs,* owe not only the restoration of the Republic in 1944 but the saving of the Republic in 1958, and again at the Algiers barricades in 1960, and again in 1961, during the *Putsch* there, and it is not six months since he surmounted the offensive of the O.A.S. Even on the evening of the recent assassination attempt, there was no one who did not feel that with him liberty nearly died. I beg of you at least to temper your words against him with gratitude."

When it was all over, the winning deputies left the Chamber shouting the "Marseillaise," with no unity of rhythm or pitch. In the courtyard outside on the *quai,* across from the illuminated spectacle of the Concorde's pale, cleansed, porticoed buildings, moon-colored just before dawn, a soldier stood in the shadows, with his cape on, his feet spraddled far apart, and his machine gun at the ready in his hands in case there might be the beginning of trouble because of this first decisive political crisis in de Gaulle's Fifth Republic.

The painful news, just announced here, of Sylvia Beach's death sometime last week, alone and for days undiscovered in her small flat above what had been the Shakespeare bookshop premises, is another American epitaph to engrave on the historic Left Bank Epoch of the Twenties, to which she was the hard-pressed presiding hostess, book publisher, book lender, bookseller, and friend, who never failed in any line. Without her, some of those who were becoming great writers could not have written so well, and certainly without her James Joyce's "Ulysses" would not have been published as early as it was. Her eyesight had never been good, and deciphering Joyce's curlicues of crabbed handwriting and interlinear scribblings on his manuscripts and proofs was an exercise of devotion and loyalty that her eyes never recovered from. She was a friend to all of us in Paris who used the pen, no matter how modestly. She was a friend to writing.

October 24

France's present crisis in government seems malapropos. It is a moment when no trouble at all in France would be welcome news. Actually, France's brief and bloodless current difficulties—or at least the first part of them—should be settled over the weekend. On Sunday, the French are to vote yes or no in President de Gaulle's referendum (which proposes the direct election of future Presidents). But this referendum has in the last ten days unfortunately turned into something quite different. It has been transformed into a bitter, explosive plebiscite on the popularity and the merits of de Gaulle himself, and into a violent fight against him personally, which has been nicknamed *La Bataille du Non*. It was launched and is being carried on by the five traditional main political parties of France, temporarily united in this effort of destruction, an all-out national attack of criticism, derision, and even insult against him—by word of mouth, by print and press, and by public meetings—with the politicians battling against him both as a legend and as a leader, and showing a frustrated fury and pent-up hatred that they have never dared to show until now, and whose revealing violence has been a startling surprise. What the politicians actually aim at is to denude him of his glory, to push de Gaulle askew on his pedestal, to drape him in ridicule and precisely laid-on criticism so voluminous that his image can never again seem the same to the voters of France. This iconoclasm is certainly a not unintelligent part of their power struggle going on here, and is due to come to its real head in the November elections of deputies to the new Parliament. This new Parliament cannot be dissolved by de Gaulle for one year, so it is of acute importance politically. What the politicians quite naturally want is to fill this Parliament—to cram it, if they can—with anti-de Gaulle deputies, who will continue in the hemicycle the power struggle over who will govern France: he or they.

To the voters, the de Gaulle referendums are like personal dialogues between him and them, in which he asks them to give him something he especially wants, and over four years they have developed a majority habit of giving it to him, loyally. The only thing that could make the Sunday referendum very serious indeed would be a failure of the affirmative majority to be massive enough to satisfy de Gaulle's present need for increased prestige. In this case, as he candidly threatened in his national broadcast last week, he would at once quit the public scene, never to return from his retirement at, supposedly, Colombey-les-Deux-Eglises.

Either the Gaullist regime or France's outworn but still ambitious political-party structure, now nearly a hundred years old, is bound to be seriously weakened in the next four weeks. What may happen is that the people, out of their proved personal devotion to de Gaulle, will vote this Sunday to keep him in power, and then next month, out of their inherited political affiliations, will elect a strong opposition majority against him in Parliament. Once again, de Gaulle might be able, as he has been over the past four years, to keep them under wraps and quiescent—to dominate them at his distance—but with greater human difficulties this time. He may remain in the saddle, but they will be in rebellion.

In the reports on the Battle of No in the daily Paris press, de Gaulle's detractors have angrily defined him as, variously, a megalomaniac, an egomaniac, a tyrant, a suborner of justice (since he has not obeyed his own decrees), a violator of his own constitution and therefore an illegitimatist, a leader who stuffs the public's head with nonsense, a demagogic flatterer, a strangler of the Republic, an adventurer, an absolutist, an autocrat, a misanthrope, a dictator, and a camouflaged monarch. M. Daniel Mayer, a leading Socialist, has just stated, "De Gaulle risks becoming the von Hindenburg of France." *L'Humanité,* citing his last TV speech, in which he threatened to leave if not supported, riposted with "The sooner the better," as the title of its answering editorial. The morning *Figaro,* though it prints certain polite anti-Gaullisms as part of today's normal news, has tried to remain editorially quasi-loyal to him, but wishes that he had not made so much trouble for himself and everybody else by setting the yes and no French at each other's throat. *Le Monde* also treats him rather strictly. In its Saturday editorial, it frankly said that the yes and no were like Scylla and Charybdis, and that everything depended on whether or not the new Parliament would set up a modern Republic "after the passage of de Gaulle's bulldozer," meaning his referendum. It then added, in insistence, "The referendum's true problem is not to save de Gaulle or to throw him out but to determine the future of the Republic. The worst consequence of a no vote would not be the departure of the General but the inevitable return to the traditional Parliamentary regime—to the certain restoration of the Fourth Republic." The only purely pro-de Gaulle paper in all Paris is the limp, one-page daily *Nation,* operated by the General's rather browbeaten political party, the Union of the New Republic. All the close to a dozen other Paris papers are, if not openly against him, at least not devotedly or continuously for him these days—not by a long shot.

November 7

It is not too late to mention how Paris reacted to the alarming world crisis between President Kennedy and Chairman Khrushchev of two weeks ago, because the Parisians themselves have been so late in putting their minds on it that they have expressed their full opinions only over the last few days. There were, it is true, some earlier snap judgments by the conventionally anti-American intellectual left-wing voices and periodicals here, shouting to the White House "Hands off Cuba!" and jeering at what they called Kennedy's obvious buildup of the whole affair as an electioneering move to help his party in this week's elections. Actually, the only President who used the Cuban tension in this fashion was President de Gaulle, who, in a final TV speech to his own electorate in his recent referendum campaign, alertly warned them that they were living in a dangerous world and had better vote for him massively, so he could take care of them. Indeed, the initial Paris political reaction to the Cuban crisis was a fear not that the whole world might blow up on Monday or Tuesday but that on Sunday Cuba would be a gift of the gods to de Gaulle's referendum, bringing him millions of otherwise wavering votes, which it probably did.

November 21

The single dominant figure in last Sunday's preliminary parliamentary elections, who was not even a candidate and yet won with a landslide of ballots all over France, was President Charles de Gaulle. Actually, it was, of course, his party, the Union pour la Nouvelle République, which, as the political go-between, received the millions of votes, but since they were meant strictly for him, they made him the utterly unexpected transcendent and spectacular winner. The U.N.R. received five and three-quarters million votes, or almost thirty-two per cent of all those cast—a startlingly high figure for France at any time, and especially now, considering the complexities of the competition. Of all the traditional old-line parties, only the Communists gained, and even the Communists—for a decade called *"le premier parti de France,"* because incomparably the most numerous—lost their title to the Union for the New Republic, now become France's first party.

According to the dazed Paris interpretation of all this, de Gaulle's victory can be attributed in part to his intelligent sense of provocation, which made of this election a national crisis, and to his brilliant, classic capacity for aloof, superior planning. Already it seems clear that he did not win the election on his legendary personal popularity alone, today worn thin by the pressures of ingratitude, legitimate criticism, and time. He won, in great part, on the unpopularity of Parliament. There is here a long, unabating antiparliamentarianism, a form of political non-belief held by millions of French citizens of all classes, lodged in their minds by memories of the shambles and national humiliations in governing that were perpetrated by parliamentary politicians during the inefficient, confused Fourth Republic—and the scandalous, wicked Third Republic, if their recollections go back that far. This week's shattering blow against Parliament—at least in its previous, too familiar form—was the result of a manifest lack of faith or interest or hope in it as the quasi-sacred political machinery of France. As soon as the election results were published on Monday morning, the Paris Bourse rose four per cent, and Switzerland cancelled its weekend selling orders.

December 6

As if in sudden recognition of the fact that there are more women in France than men (they outvoted the men seven to six in the recent parliamentary elections), for the first time in French publishing history three of the main year-end literary prizes, including the Prix Goncourt, have been given to women writers. The most stimulating literary criticism annually connected with the Goncourt Prize rarely concerns the novel that has just won it. The criticism is almost invariably directed against the Prix Goncourt itself as an institution—a vestigial, erratic, and powerful publicity enterprise that, merely by tradition, can once a year turn a book into the national best-seller. As preparation for the recent Goncourt Prize day, a round robin of critics publicly declared that no intellectuals ever read the Goncourt selection anyhow. In the literary, and even in the political, weeklies, critics vented their customary vexation at the Goncourt's basic weakness—the mysterious lack of critical acumen displayed by the Goncourt jurymen, themselves respected writers, playwrights, and academicians. In *Les Nouvelles Littéraires,* France's most notable literary critic, Pierre de Boisdeffre, sarcastically inquired, "When a writer of talent is given the Prix Goncourt, isn't it because of some misunderstanding? Have Gide, Mauriac, Giono, Montherlant, Saint-Exupéry, Sarte, and Camus been the losers in any way in never having been distinguished by this honor? The novels that in September start piling up"—three hundred is the average number submitted by their publishers for the various November prizes—"are not books but lottery tickets," in which luck, not literature, will win.

This new Prix Goncourt novel bears the bitter title "Les Bagages de Sable," or "Luggage Filled with Sand," and was written by a Polish émigré, Mme. Anna Langfus. Under the heading "A Charity Goncourt," one critic exceptionally and cruelly wrote of it and of her, "The story is poor, the writing is poor, and the author is also poor, no doubt." The Goncourt Prize automatically sells around a hundred and fifty thousand copies, bringing in royalties equivalent to about forty thousand dollars—perhaps the only cheerful item that can be associated with this painful and obviously truthful book. It concerns an impoverished Polish refugee in Paris, so scarred and sickened in her memory and body from the brutalities suffered during the war in Poland that even love, when offered to her—only by an elderly lover, it is true—fails to heal her.

With the opening today of the Fifth Republic's recently elected new Parliament, which contains, for practically the first time in the history of all of France's Republics, a majority party—de Gaulle's, of course—it is conceded here that France's republican system, as it has interruptedly been known for the past hundred and seventy years, has now come to a full stop. Something fundamental is changed in France. The three elements of French history that the French today still seem proudest of are Louis XIV, the French Revolution, and the fact that France is a republic. Yet the French have always experienced a great deal of difficulty living in and with their Republics, which so far have always turned into something else. The First Republic, of 1792, in twelve years turned into Napoleon's Empire. In 1848, the Second Republic, of almost four years, turned into another Bonaparte empire, enthusiastically voted for by a landslide of Frenchmen. In 1870, France began "going into the Third Republic backward," as the phrase then was—meaning reluctantly, since another monarchy had been hoped for by most leaders except Gambetta. The corrupt, tough Third Republic (nicknamed "La Gueuse," or "The Slut," and the longest regime that France has ever known since that of that great Louis XIV) ended in 1940 in the Vichy state of Maréchal Pétain, the only Frenchman who ever survived a hundred and seven French governments and founded one of his own, the hundred and eighth. In 1944 came de Gaulle's Provisional Government, and in 1946 came the Fourth Republic, which lasted twelve weak and addled years before it fell into de Gaulle's Fifth Republic, now four and a half years old. The general tenor of the current political commentators has been that the weakness of this country's Republics and Parliaments lies in the fatal gift of the French for individualism and for never agreeing with one another. As de Gaulle himself dryly said, "How can you govern a country that has two hundred and forty-six varieties of cheese?"

1963

January 2

The worst of the exceptional cold snap here, and all over Europe, exactly filled the holiday week from Christmas Eve through New Year's Eve, delaying letters, greeting cards, telegrams, and telephone calls, stalling buses and trains on frozen roads and rails, closing down airports crippled by icy runways, and somewhat freezing the travellers' seasonal spirit of joy and good will. Snow avalanches impeded the journeys of impatient skiers; snowslides closed the St.-Gotthard Tunnel, stranding thousands of home-going Italians. Italy had its worst cold wave in a hundred years. France had its own South and North Poles of cold: the southwestern part of the Côte d'Azur, centering on Marseille, which was snow-bound, and the northwestern slice of Brittany, where, as the French phrase it, *il a gelé partout à pierre fendre*—it froze hard enough all over the place to crack the very rocks. The canal that connects the Rhone and the Rhine was frozen between Strasbourg and Neuf-Brisach, and the waterway that runs from Belgium down into France was clogged with hundreds of barges of coal, which Paris needed, sitting paralyzed. The city had the coldest Christmas Day that it has ever known. To Paris motorists, little used to struggles with ice on forest highways or to skirmishes with snow, such weather seemed dramatic. Guests from the city arrived belated and extra-hungry for the midday festal turkey dinners in suburban country houses, where the bathroom pipes were mostly frozen. Because of thawing and refreezing, provincial roads became so dangerous for motoring that President de Gaulle, after his holiday at his house in Colombey-les-Deux-Eglises, which has no railway connection, returned to Paris in a special train on the nearby Troyes-Chaumont line. The ice on the ponds was thick enough to give young people happy days of skating, and the deer in the various forests had a quiet holiday, since hounds could not follow their scent where it had snowed, and the frozen ground was too dangerous for horses to jump or gallop on.

June 19

President de Gaulle is periodically still the most interesting Frenchman of all France to the French, and doubtless to himself as well, almost constantly. For nothing interests him like French history, and he is the only one with the power to continue making it. If one returns to France after a six-month absence, one finds that nothing consequential has changed in the interim except under his impulsion. He has all the causal elements between his large hands and within his broad imagination, and he represents the successful results. This last week, he made a vital segment of new history, which is not only French history but also European. After Parliament spent all last Thursday in often brilliant scathing debate, led by the minority old-guard Opposition—an opportunity for recrimination against de Gaulle, his deputies, and his policies such as the minority rarely has a chance at—the Chamber, balloting at midnight, gave a strong three-to-one vote (with the minority's unexpected assistance) for the ratification of de Gaulle's extraordinary Bonn treaty of Franco-German collaboration, which Parliament had been called together to consider. This treaty not only buries the hatchet on paper between France and Germany but invokes the establishment of Franco-German friendship like a new bridge across the Rhine. Many deputies and also many bourgeois sections of French society felt cold, suspicious, and grudging about offering even to the Western remnant of the former Nazi nation this Treaty of Coöperation, its official title. The former French Premier, old Guy Mollet, the Socialist Party Chief, opened the attack by caustically telling the Gaullist government bench, "Your only interest in Europe is in a balance of power—an English-style Europe without the English." Then de Gaulle's Prime Minister, Georges Pompidou, the former Rothschild banker who in a short time has become an alert, able Chamber debater, invoked the United States' Cuban crisis as proof that the free world's situation in the nineteen-sixties has changed. Pompidou explained that in the United States' recently revised defense program for herself and for her allies, the proportion seemed like that in the recipe for the legendary old-world lark pâté —one lark to one horse—and added, "I must say that a lark for our defense is not a sufficient guarantee." To American and English listeners present, Premier Pompidou's most dazing contribution to this public session, which aired the Opposition's many criticisms of the Franco-German coöperation treaty (although the deputies had no power either to change or to amend it), was his patient, courteous reminder to one captious anti-Gaullist deputy that, after all, "the government need not have submitted this treaty to Parliament. But it has done so." It is with such a sovereign free hand that President de Gaulle can create his continuing French history.

This year, the government's annual estival art attraction for Parisians and visitors is a centenary exhibition of the works of the prodigious Romantic painter Eugène Delacroix, who died here in the summer one hundred years ago. It is an extremely thorough collection. Five hundred and twenty-nine items, featuring his major grandiose pictures surrounded by their conceptual sketches, are on view in the Louvre's Salon Carré and Grande Gallerie (both badly lighted); his drawings are displayed in the Cabinet des Dessins; across town, his black-and-whites are on show in the Bibliothèque Nationale; the Parliament and Senate libraries are open to show his frescoes; his studio in the Place Furstenberg has been unlocked for sightseers; and a provincial exhibition of his paintings is in the Beaux-Arts at Bordeaux, where his father was a prefect under Napoleon, when the painter was a little boy. Because none but normal attention has been paid Delacroix for years, Paris cultural weeklies have gone into a Delacroix delirium. *Les Nouvelles Littéraires* featured him on thirteen of its vast pages, offering articles on Delacroix the Romantic painter, the writer, the dandy, the political revolutionary, and the colonial traveller; on his love affairs (which were few); on his paternity (apparently he was not the bastard of the famed Talleyrand, as was rumored by Mme. de Staël, but the son of his own dull, officious father); on his portraits and his battle scenes; and on his love for the music of his young friend Chopin, whose piano he had brought over to his own studio, so that the hypersensitive Pole could compose there in peace, away from the embraces of George Sand.

"My pictures achieve tension," Delacroix wrote. According to French analyses, he melted neoclassic formalism into light, subjected form to color, started the modern evolution in French painting that culminated in Monet, and affected Impressionism, Fauvism, van Gogh, and Cézanne. His compositions were too strong but glorious, whether depicting man, beast, or history—ancient or of his own time, for he was sensitive to both. It is these familiar history scenes that are the most popular and worthy in the Louvre show. He used the 1830 Paris revolution, which he saw but did not participate in, in his canvas called "July 28, Liberty Leading the People," with a top-hatted citizen on the barricades bearing a musket, and bare-breasted Liberty triumphantly holding the French flag. His sumptuous "Death of Sardanapalus," most grandiose of these anecdotal masterpieces (some of which need cleaning), with its amplitudes of scarlet, female flesh, and drama, was the scandal of the 1827 Paris Salon. When His Majesty Louis-Philippe, who bought Delacroix pictures for his royal gallery, sent the Comte de Morny to Morocco after the French conquest of Algiers, the artist accompanied him, and was thus the first French colonial painter—of caïds, of warriors in burnouses and sashes, of Arab horses. The odalisques that Matisse later imagined and painted in Paris, Delacroix painted in their corporeal reality in North Africa.

August 6

Since the first of this week, Paris has been what is annually called empty, about two million of its three million inhabitants being someplace else. August is like a form of restful paralysis for Paris, left with almost no motion: with nearly no traffic (including nearly no taxis) and nearly no modest restaurants open; with most grocers, butchers, bakers, and small shops of all sorts padlocked tight; with those minority Parisians who are still in residence seeming to remain indoors, as if under a permanent curfew; with parks almost naked of children; but with the stony, shady riversides of the Seine still trodden by a small parade of lovers, arm in arm—the perpetual fiancés of France, embracing and murmuring, content in their quasi solitude.

The widow of Georges Rouault has donated to the French state nearly all the works left unfinished at his death, some lacking only his signature to look completed—an edifying collection, to be added to the Rouaults already owned by the Musée National d'Art Moderne, and thereby make a nucleus for entire Rouault rooms in the new Musée du Xème Siècle, inspired by Minister of Culture André Malraux, which will be constructed, it is now announced, at the Rond Point de la Défense from a design by Le Corbusier. This will be the first great post-war museum in Paris. M. Malraux's other Ministerial triumph this week is the announcement that his anachronistic project for a painting by the fantasist Russian modern Marc Chagall to be affixed as a new false ceiling over operagoers' heads in the Paris Opéra will soon be under way. Envisioned by the Minister two years ago, the idea aroused such widespread shock that some leading British architects even signed a petition against it, since the Opéra is a unique example of Second Empire theatrical architecture—contestable, perhaps, but homogeneous. The present, original ceiling, by a *pompier* artist named Lenepveu, who also contributed, without distinction, to the decoration of the Panthéon, is so pleasantly innocuous that its subject matter always escapes one. What operagoers fear from Chagall is something characteristically recognizable—a green-faced violinist, perhaps, or donkeys floating in the air.

September 4

Modern French art has proved a remarkable preservative for its three original creators, that historic trio of elderly painters who, when young, fathered it in a triple paternal relationship—Matisse, who engendered the high-colored Fauves in 1905 and lived to be almost eighty-five; Braque, who created the first pure Cubist canvas, "Les Maisons à L'Estaque," in 1908 and died only last week at eighty-one; and Picasso, a few months Braque's senior, who begot proto-Cubism in "Les Demoiselles d'Avignon" in 1907 and still flourishes down in the Midi with mythological protean vigor, the one who has outlived everyone and everything, including his own euphoric painting epochs. Of the three painters, Braque was regarded as the supreme master of composition. In the purely French qualities of taste, measure, and refinement in his still-lifes, so perfectly posed as if to rest in changeless balance through time, he is ranked as the most essentially Gallic artist since Chardin, who died in 1779. By a sort of mimetism, Braque grew to resemble his own pictures, with his paint-white hair and the reminiscent cubic outline in the angular pattern of his handsome face. He was the son and grandson of housepainters and paperhangers in Argenteuil, a Seine river town near Paris, and was fortunately trained in the family trade. Expert in sign painting, he introduced the alphabet into his art like an abrupt intrusion of reality—as in the word "BAL" in his famous "The Portuguese"—and made it almost as distinguishing a mark of early Cubism as the cubes themselves. Accustomed to wallpaper and paste, his artisan hands were expert in the fabricating of those astonishing, impractical Cubist collages of paper pasteups that he and Picasso delighted in.

It was in 1907 that Cézanne's didactic maxim was posthumously published in Paris: "You must see in nature the cylinder, the sphere, and the cone," without mentioning the fourth geometric shape, which led to Cubism. That year, more than half a hundred Cézannes had just been shown in the Paris memorial exhibition that had finally given that dour painter a living public reputation, like an obituary. In the spring of 1908, Braque, who was by then a belated, dissatisfied Fauve, wrestling with wild, bright colors, went to the village of L'Estaque, on the Bay of Marseille, where Cézanne himself had worked, and, in a burst of extended comprehension, painted the revolutionary "Houses at L'Estaque"—brownish cubes floating in levitation among conical green trees. Back in Paris, Picasso was also approaching Cézanne's geometries with "Landscape with Figures," the human beings in it belonging to a new, cylindrical race, embracing in a conical glade. Unbeknownst to each other, the two young artists, both aged twenty-six, were moving toward something that was in the air but that only they were recording. It was later defined by scientists as the "space-time continuum," of which neither of the painters had even heard, nor did they ever define it aesthetically to outsiders, at least during the six years that they subsequently worked and talked together daily in Montmartre. "We said things that nobody else would understand any more and that will end with us,"

Braque declared much later of their conversations while they were painting, under various titles, what looked like Euclidean cubes and sectioned spheres against a background cascade of other cubes, producing an effect of immediate distance and the surprise of space. Among the Cubist masterpieces that Braque painted in 1910—all in museums or great private collections today—were "Still-Life with Guitar," "Woman with a Mandolin," and "Still-Life with Piano (with the keys already like nudes descending a staircase). By 1911, every avant-garde artist in Paris was a Cubist of sorts, to Braque's disgust. By 1912, Cubism had spread around Europe. Braque's works were shown in Munich with the Blue Riders. This analytical Cubism, so hermetic that it was no longer legible even to initiates, was followed by synthetic Cubism, which looked like plane geometry in bright colors—a flat, seductive, decorative patterning of commonplace objects, such as cigarette boxes or rum bottles, that even a child (an artist's child, at any rate) could have identified. Heroic, austere Cubism in space, as Braque and Picasso had practiced it, was already defunct when the war started in 1914, and their intimacy and friendship also failed to survive, perhaps because the epoch itself had perished. Doctrinarily, none of it had lived long. The Fauves—all except Matisse, who had invented them—had ceased being the Wild Beasts of bright colors. Cubism, in its inexplicable mystery and popularity, lasted in its opening unities only a few years. But it lasted long enough to start the death of representational painting, and led to the disappearance of the human being in the abstract painting that finally followed and that both Braque and Picasso, with no notion of guilt, thought pointless as painting and not art in any way. Synthetic Cubism, however, remained in general the personal style of Braque's future art life, in which his *natures-mortes* gave him worldwide fame. Whereas Picasso grew very rich, being protean as time went on, Braque, in his fidelities, became only very well-to-do. When Picasso dies, he will leave a fortune in his enormous collections of his own works. Braque at his death owned few Braques, and not even of the best.

Tuesday night, a spectacular national honor was vouchsafed Braque before the portico in the cleaned, gleaming-white Cour Carrée of the Louvre, opposite St.-Germain-l'Auxerrois, the church of the former kings, which tolled its bells as his bier was placed on a catafalque covered by the tricolor. He had been carried into the Cour Carrée by selected guards from the state museums, flanked by soldiers with torchlights. The Garde Républicaine band played Beethoven's "Funeral March." A silent crowd of many thousands stood assembled in the rain in a touching tribute of adieu. Minister Malraux had created this dramatic tableau of farewell to the painter he so greatly admired as a tribute to him and also to France. In his strange, brief eulogy, the Minister said, "Never before has a modern country rendered such an homage to one of its dead painters. The history of painting has been a long history of disdain, misery, and despair." In Braque's magisterial career and this governmental tribute to it, Malraux said, "the impoverished obsequies of Modigliani and the sinister burial of van Gogh"—one a penurious victim of tuberculosis and the other a suicide—"are revenged."

September 18

President de Gaulle, in his late-July press conference, declared, "France is advancing in great strides along the road to prosperity, and thus to power." "And thus to inflation" was the immediate corollary he should have drawn, to judge by the present hasty efforts of his Cabinet to halt France's dangerously high prices, up sixteen per cent over the past three years, and six per cent in the current twelvemonth. Paris has now been finally appreciated by its own government as the most costly capital in Europe. Because the French people are gourmets and skeptics, what first caught their national eye in the elaborate Gaullist price-stabilization project announced last week was the government promise to hold down the price of beefsteak; their immediate second reaction was to doubt that it could or would be done. To the free-spending French of today, the daily beefsteak has become what Henri IV had in mind when he optimistically talked of a chicken in the pot every Sunday. Other popular general promises are to cancel the rent raise scheduled for January and to punish the scandalous speculators in housing-project real estate by heavily taxing their capital gains. The Communists regard the whole stabilization program as *vernis,* or varnish, meaning eyewash—a cover for the major inflationary cause, which to them is de Gaulle's astronomically costly *force de frappe,* resented not only by Washington but by Moscow (and by a great many pro-NATO French, too) and loyally excoriated by the Communist Party here. The Socialists have called the government inflation-control plan a *"chef d'œvre de duplicité."* *Le Figaro,* the breakfast newspaper of the well-heeled bourgeoisie, merely called it "coherent but timid." This complex plan to check some people's spending and other people's profits from manufacturing what those purchasing people will buy cannot hope to succeed unless it is backed by the majority of the French population. It is taken for granted that no estimate of the plan's possibility of success can even be approximated until de Gaulle appeals to the nation on television, in what may once again be one of the most important addresses of his Presdential career, demanding all his authority, leadership, and powers of persuasion.

October 1

The *nouveau-roman* group has received special notice this year. "La Jalousie," by Alain Robbe-Grillet, which sold about seven hundred copies when printed six years ago by Les Editions de Minuit, is now coming out in a French paperback edition of fifty thousand copies. Mme. Nathalie Sarraute has just published a new book, "Les Fruits d'Or," and it is one of the most interesting that the group has ever produced. She and Mme. Marguerite Duras, the other woman member, seem more gifted at writing than at theorizing about writing, like the new novelist men. The Sarraute book is disconcerting, odd, absorbing. It is a novel about a novel—a novel just published and called "Les Fruits d'Or" ("The Golden Fruits")—and it tells how a coterie of literary French react to this new book, showing as much social intimacy, admiration, spite, flattery, and dislike as if it were a new personality, a person, a lover they wished to cosset or a bore they wanted to shed. The novel becomes a symbolic entity because of the way it is dealt with. Soon it is treated like a work of art—is it one, isn't it one, why or why not? This conception of it allows all the talkers to open up fully, for now they can air what they think about *l'art, la beauté.* All the tinsel, idiocy, or impressive good sense inside their minds comes out in declaration or argument; they talk louder and try to shout one another down, for each person has his or her own truth and tries to destroy the opponent. The struggle is by turns comic, snobbish, shameful, and inspiring. Mme. Sarraute (who was born in Russia) has written with such balance, subtlety, and modulation, such high rushes of mind, that the reader does not tire but floats upon all the words. In the end, the new novel is decided to be *not* a work of art, and is dropped by all except one familiar—one man who thinks that someday, in some way, he can revive it and make it a success once more, for taste is a form of time. This is the end of the book. Its inner technique descends from Virginia Woolf's "Mrs. Dalloway," Mme. Sarraute hopes, "Mrs. Dalloway" being one of her continued admirations. The book is hortly to be published in New York. It must have been very difficult to translate, but Mrs. Maria Jolas (who had much to do with the publication of Joyce's "Finnegans Wake") has put it into English of such verisimilitude that it seems merely orchestrated in another key.

October 23

Edith Piaf died at seven o'clock in the morning in Paris, and a few hours later on that same recent Friday her friend Jean Cocteau, in his nearby country house at Milly-la-Forêt, suffered a final heart attack, provoked by the news of her demise, and himself died at one o'clock. Yet at noon his incisive, familiar voice, already quasi-posthumous, was heard on the national radio among the hastily collected *hommages* to Piaf's memory, saying, "She died as if consumed by the fire of her fame." This epitaph for her had, in fact, been premature, originally prepared and recorded by him a few months earlier, when, as had been frequent lately, she seemed to be perishing and was given up as lost. But on this precise Friday, by a melodramatic coincidence, her intended epitaph suddenly became apropos for them both, in a confusion of mortal destinies.

In their opposite places in the French entertainment world, Piaf and Cocteau were known to millions, and in many cases to the same millions, both being legendary *monstres sacrés* for which the French public, from its intellectual summit to its sentimental depths, tends to share an appetite. In her last Paris triumph at the Olympia Music Hall, all that was left of Piaf was all that had ever counted—her immense, infallible voice, which rose to the roof, carrying its enormous, authentic outcry of banal phrases of anguish over lost loves, and poignant despair of happiness that would never arrive. Ravaged, ill, bundled in her customary modest black dress, her pallid little moon face set in its sad, nocturnal smile, she tottered—her thin legs supporting her in faltering obedience to her courage—across the stage to the microphone, to which she clung, and then her voice, that great remnant of her life, burst forth. Her rhythm was always like a beating pulse; she was the unassailable artist, raucously singing her *véridique* songs of truth about her own ancient class, the Paris poor. The misery of her youth became her repertoire. She was born on a sidewalk in Belleville, with two policemen acting as midwives; was brought up by her grandmother, who ran a brothel; and first sang on Montmartre street corners for sous. Highest-paid of the music-hall *vedettes,* and a tremendous favorite among record fans, she always remained poor through squandering her earnings vainly on her young men and hangers-on. The only love and fidelity she aroused were in the hearts of the vast French public—*la foule,* which retained its passion for her over the years, packing into the music halls to listen to her in delight, playing her records in lonely, shabby rooms: "Milord," "Le Légionnaire," "L'Accordéoniste," and the recent chef-d'oeuvre of them all, "Je Ne Regrette Rien," with its bold refrain, "Farewell to love with its tremolo, I start again at zero." Lately, she married a handsome Greek hairdresser, Théo Sarapo, young enough to be her son, now also turned into a singer. At her burial, in Père-Lachaise, forty thousand of *La Foule Parisienne* assembled in loyalty and curiosity to see her to her grave. On the weekend of her death, her records were totally sold out in Paris—three hundred thousand of them. As Cocteau said in that Friday epitaph, "Her great voice will not be lost."

In his elegant fashion, Cocteau was in a way the *agent provocateur* of that phenomenal revolutionary epoch of the creative mind just after the First World War, of which Paris was the geographic brain center, and which became the first—and still remains the only—style period of this century. He was a Protean, even a Procrustean, multiple-talented Frenchman, every so often cutting off the basic feet of one gift on which he was progressing toward more serious perfection so as to increase the headroom for another, which he then swelled to successful bursting with his genius for alternation, reinterpretation, and dimensional change. Essentially, he was always the same, dually composed of the brilliant lightning of his vision, in which he always clearly saw himself, and the minor thunder of his printed word, most resonant when it echoed only what he had felt in his own entity. As a precocious small boy, illicitly leaning in the early night from a window in his widowed mother's fashionable apartment near the old Théâtre du Vaudeville, he gazed down on the delicate, well-bred little mules in the private equipage that was fancifully used by and waiting for the fabulous actress Réjane, and his addiction to the theatre world began. Always in advance of the avant-garde and (though no musician himself) early tired of Debussy, Cocteau, with his infallible instinct for timing, was the organizer of Les Six, who as composers created a new, but less important, non-Debussyesque music, more useful for the Paris ballets that followed the Russian supremacies of Stravinsky and Diaghilev—to whom, in a historic liaison, he introduced Picasso as the dominant new discordant note in Paris painting. From his educated, legitimate inheritance of the Greek classics Cocteau created his own romantic bastardy, bringing the classical Greek personages down in impossible haste to the procreation of his stimulating personal mythology, which he used to people his plays and films, with their old truths and mysteries of misconduct—the Sphinx, Oedipus Rex, Antigone, Orpheus—and from there farther down to earth, among mere human beings and the old filial and parental errors of "Les Enfants Terribles" and "Les Parents Terribles." He began the fashion for the absurd in his creation of "Les Mariés de la Tour Eiffel," and enlarged the modern appreciation of death in the suicide-by-hanging of the *premier danseur* in the ballet "Le Jeune Homme et la Mort." The vogue for violence was early manifested in his film "Le Sang d'un Poète," disapproved of by the Church. Films were pristine material then. On them he left his elegant thumbprint. He illustrated some twenty-five books, mostly his own; his familiar profile drawing of a round-eyed, short-lipped Orpheus was so famous that in Cocteau's honor the French state engraved it on a twenty-centime stamp, as if it were his own portrait. His most serious volume of poetry, "Plain-Chant," should long outlive him. "Thomas l'Imposteur" was his earliest, most important novel; "La Difficulté d'Etre" was his richest autobiographical report. And in the realm of phantasmagorial reality in that strange 1930 Paris literary epoch of drug addiction, the text and frighteningly informative physiological drawings of his book "Opium," created in a disintoxication clinic where he did not sleep for twelve days, are of a rare literary as well as psychiatric importance. In this book he defined opium as "the sole vegetal substance which communicates the vegetal state; through opium we obtain an idea of that other speed known to plants." As a painter, he decorated two country Catholic chapels, one of them St.-Blaise-des-Simples, a twelfth-century lepers' retreat in his village of

Milly-la-Forêt, on whose walls he painted frescoes of herbs and simples formerly deemed helpful to the sick—the polydore fern and *absinthe artemisia*. He was buried in its churchyard. His beautiful hands, which he displayed in narcissistic admiration during life by wearing his cuffs rolled back to uncover the artistry of flesh and bone, were on view for the last time in the pictures taken of him on his deathbed.

November 26

Never before in our time have the French been so unified in a sympathetic public emotion as in their grief and shock at the assassination of President Kennedy. Not a sentimental people, but experienced in tragedy, they seemed to feel that his death summed up, like a legend, all that must be mourned—the young leader of his country vilely, treacherously cut down in his vigor and prime; his wife, in her beauty, a widow; his small children fatherless, the melodrama of his dying a reproach to his own land; and what he left behind him still undone in his pursuit of his hopes a loss to all men of good will. These were the causes of their grief, which Parisians talked about, often with visible tears. His death loosed emotions here, and also suddenly clarified appreciations. About these the humbler French were especially explicit, giving the reasons for their faith in him. They said he had worked without rest for peace between West and East. A rich man of the richest nation, he had had compassion for the poorer nations, had shown wiser statesmanship and more diplomatic patience than men nearly twice his age, and, above all, had fought as much as he was allowed to for civil rights, for equality between men regardless of color. And he had had faith in God. This last, coupled with the French knowledge that he was our first Catholic President, made him seem more comprehensible to them, more touched by grace, than Franklin Roosevelt, heretofore their favorite President of this transatlantic epoch.

Now, less than a week after the fatal event, already a certain realistic alarm amplifies the French grief. Whatever President de Gaulle's cumulatively successful projects for the self-domination of France and for its domination of Europe, Kennedy, as President of the United States, was the actual leader of the Western alliance, which includes France within Europe, and in his death the French feel temporarily uncovered, almost denuded. Parisians, in their cynical acuity, saw the irony of de Gaulle's attending President Kennedy's funeral in Washington after having earlier discouraged his proposal of a visit here. But to the majority of the French, de Gaulle's presence at Arlington was no mere formality between heads of state, living and deceased. It was a natural family gesture of sympathy between France and the United States, which, had he failed to make it, would have shocked his people as an omission of respect for the admired dead President. The only lessening here in the tragedy of Kennedy's assassination is that it has helped restore the feeling of Franco-American amity.

His noblest epitaph, from the pen of the French poet and former diplomat St.-John Perse, has just been published by *Le Monde,* entitled "Grandeur de Kennedy." It opens thus: "History created no myth. Face to face, he was a man simple, close, and warm, prompt to the activity of each day." It continues, in part, "He was the athlete racing toward his meetings with destiny. He fought always with his weapons unhidden, and in his meeting with death his face was uncovered. Upon events he imprinted a mark of progress that was his own and that leaves us following his path. At the service of a great people in love with liberty, he was a defender of all rights and all freedoms. No one was more the enemy of abstractions or more carried by instinct to the heart of things. He had the clear, direct gaze of those young chiefs formed for friendship with mankind. When fate lifts so high the burst of its lightning, the drama [of death] becomes universal, and the affliction of one nation becomes that of all."

1964

February 11

At his recent Palais de l'Elysée press conference, President de Gaulle appeared for the first time to have aged, at one moment resting his face on his hand in the way a reposing old eagle leans his beak on his neck plumage. During the first forty minutes of his monologue, or until he started talking of his recognition of Communist China, the foreign journalists present were politely restive and bored as he concentrated on his ideas of his supreme Presidential and Constitutional powers over France—ideas that, because of their extreme candor, were of considerable interest to the French listeners, at least. What he was saying was, in reality, directed at specifically one Frenchman, who was not even present. This single Frenchman was M. Gaston Defferre, Socialist mayor of Marseille and sole announced candidate so far for the Presidential elections to be held at the end of next year, probably against the unbeatable de Gaulle, who will then be seventy-five. In all that de Gaulle said for Defferre's information on how republican France has to be handled, "rarely," commented *Le Monde* the next day in a stern, scandalized editorial, "has the theory of absolute power been revealed more complacently, clearly, or rigorously." The paper continued, "It is a good thing to vituperate against the impotence of government by parliament and to recall its miseries, but it is no less necessary to denounce the dangers of reactionary excess. If one admits that everything in a country may depend upon one man only, a more or less totalitarian dictatorship is already present in germ."

On this past Saturday, Defferre opened his Presidential campaign by stumping in Bordeaux, a Gaullist stronghold. There, according to reports, he seemed both successful and unusual as a candidate. (He had already stated, with a sportsmanship rare in French political circles, that to be defeated by de Gaulle would be "no dishonor.") In his afternoon speeches, he intelligently chose to talk to college students from the Institut des Sciences Politiques and to workers from the Socialist labor union and the Catholic labor union, workers from the Communist-led C.G.T. union having refused even to come listen to him. That night, he collected an audience of nearly four thousand average citizens in a Bordeaux suburb, to whom he courageously declared that, as of that evening, they were no longer faced with the prospect of "de Gaulle or nothing." He rejected de Gaulle's notion that the Presidency should furnish the control and also the source of all power, which Defferre said sounded like "an absolute monarchy," as if French history had not already shown what that led to. His keynote policy was against "false French grandeur," and he further declared that he was against the French *force de frappe,* preferring a common nuclear policy for a powerful, economically and politically united Europe, including Britain and Scandinavia, which would be of a Socialist character and would favor the common interests of all countries rather than the special interests of a couple of powerful states. As for his far-off electoral struggle against de Gaulle, Defferre optimistically referred to that ancient combat between David and Goliath.

Thus, the end of 1965 will furnish France with the first direct popular election of a President since that of Louis Napoleon in 1848, who for good measure was elected Emperor four years later. Defferre is modelling his campaign on that of Senator John Kennedy in 1959–60 and, in imitation of Kennedy, has started nearly two years before the election date, in a country where campaigns for senators and deputies—about all the French are accustomed to elect—rarely last more than a fortnight. Again in contrast to usual French political practice, Defferre has actually got his Socialist Party (of which he is, after all, the Parliamentary whip) to agree that he, as the candidate, will set the campaign policy, and he has already turned thumbs down on the diehard Socialists' fatuous hopes of a return to the fatal system of government run by Parliament. Like most anti-Gaullists, he was flatly opposed in 1962 to de Gaulle's Presidential innovations. Now, like most of the more modern-minded middle-aged French, who have had to learn their modernism quickly, he believes the

Presidential system is here to stay in France. If he were to win, Defferre says, he would not even change the number of the republic; it would continue with the title that President de Gaulle gave it—*la Cinquième République Française.*

"Parlez-Vous Franglais?" is the title of an entertaining, if repetitious, book that is causing a lot of chatter here. Its author is M. René Etiemble, professor of comparative literature at the Sorbonne, until now best known for his studies of the poet Rimbaud but lately launched against the corruption of the French language by its postwar inclusion of Americanisms, which produces a bastard transatlantic tongue that he calls Franglais. "Language is the blood of a nation," he solemnly declares. "Since the Liberation, our blood has been much diluted. The vocabulary of the young generation that will be twenty years old in 1972 is already one-fourth composed of American words. At twenty, these young people will not be able to read Molière, let alone Marcel Proust." His book cites hundreds of Franglais words or phrases used in every walk of French life today, beginning with his opening chapter about *les babys* and the *coin de teens,* or teen-agers' corner, from which it moves easily to bar drinkers' requests for *"un baby Scotch sur les rocks." Le sport,* which the French took up late compared to the British and Yanquis, as Etiemble calls us, is rife with Franglais, such as *"les trottings"* at the race track, *"un crack,"* for a topflight jockey, *"un catcheur," "le karting,"* and *"les supportères"* of the home Rugby team. There is also the old Franglais phrase *"faire du footing,"* which means merely to take a walk (on your foots, naturally). Big business in Paris now features a weekly *réunion de briefing* in office buildings *de grand standing.* A millionaire executive's yacht is called that but is pronounced to rhyme with "watch." Hollywood camera terms are used even by teen-age movie fans here, such as *"un travelling,"* and so on. In the intermission between films in the Champs-Elysées movie houses, the girl ushers now sell a nut candy they loudly offer as *"noots,"* which always breaks up us Yanquis present. What most enrages Etiemble, probably a refined, slow-eating gourmet, is the old *bistros* modernized under neon signs as *"le snack," "le quick,"* even *"le queek"* or *"le self,"* which means a cafeteria, and even *"le self des selfs,"* on the Boulevard des Capucines, which means nothing on earth. As a philogist, he seems not to note that French language and cooking lack the word and the celerity for out snack-bar fare, which young Paris office workers immediately developed an appetite for at Le Drugstore, on the Champs. Etiemble concludes dispiritedly that the future of the French language is English. Alas, we Anglo-Saxons don't export it; it is the French who import it. This is an aspect of the Franglais problem that the Professor neglects to mention.

An exhibition of sixty-eight new Picasso pictures, from 1962 and 1963, has just opened at the Leiris Gallery, under the aegis of M. Daniel Kahnweiler, his early art merchant, who knew him just before his Cubism began, in 1908. There are still traces of it half a century later in what the painter has painted in his early eighties. For the past ten years, perhaps, he has been painting in a consistently convulsive manner, with traces of everything consequential indicated, if not expressed. What astonishes in these new pictures is their aesthetic energy, which the viewer can see with his eyes just as surely as he can hear with his ears, at a concert, the musical energy blaring forth from Verdi's trumpet scoring—a thrilling creative vigor being part of the sights offered by the Spaniard just as it is part of the brassy sounds supplied by the Italian. Picasso's special repetitive theme this time, of which he shows thirteen versions, is that of the painter and his model. Some Paris critics have fallen to ruminating about monotony in this 1964 Picasso exhibition. The truth probably is that Picasso is an old re-creative virtuoso, and his critics are now only wearied, practiced onlookers where he is concerned.

February 26

When President Antonio Segni, of Italy, was here on his recent official visit to General de Gaulle, it was planned that the visitor, who is a distinguished former professor, would visit the Sorbonne and be welcomed by its students. They, on their side, planned to greet him with the cry "Monsieur le Président, behold our university in ruins!"—referring to the dilapidation and crowded classrooms of their august institution of learning, which was founded in 1256. So the university authorities ordered a one-day lockout, and last Friday, when Segni called, all the Sorbonne's buildings were closed against its scholars and the students retaliated with a one-day strike—their customary retort to official pressure in their running quarrel with the state and municipal authorities. Yesterday there was a monster protest meeting of students in the court of the Sorbonne, and today the government's Conseil des Ministres took up consideration of the long-awaited plan for a general bureaucratic overhauling of French national education proposed by the unpopular Ministre de l'Education, Christian Fouchet. It certainly seems inappropriate that in a country haughtily proud of its cultural superiorities and tradition the normal relation under the Fifth Republic between the scholars and the state whose colleges furnish the means of culture should be that of a perpetual cat-and-dog fight. Students old enough to vote, and their parents, have been waiting to see whether Gaston Defferre, the Socialist candidate for President in next year's elections, would include in his platform, criticizing the de Gaulle policies, a plank that would deal with the Sorbonne scandal and offer a way out of the impasse.

As a matter of fact, Defferre, except through provincial newspaper reports of his speeches in the southern country towns where he has been stumping, is not having an easy time letting the French people know what any plank in his platform will be like. In Trèbes near Carcassonne, on Sunday, at a Socialist Party luncheon attended by twelve hundred members, he declared that the government had given orders to both state-run radio and television to boycott his meetings and speeches. Spotting two TV cameras aimed at him, as if in rebuttal, he called out, "They're not French! One is for a German news program, the other is English!" He also made a speech at Narbonne, but citizens who were listening to the radio never found out what he said in it, for that was not put on the air, only the fact that he spoke at all being considered unavoidably newsworthy. Ever since French radio and, especially, television began expanding in political and newscasting importance, as a result of the brilliant use that de Gaulle made of them, French citizens have become increasingly conscious that these not only constitute the most powerful government monopoly of mass media but also are controlled—meaning censored. The sudden national political existence of Defferre as a candidate who is criticizing the President's policies in his speeches has subjected the whole situation to heated controversy. It was noted that when he announced his candidacy, a month ago, and said that the French, aside from the citizens of Marseille, where he is mayor, did not even know what he looked like, the state television showed only a most fleeting glimpse of his face, as a national introduction, and finished its camera shots of him from behind his back. Criticism of the party uses that the state television and radio are put to here is, naturally, not new. When Guy Mollet, a Socialist, was Premier, during the Fourth Republic, the tomatoes thrown at him in Algiers by the angry Algerian French were reported on fully in the French newspapers and pictured there, too, but certainly were not featured on radio or TV. The heated discussion right now about unfair radio and TV coverage for Defferre is probably overhasty, especially since it has already been announced that the 1965 campaign will officially last only two weeks, with each candidate being given two hours' radio and television time, to be spread over the fourteen days. De Gaulle, of course, can always procure the lion's share by, in addition, giving one of his twenty-minute TV talks to the nation, as the incumbent President.

Actually, the government broadcasting monopoly is by no means ironclad as far as listening is concerned. It has lively competition from Radio Luxembourg; from Europe No. 1, whose station is in the Saar; and from Radio Monte Carlo—not to speak of the B.B.C., which ever since the war days has been the French favorite for honest news. But there is no kind of TV here except the Fifth Republic's TV. There are now five million television sets in use here, and the number is constantly increasing, which means that more than half the French can be reached visually on the screen—and influenced. However, even this absolute monopoly, sinister as it is in principle in a republic, has its comic side here in France. Government officials privately insist that the state control of television only evens things up for the regime; because the majority of the newspapers are against the regime, monopoly TV is the only chance it has of giving itself a fair show.

March 11

Local diplomatic circles are now saying, in their professional undertone, that Franco-American relations have deteriorated to a point where little is left of them except formal recognition. There is supposedly a governmental anti-American atmosphere that is à la mode in Paris. As yet, this erosion on the government level of the transatlantic national friendship has in no perceptible fashion influenced the nationals themselves here—the vast population of

Parisians and the small colony of resident Americans, who continue to get along in their relative separateness exactly the same way and exactly as well as they did before General de Gaulle recognized Peking, which is where it all started. No sooner had the Chinese delegation settled down temporarily on the second floor of the Hôtel Continental, across from the Jardin des Tuileries, than de Gaulle gave a particularly cordial welcome to M. Nicolai Podgorny, Secretary of the Soviet Presidium, as head of a Soviet delegation that enjoyed a gala visit in Paris, with Podgorny recalling that President de Gaulle had a standing invitation to a gala visit in Moscow. Then, this last weekend, millions of French TV watchers saw and heard Dr. Castro, of Cuba, where de Gaulle is to visit in a few days, give a televised, translated interview in which he was warm indeed in his admiring references to the Fifth Republic's chief. "There are several things in General de Gaulle's foreign policy with which I am in sincere sympathy," Dr. Castro said, and and enumerated them. First of all was the French leader's independence of attitude in regard to the United States, then his opinions on how to settle things in Southeast Asia, and finally, of course, his decision to send a French Ambassador to Peking. For all three of these anti-American compliments to be programmed in French on the French-government-controlled TV was like a triple massage of salt in Washington's wounds.

In confused and worrisome periods like this last fortnight, with Ambassador Charles Bohlen known to be back home talking over the Franco-American rift with the State Department, Parisians have been extra diligent in their perusal of the papers to find out what is going on in national policy matters—any papers, even the British press when it contains special pieces on French affairs. This Tuesday evening's *Monde* hastened to print in translation a Monday-morning editorial from the London *Times* entitled "De Gaulle Leans Left." With dry humour, the *Times* said, "Suddenly President de Gaulle seems to be the only active revolutionary in Europe. He has just completed a remarkable double in recognizing Peking and acting as host to a high-powered delegation from Moscow. From many a foreign spokesman of the militant Left come tributes both to the historical role of France and to the President's reinterpretation of it. At first sight it is an odd part to be played by a man whose own domestic opponents caricature him as the reincarnation of Louis XIV."

Also on Tuesday, there was a bold, analytical anti-Gaullist editorial in *Figaro* by M. Raymond Aron, Sorbonne professor of sociology, a graduate in philosophy, and a multilingual intellectual of the type that the French admiringly call *un mandarin,* who was formerly a Gaullist himself and is today the French commentator on national and world affairs best known in Paris and also in Washington. Aron titled his editorial, as if in inquiry, "The Infantile Malady of Old Nationalism?" and began his analyzing with several other pertinent questions. "Are the French in 1964," he asked, "more nationalist or less nationalist than in 1958?"—when de Gaulle came to power. "Are they more or less favorable to a united Europe? More or less hostile to the Atlantic Pact and the United States? Personally, I would not presume to decide, though in political milieux the opportunists seem convinced that to tag themselves as anti-American is the best way to court the Prince"—as de Gaulle is semi-ironically called. "What characterizes French nationalism today is less the state of mind of the French than the diplomacy of the Republic's President," he went on. "At every turn, it keeps Washington at a distance. Faced with the Soviet's exigencies, it seems ready, despite everything, to renew the traditional old game on the planetary system of drawing near first to one body, then to another—the only principle being never to be definitely tied. [In this] neo-nationalism of *la France éternelle,* she is on the hunt for a first-ranking role on the world scene [and appears as often as possible as] a lone rider, so as to wipe out any appearance of a connection with the Atlantic Pact." Aron added, "Thus, the world sees what she does as an expression and a justification of the revolt against 'American imperialism.' That France is concerned about herself, everywhere and always, is too well known to need repeating. The question the bystander asks himself is: What good do some of these decisions do for France, aside from their undeniable merit in irritating both allies and adversaries at the same time? What will France gain by making the People's China a member of the United Nations and exasperating an important segment of American opinion—aside, of course, from the glory derived from showing her indifference to the susceptibilities and preferences of an ally whose major error is that it is in possession of the reality of power?" Aron's last, highly important, question was to ask, "How does Gaullist France see the international future? In terms inherited from the Common Market and the Atlantic Pact? Or, rather, in terms that suggest the exaltations of nationalist grandeur and the subtleties of a diplomacy born in the Italian cities of the Renaissance? If France herself shows today certain symptoms of the infantile sickness that is nationalism, what country tomorrow will escape contagion?"

Ideas on the future of France, but of a very different sort, were delivered last week (and much commented on) by another highly esteemed intellectual, who is professor of law and economics at the Sorbonne and director of social research at the *Sciences Po'*—M. Maurice Duverger, ordinarily a front-page political analyst for *Le Monde*. What he had to say on Franco-American affairs was printed as an interview in the stimulating leftist weekly *L'Express,* which is anti-government and, indeed, anti-everything except criticism and vigorous information. The essence of what Duverger passionately declared was "It must be said, it must be written! There is only one immediate danger for Europe, and that is the American civilization. There will be no Stalinism or Communism in France. They are scarecrows that frighten only sparrows now. Today, all that belongs to the past. On the other hand, the pressure of American society, the domination of the American economy—all that is very dangerous. Why do you make such a face?"

To this, the *Express* reporter replied, "Because anti-Americanism gets on my nerves. Everybody in France has become anti-American. De Gaulle, Etiemble and his 'Parlez-vous Franglais?,' all that talk about 'Oh, my dear, China!,' and 'The Americans, those barbarians!' *Zut!*"

"Granted," Duverger replied. "Nothing is stupider than stylish anti-Americanism. But at the base of it all there is, just the same, a real question. America is a different society from ours. It was built by pioneers who for their cultural baggage had the Bible and a sense of adventure. With these two elements, they succeeded in making a body of men for whom money is the essential criterion—the basis of their system of values. In a country like France, the employee who reads your gas meter possesses a scale of aristocratic values. He can distinguish perfectly among a *nouveau riche,* an intelligent man, and a poet. Whether he knows it or not, the cultural ensemble that is at the bottom of his attitudes is shaped by an accumulation of history different from that of the Americans. I think that this element will help us to resist the American pressure. But don't forget one thing: America is evolving. As Russia is liberalizing itself, so is the United States civilizing itself."

"It is doing it pretty rapidly," the recalcitrant reporter interjected.

"In some sectors," Duverger admitted. "But it will probably take as long for America in its entirety to reject a system of values based on money and gadgets as it will take Russia to reject a political system based on dictatorship. For us, the essential is to escape both of them. Our luck, as Europeans, is that we are behind the times—in planned consumption in relation to the United States and in planned socialization in relation to the U.S.S.R. For us, the problem is to arrive at the abundant society when the transitory American phase is over and at socialization when the transitory phase of the proletarian dictatorship is finished. The second seems sure. The first is not sure at all. Quite the contrary. That is why America is for us the more dangerous."

Painful as many of Professor Duverger's conclusions are for many Americans, he has academically touched on basic, alarming truths for many of the French, who, even in their awareness, seem unable to do anything about them except complain—while continuing their American way of life *à la française*.

March 23

"La Damnation de Faust," which Hector Berlioz completed in the middle eighteen-forties, a weak period in French music, was indecisively described by him as *"une symphonie avec programme plastique."* For the first time in musical history, it was recently presented at the Opéra in precisely this form by the *metteur en scène* and choreographer Maurice Béjart, and the fashionable first-night audience and most critics took it to be an extraordinary mixture of splendid and shocking ballet plasticities, of scenic brilliance and muscular bad taste, of aesthetic beauty and willful uglinesses. It was a plenitude that led to noisy dissension, with outcries, catcalls, and insults being freely launched at the performers and exchanged between the spectators who applauded what they saw as something astonishingly creative, at its best, and those who booed it as merely scandalous. At the second performance, the quarrel was still going on, but more mildly. Those who disapproved shouted, *"C'est indécent!"* The admirers then shouted back, *"A la tombe les ancêtres!"*—the anathema against elderly conservatism lately popularized by the younger French and meaning, very roughly, "Off to the cemetery with all the old fogies!" So little that is remarkable ever takes place at the Opéra, aside from the amazing mediocrity of the singing, that to be credited with a scandal gave its reputation an invaluable fillip and "Damnation" a run at the box office.

What Béjart had ambitiously aimed at was to have a ballet illustrate the temptations, visions, and earthly events connecting Faust and Marguerite, which Berlioz' singers merely refer to in solos. To give his dancers room, he immobilized the choruses (dressed like medieval monks) and also made Faust and Marguerite practically stationary, as if in an oratorio—the form in which the opus used to be given. In Act I, Faust was discovered hung aloft above the footlights in a cage, from which he motionlessly viewed and sang about the sad state of the universe. It must be frankly said that Béjart has publicized his career as a stage director in part by his scandalizing imagination and his eccentric fixations, such as hanging things from the ceiling, and in his choreography he has been addicted to choruses that hop about in a semi-squatting frog position. For the famous "Hungarian March," his ballet of warriors strode in like Storm Troopers, dressed in belted khaki-colored tights and wearing what looked like motor-cop helmets decorated with death's-heads. Then, in a froglike pastiche of totalitarianism, they captured Le Jeune Homme, or Youth, who symbolized freedom, in the person of Cyril Atanassoff, the Opéra's excellent new male ballet star, who has long been needed there, as has the new star ballerina Mlle. Christiane Vlassi, a slender, ephemeral vision symbolizing the soul of Marguerite. Paris had never before seen the Fifth Republic Opéra Ballet perform as a whole with such impressive, superior technique, constantly dancing far better than the Opéra singers sang. (At the end of the first performance, when the cast made its bows, the unfortunate tenor who sang Faust was booed by the gallery gods.) In the most elaborate, poetic, and aesthetic ballet number, a half-dozen delicately bodied young coryphées wearing nothing but flesh-colored tights danced as nymphs in the half-light, in seeming innocent nakedness among the mortals. This ballet was like a Botticelli scene. Then, as Faust's tastes became more earthy, equally nude-looking girls under blowzy wigs lubriciously saddled themselves around the male dancers' waists, like infernal figurines from a Hieronymus Bosch canvas depicting antics in Hell. The décors, by Germinal Casado, Béjart's assistant, were mostly stunning—especially that of the town walls, which shone metallically, as if covered by copper. And Marguerite's small Gothic house suddenly split in two to reveal a tall silver tree beside her opened bedroom, where she sang the celebrated "King of Thule" aria.

In the last act, as an added surprise, Faust and Mephisto were seen seated on a pair of metal horses en route to damnation, contrary to Goethe's drama, of which Berlioz used the madman Gérard de Nerval's French translation as his libretto. One Paris critic was worried by the possible redundancy in Béjart's scheme of duplicating the singers with dancers, so as to make the action extra clear. For most of us there was no such pleonastic danger.

When President Nicolas Grunitzky of Togo, a worldly, smartly dressed pale African of mixed German, Russian, and African blood, made his state visit here recently, and twenty-five gigantic, costly Togo national flags (yellow and dark green, with a square upper corner of revolutionary scarlet mitigated by a big single white star of hope) flapped from the Concorde mastheads, and thousands of Togo bannerets fluttered over the Champs-Elysées and on the fronts of municipal autobuses, Parisians knew, by their ignorance of who on earth the visiting distinguished head of state might be, that he must be another remnant of European colonialism now practicing *le Présidentialisme* and come to call on General de Gaulle, his top hat doffed, for a handout—another in a regular parade of them here over the past few years. (Owing to the supposed historical fact that a prewar native deputy from one of the French colonies was invited by his tribal constituents to lunch and became part of it, some cynical Parisians now refer to these African débutant democracies as *"les républiques cannibales."*) In a series of elaborately documented articles in the illustrated, influential weekly *Paris Match,* entitled "Attention! La France Dilapide Son Argent," M. Raymond Cartier, the magazine's chief editorialist, has established the economic doctrine of so-called Cartierisme, which, as a criticism of the government's spending policy, has caused heated comment and worried smaller editorials all over France. As his main thesis, Cartier points out that France has been spending more than two per cent of her gross national product on foreign aid to underdeveloped countries—over three times what the United States has spent of hers—and that France had better look first to her own underdevelopment, which he then paints in. The Sorbonne classrooms, he says, are "as crowded as the Métro;" no new Paris hospitals have been built in thirty years; "Asiatic conditions" exist in small French villages, almost forty per cent being without running water; even in big French cities, thirty-one per cent of the apartments are without private water closets; and France's telecommunications are the poorest among all the European Community nations. Cartier ironically advises the hundreds of thousands of the French who are still waiting for their phones to be installed to "go to Abidjan, where ten thousand telephone lines, without one user," have been installed with the French taxpayers' money. In real distress, he deplores the fact that a fabulous national French fortune has been splashed over the ex-colonial lands, "with an air-conditioned Versailles palace for the Ivory Coast president, and little of the aid money in general ever reaching the poor inhabitants, who are often too illiterate to read their phone numbers and, in some places, so confused about putting ballots into urns that they add their marriage licenses." These and a myriad other costly policy errors, Cartier says, restrict the French government on its home circuit to "a Malthusian economy." As for the colonial past, he says that France should not "take the moral attitude of guilt today," for, with the possible exception of ostrich plumes, "all the colonial riches were created by European capital and work." And, as he failed to add, European capital pulled in the profits.

April 7

By the energy of his imagination and the generosity of certain of his cultural practices—frequently startling to the French, such as his having lent the Venus de Milo to the Tokyo Olympics—M. André Malraux, as Gaullist Ministre d'Etat Chargé des Affaires Culturelles, is unquestionably the most discussed and most powerful figure in European culture today, and certainly the only one backed by a government. A dazzling conversationalist who never gives interviews, he recently answered a few questions put to him, over coffee, as a luncheon guest of the Anglo-American Press Association here, the answers swelling to a brilliant, important post-prandial kind of lecture—fortunately taken down in stenotype, since the scintillating speed of his thinking and speech was beyond any of us in the way of adequate note-taking. In answer to the opening question, put by the London *Observer's* Paris correspondent, asking what M. Malraux would think of a recent suggestion that Great Britain create a Ministry of Leisure (which France had already invented and temporarily enjoyed under Léon Blum and the Front Populaire back in the nineteen-thirties), he replied, in part, "This question is one of the most important concerning the human mind and thought in this half of our century. But we must first find out whether these problems of ours should come under the heading of leisure. I think they should not. For probably ten thousand years one civilization was very much like another, with the chief of state dealing basically with agriculture, the police, the army, and finance. I will repeat what I said to President Kennedy, what I have said to the French Parliament, what I have said all my life—that throughout all that time the same things dominated humanity. If a man like Rameses II of Egypt had found himself face to face with Napoleon, they would have talked about almost the same topics. One day, all that came to an end—and that day coincides with us. What changed everything? You all know what it was. The machine, naturally. This is where the essential problem arises. If the machine is victorious, it creates spare time and, consequently, what is called leisure. The machine creates objects but it also creates the multiplication of dreams. A hundred years ago, some three thousand people in Paris went to the theatre every evening. Today, if you count television, how many people in Paris see a show every night? Probably three million. You can put unimportant things on the screen. You can also put on comedy. Comedy is so important that it alone has unified the capitalist world, doing what the will to revolution did for the Communist world. In the cinema, there is, on the one hand, Chaplin and, on the other, Eisenstein. In between there is nothing with a comparably profound effect on man's sensibilities. But, comedy aside, what remains is the essential, what I have called the eternal—to put it clearly, the realm of sex and the realm of blood. Make no mistake about it, modern civilization is in the process of putting its immense resources at the service of what used to be called the Devil. There is a great domain of nocturnal darkness in man, which none of us can mistake if he looks at himself in the mirror; even the most cretinous people, out to make money by exploiting this among defenseless children, recognize it as clearly as we do. What counts against the appeal that the power of money holds for the powers of darkness?

Here is the only great problem that exists for me behind the word 'culture.'"

The Paris correspondent of the New York *Post* then said to Malraux, "Monsieur le Ministre, a united Europe is being created culturally as well as politically. How do you envision a Europe in which nationalism has been left behind?"

To this Malraux instantly and elaborately replied, "Politically, I don't think it true that nationalism is outdated. I think we are involved in an appalling historical misunderstanding. The nineteenth century considered that nationalisms were provisional hypotheses, and that the twentieth century would be internationalist. That was not meant as a joke, since even Victor Hugo thought it childish to conceive of our century as an era of nations. Nations were what the provinces formerly had been; at the end of the nineteenth century, the provinces had become nations. Thus, the nations would become Europe. Opposed to all these ideas was somebody, who was by no means a nobody, named Nietzsche, who said, 'The twentieth century will be one of national war.' Well, has the twentieth century been one of internationalism or one of national war? Has the Soviet Union become Russia? Leather-jacketed People's Commissars have become gold-braided marshals, but is that really internationalism? Has China, the most international country, become especially internationalist? Or Italy? Or Germany? In our time, the century's dream has turned out to be nothing but the drama of nations. We are in the century of nations, and our predominant problem is how to reconcile the essential reality of nations with our hope of happiness for the world—the hope for justice, which men cannot establish except on infinitely vaster structures. To sum up clearly, I think the notion of Europe is a fundamental one. But I think that to believe that an over-all Europe will be brought about by a handful of people who simply agree about it is absolutely puerile. The destiny of the world is made by hard realities, not by good intentions. Something very strange is happening in the realm of human thought. We have been initiated into the fraternal elements of the great religions. When the great religions were great, they hated each other. But the moment they found another enemy, the wars of religion ended, with reconciliations among Catholics, Protestants, and so on. For the first time in this century, there is a domain in which fraternity is possible—a domain containing all that is most mysterious and profound in our heritage in this field of thought. It is the most powerful ferment of the future Europe."

Close to five thousand people assembled at Père-Lachaise Cemetery this last Sunday morning in the sunless, wintery cold that has marked this spring to assist at the dedication of a monument to the memory of the fifty-six thousand French deportees who died at Buchenwald. Slowly paid for over the years by public subscription, the monument is a terrifying modernist statue of two skeletal men, starved close to death but still upright and sustaining each other. It is the work of Louis Bancel, a French Buchenwald prisoner who survived. On either side of the monument, for the dedication, were placed temporary urns with little smokestacks, from which wisps of smoke emerged during the services, in faithful recollection of the Buchenwald crematories. The opening dedication speech was made by the elderly Abbé Blanc, who had been the clandestine almoner at the camp. He began by saying familially, "I am addressing the mothers and fathers, if any are still alive, of those young men who died there. I am also addressing their children who may be here, and their widows." These were many, to judge by the signs of grief manifested. Most of the middle-aged Frenchmen present (they had come from all over France) were camp survivors, who reminisced together or could be heard suddenly recognizing each other—*"Tiens, c'est toi!"*—as they met for the first time since they were liberated nineteen years ago on Saturday of this week. It was a most affecting scene and ceremony for all present.

April 23

The uglification of Paris, the most famously beautiful city of relatively modern Europe, goes on apace, and more is being carefully planned. Already, one of the enormous square blocks of skyscraper office buildings on the Boulevard de Vaugirard, which forms the first part of a huge complex of modern buildings that will be composed around and will include the new Montparnasse railroad station, is, with its eighteen stories of unmitigated cement, a solid, high eyesore on the southern skyline of Paris. It disgraces the horizon as seen from the city's upper windows giving on the Tuileries Gardens, which were formerly possessed of one of the capital's most elegant perspectives. For these ignoble changes, big business and the automobile, either squatting by the curbs or crawling or racing along the boulevards, are responsible. Now there is a plan to create a double motor highway by the Seineside, from the Place de la Concorde to the Pont Sully, along the Right Bank. Already, members of the Institut and the Academies have written eloquently in protest to the helpless Ministry of Cultural Affairs. To build the motor highway demands the sacrifice of the elderly, drooping elms that for decades have leaned over the river, opulently rooted and watered beneath the heavy cobblestones of the verge—the quietest promenade for lovers or solitary thinkers in all Paris. Cutting the elms, now in their faithful spring verdure, seems, in anticipation, a murder of nature, beauty, and art.

May 5

UNESCO held a two-day philosophical colloquy a week or so ago to mark the end of L'Année Kierkegaard, the European celebration of the hundred-and-fiftieth anniversary of the birth of the famous, eccentric Danish progenitor of Christian Existentialism. With the brilliant Tuesday-night lecture on him by Jean-Paul Sartre, which marked this French writer's return to the public scene that he formerly dominated in Paris like no other academic figure; with messages (in part recorded) in German from the German Existentialists Martin Heidegger and Karl Jaspers; and with platform participation by such leaders as the Italian Enzo Paci and the French professors Jean Wahl and Mlle. Jeanne Hersch, the handsome, modernist UNESCO auditorium became, as one philosopher admiringly remarked, an Olympus for the most eminent masters of contemporary Existentialism, still regarded in Europe as the most authentic modern philosophical thought. There was a slight hitch in the Tuesday-evening proceedings when the closed doors were assailed by a troupe of young Sorbonne *philo* students without invitations, who, upon clamoring "We are philosophers, too," were admitted. UNESCO dignitaries squeezed over on their benches to make room for youth, or else the students sat on the floor in the aisles, where they had a fine view of Sartre as he read his long address, he being the star they had come to gaze at with silent respect and to hear. He read his lecture in a quick, pleasant voice, with useful, hammerlike diction. Since Kierkegaard himself had famously said, "Truth objectively fixed is paradox," Sartre felt free to pour out paradoxes and truths like champagne. He said that the title of the colloquy, "The Live Kierkegaard," was proof that he was indeed dead but still influential; that "he was a philosopher who detested philosophers"; that "he stole the language of knowledge to use against knowledge," meaning what Hegel then stood for, "a system for thought but not for existence," from which the unorthodox little Dane's original Existentialism sprang; and that Kierkegaard "refused to the serpent the right to tempt Adam—as if God had need of sin!" Speaking personally as "an atheist of the twentieth century," and drawing largely on his own theories as laid down in his "L'Etre et le Néant," Sartre also poured out, among other shining formulas, "Contemporaries understand each other without knowing each other," "The liberty in each man is the foundation of history," and "Man is the being who transforms his existence into intelligence." In appreciation of the fact that those two so different nineteenth-century rebels, Kierkegaard and Marx, were writing their tracts of social revolt in the same years, Sartre added, "These two *morts-vivants* control our existence today." Heidegger, in his message to UNESCO from Germany, said, "The development of technology has put the finishing touch on philosophy. Philosophy comes to its end in the present epoch." UNESCO will publish the Sartre lecture at the end of the year.

May 20

Paris has grown to have such endless suburbs that the Départements surrounding it, and its own Département, the Seine, are now apparently going to be split up, and given slightly new shapes and new geographical names. There will be the Seine-et-Bièvre, the Hauts-de-Seine, and the Plaine-St.-Denis, unless one of them is more elegantly called Versailles. Similar news of modernizing is that the French telephone exchanges, with their historic and informative names, such as Gounod and Chénier, will soon become mere numerals on the phone dial—408 for the composer of "Faust" and 253 for the revolutionary youth whose statue is in the Palais-Royal Garden, where he spoke on behalf of liberty. Even Balzac will become merely 225.

June 4

This coming Saturday will be the twentieth anniversary of the English, Canadian, and American landings on Omaha and Utah Beaches in the decisive invasion of France—by them and not by the French, by their generals and not by General de Gaulle. The French citizens, often wearied by or captious about de Gaulle's standoffish reaction to the Anglo-Saxons, seem solidly behind him in his refusal to participate in this anniversary on those bloody, historic sands of his native land where he was not invited to set foot.

December 16

This year's end finds President de Gaulle on a peculiar pinnacle of lonely leadership—lonelier by far than the isolated eminence he has always contrived for himself. In a little more than a twelvemonth, through the brutal loss of President Kennedy, the unexpected sacking of Premier Khrushchev, and the sequestration into old age of Sir Winston Churchill, de Gaulle has emerged as the unique familiar, powerful political and historical figure left on the Western world's governing scene. Turned seventy-four last month, he apparently supports both time and the weight of his heavy office without any mortal weakening, and certainly with no abatement in his spiritual and intellectual concentration on the guiding of France always steeply upward, toward the floating status of international power. As encouragement, the miraculous fiscal prosperity of his Fifth Republic, now entering its seventh year, has reached new amplitudes. Today, France is one of the richest nations. In a discreet communiqué just issued by the Finance Ministry, it was made known that the country's official reserves have now reached five billion dollars, and that the gold and foreign *devises* in the vaults of the Banque de France are unequalled in Europe—except by the Bundesbank, in Bonn. Diplomatically and geographically, de Gaulle has had an especially expansive year in 1964, what with his state tour of Latin America, accompanied by Madame his wife and a suite of twenty, on which he astonished the South Americans by his bravura in making very brief speeches in Spanish—a tour de force that impressed even those compatriots back home who had become increasingly irritated by his highhanded governing methods and the accompanying Olympian manner.

In his native tongue, de Gaulle's speech last month in Strasbourg, on the twentieth anniversary of the liberation of the city from the Nazis, seems to have ranked as a real national event. It rated all over France as notable in his oratorical and thespian career—a speech still mentioned here in Paris as an exceptional example of his fine French language, his personal literary style, and his diplomatic skill. Certainly, de Gaulle's reference in it to his treaty of coöperation with West Germany after three centuries of enmity and his blunt declaration that the treaty had been aimed at "the construction of a European Europe" were intended to be heard across the Rhine by the Germans, and also across the ocean by the Americans. His distrust of the United States-sponsored Multilateral Nuclear Force (now being discussed at the NATO Council meeting in Paris) could be located behind his statement that in this push-button nuclear age there is no way "to insure the initial safeguarding of the old Continent, and, in consequence, to justify the Atlantic Alliance . . . except by the organization of a Europe that will be its own self, so as to defend itself"—and not merely to be rescued much later by others as part of their own salvation.

What de Gaulle did not mention at Strasbourg was the fact that in 1965 the West Germans will be holding their national elections. It is known that de Gaulle was outraged when the Bonn Minister of Foreign Affairs recently told his French counterpart, M. Couve de Murville, that the Federal Germans in their election propaganda will boldly contest the Oder-Neisse line, which was laid down in the Allied peace treaty as the German-Polish border. It is interesting to recall that in the third volume of de Gaulle's memoirs he recounts how in 1944, on a hasty and probably unwelcome visit to Stalin in Moscow, with the war not yet over and with him, as the French Resistance leader, still practically a nobody, he rejected Stalin's peace proposal that all Poland be sacrificed, and retired to his quarters in a dudgeon, to be awakened in the middle of the night with a message to return to Stalin, who then accepted de Gaulle's position. Another German irritant to de Gaulle has been their telling him that despite the Franco-German amity treaty, they have no intention of giving the go-by to their dear, generous old Uncle Sam. This semi-infidelity has been the major setback to de Gaulle's still precious project of a new Europe in which France—if she is to lead it and remain safely in first place—requires a half Germany as her second fiddle. Certain diplomats here believe that it is as an elderly historian expert even on modern history that de Gaulle has so well understood France's position in it—a relatively weak power playing the part of a first-class one.

France, too, will be holding her national elections in 1965, and nobody in his right mind here thinks that President de Gaulle will not be reëlected next November—if he runs for office. Since he will be eighty-two in 1972, when his new term would expire, the only serious curiosity now is about the succession, which would surely start operating before that date, and about exactly how Premier Pompidou, his present choice as his *dauphin,* might be legally inserted as the succeeding member of the Gaullist dynasty. The other, even greater question, looking ahead to the time when de Gaulle himself will no longer be in personal control, is how didactically reëducated the French Parliament will prove to have been by these last six enforced do-nothing years, during which the General, who did not trust it after its Chamber-wrecking activities in the two previous republics, practically put it out to grass, to ponder. The editor of a liberal-left Paris weekly, always in opposition to de Gaulle for his complete holding of power in his enormous hands—his thumbs looking as big as a pair of upright bananas in his famous gestures on television—has just admitted that no modern democracy, like France or Italy, has been able to function efficiently with a multi-party government. The final question is: Has the Fifth Republic's Parliament finally settled that fact firmly in scattered comprehension?

Actually, this may be the right moment to set down a kind of rough-and-ready approximation of the vital differences between the two preceding Republics and de Gaulle's, so as to obtain a year-end notion of where contemporary republican government in France has been, is, and may be going. As Anatole France said of the Third Republic (1871–1940), in which he lived and died, its main characteristic was *la facilité.* It was the easygoing *République des Camarades*—of pals—with financial and political scandals that enriched politicians and shook down governments and unfortunate petty investors like sere autumn leaves several times a year. Some of its nineteenth-century scandals were like bold, melodramatic, up-to-date farces—such as Mme. Présidente Hanau and her bank scandal, followed by her suicide in prison, where she slept on her own linen sheets and under her own mink coat. Then in the nineteen-thirties came the really alarming Stavisky scandal, with its government-backed provincial pawnshops and bogus pawned emeralds, which involved both France's Premier and his Cabinet and led to the notorious Place de la Concorde riot of February 6, 1934, when eighteen protesting citizens in the mob trying to assault the Parliament and the deputies were shot down and killed by the Garde Mobile, and the Paris climate smelled like the beginning of a Fascist civil war. In the Fourth Republic (1944–58), political morality became close to impeccable, despite the unbridled Ballets Roses scandal of the one-armed Speaker of Parliament, André Le Troquer, and the wine-trafficking scandals of a Socialist Minister. Few republics in our time anywhere have had a public servant so intelligently used as M. Jean Monnet, father of the European Common Market, though the Fourth Republic and its young technocrats had little praise in France for their farsighted faith in him. Many anti-Gaullists of the upper class still contend that it was the Fourth Republic that brought salvation and order to France's opaque finances, and should thus claim the credit for founding the base of the Fifth Republic's prosperity. Actually, the prosperity resulted more from the ending of the Algerian war, which the Fourth could neither win nor finish—the economy of no longer shedding blood and money in a colonial war. It is true that the technical handling of French finances had already improved under the Fourth's technocrats, but the improvements continued, with compounded results, in the Fifth. The great amelioration in politicos' brains from the Third Republic on lies in the fact that it was the graduates of the Ecole Normale who dimly shone as Ministerial lights in the old days, whereas in the Fourth and Fifth it has been brilliantly educated men from the Polytechnique, the severest scientific training ground in France. French higher education, starved as it is for decent classrooms, properly equipped laboratories, and decently paid faculties, has nevertheless managed to improve the quality of the students' intelligences, probably because they are still obstinately determined to achieve knowledge and culture, and study to obtain both. The whole level of economic knowledge has enormously risen since the Third Republic days, when France's economic teaching was rated by the English and Germans as among the most backward in Europe. The financial experts' level in the Fifth Republic is now high and sharp indeed, according to British bankers who had to deal with them in the recent loan, via the International

Monetary Fund, to tide over the Bank of England in the vulpine international speculators' attack on the staggering British pound.

What certain veteran foreign visitors, familiar with France during all three Republics, say of France today is that the most important fact now is not the age of its General de Gaulle but the increasing youth of its population—a refreshed situation apparently not known in this country for the last hundred years. It is they who will make the new France, whatever it turns out to be.

INDEX

Index

Janet Flanner

Janet Flanner was born in Indianapolis and attended the University of Chicago. Between 1921 and 1974 she lived in Paris. She signed "Genêt" to her first Paris letter for *The New Yorker* on October 10, 1925, the year of the magazine's founding, and her "Letter from Paris" has continued to be one of its regular features. The first volume of her *Paris Journal,* spanning the years 1944–1965, won the National Book Award. Miss Flanner is also the author of *The Cubical City, An American in Paris, Pétain: The Old Man of France,* and *Men and Monuments,* and she has translated books from the French, including two by Colette. A member of the National Institute of Arts and Letters, Miss Flanner has been decorated with the Legion of Honor. She now divides her time between Paris and New York.